P9-DBQ-040

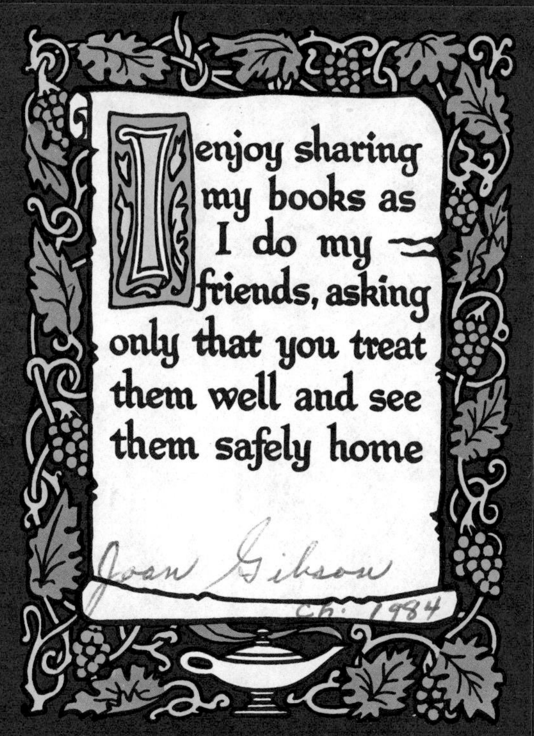
I enjoy sharing
my books as
I do my
friends, asking
only that you treat
them well and see
them safely home
Joan Gibson
Ch. 1984

THE PRIVATE CAPITAL

Ambition and Love in the Age of Macdonald and Laurier

SANDRA GWYN

THE PRIVATE CAPITAL

McClelland and Stewart Limited

Opp. title page

"The Private Capital." Then as now in Official Ottawa, information was power. This exchange was captured by Globe *reporter M. O. Hammond on a Saturday morning in February 1905 in front of the main gateway to Parliament Hill.*

McClelland and Stewart Limited
The Canadian Publishers
25 Hollinger Road
Toronto, Ontario
M4B 3G2

Canadian Cataloguing in Publication Data

Gwyn, Sandra
The private capital

Bibliography: p.
Includes index.
ISBN 0-7710-3736-8

1. Ottawa (Ont.) – Social life and customs.
2. Ottawa (Ont.) – History. 3. Meredith, E. A. (Edmund Allen), 1817-1898. 4. Canada – Officials and employees – Biography. 5. Amaryllis (Journalist).
I. Title.

FC3096.394.G88 1984 971.3′8403 C84-099319-6
F1059.5.09G88 1984

Printed and bound in Canada by T. H. Best Printing Company Limited

PICTURE CREDITS

Principal sources are credited under these abbreviations: Public Archives of Canada (PAC), National Library of Canada (NLC), Ontario Archives (OA), Thomas Fisher Library, University of Toronto (TFL); *Types of Canadian Women*, a 1903 reference book by Henry J. Morgan (TCW).

All material credited to the National Library was photographed and processed by Judy McGrath. So also was material from *Types of Canadian Women*, the pages from Meredith's diary, the sketch from Ethel Chadwick's diary, and Agar Adamson's letter, all in the holding of the Public Archives, and the snapshot of Florence Randal in the Transvaal provided by Dorothy Livesay. Material from the Thomas Fisher Library was re-photographed by Karen Hendrick.

Frontispiece: OA S8761
Chapter 1: p. 20, PAC 33230; p. 22, PAC; p. 27, from *Mary's Rosedale* (1928); p. 30, Metro Toronto Library.

Chapter 2: p. 36, PAC C773; p. 39, PAC C1185; p. 40, PAC C494; p. 42, PAC C1185; p. 43, PAC PA41323.

PICTURE CREDITS CONTINUED:

Chapter 3: p. 50, PAC C11384; p. 53, PAC C8604.

Chapter 4: p. 62, W. J. Topley, PAC A1910; p. 64, Jarvis Studio, PAC PA135072; p. 65, PAC PA25385.

Chapter 5: p. 69, Private Collection; p. 70, PAC PA27198; p. 80 (top) W. J. Topley, PAC A2447, (bottom) W. J. Topley, PAC A2415; p. 81 (top) W. J. Topley, PAC B34573, (bottom) J. D. Wallis, PAC 135071; p. 82, J. Fraser Bryce, PAC 135069.

Chapter 6: p. 85 (top) PAC C5324, (bottom) PAC PA33231; p. 86, PAC PA5328; p. 87, PAC PA26300; p. 92, PAC C5437; p. 93, PAC PA134195; p. 96, PAC PA12512.

Chapter 7: p. 100, PAC C8252; p. 104, PAC C21541.

Chapter 8: p. 123, PAC PA26438.

Chapter 9: p. 126, *The Royal North-West Mounted Police* (1906); p. 136, PAC PA26522; p. 138, PAC C6341.

Chapter 10: p. 148, PAC PA8485; p. 151, PAC PA25572; p. 152, PAC PA26462; p. 155, PAC C6865.

Chapter 11: p. 159, TCW; p. 161, from a contemporary engraving; p. 164, PAC PA26688.

Chapter 12: p. 166, PAC PA134726; p. 169, *My Canadian Journal*; p. 175, PAC PA8480; p. 176, PAC PA8492.

Chapter 13: p. 180, TCW; p. 183 (top) PAC 12421, (bottom) PAC C21570; p. 188, PAC PA13172.

Chapter 14: p. 192, PAC PA25341; p. 197, Webster Bros., TCW; p. 199, PAC PA33465; p. 201, PAC PA12694; p. 202, NLC; p. 203, PAC PA25530.

Chapter 15: p. 207 (top) PAC, (bottom) PAC C8575; p. 209, PAC PA8454.

Chapter 16: p. 216, Jarvis Studio, PAC PA135070; p. 219, Farmer Bros., PAC PA135068.

Chapter 17: p. 226, PAC C5350; p. 234 (top) PAC C51773, (bottom) NLC; p. 237, NLC; p. 238 (top) NLC, (bottom) J. Woodruff PAC C8525; p. 241, PAC C3009; p. 242 PAC PA8979.

Chapter 18: p. 247 (left) PAC C1969, (right) PAC C15558; p. 248, PAC PA12183; p. 250, unidentified; p. 256 (top) PAC PA25390, (bottom) PAC PA135125; p. 257, W. J. Topley, TCW.

Chapter 19: p. 262 (left) Livernois, Quebec, TCW, (right) NLC; p. 267, PAC C15562; p. 269, PAC PA25909; p. 271, Quebec Archives.

Chapter 20: p. 274, NLC; p. 275, NLC; p. 277, PAC PA28026; p. 279, PAC PA27917; p. 281, TCW; p. 284, NLC; p. 285, Pittaway Studio, PAC PA11042; p. 286, PAC PA27871; p. 287, NLC; p. 288, PAC C7214; p. 291, NLC.

Chapter 21: p. 294, PAC PA8988; p. 295, NLC; p. 296 (left) PAC PA28049, (right) PAC PA28046; p. 299, PAC PA28045; p. 300, PAC PA28203; p. 304, PAC PA110038; p. 305, W. J. Topley, PAC E90346; p. 308, W. J. Topley, PAC C82433.

Chapter 22: p. 316, PAC PA28066; p. 317 (left) PAC PA27930, (right) PAC PA25922; p. 319, PAC PA28151; p. 322 PAC PA33801; p. 323 (top) PAC PA134194, (bottom) PAC PA33786; p. 325, NLC.

Chapter 23: p. 334, Pittaway Studio, TCW; p. 335, NLC; p. 336, PAC PA28911; p. 337, PAC MG30 D258; p. 338, PAC C6359; p. 339, PAC PA57332; p. 340, PAC C7982.

Chapter 24: p. 346 (both), NLC (*Book of the Victorian Era Ball*); p. 348, Pittaway Studio, Courtesy Anthony Adamson; p. 351, Pittaway Studio, Courtesy Anthony Adamson; p. 353 (top) PAC PA128778, (bottom) PAC PA16431; p. 361, PAC C17553; p. 365, PAC C24614; p. 368 (top) PAC PA16417, (bottom) PAC MG30 E149 Vol. 1.

Chapter 25: p. 372, Courtesy Dorothy Livesay; p. 380, Courtesy Dorothy Livesay; p. 382, PAC C25050; p. 386, University of Manitoba.

Chapter 26: p. 390, OA S8799; p. 391, OA S8986; p. 394 (top) OA S9107A, (bottom) OA S9068; p. 397, PAC PA8436; p. 399, OA S8762; p. 400, PAC C14582; p. 401, PAC PA9023; p. 403, OA S9461; p. 404, OA S8802; p. 405 (top) OA S8772, (bottom) OA S9022; p. 406 (top) OA S8834, (bottom) OA S8835; p. 407, OA S8840; p. 408, OA S8769; p. 409, OA S8814.

Chapter 27: p. 412 (left) OA S9546, (right) OA S9547A; p. 414, PAC C52405; p. 415, PAC C15561; p. 421, OA S9043; p. 422 (top left) OA S9047, (top right) OA S9055, (bottom left) OA S9048, (bottom right) OA S9044; p. 424 (top) OA S9041, (bottom) OA S9058; p. 425, OA S9060; p. 426 (both), NLC; p. 428 (left) OA S9599, (right) OA S9597.

Chapter 28: p. 434, PAC PA27053; p. 435 (top) PAC C51835, (bottom) PAC C70468; p. 436 PAC C68857; p. 442, PAC C56072; p. 443, TFL.

Chapter 29: p. 448, NLC; p. 449 (top) PAC PA122336, (bottom) W. J. Topley, PAC B76753; p. 456, PAC PA27209; p. 457, TFL; p. 459 (left) TCW, (right) NLC; p. 461, NLC; p. 462, NLC; p. 463, TFL; p. 464, TFL; p. 468, TFL.

Chapter 30: p. 473 (all three) TCW; p. 478 (top) PAC PA25786, (bottom) TCW; p. 480 (top left) W. J. Topley, PAC D52541, (top right) W. J. Topley, PAC C52115, (bottom) W. J. Topley, PAC C56590; p. 481, PAC C86296; p. 482, NLC.

This book is for my mother, with love.
It is also to the memory of my father Claude Fraser (1905-1944) and my stepfather Frank Harley (1914-1972).

CONTENTS

PREFACE

There are characters from Canadian history at hand, and in search of an author. There is a world now scattered in the archives and the dust, waiting for whoever wants to try putting it together again.

William Kilbourn, *The Firebrand*

This book began in the autumn of 1977, although I didn't know it at the time. *Saturday Night*'s ninetieth anniversary issue was coming up; as a staff writer, I'd been assigned to plough through back issues and produce an article on the changing style of Official Ottawa as reflected in the pages of the magazine. I'd got well into the issues up to March 1897 without much inspiration, when a column by a new reporter who signed herself "Amaryllis" caught my eye.

> "*Le roi est mort, vive le roi*" has been the cry in Ottawa since Laurier's election on June 23. The very people who hoped "those horrid Grits would not get in as it would ruin our society" have been the very first to establish an *entente cordiale* with the new ascendency.

Instantly, I was hooked. What fascinated me was that this pseudonymous, turn-of-the-century journalist seemed to be a kindred spirit; I could relate immediately to the way she wrote about Ottawa. What interested Amaryllis all those years ago was precisely what had always interested me as a magazine writer: not so much the flow of political events as the *texture* of those events – how people actually live and behave as opposed to the specifics of what they actually accomplish. Amaryllis's columns ended in 1902, and I was able to weave them into a pleasantly nostalgic magazine piece. That assignment done, I gave one to myself: to write this book. In the autumn of 1980, I set out on a voyage of discovery into the past that has lasted nearly four years.

Now that my journey is over, I'm not at all sure how to explain what it has produced. Researching and writing *The Private Capital* was a good deal easier than describing it. Broadly speaking, it fits into the pigeonhole marked *Social History*, yet this category encompasses everything from Fernand Braudel's gargantuan chroniclings of everyday life before the industrial revolution to the work of the miniaturist Ronald Blythe, in his lovingly detailed account of life in a Suffolk village of the 1950s, *Akenfield*.

Another social historian, Theodore Zeldin, from whom I have borrowed my subtitle, provides a sharper definition. In the preface to *Ambition and Love*, the first volume of his massive study of France between 1848 and 1945, Zeldin writes, "Historians have by custom concerned themselves mainly with public lives, with issues and movements. So they have left private lives, the emotions of the individual, to the novelists. . . .I have tried to combine the preoccupations of the historian with those of the novelist." So have I. This book is an attempt to call back yesterday, as yesterday really was. I have tried to describe and to bring back to life as vividly as is possible, out of diaries, letters, scrapbooks, and contemporary newspaper accounts, the private face of public Ottawa, from just before Confederation to just before the First World War, when Laurier was defeated.

Like characters created in the imagination of a novelist, the people I was writing about insisted time and again on having their own heads and leading me down corridors I'd never envisaged–all the way out to the South African veldt in 1899; three decades earlier, at the time of the Fenian scare, into a capital whose nervous and paranoid mood uncannily prefigured the atmosphere in Ottawa during the October Crisis of 1970. Yet everything that happens in this book really happened, except in the case of a few passages, usually prefaced apologetically, "We can picture . . . ," in which I have tried to recreate a scene that probably took place, or to deduce a relationship–as for instance between Laurier and his close friend Emilie Lavergne–about which the available record is too scanty for certitude.

"The past is a foreign country; they do things differently there," wrote L. P. Hartley, in the haunting opening sentence of his novel of Edwardian England, *The Go-Between*. In the course of my research, I talked to a number of people who could remember, from their own youths, some of the characters who appear in this book, at later stages of their lives. But no one could remember the times I was writing about, except as a very small child, for even the later Edwardian era has now almost slipped away to join the Victorian era, in the recesses beyond living memory. Exploring the Ottawa of those times, I felt myself both at home and a stranger. Then, as now, in a city in which the pursuit of power is the organizing principle, people worried about scrambling up the career ladder and about getting asked to the right parties. They also worried, as people do not worry now, about attending the right church and about coping with their blocked and smelly drains. Ambition then was as potent a motivating force as it is today, but love, although if anything even more potent, had to find its way within the accepted conventions. As for the style of the city itself, one of my most interesting discoveries was that that Ottawa, despite the smells and the discomforts, was a more richly textured capital than the one-industry, civil-service place it is nowadays. It was, on the one hand, a raw and boozy lumbertown; on the other, thanks to the viceregal court at Rideau Hall, it was a glittering, proconsular society that had no rival in North America.

Amaryllis was my original entry point, but she quickly led me to a host of other people who quite literally demanded to be written about. She and one other central character in particular have served me as "prisms of history," in Barbara Tuchman's phrase. He is Edmund Allen Meredith, a deputy minister from 1865 to 1879, a pioneer mandarin who kept a daily diary in which he described a Trollopean world of church-going, money-worries, croquet games, and, ringing a more contemporary bell, endless power struggles, most of which pitted him against John A. Macdonald. Because of Meredith's own diligence as a diarist, because his wife Fanny wrote a chatty memoir, because their son Coly, who lived until Centennial year, was also a scrupulous keeper of family records, I got to know the Merediths and their circle almost as well as, say, the Pallisers.

As for Amaryllis, she left behind neither diaries nor letters nor descendants, and, indeed, it took me a long time to find out who she really was. But in her society columns, witty, graceful, and often surprisingly daring, she recreated the ambience that prevailed in political and social circles as Edward VII succeeded Victoria. Further, as a New Woman of the era, Amaryllis revealed an important theme: for a few heady years at the turn of the century, Ottawa was a capital in which a number of remarkable women – Emilie Lavergne, in terms of her influence upon Laurier; the Countess of Aberdeen, in terms of her attempt to use the governor-generalcy as an instrument for social reform – wielded surprising power.

Within and between the acts of these two principals, supporting characters play out their own roles. There are Emilie Lavergne and the Countess of Aberdeen, who have already been mentioned. The flamboyant Earl of Dufferin created the Office of Governor General in his own stagy image; the luscious Lola Powell, some said, and with reason, was on much too intimate terms with another

Governor General, the Earl of Minto; Agnes Macdonald was the complex, difficult, brave, and ultimately tragic wife of Canada's first prime minister; Agar Adamson, neither tragic nor complex, was irresistibly attractive, an elegant buck-around-town who proved his mettle on horseback during the Boer War; Florence Hamilton Randal, the remarkable young journalist, another of Ottawa's New Women, also showed her stuff in South Africa. M. O. Hammond, the eager-beaver political correspondent for *The Globe* during the middle years of Laurier, unveiled the long-vanished Ottawa of the "Sessional People" – fellow journalists, backbench MPs, lobbyists, and job-seekers – who were in town only when Parliament was in session, and who inhabited the dingier fringe of boarding-houses and hole-in-the-corner lunch parlours.

To all of these characters, there is a common thread. They may have had their faults – but none of them was dull. They reflected both the capital and the nation of their times: they were mostly WASPs, but a surprising number were either of Irish or Anglo-Irish extraction. They were colonials all, citizens of a country that was still umbilically tied to Britain, and yet, as demonstrated in the writings of a pair of civil service clerks whom we will also encounter, Archibald Lampman and Duncan Campbell Scott, they were aware that they were present at the creation of a unique national experiment.

In writing about them all, my greatest challenge, as social historian, non-fiction novelist, documentary dramatist, or whatever, was not to get the facts straight – the records are all there for the looking, in the Public Archives or in other research institutions – but to get the context right. Being truthful, as I discovered long ago as a journalist, is much more difficult than being accurate. Often, while I tried to reconstruct all these lives and times on my typewriter, I had the uneasy sense that ghosts were peering over my shoulder, saying, "You've got it all wrong. You're doing violence to my spirit." My rationalization is that after all these years of being forgotten, they would all have preferred being brought back on stage, even with imperfect scripts, than being left in the wings, uncalled for.

In any event, I like to think so – for I think of them all as my friends.

Part 1

PIONEER MANDARIN

THE WORLD OF EDMUND ALLEN MEREDITH, DEPUTY MINISTER 1865–1879

CHAPTER 1

Edmund and Fanny

Bid goodbye to Quebec. Leave by ferryboat at 4:30. Reached Pointe Levis hotel, intending to go on. Detained at hotel, in consequence of accident to Arthur, who fell down steep, zinc-shod steps. Poor Fanny dreadfully frightened. Arthur bled profusely; sent for a doctor who exhibited sticking-plaster. Trip had to be delayed twenty-four hours.

Edmund Meredith;
diary entry; October 20, 1865.

It was a dejected little family party that at last embarked by train for Ottawa from the Grand Trunk Railway depot at Pointe Levis on the following evening. Yet, even when creased and out of sorts, Edmund and Fanny Meredith carried themselves with the natural assurance of people of consequence. He, as Assistant Provincial Secretary for Canada West, was one of the most senior of about three hundred and fifty civil servants sentenced to move from the settled, convivial capital at Quebec City to the raw, new capital at Ottawa nearly three hundred miles to the west. Fanny was a daughter of the Family Compact, which in those days in the Province of Canada was all one really needed to say. Apart from the accident-prone Arthur, who was going on three, the Merediths had three other children: Mary and Alice, who were respectively nine and seven, and Ethel, a six-month-old babe in arms. The last member of the family was a large, unruly mastiff, straining away at the end of a leash. His name was Rab.

Two weeks earlier, on October 7, Meredith had turned forty-eight. He cut a figure both commanding and graceful, just under six feet, and well set up at 165 pounds. The striking, jet-haired, almost flamboyant good looks that had dazzled everyone in his youth had yielded to a more sombre, bald-pated, paterfamilias

Edmund Allen Meredith, 1869: Anglo-Irish gentleman, pioneer mandarin.

distinction. His narrow, intellectual head, handsome Roman nose, and fine, slightly mournful hazel eyes set wide apart, were the features people noticed.

Meredith's flowing dundreary whiskers, at a time when most Canadian men either clung to the Georgian tradition of going clean-shaven like Macdonald and Cartier, or went in for full beards like Alexander Mackenzie, suggested a hint of the dandy – though, this being the colonies, Meredith's were a trifle longer than would have been the fashion in London that year. Clothes concerned him. The choice of a frock coat, the press of his trousers, the right hat for the occasion – in summer a floppy Panama straw, on Sundays a silk topper, for winter an astrakhan pillbox he fancied so much that he wore it when sitting for his photograph by Topley – these were matters of moment. He never went out without spats. Yet Meredith was also a man brimming over with energy, a man who walked with a bounce in his stride and who would take up the new game of lawn tennis with enormous vigour when he was over sixty. He was also healthy as a horse; he lived to be over eighty and his only serious illness came in the Confederation summer of 1867, when an attack of jaundice, or, as he put it, "biliary derangement," forced him to miss all the ceremonies.

Above all, it was Meredith's voice that people would remember. "Rich, clear, wonderfully pleasant," his younger son Coly recalled years later. "A voice to coax the birds off the bough," in Fanny's words. Against a backdrop of untutored Scotch burrs and rough brogues, Meredith spoke the kind of English that nineteenth-century connoisseurs of the language prized most: the mellifluous, slightly theatrical English of southside Dublin, Dublin of the Castle, of Trinity College, of St. Stephen's Green. Like a small but surprisingly influential number of the men who in one way or another would leave their mark on Canada, including his contemporary, the Liberal leader Edward Blake, Meredith was Anglo-Irish. Established in Ireland since Cromwellian times, the Merediths, who enjoyed tracing their ancestry back to a seventh-century Welsh warlord named Cadwalader, were the kind of minor gentry who, lacking in land, had turned to the Church. Like many such families in Ireland, the Merediths were also intellectuals and scholars. Edmund himself, on Sunday mornings before going to church, always read over the lessons in the original Greek and Latin. He was also a compulsive reader who, as his son Coly informs us, "generally had a book in his office in case he had a spare moment, another in his dressing-room and a third on the stand beside his chair in the drawing room."

Meredith's childhood in Ireland had not been easy. He was born in County Tyrone in cosy enough circumstances, the youngest of seven children of the Reverend Thomas Meredith, a distinguished mathematician and Church of Ireland parson. But when Edmund was barely two, his father died suddenly – of apoplexy, according to the official record, of "a sudden, awful visitation," it was whispered in the parish. Within the year, his mother had married another parson and had embarked for Montreal with all but her eldest and her youngest. Edmund was left alone – his oldest brother having already taken Holy Orders – in the care of an elderly bachelor uncle. At nine, he was sent to boarding school at Castleknock, just outside Dublin; at sixteen, he entered Trinity College, where he

For Meredith, keeping a diary was a way of defining himself.

won a classical scholarship in his first year and, later on, prizes for political economy and science. Then he commenced a career in the law.

In 1842, just a jump ahead of the potato blight, Meredith emigrated to Canada. At first, he struck off on his own to Toronto with the idea of becoming a professor at Trinity College, but in the autumn of 1844, he moved to Montreal where his elder brother William was already well-established at the bar, had a fine house on Sherbrooke Street, and would, in due course, become Chief Justice at Quebec. That same season, on his twenty-seventh birthday, he started keeping his diary, a small morocco-bound volume with marbled end-papers, that he'd purchased in London three years earlier. He began awkwardly, and a bit coyly, as if he did not quite know how to deal with this new companion. "Lest the matter should puzzle my future biographers (doubtless they will be numerous) I should afford them a solution of the puzzle. I have selected this day for making my first jottings as being one of the most important dates of the present century, viz., the birth of Edmund Allen Meredith." But for Meredith, as for so many Victorians, a diary

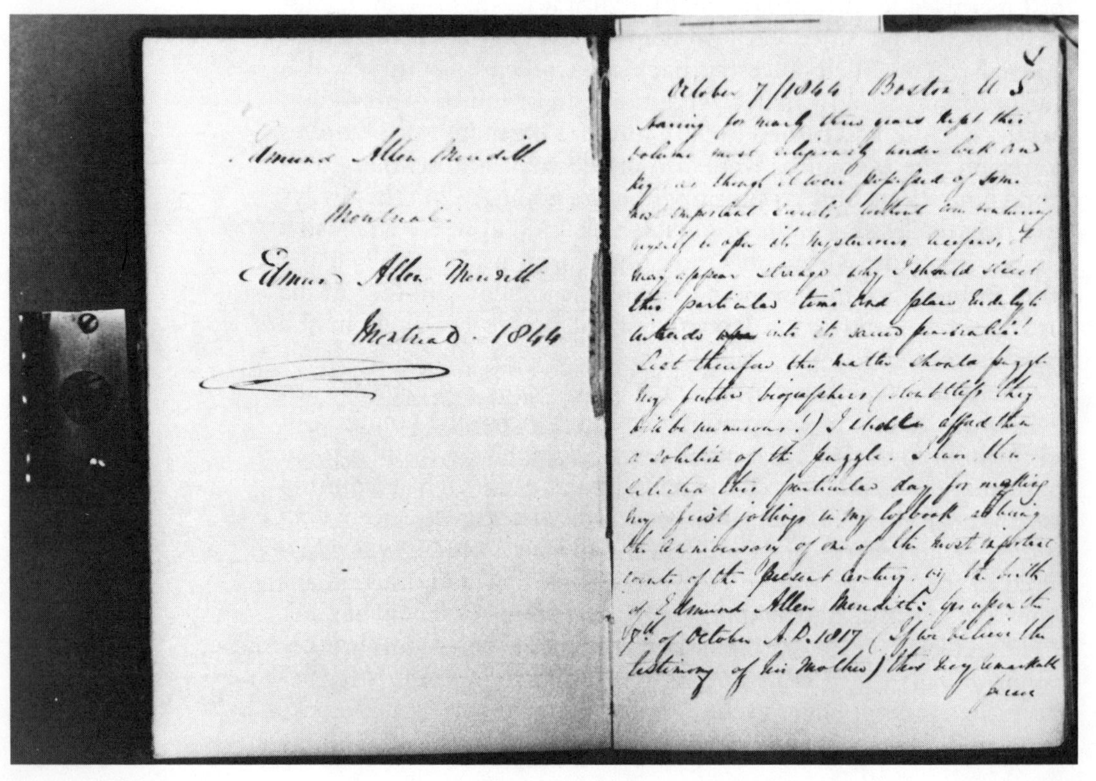

Edmund Allen Meredith

Montreal

Edmund Allen Meredith

Montreal 1844

October 7/1844 Boston U S

Having for nearly three years kept this volume most religiously under lock and key as though it were possessed of some most important secrets without even venturing myself to open its mysterious recesses, it may appear strange why I should select this particular time and place suddenly to intrude [illegible] into its sacred penetralia! Lest therefore the matter should puzzle my future biographers (doubtless they will be numerous!) I should afford them a solution of the puzzle. I have then selected this particular day for making my first jottings in my logbook as being the anniversary of one of the most important events of the present century, viz the birth of Edmund Allen Meredith: he upon the 7th of October A.D. 1817 (if we believe the testimony of his mother) this very remarkable person soon became an extension of his personality, a means of fixing his experiences, and a way of defining himself. He was rarely a voluminous writer; most of his entries run no more than ten or a dozen lines. Even so, by the end of his life in 1899, he had filled twenty-five volumes with a spiky Victorian script that at first almost defeats the modern reader but then, as one enters deeper and deeper into Meredith's world, becomes as familiar as one's own. It was a measure of both Meredith's orderly approach to life and of the importance he attached to his journals that he always took pains to find volumes that matched – although only the first volume boasts the "beautiful brass lock" that first attracted his attention, as he tells us, "in the Arcade leading off the Strand."

"It now seems strange to me," Meredith continued in that first diary entry, "that I could have dreamed, even for an instant, of banishing myself from the society of my brother, and setting up on my own account among complete strangers."

This sentence is revealing. For all his good looks and cleverness, Meredith's lonely and uncertain childhood had left him with a self-doubting diffidence, a certain lack of mettle that would leave him, in the end, somewhat disappointed and unfulfilled. But in the beginning, as a clever young barrister with a natural flair for fun and games and an Irish talent for making friends, he and Canada got on like a house on fire. Though a late-bloomer on skates, he turned out to be a whiz at hockey, playing on the frozen St. Lawrence, with the goals a mile and a half apart and a piece of oak for a puck. More significantly for his career, he also developed a notable flair for administration and for quiet diplomacy: appointed to the unpaid but prestigious part-time post of Principal of McGill College in 1846 when he was only twenty-nine, he made an impressive start on clearing up a deficit of $15,000, reorganized academic policy, and drafted a new charter. A year later, having caught the eye of someone with influence (the diary does not tell us who) he was offered the full-time civil service post of Assistant Secretary for Canada West in the government of the Province of Canada. Meredith joined the civil service on May 20, 1847, five months short of his thirtieth birthday. His salary was $2,600 per annum.

The next eighteen years, until he left for Ottawa in 1865, were Meredith's most productive. They were far from comfortable years; working for government in that era was a bit like working for a travelling roadshow. At first, all seemed easy enough; the capital was at Montreal; Meredith could even keep on teaching mathematics part-time at McGill. But in 1849, after an anti-French mob burned the Parliament Buildings, the seat of government began a hobbledehoy period of shifting back and forth between Quebec City and Toronto every five years. Even senior civil servants like Meredith were expected to pack up their own offices and to meet all the costs of removing their personal effects. On one of his endless removals, Meredith found himself aboard a train with the Christy Minstrels, "including the Hideous Monster, a huge-headed Negro dwarf named Japanese Tommy."

Even if it had remained anchored in one place, the Government of the Province of Canada would have been a demanding master. The two Canadas, Upper and Lower, renamed Canada West and Canada East, had been united in a single province since 1841, as suggested by Lord Durham. But far from solving the problem of "two nations warring in the bosom of a single state," the new system produced mostly deadlock, a parade of administrations that almost as often as they actually fell, expired of simple exhaustion. Meredith served all of them ably and well. Though by inclination and family connections a Tory, he got on excellently with Reformers and Grits. In the mid-1850s, he acquired an alternate hat, and a job he cared passionately about, as Inspector and later Chairman of the Prison Board. It was largely due to his reforms that male and female prisoners came to be separated and that children under fourteen were no longer sent to the common gaols.

By 1865, when he arrived in Ottawa, Meredith was one of the most capable and experienced civil servants around. The Ottawa years should have marked the pinnacle of his career. Yet somehow, he failed to ascend it. The notices in his diary every May 20, marking the day he first joined the civil service, grew progressively more rueful. "Alas, alas," he wrote in 1872, on his twenty-fifth anniversary in the service, "the idea forcibly suggests itself whether I might not have more profitably employed my time and talents elsewhere."

The reasons for his difficulties can be deciphered from his diaries and from the memories of his descendants. Meredith, by nature, was the very model of an up-to-the-minute, moral, and earnest mid-Victorian gentleman, intellectually curious, scientifically-inclined, a man who would have been quite at home in the pages of Trollope discussing decimal currency with Plantagenet Palliser. If he could sometimes be the most appalling prig – the reader winces and stifles the impulse to shout "STOP" when Meredith picks up his pen to chastise his brother William about the "forward conduct" of

William's daughters with young militia officers – this was redeemed by an endearing self-irony. "I have mentally resolved to give up playing at soldiers," he wrote of his own brief experience in the militia during the Fenian Scare of 1866-68. "I did not get on very well with my first drill with the sword." As endearing (and this was the aspect of Meredith in which the Irish in him could not be suppressed) was his appetite for taking costly financial flyers, all of which crashed horribly. In 1865, a fortnight before leaving for Ottawa, he'd invested $1,000 he could ill afford in ten acres of "oil lands" at Sarnia.

For Meredith, as for so many forward-looking Victorian gentlemen, leisure was serious business. He not only attempted to institute major social and prison reforms while at work, he applied his prodigious energies to setting out his views on these subjects in an unending series of pamphlets: "The Crofter System"; "Miss Dix, Philanthropist"; "Essay on Friendless and Neglected Children." Nor did he stop at writing. He invented an earth-closet; he helped his friend Sandford Fleming plot out the system of Standard Time; he founded and served as president of scientific and literary associations innumerable.

Three-quarters of a century later, when Official Ottawa came to be dominated by sound, earnest makers of public policy after Meredith's own heart, all this energy and intellect would have assured him of great bureaucratic success. But in his day, the civil service amounted mostly to a higgledy-piggledy amalgam of the old nepotistic Colonialist administration as it had existed at the time of the Family Compact, and, imported from south of the border, the Jacksonian philosophy; to the victor belong the spoils. In such a system, Meredith was destined to be a man forever ahead of his time.

Fanny Meredith, for reasons quite different, was also destined to be out of joint with mid-Victorian Ottawa. She was a child of a sunnier, more carefree, above all, a more extravagant time and place. In 1865, at thirty-five, having borne five children of whom four had survived, she'd lost some of the exquisite prettiness she'd had as a bride. (She would later bear three more children, of whom two would live beyond infancy.) Fanny had not, however, run to fat, in the way of so many Victorian matrons. She was still slim and dark, with a delicate, heart-shaped face. Nor had she lost the indefinable air of breeding, that slight air of arrogance, that came as second nature to a woman born a Jarvis, born into that tight little oligarchy that even as late as the 1860s considered itself the ruling elite of Upper Canada.

Anne Frances Jarvis, Fanny, had been born into the heart of the Family Compact. Her maternal great-grandfather was William Dummer Powell, Chief Justice of Upper Canada. Her paternal grandfather was Colonel Stephen Jarvis, a fire-breathing United Empire Loyalist who during the Revolutionary War had escaped by canoe from New York harbour across Long Island Sound to join a British sloop. Fanny's father was William Botsford Jarvis, High Sheriff of the Home District, that same, cool-as-a-cucumber Sheriff Jarvis whose impervious line of pickets, placed approximately where Maple Leaf Gardens now stands, had, on the night of December 5, 1837, ended William Lyon Mackenzie's revolution even as it was being born.

Fanny's doting parents had spoiled their eldest, prettiest daughter rotten. Reading her own charming memoir of her childhood – "a blessed childhood, with love on all sides" – evokes nothing so much as the ante-bellum Old South. Rosedale,* the Jarvis's 120-acre estate from which Toronto's best residential district later took its name, was almost a northern translation of Scarlett O'Hara's Tara; a wonderful, rambling villa perched on the edge of a ravine, with a grape house and a peach house, a wildflower garden, a conservatory full of hothouse flowers, and, the envy of Toronto, a magnificent curving double staircase that descended to a foyer panelled in richest walnut. Thanks to Fanny's whim, Rosedale even encompassed an old darky family retainer named Uncle Josh. "I at once lost my heart to this old Negro who ran away from his master in the States," she tells us. "I begged to have a house built for him at Rosedale, which was done."

On Fanny's fifth birthday, May 4, 1835, her mother marked the occasion by planting a sapling that grew into the famous Rosedale Elm. When she was seven, she crept downstairs in her nightie to watch a magnificent masquerade ball that a whole generation of Toronto party-goers would hold as benchmark the rest of their lives. Fanny's mother, Mary Jarvis, ruled over the revels as Mrs. Leo Hunter, the lady patroness in the book that was all the rage, Dickens's *Pickwick Papers*. "My father was a Welsh noble . . . Judge Haggerty had an asses' head and a lawyer's gown . . . George Wells . . . came as a squaw with a papoose, the head and face made of an apple. . . . "

Far from being a delicate, prunes-and-prisms miss, Fanny grew up in the expansive, unfettered late-Georgian style of the 1840s,

* Rosedale House stood at approximately the intersection of today's Cluny Drive and Rosedale Road, facing west to Yonge Street.

Sheriff William Botsford Jarvis and his three daughters, l. to r., Fanny, Louisa, Sara.

when the Queen herself was only in her twenties, a spirited young monarch, head over heels in love, who loved riding and dancing. When not actually eating or sleeping, Fanny was usually on the back of her mare, Juliet, sporting a low-crowned beaver hat with a green veil, a "habit shirt" made of finest lawn, and trousers made of the same fine broadcloth as her habit, naturally hidden by a long, trailing skirt. Fanny also had her own matched pair of carriage horses, named Rattler and Prince, to drive. "In summer," she informs us, "there were constant riding parties and picnics, the Toronto Island and the Humber were favourite places." One magic summer, on a visit to cousins at Hawkesbury on the Ottawa River, there was a "never-to-be-forgotten adventure: Bark canoes paddled by Indians through five miles of rapids." In such a golden cocoon even the day Mackenzie's rebels came to town seemed more an adventure than a nightmare:

> The day the rebels came into town, my brother William and I were rather seriously ill. . . . My father was obliged to hurry away to join the troops, and my poor brave mother was enjoined not to move her sick children unless absolutely necessary.
>
> A carriage with blankets was kept in readiness. Later in the day,

> many rumours were brought in – first across the Ravine, Dr. Horne's house could be seen in flames. . . . At last the rebels rushed down Yonge Street, calling out, "Down with the Sheriff, down with Jarvis."
>
> My mother thought it was time to fly. We were carried to the carriage and found our way down behind Rosedale, round Bloor's pond and through Mr. Allen's property to King Street, and on to my great-grandmother's house in York Street. Later on, my father heard it was Lount, one of the rebel leaders, who saved Rosedale from destruction. He halted at the hill and said if the people did not stop, he would leave them, that he was not there to fight women and sick children. . . .
>
> The other thing I recall during the rebellion was our being sent with my mother and the other Toronto ladies, on board a steamer on the Bay, as it was feared the city might be burnt. I remember one amusing thing, that I did not understand til later, one gentleman of Toronto was found hiding in the steamer – the only one on board.

Fanny's destiny seemed clear. She would marry into the military, an officer from one of the smartest regiments. This was the era when all the principal British North American towns – Quebec City, Montreal, Toronto, Halifax, Kingston, and Hamilton – were garrison towns and, as Luella Creighton has written in her delightful period pastiche, *The Elegant Canadians*, "The British soldier, smart as paint, brought a sword-swinging fascination to the social picture." But Fanny ignored such swashbuckling admirers as Lord Elgin's aide, Captain Grant, "who always wore his kilts and was very au fait at dancing the Highland Fling," and Major Jimmy Gore, "who always handed me the reins." When only thirteen, she'd set her cap for the elegant intellectual, Edmund Allen Meredith. There was of course, his jet black hair and the voice that beguiled. There was, in eloquent contrast to all the glittering gold braid, "the dark blue suit of broadcloth in excellent taste and worn with an air." In the end, though, as Fanny recounted in her memoir, it was Meredith's splendidly chiselled Roman nose that impressed her most. "In the summer of 1846, my mother had a letter from the then much admired Friend Mr. Meredith, asking her to go to the school where his half-sister was, and look her up . . . I said that if she had a nose like her brother, I would go. . . . "

Edmund and Fanny had met in 1843, when Meredith had turned up at Rosedale with a letter of introduction to Sheriff Jarvis. Young Fanny had fetched him some grapes from the grape house. He'd remarked her as "a pretty child." Five years later, when Fanny, now eighteen, returned from two years' finishing school in Paris (in the course of which she'd observed, with more interest than terror, the barricades flung up in the streets during the Revolution of 1848), the courtship began in earnest. In the winter of 1848-49, she set out on a lengthy visit to the family of Edmund's brother William Meredith in Montreal. "Get yourself a white tarlton lutestring and have it made fashionable . . . also any ornaments you like," urged her mother who clearly favoured the serious, well-connected barrister over any number of galloping majors.*

The wedding took place on July 17, 1851, at St. Paul's Church on Bloor Street. Fanny was twenty-one; Edmund, thirty-three, "On THE DAY," wrote Edmund, "the sun shone in unclouded majesty, and we had the most delightful breeze." Old Josh, who turned out for the wedding breakfast wearing "a whole tablecloth around his neck for a tie," was formally introduced to her bridegroom by Fanny. "He joined our hands with much gravity and delivered himself of an oration in which he likened the bride to a bright new dollar, and hoped that she might shine forever." After a wedding trip to Niagara Falls, where, robed head to toe in bright yellow "Gutta Percha," they took a thrilling trip on the *Maid of the Mist*, bride and groom set out for their new home at Quebec.

Those early years of married life, "in a very pretty cottage on the Grande Allée," in Fanny's words, were years of sheer bliss. With the exception perhaps of New Orleans, Quebec in the 1850s was the gayest city in all of North America. The twisting, cobbled streets were crammed with officers from all the best British regiments: the vivid red coats of the Guards; the spruce-green jackets of the Rifle Brigade. There were reviews on the Plains of Abraham and band concerts. For the Merediths (especially as Lord Elgin, the Governor General, was a close friend of Fanny's father), there was an endless round of dinners and balls at the lovely viceregal seat at Spencer Wood.

Above all, in Quebec in the 1850s, winter was a magic season, a never-ending holiday, played out against the wild, sweet music of sleigh bells. It was in the garrison days at Quebec that the mythology of the Canadian winter that will run as a leitmotiv through this story first began to take hold. Every officer worth his epaulettes swanked around in a low-slung cariole sleigh built to his own specifications, painted scarlet, and trimmed with the colours of his regiment. The buffalo robes and bearskins that lined the sleighs were also trimmed with regimental colours. In winter, every girl in

* *Tarlatan*, as it was more usually spelled, was the fashionable material of the period: first introduced in 1840, it was a fine, transparent muslin, often embellished with stars and spots. *Lutestring* was fine taffeta. So what Mary Jarvis was encouraging her daughter to do was to indulge in the most exquisite possible of ballgowns, tarlatan over lutestring – no expense spared. Other passages in the same letter embellish the point. "I hope to forward today a silk and also a merino dress. . . . I enclose in the same parcel three skins for lining something nice for you to wear in going out at night or driving. . . ."

Quebec yearned to be a "muffin," as the officers dubbed their sleigh-riding companions. "It might be expected that the bishop's daughter would move in a different class of society, but no," wrote a disapproving visitor from England. "Miss Mountain is a muffin, and received officers all morning while pretending to be crocheting."*

Muffins had their own distinct uniform for sleigh-riding: a perky little cap made of sealskin and velvet; a scarf of finest wool, two and a half yards long, wrapped round and round the forehead and neck and called a "cloud." Cloud-ends trailing ice-crystals in the wind, the muffins with their officers sped over the bumpy ice of the St. Lawrence to marvel at the wondrous ice cones formed from the spray at Montmorency Falls, and to risk their necks tumbling down them on little wooden sleds. The largest of the cones was always hollowed out to form a chamber, full of ice sculptures. "There is an ice sofa and a table," marvelled one visitor of the era, "a bird, a dog, and two mummies." Mr. Russell, of *The Times* pushed further and found to his amazement, "an Americanized bar and as much want of air as one would find in the Fifth Avenue of New York." At least once or twice a season, there were wonderful ice picnics

* Another visitor from England, William Howard Russell, the famous correspondent for *The Times* of London, provided a definition. "A 'muffin' is simply a lady who sits beside the male occupant of the sleigh," he informed his readers. "All the rest is leather and prunella."

Picnic at Montmorency. "Captain Buzbie drives Miss Muffin," 1868. Fanny Meredith was as skilled a driver as any of the swashbuckling officers.

at Montmorency, with bonfires, hot soup, and even dancing to military bands.

For Fanny Meredith, this was the best of all possible worlds. As a young married woman with unquestioned entrée to Government House, she could have all the fun of being a muffin without a single eyebrow being raised. For a girl to whom driving came as naturally as breathing, Quebec was very heaven. "I had never been without horses before and I missed them hugely, so Captain Cotton, one of the aides de camp, insisted upon sending his sleigh and lovely pair several times a week for me to use. I remonstrated with him for allowing me to use them so much, but he said, If I did not use them, he would send them to stand two hours daily at my door, so *que voudriez-vous*?" The next winter – perhaps some eyebrows *were* being raised – Sheriff Jarvis sent down Rattler and Prince. "The roads were so narrow in winter that there was great difficulty in passing other vehicles with a pair, so I determined to try my hand at driving tandem. My Edmund was very nervous about my trying to teach the horses a new accomplishment, but I was very successful and I had many compliments paid me on my driving capacities by Lord Elgin."

Not even Quebec City's dreaded *cahots* or potholes, which overturned nearly as many carioles as negotiated them, deterred Fanny and Rattler and Prince.

> One quite horrible adventure happened when one day I was out driving on the St. Louis Road. We came upon Judge and Mrs. Duval about five miles from Town, standing by the roadside: Mrs. Duval with a bleeding gash in her forehead, and the poor Judge in despair. We found their horses had run away. I assisted the poor lady into my sleigh when she instantly laid her head on my shoulder and groaned, *Je suis morte*, which little lament she kept up all the way into town; if she was quiet for an instant, I thought perhaps she was *morte*. I was obliged to receive loving kisses for many years afterwards from Mrs. Duval and also to dance many slow quadrilles with the kind Judge with his wooden leg.*

* Duval at this time was Chief Justice at Quebec. His wife Adelaide was the city's leading hostess.

The day of all days in Quebec was New Year's Day. By custom, the ladies stayed home by their firesides in their best clothes, presiding over tables groaning with oysters, both on the shell and scalloped, cold meats, salads, fruits, pound cakes, hot whiskey punch, and mulled wine. The gentlemen drove round in their sleighs to exchange greetings with the ladies and with each other. On her second New Year's Day in Quebec City, instead of staying home like a proper young matron, Fanny got up to a great lark that made her a legend among muffins. "I dressed in a fur coat of Edmund's, and a fur cap, and with the high collar of the coat and cap I was quite disguised, and I drove my dear husband all over Quebec to pay his numerous visits."

If there was a cloud on the horizon these happy, golden years, it was only a very tiny one. "My dear father paid the groom's wages, as we could not afford to do so."

By 1865, Quebec was gayer than it had ever been, thanks to additional regiments summoned to the garrison because of the War Between the States. Yet Fanny now was somehow out of place in it. For one thing, she was no longer a high-spirited bride, but a matron of thirty-five with four children. For another, she and Edmund could no longer afford to live beyond their means. Not only had Sheriff Jarvis died the previous year, he'd left behind such a welter of debts that soon even Rosedale would have to be subdivided and sold. Deprived of its patriarch, the Jarvis family had begun to fall apart: a younger brother, Willy, was soon to disgrace both it and himself by separating from his wife; Fanny's favourite sister, Louisa, it was turning out, had married a charming drunk.

All these events, coupled with the tragic death, in 1862, of Fanny's infant daughter Maude, the Merediths' third child, had left their mark. From then on, until the end of her life in 1919, Fanny became prone to mysterious headaches and "sick spells," to the point that the words "Fanny poorly" appear more frequently in Meredith's diaries than any others.

Since she lived to be nearly ninety, the precise nature of Fanny's trouble is difficult to pin down. Frequent childbearing, though always dreaded and debilitating, seems not to have been the core of the problem: almost always, after a confinement she felt sprightly enough to go out for a carriage drive within ten days and once, by her own account, with a baby barely a fortnight old, she scandalized one of Edmund's colleagues by proposing to set off on a jolting, two-hundred-mile journey to visit a sister at Cobourg. "Mr. Fennings Taylor was so shocked by such a proceeding that much against my wishes, I had to give it up."

Much of the trouble may have been psychosomatic, for although the rheumatism and swollen joints Meredith frequently describes were unquestionably agonizing and real, there is not much evidence that any other of Fanny's indispositions kept her from doing anything she really wanted to do. Time and again in the Ottawa years, an account in Edmund's diary that begins with Fanny spending the day lying down in a darkened room ends with Fanny parading into dinner at Rideau Hall on the arm of the Governor General, cutting a swathe in white satin and black lace. No doubt, for a woman of breeding in mid-Victorian times, as the Queen herself lapsed into torpid widowhood, it was the proper thing to be migrainous. No doubt, since Sir Charles Tupper, Father of Confederation and later prime minister but more important in this story as Fanny's physician, was so free with it, it was equally proper to become just a bit dependent on a drug called chlorodyne, a chloroform derivative.

Perhaps, though, the real trouble lay deeper. The constrained, circumspect life of the wife of a brainy, earnest, but impecunious civil servant very likely bored Fanny silly. She'd been bred to a life of adventure. "We went in a canoe, drawn by a horse, the canoe in case the ice would break," she wrote in her memoir, describing a trip across the ice bridge over the St. Lawrence in the spring. Reading this, one can't help but read into it Fanny's regret that the ice did *not* break.

The men Fanny had grown up with, moreover, were all men of action on horseback; for all that Edmund was Irish, horses bored *him* silly, and while her intellectual horizons began and ended with the novels of Ouida, he was fascinated by the world of ideas. Without Rattler and Prince and with no hope on a civil servant's fixed income of ever replacing them, one might as well take refuge in hypochondria. All the more because Tupper, quite apart from being liberal with his prescriptions, was also, as we shall see, such a tower of strength.

Even by the standards of their own time, Edmund and Fanny were not a well-matched couple. He should have married a bluestocking; she a dashing major with private means. Yet their marriage was a happy one – a union, not an accommodation. All his life he loved her passionately and she loved him, with perhaps a little less passion, a little more sense of Victorian wifely duty. "It is said that occasional absences from each other are desirable for married people," he wrote on their thirteenth wedding anniversary in 1864, when Fanny was out of town visiting a sister. "There is some truth, I think, in this: I have certainly been waiting most impatiently for the return of my 'cara sposa' and it seems to me that I love her more than I ever did before, and all her letters to me are full of the most perfect love and longing."

In 1881, once again living in Toronto, with the Ottawa years behind them, Fanny, who was then over fifty, set off for a morning canter on a borrowed horse. Edmund stood at the gatepost and fondly watched her go. Then he went indoors and took out his diary.

"F. looked like a girl of eighteen."

CHAPTER 2

An Idea in the Wilderness

Keep out of it [Ottawa] as long as you can. . . . What can you expect of a place that has no water?

Sara Adamson, wife of the Librarian and Chaplain
to the Senate, to Feo Monck,
sister-in-law of the Governor General.

Like all the other civil service families in Quebec City in 1865, Edmund and Fanny Meredith reacted to their marching orders to Ottawa with distaste and foreboding. They'd reacted, that is to say, much as civil service families in Ottawa would react today, if informed that, in the interests of keeping the nation together, the entire paraphernalia of the federal government had to be relocated at the exact geographical centre of the country – at, say, Thunder Bay.

The cabinet memo, when it finally arrived after years of delays, had been short and to the point. Except for "balusters and bells," the Parliament Buildings were "so far completed as to render them fit for public offices." The transfer must proceed forthwith. "Great indignation at time allowed for removal," wrote Meredith on October 9, 1865, the day he began packing up his office. "Close at Quebec 20 Oct.; open at Ottawa 25 Oct. Sharp Work!"

Meredith, indeed, had more reason than most of his colleagues to wish to drag his heels. He'd visited Ottawa on prison board business in 1861, tramped round the dreary construction site, where not much more than the arched cold-air ducts for the parliamentary heating system were yet apparent, and had been appalled at what he'd seen. "The whole surroundings of the place are rough,

The Parliament Buildings under construction, 1861. The novelist Anthony Trollope could visualize "the noblest architecture in North America. . . ."

wild and unfinished," he wrote. "Everything looks raw. Possibly the place may be fit for habitation in fifty years time, but certainly not before. I must confess my aversion to the notion of settling here is very decidedly strengthened by my visit."

Goldwin Smith, the peripatetic and highly-opinionated Oxford don, had never visited Ottawa – nor would he until 1872 when, having feathered his nest as the bridegroom of a Family Compact widow in Toronto and taken up roost as a permanent citizen of the Dominion, he took Meredith aback by dropping into his East Block office for a leisurely chat. Yet Smith's devastating putdown, "sub-arctic lumber village transformed by royal mandate into a political cockpit," said most of what there was to say.

It was only as Meredith and his colleagues straggled in, by rail and by paddlewheel steamer, that Official Ottawa, symbol of a nation, began its life. From now on, its dynamic would be the pursuit of power. A more ridiculous venue could scarcely be imagined. And yet, as Napoleon had remarked half a century earlier, power is *never* ridiculous.

Instant capitals, today, are common enough: Ankara, Bonn, New Delhi, Canberra, Brasilia, Islamabad. But in the mid-nineteenth century, Ottawa's only role model was Washington. According to one delicious rumour current at the time, Queen Victoria had selected the site for her rival to Washington by putting on a blindfold and playing Pin the Tail on the Donkey with the map of British North America. This story can be supplemented by a better one that has at least a grain of truth, recounted by Lilian Scott Desbarats, a member of one of Ottawa's founding families, in a charming book of reminiscences published privately in the 1950s.

Back in 1857, according to this version, just as inter-city competition between Toronto, Quebec, Kingston, Montreal, and Hamilton to become the capital was reaching the boiling point, Lilian's father, Richard Scott, a former mayor of Bytown (as Ottawa was known until 1855) and a great civic booster, was elected Ottawa's Member of Parliament. In the early autumn of that year, when Ottawa, as always, was looking its most spectacular, Sir Edmund Head, the Governor General and the Queen's principal adviser on choosing a capital, arrived in town with his wife to look the place over. The high point of the visit, Lilian informs us, was a lavish "luncheon under canvas" on Major's Hill, high on a bluff overlooking the Ottawa River. "My father, being the member for Ottawa presided, and Lady Head sat on his right. He pointed out to Lady Head the attractive surroundings of Barracks Hill [now Parliament Hill] clothed in beautiful foliage and the sloping bank going down to the water's edge. The day was bright and clear. They had a fine view of the Chaudière Falls. Lady Head was so impressed with the picturesque scenery that she made a sketch of it. My father always believed that this very sketch was shown to the Queen, as Sir Edmund and Lady Head visited England that year, and Lady Head was a friend of Her Majesty."

Who knows? Perhaps the Queen, herself a skilled and ardent watercolourist, really was taken with Lady Head's sketch. But there are other, less romantic reasons why the royal favour descended on Ottawa. Poised precisely on the boundary between Canada East and Canada West (soon to become Quebec and Ontario), Ottawa won so that no other contender could be seen to have lost. As a bonus, Ottawa was several marching days distant from the American border.

In fact, with a population of some sixteen thousand, Ottawa could claim to be a little more than just a "lumber village." The settlement itself dated back to the turn of the century, when a canny Massachusetts Yankee, Philemon Wright, discovered that loads of majestic white pine could be rafted all the way from the Ottawa Valley to tidewater at Quebec. By the greatest good fortune, Wright had made this discovery in 1806, just a year before Napoleon sealed off the Baltic ports, separating the Royal Navy from its timber supply. All too quickly, the best of the Valley's trees vanished. However, in 1854, a Reciprocity Treaty with the United States opened up an almost limitless market for sawn lumber. A second wave of Yankee entrepreneurs, quickly dubbed "The American Colony," rushed in to exploit this opportunity, using the turbulent Chaudière Falls just to the west of town as a source of cheap waterpower for their sawmills.

Both the name, Bytown, and a certain civility had been introduced to the place by Colonel John By. A stout senior staff officer of the Corps of Royal Engineers, he arrived in 1826 to establish an internal military supply line, a kind of nineteenth-century autobahn, connecting Kingston to the Ottawa River, and thereby to Montreal and Quebec, by way of a route well clear of the border. A lonely visionary, By built a 126-mile canal terminating at the Ottawa, a waterway that, with its forty-seven locks, still functions flawlessly a century and a half later. The Scottish stonemasons who came with By stayed on to build, in the settlement itself and on surrounding farms, some of the most naturally graceful stone houses anywhere in the country. John By himself became a victim of power politics. In 1832, he was summoned back to England to face prosecution by a Committee of the House of Commons for having exceeded his budget by £82,576. He defended himself successfully, but knowing his reputation was tarnished irreparably, he retired from the army. Four years later he died, disappointed and unknown. Almost a century passed before By's genius was recognized, and a statue to him erected, in Major's Hill Park, just behind the Chateau Laurier.

The construction of the Parliament Buildings for the new capital was as ambitious a project as By's canal. It was also no less controversial. By 1865, the three blocks, East, West, and Centre, were still unfinished, and the money spent on them had risen from an original estimate of about $500,000 to about $2.6 million. Eventually, the cost would rise to an unimaginable $4.5 million. Perched on their bluff, still surrounded by piles of debris, the tryptych of buildings, designed in the à la mode Gothic Revival style, constituted a visionary, if slightly uncertain, idea in the wilderness. "The noblest architecture in North America," wrote the novelist Anthony Trollope, happening by on a lecture tour in 1861. "The glory of Ottawa will be – and indeed already is – the set of public buildings which is now being erected on the rock which guards the town from the river . . . I know no modern Gothic purer of its kind, and I know no site for such a set of buildings so happy as regards both beauty and grandeur."

Edmund Meredith, arriving on his business trip the same year, found no such appeal to his imagination. He dismissed the buildings "as unsuited to the present circumstances of the locality as to the provincial condition of the country." Lord Monck, the first Governor General to live in Ottawa, shared Meredith's views – and pushed them further. "He thinks that the fact of the seat of government being in such an isolated place will have a damaging effect on public men," reported Meredith of a conversation across the Rideau Hall dinner table in June 1866. "He spoke very decidedly about the probability of an early removal." On another occasion, Monck suggested jokingly to Fanny Meredith that she join him in a plot to blow up the Houses of Parliament.

Ottawa and the completed Parliament Buildings, 1866: "a subarctic lumber village transformed by royal mandate into a political cockpit."

The real trouble was that, away from the immediate confines of Parliament Hill, Ottawa as a community was quite unfit for gently-bred city folk to live in. "Very desolate," wrote Governor General Lord Dufferin in 1872, "a jumble of brand new houses and shops, and a wilderness of wooden shanties spread along either side of long broad strips of mud." In 1865, when the Merediths arrived, they found no gas system, no sewers, and, worst of all, no water supply. Instead, barrels of water were delivered to doorways by horse and wagon. Stinking piles of garbage and "night soil" accrued behind houses all winter, to be hauled away in April, and dumped on the river ice. Along with being excessively dirty, Ottawa was also excessively noisy. The sawmills at the Chaudière whined and yammered incessantly. Huge teeter-tottering piles of lumber and mountains of dirty yellow sawdust towered everywhere. "I see little beauty in the scene near Ottawa except in its river and its riverbanks,"

The corner of Rideau and Sussex streets, the heart of Ottawa, c. 1865.

wrote Agnes Macdonald, the wife of Canada's first prime minister. "But even these are disfigured with piles of sawn timber, great rough pine boards piled in huge stacks, and the ground in every direction littered with shavings and splinters." Somehow, there always seemed to be an acrid, choking smell of smoke in the air, for the sawdust caught fire frequently, and so did the surrounding forests, every summer without fail.

To make all this that much worse, Ottawa was only just beginning to live down a reputation for being one of the roughest, booziest, least law-abiding towns in all of British North America. In a harbinger of all the racial and language tensions to come, gangs of Irish "Shiners," so-called because they slicked down their forelocks with bars of rough yellow home-made soap, brawled for supremacy on the river with burly French-Canadian shantymen. Not infrequently, members of opposing factions tossed one another into the falls at the Chaudière. The aggressors were seldom punished, because it wasn't until 1865 that even a rudimentary police force was organized. The week the Merediths arrived, the Ottawa *Daily Citizen* reported a stabbing on Sparks Street and the arrest of a pair of layabouts for "throwing stones at peaceable citizens."

Such polite society as existed at all in Ottawa, pre-1865, was comprised of only a handful of professional men and merchants and the more couth among the sawmill operators. Yet these few were not swamped by the *arriviste* politicians and bureaucrats. As already remarked, there were only about three hundred and fifty civil servants, of all ranks. Most politicians were in town for only about four months of each year. Ottawa's transformation into a one-industry town, in which not to be in government was to be nobody, happened only during the Second World War. Until then, local society made up much of Official Society. Professional people and lumber barons were invited to Government House as readily as were the most senior mandarins, like Edmund Meredith. Ottawa, thus, was a much less self-important place than it is nowadays, much more of a piece with other comparably-sized Canadian communities.

There was, however, quite apart from the presence of Parliament and of Government House, one characteristic of the Old Ottawa that did set it apart from other cities of the era. To an astonishing, if entirely accidental degree, comparatively few members of its local society were Scottish and fewer still were Loyalists. French-Canadian society, for its part, though quite sophisticated, was fiercely self-contained. A couple like the Queen's Printer, George Desbarats and his wife Lucianne, who moved easily in both circles, were an exception to prove the rule. Ottawa, on the brink of becoming the capital, had, rather, a distinctively Irish flavour. To the ranks of such prominent local Irish families at those of the MP, Richard Scott, of Michael Davis, a wealthy contractor, of Daniel O'Connor, a leading lawyer, there would shortly be added, with the arrival of government, such Anglo-Irish families as the Merediths, the Agar Adamsons, the Fennings Taylors, the Bedford-Jones's, such Irish-Catholic families as the Anglins, the Fitzpatricks, the Griffins, the Chadwicks, the Moylans, and the McGees.

This quality of Irishness, though almost wholly vanished today, defined Official Ottawa until well into the twentieth century. It lent to Official Society a somewhat less dour and more tolerant tone than prevailed either at Montreal where, although the Irish were numerous, Scotch-Presbyterianism and mercantilism ruled the roost, or at Toronto, where Irishness tended to be of the narrow-spirited northern variety that went in for riding white horses and waving Orange flags, as exemplified in the persons of the politician D'Alton McCarthy and the merchant, Timothy Eaton. In Ottawa, as was hinted at by those early epic battles between the Shiners and the French-Canadian lumbermen, more friction existed between Irish and French Catholics than between Irish Catholics and either Irish or English Protestants. Perhaps because so many of the early governors general – Monck, Lisgar, Dufferin, Lansdowne – came from the relatively broad-minded, easygoing ranks of the Anglo-Irish aristocracy, the leading Irish-Catholic families of Ottawa moved easily in the Government House circle and at some periods came close to dominating it. Indeed, the well-connected society journalist, Amaryllis, who succeeds Edmund Meredith as our guide to the capital at the turn of the century, was herself a local archetype of the breed who in Dublin were known as "Castle Catholics."

Far removed from the castle, however, were those many Ottawa Irish working-class families who, in 1865, co-existed in sullen and often explosive enmity with their French-Canadian opposite numbers in the shacks of Lower Town. This was far and away the most thickly-settled section. Here, Mrs. Mary Ann Campau, among numerous other "unfortunate frail ones," in the journalistic euphemism of the day, kept a well-known house of ill-fame. Wellington Street, nowadays a windy stretch of monolithic government buildings but in those days a bustling conglomeration of houses and businesses, connected Lower Town, and also the new bedroom suburb of Sandy Hill, with the industrial centre at the Chaudière. The Chaudière, as much as government, was Ottawa's organizing principle and would continue to be so for another half century. The lumber trade was the real growth industry. Already, by 1865, ten thriving mills employed about six hundred and fifty men. That year, the largest of these mills, Harris Bronson, produced fifteen million board feet of sawn lumber. Twenty-five years later, the mills of the legendary John Rudolphus Booth, greatest of all the lumber barons, would boast the highest daily output of sawn lumber in the world.

Wellington Street looking west from Parliament Hill, c. 1865. The spire of Christ Church Cathedral is visible in the background.

Only very slowly, and not really until the expansive and prosperous Edwardian era, did Ottawa even begin to take on the appurtenances of a capital, the Parliament Buildings aside. It wasn't until the turn of the century that even the main thoroughfares of the city were paved. "Sparks Street, the principal mudpath, looks like a canal of peasoup," a bouncy young gentleman immigrant draftsman, James Seton Cockburn, wrote home to his parents in 1884. "It is covered from one end to another with about three inches of liquid mud. One enterprising shop has rigged up a canoe and secured it to the sidewalk all decorated with flags and with 'boats or yachts for hire' painted in large letters." In 1882, Oscar Wilde, in town for a lecture, taunted his audience about the hideous piles of sawdust.

Yet, as even Edmund Meredith was forced to admit in 1865, there were a handful of grace-notes. Spring came a full fortnight earlier than it did to Quebec, he noted that May, on a hasty reconnoitring mission to find himself a house; already the lilacs were "everywhere in flower." The town had two fine stone cathedrals: Notre Dame in Lower Town and Christ Church, overlooking Wellington Street. It had a scattering of handsome mansions, most notably Rideau Hall, the rambling Regency-style villa out at New Edinburgh, built by the Rideau Canal contractor, Thomas Mackay, which, complete with such up-to-the-minute luxuries as a hot-air

The Russell House hotel, Sparks and Elgin streets, 1865. Meredith admired the cuisine.

furnace and hot and cold running water, was being refurbished to accommodate the Governor General. Equally handsome, in the Gothic Revival style, although uncomfortably close to the railway depot, was the mansion on a bluff overlooking the river that John A. Macdonald eventually bought and christened Earnscliffe. Already an institution that would soon become central to the Ottawa style had begun to take shape: John A. and George-Etienne Cartier, both eminently clubbable gents, had hired a room in Doran's Hotel on Wellington Street and had christened it the Rideau Club. Meredith himself became one of its earliest members.

The best grace-note of all, in Meredith's opinion, was the Russell House hotel, a stone building which stood at roughly the same spot in Confederation Square where the War Memorial stands today, and which was in the process of being expanded to cope with the influx of government people. Stopping over there in May, during his house-hunting foray, Meredith was quite frankly amazed. "And now, after dinner," he wrote, "let me observe that this hotel excels by far all others in Canada in its cuisine. Everything is served hot, and nicely cooked."

CHAPTER 3

"Drains, Drains, Nothing but Drains"

The more I see of Ottawa, the more do I dislike and and detest it.
Edmund Meredith
diary entry; November 17, 1865.

Meredith's original intention, having measured the comforts of the Russell House against the excruciatingly short list of houses for rent, had been to take a room there for the winter while he looked for a decent place to live; Fanny and the children remaining behind in Quebec City until the spring. But Fanny would have none of it. "I would not agree to such a long separation," she wrote in her memoir. "We had to make the best of it." On October 27, 1865, in pouring rain, they moved into the best dwelling they could find – a mean little house on Ashburnham Hill, then on the city's western fringe. "My unhappy furniture," wrote Meredith that evening, extending his own feelings anthropomorphically. "It was moved to the cars* in rain, and moved from the cars in rain also."

Winter came early that year, and the house turned out to be freezing cold. "Windows blew out in the night," Fanny tells us, "stoves had to be replenished in the dark hours." Their first local purchase, on November 7, was a "new open stove for the dining-room." Just to maintain the woodpile was a never-ending problem; their logs were constantly being purloined. To deter pilferers, the Ottawa *Citizen* recommended "making an augur hole in a sufficient number of billets, and plugging these with gunpowder."

Meredith's office in the East Block was handsome and roomy. Yet, there he shivered no less miserably. Despite the burning of four

* "Cars," short for steam-cars, was the common mid-Victorian usage for trains.

cords of wood a day, the much-heralded forced-air heating system could guarantee an average temperature of no more than fifty degrees, for the hot-air vents were placed at the tops of the walls. "The more I see of Ottawa," wrote Meredith on November 17, "the more do I dislike and detest it."

For all that they never warmed to Ottawa during their stay of fourteen years, the daily family life the Merediths began to live there, once they'd found a permanent roosting-place and settled into the local society, was much the same as the daily routine lived by other families of the Canadian gentry in other Canadian cities. Urban life was still almost rustic in character. Like everyone else who wanted a supply of fresh clean milk, the Merediths acquired a cow, at a cost of $40; like everyone else's Rosy or Daisy or Buttercup, she was forever wandering off, usually at the most inconvenient times. One Christmas Day, for instance, Meredith crossly reported spending the whole afternoon walking "three miles into the country in search of her," and having, even so, to pay a dollar fine. He also kept hens, and, in an era when the pleasures of fresh vegetables were brief and fleeting, he grew his own Indian corn, "pease," beans, and tomatoes, not always with the greatest success. "Going out to garden this A.M. at 6," he writes on July 25, 1868, "found the fence swept clean away by cows and pigs and the garden land desolate. Not one blade of corn standing, pease all destroyed." Other years were more rewarding. "Picked the first ripe tomato," he notes with a flourish on July 24, 1870. "The earliest on record."

One of the charms of the capital, even this early on, was its easy access to the countryside around. In summers, when they could afford it, the Merediths would sometimes hire a carriage and with Fanny at the reins, drive out to the Chelsea Hills for a picnic. Or they would hire a skiff and row up the Rideau Canal to the first set of locks at Hog's Back. "I rowed the whole way to and fro," reports Meredith on August 5, 1869. "Felt a little tired and sickish on my return home, a coup of brandy restored me and I went early to bed." Most often, they simply went for walks. Like all the Victorians, Meredith was a great walker. "Took the steamer to Gatineau Pointe," he tosses off nonchalantly on August 29, 1874. "Walked up the Gatineau to the bridge, and crossed to Chelsea, back by Hull, a tramp of ten miles." On the first warm Sunday in May, a date that nearly always coincided with "setting aside winter flannels," he and the children would foray far into the woods in search of flowers for Fanny; great swaying armloads of mayflowers and wild violet

"DRAINS, DRAINS, NOTHING BUT DRAINS"

and bloodroot. On June 6, 1869, the entire Meredith family set out to ramble "round the new walk round the Parliament Building cliff, commonly known as Lover's Walk."*

More inviting still were excursions by paddlewheel steamer. If travel by rail was a miserable purgatory of dirty, jolting coaches, constant derailments, and cinders in the eye, travel by steamboat aboard the *Prince of Wales*, the *Queen Victoria*, and later the magnificent iron-hulled *Peerless* which could accommodate a thousand passengers, offered a mode of transportation that was as enjoyable as it was efficient. Travellers who took the day-long trip to Montreal – the return fare was $4 with excellent meals included – had a splendid adventure in store. At the Lachine Rapids, the steamers shot down the rapids, like large, ungainly canoes. "The steering was the best part," reported the draftsman, James Seton Cockburn. "The channel is sometimes no more than 20-30 yards between the rocks."

For the Meredith family, the most memorable trip was one that Meredith himself organized on June 11, 1868, in his capacity as President of the new Natural History Society. This was an excursion forty-five miles downstream to Papineauville, to call on the great rebel, Louis-Joseph Papineau himself, at his seigniory at Montebello. They set out at 11:30 in the morning, with about a hundred excursionists on board:

> Reached Papineauville at 1. Did not know whether Mr. P. wished the party to visit his grounds. He had sent a message to meet the party and point out a picnic ground *not* on his property. To this ground (a very uninviting place) some of the party went. The rest, including myself, went to Mr. P.'s. Mr. Roper introduced me to the venerable gentleman; I asked permission for the party to visit his grounds to which he very politely assented; they are very beautiful and laid out with much taste. The house is built after the fashion of the French Chateaux and is quaint and curious. The views up and down the river and also inland are very beautiful. The old man, the victim of Canadian politics, is a firm, hale and most courtly old gentleman. I was requested to present the thanks of the Natural History society to Mr. P. which I did in my best French.

We can suppose that Meredith, in his diplomatic French, refrained from mentioning to "Mr. P." that his own father-in-law had been that spoiler of revolutions, Sheriff William Jarvis.

In keeping with their position in society, the Merediths went regularly to church, much less regularly to the theatre, not because they

* Until Lover's Walk was sealed off in 1935, for fear that the hunger-marchers of the Great Depression would camp there, this dream-like glade in the heart of the city served Ottawa much as Dufferin Terrace served Quebec.

did not enjoy it, but because of the poor quality of the fare afforded. "Shylock was drunk," he reports of a performance of *The Merchant of Venice* at Her Majesty's Theatre on Wellington Street, in November 1865. "All the others, save Portia, execrable." Travelling circuses generally proved more reliable: the Merediths, along with everyone else enjoyed the famous Van Amburg menagerie from Europe, including the lions that the great Landseer had painted, and the splendid "Yeado" troupe of acrobats from Japan. When P. T. Barnum came to town, Meredith took his children down to the office to get an excellent view of the dwarf Tom Thumb riding past in an open carriage. Nor was there any shortage of home-grown attractions: lacrosse matches, snowshoe races, the fireworks and military reviews that marked the Queen's birthday on May 24, the ascensions by balloon on Dominion Day that became popular during the 1870s. Most of the time, though, the Merediths, like everyone else, manufactured their own entertainment. As an elocutionist and an amateur actor, Meredith himself became a considerable local star. They entertained their friends to dinner and to tea, at the popular evening events known as "conversaziones," and the big after-dinner crushes that were called "kettledrums." Above all, their evenings resounded to the deliberate slap of cards. One game Meredith couldn't abide was the popular "Pope Joan." "Much too slow," he complained. He much preferred whist, and the new game of bezique.

In the refulgent style of the period, when a little embonpoint was fashionable, the Merediths were addicted to the pleasures of the table. Breakfasts were big ones, with porridge, ham and eggs, and hotcakes. On Christmas Day, according to Coly Meredith (always much better at setting down detail than his father) they worked their way through a massive dinner that included "a large roast of beef with Yorkshire pudding at one end of the table, and at the other, a huge boned turkey that was worth waiting a year for, with a boned chicken inside it and inside that a boned partridge with all the remaining spaces filled with oysters and stuffing." Not only at Christmas, but in every month with an *R* in it, they gorged on oysters, those splendid gigantic nineteenth-century oysters which, at the price of only twenty cents a dozen, could be had in vast quantities in every grocery store in town. "We had two great washbasins chockfull," James Seton Cockburn wrote home in wonderment of an "oyster feed" given by his boss, a prominent Ottawa patent lawyer. "I guess I did four or five dozen." The summer months without an *R* produced their own treat: fresh salmon shipped in daily from the Gaspé, and available at The Teapot on Sparks

Street for twenty cents a pound. To the unsophisticated eyes of the Meredith children, if not to their parents, the shop-windows on Sparks Street were a rare show in themselves. At Bate's grocery store, miniature steam engines drove coffee and spice grinding machines. At Miles's Parliamentary Hairdressing Saloon, where, when Coly Meredith was four he and Fanny both suffered the trauma of having his baby curls cut off, there was a magnificent "steam-driven rotary hair-brush," a kind of ancestor of the blow-dryer.

With the coming of winter, the shop-fronts along Sparks and Rideau and Wellington took on exotic dimensions. "The windows are full of snow-shoes, moccasins etc.," Cockburn informed his parents. "I hear very different stories about the winter. Some people say it is so cold that the rain freezes into icicles as it comes down, and forms pillars which you can climb up." Later, he reported, "I got a fur collar put on my monkey jacket which costs $7. When turned up it comes nearly to the top of my head. It's about six inches deep, of beaver skin which being a light brown looks simply swagger on my dark brown coat." A week later, however, he was yearning for something more ambitious: a coat of "Australian grey bear." One assumes that Cockburn achieved his wish: his first batch of letters home were privately published by his father for sale to his friends, and the proceeds sent to Cockburn in Ottawa to pay for his furs.

Little of this was in truth quite as idyllic as it sounds. These were dirty, demanding times. Hardiness, patience, and above all, a resignation to the will of providence were the mainstays of everyday life. The spectre of early death, in the words of one historian, "hung like a capricious plague over the proper and the prosperous." The Merediths, six of whose eight children lived to grow up, were quite exceptionally fortunate. Even at the most elegant parties, the air was dank with the smell of stale perspiration. Teeth, even in rose-bud mouths, were frequently snaggled and discoloured. The roads were full of mud and manure; the wooden sidewalks covered with clots of spittle, tobacco juice, and worse. The difference between Ottawa and elsewhere was that because everything here was so raw and new and overcrowded, all the difficulties of life seemed multiplied ten times over. "It seems like a tale that is told when one speaks of the horrors of those days," wrote Fanny Meredith more than half a century later. For Fanny, the incident that somehow set the tone for the next fourteen years happened just a few days after they'd arrived. Late autumn was hog-killing time. One evening, as

"The more I see of Ottawa, the more do I dislike and detest it." The corner of Sparks and Kent streets, c. 1866. Meredith lived near here until he moved to Sandy Hill in 1869.

the Merediths sat down to supper, "I was more than horrified to hear the shrieks of a pig and the next morning to see it displayed quite within sight of our windows. It made me so ill and was so shocking that Edmund lost no time in making various complaints. I believe that was the last pig ever killed within city limits."

Housing in the instant capital topped everyone's list of horrors. That first winter, there were moments when Meredith, trying to cope with the drafts on Ashburnham Hill, counted himself lucky at least to have a roof over his head. There were just too many newcomers. "Fennings Taylor [Clerk of the Senate] came in after dinner," he wrote on February 23, 1866. "Utterly disconsolate about finding himself a house." The shortage of acceptable accommodation remained a problem for several years. "Visions of clean towels and a refreshing toilet obscured all other objects," wrote the Liberal MP, George Ross, in 1873, soon after his election. Better off financially than most, Ross found a suite of rooms including a private parlour and dining room at the British Lion Hotel on Sparks Street, which he shared with a dozen other members. Some of his colleagues, including Edward Blake, swore by Mrs. Brown's cosy establishment on Albert Street. But most boarding-houses, clustered in what is now Ottawa's central business district, were mean and dingy. "The room I now occupy . . . belongs to the ancient style of architecture known as the Five Dollar Boarding House Rectangular," wrote James Seton Cockburn. "There is a stovepipe that comes in at the wall and goes out at the ceiling . . . the object of the design being the economical warming of the whole structure by the means of one stove. . . . There is also, on the opposite side of the room, an antique sofa celebrated for having been too forcibly sat on. . . ."

For permanent residents like Edmund Meredith, the housing crisis had an additional twist: it was linked, inextricably, to that equally pressing problem, the servant crisis. For a family like the Merediths, not to have, at the very minimum, a cook, a nursemaid, and an all-round manservant was quite unthinkable. Almost the instant they arrived in Ottawa, Fanny tells us, "our two maid servants who had lived with us for several years could not stand the discomforts and returned to Quebec." Worse was the defection of their faithful manservant Harris, a discharged soldier who, among other things, was a first-class cook and nanny; the kind of household treasure who, in Fanny's words, "would knock at my door in the mornings and say, 'Will I take the child off ye while ye put on ye, Mam?'" Six months after their arrival in Ottawa, Fanny continues, Harris knocked sorrowfully on her door and handed in his notice. "He said he was very sorry to say he would be obliged to leave us. He could not find any place for his wife to live. 'My wife hates Ottawa,' he said. 'She says she would not even be interred in Ottawa.'"

Harris was succeeded by a constantly changing procession of "inferior creatures" in Meredith's phrase. On April 6, 1866, he writes of "Anna the cook, rather obfuscated by liquor this morning but as she only gets drunk occasionally and is in other respects a tolerably good servant, I pretended not to notice anything being the matter." The next year, her successor, "Nora, the admirable, the excellent, was drunk on whiskey taken out of my wine closet." In 1871, there was an unnamed manservant who "seems almost equivalent to Handy Andy, he washed the *inside* of Arthur's shoes some days ago, and left the carriage out in a heavy shower because it was dusty." Not to mention a French cook hired in 1874 who "disappeared through the kitchen window, it seems to be her way of leaving on the shortest notice," and a cook and laundress of 1878 whom Meredith "found, on reaching home had turned out to be whores or something of that kind and I had the unpleasant duty of turning them out of the house."

The same problems affected the highest in rank. "I have thought of a way to keep a servant," wrote Sir John A. Macdonald to his sister Margaret on December 6, 1873. "When the wages are settled, say to the girl, 'Now, your wages are so and so; if we get on well together and I find you with me on, say June 1 next, I will make you a present of say, $10 (or any other sum). Now this is not binding on me, and if we part before that date, you will get your wages agreed on and no more.'"

A solution – Sir John on the evidence didn't apply it, but Meredith did – was to do some of the work oneself. A husband decidedly ahead of his time, he cheerfully shined the shoes, lit the fires, and, when need be, even wielded a broom. He also burped babies, helped give them their baths, and cheerfully wiped up the mess when they were sick over him.

During their first months in Ottawa, the Merediths considered building themselves a house. Spacious building sites with magnificent views abounded everywhere, for about $200 each. They had no thought of a magnificent stone mansion complete with conservatory, such as the Queen's Printer, George Desbarats, had just completed on Sandy Hill* – "handsome but not homelike," opined Meredith – but at least perhaps a comfortable Irish gentleman's house that somehow might help compensate Fanny for the loss of Rosedale. With the architect Henry Horsey, whom Meredith had met on his first trip to Ottawa to look over Horsey's new Carleton County Gaol,* he inspected several lots, including a "very picturesque point covered with cedars" on the Mackay estate at New Edinburgh that sounds very like the present-day site of 24 Sussex Drive. None of these plans came to anything. The most obvious reason was the financial setback Meredith had suffered over his oil shares. But the underlying reason was that the Merediths shared fully the general unwillingness to believe that Ottawa could actually survive as capital of the nation. At Rideau Hall, Lord Monck never let up badmouthing it every time he had an audience. "He, also Mr. Pope of P.E.I.* and Colonel MacDougall [the adjutant-general] joined forces in denouncing," wrote Meredith in the summer of 1866. "I believe now that within five years, Ottawa will have ceased to be the

* This house was called Chapel Court. When the Desbarats left Ottawa in 1869 they sold it to Sandford Fleming, newly arrived in town, for the astonishing sum of $12,000. Considerably altered, it survives today as an apartment building.

* The gaol survives, and since 1971 has been used as a youth hostel.

* William Henry Pope, Prince Edward Island's delegate to the Confederation Conferences of 1864 at Charlottetown and at Quebec. He was the father of Sir Joseph Pope, private secretary to Sir John A. Macdonald and later first Under-Secretary of State for External Affairs.

capital, and then, alas for people who have invested in property here."

"DRAINS, DRAINS, NOTHING BUT DRAINS"

Since the capital refused to budge, the Merediths moved house constantly within it. Late in 1866, they moved from their first house on Ashburnham Hill to another in the same district that was a very slight improvement. Their next-door neighbour, J. D. Lewis, was the City Solicitor. When the Meredith's rambunctious mastiff, Rab, playfully nipped Lewis's son, his father "turned quite savage . . . says that if Rab not removed he will have him destroyed at any cost. Poor Mary and Alice cried bitterly. Mary called Mr. Lewis many nasty names and Arthur threatened to get a sword and gun and kill him." To prevent such excesses, Rab was found a home in the country and did not accompany the Merediths on their next removal, across town to a semi-detached stone house on King Street (now King Edward Avenue) in the much more fashionable area of Sandy Hill, next door to an old friend from the era of sleigh bells and muffins, Lieutenant Colonel J. G. Irvine, the senior aide at Government House. At last, in September 1871, they took the plunge and paid what Meredith considered to be the rather excessive price of $1,325 for a pleasant Gothic Revival villa with a pretty gingerbread trim at 253 Augusta Street, on what was then the outlying fringe of Sandy Hill. In 1871, however, Augusta Street bore no resemblance whatever to the leafy heritage precinct it has matured into today. A photograph of the Meredith's house, taken just as it was being completed in October 1865, shows a treeless wasteland of mud in the foreground, and not even so much as a wooden sidewalk.

Meredith's house on Augusta Street under construction. The house was torn down in the 1960s to be replaced by a pair of modern bungalows. The neighbouring house on the left, which survives handsomely today, was occupied by Lester Pearson and his family during the 1940s.

On Augusta Street the family found a measure of contentment at last. There was room to spare not just for the new dogs Bang and Tiny, but for all the sixteen pets – parrots, rabbits, cats, and turtles – that by Fanny's reckoning eventually became part of the family. The family remained there until they left Ottawa. More than seventy years later in 1947, Coly Meredith remembered it with an old man's nostalgia.

> Behind the house stretched a wonderful common extending all the way to the high banks of the Rideau River. Cows grazed there and kept the grass short between the clumps of cedar trees, and wild Iris grew along the river. . . .
>
> On the southeast corner of Rideau Street and Augusta there was a barber shop. It had the regular red and white and blue barber's pole outside and I can clearly recall how, when coming home from a walk with an elder member of the family, the sight of the pole would call for "Three cheers for the Red White and Blue," as it was a sign we were near home.
>
> Sir John A. Macdonald, who in the days before he moved to Earnscliffe lived in a house called Stadacona Hall, the last house on Theodore Street*, was our nearest neighbour to the south. When the house was empty for the summertime, the children would go into the grounds to play and I can distinctly remember sitting on the front steps when all the others fled and left me alone. The front door had opened and closed, so thinking the house was haunted they had run away. I suppose a caretaker had been left in charge and was investigating the gathering of children.

* Now Laurier Avenue. The house survives as the Embassy of Belgium.

But, in early Ottawa, even the most agreeable of houses had about them one exceedingly disagreeable aspect: they stank to high heaven. Until 1874, when the capital's first water and sewage systems were installed, the smells let out by primitive wooden drains pursued everyone everywhere. The urgent imperative to get away from the putrid, overpowering stench of stagnant water and human feces that as Meredith wrote on one occasion, "nearly knocked me down," was the main reason the Merediths bought the house on Augusta Street. The same imperative had led the Macdonalds to Stadacona Hall and away from "The Quadrilateral," the stone terrace house on Daly Street in which they'd spent their earliest married years. In 1868, as Sir John wrote to his sister, the stench in his ground-floor study was so bad that he had to move his papers upstairs into his mother-in-law's bedroom. "She took possession of her son's bedroom, and he is now sleeping in the garret." Often, for Premiers and ministers and senior officials, drains outranked the problems of state and functioned as the great leveller. As late as 1906, Lady Victoria Grenfell, a daughter of the Governor General, Earl Grey, died at Rideau Hall of typhoid fever, a disease nearly always attributable to inferior drainage.

"DRAINS, DRAINS, NOTHING BUT DRAINS"

Meredith himself had arrived in Ottawa surprisingly chipper on the subject of drains. Since the absence of running water ruled out the new water-closets that elsewhere were just beginning to come into upper-class use, the problem of finding an efficient bathroom facility challenged his scientific inventiveness. In 1868, he designed a "dry-earth system," based, as he put it, on "the marvellous capability of dry and sifted earth for deodorization," installed it in his house, and, during a humdrum period at the office, wrote a "how-to" pamphlet describing it that was published as a public service under official government auspices. Overnight, he became the most talked-about man in town. "Very favourable review in the *Citizen*," he wrote on November 14, "and very great demand." Even Lord Monck himself, Meredith noted with satisfaction, asked for copies.

Diary references to the dry-earth system, however, petered out in 1869, suggesting that Meredith's solution had been overwhelmed by the pervasiveness of the problem.

By the spring of that year, Meredith had grown as morose about the drains as everyone else. "Stench intolerable," he wrote in April, "add to which the combined odours of chlorine and lime, carbolic acid and other diabolical disinfectants that I have been using freely." The next year, things were so bad that the Merediths had to decamp to a neighbour's house in the middle of the night. "I have been so downhearted and miserable about domestic troubles that for ten days I have been unable to write a line in my journal," he wrote on May 3, 1871. Even the move to Augusta Street, while it improved matters, didn't resolve the problem. "Drains, Drains, Nothing but Drains," runs Meredith's entry on June 25-26, 1872. "Garden torn up, cellar floor. Drain outside found to be choked up, pipes are of common red clay, not glazed, joints not cemented." Not until the arrival of the sewers in 1874 could the Merediths at last relax and inhale luxuriously.

Only slightly the lesser of two evils was Ottawa's concomitant domestic misery, the lack of running water. Fanny never got used to the dreadful business of having to buy puncheons of extremely questionable-looking water, at 15¢ a gallon in summer and 25¢ in winter, off delivery carts that came door-to-door a couple of times a week. As late as 1873, Meredith reports her "screaming horribly" at having encountered something that looked suspiciously like "cat's fur or worse" on top of a puncheon.

For a fastidious couple like the Merediths, the problem of keeping themselves clean must often have been intolerable, yet it was so much taken for granted that neither Edmund nor Fanny ever mentioned it. The "primitive tin bath" that Coly Meredith remembered in the attic of the house they lived in in Toronto in the 1880s had either been shipped from Ottawa, or had had its counterpart there. This was "shaped like a coffin and securely built-in with lots of woodwork; such a thing as a basin had not been dreamt of. There were hand wash stands in all the bedrooms, with jugs and basins." Like most gents of that era, Edmund relied on the messy compound known as Fuller's Earth to remove from the shoulders of his frock coats the gummy leavings of the macassar oil he used to smooth down what was left of his hair. Fanny, like all the ladies, relied on detachable collars of fresh linen or muslin and similarly removable "undersleeves" to freshen up her velvets and bombazines.

In the absence of running water, fire was an ever-present threat. Fire, as a topic of conversation, obsessed everyone – and it was no comfort to know that until 1874, for lack of money in the municipal budget, Ottawa's two hook and ladder wagons had to be pulled by men instead of horses. If and when the firemen arrived, they had to depend on water from the horse-drawn puncheons, the first carrier on the scene being paid $5 as prize money.

Unlike many of their friends and acquaintances, the Merediths never lost their house to fire. Even so, on June 22, 1868, they had a nasty scare. "Anna the cook woke up dreaming of fire," wrote Meredith, "and found the kitchen ablaze. I rushed downstairs and got it under control with the help of the few pails of water that, thank God, were in the pantry. The fire appears to have commenced behind the fireboard behind the kitchen stove, which was not sheathed with iron or tin. The fireboard communicated with the woodbox, which was placed against it."

The worst of all the fire scares came in the summer of 1870, the hottest and dustiest in memory. In mid-August, the forest fires that had been raging for weeks in the surrounding bush and that had destroyed many of the fine stone homes along the Ottawa River built by British officer-emigrants on half-pay, swept down to threaten the city itself. The City Council took emergency action, closing all stores, and calling on all citizens to prepare to flee. Only by cutting the dam on the Rideau Canal at Dow's Lake to create a water-

"DRAINS, DRAINS, NOTHING BUT DRAINS"

barrier was the city saved. As it happened, the Merediths were out of town that day, visiting relatives near Cobourg. As early as July 21, though, Meredith had remarked how "the whole city is covered by a dense cloud of pall and smoke, twilight and eclipse." By August 11, "leaves on the trees are dying; many trees quite dead." In mid-September, when the danger was past, the family drove out towards Chelsea in the Gatineau Hills. "The traces of the late fires are very plain; the beauty is much spoiled. The country will for many years show sad disfiguring scars telling of the Fire King's terrible doings."

Ottawa's other discomforts, while plentiful, were more routine. In winter the Merediths complained about the splintery wooden sidewalks from which every householder was expected to do his share of clearing away the ice and snow but which often made walking extremely hazardous, since there were many defectors. "Our street fearfully dangerous being covered with glare ice," wrote Meredith in 1877. "This proves the law that water always freezes with the slippery side up." The winter of 1867-68 was the coldest on record; that February, as Meredith noted in his diary, the thermometer stayed below zero three-quarters of the time. The next winter was far and away the snowiest: on February 11, 1869, the day the little Fenian-sympathizing tailor Patrick Whelan was hanged for the murder of Thomas D'Arcy McGee, a blizzard began that went on non-stop for a fortnight. "The usual snowstorm," wrote Meredith laconically on February 24. "No mail since yesterday. All trains stuck hopelessly." Still one gets the impression that Meredith didn't really mind all that much. "Walked into town on snowshoes," he wrote with a note of exhilaration on February 15 and again the next day.

Following the mud of spring, summer brought the dust and the annual invasions of flies. "As there was no collection for garbage and nearly everyone kept horses," Coly Meredith recalled, "the flies simply multiplied and thrived. They were simply taken for granted as one accepts rain or snow; the danger from them as carriers of disease was not understood. I have no recollection of ever seeing a wire fly screen . . . even in the best regulated households, flies were frequently passing away in the soup or the stew, or getting into the milk." Summers, indeed, were really the most unendurable of the seasons, given the thick layers of clothing everyone wore and the absence of shade trees that, although Meredith had written imploringly about them to the Ottawa *Citizen* in 1869, City Council didn't get around to planting until the 1880s. "Hot today – very hot," wrote Lady Macdonald in the sweltering Confederation summer of 1867. "A blazing summer sun shining full down on the unsheltered houses in the wide, dusty, ugly streets of this our capital. I lay on my sofa, *panting*." Meredith, in his office in the East Block panted equally. "The mercury stood at 84 degrees this afternoon," he complained as early as mid-June of 1870. "Mr. Langton's office, at the same time, was not 75 degrees." No wonder that the Macdonalds and the Merediths and everyone else of their station escaped as soon as they could every summer to the cool ocean breezes of Rivière du Loup or St. Andrews-by-the-Sea. Curiously, given the expense and discomfort the long trip by rail and/or steamer involved, it would be another generation before the lakes in the Gatineau Hills, just north of Ottawa, even began to be opened up as summer resorts.

Rats, to complete the melancholy list, were an Ottawa plague that knew no season. Rats flourished with merry abandon, Coly the architect tells us, because "the basements, if floored at all were of wood on cedar sleepers, this left plenty of room for them and the problem was multiplied by the fact that every home had a series of sheds and stables in the rear." "WAGING WAR AGAINST RATS," Meredith headed an entry in large capital letters on September 9, 1876, a year when they seem to have been particularly numerous. It was during this battle that Fanny, as he reports, "could not bear to look but was informed of twenty-eight rats lying poisoned on the sidewalk." Then – who can blame her – Fanny went immediately upstairs to lie down.

CHAPTER 4

"Good Kind Dr. Tupper"

How Dr. Tupper, one of the Fathers of Confederation, ever had time to attend to the affairs of state I do not know. He was forever being called to look down some child's throat.

Coly Meredith;
unpublished manuscript,
Some Things I Remember; 1947

Flies, rats, blocked drains, extremes of temperature, and mosquitoes made Ottawa an extremely unhealthy place in which to live. They all took their toll of the Meredith family, although Edmund himself, luckily, was gifted with an excellent constitution. Except for the attack of jaundice that ruined most of the summer and early fall of 1867, he rarely mentions even having so much as a cough or a cold. Or perhaps it was that Meredith had no time to be ill – given that everyone else in the family appears to have spent at least a quarter of their lives in bed with a high fever. "I spent a great part of the night going about administering medicines like a hospital nurse," he wrote wearily on February 1, 1870, only one of many such nights.

The endless procession of "sore throats," "putrid sore throats," bronchitis, abscesses, earaches, grippe, and, nastiest of all as a consequence of the lack of proper sewers, "summer complaint," began within a month of the family's arrival in Ottawa in 1865. "All the children ailing," Meredith noted, and sent for the most highly recommended physician in town, Dr. James Grant, whose patients included both the Governor General and the prime minister. "He sent a prescription, and informed Fanny our locality is not healthy." The procession continued with scarcely a break until shortly before the family left Ottawa in 1879, when Edmund reports "Fanny laid up with bad headache from effects of toboggan party." As for the routine diseases of childhood – mumps, measles, whooping cough, and the like – these, like the flies of summer were so much part of the scenery that Meredith hardly ever bothers to remark on them. In the summer of 1871, for instance, the only reason we know that all four children were down with chicken-pox is because six-year-old Ethel Meredith did everything but stand on her head to let people know. "As I was returning home, Ethel shouted out while I was yet on Rideau Street, 'I have got it, Papa.' The 'it' being the chickenpox. She had begun to think she was going to be passed over." A few years earlier, Ethel had horrifed her parents by coming down with "that unmentionable abomination, scabies."

In an era of rudimentary dentistry, toothache was in some ways the worst illness of all. A dentist, Dr. Martin, existed in Ottawa early on, and in Meredith's opinion, he was reasonably skilled. "He filled a huge cavity in my lower jaw, very well I think," we learn early in 1869. Young Arthur Meredith wasn't as lucky. In 1871, when he was eight, recurring attacks of toothache ruined the entire Christmas holiday season. "Arthur suffered all night terribly from his teeth," writes Meredith on December 21. "Dr. Martin came and extracted two or three. Got chlorodyne for Arthur who is suffering terribly." On Christmas Day, Dr. Martin had to be summoned yet again, "He extracted another fang, Arthur being chloroformed." This agony went on for another four days, with Arthur hiding under the bed and refusing to open his mouth, until at last "Dr. Martin got out the last tooth and Arthur was free from pain."

Yet, by the standards of the day, all the young Merediths were reasonably robust. As the children of his friends succumbed to scourges almost forgotten today, like diphtheria and typhoid and the dreaded "malignant scarlet fever" that in a single dreadful twenty-four hours in 1871 took the lives of both Colonel Irvine's pretty daughters, Maggie and Katie, Edmund counted himself extremely fortunate. It was Fanny, always Fanny, who worried him most. And if many of her illnesses were undoubtedly psychosomatic, there were three terrible years, from 1867 to 1870, when, from a combination of childbirth and miscarriages, the death of an infant, and an agonizing siege of what seems to have been a form of rheumatic fever, Fanny suffered mental and physical agony almost incomprehensible to us.

Meredith's diary entries relating to Fanny and her health provide interesting insights into Victorian sensibility. In the matter of their sexual relations, he was, of course, much too prudish ever to commit any mention whatever to paper. Only gradually, and upon frequent use, does it begin to sink in on the reader that the phrase "Fanny is afraid she is in trouble," means that Fanny is afraid she is pregnant. Yet he was not at all reticent about recording many other intimate physical details: a painful breast abscess in 1871, a "persistent hemorrhage" in 1878. He was not only present at the births of all his children but administered the chloroform and wrote down carefully exactly what Fanny said "under the influence." Indeed, in 1865, in Quebec, six months before leaving for Ottawa, he had actually delivered his daughter, Ethel. "Fearful to relate, the baby arrived when I was absolutely alone with Fanny in the house. Never did I feel more helpless. I pray that I may never again be found in such a predicament." Such entries reveal a good deal more than the actual event. They are, as the historian Peter Gay has brilliantly observed in his study of Victorian sensuality, *The Bourgeois Experience*, "precious moments of illumination resembling nothing so much as a subtle, climactic scene in a novel by Henry James, in which a great deal is clarified by spare gestures, and a few words."

For reasons that Meredith never explains, Fanny spent the first five years of marriage childless. Then, during the eighteen years that stretched between the birth of Mary in 1856 and of Coly in 1874, she was more or less constantly "in trouble." On June 8, 1867, just three weeks before Confederation, she gave birth to her first Ottawa baby, a son whom they named Clarence. Except that she "took a very great deal of chloroform, exhausting the stock Dr. Grant had brought, and nearly using all that I had previously laid by, and talked a great deal about her poor mother's death, which occurred this day 14 years ago," this delivery proceeded uneventfully; as usual after a confinement, Fanny was downstairs within a fortnight. But that October, with Edmund just barely back on his feet from his attack of jaundice, Fanny came down with an excruciating attack of "inflammatory rheumatism" that went on, almost without remission, until the following summer. "The rheumatism has attacked both arms and both hands," Meredith writes on November 4. "Her cries of agony during the night are most disturbing. I am generally called up once or twice every night to move her in her bed." In the spring, the misery attacked her feet. On April 19, 1868, "Poor Fanny passed a miserable night . . . her head shook from side to side like that of a palsied woman." It was during this illness that Fanny, like many Victorian women, began to become dependent on drugs. "She took morphine twice during the night, half a grain each time."

By early summer, Fanny, though pale and shaky, had more or less recovered; soon a pleasant six-week stay at Rivière du Loup restored her further. But much worse was to come. On August 25, Meredith came home to find her "very much frightened about Clarence; he had passed blood two or three times during the day. Dr. Grant had been sent for, ordered laudanum." The next day and the next and the next, the dysentery grew worse until, on August 29, Meredith wrote sorrowfully, "Yesterday, sad day in my household, my lovely little baby Clarence passed away from us at a few minutes after 2. The doctor thought there was no danger. Poor Fanny on the contrary had a strong foreboding, which she frequently expressed. Fanny became composed at the end and closed the eyes of our lovely boy." Calmly, she arranged, as was the custom, for the photographer Topley to take a picture of the baby in his coffin. Then, a few days later, on the melancholy journey to Toronto to bury Clarence in the Jarvis family plot, Fanny was called upon to summon up all the steely composure that Sheriff William Jarvis had left as legacy. As she recorded more than half a century later in her own memoir: "As usual we were delayed several hours at Prescott, and were obliged to remain in the waiting room with our sad little box containing the coffin with our baby boy beside us, and had great difficulty in preventing other travellers from making a seat of it." Fanny had lived out this painful scenario twice before – once in 1862, when the infant Maude had died at Quebec, and during the summer just previous, when her sister Louisa's posthumous son had died a few minutes after being born, just a fortnight after the death of his father. "I had to send to Reverend Dr. Bethune in the middle of the night to come without delay to baptize the babe," she confides in her memoir. "Then, for several days, until kind Dr. Bovell came to take the baby to place it in the grave with his father in Toronto, I had to keep the baby out of sight, as my poor sister did not wish the other children to know."

The spectre of early death haunted everyone. When Clarence Meredith died at fourteen months in 1868, Fanny arranged for this photograph to be taken.

Nor was Fanny's personal nightmare over. Even while burying Clarence, she was again "in trouble," only to miscarry in December, with extreme loss of blood. This time, because she could no longer bear the sight of Dr. Grant, Meredith sent for Ottawa's other reigning physician, Dr. Hamnet Hill. "He found Fanny in a very weak state. For a short time, during a fainting fit, he thought she was actually gone. He called me into my dressing room . . . evidently to prepare me for the worst. . . . Towards evening, Fanny rallied under the influence of champagne." For all his tenderness towards Fanny, it never seems to have occurred to Meredith to give her a rest from what they both no doubt considered to be her marital duty.

Barely ten months later, in October 1869, she miscarried again, this time of twins, a misfortune caused apparently by toxemia. "The doctor said it was providential that it happened as it did; dropsy had already begun."

It was this unending series of medical tragedies, along with Fanny's unforgiving rage at the doctor who hadn't grasped how desperately ill the baby Clarence really was, that propelled her into the sturdy, capacious comforting care of a new medical adviser, Dr. Charles Tupper.

In official Canadian annals, Tupper is remembered as one of the most important of the Fathers of Confederation; the young Premier of Nova Scotia who persuaded Nova Scotians to ratify Confederation, and who, a few years later, outmanoeuvred Joseph Howe in his attempt to pull the province out. In the famous set-piece painting of the Quebec Conference by Robert Harris, he's the striking, almost flamboyant figure with a great shock of black hair and flowing sideburns, standing just in the right foreground. In Ottawa in the early 1870s Tupper was Sir John's sturdy and blessedly sober right-hand man, serving as President of the Executive Council and later as finance minister. Later still, as Minister of Railways and Canals, he played a key role in negotiating the Canadian Pacific Railway contract, and went on from that to serve as High Commissioner in London. In 1896, aged seventy-five, he was called back to succeed Mackenzie Bowell as prime minister; after being defeated by Laurier, he moved to Vancouver. He died in 1915 at ninety-four.

Tupper was further remembered by his colleagues as a man for whom no metaphor was too dramatic. "Broadshouldered, self-contained, vigorous-looking as Wellington's charger 'Copenhagen'," wrote the MP, George Ross. "In repose, even, he looked as if he had a blizzard secreted somewhere about his person." "For fifty years he was a storm-centre in politics," wrote the journalist M. O. Hammond. "No matter how threatening the gale, he braced his feet, like a fisherman bound for the Grand Banks, and faced the danger without flinching." As recorded by Hammond, the seventy-five-year-old Tupper, when summoned back from England to assume the prime-ministership, "dashed into the fray like a regiment of cavalry." On June 23, 1896, when defeat at the hands of Laurier was obvious, he met it with panache. "Do not let a trifling matter like this interfere with the pleasures of a social evening," he told a crestfallen crowd of Conservative workers at Halifax.

As remembered by the Merediths, yet another Tupper emerges. To Edmund and, above all, to Fanny, he was "good kind Dr. Tupper," the one-time country physician who never ceased practising his profession all the while he was a politician. It was part of his no doubt carefully-cultivated mythology that, in readiness for emergency, he always kept his black bag under his front-bench seat in the House of Commons. "When I was very small," Coly Meredith tells us, "I had some gland trouble in my neck after an infantile illness; this brewed up until it had to be lanced. Dr. Tupper had promised to come and operate at any time. Of course I selected an awkward time, and he was sent for just as he was entering the House."

Fanny Meredith in the 1870s. Well into her forties, she was an attractive woman.

Tupper makes his first appearance in Meredith's diary in April 1872, writing a prescription to allay the teething troubles of Morna, the Meredith's second Ottawa-born baby, who had arrived "healthy and squalling" the previous July. That October, he "called to see Alice and Arthur who are laid up with bad colds." A few weeks later, when Fanny had one of her sick headaches, "Dr. T. called in the evening and gave her chloroform." The following March, "F. saw Dr. T. who after awful examination came to the conclusion that she suffered from overanxiety and overwork, and that she wanted rest and a change of scene."

Tupper by then had become almost a member of the Meredith family. To Meredith himself Tupper was, although four years his junior, a kind of father-confessor, Meredith's closest friend among politicians, into whose ear he regularly poured out all his frustrations about his cavalier treatment at the hands of Sir John.

But Tupper, because he understood her complicated, capricious nature as Meredith did not, was, much more, Fanny's friend. Like all good doctors, he knew which of her many complaints to take at face value, and which to look beyond for deeper reasons. A letter from Fanny, for instance, on a visit to friends at Toronto that baffled Meredith totally – "She mentions riding to hounds; she is still, however, complaining of her cough" – would not have puzzled Tupper at all. He would have guessed that the cough translated into Fanny's guilt about being off enjoying herself while away from home. He also readily prescribed for her the chloroform and the chlorodyne that were the Victorian equivalents of Valium.

More revealing of the nature of their relationship, Tupper prescribed equally freely, "changes of scene." Many of these managed, curiously, to involve her in his company.

The first of the scene-changes undertaken for reasons of health took place in the summer of 1873. Fanny and the children tagged along with the Tuppers to St. Andrew's, New Brunswick, taking rooms, she tells us, "in a boarding-house kept by a black woman. We had a fine view of the water and vessels from our window." Going out sailing "in the customs-house vessel" and riding to her heart's content in a habit borrowed from Tupper's daughter, Emma, Fanny had a fine time. "Edmund joined us, having leave from the office and was as much pleased as I was to see me on horseback." Meredith, however, did not much enjoy St. Andrew's, finding the pleasure "mostly of a negative character," as he recorded in his diary.

The next summer, though Fanny by then was seven months pregnant with her last child, Coly, she again undertook the long, harrowing journey to St. Andrew's, which involved travelling by rail to Portland, Maine, and then northwards by steamer. This time, she confides, "we had Dr. Tupper's own very pretty highland hill cottage." On September 15, however, it was not Tupper but another physician who delivered the baby. Five days previously, reports Meredith, who by then had arrived on the scene, "Dr. T. called at 5 in the morning to see Fanny. He was obliged to leave for Amherst at 8:30. Fanny very miserable and distressed at having to be attended by a stranger."

The Honourable Dr. Charles Tupper, 1874. He had a reputation for being a womanizer.

As this entry suggests, the true nature of the relationship between Tupper and Fanny may have been no more than the natural close dependency that so often develops between a nervous, hypochondriacal woman and the doctor she has come to trust, a doctor, moreover, whose calm, self-confident presence must have evoked the memory of the much-beloved father who once had indulged her every whim.

Perhaps, though, there was a bit more going on. Although, to all outward appearances a happily married husband and paterfamilias, Tupper had a reputation for being a womanizer, and, indeed, in his rambunctious Nova Scotia days had been dubbed "the ram of Cumberland." In Ottawa, among the ladies he flirted with more sedately was the pretty, witty Lucianne Desbarats, wife of the Queen's Printer, who in her own old age loved to tell her grandchildren how, long ago on Sandy Hill, Tupper used to walk a block out of his way every morning to "surprise" her watering her flower garden. In the 1870s, with the Desbarats removed to Montreal, it was Fanny Meredith who was just around the corner, still an extremely attractive woman, though by now well into her forties.

There are entries in Meredith's diary that suggest moments when there may have been question marks even his own, simon-pure, see-no-evil mind. "F. leaves for Toronto with the Tuppers," he writes, just a trifle testily, in October 1876. "F's departure somewhat sudden, but Dr. T. recommended some change." And again, on May 24, 1878. "Dr. Tupper arrived unexpectedly, paid a prolonged visit to Fanny and after giving her chloroform told me that he was going to Montreal at 2:30 and would take charge of Mrs. Meredith if she was ready to go. Fanny packed up and started." On that particular day, as it happened, Fanny had scarcely stirred out of her bed for two weeks, having undergone with "extreme agony" what seems to have been a dilation and curettage operation at home "to cure a persistent hemorrhage" with Edmund administering the anesthetic and Tupper supervising the surgeons. In any event, the treatment worked. On May 29, reports Meredith, "F. seems to be enjoying herself in Montreal." She did not return until June 12. "Decidedly the better for her visit."

Fanny, in her own "Rambling Recollections," provides no gloss to any of this. She does go out of her way to inform us, several times, that Lady Tupper was her "dearest friend." Then, right at the end of her description of the "pleasant summers" at St. Andrew's, she furnishes an anecdote that reveals, perhaps, just a bit more about her subconscious feelings for Tupper than she intended.

"To my great dismay," writes Fanny, "the Tuppers' great Newfoundland dog, Tiger, jumped on my dear little dog Tiny, and broke a rib." Then she continues. "Sir Charles was away from home and I could not call upon him to set the rib, so I had to try my own hand at it, which I did and bandaged the poor dog to the best of my ability." The treatment was successful. "When Sir Charles returned home and saw Tiny, he said he could not have done it better, and for years after in Ottawa, he always felt for the mended rib."

Our last glimpse of Tupper and Fanny together takes place in the autumn of 1879, as Fanny and the children depart to take up residence in Toronto, Edmund having already left on a trip abroad.

"When we went to the train, Sir Charles and Lady Tupper took me. Sir Charles carried our pet cat."

CHAPTER 5

"The Ashes of His Fathers, The Temples of His Gods"

And how can man die better
Than facing fearful odds
For the ashes of his fathers,
and the temples of his Gods?

Horatius at the Bridge,
Thomas Babington Macaulay

Even if they were not quite prepared to admit its existence, the electricity that unquestionably was in the air between Fanny and Dr. Tupper requires no leap of the imagination to comprehend. Nor is it difficult to empathize with Meredith's battles against foul smells and rats. The point at which Edmund and Fanny begin to demand more from us, if they are not to slip away and become only cardboard cutouts in period costume, is when we arrive at an aspect of their lives that is much less tangible: the ethical and attitudinal assumptions that determined the way they behaved.

Today, many individuals, of both sexes, define their lives by their work, and by their career successes. Meredith's life, in a society that was hierarchical, and to a considerable degree static, was defined at least as much by two other imperatives: his religion, and his and Fanny's extended family – not just the two of them and their children, but a whole private universe of Merediths and Jarvises.

Architecture is always the most reliable barometer of social attitudes. Nowadays, the dominant presence on the Ottawa skyline, away from Parliament Hill, is the conglomeration of office towers. In Meredith's day, and for a good many years after that, whenever people looked up, they saw steeples.

As early as the mid-1860s, the leading Irish-Catholic political families, the Richard Scotts at the head of the list, coalesced around St. Joseph's Church in Sandy Hill, and fashionable French Canadians did the same around the nearby *l'eglise Sacré-Coeur*. Supporters of the Church of Scotland (not formally dubbed Presbyterians until 1874), among whose numbers the Tuppers were prominent, built St. Andrew's, or "The Scotch Church" as it was usually known, in a commanding site on Wellington Street, just to the west of Parliament Hill. Here, the sermons of the young, charismatic George Monroe Grant drew large and appreciative congregations. In the 1870s, Grant was already renowned for having accompanied Sandford Fleming on his epochal survey for the Canadian Pacific Railway and for having written a best seller about it called *Ocean to Ocean*; later he became yet more renowned as Principal Grant of Queen's University.

The *crème de la crème* of official society subscribed to the Thirty-Nine Articles of the Church of England. As a senior bureaucrat, and the son and grandson of distinguished clergymen, Edmund Meredith took pride of place within this inner circle, outdistanced only (and only because of her official position) by Lady Macdonald, wife of the prime minister. It says much about Meredith but even more about the socio-political dynamics of Official Ottawa in his day that although the mark he left on the public service can only be pieced together laboriously from his diary and from a few dry-as-dust official records, his religious monument is instantly shiny and visible. On the wall at the top of the nave to the right in the Church of St. Alban the Martyr in Sandy Hill, one comes upon the plaque:

To the Glory of God
and in loving memory of
Edmund Allen Meredith Lld.
1817-1899
and of his beloved wife,
Anne Frances Jarvis
1830-1919
Who were among the first worshippers in this church.

Unchanged in all its essentials since Meredith's day, St. Alban's continues to prosper as one of Ottawa's most charming and evocative examples of Gothic Revival architecture. Although the church is small, the grace and slight eccentricity of its proportions – Why such a tall basement? Why no spire? – give it an air of being special. A visit to St. Alban's on, say, a bitterly cold Sunday morning in January following a snowfall is a shortcut into the world the Merediths inhabited.

St. Alban's, by S. H. Maw. Religion mattered even more than politics.

On such a morning, before the snowploughs have been around, the walking in Sandy Hill is no less treacherous than it was in the 1870s; the sun glitters on the snow with the same diamond-sharp intensity. That fine square stone house just opposite the church, we realize with a start, is one that Meredith himself would have passed every Sunday and noted admiringly; the home of the original landowner on Sandy Hill, Louis Besserer.

We slip deeper into the past. We hear the sound of sleigh bells, mingling with the deeper peal of church bells. We observe, hurrying up Daly Street, the commanding, if slightly ungainly figure of Lady Macdonald. As a woman born in Jamaica, she never got used to the Ottawa cold. She wears a heavy paisley shawl and over that a fur-lined cloak, but still she shivers. On an even colder Sunday morning recently, Lady Macdonald, on her way to church, encountered George Desbarats, the Queen's Printer, on his way home from Mass at St. Joseph's. She recorded their conversation in her diary. "He had a great spot frozen on his nose. I had to stop to give him the startling information. I had never seen a 'frostbite' before; it looked as if he had put a small, irregularly shaped piece of cloth on one side of his nose. Fancy our greeting with an interchange of bows. 'O, excuse me Mr. Desbarats, but I fear your nose is frozen.' "

Sir John, who likes to lie abed late on Sunday mornings, and who, anyway, has a bit of a head, has not come to church with his wife. Instead, she is accompanied by her brother, Hewitt Bernard, a rather fussy bachelor who serves as Sir John's private secretary. As they sweep into the church and take their accustomed places in the fourth pew on the left, we linger in the vestibule and watch the rest of Official Ottawa arriving for prayer. The tall imposing presence with the flowing white beard we know to be John Langton, Auditor-General, the most important member of the civil service. The shorter, more voluble figure with the mutton-chops is G. C. Reiffenstein, Confidential Clerk in the Receiver-General's office. We take note of both of these people, for we are going to meet them again. Here also is Fennings Taylor, Clerk of the Senate; William Himsworth, Assistant Clerk of the Privy Council, Horace Wickstead,

Law Clerk of the Commons, Colonel Irvine of Government House, and the bouncy chaplain to the Senate, Dr. William Agar Adamson, a sporting parson out of Trinity College renowned for his Izaak Walton-like treatise, *Salmon Fishing in Canada*.

We follow them into the church. We admire the fine vaulted ceiling, the simple pews of polished pine, the delicate stained-glass windows. We notice two that are particularly poignant, dedicated to the memory of those two tragic daughters of Colonel Irvine, swept away by scarlet fever. We notice also that it is nearly as cold in St. Alban's as it is outside, and that Lady Macdonald is surreptitiously blowing on her fingers to warm them.

At precisely five minutes to eleven, Edmund Meredith arrives, a tall, grave figure in frock coat and winter moccasins. He emerges from the basement where, as on most Sunday mornings, he has spent the past hour teaching Sunday school. Meredith is an excellent teacher, and tries to impart to his charges his own generosity of spirit. "He never recited the damnatory verses of Psalms or concurred in the cruel judgements of the Commination Service," his son Coly recalls in later years. "He always remained silent during the reading of the Athanasian Creed."

Just seconds before the service begins, Fanny Meredith, in a flurry of sealskin and "clouds," rushes down the aisle to join Meredith. He is a bit surprised to see her, for he left her at home with a sick headache. During the sermon, which today is excessively long and dry, Fanny, as we can easily tell, is not listening. She has a faraway look in her eyes.

St. Alban's interior.

For Meredith and for the rest of the St. Alban's building committee, achieving this fine new church was an achievement that resembled in miniature the building of the CPR. Church politics in that era were as Byzantine as those on Parliament Hill. In Meredith's diary and in Lady Macdonald's, the amount of space given over to *Sturm und Drang* at St. Alban's takes second place only to his accounts of Fanny's incessant illnesses, and to hers of those frequent "rather trying weeks," when Sir John got too friendly with the bottle. "This first Sunday after Easter does not seem to find the congregation of St. Alban's in a particularly good temper," she wrote in 1868. "These church squabbles are most disastrous." Seven years later, by Meredith's account, not much had improved. "Church matters *still* the only subject of discussion," he wrote in exasperation in June 1875.

Far and away the most intriguing account of the politics of St. Alban's, and for the same quality of unselfconscious prattle that makes Fanny's memoir such beguiling reading, is the memoir written at the turn of the century by its founding pastor, the Reverend Thomas Bedford-Jones.

Bedford-Jones was yet another Trinity College Irishman, like Meredith, but unlike Meredith, Bedford-Jones was also much given to putting on airs. "He objected to our praying round a table littered with eggshells," Coly Meredith writes, of an occasion when the rector dropped round unexpectedly, and caught the Merediths in the midst of the morning ritual of post-breakfast family prayers. And though Meredith, as a fellow-scholar, admired Bedford-Jones's wordy and erudite sermons, Lady Macdonald, among many others, did not. "So very unsatisfactory," she fulminated in her diary on March 29, 1868. "If only he would explain the history less." Still, as Lady Macdonald was well aware, Bedford-Jones, as Rector of St. Alban's, was nearly as significant a figure and almost as skilled a political in-fighter as Sir John A. himself.

His story, and that of St. Alban's, begins in the summer of 1865. In the way of all the best inside-Ottawa stories, it involves a conflict over jurisdiction. On instructions from his bishop, Bedford-Jones had arrived in town to establish a new "moderate High Church" parish to accommodate the influx of government people. In short order he encountered his entrenched rival, the Reverend J. S. Lauder, Rector of Christ Church Cathedral, Ottawa's existing Church of England parish. As soon became apparent, Lauder regarded the newcomer as an out-and-out poacher. "I happened to mention that the Bishop had included New Edinburgh in my sphere of work," Bedford-Jones wrote. "I was astonished to find that my information made him very angry, and he questioned the right of the Bishop to act as he did." Lauder, continues Bedford-Jones, twisting in the knife, "had not then won the well-deserved esteem and affectionate regard of all classes of churchmen." (New Edinburgh's importance to men of the cloth was that it included Rideau Hall.)

Backed by the Bishop, Bedford-Jones pushed on. He established daily services in the back room of "a small Berlin Wool shop on Sparks Street kept by two English girls." Then, on October 22, 1865, just as the government people started flooding into town, he held his first Sunday services in makeshift quarters in Ottawa's courthouse. A fortnight later, right after their arrival, the Merediths became regular parishioners. "We used to draw the two youngest children on little sleighs from Ashburnham Hill across the

Canal to the Courthouse," Fanny recalls in her memoir. The courtroom itself, in which the murderer of Thomas D'Arcy McGee would later be tried, was far from conducive to Higher Thoughts. "A dirty, dingy chamber, in Bedford-Jones's account, "brightened only by a large portrait of the Queen over the Judge's bench, which served as both prayer desk and pulpit. Underneath was the official's desk, all splashed with ink." During the services, the Rector continues, "the elite and fashionable secured sittings in the Jury and Sheriff's boxes, the bulk of the congregation climbing up the gallery seats which, when court was being held, were occupied by the great unwashed." To Bedford-Jones's immense satisfaction, the Governor General, Lord Monck, decided to join his congregation; to his astonishment the Governor General invariably chose to sit among the common herd. "Sunday after Sunday, I have seen him take his place and how he managed I do not know but he always *knelt on his knees* during the prayer." For some parishioners, the single most distracting aspect of the courtroom was that its windows directly overlooked the adjacent gaol. "I could not help watching the prisoners sitting close to the barred windows eating their coarse dinners," wrote Lady Macdonald. "There was one boy, a brown-haired child almost – and I pondered over the strangeness of prison discipline that could allow that young criminal to associate with villainous blackguards." No doubt the sight troubled equally Edmund Meredith, Chairman of the Prison Board.

Meanwhile, plans for a new church were pushed ahead. "Dr. Jones preached an excellent sermon," Meredith reports on June 17, 1866. "I myself put in $5 in aid of the new church." Even the Romanist D'Arcy McGee, in a fine show of ecumenicalism, "volunteered all he had in his purse," after Bedford-Jones encountered him at the House of Commons. "Suiting the action to the word, he took out an old purse, opened every flap and found a five-dollar bill which he handed me with a kindly benediction." McGee told Bedford-Jones to consider it "a gift from a fellow Irishman."

The site was quickly selected – in Sandy Hill, where so many of the government families were settling. Then, abruptly, and quite literally, the ground fell out from under the Building Committee's feet. Sandy Hill, it developed, had been only too aptly named. "The site had been purchased from the Besserer estate per Mr. Henry Bate for $600," Bedford-Jones explains. "It was then mid-winter, deep snow covered the ground, and only in the spring when the contractors were starting operations was it discovered that at the very edge of the streets there was a sudden dip of the blue clay into a great pit of sand. This upset everything." Instead of the large, imposing church with tower and spire that Thomas Fuller, architect of the Parliament Buildings had been arm-twisted by Bedford-Jones into drawing up the plans for, for free, a much simpler structure had to be hastily designed. Bedford-Jones was embarrassed beyond words – almost. "From Mr. Fuller's drawings, I had had photographs taken and these in two sizes had been circulated among friends all over the province and in England." Fuller was so put out that he declined to do anything more. "Instead, he advised our employing his talented pupil, Mr. King Arnoldi . . . who gave us a new design dispensing with chancel, transept, tower and spire, but providing a large basement to extend under the entire building."

At last, on May 9, 1867, the cornerstone of St. Alban's was laid. Late in September, the Merediths' doomed little son Clarence became the first baby christened at the church. "There was another baby in the same service," Fanny tells us, "but our dear friend Dr. Bedford-Jones gave our baby his name first."

A fortnight earlier, on September 8, the first Sunday Services had been held. The preacher at the evening service, Bedford-Jones informs us, was the luckless Reverend J. S. Lauder himself, now a guest at his rival's feast. Bedford-Jones, as victor in their power struggle, allowed himself to gloat. "Let me say that by this time, nearly all the disagreements had been smoothed away."

Still ahead for rector and parishioners of St. Alban's was the problem of actually paying for the church. In 1872, the parish was still $5,000 in debt; interest rates in that year of depression had risen to a heady eight per cent. To meet this challenge, Bedford-Jones had to contend with an adversary incomparably more puissant than Lauder: Lady Macdonald.

A formidable and exceedingly intelligent woman, Agnes Macdonald, like many women of ability in her day, poured much of her prodigious energies into church affairs. The sticking point between Bedford-Jones and Lady Macdonald concerned Bedford-Jones's theological principles: as a devout "Free Church" man, he would not countenance the raising of funds in the usual way of charging rent for the pews. Nor would he countenance the holding of bazaars. To give to the Lord meant a *free* gift, "not the price of a cushion or toy, a picture or an article, much less a gambling transaction."

Lady Macdonald, like all skilled power players, bided her time until Bedford-Jones had left town for a visit to Ireland. Then she moved quickly. "On my return," reports Bedford-Jones, "almost the very first news I heard was that some of the leading members of the congregation had in my absence decided to hold a bazaar on behalf of the church debt and that all the arrangements had actually been made. At the head of the business was Lady Macdonald. My protests were useless. I either had to submit or resign the parish. In the early part of 1873, the bazaar was held. . . . It was an immense success . . . I never went near, but the debt was paid."

It was Meredith, the quiet diplomat, who came up with a parallel fund-raising scheme of which all parties approved; evenings of musical selections and recitations that were known as "Penny Readings," given on Monday nights during the winter in St. Alban's basement. The prickly matter of money was solved by charging no admission, but taking up a collection. "Dr. Bedford-Jones was a wonderful reader," Fanny tells us, "and besides he could play the piano, his lovely voice and singing were always a joy to hear. . . . Then we had several lady singers and later still we used to have charades."

But it was Meredith himself who, as Fanny continues proudly was always "the bright and particular star." At most Penny Readings he stole the show, standing in front of the lectern, reciting all the great set pieces that most of the audience knew well enough to mouth along with him. Thomas Hood's *Bridge of Sighs*, for its moralistic pathos, was always a popular favourite. So were Scott's rousing *Lochinvar* and Ayrton's *Death of Montrose*, Shylock's "Ten Thousand Ducats" speech from *The Merchant of Venice* and Longfellow's *King Robert of Sicily*. Above all, it was when Meredith paused for effect, cleared his throat dramatically, took a long drink of water, and launched into *Horatius at the Bridge* by the matchless Macaulay, that a pin could have been heard to drop in the chilly, smelly air of St. Alban's basement. Meredith's wonderful, sonorous Dublin voice swept all before it.

To every man upon this earth
Death cometh soon or late;
And how can man die better
Than facing fearful odds
For the ashes of his fathers,
and the temples of his Gods.

So popular were Meredith's renditions of Macaulay that the Ottawa papers sometimes sent along reviewers. "Mr. Meredith read in a manner that would have done credit to a professor of elocution," ran one notice in the *Free Press* that he proudly pasted into his diary. Just as gratifying were the proceeds. "Collection seemed good," he noted further. "I put it down at $25 or $30."

Less conducive to good spirits, however, were the family problems that Meredith soon began to encounter. On the night of March 8, 1870, he came in from St. Alban's and was astonished to find his brother-in-law, Willy Jarvis, sitting sheepishly in the parlour along with his two sons, and Fanny in tears. This handsome, red-haired, obstreperous major in the militia, two years Fanny's junior and a veteran of wars against the Zulus in Africa, was in terrible trouble. Yet as he heard out Willy's problems with a sinking heart, it never occurred to Meredith that he would do anything other than try to solve them. Responsibility had to be accepted for all members of the extended family – its black sheep as well its snowy lambs.

As much as the church, family was the organizing principle of Meredith's existence. So wide a gulf existed between family and everyone else that the only one of his many friends that he ever referred to by Christian name was Grant Powell, his own second-in-command at the office, but also a cousin of Fanny's. Never would he have dreamt of addressing Tupper as "Charles" or Bedford-Jones as "Thomas." Nor, though Meredith was as high-minded a civil servant as existed in Ottawa, would it have entered his mind that pulling strings to get good jobs for relatives like Grant amounted to nepotism.

Luckily for Meredith, his own immediate family in Canada required little in the way of pulled strings. The Canadian Merediths were a stalwart, upright crew: his brother Henry a barrister at Port Hope; his sister Harriet well-married to a successful businessman at Cobourg; his elder brother William made Chief Justice at Quebec and soon to be knighted. Except for a few representations that needed to be made on William's behalf to D'Arcy McGee in 1866, when it seemed that an upstart judge named Caron might nose him out for the Chief Justice-ship, and a touchy little contretemps in the summer of 1869 when, shocked by the "very fast conduct" of William's daughters on holiday at Rivière du Loup, Edmund wrote to his brother "suggesting greater check on their intercourse with military men," not one of his own family ever caused Meredith a single night's missed sleep.

The Jarvises were quite another story. Shortly after the death of the Sheriff, Fanny's clan lurched into a melodramatic tailspin, with successive misfortunes played out around the Meredith's dinner table.

The first act unfolded during the years 1867-70, years that, perhaps not entirely by coincidence, were also the years of Fanny's worst siege of illness. The key player was her younger sister Louisa.

In 1855, Louisa's marriage to Augustus Nanton, a promising young barrister of Cobourg, had seemed a match as happily augured as Fanny's own with Meredith. By her account, Fanny set off from Quebec to attend the wedding accompanied by "Madeline, my French maid, the old parrot and other pets." But by 1861, like so many other young men in an era when spirits were cheap and Toronto, among many other cities, boasted a tavern for every 120 of its residents, Nanton was clearly an alcoholic. Meredith records him on June 5 of that year "arriving at table frightfully muddled. Poor Louisa was consequently in misery all dinner time. After the solemn pledge recently given by A.N. to lay off all spirituous drinks, this exhibition seemed to me conclusive as to the hopelessness of any real reformation." Meredith was right. Six years later, Nanton was dead. Almost penniless, and with four children to bring up,* Louisa tried to eke out a living as a teacher of French. In the late 1860s, she and her brood spent at least a third of its time under Meredith's roof in Ottawa. That Louisa shared Fanny's hysteric disposition did not help. Nor did the fact that her best offer of a teaching job came from the despised Reverend J. S. Lauder. "Wrote to Louisa saying I could not in all conscience recommend her to take place at Lauder's school," Meredith tells us, on July 19, 1869. It wasn't until the following year that in the best tradition of Victorian melodrama, a benefactor who preferred to remain anonymous came to Louisa's rescue by sending her $10 weekly in an unmarked envelope. "Delighted to find Louisa's letter informing me that the weekly stipend is likely to last for many years," wrote Meredith in November 1870. "The donor is still a mystery; Fanny thinks now it may be Gzowski."*

However pressing, Louisa's problems were at least respectable. The problems presented by Willy that March evening in the parlour were so appalling that neither Meredith nor Fanny dared admit them to outsiders. Women were at their root.

In 1861, Willy had married a young woman of no particular

* One of these children, Augustus Nanton the younger, later redeemed family honour by becoming President of the Winnipeg Grain Exchange.

* This was Sir Casimir Gzowski, the great Polish-Canadian engineer, who, among his other achievements, built the great bridge at Fort Erie. He was the great-grandfather of the author and broadcaster Peter Gzowski. As recorded in earlier family correspondence, Sheriff William Jarvis had been a friend of Gzowski's, but Gzowski's putative affection for Louisa is not otherwise explained.

origins named Maggie, who, as Meredith recorded condescendingly "was certainly very pretty and likely enough to turn a young man's head." A few days before Willy and his sons appeared on Meredith's doorstep in 1870, the pretty Maggie, for reasons unspecified, had committed the unspeakable by abandoning them. "There has been a good deal of scandal about it," wrote Meredith, "Fanny has had some very *hard* letters from Maggie." As was no surprise, Willy proved to be harder up than even Louisa. "He left for Toronto," wrote Meredith on March 14, "I supplied him with the funds." But Willy left behind his sons, a pair of little Hottentots who nearly drove Edmund and Fanny to distraction. "Arthur and Ethel cried all morning after the little boys," he wrote when they finally departed, nearly a year later, "I must confess that I did not."

For a long time, the everlasting problem, What To Do About Willy? preoccupied Meredith's attention. That spring of 1870, the unseen presence of Louis Riel briefly hovered in the wings as a possible deliverer: Meredith used all the influence he could muster to secure Willy a captaincy in the force being assembled under Colonel Garnet Wolseley to put down the rebellion at the Red River. But Willy's reputation as a libertine ran ahead of him. "Poor Willy's chances are gone," Meredith wrote on May 2. "Appointments made last Sat. and his name struck off and another placed in its stead. Was told today that Col. Wolseley objected, and that was fatal." Three years passed before Meredith found the right outlet for his scapegrace brother-in-law's undisciplined energies. In the wake of the Cypress Hills massacre of 1873, Lieutenant-Colonel G. A. French, a British officer seconded to the Canadian militia, had been given a mandate to establish a new force to police the Northwest; its members were to wear scarlet tunics to remind everyone of British redcoats. By now Deputy Minister of the Interior, Meredith could exercise considerable influence. "Sent in W's application for post in Mounted Police Force," he reports hopefully in May 1873. On September 20, "Willy made a senior captain of Mounted Police for Northwest . . . he is to have $3.00 a day, of which $70 a month is to go to Louisa." So Willy, in a scarlet coat, disappears into the West, leaving his sons in the charge of his and Fanny's long-suffering sister Louisa. He will, however, reappear.

Other in-laws roosted frequently in Meredith's nest with Fanny and him, or, in one way or another, required patience and forbearance. There was Colborne ("Coly") Jarvis, for instance, Fanny's youngest and favourite brother, after whom she'd named her own youngest son. He, by Sheriff Jarvis's own account was "an elegant young man, a very lady-killer," who, like so many younger sons of the Canadian gentry joined the British regulars. The trouble was, Coly hardly ever wrote home and in the few communications he did produce, managed to cause Fanny deep pain. "Fanny received letter from Coly who seemed much hurt at her letter in which she attributed his refusal to come to Canada to his want of affection for his relatives here," wrote Meredith in October 1869. "I wrote back regretting the misunderstanding between him and Fanny."

When at last, seven years later, Coly did come on leave, "looking very well and handsome but somewhat weatherbeaten," it was less than the most blissful of reunions. "On Christmas night," reports Meredith in 1876, "we had a party all told of 15 to meet him. Arthur had decorated the rooms and all looked very pretty. We had borrowed plates and other things." But Coly, still a dashing bachelor, found Ottawa so tame that he pushed on to Toronto rather quicker than he decently should have. "Fanny much disturbed at Coly's defection," wrote Meredith on New Year's Day. To Fanny's chagrin, Coly Jarvis remained a wanderer. After serving with distinction on the Northwest Frontier of India in the Afghan War of 1879-80 he retired from the army and disappeared for years into the Antipodes.

"Unlike the typical Victorian father," wrote the seventy-three-year-old Coly Meredith of Edmund, "he never ordered me to do anything; when he wanted something done, one knew that it should be done and naturally, without question, tried to do what he wished. . . . At times, the confusion made by small children must have been trying, but he never lost his temper, or showed irritation. When one considers his own very lonely life as a child, one marvels at his being able to become such a perfect father." In 1947, Meredith's youngest daughter Morna recalled for Coly's memoir an afternoon in 1877, when she was six, as if it had happened yesterday. "It was in the nursery at Ottawa; he had just returned from his office and coming to see us, he 'conjured' oranges; he snapped his fingers to the East, to the West, to the North and to the South, and suddenly, to our delight, we each found an orange in our small hands; all through the adroit entertainment, he was serious and intent on our pleasure."

Of all the faces of Edmund Meredith to be found in the family papers, by far the most beguiling is Meredith the paterfamilias.

Unlike Fanny, who was sadly self-centred and who also had a lamentable tendency to be fussily over-protective, Edmund was a relaxed, confident parent, never happier than when horsing around "having a capital time with my chicks." Though fifty-seven when his youngest son Coly was born, accounts of the great sport these two got up to together suggest a man half his age. "Quite often," writes Coly, "he would play battledore and shuttlecocks with me in the dining room; the room was long and there was a clear strip of hardwood at the side; the racquets were not strung but were covered with parchment like a drum; the shuttlecock was of cork and feathers." Even an accident that terrified Coly failed to deter Meredith. "On one occasion, my father in reaching back slipped on the polished floor and fell backwards, hitting his head on the door trim and knocking himself unconscious. When I saw what had happened, I rushed for help shouting that I had killed him . . . the concussion lasted for several hours, but the fall left no ill effects."

When the circus came to town, Meredith enjoyed it as much as the children themselves. "The giant Chang was nine feet tall," Coly tells us. "My father walked right under his arm." The style of the period was practical jokes, which meant that April Fool's Day breakfasts were almost as memorable an annual occasion as opening the stockings at Christmas. "The maid would put the hot dish in front of my father," Coly explains. "As cats frequently have their families towards the end of March, there was sure to be a supply of kittens by April. So that when my father took off the cover of what was supposed to be ham and eggs, half a dozen kittens would be wriggling inside. Father would be tremendously 'surprised' and the rest of the family greatly delighted."

Even in his diary, Meredith was scrupulous about not playing favourites among his children. Mary, the eldest, whose persistent attacks of asthma continually worried him, is always "sweet and good," a well-mannered little woman who at the age of twelve, as he reports in July 1869, "made the red currant jelly all by herself and considers it 'fun' to do anything useful." But Alice was more interesting; a clever, quicksilver child who liked to imagine she was the other Alice over in Oxford, and who, by the time she was eight, exhibited a considerable talent for inventing her own adventures in Wonderland, as well as for composing little poems that Meredith proudly transcribed in his diary. Alice was also a dab hand at fishing; on one occasion in 1871 she triumphantly brought home "10 bass, of which one alone was sufficient to feed the entire family for supper." For Ethel, the baby whom he himself had delivered, Meredith had a particular, if rueful, soft spot. "She began the night in my bed," he wrote in 1867, when Ethel was a rambunctious two-year-old, "but when I thought I had got her to sleep after about an hour's labour, she threw up on the sheets and generally made a sad mess of her and me." Little Morna, the family flirt, charmed him as she charmed everyone. After a children's party given by the Dufferins at Rideau Hall in 1878, he reports proudly that "Morna was much noticed by the Royal Party . . . when bidding goodbye to Lady Dufferin, Morna said with much emotion, 'it was just lovely' adding 'I think I should like to kiss Basil [Lady Dufferin's seven-year-old son] before I go,' whereupon Basil was hunted up and the two embraced each other very affectionately."

Of the boys, Arthur was Fanny's special pet. Though delicate, he was the only one of the family who'd inherited her daredevil talent on horseback; at the age of six at Rivière du Loup, as Meredith proudly reports, "he insisted upon riding bareback, without the leading rein." Arthur also "walked splendidly on snowshoes" and was an excellent swimmer who, under his father's watchful eye, had no difficulty making it back and forth across the Rideau River before he was ten. Coly, the baby, born in 1874 when his eldest sister Mary was already eighteen, was the "sweet Poppet" whom the whole family petted and cossetted. As keeper of the family records, Coly, in his old age, returned the compliment.

The Meredith children: above, Arthur and Mary; below, Ethel and Alice.

As a parent, Meredith had just one blind spot. To the education of his children, his attention was decidedly slapdash. Curiously, this supremely devoted father who himself had had such a splendid education allowed his brood to grow up educated just as sketchily and as patchily as the children of the lowliest clerks and messengers in his office. That neither Mary nor Alice nor Ethel nor Morna ever saw the inside of a classroom, wasn't, for the period, all that surprising. That neither Arthur nor Coly benefited from a formal education until they were well into their teens was quite out of the ordinary.

The problem wasn't an absence of schools. By 1865, the year the Merediths arrived, there were at least a dozen in Ottawa, thanks to the enlightened policies of Egerton Ryerson, the great educational pioneer of Upper Canada: small elementary schools with one or two rooms and one or two teachers in each of the city's six wards; a senior grammar school to serve the city. The problem was rather that, even for an intellectual like Meredith it was much more important that his children should be fitted to occupy their proper place in society than that they should be prepared for the working world. "It was not the thing to send a gentleman's son to the common schools," Coly wrote, "so if a more select school was not available, a governess was obtained. Some may have been trained for the work, but I doubt it."

Miss Elwell, whom Meredith travelled to Kingston to engage in September 1866, was clearly a disaster from the beginning. "Fanny does not seem much taken with her manners," he wrote within a fortnight. Six months later, "Miss E. informed me she was going. She has not managed to make herself one of the family." Miss Godard, who came the following autumn, fared better, though seemingly less as a teacher than as a kind of resident babysitter who took the children to Hanlon's Circus and to the opening of the House of Commons.

Above, Morna Meredith, mother of Escott Reid; below, Coly Meredith.

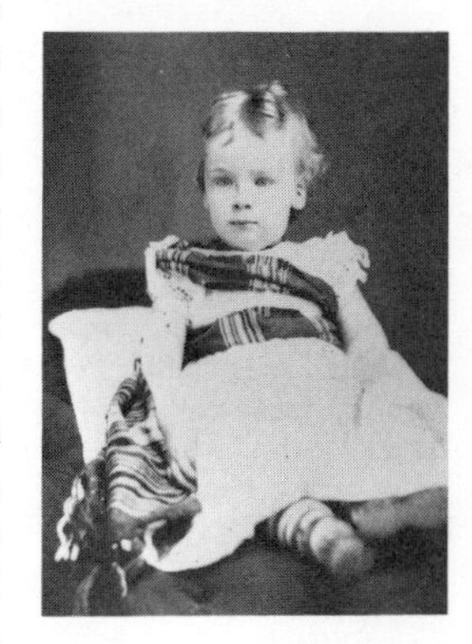

The truth is that Meredith made far more references in his diary to servants than to matters that touch on education. Only once, and fleetingly when he engaged an itinerant young Irishman as tutor, is there a glimpse of a teacher who really knew his business. "Alice and Mary in great excitement about Mr. McGrath's prize in arithmetic," he writes on October 5, 1867, when his daughters were nine and eleven. "Each declared that if not the successful one, she will run away and kill herself, or do something desperate. Mr. McG. has privately informed me that he intends them to be equal, and give both prizes."

It's easy enough, across the gulf of years, to accuse Meredith of something close to negligence. By his own lights, he likely did the best he could. The richer Canadian gentry could afford to send its sons across the Atlantic to public schools in England, its daughters to be finished in Paris, as Sheriff Jarvis had sent Fanny. For everyone else, a second-best education was a fact of life about Canada that had to be accepted. True, some colonial carbon copies of British public schools had begun to emerge: Bishop's College School at Lennoxville; Trinity College School at Port Hope; Upper Canada College at Toronto; "Barron's School" that the Reverend William Barron had established at Gore's Landing. But these were expensive, and showed no promise of being able to provide a better, or even as good an education as Meredith, the Trinity Gold Medallist, could provide at home. The rumblings that came back from Gore's Landing in 1879, in answer to enquiries Meredith made when Arthur was beginning to be a bit of a problem, bore him out. "In consequence of information received regarding Mr. B's intemperate habits," Meredith wrote, "I am obliged to abandon plan." So he drilled his children in Euclid, and tried to set an example in classics by keeping up his own Greek and Latin. Fanny, though no intellectual, did her best to pass on her own fluent command of French. He gave the children free run of his library and when the talented Alice, at fourteen, wrote "a very sensational short story," sent it off to his publishing acquaintance George Desbarats, who ran it in his *Canadian Illustrated News*. "I think Alice will be a good writer of stories," Meredith noted with pride. "Her first earnings were $7.00."

Arthur Meredith in 1893, two years before his death.

Yet he knew he was not doing enough. In 1879, when a long-awaited legacy at last came his way, Meredith exchanged the old Chickering piano for a fine new Durham, engaged a music master, and gave Mary, who was then twenty-two, the present of lessons in German. "I have not been able to do anything but token justice to the girls, or Arthur, in the matter of education," he wrote ruefully.

It was Meredith's sons – less verbal, less quick-witted than his daughters – who suffered most. Arthur tried and failed the examinations for the new Collegiate Institute in Ottawa that was just beginning to be considered suitable for gentlemen's sons. He then studied natural philosophy on and off with a young local doctor, and eventually spent a single unhappy season at Trinity College School at Port Hope. Though he was possessed of charm and good looks, Arthur proved unsuccessful as a businessman; he then set off to farm near Edmonton, in the Northwest Territories, where he died in 1895, aged thirty-three, of complications from pneumonia.

Coly, thanks mostly to gritty determination, fared better. "After far too long of this sort of teaching at home," he wrote in his own memoir, "I went at last to the School of Practical Science at the University of Toronto, before being articled as a student of architecture."

As an architect practising in Ottawa from the Edwardian era, Coly became a considerable success.* In 1912, he was elected President of the Ontario Association of Architects. During the First World War, he was Commanding Officer at Camp Petawawa, and later he served as General Secretary of the League of Nations Society in Canada. Yet even this most loving, almost worshipful of sons could never quite forgive his father for not having done more to prepare him for the world. "My education, irregular and spotty, was inclined to make me have a lack of confidence which hampered me for many years."

* Among other buildings, Coly designed in 1909 Ottawa's first structure in poured concrete, Murphy-Gamble's department store on Sparks Street, later Simpson's, and now offices for the Bank of Nova Scotia. He also worked on what is now the National Press Building, and remodelled Earnscliffe.

CHAPTER 6

Office Politics

A good deal of anxiety begins to manifest itself among officials as to the probable official position of all and sundry after Confederation. Also as to salaries.

Edmund Meredith;
diary entry; April 10, 1867

Whenever Meredith writes about office politics in his diary, we come closer to his own bone than at any other time. We are also granted an intimate glimpse into how Official Ottawa actually worked during the period immediately before and immediately after Confederation, the years of Macdonald's first premiership and of Alexander Mackenzie's brief and troubled stewardship, the years of the Fenian scares, of the Pacific Scandal, of the first tentative opening up of "the Great Lone Land."

By the standards of that era, Meredith was far from a typical servant. Unlike most of his peers, he was deeply interested in the development of what a later generation would describe as "sound public policy." He wrote half a dozen major policy papers on prison reform and pursued this passion until the end of his life. He also wrote extensively about "global" issues, such as the quarrel between the United States and Canada over the Oregon boundary ("54/40 or Fight!") and about the probable effect of the gold discoveries in California and Australia on world inflation. As Chairman of the Civil Service Board, a position to which his colleagues elected him year after year, he prepared long memoranda on such matters as the establishment of departmental reference libraries.

Yet more unusual, Meredith was renowned for being resolutely non-partisan. Between 1873 and 1878, he weathered the lifted eyebrows of John A. Macdonald and the even testier glances of his close friend Charles Tupper to serve the Liberal government of Alexander Mackenzie as cheerfully and efficiently as he had served the Tories.

Yet Meredith, like all civil servants of every era, was concerned most of the time by immediate exigencies: his title, his salary, his bureaucratic territory. Much of the routine he followed was dull and monotonous: a round of committee meetings and memos and filing cabinets. Still, as a senior deputy minister he was at the heart of events, and was well informed about most of them. He knew the Fathers of Confederation with all of their warts: Macdonald's incessant drinking; the egotism of George-Etienne Cartier, Macdonald's partner in Confederation; the bitter rivalry between Cartier and the golden-voiced prophet of Confederation, Thomas D'Arcy McGee.

Beyond all this, Meredith helped set the tone for Official Ottawa, as it began to take shape and began to acquire the forms and functions and conventions and codes that have defined the city's inner life ever since. Let us join him in his office then, on Monday, May 6, 1867, a balmy though drizzly day in springtime, when the future direction of post-Confederation events is still uncertain.

For Meredith, the day promises to be one of more than usual interest. On the weekend John A. Macdonald, still two months away from his Confederation Day knighthood, had returned to Ottawa for the first time in six months, having travelled to London to watch the final passage of the British North America Act through Westminster. Of equal, if not of more interest to Meredith and everyone else, Macdonald, who is fifty-two and has been a widower for a decade, has brought back with him a thirty-one-year-old bride, already known to many as Miss Susan Agnes Bernard, the prim, plain but undeniably clever sister of his long-time private secretary, Hewitt Bernard. "Miss B. is running a slight risk!" Meredith noted in his diary when this news reached Ottawa, echoing the sentiments of everyone in town.

Also returned with Macdonald, as is of as much import to Meredith, is Meredith's immediate political master for the past several years, William McDougall, Provincial Secretary for the Province of Canada.

The rain has let up for the moment, as Meredith steps briskly up to the East Block from Wellington Street, and the clock in the Centre Block tower measures precisely 9:30 A.M. Meredith would much prefer to begin at the more civilized bankers' hour of 10:00 A.M. –

The Parliament Buildings and the East Block as seen from Elgin Street in June 1867. Meredith's handsome office was on the second floor.

post-breakfast family prayers are a never-missed part of the daily routine, all the more so for having been a condition of his mother's will – but when he floated that balloon in a memo to his fellow deputy ministers, they overruled him. Still, the working day ends at four and includes a two-hour break for lunch. And though the working week includes Saturday mornings, on Thursday afternoons it is customary for the wives of ministers and senior officials to come in for tea. Once in a while, when she feels up to it, Fanny brings the older children. In May of 1867, however, Fanny is eight months pregnant and feeling decidedly under the weather.

Edmund Meredith. His problem was that he was a civil servant far ahead of his time.

Meredith has on his standard rig-of-the-day for the office, minus the heavy serge overcoat and thick leather mitts he wears November through April. In the manner of all men of substance, this consists of a dark, double-breasted jacket trimmed with grosgrain around the lapels, nipped in at the waist and reaching almost to the knees, worn over narrowly-cut trousers of grey worsted with (since he is a bit of a dandy) an elegant black stripe down the side. Under the jacket, or "Prince Albert" as it is commonly known, Meredith wears a double-breasted waistcoat with a heavy gold watch-chain looped over it, a stiffly-starched shirt with a high collar fixed with a large pearl stud, and a narrow black cravat. Given the circumstances of the weather, he is most likely carrying a large black umbrella; given the muddy condition of the streets, he may be wearing the new-fangled indiarubber galoshes that, like everyone else in Ottawa, he refers to as "gums." His regular, in-between-season weekday hat, now that the astrakhan pillbox he so much fancies is laid up in mothballs, has a hard, flat top and is about halfway as high as the silk topper he wears on Sundays and to go out calling.

On his way to work, Meredith has been polishing his rendition of *Horatius at the Bridge* just under his breath. The seventieth and final stanza dies unspoken: going in through the arched oak door under the southwest tower, he nearly collides with the premier-elect, the arrival of whose carriage he was too much absorbed in Ancient Rome to notice.

These two bow to one another gravely, and proceed together up the shallow stone stairs to the second floor. Meredith notes that, as usual, Macdonald is dressed a bit too flamboyantly for his own discreet taste: a dizzying array of checks, a loud glen jacket over trousers of houndstooth. It is on the tip of his tongue to offer congratulations to Macdonald on both the successful achievement of the BNA Act, and his marriage. Halfway up he decides not to: the Premier has the rumpled, cranky look of being, in Meredith's phraseology, "on the burst."

Sir John. A. Macdonald. Like Benjamin Disraeli, he dressed flamboyantly.

At the top of the stairs, Macdonald heads into his corner office with a slight lurch, pulling himself together to acknowledge, with a smile and non-committal wave of his hand, a noisy queue of office-seekers lined up to accost him. These as a hopeful gesture, shout "Hip-hip-hoorah!" Meredith turns right, and walks two-thirds of the way down the south corridor to his own office, Number Five. The room just to the immediate right of Meredith's, a small narrow space dominated by a handsome rose window, is occupied by departmental messengers; even this early in the day, they are lounging around, gossipping and playing cards. To the left of him, in Number Six, his two junior clerks – Henry Steele and Nazaire Tetu – are working on stools at tall pine desks; his Chief Clerk, Fanny's cousin Grant Powell, has his own separate office *en suite*. Meredith pokes in his head to nod good morning to all these people, and beckons Powell to come into the inner sanctum.

Powell gets out his pipe – Meredith himself does not smoke – and the two exchange a bit of family gossip, concerning firstly, Fanny's state of health and secondly, the state of Willy Jarvis's marriage which even as early as 1867 is known to be shaky. Then they move onto shop. Powell mentions that their minister, McDougall, has just a few minutes previously stomped into his own office without saying hello, banged the door, and sent out a message that he wishes to receive no one today. "He was rather ignored at the railway station on Saturday," is Meredith's conclusion.

The two go on to discuss a matter of greater consequence that may be haunting McDougall: the question of his position, as an old Clear Grit, in the new post-Confederation cabinet. Even at the best of times, they reflect, McDougall is a difficult master. He's able enough, but his manner is cold and repellent. He is also a man with some extraordinary bees in his bonnet. He keeps on beleaguering the government architects with the suggestion that the *exterior* stone of the Parliament Buildings ought to be painted, preferably green, to harmonize with the surrounding scenery.

OFFICE POLITICS

The Honourable William McDougall; a difficult man to work for.

For Meredith, the bee that has stung him personally is that it was McDougall, back in 1865, who bullied him into investing in the disastrous "oil lands" at Sarnia. Powell forbears from bringing this up. Edmund's propensity for getting involved in costly flyers would be a family joke if it weren't so expensive: post-oil, to Grant's and Fanny's horror, he has gotten himself involved in an even shakier scheme for cutting peat.

Cranky as McDougall is, Powell ventures, life in the office is smoother and simpler when he is on hand. Meredith immediately grasps the reference. While McDougall was off in London, Meredith and Powell had the very devil of a time dealing with his brother and son, to whom McDougall had given the run of his office. "The two McDougalls open all the official letters and distribute them," Meredith had written in his diary. "They insist upon having all newspapers and telegrams brought to them in the first instance. This appears to me to be a most outrageous form of impertinence as well as a gross violation of official property; the public correspondence being in this way submitted to the inspection of two perfectly irresponsible [figures] in no way connected with the government." Meredith had no alternative but to complain to Adam Blair, President of the Executive Council, the senior minister minding the shop while Macdonald was away. "Mr. Blair himself opened the letters," he noted next day. "The McDougalls very savage."

Such are the joys of serving Her Majesty's Government in the colonies, reflects Meredith, as Powell departs and he turns to the business at hand. Today's incoming letters and telegrams are piled up in an "in" basket made of woven wicker; in front of him, in the tall, leather-bound ledger that, like everyone else, he calls his "letterbook," are the copies of all his own outgoing correspondence carefully transcribed onto foolscap in the copperplate handwriting of his clerks. Opening the mail is not a task Meredith approaches with relish; most of the business contained is routine and repetitive, much the same kind of business he has been dealing with daily for almost the last twenty years. On the organizational chart of the Province of Canada, now just about to pass into history with the coming of Confederation, the Office of the Provincial Secretary has functioned much as the provincial departments of municipal affairs will in future. Among other things, Meredith has rubber-stamped hundreds of appointments to local boards and councils, and scrutinized scores of municipal financial returns. Many of these duties have concerned "matters of a merely local or private nature" as Section 92 of the new British North America Act defines them; soon, they will be transferred to the new provincial governments, leaving Meredith's future undefined.

Meredith reaches for the copy of the BNA Act that is in his in-basket, and ponders it for a while. The only part of his empire he really cares about holding onto, he reflects, is his alternate job as Chairman of the Prison Board. His annual reports on the prison system, he likes to pride himself, could stand scrutiny as models of their kind even at Westminster. As a kind of Wilberforce in the colonies he has laid the groundwork for important reforms. Ahead is the urgent need to establish reform schools, so that twelve-year-old stealers of apples and pencils will no longer be led further astray by hardened criminals.

Meredith arrives at subsection 28 of Section 91 of the new Act, rereads it, and, reaching for a pencil, underlines it. This, he reflects, is the reassuring part; to Ottawa is accorded "the establishment and maintenance and management of penitentiaries." But then, in the margin, he places a question mark, and then adds another, and another. For there is also the disquieting knowledge that after Confederation, the Prison Board, like all other Dominion-appointed bodies, will have to accommodate a huge flood of office-seekers from the new provinces of New Brunswick and Nova Scotia. By hook or by crook, Meredith remarks to himself, he must catch Macdonald in a sober moment and lay claim to his future.

All Meredith has to go on, with Confederation less than two months away, is the memory of "a long, confidential chat" of a year earlier that Macdonald, more likely than not, has forgotten. Meredith's recollection of it in his diary provides a rare glimpse into Macdonald's unmatched reputation as master of the art of "soft-sawdering" anxious and importunate colleagues.

In this meeting of May 28, 1866, as Meredith recorded it, Macdonald first played around with generalities. "He spoke much of Confederation, which he regards as a fixed fact." Then he took Meredith into his confidence, and passed on some gossip. "Lord Monck to get an English peerage. He also said a very large number of the Opposition were buyable and bought and named. . . ." When at last Macdonald arrived at something approaching the point, however, he veered off on a political tangent.

> He then told me that he was to have the arrangement of distribution of offices between the Confederate and local governments, and that he intended to hand over all the loose and doubtful fish to the local governments where they would be clearly watched and killed off like nits.

At last, Macdonald leaned forward and addressed Meredith directly.

> He spoke to me in very complimentary terms. He added that he intended to form a committee to advise with him on the subject of the distribution of the existing offices and that he intended making me one of the Committee with Bernard, and just possibly Langton [the Auditor General]. Bernard, however, had been just a little spoiled, and he did not intend to spoil him any more.

All very encouraging. Except that Macdonald had managed to end the interview without saying anything about the Prison Board. And, a year later, as of this May morning in 1867, the Advisory Committee has yet to be established.

While Meredith has been chatting with Powell, and brooding about his prospects, most of the morning has already drifted by. Today's correspondence, luckily, is not very onerous. He pulls a few sheets of paper from the pigeon-holed wooden stationery tray in front of him and drafts a few quick replies. Like most up-to-the-minute gentlemen, Meredith uses a wooden pen, with a detachable steel nib. A few of his older colleagues however – Fennings Taylor, Clerk of the Senate, for one – insist on clinging to the old-style quill. Other letters he marks for distribution and, by pressing the brand-new electric buzzer that hangs down over his desk on a long cord, summons a messenger from next door to take them round. Then he leans back in his chair and lets his eyes run round the room.

As Meredith, for all that he hates Ottawa, can't help but admit, this "Eastern Departmental Building" (as he tends to call it much more often than "East Block") is unquestionably the handsomest and most modern office building in the country. His own office is airy and sunny, a spacious high-ceilinged room, painted yellow and with an expansive view southwards towards the Rideau Canal. As a deputy minister, Meredith rates the status symbol of a tall glass-fronted bookcase where he secretes away, among august tomes on prison reform, such slender frivolities as *Aurora Leigh* by Mrs. Browning. A much more important status symbol, given that the hot-air heating system, made visible by a vent high on the wall, operated by a long tasselled cord, does not work, is the fireplace on the west wall framed with a pointed arch of sandstone. The best status symbol of all, reflects Meredith, considering the uncertain state of washing arrangements at home, is the small marble washbasin in the corner, primly hidden behind a curtain on a curved brass rod, with a tap that produces clear cold water – for the East Block is equipped with its own water-supply. Meredith, on impulse, springs up from his desk. In any event, it's nearly time for lunch and today, instead of going home for cold mutton left over from yesterday's joint, he and Powell have decided to look in at the Rideau Club and catch up on the gossip. He walks over to the basin and turns on the tap. Just for the sheer, joyful profligacy of it, he stands and watches water run.

In 1867, as in 1865, the Rideau Club occupied space in Doran's Hotel, about two blocks to the west along Wellington Street.* When Meredith and Powell arrived there that rainy Monday they were probably joined by most of the men who made Ottawa tick. Besides its leisurely pace, the most striking feature of the milieu in which they worked was how small it was. The entire Ottawa bureaucracy comprised only about three hundred and fifty clerks and officials, all comfortably ensconced within the East, West, and Centre Blocks. Meredith was one of only nine deputy ministers.*

In all its institutional essentials, the civil service was still much the same as it had been when Meredith joined in 1847. Getting in was mostly a matter of who one knew and of one's political connections. Patronage aside, seniority mattered far more than merit – to the point that Meredith, with his twenty years of service, ranked almost as a newcomer. William Henry Lee, Clerk of the Privy Council, and dean of the civil service, had joined in 1821.

Within this civil service, there was little room for either initia-

* The club remained at Doran's until 1870. Between 1870 and 1876 it occupied space above the Queen's Restaurant, and in 1876 its own premises were erected at 84 Wellington Street, just opposite the main gate to Parliament Hill. It remained in this commanding positon until 1979, when the building was destroyed by fire. Nowadays, the Rideau Club occupies a suite of rooms in a downtown office tower.

* There was also an "Outside Service" which comprised about two thousand employees scattered across the country, from steamboat inspectors, through lighthouse keepers and customs officials. Then as now, however, the only bureaucratic power that mattered was centred in Ottawa.

tive or excellence. "The price of a commission is the free exercise of a glib tongue," wrote an anonymous contributor to *The Canadian Monthly* in November 1876 who, judging both from the style and from the fact that Meredith occasionally wrote signed articles for this journal, may well have been Meredith himself. "Serve the party day and night, secure us an electoral triumph by fair means or foul, and you shall be quartered for life on the public treasury. . . . To the well-informed, trained and experienced member of the service there is little chance of advancement when one of these gentry stands in his way." Occasionally, a far-sighted politician, such as D'Arcy McGee in 1864, fulminated against the "sterile system" that advanced incompetence and repressed ability. But it simply never occurred to most politicians, first and foremost among them Macdonald, to be bothered about sound administration or managerial efficiency. As for the notion of a politically neutral civil service, this, as the premier once remarked, "was like trying to put Canada back to the age of Adam and Eve, before the apple."

Meredith, however much he chafed within the system, did have some compensations. In the mid-1860s, his pay of $3,600 a year (less $400 deducted for pension) was exceedingly comfortable, roughly the same as that for a full professor at the University of Toronto, and quite astronomical next to an average salary for teachers of about $450. And as always, the civil service invented discreet perks for itself. A letter of 1866 shows Meredith writing to Lord Monck's secretary requesting permission for senior civil servants to use the new covered tennis court at Rideau Hall when the Governor General was out of town.

There was also the fellowship afforded. Meredith, always good at making friends, moved easily among the pioneer mandarins. He organized banquets for them at the Rideau Club – "very fair," he wrote of one in 1869, "but our pleasure was marred by the constant groaning of the dumbwaiter which finally collapsed utterly." He called on their wives and daughters on New Year's Day and played whist and bezique with them during the long winter evenings. All of these individuals, as little remembered as Meredith would be but for his diary, lived much the same kind of upper-middle-class life. Two of them, because they turn up so frequently in Meredith's accounts, deserve a more extended mention. Most likely, on May 6, 1867, they were among the group who gathered for lunch at the Rideau Club.

Auditor General John Langton, the august presence with a long white beard whom we glimpsed in the previous chapter going into

St. Alban's, held the commanding position in the civil service that the Deputy Minister of Finance occupies now. Just the positioning of his office bespoke his power: Number One in the East Block, first office to the right of the main door. Like Meredith, Langton was a gentleman emigrant; he had come out in the 1830s, after the family fortunes, amassed in the mercantile business in Russia, had been lost in speculation. He had taken up land by Sturgeon Lake, not far from Lakefield where the writer Susanna Moodie and her husband were attempting to farm. Unlike his hapless, unhandy neighbours, Langton quickly got on top of events in Canada; having served as a member of the legislature, he was appointed first Auditor General in 1855.* Nor, in contrast to the somewhat diffident Meredith, did Langton shirk in asserting his authority. In a letter to his son, he explained how he managed the politicians. "An Order in Council must necessarily be authority enough for me and precludes my inquiring whether the O.C. is founded upon just grounds," he wrote. "But if I report upon a claim for money, it is not very easy for them to pass an order contrary to my report."

* Langton's letters home, published in 1926 under the title *Early Days in Upper Canada*, give a more cheerful if less riveting picture of life in the bush than Susanna Moodie's famous journals.

Langton, by Meredith's account, was a man somewhat given to taking umbrage. In 1869, for instance, there was a very sticky fortnight when Meredith, in his capacity as President of the newly formed Ottawa Literary and Scientific Society, asked Langton to give an address on the subject of a revolutionary new telescope called the "Spectroscope" and then inadvertently upstaged him by saying too much about the subject in his own presidential address at an intervening meeting. "I had no intuition that he would in the least mind my going at the subject . . . however, he was very angry indeed." It wasn't until the very day of the promised lecture that Langton was mollified, and then only partially. "Instead of delivering the promised speech on The Spectroscope, he delivered a very interesting lecture on the sun's eclipse of 1869."

John Langton, Auditor General. Meredith was always a little in awe of him.

It would have taken a saintlier man than even Meredith not to be more than a bit pleased when, a few months later, as he reports, the newspapers in Ottawa and Toronto published "several very contemptible" articles attacking Langton for the extra stipend on top of his regular salary that he received as Secretary of the Treasury Board. Civil servants in those days were fair game for press gadflys. But in keeping with the period style of partisan journalism these attacks were decidedly personal. "If Mr. Langton cannot properly be called a prig," wrote the Toronto *Telegraph*, "he is certainly the very incarnation of pedantry of the most offensive kind." Reading this, the politician William McDougall, whom we can assume that Langton with his pecksniffian questions about expenditure had crossed many times, could scarcely contain his glee. "Mr. McDougall told me that he had discovered the author of the attack," reports Meredith on July 9, 1869, "and hinted they were two men in Langton's own department. I never saw Mr. McD. so genial and communicative."

Pedant or no, Langton was tough enough and able enough to survive all assaults, ministerial or journalistic. Having laid the foundations for a system of governmental budgeting that in almost all respects endured right up to the Glassco Royal Commission of the 1960s, he retired in 1878 on his seventieth birthday, when, reports Meredith, "We all drank his health." Langton died in 1894.

G. C. Reiffenstein was the very antithesis of a pedant. He was the Confidential Clerk in the Receiver General's department, Langton's next-door neighbour but two in the East Block. But when Reiffenstein first turns up in Meredith's diary, soon after they'd both arrived in Ottawa, it is as the cheerful, voluble giver of the best parties in town. As a fellow pillar of St. Alban's Building Committee, Reiffenstein organized a raffle for the building fund and, out of his pocket, provided a pony for the prize. Often Reiffenstein appeared on the guest list at Edmund's and Fanny's dinner-parties; the Merediths apparently thought so highly of him that on one occasion he shared their table with the Minister of Finance, John Rose and his elegant wife, Charlotte.

G. C. Reiffenstein in May 1869. A month later he was arrested in the midst of giving a dinner party.

Reiffenstein's fall was catastrophic. On Sunday, June 27, 1869, the news raced round Ottawa: the Confidential Clerk had been arrested for forgery, *at his own dinner table!* After the fact, Meredith attempted to be wise. "No one much surprised at the news," he wrote, "seeing that his extravagant mode of life for years past has been the constant puzzle of everyone who knew his means." Next day at the office, Meredith got the full story. "This reads like the chapter of a novel! Singular to say, he had invited Mr. McMicken, the police magistrate, to dine with him Saturday. McMicken did not dine, but sent his police officers in his stead, who arrested."*

For St. Alban's parishioners, the whole affair could scarcely have been more embarrassing, all the more because the rest of the Reiffenstein family, demonstrating no sense whatever for the fitness of things, continued to turn up Sunday after Sunday in their regular pew. On August 8, 1869, Meredith wrote, there was a truly dreadful scene. "Dr. Jones preached a sermon on the Pharisees and the Publican, sermon . . . most telling." Near the end Mrs. Reiffenstein screamed, and threw herself on her daughter Carrie's lap. "Dr. Jones . . . was terribly distressed."

* Gilbert McMicken was commissioner of police for the Dominion, and is best remembered for establishing an efficient information-gathering network during the Fenian raids. He was, in other words, Canada's first "spook."

At Reiffenstein's trial the following spring, his indictment on forty-seven separate counts took nearly two-and-a-half hours to read. The facts brooked not the shadow of a doubt: he was convicted of having milked the municipal and debenture fund of Upper Canada of $1,687.50 and was sentenced to four years in Kingston Penitentiary. Reiffenstein, however, was nothing if not a man of style. In January 1873, he was no sooner out on parole than, to the horror of his former colleagues, he was back in Ottawa. "Meeting of deputy heads in view of Reiffenstein's return," wrote Meredith. "Feeling as to the mode of receiving him unanimous. Sir J. expressed his views tersely to Langton. 'Cut him like any other felon.' "

Yet at St. Alban's, on the next Sunday, with a sense of theatre that even Meredith, deep down, could not fail to admire, "Reiffenstein took a seat on the same bench with me, looking imperturbable." It is good to be able report that Reiffenstein managed to restore his reputation and functioned well beyond the turn of the century as, of all things, a successful insurance agent.

This, however, is running ahead of the story. We must return to the business at hand, events taking place on May 6, 1867. One of those who does not choose to join the convivial group at the Rideau Club is John A. Macdonald. For one thing, he has no wish to be buttonholed by Edmund Meredith, who he knows perfectly well is anxious to talk to him, as are so many other nervous civil servants. For another, having forsworn all morning while getting through piled-up paperwork, the Premier is sorely in need of a nip. We find him in his corner office, just rising from his handsome mahogany double-sided "partner's desk." He pours himself a generous three fingers from the decanter on the side table then walks over the window and stares out thoughtfully.

Macdonald's office, we can observe, is an extremely pleasant setting in which to have a pre-lunch drink. The walls are a rich, soothing dark green, and it boasts, among other embellishments, a handsome carpet patterned with flowers, an elaborate cream plaster cornicing picked out in turquoise, a fireplace that, while similar in size and shape to Meredith's sandstone one, is made of a much more elegant blue-veined marble, and a large red-leather chesterfield. Macdonald, in later years, will have further reason to be glad his room is so homey: in the spring of 1870, after a sudden attack of gall-stones, he will spend almost a month bedded down here. This is also a room that Agnes Macdonald will soon come to know as well as her own parlour. Often, she will drop in to collect Sir John at the end of a working day, and a few months hence she will sketch a charming picture in her diary. "Driving down in a sleigh, I really cowered from the keen wind which though light, swept over tracts of snow and brought its icy particles dashing against my face through the meshes of my cloud. I waited for Sir John, sitting meanwhile on the broad windowsill, finished *The Last Chronicle of Barset*."

Ten doors down the western corridor lies the office of Macdonald's great ally in making Confederation, the Montreal member George-Etienne Cartier, soon to become Minister of Militia.

For more than a decade, these two have shared not just a close working relationship but the warmest of friendships; they even share a taste for reading racy French novels. It would be pleasant to drop in on this liveliest and most entertaining member of cabinet, but Cartier today is out of town, and will not return for another week. Having accompanied Macdonald to London, he stayed on for railway business and then took a holiday on the continent. More likely than not, Macdonald and others suspect, Cartier is travelling in the company of his mistress, an astonishing woman named Luce Cuvillier, a brilliant sophisticate who is said to wear trousers in the privacy of her country home and to stomp around smoking cheroots in the style of George Sand.

Many in Ottawa care little for Cartier, with Agnes Macdonald at the head of the list. "Always full of life and pleasant chattiness," in her opinion, "but exceedingly egotistical." Agnes does not care much for French Canadians in general, which is a matter of considerable chagrin to Macdonald. "These divided nationalities must be wonderfully difficult to legislate for," she soon confides to her diary. "The French seem always wanting everything, and they get everything."

Out at Rideau Hall, where such prejudice does not exist, Cartier is a particular favourite. "His laugh is so funny," the Governor General's sister-in-law, Feo Monck, has recently written home, "it goes rattling on so long and loud . . . he sang, or croaked after dinner and made everyone he could find stand up, hold hands and sing a chorus."

Cartier's office, even when empty, exudes his personality. It is a room riotous with colour: the carpet a vivid turkey red; the walls a deep beige-gold. Cartier chooses to work at a table instead of a desk; his room is also equipped with up-to-the-minute Venetian blinds to keep out the westering sun.*

* In later years, beginning with Laurier and continuing through to Lester Pearson, the office then occupied by Cartier served as the office of the prime minister.

THE PRIVATE CAPITAL

Beyond the magnificent etched-glass doors at the end of the corridor lies the suite of offices that serve as the cabinet chambers. Here the atmosphere is particularly festive, almost like a ballroom. The walls are a rich ivory, stencilled with a subtle pattern of gold flowers, the ceiling is palest mauve, the cornicing a pale powder blue. Over the splendid, leather-topped table, an ornate gas chandelier of the most advanced model swoops down low over ministerial heads. Civil servants like Meredith know this sanctum sanctorum only by repute. Only the Clerk of the Privy Council, who sits off to one side

The old Council Chamber.

at a small schoolboy desk, is privileged to enter. During the most critical of cabinet debates, even he must leave the chamber. There is a hinged box, divided into two sections, at the head of the table, and when the Clerk slips back into the room at the end of the meeting, he finds proposals approved deposited in one side of the box, proposals rejected in the other.

The ante-room of the cabinet chamber serves ministers of the Crown as a small, clubby dining room. Here, at almost half-past one, Macdonald at last arrives. Along with cold beef and mutton, sherry, port, and whiskey are all available at about $2.50 the bottle. Macdonald, this day, decides to celebrate his return to the capital and the advent of Confederation. He does not return to his office. Instead, as Edmund Meredith records disapprovingly, "John A. carried out of the lunchroom, hopelessly drunk. What a prospect Mrs. John A. has before her!"

Monday, July 1, 1867, the long-awaited day of Confederation, dawned in the capital hot and sunny. At eleven o'clock, Lord Monck, the Governor General, arrived at the East Block to swear in the new Cabinet, and to inform John A. Macdonald of his knighthood. At noon, there was a splendid military review on Parliament Hill, marred only by a single mishap when, as the local papers reported, "The Civil Service Rifle Company fired a *feu-de-joie* but forgot to remove their ramrods which sailed gracefully over Sparks Street." Later, in the golden afternoon, St. Alban's parishioners and their children assembled for a Sunday School picnic at New Edinburgh at which even the Reverend Dr. Thomas Bedford-Jones got quite carried away and challenged a local judge to a piggyback race. Later still, after sunset, the Ottawa City Council put on a magnificent display of fireworks.

Edmund Meredith, alas, took part in none of the fun. He was laid up at home in bed, as he had been for the whole of the past fortnight, with a nasty attack of jaundice, the one serious illness of his life. "My liver has gone wrong," he wrote dolefully, "and I have been consequently in a sorry plight." Contemplating his yellowed countenance in the mirror, he was reminded of the American Civil War recently past, "one of those horrible photographs of the Northern prisoners in Libby Prison."

Meredith's spirits matched his physical condition. He had never had the long-sought-after interview with Sir John. Nor had Sir John had the courtesy to inform him in person of what he had long suspected: he would soon be replaced as Chairman of the Prison

Board by a Nova Scotian. Instead, on May 24, Meredith found out by the grapevine.

Early in September, after convalescing at Rivière du Loup, Meredith set out on his last duty for the Prison Board, an inspection tour of the Maritime penitentiaries now under Dominion jurisdiction. But he had attempted too much too soon. In Saint John the illness recurred and, instead of proceeding on to Halifax, he had to spend ten days holed up in a boarding house which, though perfectly comfortable, afforded nothing in the way of reading material beyond a single novel by Mrs. Gaskell.

He returned to the office in mid-October, still a bit wobbly, to find that the cantankerous William McDougall had become Minister of Public Works, with offices in the West Block, and had been replaced by a minister from the new province of Nova Scotia, the pleasant and courtly Adams Archibald. Meredith also learned that his old department had now been renamed Secretary of State for the Provinces, and that it would be responsible for correspondence between Ottawa and the provinces.

His future appeared uncertain. Equally uncertain during the tumultuous and brutally cold winter of 1867-68, appeared the future of the new Dominion.

CHAPTER 7

The Shield of Achilles

He looks like a nigger with an Irish peasant's mouth. . . . He tells capital stories.

Feo Monck, sister-in-law of the Governor General, describing Thomas D'Arcy McGee.

If there was one vision of himself that Edmund Meredith had never entertained, it was that of Meredith the soldier. In an age that worshipped all things military, the whole panoply of swords and epaulettes and fifes-and-drums left him totally cold. Yet during the first three years he lived in Ottawa, Meredith frequently had no choice but to spend the beginning and the end of his working day drilling to and fro across Parliament Hill, clad in the blue patrol coat and pillbox hat of a non-commissioned officer in a militia unit called the Civil Service Rifles. Although it often occurred to him that "playing at soldiers" was a trifle ridiculous for a scholarly fellow of nearly fifty, he kept such doubts to his diary.

During this period, from the spring of 1866 to the winter of 1869, Ottawa was a capital in turmoil. Much in the manner of Washington during the Civil War just ended, reports of planned invasions and rumours of civil strife dominated events both public and private.

The source of the unrest was the threat posed by the Fenian Brotherhood, a revolutionary secret society composed of Irish Americans and based in New York, whose aim it was to conquer Canada and to make it a base of operations for the eventual liberation of Ireland. In fact, the actual raids launched into Canada by the Fenians were almost as ludicrous and as muddle-headed as their goal. Yet they culminated in the single most dramatic event in Ottawa's peacetime history until the War Measures Act of 1970, the assassination of Thomas D'Arcy McGee.

"Mr. McGee met me going out of my room today," wrote Meredith in his diary. "He said Irish interests were looking up, notwithstanding the Fenians, and be hanged to them!" The date was June 21, 1866, the crisis had been going on now for three and a half months. By Meredith's account, it had begun on March 9, when "10,000 volunteers were called out," because of rumours of a massive Fenian invasion on St. Patrick's Day. The crisis escalated in April, when three hundred Fenians massed on the border between Maine and New Brunswick. A few days later, Meredith launched his own career as a soldier. "Our Civil Service is being organized into a Rifle Regiment," he wrote. "The Deputy Heads met until 5:30 electing

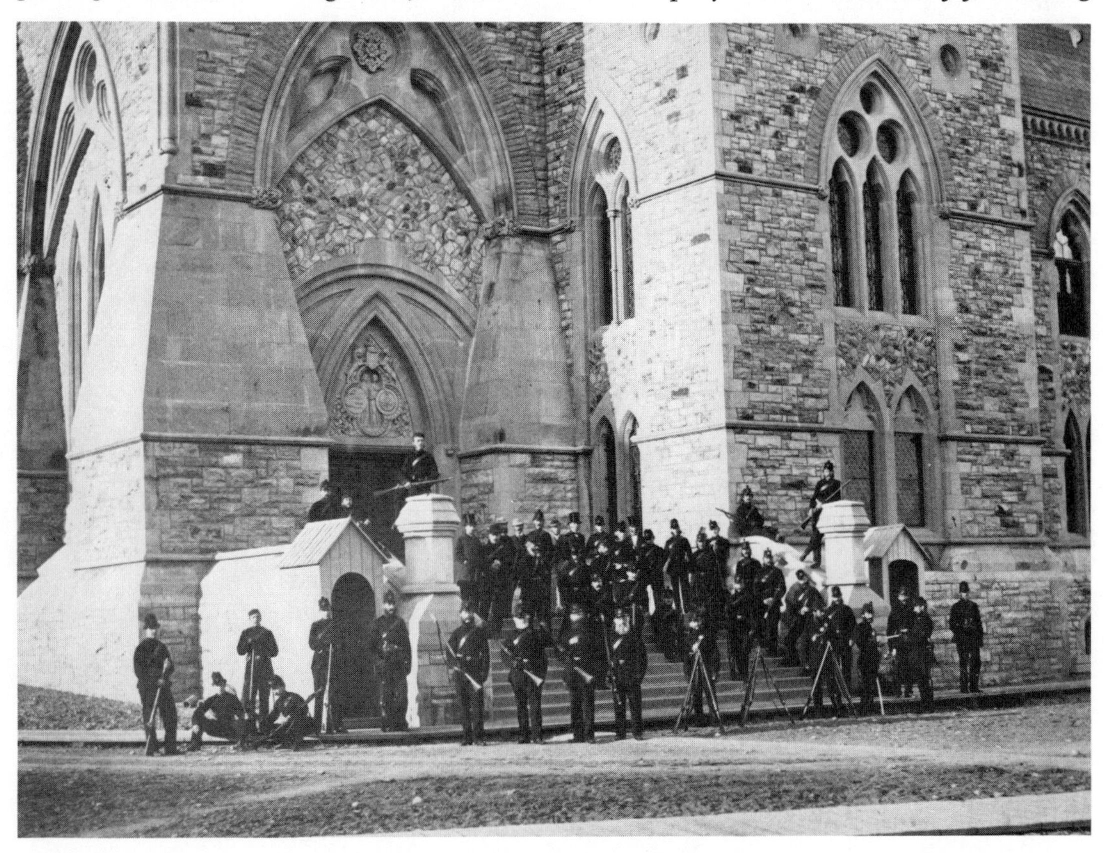

Officers and men of the Civil Service Rifles guarding the East Block.

officers." Meredith himself, as he well knew, was not officer material. Instead, he became a corporal. That same week, the regiment began drilling twice daily "at 9 and at 4; the officers have quite a military appearance and wear their uniforms during office hours." Meredith "did not get on very well with my first drill with the sword." Nor was he handy with a rifle. But he acquitted himself "quite capitally" as a marcher. Frequently, because of his height and his ability to keep in step, he was designated to be the pivot man in his company.

The real scare came late in the spring. On Friday, June 1, just before dawn, a troop of about eight hundred Fenians, mostly discharged veterans of the Union Army, under the command of a thirty-two-year-old former colonel of cavalry, John O'Neill, slipped across the Niagara River by boat, and landed near Fort Erie. Having planted the Fenian flag on Canadian soil and breakfasted at the local hotel, they spent the next two days wandering around the countryside, commandeering chickens, hams, and farm wagons. They also distributed a proclamation announcing that the Fenians had taken up the sword "to strike down the oppressor's rod, to deliver Ireland from the tyrant, the despoiler and the robber." Less like comic opera, at a spot called Limestone Ridge, a few miles west of Fort Erie, O'Neill and his men trounced a mixed force of regulars and volunteers sent out to meet them. Before the Canadians rallied and forced the Fenians to withdraw back to Buffalo, nine were dead and forty-four wounded.

An unidentified non-commissioned officer in the Civil Service Rifle Regiment. This began as a volunteer corps of clerks and officials in 1861 in Quebec City. In 1866, because of the Fenian threat, service was made compulsory for civil servants, so that Meredith had no choice but to join. The regiment was disbanded in 1868.

Canada was humiliated; Ottawa was outraged. On June 8, 1866, when Parliament met for the first session to be held in the new capital, its first act was to pass a bill suspending Habeas Corpus. "A very great assembly," reported Meredith, who had elbowed his way into the gallery. "A very great satisfaction expressed."

Walking home that night, westward along the wooden sidewalks of Sparks Street, Meredith observed a town turned into an armed camp. The streets were crammed with soldiers. Outside the East Block, a pair of sentries stood guard in wooden pillboxes, rifles at the ready. Militia units from the outlying districts marched briskly on their way to guard city hall, the railway depot at New Edinburgh, and Rideau Hall. The Carleton Blazers, the crack local unit, were mobilized at the Drill Shed on Nicholas Street. There was a sound of martial music in the air, for each time a new unit made its appearance, the ceremonial known as "crying down the soldier's credit" was carried out. A sergeant's guard with bugle and fifes and drums playing marched throught the streets; at the main corners, the sergeant, in his best parade-square voice, bawled out a warning to shopkeepers not to extend credit of more than a day's pay.

McGee was forty-one in 1866, risen to the post of Minister of Agriculture and with the excesses of youth far behind him. In 1857, after nine years as a journalist in Boston and New York, he'd found himself powerless against the tide of Know-Nothing prejudice against Irish-Catholic immigrants and had moved to Montreal. Here, where the post-famine flood of immigration had boosted the Irish to one-third of the total population, the tide of events was his for the taking. Within a year, he was elected to Parliament as representative of Irish interests. Before long, the idea of the union of all the British North Americas seized his romantic imagination.

More than Macdonald, more even than Cartier – who never got on with McGee, mostly because the Irishman was even better at singing and telling funny stories – it was McGee who became Confederation's golden-tongued prophet.* To find his metaphor, he reached far beyond the pettifoggeries of who would run lighthouses and collect taxes, beyond even the commanding vision of railways. "I see in the not remote distance, one great nationality bound like the shield of Achilles by the blue rim of the ocean," McGee told his spellbound audiences.

> I see it quartered into many communities, each disposing of its internal affairs, but all together by free institutions, free intercourse and free commerce. I see within the round of the shield, the peaks of the western mountains and the crests of the eastern waves – the winding Assiniboine, the five-fold lakes, the St. Lawrence, the Ottawa, the Saguenay, the St. John, the Basin of Minas, by all these flowing waters, in all the valleys they fertilize, in all the cities they visit in their courses, I see a generation of industrious, contented moral men, free in name and in fact . . .

It was all wonderful, blood-rousing stuff. In the minds of many British North Americans, the very name *McGee* had become almost a synonym for Confederation. Yet now, south of the border, fuelled by rifles that demobilizing Union soldiers could carry off with them for $6 each, a new force was mustering to kill the dream. For an old revolutionary, it was surely the height of ironies that Fenianism had been born out of the debacle of the Young Ireland movement of 1848 and then transported to the United States.

McGee, in fact, feared insurrection at least as much as actual invasion. Although the strength of the Fenians within Canada was never precisely known, some reports suggested that as many as

* Among many sore points between them, Cartier could never quite forgive McGee for teasing him unmercifully, time and again, and often in public. In 1860, for instance, as Alastair Sweeny reports in his biography, *George-Etienne Cartier*, McGee rose in the House to prick Cartier's vanity for having attempted to steal the show during the recent visit of the Prince of Wales:

> He has told us himself of one of the functions he discharged during that historical period – his dancing – but he modestly suppressed all references to the other constitutional duty he discharged, namely, his singing. Yet we have it set down in sundry places in a history of the visit . . . how the honourable gentleman transformed himself both on the St. Lawrence and the Ottawa from a severe Prime Minister into an amusing Primo Boffo. At one place . . . volunteering a very earnest Canadian song of emphatic accent and tender purport. Oh, Mr. Speaker, if he would only have his speeches set to music and sing them from the Treasury Bench in the manner of an operatic hero, what a saving it would be to our ears. . . .

"Baboon," muttered Cartier.

eighty of the society's seven hundred cells could be found there, principally within Irish Montreal. "He knew only too well the fascination that schemes and fantasies had for the Irish temperament," writes Josephine Phelan in her biography, *The Ardent Exile*, "and he knew how grievously Fenianism could prejudice the position of the Irish in Canada."

Not for more than another century, until the crisis of October 1970, when armoured vehicles and troops prowled the streets and sheepish lance-corporals guarded ministerial wives out shopping for groceries, would Ottawa appear as warlike as it did during the Fenian scare. These two crises strangely resemble each other. In each instance, in response to an "insurrection apprehended" the instinct for "peace, order and good government" triumphed over the bedrock principle of the common law. Like the *Front de Libération du Québec*, the Fenian Brotherhood was a conspiratorial society organized around the device of the individual cell. Fenians and *Felquistes* alike contained in their ranks muddled idealists and gangsters greedy for licence to murder. Both movements were motivated by a hatred for the British – or, as the British had become by 1970, *les maudits anglais*.

Most remarkable of all, the Fenians, as much as did the *Felquistes*, found their most dangerous opponent not among the ranks of the enemy but in one of their own kind, himself a former revolutionary turned mainstream politician, who yet considered himself an equally passionate defender of his race. The difference across a century is that unlike Pierre Elliott Trudeau, who survived the FLQ to fight many another day, Thomas D'Arcy McGee did not survive the Fenians.

Although McGee's office was just down the hall from Edmund Meredith's and they frequently passed the time of day in the East Block corridor, the two were not close friends. As a broad-minded churchman, Meredith might have been able to cope with McGee's being a Romanist – the fellow after all had been uncommonly decent about contributing to St. Alban's – but, as mattered in particular because the two were Irish, McGee, as the son of a coast guard in County Wexford, did not rank as a gentleman. Even less could Meredith, as a member of the increasingly threatened Protestant Ascendancy, erase from his memory the fact that McGee, as a fiery young journalist on the Dublin paper, *The Nation*, had gotten himself mixed up in the Young Ireland revolutionary movement of 1848 and been forced to take ship for Boston disguised as a priest. We can speculate further that Meredith, whose only real vanity was his voice, was less than charmed by the fact that McGee had an even more splendid one, and a fine florid talent for writing poetry to boot.

Thomas D'Arcy McGee. His charm was greater than his looks.

Still, by 1866, like everyone else in Official Ottawa, Meredith had come to respect and admire this squat, swarthy little figure with the map of Ireland written all over his face, whose plainness was so extreme that McGee's wife Mary, living in Montreal, was even blunter about it than Feo Monck. When a friend suggested to Mary McGee that it might be dangerous to trust a charming husband on the loose in Ottawa, she is said to have replied, "Sure, I've great faith in his ugliness." For his part, Meredith appreciated McGee's having interceded on his brother William's behalf in the matter of the Chief Justiceship at Quebec. That a formal offer of this job was just that day on its way to William had been, in fact, the hard currency of their conversation on June 21.

McGee communicated his fears of Fenian infiltration to everyone he met. "The feeling is growing that there is a large number of ruffians in our midst who sympathize with them and would join on the first outbreak," wrote Meredith after their June 21 encounter. "It is said that any day large numbers of rowdies are being brought into the country by the Grand Trunk railway and scattered all over the frontier in towns and villages."

Well into 1867, the alarms continued. For lack of any real excitement, the young bucks among the Civil Service Rifles sometimes manufactured their own. "Some of the young gentlemen of the Regiment got into a row last night, beating a policeman," Meredith noted in April. Yet, by now it was becoming apparent that the raid at Niagara had been the high-water mark of Fenianism; after that, as embarrassed American authorities reasserted control and prevented potential troublemakers from crossing the border, the movement lost its effectiveness. It helped further that one of the key members of the Fenian inner circle, a certain Henri Le Caron AKA Thomas Billis Beach, was in reality a British secret agent; at the rate of $76 a month, Le Caron provided the Canadian government, through the Chief Commissioner of Police, Judge Gilbert McMicken (that nemesis of G.C. Reiffenstein) with almost daily reports of Fenian activity. By May of 1867, Meredith had pretty well given up attending drills and was confiding tongue in cheek to his diary, "Clearly, my genius is not military." At the end of the year, on an official visit to Kingston Penitentiary where some Fenians taken prisoner at Fort Erie were being held, he was relaxed enough to be generous. "Colonel Lynch is a rather decent-looking fellow, for a Fenian."

Not so D'Arcy McGee, for whom the only decent Fenian was probably a dead one. He maintained his attacks relentlessly. He ridiculed the Fenian leaders – who were pleased to grant themselves titles like "President" and "Senator." "If their leaders were *real* rulers at Washington, would they be playing at governments?" he asked his audiences, by implication pointing to himself as an Irishman who, as a cabinet minister, wielded real power. It was also widely suspected that McGee had deliberately engineered the New Brunswick invasion scare of April 1866, in order to swing a reluctant New Brunswick into Confederation.

By now, McGee had overreached himself. His unsparing attacks on the Fenians had exposed a streak of fanaticism in his own nature. "He would admit of no compromise," writes Phelan, "no weak, hesitant sympathy. Fenians were lepers and pariahs whom Irish Canadians must thrust out, or be destroyed by them." Still more dangerously, by making no secret of being ready to play the hated role of informer, he trifled with that most cherished of all Celtic qualities: tribal loyalty. "I know many of the men who are associated with Fenianism," he bellowed. "And I say this, that if they do not separate themselves from that organization, I will denounce them to the government. There is evidence enough to hang them."

Even Macdonald, although grateful to McGee for having undermined the Fenian threat, had started to worry about overkill; in particular, Macdonald feared the damage that McGee might inflict on the Tory party by alienating the Irish vote. In the summer of 1867, as the first post-Confederation election drew near, the Prime Minister sounded distinctly dubious while writing to a prospective candidate who was also a close friend and associate of McGee's. "In consequence of your bold and patriotic course in the Fenian matter, you have alienated so many of the Catholic laity that it would be impossible to elect you." McGee himself was re-elected that year by the smallest majority of his career.

If Official Ottawa was talking much less of Fenianism by the spring of 1868, it was talking even less of McGee. Abruptly, he had become yesterday's man. He was no longer a member of cabinet, having withdrawn, none too graciously, at Confederation to make way for the additional French-Canadian representation that Cartier insisted upon. He was muttering about resigning his seat before the next election. He was in indifferent health, troubled by a painful circulatory ailment, and he was bothered by strange, portentous dreams. Still, McGee was the same charmer of old. The first week in April, when the Merediths took Louisa Nanton and her children on a tour of the Parliament Buildings, it was "kind Mr. McGee who placed little Herbert Nanton in the Speaker's Chair," Fanny recounts in her memoir.

Nor, when it came to events threatening his beloved Confederation, had McGee's enthusiasm waned. Near midnight on Monday, April 6, 1868, just as the House was about to adjourn for its Easter Recess, he rose to deliver a passionate defence of national unity, now under attack from disaffected Nova Scotians led by Joseph Howe.

After his speech, McGee accepted everyone's congratulations. He put on his overcoat and a new white top hat, and paused, at the front door of the Commons, to light a cigar. It was a clear, icy night with a full moon. He walked down the Hill in the company of another MP, said an affable goodnight, then turned right to walk alone half a block down Sparks Street, to his digs at the Widow Trotter's boarding house.

Just as McGee stooped to insert his latchkey, a shot rang out. It was fired at such close range that the powder singed his hair as the bullet entered his temple. He fell over backwards onto the wooden sidewalk. There he lay without moving, in a widening puddle of blood.

At that precise moment, Edmund Meredith was at home in his bed, sound asleep. But Lady Macdonald, in the most carefree of moods, had been sitting up by her dressing-room fire, waiting for Sir John to come home from the House. "Midnight," she'd written in her diary, "the fire is crackling and the gas singing; all else is silent and outside the soft moonlight is lying as if asleep." Then, as she added later:

> about 1/4 past 2, I heard the carriage wheels and flew down to open the door for my husband. We were so cosy after that – he coming in so cheery – with news of the debate – and sitting by my dressing room fire with his supper. . . . I was almost half asleep when I was roused by a low, rapid knocking on the front door – in an instant a great fear came

> upon me – springing up I threw on a wrapper – just in time to see John throw up the window, and hear him call out, "Is anything the matter?" The answer came up fearfully clear and hard, "McGee is murdered – lying in the streets – shot thro' the head."

All next day, Lady Macdonald "lay paralyzed" on her sofa, too distraught even to contemplate going up to the House. But Edmund Meredith, grave and sombre, shouldered his way into the galleries. "The members sat in their seats as motionless as statues," he reported, "many of them with their heads down, not a whisper was heard in the House, save the Speaker's voice, broken with emotion . . . Sir John had spoken, but was barely audible in the gallery." In many accounts, Cartier is described as having given the most eloquent tribute in which he proposed a state pension for McGee's wife and daughters and a state funeral at public expense. But Meredith, perhaps because he knew these two had never been easy in each other's company, saw things differently. "His [Cartier's] hard and unmusical voice was ill-fitted for such an occasion, and it was a relief when he sat down."

A more heartfelt tribute to McGee, because it was private and unsolicited, was paid by the Governor General, Lord Monck, in a letter back home to his son. "Never was there a more fearful occurrence . . . I always liked him *so much*."

The loss of McGee and, in Meredith's words, "his large-hearted Catholic principles," made Canada, for generations after, a narrower nation in which to live. In the spring of 1868, his death sent waves of panic through the town. "We talked of Fenianism till my blood ran cold," wrote Lady Macdonald. The next week, "Lord Monck came in after service to tell John that the Duke of Edinburgh had been fired at by a Fenian in Sydney, Australia; the feeling here is very intense." Each day now, her brother, the faithful Hewitt Bernard, accompanied Macdonald back and forth from the House as a body-guard. "I feel so much more satisfied," she wrote, "for that dreadful shadow of the murder is ever on one's mind."

Rumours of plots and counterplots and accomplices surged through parlours and East Block corridors. Even Meredith, that calm man of reason, "formed the idea that it must have been done by . . ." – but luckily for this no doubt entirely innocent citizen's posterity, the name Meredith has written is indecipherable. Among the many accounts of how people reacted, perhaps the most descriptive is that related by Lilian Scott Desbarats in her 1957 book of reminiscences. "Please remember," Lilian insists scrupulously, "I wasn't born for some years yet." Her elder sisters Fanny and "Saney" Scott, however, were already eleven and twelve, and they had told her how it had been:

> At that time, they went to school at St. Mary's Academy, which was on the south side of Wellington Street between Bay and Lyon. . . . After their lunch, they often walked to 47 Daly Street, where my grandfather lived. This they did, the morning after the murder, and Fanny described to me how, going along Sparks Street, they saw the space roped off where the ground was stained with blood and the awful horror that came over them when they were told that here their father's dear friend had been murdered. For Mr. McGee had spent the last Sunday of his life at our house and had gone away leaving his walking stick behind him. . . . I myself well remember looking at the black thorn stick and looking on it with awe as having belonged to a murdered man.

The boarding house where McGee had been living, Lilian continued, had actually belonged to Queen's Printer George Desbarats, her future father-in-law, and was part of the block that housed his printing works. "The planks of the wooden sidewalk saturated with the blood of this good and noble man belonged also to Mr. Desbarats, as they were on his property. At the request of the Mayor of Ottawa, Mr. Desbarats allowed the City to take up these planks and burn them. It would have been desecration to have them again trodden on." But as of April 15, nine days after the murder, the planks had not yet been destroyed, and were resting in Desbarats's office. On that day, as Desbarats's wife Lucianne wrote in her diary,

> . . . the brother of Mr. McGee, a young man of 25 came to the office to ask George to let him see the two wooden planks that had been soaked by the blood of his poor brother. When [George] brought them to him, the young man took off his hat, knelt down and kissed the bloodstained planks and wept. Very few of the office assistants had a dry eye.*

Desbarats, who also put up a commemorative plaque to McGee on the front wall of his printing works, suffered for his pains. Nine months later, on the night of January 20, 1869, he and Lucianne were presiding over a fancy-dress ball at their majestic stone mansion on Daly Street. This was the most glittering event so far to be

* John McGee was, in fact, McGee's half-brother. He later became Clerk of the Privy Council.

held in the new capital, for the Desbarats were a gregarious couple who enjoyed spending money. Even the new Governor General, Sir Francis Young (soon to be elevated to the peerage as Lord Lisgar), had been pleased to accept the invitation. Just as Lucianne was leading the Governor General into supper;

> A man from the printing works rushed in shouting, "your building is on fire." George tore off his costume and rushed away. Left alone with all the guests, the centre of attention, I was in an awkward position. I gave the signal to the band to play "God Save the Queen."

Nothing was left of the four-year-old building but smouldering ruins. (The plaque to McGee was found years afterwards, when foundations were being laid for the building that housed the Ottawa *Citizen* until the 1970s.) Soon after, too heartsick to contemplate the fearful cost and bother of rebuilding, Desbarats moved his family to Montreal; there, he founded *The Canadian Illustrated News*. No one knows for certain, but according to George and Lucianne's great-grandson, the television journalist and author Peter Desbarats, it is family folklore that the Fenians lit the fire as an act of revenge.

Neither is it known for certain whether or not the little tailor's ironer Patrick Whelan, one among half-a-dozen known Fenian sympathizers rounded up after the murder, actually shot D'Arcy McGee or was framed as the villain most convenient. To the very end, Whelan protested his innocence. But the fact that the bullets in the revolver found among Whelan's belongings matched precisely the bullet found lodged in Mrs. Trotter's door was accepted as irrefutable circumstantial evidence. Nor did it help his case that Whelan was alleged to have bragged to fellow prisoners, "I shot that fellow like a dog . . . there was three of us, but the others skedaddled home." Doubts lingered for years about the identity of the two others – if indeed they existed at all. "My mother would never engage the cabman Pat Buckley," writes Lilian Desbarats, "feeling he knew too much."

The outcome of Whelan's trial, which took place at the September 1868 assizes and lasted nearly a fortnight, was a foregone conclusion. The trial was also, in an era marked by a blood-lust fascination for gory detail that was no doubt an outlet for Victorian repression, the biggest melodrama to play in Ottawa for many a year. Admission was by ticket only, and virtually the whole town lined up for them. Among those few who did not try to attend –

perhaps because they were suffused with private grief for baby Clarence – were Edmund and Fanny Meredith. Lady Macdonald, however, sat through it all from first to last, in a seat close to the Chief Justice of Ontario. She has left us a moving account, not just of a "deeply, fearfully interesting" public event, but also of the play of emotions that all who witnessed it underwent.

The trial itself took place in the same shabby courtroom where the Merediths and the Macdonalds had so often bowed to each other while attending Sunday services. Now, though, it was "the ponderous judge with his ponderous notebook" and not the Reverend Bedford-Jones who presided at "the shabby desk, under the haunting picture of Her Majesty, life-size in oil, whose splendid satin robes and diadem showed strangely against the dingy wall." Whelan's defence counsel, curiously enough, was a leading Orangeman, Hilyard Cameron. But, so that justice might clearly be seen to have been done, the chief counsel for the prosecution was an Irish Catholic from Kingston, James O'Reilly, QC.

Lady Macdonald continues the chronicle:

> Shall any of us forget the scene, the shabby, anxious, gazing crowd; the ragged homespun lines of attentive jurors . . . and last but certainly not least, *The Prisoner*, sitting with folded arms within the wooden dock, listening silently hour after hour to the deliberate unfolding of his *doom*! He is a small, mean-looking yet determined man of some eight and twenty with a largish head and brownish hair brushed back, a low-wrinkled fore-head, blue, intent, cunning eyes, coarse Irish features and a long reddish beard. He dressed in black neatly with a small black tie except that on the last day but one of his trial, he wore a bright green cravat. I think that there is but little doubt that he is one of that unfortunate, misguided fraternity, the Fenians. I believe him to have been a tool in the hands of maturer and worse men, but that he was also a ruffian, a low foul-mouthed whiskey-drinking idler the evidence fully proved. Patiently, did the broad-shouldered counsel tell link after link of the chain of evidence and as each witness stepped out of the box, the impression of the prisoner's guilt seemed to increase and deepen. There was dead silence while the witnesses spoke, anxious, straining silence after the Formula of the Oath had been hurriedly given and hurriedly taken until the counsel said, "you may go," and then everyone breathed and moved and many whispered until another figure appeared in the little yellow box and the clerk began shuffling out, "You shall well and truly etc. . . ."

Like everyone else, Lady Macdonald became transfixed by the

figure of Whelan, who even to her, "after many long days," assumed a certain dignity:

> Still sat the prisoner, wonderfully collected with all eyes generally fixed on him and with the narrow margin of hope he must have had at first growing narrower as the sun went down. Once or twice, when one of the principal witnesses for the defence palpably exaggerated, or by clever cross-questioning showed that some statement was incorrect, I saw a sort of shade pass over his face, and tremor of the lines below his mouth. Occasionally too, he bit at his moustache, and stroked it roughly with nervous fingers. But he munched apples too, at intervals, and watched the flies creep on the ceiling and laughed when the Constable's foot slipped as he was about to lead him [Whelan] forth for his dinner.

On September 16, at around half-past five, the jury adjourned to its deliberations. Since the Macdonalds, like everyone else, "knew how the verdict would go," they left and drove over to the East Block, where Sir John had some papers to attend to, and then, around seven, started home for the Quadrilateral, where guests were expected for dinner at half-past the hour. Yet, as their carriage passed the court house, Sir John leaned forward and bade the driver stop:

> My husband said we would go in; we did so and nothing ever struck me more painfully than the aspect of things at that hour, in contrast to what had been going on all day. The people, finding the excitement over, the trial virtually at an end, the man's doom fixed, had gone as the people always go, their separate ways to dinner, to eat, drink and make merry, to walk, to gossip, to lounge, to chat, to sleep, who knows, leaving the wretched human thing they had so long gazed at to its lonely misery.
>
> The poor walls of the courthouse looked horribly blank and bare; some few late stayers, rough-looking men, half asleep, were doubled up on the common wooden benches of the gallery; the chairs which the ladies had occupied were empty and thrust aside. Scraps, of paper, torn envelopes, crumpled journals lay about the dusty floor; the two great staring windows made great white blanks in the darkening room. Twilight filled it, the corners were already night; two lights glared steadily, one over the judge's desk and the barrister's semi-circular table; the other a large gaslight just opposite the prisoner's box.

At this spooky, crepuscular hour, Lady Macdonald took her last look at the prisoner. The scene she sketches is out of Daumier:

> There he sat, a living pallid face against the dull background, he in the full light, a solitary figure; his guards mere masses in the gloom; with wide opened, unwinking eyes, a set face, the lines hardened by intense restraint, motionless, yet fearfully active; silent, yet passionately speaking. They tell me he cannot feel. Cannot feel! Perhaps not in the refined sense of our word, not perhaps with the details of cultivated suffering but . . . can a living healthy man, young and active, in whose veins the blood bounds quick and strong, can he know he shall be sentenced to hang by the neck until his body be dead and *not feel!* If men then do not feel then capital punishment is useless murder.

Five months later, at half-past ten on the snowy morning of February 11, 1869, Patrick Whelan was hanged. His last words, reported Meredith, who attended in his capacity as a former Prison Board Chairman, were " 'God save Ireland and God save my soul.' He showed no nervousness nor fear. He acknowledged the sins which he had committed and asked forgiveness for them."

Meredith then turned briskly to other business, as did everyone else in Ottawa. In this case, it was the matter of some distant connection of Fanny's who had recently died intestate and from whose estate there was some faint hope of a legacy. Lady Macdonald, having given birth to a daughter four days earlier, made no comment about Whelan's death in her diary.

CHAPTER 8

Undone by Sir John

Our life is like a German confederacy, made up of petty states, with its boundaries forever fluctuating.
Henry David Thoreau, *Walden*

Tuesday, July 1, 1873. A gorgeous early summer day. The blowsy peonies are dripping their last petals in Sandy Hill; the mingled scents of mock orange, sweet pea, and lavender are heady in the air. Because he has nothing whatever to celebrate on this, the Dominion's sixth birthday, Edmund Meredith has decided to spend the holiday tending his garden. These last several years, he has begun to use his diary less as a simple *aide-mémoire* than as an emotional outlet; more easily than before, we can enter his thoughts.

If very little in his official life has gone right lately, Meredith reflects, home is at last becoming habitable. By dint of much levelling and sodding and endless back-breaking rolling, he has created out of a sea of mud an admirable croquet-lawn – the greenest and most velvety in town, but for the Governor General's. Often of an evening, Dr. Tupper, by now almost a member of the family, strolls the three blocks round from his house on Daly Street for a game. Lucky indeed the previous May 13 that Tupper was on hand: Arthur, no less accident-prone at ten than at two, managed to get his eye "quite sorely cut by a mallet." But a fortnight ago, the Tuppers journeyed east to their summer place at St. Andrew's, taking Fanny and the four younger children with them. Save for the servants, and for Willy Jarvis, who is cooling his heels while waiting for word on his application for a commission in the new North West Mounted Police, Meredith and his eldest daughter Mary, who at sixteen has blossomed into an extremely capable little chatelaine, are alone in the house.

Having Willy around nowadays, Meredith reflects, as he measures the height of his Indian corn with a practised eye and counts the flowerlets on the tomatoes, almost counts as a pleasure. For Willy's problems, as recounted for the umpteenth time a couple of nights ago over "dishes of strawberries and cream at the Russell Hotel" are of the cosmic nature that make Meredith's own pale into insignificance. "He stated he could never again live with Maggie," wrote Meredith. "Poor fellow, he is very much to be pitied."

As for Meredith, his own solace of late (though generally speaking he is not much of an admirer of the Yankees) has been the writing of the reclusive New Englander, Henry David Thoreau. It is perhaps, a line from *Walden* that commends itself most. "Our life is like a German confederacy, made up of petty states, with its boundaries forever fluctuating."

Canada between 1867 and 1873 had been growing apace. Manitoba became a province in 1870, British Columbia in 1871; this very Dominion Day of 1873 the nation was celebrating the entry of Prince Edward Island. This last acquisition George-Etienne Cartier had not lived to see. He had died in London in May, of Bright's disease, with Luce Cuvillier at hand. But the boundaries of Meredith's own office empire had been shrinking. Within months of Confederation, as he'd suspected would be the case, he had very little to do. Despite his fancy new title, Under-Secretary of State for the Provinces, Meredith had been "rendered a fifth wheel to the State Coach," as he wrote gloomily in his diary. More often than not, when he came into the office he found a bare desk. "Not a single letter, official or private received today or Saturday," he noted on October 19, 1868.

As early as the spring of 1868, Meredith had set out to look for a new job – preferably a job that would take him far, far away from Ottawa and the stench of its drains. "I begin to have some notion of trying to get the Collectorship at Toronto," he wrote on March 26, 1868. This was aiming rather high, for Customs Collectorships at the major import-export centres were among the richest and juiciest of all the patronage plums in the gift of the prime minister. No doubt, having suffered manfully and without complaint the loss of his position on the Prison Board, Meredith felt that Sir John owed him one. Macdonald, for his part, while not unappreciative of Meredith's abilities, would not have had the slightest inclination to dispense such a goody to someone unable to pay for it in cold hard cash to party funds. Nor, for that matter, would Macdonald have wanted to lose from the civil service one of its best and brightest members. Between the two of them, that spring of 1868, there began a period of psychological warfare that would last for a decade and that would end in a draw.

During his seven-month campaign for the Toronto Customs Collectorship, Meredith used every ounce of influence he could summon up – and so he provides a case study of how prize jobs were bargained for. His first step, on March 28, was to send out an informal note of application to Macdonald. The Premier responded promptly, if not precisely encouragingly. "Sir John says there is a fierce fight and he does not know if he is strong enough to get it for me." By way of reinforcement, Meredith rounded up such support in the financial community as he could muster: a letter from his brother-in-law at Cobourg, and one from the Toronto businessman, R. C. Hampson. From there, he turned to the politicians: first, his former minister, William McDougall, whose moral debt on account of the money lost on "oil lands" was still outstanding; second, Alexander Campbell, the steady and thoughtful Postmaster General, who also was one of Macdonald's closest friends. Next, there was finance minister John Rose, chummiest of all Macdonald's cronies, with whom, long long ago, the prime minister had once got up to a great lark. On holiday south of the border, the two had pretended to be strolling players: Rose capering around as a dancing bear, Macdonald playing the musical accompaniment. Meredith, on May 29, 1868, found an older and wiser Rose confined to bed with lumbago and not best pleased to be importuned. "He says he has seen Sir John and done all he could for me. He says Sir J is *The Man*!" For good measure, Meredith turned to an acquaintance in Opposition, the Liberal member, Thomas Workman. "He says he feels satisfied that the appointment would be the most popular that the government could make, that all those who had had any official relations with me would support it, be they Tory or Radical."

Meredith saved his best card for last. On June 7, in the guise of saying goodbye to him, he took it upon himself to call on the Governor General, Lord Monck, soon to return to England. "He said he would speak to Sir John. He added he thought he might say, without flattery, that the government owed me something." But on June 16 – had Monck spoken or no? – Macdonald, when encountered in the East Block corridor, continued to sound evasive. "Nothing can be done about the Collectorship until he goes to Toronto. He says he is haunted about it." Soon afterwards, Macdonald left town – but not for Toronto. Instead, he journeyed to Halifax, to deal with the incomparably more haunting problems posed by the secessionist agitations of Joseph Howe.

By early autumn, all this prevarication should have warned Meredith of the way things were going. But, consumed by grief for baby Clarence and wanting more desperately than ever to get out of Ottawa, he chose not to notice. All through September and into October, he kept up his barrage. On September 10, when Peter Mitchell, the Minister of Marine and Fisheries, called at his office, "I took the opportunity of talking to him about the Collectorship. He said he thought Sir John . . . was very favourably disposed towards me." On October 12, Sir John having at last embarked on the long-delayed trip to Toronto, Meredith called once more on Rose. "He anticipated me, referring to the Toronto Collectorship. When I told him of my performance as being an argument that ought to have weight in my favour, he telegraphed the fact to Sir John at Toronto." On October 18, with Sir John returned to Ottawa, there was still a straw to clutch at. "Collectorship not given away!"

Perhaps Rose never sent the promised telegram. Perhaps none of Meredith's business supporters fattened their testimonials with contributions to party funds. As seems most likely, Sir John had never had the least intention of giving Meredith the Collectorship and had simply allowed him to hope as punishment for being so importunate as to ask for it. On October 20, the long agony was over. "The Toronto Collector is named at last. One of the great family of Smiths! Poor Fanny is greatly disappointed, so indeed am I." When Macdonald offered as consolation prize the chance to serve as one of the federal commissioners to an Intercolonial Railway Conference soon to take place, Meredith turned it down in a fit of pique. Instead, he turned his attention to matters domestic, and during November and December of 1868, spent most of his office hours preparing his pamphlet on dry-earth sanitation systems.

Round one to Macdonald. Yet for Meredith, life at the office improved considerably in 1869-70 thanks to the tide of political events. The acquisition of the new territory of Rupert's Land, soon to be renamed Manitoba, from the Hudson's Bay Company, and the appearance of the strange, messianic Métis leader Louis Riel pushed the somnolent Department of the Secretary of State for the Provinces to the forefront of events. Suddenly, Meredith was sending and receiving no end of telegrams and despatches to and from the troubled Northwest.

UNDONE BY SIR JOHN

On September 28, 1869, his former minister, William McDougall, left for Fort Garry as Lieutenant-Governor of the new territory. (The week before, to Fanny and the children's great delight, McDougall sent for his former deputy and, as final compensation for the oil lands, bequeathed him his "little horse" for the fire-sale price of $50.) By late autumn, as Riel's rebellion began to erupt, the short, staccato entries in Meredith's diary reflect the tension that gripped the capital. *November 19*: "News that Mr. McDougall has been stopped on the edge of his own territories by the halfbreeds confirmed by letter . . . this is an awkward beginning of his government." *November 20*: "Further letter from West of War. Mr. McD. in a very ticklish position; Fenian sympathizers in his rear and halfbreeds in his front." *November 21*: "So busy at the office with the Northwest disturbances that I did not take the Saturday half-holiday; matters very serious indeed." *November 22*: "News received that the halfbreeds have taken Fort Garry!"

There were times during the next few hectic months, all the way up to the summer when Colonel Garnet Wolseley and his troops put paid to the whole affair, when Meredith functioned more as minister than as deputy; the reason being that his new political chief, the old lion of Nova Scotia, Joseph Howe, rewarded with the position for having agreed to be "pacified," could hardly have been on worse terms with McDougall. Their enmity went back to a chance meeting in the wilds of Minnesota in mid-October: Howe, on his way back from a fact-finding mission to Fort Garry during which he'd encouraged the Métis to hold firm in their demands, had not stopped to warn McDougall of trouble ahead. According to McDougall's account "Howe knew that he had done me an ill turn and was ashamed to meet me." In Howe's version, "A cold north-west wind was blowing in the face of McDougall and his party," and "it would have been barbarous to have stopped the cavalcade."

Whatever the rights and wrongs of the argument, there was no doubt in Meredith's or anyone else's mind that when McDougall finally arrived at Fort Garry, on December 1, he blew his mission badly. Instead of trying to conciliate the Métis, he pushed them still further by issuing, without instructions, an illegal proclamation annexing Rupert's Land to Canada. Riel's answer was to trounce McDougall's handful of troops without a shot being fired, and to issue his own proclamation establishing his own provisional government. As Macdonald wrote in fury, "McDougall has done his utmost to destroy our chance of an amicable settlement with these wild people." In Meredith's less highly coloured version, McDougall's action had been "somewhat premature."

In January, when McDougall slunk back to Ottawa in disgrace, "very chop-fallen and sulky" in Macdonald's words, it was Meredith, now in the agreeable position of holding the upper hand, who went round to debrief him at the Russell House. "He describes the Rebellion as a Priest's Rebellion, encouraged by the Yankees . . . he has seen a copy of a letter from the U.S. Senator Sumner, encouraging the insurgents to hold out." All that winter and spring, Meredith buzzed merrily around town as the man who got to see the despatches from Red River first. "News of the shooting of Scott by Riel at Fort Garry!" he wrote on April 2. "This is crossing the Rubicon!" A fortnight later, he called round to the Hudson's Bay Company offices at Rupert House to get first-hand information from the Chief Factor, Donald A. Smith, just back from Fort Garry where he'd acted as the government's special commissioner. "He spoke freely of the great gravity of the crisis . . . introduced me to Judge Black* from Red River who says it is hardly possible to estimate the horrors through which the people have passed during the past few months, not knowing for a moment what would happen next." A month earlier, in March, there had been a heady if uncomfortable twenty-four hours during which Meredith himself became the centre of events as the result of a leak to the newspapers. "Appeared before Committee of the House of Commons on breach of privilege connected with the publication of certain Red River papers before these were laid before the House," he wrote on March 12. Luckily, Colonel Stoughton Dennis, McDougall's hot-headed lieutenant at Fort Garry, "satisfactorily cleared the affair by sending a telegram stating that it was he who had supplied the correspondence to the newspapers."

Judge John Black was one of three delegates sent to Ottawa to negotiate the terms of entry by which Manitoba would become a province.

Eventually, the action moved on. By mid-summer 1870, with Colonel Wolseley's troops departed for Red River (minus Captain Willy Jarvis whose appointment Wolseley had personally vetoed), Meredith's "In" basket once again dried up. As partial consolation there was the pleasure of chatting with Howe, who, unlike the moody and taciturn McDougall, delighted in passing on gossip: the tidbit, for instance, that Meredith recorded on May 30, 1870, when Sir John lay ill in his East Block office:

> Mr. Howe told me he was urging Sir J. to take the post as Chief Justice in the proposed Supreme Court as a suitable and dignified office to retire upon. Sir John said, "I would as soon go to Hell!"

As the months went by, and it became more and more obvious that, in the words of the MP George Ross, Howe's "intellectual windows had grown frosted," Meredith grew fiercely protective of his minister, recording sadly on December 13, 1872, how "the grand old man showed some indication of failing powers by relating the same anecdote three times during dinner." Four months later, when the Howes left Ottawa for good, Meredith went to the railway depot to say goodbye. Sensing somehow that Howe had not much longer to live (in fact, he died within weeks) his diary entry was a tender epitaph:

> The Old Man Eloquent is, I think, a most lovable man in whom the coarseness, etc., of early years has been mellowed down or altogether disappeared. We ne'er shall look upon his like again.

Howe, though, was entirely in command of his faculties on November 6, 1872, when he confronted Meredith with what would prove to be the great missed opportunity of his career. "He asked me, how I should myself like to be Governor of Manitoba. I said, God forbid, and then said that irrespective of other considerations the salary was insufficient: that Mr. Archibald* had spent $13,000 and received only $8,000. I did not consider that Mr. H. was making me a serious offer of the post, but I did think he was sounding me out as to the matter."

Had Meredith accepted, he would have gone down in history as the man who, between 1873 and 1877, negotiated the five great treaties between the Dominion and the Indians of the Northwest, a work that instead fell to Alexander Morris, one-time revenue minister and an early promoter of the metric system. Neither then nor later does Meredith ever appear to have regretted the road not taken. In 1876, when Morris was in Ottawa on business and the two lunched together at the Rideau Club, Meredith's diary comment is terse and to the point. "He says that last year, he spent $4,000 over and above his official income."

* Adams Archibald of Nova Scotia, who, after serving as Secretary of State for the Provinces from 1867 to 1869, succeeded McDougall as Lieutenant-Governor of Manitoba in 1870. He later served as Lieutenant-Governor of Nova Scotia.

Money, or rather the lack of it, came to preoccupy Meredith to the point of obsession. In the 1870s Canada was mired in a deep depression yet interest rates were steep: eight per cent as we know in the case of the debt on St. Alban's. In Meredith's opinion, set forth in a long paper he prepared on the subject and published in *The Canadian Monthly*, the cause of the inflation was "the extraordinary influx of gold into the world from the apparently inexhaustible mines of California and Australia."

For Meredith, and for all other deputies without private means, the once princely salary of $3,600 (minus $400 deducted for pension) now barely covered expenses. In 1874, with the Rosedale estate long since carved up into lots and sold, Meredith felt he had no choice but to arrange secretly with Fanny's brothers Willy and Coly to sell the house itself. The decision provoked the worst crisis in his marriage. When Fanny found out, "accidentally, from a letter which without thinking I had handed to her, she threw the letter from her as if it had stung her." A few months later, at St. Andrew's, while under chloroform during Coly's birth, "She moaned that the sale of Rosedale had killed her. God knows I would have avoided the unfortunate business had it been possible to see my way towards keeping the family out of debt." A year later, in order to pay the annual taxes of $112.50 on the Augusta Street house, Meredith had to dip into an insurance policy that was rightfully the property of his eldest daughter Mary on her twenty-first birthday. And he still owed $400 on the mortgage.

As early as 1871, with his career going nowhere and not much to lose, Meredith had determined to make higher pay for deputy ministers his personal crusade. An unpopular cause, but he pursued it relentlessly.

He began at the top, buttonholing Lord Lisgar himself at an official dinner party for deputy heads at Rideau Hall on January 31, 1871. "He spoke of the D. Heads being underpaid; a fact that I admitted." A week later, Meredith took the lead in organizing a round-robin "memorial," signed by all ten deputy heads, setting out the case for increases. A year later, when nothing had come of this, he took the bull by the horns and on March 5, 1872, confronted the Postmaster General, Alexander Campbell. "I reminded him of the subject of the memorial and asked if it had been burned. He promised to have the matter brought up, saying he had never seen it." At the end of April, there was a glimmer of hope: civil service salaries were the topic of a debate in the House. "Tone favourable on the whole. Several members urged the benefits of an increase."

By autumn, when nothing more had happened, Meredith decided to hang it all and go public. On November 28, at a meeting of the Ottawa Literary and Scientific Society, in front of a "room crammed with anxious civil service men," he read a long paper titled *Wages, Prices and Fixed Incomes*. In for a penny, in for a pound, he described Ottawa as "the most expensive and least attractive city in the Dominion." "Some took exception," he wrote in his diary. "Verité hurts!" Meredith's paper appeared in *The Canadian Monthly* of January 1873, exactly as he'd delivered it but for a tactful insertion by the editors that read, "We readily admit that Ottawa boasts many natural beauties but few, besides the natives of the place will contend that compared with other cities in Canada it possesses any permanent attractions as a residence." Carefully documented and closely reasoned, written in graceful, fluid prose, the paper commands our attention as an example of Meredith's skill as a draftsman. Easy to picture the audience nudging each other, nodding, and sometimes clapping as Meredith raised his fine Dublin voice in indignation:

> *Even in Tasmania*, with a population under 100,000, with only 20 miles of railway and a revenue not equal to the Customs duties collected at the port of Toronto, and only about a quarter of those collected at Montreal, the scale of public salaries is generally higher than in Canada.

So strong were his feelings on the subject that when it came to making the inevitable comparison with the private sector, Meredith, notwithstanding a trace of self-pity, led his audience into his inner self, his frustrated hopes and thwarted ambitions.

> In Canada assuredly, the most successful official of 20 or 30 years standing – the envied possessor, it may be of one of the few prizes which the Service has to offer – even he can hardly find much reason for self-congratulation, when he compares his position with that of others who started in life with him. He cannot fail to see, on every side, many of his contemporaries at school and college, say, many of his juniors, who have already earned for themselves in their profession or in business a proud name and honourable rank, and have secured for their families a comfortable independence, while he is obscure and utterly unknown and his family, hardly, if at all, raised above actual want – and all the while he may feel keenly conscious that had he followed any other career, had he devoted to business or to any of the open professions, the same energy and zeal which he has expended on the Public Service, he, too might ere this have secured a name and position for himself and a comfortable maintenance for his family – that had he done so he would not be, as he now is, ever haunted by the feeling that at his death his wife and children must be left inadequately provided for, if not entirely destitute.

At last Macdonald, whether or not propelled by Meredith's speech, acted. On April 22, 1873, he put forward a resolution in the House to provide a cost-of-living bonus in lieu of an actual salary increase: for those in Meredith's income bracket, this would amount to about $300. Macdonald, as usual, had thought of everything.

"As the members of the Senate and H of C have their indemnity increased from $600 to $1000 and as that is embodied in the resolution," reported Meredith, "it is quite clear that there will not be much opposition to the scheme." Nor was there.

Round two, or at least a split decision, to Meredith. A split decision, however, was not enough for one in his financial straits; much better would be a new and higher-paying job. This time Meredith sought out, as principal ally, one of the most compelling of the new personalities in Ottawa: Sandford Fleming.

Of all the many gifted individuals who have served the Government of Canada, few have been more gifted than Fleming. He was a true polymath: the inventor of Standard Time; the surveyor and engineering genius behind the coast-to-coast Pacific Railway; the designer of the first Canadian postage stamp; the kind of protean figure that Edmund Meredith would have wished to be. He was also a hearty and vigorous figure who thought nothing of swimming in the Northwest Arm, at Halifax, as late as November. The other side of Fleming, as he emerges from Meredith's diary and from other accounts, is that he was probably the single most charming individual ever to wield power in Ottawa.

As Fleming's only surviving granddaughter can remember today, he always ate his breakfast porridge with a dollop of marmalade in it. He was a man who loved children; instead of trying to remember the individual birthdays of his many grandchildren and their young friends, he always sent them presents on *his* birthday instead. And these were generous presents. As we discover from Fleming's own *aide-mémoire*, when he turned seventy in 1897, he sent £3.10 in sterling to 111 people, to commemorate his own three score years and ten. Fleming was a thoughtful soul, who as Lilian Desbarats has recalled, when making a present of "gorgeous roses" from his conservatory would also make you the present of a vase in which to hold them. No one could have been more tender and loving towards the Macdonalds' painfully handicapped daughter Mary than Fleming. At childrens' parties, as Lilian Desbarats remembered, "he would hold her under his arms and make her join in the ring when we played cushion dance." At the same childrens' parties, when faced with a rascally pair of identical twin brothers named Owen and Willie, "Sir Sandford would get pen and ink out and write O on Owen's cheek and W on Willie's."

In the winter of 1873, Fleming was forty-five, a decade younger than Meredith, just on the brink of his fame. These two had been good friends since 1869, when Fleming had arrived in Ottawa and bought Chapel Court from George Desbarats. Standard Time, for instance, fascinated both of them equally. In mid-February 1873, recently returned from his epic trip from the Atlantic to the Pacific to select the route for the new railway, Fleming asked Meredith to help him prepare his confidential report to the government. By February 22, when Meredith, by his account, "had finished the confidential report to Mr. F.'s satisfaction," a new idea had begun to sprout in his mind. With Fleming's support assured, he would apply for the "Secretaryship of the Railroad," a job tailor-made for his administrative and diplomatic skills. Quickly, he enlisted the additional support of Tupper, who promised to bring all his own influence to bear.

Sandford Fleming in 1874. He was Meredith's great friend and neighbour.

In the spring, as rumours began to float round Ottawa of questionable financial dealings between Macdonald and Sir Hugh Allan, president of the railway syndicate, Fleming warned Meredith of potential dangers. "He came to see me," wrote Meredith on April 30, "expressed confidentially his grave doubts of CPR company; he thinks they have attempted to raise too large an amount of money." Meredith was unperturbed. "Had a few words with Dr. Tupper re Secretaryship," he wrote on June 19. "He told me confidentially that Sir Hugh had telegraphed that he had made arrangements for the railroad subject to approval of the Directors and the Government."

Approval by government meant the approval of only one man. On June 27, Meredith called on Macdonald. The Premier, as usual, "was very kind and polite; he talked very pleasantly about general matters." But to the only matter that counted, Macdonald gave an unequivocal "no." "He quite upset my proposed arrangements, assuring me that the government could not possibly give me my retiring allowance if I left the service now." It was equally clear that even if Meredith could have afforded to waive the allowance, Sir John would not approve the appointment. The rest of Macdonald's conversation, which only six months ago would have come as music to Meredith's ears, he barely heard. "He said he intended to recommend a large increase to the salaries of deputy heads, adding he thought much of the service was sufficiently well paid, but that responsibility was not paid enough, and that there should be a marked difference between the Deputy Heads and the next rank."

It requires no stretch of the imagination to suppose that while he weeded his garden on the morning of Dominion Day, 1873, the words uttered by Macdonald in his slightly nasal Scottish burr – "I'm afraid the decision is final, Mr. Meredith" – were playing around Meredith's mind like an angry buzz-saw. Round three to Macdonald.

Troubles never come singly, as Meredith would tell himself later that day. At noon, while Meredith is enjoying a leisurely lunch with Mary and Willy – possibly a cold chicken, some new green "pease" that Meredith just this morning has picked from the garden along with the last of the fresh strawberries, and, perhaps, since this is a holiday, a bottle of hock – the three are surprised by the clank of a carriage driving up. Yet more surprising, as Mary reports on dashing to the window, alighting from it is the short, slight, but all the same imposing figure of the Postmaster General, Alexander Campbell. Campbell and Meredith are Rideau Club acquaintances, but far from the kind of intimate friends who drop in on each other without advance warning on holidays. Something has to be up.

Campbell enters the drawing room and bows gravely to Meredith, who gestures to Mary and Willy to leave them alone. For a few minutes, the two exchange pleasantries about the fine weather and about the excellence of the croquet lawn. Then Campbell arrives at the point. There has been a major reorganization of government business, he informs Meredith, in keeping with the rapid growth of the country. A new department has been created, to be named the Department of the Interior. It will absorb both the Indian Affairs Branch and the Dominion Lands Office. It will also absorb some of the work of the Department of the Secretary of State for the Provinces. He himself has been named minister of the new department. He is extremely pleased to add that Meredith has been appointed as his deputy.

Far from feeling honoured, Meredith receives the news with bleak fury. "I am not *at all* pleased with the appointment," he writes later in his diary. "I had not heard anything of the matter before, which brings me into new work entirely."

It is all he can do to bid a polite farewell to Campbell, and to see him into his carriage. Immediately, he strides over the croquet lawn, grabs up the nearest mallet, and plays "a very fast game with Mary and Will."

CHAPTER 9

"The Superannuated Man"

I have of late become very down in mouth and weary of the sun.

Edmund Meredith; diary entry; 1877.

Had he been the least bit inclined to look on the bright side, Meredith might have realized that Macdonald and Campbell had paid him no mean compliment by naming him Deputy Minister of the new Department of the Interior. The nation, that summer of 1873, was poised on the brink of a transformational surge westward. The great era of railway-building was about to begin. "The iron horse has opened up a new era," as a newspaper of the period put it, "and the blessings of civilization will flow."

The title alone, Deputy Minister of the Interior, had a resonance. More than just the instrument of westward expansion, the new department was virtually the government for the entire Northwest. For a start, there was the Indian Affairs Branch to be administered, involving the fortunes of some hundred and forty-five thousand Indians. At the time Meredith took over, Treaty Number 3, between Canada and the Ojibways of the Northwest Angle around Lake Superior was about to be signed. More substantial were the responsibilities of the Dominion Lands Branch, which encompassed the massive trail-breaking surveys of prairies and foothills, as well as the administration of the epochal Homesteading Act of 1872, which, by providing a quarter-section of free land to anyone prepared to work it for three years, prefigured the endless miles of waving golden wheat that, by the turn of the century, would make the plains of Canada "the breadbasket of the Empire."

For many an adventurous easterner, the opening up of the West proved the making of the man. Among them, it is good to be able to report, was Fanny's brother, Willy Jarvis, who in mid-July 1873 had received his summons to join the embryonic North-West Mounted Police at Fort Garry. Within little more than a year, Willy had become a hero. In the summer of 1874, he was one of four newly-appointed inspectors who led the first troop of three hundred Mounties on their legendary march towards Fort Whoop-Up, lair of wicked whiskey traders. At Roche Percée, in what is now Saskatchewan, Willy and "A" Division split off from the main party to trek nearly a thousand miles north-westward to Edmonton, a journey that took eighty-eight days. In the official report he sent back, which Meredith took home from the office for Fanny to pore over proudly, Willy spoke no longer with the voice of a scapegrace but in the confident, tone of a commander who'd been through the fire.

> I may state that on looking back over our journey, I wonder how we ever accomplished it with weak horses, little or no pasture, and for the last 500 miles no grain, and the latter part over roads impassible until we made them. That is to say, I kept a party of men in advance with axes and when practicable, felled trees and made corduroy over mudholes, sometimes 100 yards long, and also made a number of bridges and repaired all the old ones. . . .

Willy established Fort Saskatchewan just outside Edmonton and commanded it until 1879, when he was transferred to command Fort Macleod at Calgary. He retired a few years later, to settle at Edmonton, and on his occasional visits to Toronto was received as a conquering hero. "He was the sort of uncle nephews like to have," Coly Meredith remembered, "one of his ways of entertaining me was to have me run round the lawn and he would lasso me on the run." Both of Willy's sons, adds Coly, also joined the Mounties.

Willy Jarvis – Superintendent W. D. Jarvis of the RNWMP. By now, he was a giver of advice instead of a taker.

Meredith, the unseen architect of Willy's triumphs, rejoiced in them. Yet sadly, the romantic dimension of other events he was dealing with from behind the scenes failed to capture his imagination. Perhaps, at fifty-five, he was simply too old for new challenges. Instead, he applied much of his energy to railing against his fate. "Have been during the last week so busy with the work of the new department, and so sick of everything that I have neither heart nor time to write," he informs us on July 10, 1873, just a week into the new job. Five years later, in October 1878, he was still at it, complaining of "having been pitchforked into a position most disagreeable in many ways . . . literally, a hornet's nest." First and foremost a scholar and intellectual, also a city man who had never visited the Great Lone Land nor ever evinced the least interest in doing so, Meredith in his way was the prototype of all the generations of Ottawa mandarins whose attitudes towards them westerners have raged against as uninformed and condescending.

Nor, despite his compassion towards prisoners, could Meredith empathize with the problems faced by native peoples who were being displaced from their land by the relentless push westward. Dismissively, he described them as "red children." Reading his diary account of the one occasion on which he actually dealt directly with Indians, in August 1876 while vacationing at Rivière du Loup, we can only reflect that, fond as we are of Meredith, it was just as well that the chance to become Governor of Manitoba did not appeal to him.

> Fanny and Alice drove with me to Cacouna. I found about 12 families there; they earn their living during the summer making baskets and other Indian work. They are squatters and are tolerated by the people of the village as being an attraction to the summer tourists. They are anxious to have some land secured for them in the immediate neighbourhood of the village where they can put up permanent houses for themselves. The wigwams which they occupy at present are miserable things, but they say it is not worthwhile to put up anything better on land which does not belong to them. They complain that the government does not allow them to catch fish as they used to do, nor deer, nor other game – all of which is true.
>
> They are, I fear, a very lazy crowd. Just now, when it is difficult to procure labourers to cut the grass, it never occurs to these lazy lubbers to earn a few dollars for themselves in that way.

Still, Meredith was much too much a professional not to do the best job he could, by his lights. Mostly, this involved blizzards of paperwork. "Every day reveals still further depths of arrears and hopeless muddle in the Indian Branch," he wrote on July 17, 1873. "I am well nigh in despair." Eighteen months later, with the crucial Qu'Appelle Treaty with the Saskatchewan Indians recently signed, he had almost given up hope of *ever* catching up. "The work is now of a highly responsible character and involving enormous expenditures in the Indian branch." The sheer logistics of treaty-making, all of which had to be monitored back in Ottawa, were staggering. The Fort Carlton Treaty, on which he was pleased to see the signature of Inspector W. D. Jarvis appearing as witness, took a full week of meetings to negotiate. The supplies of food, clothing, and treaty money (usually in the form of uncut sheets of one-dollar bills) that had to be accounted for were endless, and the work of making sure the right Indians received the right goods was exhausting.

Some of his subordinates compounded Meredith's problems. William Spragge, Superintendent-General of the Indian Branch was particularly irascible. After two decades of running his own empire in whatever haphazard fashion he chose, he did not take kindly to the new order. "Spragge talked today very wildly about Mr. Campbell," wrote Meredith, three weeks after taking over the job, "saying he would not mind putting a bullet through him and other things of that kind. He is really dangerous." Nine months later, the sudden death of Spragge, which Meredith found out about "from the greengrocer, while walking to the office," would have been a happy release except that his successor, Lawrence Vankoughnet, son of a great political friend of Sir John's, was no great improvement. "Spent the last several evenings rewriting Vank's report," he reports in 1875. "It was very much in need of changes." It may well have been Vankoughnet, described by the Toronto *Mail* as "an imbecile," whom Meredith had in mind when he scrawled across the bottom of one official memo, "Can't this man do anything right?"

Somehow, Meredith coped. Just how well he coped was revealed three-quarters of a century later (in 1952) when Coly Meredith, while in the course of researching his family history, received an intriguing memo from an official in what by then had become the Department of Mines and Technical Surveys. "Your father's restructuring of the Dominion Land Branch, the enormously expanded Indian Affairs Branch and the nucleus of the Mines Branch was clearcut and logical," wrote this official, who is identified only by the initials K.D., but who was clearly a man after Meredith's own heart.

> His own organization was so successful that it ran until sometime in the first decade of the 1900s, when an attempt was made to reorganize . . . a few years experience showed this was quite unnecessary. Mr. R. E. Young then reorganized and followed the lines originally laid down by your father. A few years later, another Minister with new broom ideas made an attempt to reorganize, but again an unnecessary mess resulted and the original set up was once more followed. A third attempt was made, and also failed, and I am now interestedly awaiting the fourth reorganization to the original set up.

Once in a while, even Meredith was forced to admit that the new job had its compensations. Visitors from the Great Lone Land constantly passed through Ottawa, with strange and wondrous tales to tell. "The Reverend Mr. [name indecipherable] arrived from the Mackenzie River," he wrote in January 1874. "He has been years in the wild regions and has apparently acquired the way of speaking peculiar to the Indians." The next summer, "Mr. Wagner, a rough and bluff German from Manitoba took tea with me. I took down information of interest which he gave me about men and things in the Northwest. Donald A. Smith he speaks of as a hard man, a tyrant to his subordinates." The next year, by virtue of his position, Meredith received a summons to dinner from the tyrant himself: "About 20 in all, the dinner was very northwestish; on the bill of fare was pemmican and champagne and Hudson's Bay salmon . . . slipped away about midnight . . . learned in the morning that the party was still in form at 2:30 A.M., everyone proposing everybody's health."

Sometimes, as in the case of "Mr. Duncan of B.C., famed for his labour among the Indians," a visitor proved so intriguing that Meredith, in the interest of broadening his children's horizons, took him home for lunch. In 1877, when the great naturalist and botanist John Macoun arrived from the Peace River district bearing sheaves of prize-winning wheat raised at Lake Athabaska, Meredith took him round to Sandford Fleming's conservatory where, as Macoun stood proudly by, he and Fleming put the wheat under a microscope and remarked, to their amazement, that "some ears numbered 96 grains." Most rewarding of all, in June 1878, was the first visit back home of Willy Jarvis, now become an NWMP Superintendent and a giver of advice instead of a taker. "He looks very fat and has an enormous red beard. . . . He thinks matters in the Northwest are in a very critical state." So indeed they were, as the great buffalo herds, livelihood of the Métis, began to disappear.

In his earliest months in the new job, Meredith's greatest compensation was his new minister, Alexander Campbell. Though a loyal and close friend of Macdonald's, having articled in his law office in Kingston, Campbell was never one of the Premier's drinking cronies. Like Meredith, he was conscientious, thoughtful, intellectual. The two quickly became close friends, so close that in 1874 Meredith invited Campbell to become godfather to the baby Coly. Like Howe before him, Campbell passed on all the political gossip to his deputy; during the stormy political autumn of 1873, this information, as recorded in Meredith's diary, provides a vivid glimpse through the keyhole into one of the most tumultuous and conspiratorial events in Ottawa's political history.

Early in April 1873, at the same time as Meredith was angling to achieve for himself the secretaryship of the Canadian Pacific Railway syndicate, Lucius Seth Huntington, the tall, imposing Opposition member for Shefford, in Quebec's Eastern Townships, had risen in the House to accuse Macdonald of having received large sums of money from Sir Hugh Allan, the Montreal shipping magnate who headed the railway syndicate.

On July 1, as Meredith smashed his way round the croquet lawn in blind fury on hearing he was to become Deputy Minister of the Interior, Macdonald was skulking around Montreal with a bottle, awaiting the initial hearings of a Committee of Inquiry he'd been forced to appoint to look into the affair that, accompanied by headlines blazoning his "smoking-gun" telegram to Allan – "IMMEDIATE. PRIVATE. I MUST HAVE ANOTHER TEN THOUSAND." – was about to be christened the Pacific Scandal. Soon after, the Premier disappeared for most of the summer – not even Lady Macdonald knew where. "Horrible rumour today," wrote Meredith on August 5, "that Sir J. had jumped off the wharf at Rivière du Loup." He hadn't. Or if he had, he'd thought the better of it at the last moment and had speedily swum ashore. But by late October, when the House reconvened, it was clear that Macdonald had been drinking more heavily, more consistently, than ever before. It was equally clear that his parliamentary support was evaporating. Worse still, the new Governor General, the activist Lord Dufferin, was threatening to take matters into his own hands. "Your personal connection with what has passed," Dufferin wrote to Macdonald on October 19, "cannot but fatally affect your position as minister."

Thanks to Campbell, Meredith knew almost from moment to moment what was going on. As it happened, every morning on his way to work, he walked past his minister's front door, at 108 Daly Street. "Mr. Campbell stopped me when passing his house to give me some instructions," he wrote on October 22, the day before the House opened. "Spoke of things as stormy; said that he and Sir J. were going out to Rideau at 1." Later that afternoon, "Mr. C. looked more cheery than for some time past. On coming to the office he said that all was right; that they were going to hold onto the government, giving me to understand that they had thought of abandoning the field."

Meredith understood quite rightly. The day before, in response to Dufferin's threat of dismissal, Macdonald had indeed seriously considered pre-empting him by resigning. But by the time he and Campbell arrived at Rideau Hall the weekly diplomatic pouch from London had already arrived by "the English mail." It contained, as Dufferin told them frankly, a letter from the Colonial Secretary that had caused him to think twice about intruding into business that better belonged to the Dominion Parliament. Macdonald might consider his previous letter "as in some degree cancelled."

Within a fortnight, however, Campbell was looking gloomy again. On Sunday, November 2, he lunched with the Merediths at Augusta Street and told them, as Meredith tells us, "the government very shaky; 'ratting' goes on daily." The trouble was that the Premier, for the first time in anyone's memory, was manifestly incapable of pulling himself together to deal with a crisis. Instead of rising to defend himself and his government while one after another of his MPs defected, Macdonald slumped white and shaky in his seat, "showing to everyone," as Lord Dufferin wrote, "as his colleague and doctor, Tupper, admitted to me, that he was quite tipsy." Nor did it help that when, on the night of November 3, Macdonald at last rose to the occasion with a fitfully brilliant five-hour oration, he fortified himself with tumbler after tumbler of gin-and-water, supplied, by previous arrangement, by the Minister of Fisheries. On Wednesday, November 5, as the last of his "loose fish" slithered away, Macdonald rose in the House to announce his resignation. "The Opposition," Lady Dufferin reported home to her husband, "directly crossed the House to their new desks." Later that evening, in the Commons smoking room, as the Liberal member George Ross recounted, he and his fellow backbenchers sang, "Sir John is dead and gone forever," to the tune of "My Darling Clementine."

Two days later, while clearing out his office, a dejected and bitterly angry Campbell beckoned in Meredith to say goodbye. "He said that had Sir J. kept straight during the last fortnight, the Ministry would not have been defeated." After Macdonald's restoration in 1878, Campbell again served his chief as Minister of Justice and as Postmaster General, but he never regained his respect for his old mentor.

"All the offices are crammed with hostile people so that we can trust no one," wrote the new Premier, the former stonemason Alexander Mackenzie, on November 11, 1873. Luckily, Meredith, who like all civil servants was nervous enough already about the takeover, was not privy to this communication. Bad enough that when he arrived at the office on November 8, "Mr. Laird, the new Minister of the Interior had already been in my room." David Laird, a member of no particular distinction from the new province of Prince Edward Island, was "a long, lanky, conjointed creature who seems a very rough specimen," in Meredith's opinion. "*On dit*," he added, in some trepidation as to what might be coming next, "that the new Ministry has cancelled all the recent appointments made by the late Government, including the Lieutenant Governors of Ontario and New Brunswick."

But the Mackenzie government in fact made surprisingly few civil service changes. For one thing, Mackenzie had no wish to antagonize those defecting Conservative members who had put him in office. For another, he himself was opposed in principle to the idea of a purge. "I am no believer in a retaliatory policy at any time," Mackenzie wrote. "Every officer will receive ample protection."

For Meredith, therefore, life under the new regime continued much as before. There were letters to be opened, treaties to be signed, and, for the man who by now was renowned as the most skilled draftsman in Ottawa, endless memos to be prepared. In November 1874, when the government of the new province of British Columbia caused difficulties by refusing to negotiate treaties with the Indians before taking possession of Crown lands, Meredith was gratified to be summoned personally by Lord Dufferin to discuss the problem directly, still more gratified when "the Governor General was commendatory of the memo which I prepared for the Council which Mr. Laird signed." Nor was Dufferin just being polite. On December 3, he sent Meredith's memo off to the colonial secretary, Lord Carnarvon, with scarcely a comma changed, describing it as "a very important despatch." As for Laird himself, if the lanky, bearded Prince Edward Islander was not quite the sort of fellow Meredith would care to invite to his own table, in the end he wound up liking his minister well enough. "I shall be sorry to lose so hardworking a chief," he wrote in October 1876, when Laird was appointed Governor of the Northwest. In Laird's successor as Minister of the Interior, the earnest and studious David Mills, who in later years served as Laurier's Minister of Justice, Meredith found a true kindred spirit. "The new minister works famously . . . very pleasant and intelligent," he wrote in December.

Unchanged from of old – and no more successful – was Meredith's constant agitation for higher pay. "Informed that the Act amending the Civil Service Act is now in type," he wrote gloomily in February

1875, "but the Dep Heads maximum has been fixed at $3600 not $4000." There was also his work as Chairman of the Civil Service Board, an elective position which he'd first attained in 1865, and which by the late 1870s had at last gotten round to the crucial business of addressing "superannuation to civil servants, and widows and orphans." There were the fortnightly meetings of the Ottawa Literary and Scientific Society which served almost as an extension of the office for public servants of scholarly bent. In November 1877, Meredith gave a "very well received" paper on his consuming passion for prison reform, "the audience being very large, even though a dank miserable night." The next year, he debated "The Future of the New Science of Political Economy," with William Dawson LeSueur of the Post Office. On another occasion, he listened intently while LeSueur presented a paper "containing the most advanced views of Herbert Spencer."* Nor had Meredith, though now approaching sixty, lost his zest for churning out pamphlets. In 1875, having produced one on the unlikely topic, *The Question of Military Drills in the Schools*, he was enraged to hear one of the Ottawa Members of Parliament, "bring the subject forward in the House, paying me the compliment of reading a large portion of my pamphlet, without crediting me for it."

* LeSueur became a *cause célèbre* in 1909, when Mackenzie King, then Minister of Labour, arranged to suppress his revisionist biography of King's grandfather, William Lyon Mackenzie.

None of this was enough for what had become, by 1876, "the horrid grind of office work." "I have of late become very down in the mouth and weary of the sun," he wrote, "I think I must have a total rest from work for 2 or 3 months." Just how jaded he had become in as much evident in what he leaves out of his diary as in what he records.

In the summer of 1877, for instance, Meredith has nothing whatever to say about an incident that not only had the whole town talking but must also have absorbed much of his time as Deputy Minister of the Interior: the arrival into the Canadian foothills of Chief Sitting Bull and a party of eight thousand American Sioux, fleeing northwards from the U.S. Cavalry after having decimated General Custer and his troops at Little Big Horn. Nor, even more out of character for a man so fascinated by scientific inventions, does Meredith make note of the wondrous event that took place in the East Block on September 3, 1877, when, thanks to a wooden hand telephone installed in Mackenzie's office, the Premier was able to communicate directly, by voice, with his secretary out at Rideau Hall. (On this occasion, Mackenzie recited the Lord's Prayer.)

Unable to shake off his depression, Meredith decided abruptly in late autumn to chuck the whole thing in. "Called by appointment on Mr. Mills at his house," he tells us without warning on November 11, 1877. "Propounded to him for the first time my desire to be superannuated. He received me most kindly, and listened very pleasantly . . . expressed his regret to learn that I wished to leave and he was pleased to say that he would be extremely unwilling that I should go but thought at the same time, that if I insist on leaving that the government should not compel me after so long a service to remain. . . . I was very much satisfied with the interview."

So indeed Meredith should have been; Mills, in the way of all skilled handlers of subordinates, had kept him talking for more than an hour. Then, in the style of all managers unwilling to lose a good man but unable to offer more pay, he sought around for a plum. By December, thanks to the good offices of his colleague Richard Scott, the Secretary of State, who by luck was also a considerable friend of Meredith's, Mills had found a prize that could scarcely have been more to his querulous deputy's taste. "Had letter from Scott informing me that he had written to Lord Dufferin urging my appointment as a delegate to the Congress on Prison Reform at Stockholm to be held next August," Meredith wrote in surprise and delight on December 8. "Scott urged my claims in very complimentary not to say flattering terms."

Alas, though, it was not to be. Instead, it was the story of the Toronto Collectorship all over again, except that this time it was Mackenzie instead of Macdonald who cast the dissenting vote. On June 15, 1878, after six months of cheerful, expansive entries, Meredith once again was plunged into gloom. "Mr. Scott informed me today that my chances of visiting Stockholm this year were gone. He had submitted a memo to Council on Friday recommending that I should be sent as the delegate of Canada and the Council declined on the sum of the expense: $750. I am very much disappointed. I have looked forward not only to having a chance of seeing my kinfolk whom I have not seen for nearly a quarter of a century but also to the chance of finding at the Congress an opening to some new field of remuneration and labour after my proposed retirement. Had I the money to spare, I should go willingly at my own expense!"

Mills tried hard to get the decision reversed. But on July 15 came the final blow. "It is not for me to reach Stockholm," wrote Meredith. "The government has resolved itself to avail itself of the services of Mr. Blake,* now in Europe. . . . Mr. Mills is very much disappointed on my account and somewhat mortified on his own account, I think, that his recommendation has not been acted upon." Mills, however, had seized the moment to wring a concession on another front. "He tells me he profited by the occasion to bring up

* This was of course, Edward Blake, the former Minister of Justice, who had resigned from Mackenzie's cabinet in January, and who had sailed for Europe on July 4, to spend a long, leisurely holiday.

the matter of superannuation, hoping that given the disappointment in the Stockholm matter, the Council might be disposed to take a favourable view of other things affecting me. This, he says, seems the case and he hopes that I may be allowed to retire on an allowance based on a salary of $3600."

There, "but for an extraordinary turn of the political wheel," in his own words, might Meredith's civil service career have ended. Instead, as Macdonald rose phoenix-like from the ashes of defeat, in the closing months of 1878 Meredith was dragged willy-nilly into a series of events that provided him with far and away the most dramatic moments in all his thirty-odd years in government.

"The day of the General Election," writes Meredith, just returned to town from a holiday at Rivière du Loup, on September 17, 1878. "Arthur brought home the startling news that the Conservatives had triumphed." So amazed was Meredith, along with everyone else – the Conservatives included – that it wasn't until the next day that he really believed what had happened. "The Conservatives would appear to have a large majority, say 40." But Macdonald himself, as Meredith couldn't resist adding with a certain relish, "has been defeated by a large majority at Kingston!" In the end, by the time the last ballots from faraway Manitoba and British Columbia had been counted, and Macdonald himself acclaimed hastily to a seat at Victoria, the Tory majority had mounted to the incredible figure of 78. At half-past one on the afternoon of October 9, Macdonald, seemingly a very different Macdonald from the trembly, ashen-faced figure who'd surrendered his government five years earlier, was once again sworn in as Premier. "He can certainly drink wine at dinner without being tempted to exceed which hitherto he has never been able to do," wrote Dufferin to Carnarvon.

For Meredith, the week which immediately preceded the Tory takeover and the week which followed it were filled with agonizing tension. He remembered only too well his interview with Macdonald five years earlier, when the Premier had refused his request to be allowed to retire. At all costs, his resignation *must* be a *fait accompli* before the Liberals left office.

On October 4, by appointment, Meredith called on Mills. "I handed in my desire to carry out the preference that I should be allowed to retire. This was done at Mr. Mills' suggestion, who at the same time expressed himself as greatly pleased with our official relations, and as being desirous always to do anything which would be in his power hereafter to promote my interests." As a token of esteem, "Mr. Mills gave me for my young people, framed likenesses of Lord and Lady Dufferin." Even more to Meredith's gratification, Mills also remarked "that nothing has occurred since he took office which so much annoyed him as my not being sent to the Congress."

So far, so good. Three days later, on his sixty-first birthday, Meredith got the word that his retirement had been approved and would date from that day. "Strange coincidence," he noted, "a strange way of celebrating my birthday." There was, however, one slight hitch. On being summoned to see Richard Cartwright, the retiring Minister of Finance, about financial arrangements, Meredith was informed that "all the members of Council were much grieved that they were not able to grant me the three months leave of absence I had asked for, but that being about to resign and desiring to appoint my successor at once, they could not do that." The Liberals, in other words, were anxious to take care of one of their own – and quickly. That very day, Mackenzie's own private secretary, William Buckingham, was appointed to Meredith's job.

Still, in the gift of the departing Grits, however, was an honour that would mean far more to Meredith than three months' lost salary. On the morning of October 9, with just an hour or two left to him as Prime Minister, Alexander Mackenzie walked down the East Block corridor to call on Meredith, who was engaged in cleaning out his office.

Alexander Mackenzie in 1878. On his very last morning as prime minister, he amazed Edmund Meredith.

The Premier found the Deputy in shirtsleeves, cravat askew, almost dropping an armload of books on the floor in astonishment as he beheld this short, slight, bearded, and pale-faced visitor with whom, up to now, he had scarcely ever even passed the time of day.

> He walked into my room very smilingly. After some five minutes conversation about ordinary matters, he told me that he had thought it right before retiring from office to recommend some gentlemen in the Civil Service for recognition of their services and that he had submitted my name for the CMG and that Lord Dufferin had heartily coincided in the recommendation.

Commander of the Order of St. Michael and St. George! Next best thing to a knighthood! The decoration for which all civil servants yearned. When Sir John, in 1872, had bestowed this honour on his brother-in-law, Hewitt Bernard, then Deputy Minister of Justice, Meredith had noted it in his diary wistfully as something he himself was unlikely ever to achieve. For an instant, Meredith was almost too overcome to speak. Then,

> I thanked Mr. M. very sincerely, and said that I felt very much gratified

> that he should have thought my services desiring of such honourable recognition. That I valued the distinction not a little and that I had endeavoured to perform my official duties as loyally to his government as to that of their predecessors.
>
> He said that all his colleagues had always had the greatest satisfaction in their official relations with me – he added that his government has had much difficulty in their administration owing to the conduct toward them of some men in the service, but that with regard to the upper rank of the Service, with but one exception (Mr. Langton?) they had been entirely satisfied. Mr. M. also said that as regards my official services, he would take care when the proper time came to state *publicly* his appreciation of them. He said he had not spoken to any of his colleagues, except Mr. Mills of his recommendations respecting the CMG and that of course it was to remain a secret until announced publicly.

The official business was over – yet still Mackenzie lingered. Perhaps – with Macdonald already on his way to Rideau Hall for the swearing-in – he preferred not to be alone with his thoughts. Perhaps he recognized in Meredith another disappointed man, someone else whose hopes and ambitions the devious and wily Macdonald had thwarted. Perhaps, always a man of conscience, he simply felt guilty at having cheated Meredith out of the trip to Stockholm. In any event, there seemed no end to his compliments.

> Mr. M. also said that he had matured a scheme for the reorganization of the service – one of the leading features of which was a higher remuneration of the upper ranks of the service. I told him that I certainly concurred.
>
> He then bade me an official farewell. His last official act certainly surprised me and pleased me very much, the more so as I somehow was always under the impression that Mr. Mac was not particularly friendly to me, and secondly, I knew that he was very choosy in paying compliments, and saying pleasant things.

The following Saturday, October 12, 1878, with a spring that had been absent for many months restored to his stride, Meredith took his successor Buckingham on an introductory tour round the offices. Later that afternoon, *faute de mieux*, he and Fanny drove round to call on Macdonald, who was staying with his close friend, Thomas Reynolds, the railway magnate, at the handsome stone house overlooking the Ottawa River for which Sir John had already suggested the name *Earnscliffe*, which meant "Eagle's Nest" in the Cornish dialect. Within moments of their meeting, all Meredith's newly restored buoyancy had vanished.

The drawing room at Earnscliffe in 1878. The mise en scène *for Meredith's difficult interview with Macdonald.*

"Well, you Superannuated Old Man, how are you?" boomed Macdonald, striding into the drawing room, as Fanny and Meredith exchanged an anxious glance. "Look my boy," he continued, "you must take that back." When Macdonald left the room, Meredith informs us, "Mr. R. said that Sir John had been talking over the changes since he left, and that Sir J will not let me go from Ottawa!"

"Look my boy, you must take that back." Above all, "*Look my boy*." All the bumpy ride back to Sandy Hill in the carriage, that deliberately condescending phrase of Macdonald's uttered to a man barely two years younger than he reverberated over and over in Meredith's ears. Nothing now would persuade him to come back – not even a doubling of his salary. The next day, "a lovely fall day, warm and balmy as July," he entreated Tupper to come over for early Sunday dinner.

As Tupper well knew, this was not a casual invitation. Before dinner, pacing around the croquet lawn, Meredith poured out all the frustration and fury he'd been storing up for years:

> Dr. Tupper asked me if Sir John had said anything special to me yesterday and "on that hint I spoke" having made up my mind to speak very plainly to Dr. T. I told him that although neither infirm or weak in body, I thought I had fully earned my retiring allowance and that I

> certainly would not voluntarily resume the duties of my old office. I explained to him how I had without my previous consent being asked, been deprived of my own office, in order that it might be given to an ignorant creature whom Sir John felt compelled to provide for and how I had been pitchforked into a position most disagreeable to me, where the work and responsibility was 10 times, nay, immeasurably greater than in my former office; that I had protested against the posting the moment I was first informed of it by my friend Mr. Campbell . . . I told him moreover how Sir John had promised me special remuneration for my services as Secretary of the Board of Inspectors and that after my nine years service in that capacity, when I applied for compensation, I got nothing. I told him that I did not feel under any obligation to Sir J and that I felt I owed the Service nothing!
>
> After dinner was over, and I had recovered my equanimity (for I pressed my case very warmly during my tête-à-tête with Dr. T) I walked with Dr. T. out Rideau Street. He said that he would see Sir J on the subject and that he thought I might leave the matter in his hands. . . .

The actual words that Tupper used to Sir John are lost to history. But as usually happened when Tupper was seized of an issue, his magic worked. Although for the next few days Meredith lived on his nerve-ends – "I felt somewhat uncomfortable walking through the streets," he wrote, "as if people were staring at me as 'The Superannuated Man' and surprised at my not being blind or halt" – there was no further strongarming from the Premier. Instead, when the two next met, on October 22 at the Privy Council Office, the conversation was crisp and businesslike: "He asked me about the circumstances connected with my resignation; which I fully explained to him as I had to Dr. Tupper." Though Sir John was unable to resist remarking "that the late government should not have superannuated me, under the law," he did not threaten to rescind it.

Even so, that canny old fox, Macdonald, had a few last cards to play. "Received a note from Sir John asking me to call on him," reports Meredith on October 26. "Walked down after lunch, found Sir J at the Rideau Club, walked with him to the Privy Council." In his manner of old, Macdonald prefaced his entreaty with a few juicy tidbits of gossip.

> At the Club, Sir J. talked of Gladstone, Lord Russell and Palmerston. He said he thought the former two were among the greatest scandals of the century and that the only excuse for Gladstone was that he was mad.

He added that Lady Head had told him twenty years ago that Gladstone was then mad, and that Mrs. G. was his keeper.

During their formal interview at the Privy Council Chambers, Meredith for once had the oddly pleasurable sensation of having the upper hand.

> Sir J. asked me whether I would be willing to return to my old office; he said that he could not promise any increase of pay but that, speaking generally, he hoped that the position of Deputy Head as a class would be improved within the next few years. Sir J spoke of his intention of opening another Commission to enquire into the Civil Service and said that with that view he had already authorized Bernard to collect all possible information about the civil service in England. This was, of course, *confidential.*

For Meredith, all of this was an old, old story. Politely, but firmly, he turned Macdonald down.

> I told Sir J that . . . I could not return to the office on the terms proposed by him. To do so would be to stultify myself. If a decided increase in pay had been offered there might have been something to justify it, but without that, nothing.

Macdonald at last retreated and changed the subject. Of the fate of Meredith's successor as Deputy Minister of the Interior, the Liberal appointee Buckingham, he left no doubt. "He said that he was going to send for Buckingham, to inform him that his services would not be required by the Department." Then, just as Meredith was getting up to go, the Premier, not best pleased at having been outmanoeuvred, was unable to resist one last parting shot.

> Sir J asked me how I hoped to eke out my retiring allowance and said that he thought I should have some difficulty making up what I gave up.

This was a blow beneath the belt – and one that hurt. Meredith made no reply. Instead he drew himself to his full height, bowed stiffly and correctly, and, hesitating just a fraction of a second, accepted Sir John's outstretched hand.

On Sunday, February 11, 1879, thirty-two years less two months after he'd joined the Government of the Province of Canada, fourteen years and a bit after coming to Ottawa, Meredith bade his formal farewell to the civil service. In the office of his Conservative-appointed successor as Deputy Minister of the Interior, Colonel Stoughton Dennis, in front of a company of about two dozen colleagues, he was presented with a silver epergne, a tea kettle for the breakfast table "worth $80 or $90," a handsome fruit basket (included especially for Fanny), and an illuminated address composed by "my dear old friend Horace Wickstead," law clerk of the Commons whom Meredith had known from his earliest days in the service. "We have seen in you," his address read in part, "a bright example of the way in which education and learning and the cultivation of polite literature can throw a charm and grace over the performance of public duties and make themselves pleasantly felt even in the dry and sometimes irksome work of official life."

The words could scarcely have been more gracious. It also touched Meredith deeply that Sandford Fleming had interrupted his Sunday at home to attend. So had Grant Powell, Meredith's old Chief Clerk and cousin-by-marriage, nowadays a deputy minister in his own right, as Under-Secretary of State. Somehow, though, the ceremony fell flat. "I felt rather uncomfortable," wrote Meredith, "and very glad when it was all over and I had shaken everyone by the hand. After the ceremony, I called for Fanny in a covered sleigh and drove home with our precious gifts."

The real source of Meredith's malaise was that the promised CMG had not materialized. Nor would it ever, despite an anxious note from Meredith to Mackenzie a couple of months later and Mackenzie's courteous reply. "He stated that he had not lost sight of the matter and that he had been surprised at the delay and had written to Lord Dufferin on the subject, and had heard from him that it would probably be attended to about the Queen's Birthday." But on May 24, when the Birthday Honours list arrived, though Meredith's friends Tupper and Campbell received knighthoods, his own name did not appear. In his diary he never referred to the subject again.

Perhaps, as Coly Meredith wrote years afterwards, it was the British who were the spoilers. "When the list was forwarded, Sir Michael Hicks-Beach considered the list too long and omitted this recommendation along with a number of others." Or perhaps, as it is impossible not to speculate that Meredith himself might always have suspected, it was Macdonald who had undone him again.

Nothing remained to hold the Merediths in Ottawa. Yet instead of departing immediately, they lingered on for nearly another year. One reason – Macdonald had been right – was lack of money;

pulling up stakes was expensive and though Meredith now had expectations of a handsome legacy from an elderly Irish relative, this had yet to appear.

The other reason was that Ottawa had become, in some respects, an agreeable place in which to linger. These last few years Edmund and Fanny, and also Mary and Alice now that they were of an age to put up their hair and don ballgowns, had been caught up in a splendid social whirl. The arrival of Lord and Lady Dufferin at Rideau Hall in 1872 had created a sense of social excitement in the capital that made it the envy of all other Canadian cities. Ottawa, in a way, had become like the Dublin that Meredith once had known.

CHAPTER 10

"O What a Merry Company We Were!"

It was a ball on a scale so magnificent that it had been talked about ever since Parliament met. . . . Some people had expressed an opinion that such a ball as this was intended to be could not be given successfully in February. Others declared that the money which was to be spent – an amount which would make this affair quite new in the annals of ball-giving – would give the thing such a character that it would certainly be successful.

The Way We Live Now, Anthony Trollope, 1875

W*ednesday, February 23, 1876.* A mild, soft winter evening; a few damp snowflakes falling. As the gaslights begin to glow in the Meredith household at 253 Augusta Street, pandemonium reigns. Squeals of approbation; shouts of disapproval. Urgent calls for needle and thread and the pincushion, yet more urgent requests for the gluepot. There is also the sharp, scorching aroma of singed hair in the air, as the curling tongs, heated by candle-flame, are held in place just a fraction too long.

The Meredith household, augmented this evening by a bevy of relatives in from London, Ontario, and from Port Hope, is preparing itself for an event quite extraordinary: a fancy-dress ball so lavish in its arrangements that it rivals the ball at Grosvenor Square in London, given by the financier Melmotte, described in Mr. Trollope's controversial new novel, *The Way We Live Now*. Except that the Ottawa event has immensely more cachet, for it happens at Rideau Hall, by command of the Earl and Countess of Dufferin. During their four years in Ottawa, this pair of Anglo-Irish aristocrats from County Down have seized hold of the capital and stood it on its ear. They haven't so much embroidered upon the office of Governor General as reinvented it.

Here, as in capitals all over the British Empire, a glittering new era, the age of Imperialism, is beginning to dawn. At Westminster, Benjamin Disraeli, in the description of the historian James Morris, sees the Empire "as an Eastern pageantry, a perpetual durbar, summoning the British people away beyond the dour obsessions of Europe to a destiny that was spicy and gilded." The first Earl of Dufferin, Dizzy's lieutenant in the west, beholds Empire equally romantically–but with a coronet of ice and a mantle of snow.

All of which, from the point of view of Edmund Meredith, is the universe unfolding as it should. No one likes theatre better than this Anglo-Irishman. Around eight o'clock, on this epochal evening, as the Merediths and their guests assemble one by one in the front drawing room, to the oohs and ahs of the younger children, they resemble an eclectic cornucopia of literature and legend. Nineteen-year-old Mary is draped *à la Greque* as the Maid of Athens in Lord Byron's poem. "Very beautiful, very becoming," in her fond Papa's estimation. Seventeen-year-old Alice is also "very pretty," covered all over with spangles as the Queen of the Butterflies. Anne Meredith, a sister-in-law from Port Hope, is decked out magnificently as Marguerite de Valois; Annie Meredith, a cousin from London, is equally splendid as the ill-fated Amy Robsart from Sir Walter Scott's *Kenilworth*.

Yet, to Meredith's mind, it is Fanny, the last to descend the stairs, all sparkly and shimmery, who steals the show. As we are not surprised to discover, "Fanny has been very ill for some days, but got out of her bed to dress for the ball." No matter that, at forty-six, Fanny's wonderful dark hair is speckled with gray; she has powdered it over liberally to complement her panniered costume as "a very elegantly dressed lady of the last century," the Duchess of Rutland. As for Meredith himself, while some of his Rideau Club confrères have grumped that while fantasy for the ladies is all very well, they will come in their usual evening garb as sedate black-and-white penguins, he has decided to go all-out for the occasion. The last several hours, fussing more than anyone else in his entourage, he has spent arraying himself as Jacques Cartier. "Not at all bad," he informs us. "But the artificial beard and moustache were *very* uncomfortable."

Usually, when they sortie out from Sandy Hill to Rideau Hall, the Merediths hire a carriage or sleigh from Coleman's Livery Stable, or else, since the return fare is a shocking $5, they chip in with friends, the Grant Powells and the Bedford-Joneses, on the big van from Coleman's that holds three or four parties, and can travel on wheels or runners according to the season. But tonight, by special viceregal fiat, two of the horse-drawn streetcars that began plying Ottawa's streets six years ago have been commandeered to serve those guests of the Dufferins who do not have transport of their own. "The drive out to Rideau Hall was most amusing," Fanny tells us in her memoir. "The carriage was crowded with costumes from many parts of the world and of many ages. O, what a merry company we were!"

As much as it was merry, this company advancing on Rideau Hall was also exceedingly select. Hand-in-hand with the New Imperialism had arrived a new and much more rigid social structure. In the immediate post-Confederation years, when everyone was struggling with their drains, Ottawa society had been cheerfully hugger-mugger. Lady Monck and Lady Lisgar had advertised their At Homes in the newspapers. Now, with invitations sent out six weeks in advance, cards a profligate six inches by four, wrapped in tissue paper inside parchment envelopes, society was becoming stratified into a pecking order that, in most of its essentials, remained intact right up to the Second World War.

Thanks to the Ottawa *Daily Citizen*, which on February 24 printed the guest list for the fancy-dress ball in full (in an edition of which three and a half of the normal four pages were devoted to that event), we have an elaborately detailed guide to capital society as it existed in 1876. Those who had the entry, it can be discerned, fell into one of three general categories.

There were, to begin with, the lumber barons; not all of the barons to be sure, only those dynasties who had been in the game long enough to have acquired a certain social gloss. Included were the Perleys, the Pattees, and the Bronsons, all members of "The American Colony" who had arrived in Ottawa after the Reciprocity Treaty of 1854; and the Egans of Aylmer and the Maclarens of Buckingham, two neighbouring towns on the Quebec side of the river. The cream of this crop were the Curriers, who'd built for themselves the fine stone house overlooking the Ottawa River that nowadays is 24 Sussex, and the Gilmours, whose mansion on Vittoria Street, approximately where the Supreme Court of Canada now stands, encompassed both a conservatory and an art gallery. Ezra

Butler Eddy of Hull, the transplanted Vermonter whose mills were already producing nearly a million matches a year, had squeaked onto the list, though known to be eccentric. Not so, however, Eddy's great rival, John Rudolphus Booth. No matter that Booth's acquisition of the richest timber stands in the Valley had already made him far and away the wealthiest of the lumber-lords; his rough language and unfortunate habits with tobacco juice put him decidedly beyond the pale.

One rung higher on the scale – so, at any rate, this next group liked to think – perched the families of the leading professional men, many of whose antecedents, they prided themselves, far predated the lumbering families. *Primus inter pares* were the Keefers, a family of gifted civil engineers, related by marriage to the Rideau Canal contractor Thomas Mackay; the achievements of the Keefers included building the fine suspension bridge across the Chaudière and Ottawa's long-delayed water and sewer system. Other "Old Ottawa" clans included the Clemows, the Cambies, the Cassells, the Sparks, the Slaters, the Sherwoods, and the families headed by Sheriff W. F. Powell, and the physicians James Grant and Hamnet Pinhey Hill.

At the top of the pyramid stood, not the politicians, even though, well, *politics* demanded that cabinet ministers and a few Opposition frontbenchers be asked – but the top government people. "It is the government and House Officers that form the better class," wrote Achille Frèchette, a young poet and House of Commons translator, to his fiancée in Boston in this same year of 1876. He might have embroidered the point to add that the "House Officers" – Gentlemen Usher of the Black Rod René Kimber; Sergeant-at-Arms of the Senate St. Denis Lemoine; Clerk of the English Journals at the Senate James Adamson, among others – were considered to have a trifle more *élan* than deputy ministers like John Langton and Edmund Meredith. Frèchette himself, only a humble translator who owed his position to good Liberal connections, didn't really qualify. It was probably because it was already common knowledge that his Bostonian bride-to-be, Annie Howells, was the sister of the distinguished American novelist and editor, William Dean Howells, that his name got onto the list. For all practical purposes, this social ranking of "Government and House Officers" ahead of politicians persisted for years. Well into the Edwardian era, elected officials were still being disparaged as "Sessional People," who, for form's sake, had to be entertained, but who repeatedly demonstrated a regrettable inability to use the right fork.

That year of 1876, the establishment of the Supreme Court had added six new stars to the social firmament.* Only Sandford Fleming, who was *sui generis*, almost on a pedestal with high-ranking officers of the Imperial military, outshone Chief Justice William Ritchie and his associates. With amazement, one discovers Fleming's name absent from the list in the *Citizen*. With relief, one discovers from Fleming's own *aide-mémoire* that his wife had been grievously ill for many weeks.

As much as by its inclusions, the *Citizen* list is revealing for its omissions. No dentists were invited to the ball, nor any teachers, and only the most select among ministers of the cloth. And while merchants in wholesale were generally acceptable – witness the appearance of the grocer-king Henry Bate – those in retail, at this date, were generally not. "All talk of the ball at Rideau Hall . . . the most brilliant affair that has ever taken place in Ottawa," wrote Janet Anna Hall, nineteen-year-old granddaughter of a leading local hardware merchant, Alexander Workman, in her own diary on February 23. It was a measure of the social style now ascendant in Ottawa that although accounts of goings-on at Rideau Hall occupy a good third of Janet's diary entries, she herself was never invited there, nor ever expected to be.

As the horse-drawn streetcar containing the Merediths approaches New Edinburgh, it joins a long, restive queue of sleighs and carriages backed up nearly to the bridge over the Rideau River. Inside the gate of Rideau Hall, coming up the winding avenue, the company can hear the band of the newly-formed Governor General's Foot Guards playing sprightly military rhythms in the hall. As has been much talked about, a *second* orchestra, Gruenwald's Quadrille Band, has been imported from Montreal to play for the dancing. In the foyer, as his five ladies twitter off to titivate in the dressing room – "a chamber which is pregnant of the whole form and vista and beauty which is so soon to overpower with its brilliance and ravish us with its grace," scribbles the reporter for the *Citizen*, getting somewhat carried away – Meredith pokes his head into the new Tent Room, just off to the right, barely completed in time to serve tonight as supper room.

Here is an indoor marquee such as neither Meredith nor anyone else had ever seen before, swagged with red and white draperies that are studded with shields bearing the coats-of-arms of the United Kingdom, the Dominion of Canada, the seven provinces, and last

* The original Supreme Court comprised only six members. It was not until 1950, a year after appeals to the Judicial Committee of the Privy Council in Britain were abolished, that the number of justices was increased to nine.

The Tent Room at Rideau Hall, as Meredith would have seen it on the night of the Dufferin's fancy-dress ball. The room is still used for receptions.

but not least, "The Arms of Blackwood, Hamilton and Temple, being the quarterings of the Governor General." This Tent Room contains three long tables each capable of accommodating eighty or so guests, each set out with fine napery and plates of exquisite vermeil, with three crystal wineglasses at every place. Myriads of spring flowers from the viceregal conservatories adorn the tables; supplementing the candles (a candle for every guest, goes the formula) are tall flaring gas standards every half dozen or so places. Noted equally by Meredith and by *The Canadian Illustrated News* is "a centrepiece of massive gold, which featured at Imperial banquets when France was an empire." The menu card informs the guests they will soon be partaking of *Saumon au mayonnaise*; *Les petits aspics de Volailles a la Reine*; *Les Biscuits de Savoie a la Vanille*, not to mention a plethora of jellies, spun sugar roses, and apricot and strawberry *glacés*.

As he waits for his womenfolk, Meredith is reminded of a chance conversation he had with Sir John Macdonald aboard the steamer *Peerless*, *en route* to Cartier's funeral in Montreal in 1873, six months after the Dufferins had arrived. "Talking of Lord D., he said he very much feared that his extravagance would do him in." (So it would, but not for another quarter-century.)

The scene presented inside the ballroom itself, as the bewigged footman in the livery of the House of Dufferin bawls out the names of the Meredith party, occasions yet more astonishment. Mary and Alice are wide-eyed in wonderment, Fanny, more composed, measures it against the ball that she watched as a child on the staircase at Rosedale, oh so many years ago. Like the supper-room, this splendidly-proportioned chamber, first unveiled in 1873, is another embellishment of the Dufferin era. Tonight it glitters as never before, with hundreds of newly-lit candles supplementing the gas lights, wreath upon wreath of pink and white flowers festooning the pilasters and at the far end, a dais of three crimson-carpeted steps ascending to a throne surmounted by an imperial crown.

Yet tonight, it is much less the splendour of the ballroom than the splendour of the company that takes the breath away. "Dazzling and perplexing as a kaleidoscope," in Meredith's view. "Uniforms will not be admissible; nor will fancy dresses imitating the costume of any religious order," had read the card that accompanied the invitation, but that left plenty of scope, and for the past six weeks, everyone having first ploughed through the numerous volumes on costume design that the librarian of Parliament, Alpheus Todd, had thoughtfully stocked up on, the sewing rooms of Ottawa have resembled a theatrical costumiers. In a depression year joyful milliners and bootmakers and dressmakers have found themselves swamped with orders. "In the present tightness of things monetary," noted a correspondent in *The Canadian Illustrated News*, "the ball has been a perfect godsend to tradesmen innumerable."

Here to begin with, as reported by the *Citizen*, is the Empire unfolding in all its gathering glory: a khedive from Egypt, several maharajas from India, a pasha, "his scimitar gleaming," and a panjandrum, "all plumed and stately." Here, closer to home, is a north-woods trapper, "in a shirt of caribou-smoked skin, embroidered in silk to represent the flowers of the forest, cuffs and collars trimmed in ermine and mink fur, scarlet silk sash and tomahawk." Here further, since the stricture against uniforms has not been interpreted to apply to glorious history, is the full complement of the old (British) guard at Quebec, circa 1759. Here, above all astonishing, is Mme Juschereau St. Denis Lemoine, wife of the Sergeant-at-Arms of the Senate, sweeping into the ballroom as the Dominion of Canada, "in a white satin skirt with gold tunic, surrounded with a wreath of maple leaves." Other accoutrements include "the flag of the Dominion worn as a scarf, fastened on one shoulder with a gold beaver, and small British flag in the hair."

Missing from the Lady Dominion – as perhaps the observant young poet Achille Frèchette is the only one to notice – is so much as even a single *fleur-de-lis*. Edmund Meredith certainly does not notice. Instead, he is overcome with consternation to see that the gentleman accompanying the Dominion, St. Denis LeMoine, has chosen to deck himself out as a fellow Jacques Cartier. LeMoine's costume – he married money, the daughter of a munificently rich lumber baron at nearby Arnprior – is infinitely more resplendent than Meredith's: "jacket and knee breeches of white satin," according to the *Citizen*, "buckskin boots trimmed with lace and ribbons, black velvet cap with ostrich feathers."

Even so, and even as the glue on his home-made moustache begins to tickle unbearably, Meredith has no need to feel upstaged. If there are Cartiers in duplicate there are also, among Shakespearean characters, three Tybalts, two Mercutios, and four Falstaffs, not to mention several Portias, and a trio of Kates from *The Taming of the Shrew*. Mrs. Edward Blake, wife of Mackenzie's senior lieutenant, is Katherine of Aragon, and the prominent Ottawa lawyer, R. S. Cassells, appears as Hamlet. Curiously, though, there is not a single Macbeth nor a Lear, not even – as a character for a costumier to have fun with – a single hunchbacked Richard III. Nor, though the night would appear to have been made to order for hijinks, is there an Ottawa damsel nervy enough to brazen it out in doublet and breeches as Rosalind.

Characters from popular novels bristle off the pages all over the ballroom. Out of Dickens and Thackeray, with the noteworthy exceptions of Fagin and of Becky Sharp, virtually everyone who is anyone is on hand, including Esther Summerson, Mr. Micawber, Mrs. Leo Hunter, and Henry Esmond. Not to mention, from other bestsellers, the Count of Monte Cristo, the Hunchback of Notre Dame, Fra Diavolo (five of him), and Jane Eyre. Characters from Trollope, it would appear by their absence on a night that would seem to have been made to order for John A. Macdonald's favourite fictional politician, Phineas Finn, cut a little too close to the bone. So also do those from Jane Austen, given that so many of the company, including Edmund Meredith, have been burdened with houses full of marriageable daughters.

A number of guests, perhaps with an eye to their own futures, have chosen to salute their hosts. One "Mr. Nettle," otherwise unidentified, has got himself up as a sailor aboard Lord Dufferin's sailing yacht, the *Foam*, on which the Earl made a daring trip to Iceland in the 1850s. The Merediths' relatives, Mr. and Mrs. Grant Powell, have come as Sir Peter and Lady Teazle from *The School for Scandal*, whose author, Richard Brinsley Sheridan, was Lord Dufferin's great-grandfather. If Prime Minister Alexander Mackenzie and his chief lieutenant, Edward Blake, look a trifle dour in the official dark blue Windsor Uniform of members of her Majesty's Privy Council in the Colonies, they considerably outshine their colleague, Secretary of State Richard Scott who, of all choices for a Catholic Irishman, has decked himself out as that puritan hero from Longfellow, Miles Standish. Still, because this is Centennial Year south of the border, stars and stripes are all *au fait*: the Perleys and the Pattees and other members of "The American Colony" salute their patrimony by appearing as members of the "Republican Court of George Washington" in black velvet coats, powdered hair, and knee breeches.

Many who come to the ball tonight will remember down the years the extraordinary sight of Dr. Hamnet Hill appearing, a trifle out of season, as Santa Claus, all decked out in holly leaves and carrying, like a shield, a six-foot decorated Christmas tree. Others will recall Mrs. F. W. Mills, wife of the organist at Christ Church Cathedral, as "The Canadian Press," in a costume constructed entirely out of newspapers. Curiously, though their names appear on the official guest list, no one (neither the *Citizen* reporter nor Edmund Meredith at any rate) can recall seeing Sir John and Lady Macdonald at all. Perhaps, not wishing to be upstaged by the incumbent, if easy-to-overlook, Prime Minister Mackenzie, they begged off at the last moment. There is also the fact that Lady Macdonald, as is well-known, does not approve of balls.

Frederick Temple Blackwood, fifth Baron and first Earl of Dufferin, in costume as James V of Scotland. The elegance of his attire made everyone else feel tawdry.

At precisely half-past nine o'clock, prefaced by much capering by a court jester in cap and bells, and by a great burst of music from the military band, the viceregal party sweeps into the ballroom. All of a sudden, as undoubtedly was the master strategy all along, all the brilliant costumes that everyone has worked on so hard for so long, suddenly seem too flamboyant, even tawdry. For Lord Dufferin's costume, "though very rich is perhaps the plainest in the room," as *The Canadian Illustrated News* reports.

Frederick Temple Blackwood, fifth Baron and first Earl of Dufferin, lacks the gift of height. In all other respects he has the presence and bearing of a proconsul. His rich black hair, worn down over the ears in the manner of southern colonels of cavalry, is in keeping with the character he has chosen to play this evening: James V of Scotland, the father of Mary, Queen of Scots, a figure much more popular with romantic and chivalrous Victorians than any of the conniving and calculating Tudors.

Lady Dufferin as Margaret of Guise. She wears the famous shamrock tiara of the Dufferins.

Lady Dufferin, some inches taller than her spouse, fair and willowy though not a beauty, suits admirably her character as James V's consort, Margaret of Guise. She wears, as the *Citizen* reports, "a petticoat of crimson satin; white satin train with two rows of gold embroidery; huge sleeves of white satin puffed in crimson, crimson velvet robe lined with white satin and bordered with ermine." The *coup de foudre* is Lady Dufferin's hat, crimson velvet with a white feather, encircled, a trifle anachronistically, by the famous Dufferin tiara, a coronet of diamond shamrocks. Flanking their parents are the Dufferins' two eldest children, barely into their teens; Lady Helen Blackwood as the young Mary, Queen of Scots and Archie, Viscount Clandeboye, as Lord Darnley, her cousin and future husband.

The viceregal party settles itself on the dais and beams serenely at the assembled company. Then, at a pre-arranged nod from Dufferin, the Quadrille Band from Montreal begins to play. As alway on such occasions, in a custom that will endure at Government House until the 1920s, the dancing begins with a formal state quadrille, tonight to the up-to-the-minute music of *La Fille de Madame Angot* by Charles d'Albert. In keeping with protocol, His Excellency leads out the wife of the Prime Minister, while Alexander Mackenzie partners Lady Dufferin. Such moments on public display are a source of great trial to the plain, unvarnished Mackenzies for, as Fanny Meredith tell us in her memoir, a bit waspishly, "Mr. Mackenzie was not as clever a dancer as he was a politician, and good kind Mrs. Mackenzie was not over *au fait* with it either." Dufferin, though, is extremely *au fait* both at small talk and at easing the burden of his own greatness for those for the moment inflicted with it.

Tonight, however, hardly anyone bothers to poke fun at the prime-ministerial couple bumbling their way through the intricate steps: instead, everyone is eagerly awaiting the *pièce de resistance* of the evening: the four "Singing Quadrilles" that the viceregal party and a handpicked few of Ottawa's beaux and belles have been rehearsing for weeks. "These singing dances appear to have been quite the rage in aristocratic circles in England during the last season," reports the *Citizen*. "The idea consists in setting to light music the words of familiar nursery rhymes which are sung by those taking part." In order that everyone may be letter-perfect, the Countess of Dufferin herself has helped the aides-de-camp copy out all the parts. "You may imagine the confusion and difficulty of arranging all these separate bits of paper," she wrote to her mother in Ireland. Still, the finished production turns out to have been worth all the tired fingers: the hit of the show, reports the *Citizen*, "was the waltz in three parts, that commenced with *Humpty-Dumpty*, continued on through *Pussy Cat, Pussy Cat Where Have you Been?* to the history of *The Spider and the Fly*, which last was executed to the steps of that exceedingly fashionable waltz, the *Boston*."

At last, towards eleven o'clock, the real dancing begins. Mostly, the programme tells us, it is the waltzes by "Johann Strauss of Vienna" that predominate, with the lilting "Blue Danube" the most often requested. Every now and then, an old-fashioned *galop* is thrown in for good measure. Lady Dufferin, as usual, keeps a queenly distance from her partners, dancing only the stylized quadrilles and lancers, or "square dances" as she describes them. But His Excellency, so *bravura* in his footwork that he might easily be a dancing master, twirls and whirls through everything on the programme. To Mrs. Mackenzie's horror, he insists on leading her onto the floor yet again – this time for a waltz. More of a pleasure than a duty for Dufferin are the lancers he dances with Mrs. Richard Scott, the wife of his Secretary of State, for, though now of an age to dress as Mrs. Page in *The Merry Wives of Windsor*, she was once upon a time the ravishingly beautiful professional singer Mary Heron, a member of the merry Irish troupe of sisters, The Heron Family, who beguiled audiences throughout North America and sometimes titillated them by appearing in male attire. Even for two such surefooted partners the dancing is tricky tonight; one of the most amusing features as the evening wears on, reports *The Canadian Illustrated News*, "is the discarded paraphernalia that adorned all corners of the room. Father Christmas set down his tree; Britannia her shield and trident; the buxon fishwives their nets full of papier-mâché mackerel."

As for the Merediths' progress through the evening, Fanny, it must be said, was a little chagrined that His Excellency did not invite her to waltz, and remembered ruefully how, with his predecessor Lord Lisgar, "it was sort of an understood thing," as she wrote in her memoir, "that after receiving guests at an afternoon reception, he would come over to me and say, 'now let us go and have a cup of tea.' " Still, as the ballroom grew stiflingly hot, and the damp smell of perspiration began to pervade the air, Dr. Tupper appeared, all splendid in knee breeches, to take her into the Tent Room for supper, and thence on a stroll through the conservatories bedecked with Chinese lanterns.

Not until the clock struck four did the Dufferins, by leaving the ballroom, indicate that it was time for the affair to end, and for everyone to go home. "The people seemed extremely pleased," yawned the Countess over her diary. The Merediths didn't get back to Augusta Street until nearly five, with the first cracks of dawn already in the sky.

Leave the last word to the *Citizen* reporter, searching for a way to write finis to the long, long story, as the printer waits impatiently. "A ball is like a piece of statuary . . . if you press on for details, you lose the matchless whole . . . an epitome of wit and beauty and hospitality."

The revels, in fact, had yet to end. Not to be outdone by the Governor General, the Quebec Members of Parliament, five nights later, invited everyone to climb back into their finery yet again for an equally magnificent party celebrating the completion of the Library of Parliament. Among the members of the organizing committee was the up-and-coming young member for Drummond-Arthabaska, Wilfrid Laurier. He had his work cut out for him, for, according to the indefatigable *Citizen* correspondent, "several men were engaged not simply to decorate but also to clear out the last of the workmen's debris." The result was worth it. "No finer room could have been secured . . . to form an idea, the reader must imagine himself in a room 80 feet in diameter, with a ceiling something like 130 feet in height; blue tinted, enriched with dark tooth moulding, groined ribs, supported by marble columns."

At the height of the Victorian craze for the trappings of chivalry and for the sentiments of Camelot, no setting could have been more dramatic for a costume ball than this Library which had been designed specifically to resemble a medieval Chapter House, and which remains today one of the finest examples of the Gothic Revival to be found anywhere in the world. Much of this chapter has been researched there, and for the writer a century on, it was an enchanting experience to gaze up at the serried galleries that today are lined with books and to try to imagine, down to the last flickering gas jet, how it all was on that dazzling evening. Once again, the *Citizen* reporter is our best guide back into the past:

> The management had two bands painted round the side of the wall with green rosettes and eight triumvirates of flags placed at intervals. . . . A dais was erected for their Excellencies facing the chamber. It was covered with green, with lounge and chairs upholstered in crimson damask. Immediately above the dais was a niche in which was placed a handsome bust of the Prince of Wales. In the opposite side of the

> building was a bust of the Princess of Wales and on the right hand side of the chamber appeared one of Sir George-Etienne Cartier. . . . Almost opposite the dais was a stand for the orchestra decorated with flags.
>
> The room was magnificently illuminated with some 300 gas jets. In the lantern, there was a circle of 200 jets and suspended from the summit was a star-shaped gasolier and ten feet under it, another circle of light. The heating apparatus was well regulated and in fact, everything worked to perfection.

If anything, according to Fanny's memoir, the Merediths had an even more splendid time than at Government House. The point was, this time they had the great honour of being invited to take part in the opening quadrille along with the Dufferins and the Mackenzies. "I think it was the Lancers I danced with Colonel Fletcher, Military Secretary to His Excellency, your father with his wife, Lady Harriet Fletcher." Later, there were more lancers, the "Blue Danube" again, and, the Quebec members liking to kick up their heels, rather more *galops* than at Rideau Hall. Once again, the dancing continued until four in the morning.

Wistful Janet Hall, the diarist who lived over the hardware shop on Wellington Street, did not get to attend this ball either, even though one of her uncles, Thomas Workman of Montreal, was one of the Quebec members, and a Liberal at that. Instead, she got most of her information from a long gossip with her friend, Mrs. John Bourinot, wife of the Assistant Clerk of the House of Commons.

This composite portrait of the fancy-dress ball took the Ottawa photographer, William Topley, three months to produce. The complicated technique involved photographing each person separately, and then assembling these against a painted backdrop for re-photographing. Seated under the arch, the Dufferins demonstrate the emerging viceregal style.

A few weeks later, on a bright spring morning, Janet walked up to Mr. Topley's photographic studio on Wellington Street, only to find that "the large photo of the Fancy Ball was not yet finished." It was not until June that the huge composite portrait of the Dufferin Ball, in which one can even pick out Dr. Hamnet Hill's discarded Christmas tree standing against the far wall, was unveiled with a flourish. By pressing her nose against the glass, Janet Hall could at last see for herself how truly memorable the evening had been. Had she been reflective (and nothing in her diary suggests that she was), she might have wondered how, in less than a decade, this raw backwoods capital could have advanced so far in social grace and extravagance.

CHAPTER 11

The Dufferin Style

Do not be too Irish or too Sheridanish. . . . It is an awful combination.

The Duke of Argyll
in a letter to Lord Dufferin, 1874.

The fancy dress ball given by the Dufferins stood as a benchmark among Ottawa social events for a full generation. But the viceregal style established by the Dufferins lasted far longer – indeed, in some respects, it lingered for another century. Dufferin style amounted to an Imperial Stewardship – an elevation of the Governor General's responsibilities from unobtrusive go-between and gatherer of loose ends between Crown and Dominion to social arbiter for the nation and, only slightly less arrogantly, political referee.

In the matter of politics, the kind of governor-generalcy Dufferin invented came to its end during the King-Byng crisis of 1926. As wielder of social power, though, the Dufferin style persisted right up to our own time. Indeed, some of the difficulties that Governor General Edward Schreyer experienced between 1978 and 1984 in his efforts to impose a more populist and lower-keyed approach to the office, stemmed from the fact that Canadians, without realizing it, had come to expect that their governors general would forever behave as the Dufferins had once behaved.

In sculpturing their style, the Dufferins adapted freely from a model they both knew at first hand: the viceregal court at Dublin. "A strange, theatrical institution," in the words of the historian Sir Charles Petrie, "of which the influence affected everything in the country down to the commonest little tradesman." Canada, unlike Ireland, was a self-governing Dominion, yet, just as Dublin revolved round the Castle and the viceregal lodge at Phoenix Park, so Ottawa revolved around Rideau Hall, to the point that what happened out at Rideau (just that single word, Rideau, was the commonest usage) meant far more, not just to Official Ottawa but to *all* of Ottawa, than anything that happened on Parliament Hill. Each year, beginning in the Dufferin era, all the cabmen in the city would club together to present a testimonial of thanks to Their Excellencies for the brisk trade afforded by viceregal functions. As we have seen, even the city's streetcar system could be pre-empted to serve viceregal whim, and social events at Rideau crowded political events off the front pages. Like Janet Hall up over the hardware store, most Ottawans were doomed by accident of birth or choice of occupation to live forever on the outside of Rideau looking in, yet the thralldom that Rideau exerted, no one dared challenge.

Much that took place at Ottawa's ersatz court was puffed-up folderol. Mean little snobberies imported across the Atlantic flourished with peculiarly nasty vigour in the northern air. As mattered more, by their insistence on pomp and circumstance and by the mystique they consciously wove around themselves, Ottawa's viceregal rulers and courtiers helped also to detach the capital from the nation it existed to serve. The arrogance of the viceregal court cowed Canadians and so, by extension, prolonged the nation's immaturity. It took us until 1952, only fifteen years short of our centennial, to summon up sufficient nerve to appoint a Canadian-born Governor General. Even then, Vincent Massey was so much an English aristocrat in all but the geographical circumstance of his birth, that the British Foreign Secretary, Lord Cranborne, once remarked, "Fine chap, Vincent, but he does make one feel a bit of a savage."

There is, however, another way of looking at all of this. The viceregal court lent to Canada a touch of class. For all that its ruffles and flourishes were out of phase with the nation, Rideau Hall, just by existing, provided Ottawa, and indeed the whole of the nation, some grace-notes that Washington, though an incomparably more energetic and powerful capital, conspicuously lacked. At the White House in the 1870s, as contemporary accounts reveal, the entrance hall was always jammed with noisy office-seekers clustered round spittoons; on the china used for state occasions, crudely painted coyotes glared up through the soup. In the cool shadowy reaches at Rideau, there were powdered and liveried footmen behind every chair, elegant vermeil to dine off, and never, ever, a single spittoon.

This role model made a difference. Our politicians may not have been any more skilled than their counterparts in Washington, and, if anything, they were even more friendly with the bottle. They were, however, even in their excesses, a trifle classier. "I know enough of the feeling of this meeting to know that you would rather have John A. drunk than George Brown sober," Macdonald once claimed. Somehow, one cannot imagine John A.'s contemporary in the White House, Ulysses S. Grant, possessing either the daring or the panache to come up with that line, for all his military prowess.

The defining characteristic of the governor-generalcy created by the Dufferins was its most obvious characteristic: its *Englishness*. The Castle at Dublin may have provided the conceptual framework, but in Dublin, as everywhere else in the Empire, London was the place to which everyone looked for guidance on how to behave. By 1872, the year the Dufferins arrived, English attitudes towards the colonies were undergoing a fundamental change.

In the 1850s and 1860s, in Canada as in all the other colonies, an easygoing, almost Georgian air of informality prevailed between the British governors and their overseas subjects. "There was much less formality then," Fanny Meredith reminisced years later, of her early married life at Quebec. "[The Governor], Sir Edmund Head and Lady Head frequently dined with us, or came for tea." In the immediate post-Confederation years, the "Little Englanders" under Gladstone had little interest in what went on beyond their shores, across the Channel let alone across the oceans in India, Australia, Canada. As the historian Frank Underhill has noted, Gladstone himself "was generally suspected of not being averse to seeing the self-governing colonies, of which Canada was the chief, become separate independent states." As a result, the proconsuls Britain sent out to Canada had neither motivation nor inclination to think of themselves as anything other than senior colonial administrators. So unattached to fuss and feathers was Lord Monck that on July 1, 1867, he had turned up at the Parliament Hill ceremonies marking Confederation in an ordinary, everyday frock coat, while Macdonald and his incoming cabinet were resplendently arrayed in full court uniform.

Lady Lisgar. Meredith found her "very theatrical."

Monck's successor, Lord Lisgar, was cut from the same workaday mould. Though Lady Lisgar had a tendency to be, in Meredith's words, "very theatrical," once receiving Lady Macdonald (as the prime minister's wife tells us) "while reclining on a padded chintz sofa in a room heavy with the scent of hyacinths, arrayed in a rich robe of violet satin, thickly quilted and trimmed with swansdown," Lisgar himself liked nothing better than whiling away the hours in his study, working out quadratic equations – much in the manner of Edward Schreyer ploughing through the *Encyclopedia Britannica* from *A* to *Z*. One day in February 1872, when Meredith called at Rideau and found the Governor General thus engaged, the two had a chat about Canada's political future. From Meredith's account, Lisgar was extraordinarily far-sighted. "He said it was the duty of Canadians now to consider what means could be found of uniting the Dominion to Great Britain by some sort of alliance by which the Dominion would be unaffected by any sort of trouble between Great Britain and the United States, and yet might enjoy the benefit of England's protection in the event of aggression from neighbours." Canada, in other words, should be responsible for its own foreign policy.

Frederick Temple Blackwood, fifth Baron and first Earl of Dufferin, thought directly the opposite. This strong-willed aristocrat was easily the most vigorous and flamboyant figure ever to occupy Rideau Hall. In 1877, the quite minor matter of Alexander Mackenzie sending his Minister of the Interior down to Washington to negotiate the fate of Sitting Bull without first asking the permission of the Governor General sent Dufferin into a fearsome rage.

No sooner had Dufferin arrived in Ottawa in 1872, than he asserted his authority by establishing a viceregal office at the government's nerve-centre, the East Block, reached by a private entrance and a curved sweeping staircase that no one else was supposed to use.* Though officially a Liberal, and an appointee of Gladstone, Dufferin's ideas about Britain's relations with her colonies were much closer to the new creed of aggressive imperialism that Disraeli was beginning to weave into the Tory platform. But while Disraeli, on reaching office in 1874, was chiefly interested in Britain's eastward empire – India, Suez, and all the rest of it – Dufferin was the proconsul who carried the philosophy westward. "His fundamental conception of society was a territorial one," Dufferin's nephew-by-marriage, the British man of letters Harold Nicolson has written. "His Utopia was one in which a small caste of philosopher-landowners would, while maintaining among themselves a high standard of exclusiveness and culture, devote much of their time and some of their profits to the physical and religious well-being of their less fortunate brethren." Not that Dufferin, who was an extremely skilled diplomat, was ever so tactless as to allow such feelings to show. "Were the curb pressed too tightly," he wrote to the Colonial Secretary, Lord Carnarvon, "Canada might soon become impatient, the cry for Independence would be raised. . . ."

* Governors general maintained this East Block office until 1942.

Dufferin's method instead was to apply the carrot, firing the imagination of Canadians with his charm and rhetoric, and most of all binding Canadians to Britain by the sheer force of his persona. Just before Dufferin left for Canada, a friend approached him at his club and remarked, as he himself wrote later, "Now, you ought to make it your business to get rid of the Dominion. . . ." To which Dufferin, prefiguring one of Winston Churchill's most famous and most defiant comments replied, "I certainly did not intend to be handed down to history as the Governor General who had lost Canada."

When Dufferin arrived in Canada in the summer of 1872, he was forty-six, a slight, swarthily handsome figure whose exotic and florid manner – a drawling lisp, a stagy deportment, a monocle that dangled before him on a black ribbon – so uncannily mimicked that of Benjamin Disraeli that many were convinced he was Dizzy's natural son.* Such speculation quite apart, Dufferin's maternal great-grandfather had been every bit as flamboyant – Richard Brinsley Sheridan, greatest of all eighteenth-century playwrights. Dufferin's mother was the ravishing, raven-haired Helen, eldest of three gorgeous Sheridan granddaughters who took London by storm in late Regency days. (Georgiana, the youngest, having reigned as Queen of Beauty at the famous Eglinton Tournament of 1839, helped launched the Victorian craze for things medieval that even in faraway Ottawa had inspired the Parliament Buildings. Caroline, the middle sister, following a disastrous marriage that had culminated in a notorious divorce case in which Prime Minister Lord Melbourne had been named as her lover, metamorphosed into the fiery feminist writer, Mrs. Norton, whose agitation helped produce that landmark of female emancipation, *The Married Woman's Property Act.*)

Lord Dufferin. He was a pioneer of Imperialism, Disraeli's lieutenant in the west.

In Dufferin's veins, as Nicolson has written felicitously, "the Sheridan blood seethed and tingled like champagne." It showed in his wild extravagance. "I hear *terrible* things about your expenditure," wrote his mentor, the Duke of Argyll, when news of the lavish goings-on in Ottawa reached London. "Do not be too Irish or too Sheridanish; it is an awful combination." It showed in his love of things theatrical: for amateur productions at Rideau Hall, as Fanny Meredith's memoir tells us, Dufferin himself rouged and powdered the actors. It showed above all in his passionately romantic nature. Dufferin was in the vanguard of those many Victorian gentlemen who adopted the rekindled myths of Camelot as inspira-

* To kill a romantic tale, Disraeli, according to his own diary, had first encountered Dufferin's mother when her son was already six years old. Dufferin's father was Price Blackwood, fourth Baron Dufferin, quite without distinction except as a one-time naval officer.

tion for their own behaviour. In his twenties, as a young Lord-in-Waiting to Queen Victoria and very handy at driving a curricle, Dufferin commenced a long, chivalric attachment to one of the Queen's married ladies of the bedchamber, Lady Frances Jocelyn. All his life he was enormously attractive to women: Nicolson writes of how, during the 1890s, when Dufferin was in his seventies, he swept Nicolson's own straight-laced governess off her feet by treating her "as if she were an exiled member of the House of Bourbon and would rise from his chair (that brown hand upon the arm of the chair – that slow and stately smile) whenever she entered."

Dufferin's most remarkable affair of the heart, though, was the relationship he shared with his mother.

When Dufferin was born in 1826, the lovely Helen was barely eighteen. There were no other children. His father, ever a shadowy figure, died of a mysterious overdose of morphia in 1841. Between son and mother there developed the kind of intense, hothouse relationship that, however unhealthy it sounds in our own time, was praised by the Victorians as an example of filial devotion. "She shared his interest and his every pleasure. They enhanced each other's merriment and inspired each other's wit," Nicolson wrote, half-thinking, perhaps, of his own extraordinarily rich but asexual marriage to Victoria Sackville-West. To Dufferin, Helen was forever the wise and gracious lady in the tower; he her devoted squire. At times, the mocking Irish strain in Helen couldn't be repressed. "You are very careless in your spelling," she wrote when he was at Oxford. "My grandfather Sheridan always affirmed that no Irish peer could spell." (Dufferin never did learn to spell.) No gesture, when it came to celebrating Helen, was too flamboyant or too expensive. In 1860, when he was thirty-four and she fifty-two, he designed and built a fantastical tower to her glory, a tall slender Gothic spire that still beckons on the Dufferin estate, Clandeboye, just outside Belfast, as one of the most charming of Victorian architectural follies. A chamber near the top was inscribed with specially commissioned poems. That by Tennyson begins:

Helen's tower here I stand
Dominant over sea and land
Son's love built me and I hold
Mother's love in letter'd gold.

In 1862, when he was thirty-seven, Dufferin at last chose a bride: the shy, golden-haired, nineteen-year-old Hariot Rowan

Hamilton, daughter of a neighbouring landowner. He carried her off to a bridal chamber enlivened, Nicolson informs us, "with copies of the more decorous among the Pompeii frescoes." A few months later, his mother Helen electrified all of England by embarking on an impulsive second marriage with one of Dufferin's own contemporaries, the thirty-seven-year-old Earl of Gifford. Of Dufferin's reaction, suffice it to say that his official biography, written three years after his death in 1902, contains no mention whatever of Helen's marriage to Gifford. As late as 1937, Harold Nicolson, in his own anecdotal memoir of Dufferin, titled *Helen's Tower*, skirts the matter with extreme delicacy. "This had come as a lasting shock . . . we were all aware that the heroine of Helen's tower must not be associated with any second marriage." In the event, the unfortunate Lord Gifford survived the marriage by less than a year. Helen herself died in 1867, after an agonizing two-year siege of breast cancer. One can't help speculating that to the new Countess of Dufferin, the news came as a happy release in more ways than one.

And yet, to confound our post-Freudian consciousness, the Dufferin marriage bloomed and prospered. By the time they set out for Canada, there were five high-spirited children, with two still to be born. Lady Dufferin's weekly letters home to her mother, published in 1891 as *My Canadian Journal*, and our primary source of information on their life in Canada, are unmistakably the accounts of a supremely happily married woman, albeit one always more than a little in awe of her brilliant husband. "My aunt would never refer to my uncle by his Christian name," Nicolson tells us. "It seemed curious also that she should suddenly cease speaking the moment he appeared." As for Dufferin, "his own attitude was one of old fashioned chivalry. . . . He would pay her little compliments which brought the blush to her cheeks. 'O little Lal,' he would say when he was over seventy, 'How well that gown becomes you! How beautiful you look tonight.' " If Hariot never quite supplanted the gorgeous Helen in Dufferin's affections, and if she remained to him in some ways forever a child-bride, he yet encouraged her to grow into a considerable figure in her own right: stately, handsome, and slender, always a trifle shy and reserved, yet so queenly a presence that the King of Greece once remarked, as Dufferin in his *éblouissant* fashion liked to tell everyone, "No one in the world can enter a room like Lady Dufferin."

Of all the capitals Hariot Dufferin eventually came to grace – New Delhi as vicereine; Rome and St. Petersburg and Paris as ambassadress – it was that first diplomatic posting to shabby little Ottawa that agreed with her best. Of all the many photographs that survive, the one that shows her to best advantage is a portrait by the Ottawa photographer Topley. In it (for it was the 1870s fashion in Canada to pose in one's furs), she is wearing a perky little sealskin cap, much the same kind of cap Fanny Meredith had worn as a muffin, with the ever-present wintertime "cloud" of fine wool draped around her shoulders. In the pages of *My Canadian Journal*, knowing what we do of Lady Dufferin's background, it is impossible not to read between the lines the exhilaration of a woman who, in her early thirties, has been liberated at last from the ghosts of the past.

Lady Dufferin. Canada agreed with her.

At least as much, Canada agreed with Dufferin himself. The truth was, the governor-generalcy was the first job to which he had seriously addressed himself. Though gifted with a fine, far-ranging mind, an ability to wield an elegant pen, and an intellectual curiosity that set him to learn Persian when he was over seventy, he'd frittered and dreamed away his youth no less profligately than any Regency fop. After a huntin'-fishin'-shootin' sojourn at Oxford and a term as Lord-in-Waiting to Queen Victoria, there'd been a daring trip to Iceland by yacht that had produced a charming, high-spirited travel book, *Letters from the High Latitudes* (over which Edmund Meredith roared laughing on a train journey to Sarnia in 1864), followed by a desultory decade in the House of Lords. Then, in the spring of 1872, just as he was about to retire to his estates to write a definitive history of Ireland, the course of an assassin's dagger that struck down the incumbent Viceroy of India, Lord Mayo, changed the direction of Dufferin's life and of Canadian history. At Gladstone's hurried insistence, Dufferin allowed his name to be put forward on the short list of possible replacements. Another peer, Lord Northbrook, got the job; as consolation prize, Dufferin was offered Canada. He set sail in June aboard the Allan liner *Prussian*, together with his Countess and their five children. Also aboard and reflecting a very different sort of Canadian reality were, as Lady Dufferin tells us, "107 street-arabs from London and Liverpool," *en route* to adoption in Canada.

CHAPTER 12

Bombasto Furioso

I am inclined to believe I should have made a better actor than anything else.

Edmund Meredith;
diary entry; April 19, 1879

"Rather too gushing for my taste," wrote Macdonald to the recently departed Lord Lisgar of his first impressions of the Dufferins. "It was amusing to see the dismay with which they first saw Ottawa and Rideau Hall."

In their own letters home, the Dufferins recorded that dismay. He wrote that Government House was "nothing but a small villa such as would serve the needs of a country banker." Lady Dufferin was equally cast down. "The first sight of Rideau Hall did lower our spirits," she confessed to her mother. "The road to it is rough and ugly, the house appears to me to be at land's end, and there is no view whatever from it, though it is near the river – and we have come through hundreds of miles of splendid scenery to get to it."

Central to Dufferin style, however, was brisk, up-with-the-sun optimism. "I am always at my best in the morning tapping my egg," the Governor General once confided to a friend. "The morning has brought more cheerful reflections," wrote Lady Dufferin in a quick postscript to the letter quoted above. "We are not intended to live here at midsummer and I daresay that in winter the place looks lovely . . . the Houses of Parliament which after all I do see from my windows are very beautiful . . . so why did I grumble?"

Within a week, the famous Dufferin charm had cajoled the parsimonious Department of Public Works into ordering acres of "carpets and cretonnes," drawing up plans for a cricket pavilion

Rideau Hall in 1878. "Nothing but a small villa such as would serve the needs of a country banker."

and a new ballroom, and installing new-fangled buzzers and gasoliers. Similarly, Lady Dufferin had discovered the sybaritic pleasures of that fixture already well established at Government House: the aide-de-camp. "I find the ADC is a charming institution," she wrote. "They ask me if I will 'drive' or 'walk' or 'boat' or 'If I want anything from town,' and if I turn my head they find out what I am looking for and get it for me." In years to come, the ADC with his shoulderful of braid and his blue revers, nearly always an officer in a smart regiment, if not with a title then at least with a listing in *Burke's Landed Gentry*, usually handsome, and always under thirty-five, became almost as glamorous a figure on the Ottawa social scene as the Governor General himself and indeed, as far as Ottawa belles were concerned, aides were incomparably *more* glamorous. At the peak of viceregal splendour the complement of aides would grow to half a dozen or more; at the start of the Dufferin era there were two, plus the senior aide, or Military Secretary, Colonel Henry Fletcher of the Scots Guards, whose imminent arrival, plus wife and five children, made necessary the immediate installation of a second storey on Rideau Cottage, the pleasant square red brick villa on the grounds of Rideau Hall which even today remains the grace-and-favour residence of the Governor General's Secretary.

Setting a pattern of uninhibited aristocratic nepotism which lasted until the Second World War, when one of the kin of the then Governor General, the Earl of Athlone, grievously embarrassed the Household by being found dead in a snowbank, Lady Dufferin arranged to import her own younger brother, Captain Fred Rowan Hamilton of the 9th Regiment of Foot as a replacement for one of Lisgar's leftover aides. Fred's first duty of the day, she informs us, was to inspect the stables. After that, he got on with the real work of addressing invitations.

In early July of their first summer, the Dufferins embarked on the midsummer exodus to the lower St. Lawrence ports along with the rest of fashionable Ottawa. At Rivière du Loup, they encountered the Merediths. "I suppose meeting so often and so informally at Rivière du Loup," wrote Fanny, "was the *raison d'être* of somewhat of an intimacy which lasted while Lord and Lady Dufferin were in Canada." It helped the acquaintance along that the Dufferin children were more or less of an age with the nicely brought up young Merediths. As a summer resort, however, the Dufferins much preferred Tadoussac at the mouth of the Saguenay and in their customary extravagant style ordered a summer house to be built there, a pretty cottage with red roof, green shutters, and white walls that can still be seen today. Then, early in August, the Dufferins embarked on the task that would absorb most of their time and energy for the next six years: the serious business of writing their own names, and by extension that of *Victoria Regina*, across the length and breadth of the Dominion. It would be a challenge both exhausting and time-consuming, for the nation was growing ever larger. Seven provinces now, stretching *a mari usque ad mare*, much as D'Arcy McGee had dreamed, from tiny, pastoral Prince Edward Island in the east to vast and only partially explored British Columbia in the west, with the great untamed sweep of the prairies in between.

They began where Canada itself had begun, in Quebec City; the city they'd both fallen in love with the instant they'd stepped ashore from the *Prussian* on June 25, 1872. Acting, as always, on impulse, they decided to transform the old military barracks known as the Citadel, with its magnificent view of the St. Lawrence, into an additional viceregal residence – one in which all succeeding Governors General have lived for part of each year. For Dufferin, creator of Helen's Tower, Quebec's brooding mystique of history and of tragedy was the perfect *mise en scène* for his romantic imagination.

In short order, he was plotting ways of restoring the city's stone walls and before long had imported the Irish architect, W. H. Lynn, to develop plans which, had they been carried out, "would have transformed the city into a modern Camelot or Carcassone, encircled with cliff-top walls and towers," as the British architectural historian, Marc Girouard, has noted recently. In the end, neither the budget of Public Works nor Dufferin's own not very extensive personal treasury would extend quite that far; instead, apart from the Citadel, his legacy to Quebec was the superb wooden terrace bearing his name that winds around the cliff-face.

In the case of Lady Dufferin, it was the old seigneurial privilege by which the Governor General might visit the cloistered convents that appealed to *her* sense of the exotic. "We looked at Montcalm's skull til all was ready," she writes of a visit to the Ursuline Convent, "and then went to the great door of the convent and knocked. Some nuns opened to us and conducted us to a large room where we found all the pupils dressed in white, with wreaths of flowers in their hands." Yet more intriguing was a second visit to the Convent, with the Dufferin children in tow, during which they conversed with the nuns through iron bars. "It was quite funny to hear them all buzzing inside their cages, laughing and talking and handing sugar to the babies and admiring them."

By the time they left Quebec in mid-September, the Dufferins were already well on their way to accomplishing their objective. "When we arrived," wrote Dufferin, "the inhabitants showed neither interest nor curiosity . . . but on leaving the whole population lined the streets, the sky was darkened with flags, we ourselves were deluged with bouquets and half a dozen steamers crammed full with the society of the place escorted us twelve miles up the river. Ever since, we have never entered a town without being met by horse, foot and artillery and all the paraphernalia of a triumphal progress." It was the next best thing to *Vive La Reine*!

Southern Ontario, where they arrived at the peak of the season of fall fairs, put on an equally good show. At Hamilton, Lady Dufferin tells us, "we examined prize horses and pigs . . . then drove to City Hall and received a deputation from the Six Nations. The chief 'Chief' was finely dressed and wore feathers in a hat and many medals on his breast. He carried the silver pipe of peace and he also had a scalping knife, a tomahawk and a dagger." At Niagara, there was the customary voyage on the *Maid of the Mist*, and a visit to the Cave of Winds. "I was surprised to find that we were expected to array ourselves in yellow oilcloth trousers with jackets and hoods of the same material," she continues. "We did look a funny yellow party, dripping with water." It was at Fort Erie, where Casimir Gzowski was constructing the magnificent Peace Bridge over to Buffalo, that the Dufferin's chief aide, Colonel Fletcher, scored a coup. "He put on diver's dress and went down eighty feet to the depth of the piers, bringing us some stones from the bottom." A few days later at Petrolia – though, sad to say, not on the "oil lands" owned by Edmund Meredith – "we saw the process of looking for a 'well'; all the machinery used and saw the oil as it comes up through the pump – thick, black and mixed with water." Arriving at Toronto, the Dufferins were overwhelmed by the hospitality of their hosts. This is a great place for presents," wrote Lady Dufferin, "I have fruit, flowers, butter, fancy bread, fish and game sent to me constantly." Dufferin himself wrote as enthusiastically, if with a hint of aristocratic condescension. "Both men and women are dignified, unpretending and polite, very gay and ready to be amused, simple in their ways of life and quite free from vulgarity or swagger."

Never before had a British proconsul plunged so enthusiastically into the life of Canadians. Never before had a Governor General taken his wife along as consort. Yet the foray of 1872 was only a curtain-raiser to what would follow. In 1873, right after Christmas (though Lady Dufferin was by now four months pregnant all references to this would be carefully expunged from her published journals) they held court at a glittering two-week season at Montreal which included, among other festive events, a torchlight procession up Mount Royal on snowshoes. "They wore white blanket coats, tight leggings and red caps. The procession walked up the mountain and we drove around it, watching the fiery serpent winding among the trees." On a visit to McGill College a crowd of exuberant students met the viceregal sleigh at the gates, unharnessed the horses, and pulled the Dufferins up the avenue to the doors. "While D. was taken to the dissecting-room, I went to have tea with the ladies."

The following summer (the birth of a daughter, on May 17, to whom Queen Victoria herself agreed to be godmother, is mentioned only as epilogue to a tea-party the day before) they embarked on a tour of the Maritimes and, while salmon fishing on the Miramichi, encountered those twin scourges of Canadian sportfishermen, "the terrible flies and the salmon who do not rise." At Charlottetown, they attended a grand ball at the Parliament Buildings, held to celebrate that province's entry into Confederation. Here, the decor featured a bold array of the flags of the seven provinces, and, striking a note of hope for the future, "the flag of Newfoundland still rolled up." On August 9, when the unfolding Pacific Scandal

A viceregal fishing trip. The sketch is by Lord Dufferin.

forced Dufferin to return post-haste to Ottawa, Lady Dufferin conquered her shyness and continued the trip on her own. "Never was I so stared at as today," she reports of the trip by rail to Saint John. "At the stations, the people looked in the windows and gazed at me while I ate sandwiches."

A year later, in the summer of 1874, they travelled west: by rail through the district of Muskoka, and then on by steamer as far as the Lakehead. Though pregnant yet again, Lady Dufferin much enjoyed the north-woods custom of sleeping in tents. "The whole floor is spread with firboughs which are laid down most carefully and scientifically and make a most delightful carpet and spring mattress."

On February 26, 1875, back in Ottawa, the birth of the Dufferins' seventh and last child Frederick was treated with customary insouciance: it occurred in between "a large dinner party for married Ministers and Wives" on February 12, and a performance of amateur theatricals on March 31.*

Then, on July 31, 1876 ("as I write these words," noted Edmund Meredith in his East Block office, "the cannons are firing a salvo on the departure of Lord Dufferin for British Columbia") the viceregal couple set out on their most ambitious progression of all – clear across the continent by train to San Francisco; up the Pacific Coast by British man-of-war as far north as the Queen Charlotte Islands where they marvelled at the totem poles; then back through Salt Lake City (where although they declined the offer of an interview with the polygamous Mormon leader Brigham Young, Lady Dufferin was not above recording in fascination a chance glimpse of "Amelia, the most powerful of his wives") and on to Winnipeg, and then back to Ottawa through Lake of the Woods.

Power politics, as the booming guns bore witness, had dictated this most important of all the Grand Tours. Dufferin had plunged headlong into a delicate exercise in what a later generation would describe as "federal-provincial diplomacy." Indeed, the fact that the Dufferins had had to detour through the United States in order to arrive at Canada's westernmost province set the burning issue of the day in sharp relief.

On one side of this federal-provincial fracas stood British Columbia, which had been cajoled into Confederation in 1871 on the condition that the transcontinental railway would be completed within ten years. On the other side stood Ottawa, in the form of the financially hard-pressed government of Alexander Mackenzie, which by now had made clear that it had no intention of abiding by this

* Frederick, the Dufferins' only Canadian-born son, succeeded to the title in 1918, after two of his elder brothers, Archie and Basil, had been killed, respectively, in the Boer War and the First World War, and after a third, Terence, had died of natural causes. Frederick died in 1931, in a notorious "society air-taxi crash" over Kent, *en route* home from Le Touquet. According to contemporary newspaper accounts, "Over £65,000 worth of jewellery was said to be scattered over the countryside." Frederick's son Basil, an individual of enormous promise who served as a junior minister in the government of Stanley Baldwin, was killed in Burma in 1945. His son, born in 1938, the present Marquis of Dufferin and Ava, whose christian name Sheridan evokes the heyday of family history, is a London patron of the arts.

promise. In between the two, as harsh words and threats of separation flew back and forth, stood Dufferin who, much to the dismay of his Canadian advisers, had decided to carve out for himself the role of domestic diplomat.

As he later reported to Lord Carnarvon, Dufferin spent his first week in Victoria "receiving visits from every soul in the place. I began at nine o'clock in the morning and never left my room until seven in the evening; the whole immediate ten hours being passed in listening to the same stories of abuse of Canada and of the Canadian premiers." Having got nowhere with quiet diplomacy, Dufferin went public on September 20, 1876, in an epochal speech that lasted two and a quarter hours and that combined, in roughly equal parts, a defense of Mackenzie's position and a "soft-sawdering" of British Columbia. "I may say frankly," said Dufferin, amid much other hyperbole, "that I think British Columbia is a glorious province . . . whose association with the Dominion she ought to regard as the crowning triumph of federation."

To his west-coast audience, the Governor General's message went down tolerably well. Back in Ottawa, however, word of it unleashed the furies on both sides of the House and it escalated into one of the few serious blunders in all of Dufferin's long diplomatic career. For the outrage of the Opposition Tories at Dufferin's seeming softness to Mackenzie, we have Meredith's account of a conversation on the croquet lawn with his friend, Charles Tupper. "He said that Lord D. went far beyond the proper bounds in defending the conduct of Mr. Mackenzie, and that his speech means misery for the Governor General next session. He told me to *mark his words*!" For the reaction of the ruling Grits at the intrusion of the Governor General into strictly Canadian matters, we have Dufferin's own account to Lord Carnarvon of "a most stormy interview" with Mackenzie and Blake on his return to Ottawa, in which this trio "nearly came to blows." "Mackenzie was simply pitiable," Dufferin continued, "and Blake was on the point of crying, as he very readily does when he is excited."

For the first time, but by no means for the last, a Governor General discovered that while Canadians revered the Crown, they wanted it to float well over their heads as a sort of iconic halo. Dufferin weathered the storm, but he never again made the mistake of confusing influence with power. In the event, the CPR didn't reach the west coast for another dozen years. On the other hand, British Columbia didn't separate. As for Lady Dufferin, other matters were of greater concern to her. Her diary for September 20,

1876, the day of her husband's epic speech, records only her pleasure at the concert got up by the officers of H.M.S. *Amethyst*, the Dufferin's west-coast home afloat, "and afterwards some Christy Minstrels which were very amusing."

Back in Ottawa, the Dufferins did their best to rectify what the Earl described in a letter to Carnarvon at Whitehall as "the solitude, desolation and incompleteness of the capital." The going wasn't easy. Ottawans proved awkward, and difficult to entertain. "My guests fidget off by ten," Lady Dufferin expostulated in a letter to her mother. "When one person moves they all go, and it is useless to say, "Do stay."

There was also the equally pressing problem of assuaging their own cabin fever. "There is a terrible want of society," wrote Dufferin to Carnarvon, "and one's life at times is dull and lonely." In an era when Parliament, during the three or four months it was in session, provided the only live entertainment in town, Dufferin's life often was duller than his wife's. She, like all the other ladies, could dash off to the House to hear all the exciting debates. Viceregal etiquette required him to remain sequestered in his office, touching up the exquisite pen and ink sketches he'd taken to making during their travels, and reading Plutarch in Latin. In between times, he received the briefings of his successive prime ministers, Macdonald and Mackenzie. There was no doubt about which one Dufferin preferred. Macdonald, for all his bouts of "transient weakness" as the Governor General tactfully described them, was, as he put it in a memo to his successor, Lord Lorne, "a thorough man of the world, charming in conversation, gentlemanlike, with excellent manners . . . ," and this even though "his political morality, at least as far as bribery and corruption are concerned was learned in a school far less straight-laced than that in which we have been brought up."

Mackenzie, by contrast, Dufferin described in a letter to Carnarvon as "a small man without creative genius or any real initiative or power of forecast."

By the end of their first winter in Ottawa, the Dufferins had discovered the means both of energizing their own existence, and of breaking the ice with local society. The trick, they found, was to institutionalize, as the two mainstays of their official entertainments, the pastimes they each enjoyed best: her passion for amateur theatricals; his for winter sports. In so doing, the Dufferins established an organizing principle for off-duty Ottawa that obtains to this day, demonstrated by such quintessential institutions as the Little Theatre, and the wintertime obsession with skating and skiing.

At Rideau Hall in the 1870s, amateur theatricals in themselves were nothing new. Even in the humdrum era of the Lisgars, Edmund and Fanny Meredith had been invited to a "set of charades" during the 1870 visit of Prince Arthur, future Duke of Connaught, in which, much to Meredith's amazement, "the Prince himself took the role of a servant." The difference was, never before had there been a vicereine – never for that matter, would there be again – whose attack was so enthusiastic and who herself was such a vivacious actress. As if the Sheridan blood had somehow been transfused osmotically into her own veins, Lady Dufferin used to hone her technique in front of an audience of one. In the small hours of November 4, 1873, for instance, when the Macdonald government was in its death-throes over the Pacific Scandal, she rushed home from the House of Commons to the viceregal bedroom to replay, virtually *in toto*, and perhaps even including gestures to suggest the sips of gin-and-water, Sir John's brilliant though ultimately unsuccessful last ditch speech. "She was pleased to keep me awake from three to five," Dufferin wrote to Macdonald, "repeating it with appropriate actions." Around the breakfast-table next morning she ran through it again, "to a continuous chorus of admiration from all my English friends."

With Lady Dufferin and her brother, Captain Fred Hamilton, as principal stars, with Dufferin himself in charge of make-up, and, for supporting cast, a bevy of talented locals who included most notably René Edward Kimber, the dapper and polished Gentleman Usher of the Black Rod, and Mrs. Anglin, wife of the Speaker of the Commons, the Rideau Hall Players shortly burst onto the Ottawa scene as the next best thing to a resident repertory company. The first gala performance, of a comic warhorse of the Victorian stage, *To Oblige Benson*, took place on March 13, 1873, in the newly completed Rideau Hall ballroom. Since Lady Dufferin at the time was seven months pregnant, this was one of the few occasions on which she herself did not act. Instead, she hovered over the scene like an anxious theatrical angel. "The guests assembled at nine," she reports, "and after having some tea were conducted through unknown passages to their future ballroom where they found 300 chairs in rows, arranged in front of a very pretty little stage and a band dressed in the gorgeous uniform of the Governor General's Guards. The entertainment went off admirably." Ottawans, for once, did not go home too early; indeed, they lingered almost too long. "We went into the supper room afterwards, and it took time to 'feed and speed' the parting 300."

Each year thereafter, during Lent, the season when balls were frowned on, two or three plays were produced, with an additional pantomime for the children at Christmas. More important than the content of anything that was performed – the exception being an original operetta, *Le Maire de St. Brieux*, produced in 1875 with lyrics by the Dufferins' children's tutor and with music by the Cathedral organist, F. W. Mills – was the galvanic effect these productions had on Ottawa. The dutiful diarist Janet Hall, although never invited to any performance, never failed to note each one, "Private theatricals at Rideau, Uncle went," runs a typical entry on April 8, 1876. By the end of the decade, as the passion for play-acting spread through the town like wildfire, she was able to buy a ticket to see and enjoy the ineffable Dr. Hamnet Hill, he of the six-foot Christmas tree at the Fancy Dress ball, playing Sir Joseph Porter, KGB, in a full-scale production of *H.M.S. Pinafore*, that wildly popular operetta by Gilbert and Sullivan first produced in London the year before. "All very good," she wrote, "except that the Admiral could not be heard." Meredith, who went the same night, April 23, 1879, was also impressed – to a point. "Dr. Hill, the First Lord of the Admiralty, would have been excellent if he had any voice," he wrote in his diary.

Meredith had plenty of reason to preen himself as a critic that night. Earlier that very week, he himself had "trod the boards" in front of an invited audience of nearly a hundred in a leading role in a confection called *The Honeymoon*, "a play very rarely attempted by amateurs being considered too difficult," as he proudly wrote. This production took place in the back drawing room of the Merediths' house on Augusta Street, on a stage constructed by sixteen-year-old Arthur, with sets, also by Arthur, that included "two different street scenes."

No family in the city had been more inspired by the Dufferin passion for theatre than the Merediths. If anything, the productions of "The Nemo Troupe," as the family collectively styled itself, were considerably more ambitious than anything ever attempted at Rideau; the first of these, at Christmas 1877, was nothing less than an adaptation of *Bleak House* prepared by the talented nineteen-year-old Alice. On that occasion, only three outsiders were invited to watch, but by the next Christmas the Nemo Troupe had grown much bolder, thirty friends and neighbours were invited in to see a production that the programme, carefully transcribed in Fanny's memoir, describes as "The Celebrated One-Act Burlesque, *Bombasto Furioso*, starring The Incomparable Tragedian, 'Mr. Blank' from Geddo." "Mr. Blank's" initials were E.A.M. Like all inveterate hams, "E.A.M." made a great show of reluctance. "I find my part horribly long and troublesome to learn," he protested in his diary. Nonetheless, he had more fun playing a character named "Artanonimous" than even when reciting *Horatius at the Bridge*, which anyway, in the new heady atmosphere, seemed now very old hat. The following April, he enjoyed playing "the comic role of a servant" in *The Honeymoon* even more. "Some persons said that our performance was worth ten of them at Rideau. Dr. Tupper and several others opined that I had mistaken my vocation and should have been an actor."

"I am inclined to believe," Meredith added sadly, having by now left the government, "that I might have made a better actor than anything else."

For all her infectious enthusiasms and her hearty County Down habit of stomping cheerfully along the muddy roads of Ottawa in heavy hobnailed boots, there was one aspect of life in Ottawa that Lady Dufferin, however hard she tried, could never adjust to: the bitter cold of winter. "Thermometer 20 below zero," she reports in horror on their first Christmas Day in the capital in 1872. "Must go to church in sealskin turbans . . . we are devoted to our 'clouds' in which we wallow." By contrast, Dufferin wallowed in winter, the colder the better. "D. wears less than he used to do in May at home, and scarcely seems to feel the cold at all." Even more than by the Canadian wilderness, Dufferin's imagination was captured by snow and ice. He became the first in a long line of proconsuls who, accustomed to an empire that nearly everywhere else was steaming hot, with punkahs waving, found winter and all its panoply of blanket coats and bright red tuques romantic and exotic. In Ottawa, thanks to Dufferin, winter became as it had been in Quebec during the era of the muffins: the fashionable season.

Lord Dufferin, his daughter, and a friend depicted on the new Rideau Hall toboggan slide. He wears a habitant *tuque and Lady Helen Blackwood wears a Hudson's Bay Company blanket coat.*

Just as for Fanny Meredith in Quebec in the 1850s the *sine qua non* of muffinhood had been the ability to drive Rattler and Prince dashing in tandem over the ice of the St. Lawrence, so for her daughters, in Ottawa in the 1870s, the key to social success became the ability to instruct the viceregal court in the intricacies of the waltz and the "outside edge" on skates, on the private rink at Rideau Hall. Even more fun, from Lady Dufferin's point of view, was the new toboggan slide that the Dufferin children prodded their

A composite photograph of a Dufferin tobogganing party.

parents into installing in 1874. "Most exciting," she reported back home. "A long flight of stairs now leads to the top of a high wooden slide and as this is almost perpendicular, the toboggan starts at a great rate." Guests of the Dufferins, over from Britain, were equally enthralled. "Tobogganing is a most favourite amusement," Lieutenant William Galwey of the 49th Parallel Survey Party wrote home to his mother. "Ladies go in for it. I think they like rolling over and over with the gentlemen." Even the supposedly fragile Fanny Meredith, egged on by her children, went in for it. "Fanny laid up with the effects of the toboggan party," Edmund reports in the winter of 1879. "I go for Dr. Tupper."

As for Dufferin himself, it was the sport of curling that captured his fancy. Indeed, on February 23, 1876, instead of resting up for the Fancy Dress Ball, he spent most of the afternoon wielding a broom. Writing of a boyhood visit to the Dufferin family seat at Clandeboye in the 1890s, Harold Nicolson describes the stairway leading down from the entrance to the front hall as, "flanked by a double row of curling stones."*

* In 1984, reports Dufferin's great-grandson, the present Marquis of Dufferin and Ava, these curling stones continue to flourish at Clandeboye, and in the same location.

In the autumn of 1878, amid a great show of emotion on both their parts, the Dufferins left Ottawa forever. Dufferin's last official act, on October 9, while Alexander Mackenzie, seeking out company in his misery, dropped by Meredith's East Block office, was to swear in Macdonald as a prime minister reborn. They left behind an Ottawa quite different from the one they had found in 1872. "It was considerably livelier, and had some awareness of its destiny,"

Robert Hubbard has noted in his history, *Rideau Hall*. Dufferin himself went on to far greater Imperial glory: his immediate posting after Ottawa was to St. Petersburg as Ambassador; after that he served as ambassador to Constantinople, in India as viceroy, later as ambassador to Rome and to Paris. In September 1888, on leaving India, he was created a marquis and it was this elevation, as much as the curling stones, that demonstrated the manner in which his six years in Canada had captured his heart. For the second title a marquisate required, he wished to take the name, Quebec. "The town owes its preservation to me," he explained, "as I saved its walls from destruction. Moreover, so many of my happiest associations are connected with it." Much to Dufferin's chagrin, Queen Victoria did not approve; probably she was influenced by the same edginess about public opinion in the United States that, back in 1867, had prevented Canada from being styled a "kingdom" as Macdonald had wished, so that instead we became a Dominion. For his additional title Dufferin instead chose the old Burmese capital of Ava, to commemorate the fact that Burma had been annexed to the British Empire during his term as Viceroy of India, and so he became the First Marquis of Dufferin and Ava.

The last years of Dufferin's life, in retirement at Clandeboye, were a sad finale to a sunny and fruitful life. In January 1900, his eldest son Archie, Lord Ava, Arthur Meredith's special friend in Ottawa, who kept up his ties with Ottawa into his dashing young manhood, was killed in the war in South Africa. In 1901, the "awful combination" of Irishness and Sheridanishness at last caught up with Dufferin: a company of which he had agreed to be chairman went bankrupt owing its shareholders hundreds of thousands of pounds. Dufferin died at seventy-six in February 1902, at least as much of grief over Archie and humiliation over his financial failures as of natural causes. Lady Dufferin, for whom the sun never shone again, lived on until 1936.

In Canada, in 1878, some people did not in the least regret Dufferin's taking his leave. "Our terribly prosaic people were just beginning to get tired of the illimitable sweetmeats and soap-bubbles, and even to fancy that the magician was partly advertising himself," wrote that sturdy, no-frills Presbyterian, Principal George Grant of Queen's University. In Toronto, the annexationist and Republican Sage of The Grange, Goldwin Smith, poked fun at Dufferin's habit of handing out verbatim texts of his speeches to the newspapers, "with notations such as 'applause' and 'hear, hear' marked at proper intervals."

Not among this company was Edmund Meredith. Thanks to the Dufferins, the years of his greatest frustrations at the office had been the years of his – and also of Fanny's – greatest social success. With Arthur and Archie, the future Lord Ava, enrolled in the same dancing class and driving round together as the greatest of chums "in a sleigh drawn by our two dogs, Bang and Tiny," as Fanny tells us, and with little Morna Meredith at six the earliest recorded conquest of Lord Basil Blackwood, already a devilishly handsome lady-killer, the Merediths had been right at the heart of the Rideau Hall circle. In October 1878, when Meredith was in the midst of his battle to get his superannuation, it touched him deeply to come into his office one day after lunch and discover that "Lord Dufferin had been sending messages wishing to see me; I decided to go to the station to wish him goodbye." It touched both the Merediths yet more deeply that, at the railway depot, Dufferin singled out fifteen-year-old Arthur from the crowd, and gravely shook his hand. "He said, 'Arthur, my boy, God bless you,' " Fanny wrote, "I shall always be glad to hear of your welfare."

Meredith's own time in Ottawa was, by now, winding to a close. He had just time enough left to witness the opening scenes of that most curious of all governor-generalcies, the troubled and querulous years of Princess Louise and the Marquis of Lorne.

CHAPTER 13

The Gay Governor General

Tomorrow night I lecture Lorne on dadoes at Ottawa . . .
Oscar Wilde, in a letter
to Norman Forbes-Robertson, May 15, 1882

Wilde in fact, was dreaming in colour. During his two-day stopover in Ottawa in the midst of a lecture tour of North America, he did not set eyes on the Marquis of Lorne. Not only was he not invited to dine at Rideau Hall, the Governor General did not even bother to interrupt a round of golf to ask him to lunch. Nor did Lorne attend Wilde's public lecture at the Grand Opera House. (Neither, for that matter, did Edmund Meredith, for the uncomplicated reason that he by then was no longer living in the capital.) Yet Wilde's visit to Ottawa is worth a slight digression, for it was here, of all places, that he made the chance acquaintance that changed the direction of his life.

Wilde's appearance on stage at Ottawa, clad in his customary platform rig of black velvet suit and knee breeches, hair waving *en bouffant* over his ears, was far from the most auspicious of his tour. Though he was sufficiently newsworthy to rate a front-page story in the *Daily Citizen*, and this on the very same day that Macdonald prorogued Parliament for an election, the reviewer was profoundly unimpressed. "Of more than ordinary height, Wilde would present a good appearance were it not for the outré manner in which he wears his hair," the unbylined account was prefaced. Then it continued:

> As a lecturer, he is anything but an unqualified success. His style resembles very much the dull monotone so common in some of the pulpits. . . . Although a native of "The Green Isle," Mr. Wilde's speech resembles the English cockney more than it does that of the Dublin born and educated gentleman. . . . The ideas promulgated by this gentleman might be excellent if all people were either millionaires or savages, but in the practical 19th century and in a practical country like Canada, he is not likely to find many followers.

Wilde's fatal error, however, was to have inserted a verbal hatpin into Ottawa's boosterish pride.

> His local suggestions were by no means new, though no practical man would have expressed them so extremely. That it is a pity that Ottawa should be dirtied with sawdust has long been admitted, and that pure sky should be dirtied with smoke may also be a pity. But Mr. Wilde goes too far when he advocates that no man should be allowed to carry on a business which produces either of these results.

There were, however, consolations. Wilde dropped in on a late-night sitting of Parliament after his lecture and, as a visiting celebrity, was invited to sit on the floor of the Commons, next to the Speaker. Next morning, at the Russell House, he held court to a crowd of "female autograph hounds," as a reporter for *The Globe* described them. The most beguiling supplicant, who brought along her Birthday Book for him to sign, was a certain Miss Frances Richards, a young Ottawa portrait painter. Then thirty, she was a young woman of pre-Raphaelite looks and impeccable antecedents, the daughter of a former Lieutenant-Governor of British Columbia, niece of a former Chief Justice of the Supreme Court. She was also a woman of considerable sophistication. In the 1870s, she'd spent three years studying art in Paris in the studios of the best-known teachers of the era, Robert Fleury and Carolus Duran. One of her fellow students had been the doomed consumptive painter Marie Bashkirtseff, whose feverishly introspective *Journal of a Young Artist* made her a cult figure of the 1880s when it was published posthumously. Bashkirtseff had painted Frances's portrait and mentioned her in the diary. In 1882, having spent a year back home running the newly-established Ottawa Art School, Frances was on the point of returning to Europe for further studies.

Frances Richards. Her portrait of Oscar Wilde was probably the inspiration for his novel The Picture of Dorian Gray.

Wilde was entranced by her, and went round to her studio. "I wish I could be in London to show you a few houses and a few men and women," he told her. "But I will be in Japan, sitting under an almond tree, drinking amber-coloured tea out of a blue and white cup and contemplating a decorative landscape." Then he dashed off a letter of introduction to his close friend, the American expatriate painter in London, James McNeill Whistler:

My dearest Jimmy,

> I want you to know, and to know is to delight in, Miss Richards, who is an artist, and a little oasis of culture in Canada. She does really good work and has already civilized the Marquis of Lorne.
>
> She is devoted to your pictures, or rather to my descriptions of them, which are just as good, I often think better. She is quite worthy of your blue and white china, so I send her to you with this letter; I know you will be charming to her. *Toujours*,
>
> Oscar

Whether or not Frances actually appeared with the letter at Whistler's studio in Chelsea is lost to history. Certainly, though, Wilde saw her in Paris the following spring and, in 1887, when she moved permanently to London, she became for a time a regular member of his circle. That same year, around Christmastime, she painted his portrait, and according to a contemporary London art critic, Christopher Millard, this was the inspiration for Wilde's novel, *The Picture of Dorian Gray*. "When the sitting was over and Mr. Wilde had looked at the portrait, it occurred to him that a thing of Beauty, when it takes the form of a middle-aged gentleman, is unhappily not a joy forever," Millard wrote in 1890. "'What a tragic thing it is,'" he exclaimed. "'This portrait will never grow older, and I shall.'"*

Frances Richards never returned to live in Canada. Instead, in 1888, she married into the landed gentry – one W. E. Rowley, Esq. – and thereafter divided her time between a *pied-à-terre* in Cheyne Walk in Chelsea, and a country house named Glassonby in Cumberland. But her lingering connections with Canada were the source of her most profound influence on Wilde.

By way of keeping up her ties with home, Frances had formed a close friendship with another expatriate living in London, a widow named Augusta Ross. Mrs. Ross was the daughter of Robert Baldwin, the great Reform leader who served as premier of the Province of Canada in 1848-1851, and who is best remembered for having achieved Responsible Government. It was almost certainly through Frances that Wilde made the acquaintance of the Ross family and, in particular, the acquaintance of Augusta's third son, nicknamed "Robbie." Until this meeting, as most of Wilde's biographers agree, the homosexual side of his nature had never asserted

* This portrait, sadly, has long since disappeared.

itself overtly; rather he had a reputation for being quite a ladies' man. Robbie Ross, "a small, slight, attractive man with an affectionate, impulsive nature and considerable charm of manner," in the words of the British writer Hesketh Pearson, became Wilde's first recorded male lover. It was the same "faithful Robbie" who was with Wilde when he died in Paris in 1900, in penury and disgrace.

Perhaps, even in 1882, the Marquis of Lorne's reason for avoiding Wilde so studiously was the need to be circumspect. Already over his governor-generalcy there hovered a whiff of heliotrope, a lingering scent of the green carnation. There is no other viceregal tenure about which so many delicate questions remain unanswered. What was the true nature of the relationship between Lorne and his wife, the Princess Louise? Was it because Louise detested Canada or because she detested Lorne that she spent so little time at his side here? Quite apart from the matter of her troubled marriage, was the story of Princess Louise's bitter quarrel with Sir John and Lady Macdonald based on fact – or was it only the product of malicious gossip?

In hindsight, the years of the Lornes at Rideau are a conundrum. In terms of tangible results, few governor-generalcies have been more productive: during their term, and boosted by a brief, buoyant surge in the economy, Official Ottawa embarked on a heady Golden Age. Thanks to direct viceregal initiative, two landmark instruments of Canadian culture, the National Gallery and the Royal Society were established in the space of two years. Yet not even during the King-Byng crisis of 1926 has a governor-generalcy been marred by so much acrimony in public and nasty whispering in private.

In the autumn of 1878, the news that the Marquis of Lorne and the Princess Louise would succeed the Dufferins had seemed to Ottawans like a gift from the gods. In truth, it was a gift from that canny old bird Benjamin Disraeli, now well advanced on the road to creating a glittering Empire. In Disraeli's view, as the historian W. S. MacNutt has noted, the appointment represented "a continuation of his experiment in statecraft by which the Crown was employed as an instrument to proclaim the greatness and unity of the Empire." The previous July, when Dizzy had travelled to Balmoral to broach his bright idea, the Queen had agreed with alacrity. For public consumption, Victoria made all the proper maternal noises about the pain of parting with her daughter. One can't help speculating, though, that in private she appreciated Disraeli's suggestion as the best possible solution to a difficult and continuing problem. For, as everyone in court circles was only too well aware, the marriage of the Queen's fourth daughter was in serious difficulty.

Louise, in 1878, had just turned thirty. Though by no means the most brilliant of Queen Victoria's five daughters – her eldest sister Vicky, mother of the future Kaiser Wilhelm was unquestionably the intellectual in the brood – she was far and away the best looking; "a tall, slight, handsome figure who wore black velvet with diamonds in the evenings," in the words of a contemporary. Louise was also the most creative of Victoria's children, a talented painter and sculptor whose work – as in the portrait of her friend Clara Montalba, executed at Rideau Hall – far transcended that of a gifted amateur. To her own later great unhappiness, Louise was also Victoria's most capricious child. In her late teens, she'd regarded with horror the plump, dull German princelings to whom her elder sisters had been married off. She declared that she would marry an Englishman. In 1869, when she was twenty-one, and with the Queen's approval, she set her cap for the twenty-three-year-old Marquis of Lorne, eldest son and heir of Dufferin's great friend and mentor, the Duke of Argyll.

H.R.H. Princess Louise in furs and a "cloud." She was Queen Victoria's most difficult daughter.

Though the court ladies whispered that Louise was not in love with Lorne, her choice on the face of it seemed sensible enough. Lorne's blond, dreamy, slightly abstracted good looks counterpointed her own dark, intense elegance. Better still, Lorne shared her artistic tastes: the painters Landseer and Millais were among his friends; he himself, though much less proficiently than the Princess, enjoyed dabbling in watercolours – and also in verse. He was also a romantic who, no matter that by the time he arrived in Italy all the excitement was over, had at least made the attempt to join Garibaldi.

But Lorne was, almost certainly, a homosexual, and not always one who remained in the closet. As a schoolboy at Eton, as the British scholar Timothy D'Arch Smith has revealed in his book, *Love in Earnest*, he had been involved in a relationship with another sprig of the aristocracy, Frederick Wood, the future Lord Halifax – a relationship so tender that one of their masters, the poet William Johnson Cory, had apotheosized it in an underground poem titled "An Epoch in a Sweet Life." In later years, Lorne was well-known as an habitué of certain illicit London clubs and to attend what were discreetly described as "masculine parties."

The Marquis of Lorne. Many of his best friends were painters.

Louise, in unhappy contrast, had inherited beyond doubt the Queen's own highly sexed nature. In the mid-1890s when she was nearly fifty, it was rumoured in court circles that her ceaseless pursuit of Prince "Liko" Battenberg, husband of her younger sister Beatrice, had forced that unfortunate man to seek refuge in an Imperial expedition to Ashanti in West Africa, where he promptly died of fever. Years later, Princess Alice, Countess of Athlone, who was both Louise's niece (daughter of her favourite brother Leopold) and vicereine at Rideau Hall during the Second World War, reminisced quite uninhibitedly to the British writer Nina Epton about Louise's predilection. "She got on well . . . with any man – she ran after everything in trousers. Louise liked Louis Battenberg too . . . oh, all the men." About Lorne, Princess Alice was a trifle less candid. He was "a dear . . . good-looking, kind, vague . . . too soft with her . . . he was a little odd in his behaviour; he would wear a Norfolk jacket for a formal occasion and at other times appear at breakfast wearing the Order of the Garter."

Louise and Lorne married in 1871, with splendid ceremony that included a cake five feet high, decorated with figures representing the Fine Arts, Science, Agriculture, and Commerce, that had taken three months to build. The only note less than rapturous was sounded by Lorne's doting mother, the Duchess of Argyll. "You must not expect Louise to look young enough for him," she wrote to her sister-in-law – a curious comment given that the Princess was only twenty-three and two years Lorne's junior. But perhaps the real problem was that Louise with her elegant ways made all her dour Scottish in-laws feel clumsy. "I think Princess Louise made my mother discover how handless we were," wrote Lorne's younger sister Frances, who later married the younger brother of Prime Minister Arthur Balfour and became a noted suffragist. "We did not excel in the arts."

Within a year or two, the absence of a pregnancy was causing tongues to wag. It was also noticed at court that Louise was no longer as bright and lively as she once had been. One rumour had it that she had never had a menstrual period and was unable to bear children. By 1875, when the Queen paid a visit to the Lornes at Inveraray Castle, seat of the Argylls, it was obvious that their relationship was out of kilter. Even the Queen found it curious that Louise had so arranged things that Lorne almost never joined them for meals. The Queen's trusted private secretary, Sir Henry Ponsonby, confided to his wife in a letter: "It is absurd talking of two dinners in a private house; she has married into a Duke's family and must live with them as a relation."

No doubt, as Ponsonby continued, Louise *was* "a mischief-maker, who plays old Harry with every household or person she touches." No doubt she did henpeck Lorne quite unmercifully, as everyone noticed. "If anything, Lorne's manner to women was *too* chivalrous," wrote his devoted sister Frances in a veiled criticism of her sister-in-law. "It was said of him that he could never be waited on by a woman without offering to take the dishes out of her hand." Yet, to withhold sympathy from Louise is impossible. In an era when homosexuality was "the love that dared not speak its name," what on earth could she say to explain?

In the autumn of 1878, Lady Dufferin was one of a handful of shrewd observers who wondered privately whether shipping Louise and Lorne out to Canada was all that good an idea. Stopping off in London *en route* to the Dufferins' new post in St. Petersburg, she confided to Ponsonby, as he recorded, that "Lorne was very vague in his conception of the duties of his office but the real difficulty was, how Louise would treat people in Canada – if as royalty, there will be trouble, but if in the same way Lady Dufferin did, they will be flattered."

For the first few months, however, the new viceregal universe unfolded exactly as Disraeli and Queen Victoria had hoped. The change in Louise's surroundings appeared to have perked her up. She arrived at Halifax after a brutal late-November crossing aboard the *Sarmatian* looking only slightly pale. (While Louise had kept to her berth, Lorne had occupied himself sketching seagulls.) And if Sir John, in the welcoming party, looked visibly the worse for wear, having only recently rallied from one of the very worst of all his drinking bouts, she made a point of not noticing. Far from insisting on having a separate dinner served in privacy aboard the viceregal train as it steamed up to Montreal, she was seen by the press party tucking into her food with hearty appetite, and demonstrating, as the man from the *Montreal Star* noticed, "a decided partiality for mutton chops." At Montreal, when the orders of an over-zealous aide provoked a teapot tempest over the proper dress for ladies to wear when being presented at the viceregal drawing room – he'd prescribed full court decorum, which implied low-necked dresses and these, to the Quebec clergy, were anathema – she deflected it with a shrug. "I should not have cared it they had come in blanket coats."

In Ottawa, when they arrived on December 2, the weather was so abysmal that all the official ceremonies of welcome had to be postponed for twenty-four hours. Even so, on the next day, a murderous mixture of rain and sleet continued to drip from the magnificently turreted civil service arch of welcome erected on Parliament Hill at a cost of $1000. Wisely, the Princess skipped the "presentation of twelve addresses in the Senate Chamber" and let Lorne go alone. (Fanny Meredith and her daughters braved the crush and "saw nothing, but felt a good deal," as they reported to Edmund, "to wit, two or three fat men who nearly crushed them to death.") But within a day or two, to the general delight, Louise was seen striding around the town no less enthusiastically than Lady Dufferin. On December 8, Janet Hall, always punctilious about recording the to-ing and fro-ing of Ottawa's vice-royals, looked out of her window over Wellington Street and was astonished to see the Princess and her party stepping briskly by. A few days later, the two almost bumped into each other on Sparks Street. "I got a very good view, and she seems rather good-looking." Then, early in February, the Merediths, who had worried that their names might have been struck off the "inner circle" list now that Edmund had retired from the government, were delighted to receive an invitation to dinner. "Great excitement! Old dames draw us out," wrote Meredith. On February 8, more exciting still was the discovery that only about thirty of the select had been invited and that Major de Winton, Lorne's private secretary, had been delegated to escort twenty-two-year-old Mary Meredith in to dinner. Most exciting of all, "after dinner, the Princess talked to Fanny during the greater part of the evening and F. was greatly charmed with her."

No less charmed, after a curling match at Rideau Hall in March, was former prime minister Alexander Mackenzie – now six months into Opposition. As if she recognized instinctively that here was a man in need of cheering up, the Princess went out of her way to inform him that her mother had visited his birthplace, Dunkeld in Scotland, and had remarked to Louise that it was the most beautiful place she had ever seen. Both she and Lorne, the Princess confided, felt as much at home in Ottawa as in Argyllshire, "because we meet so many Scotchmen."

In a way that no viceregal couple had ever done before, Louise and Lorne, during those first pleasant months, also made inroads into Ottawa's French-Canadian society – a small, self-contained world of whose existence Edmund Meredith was barely aware, but which, centred round the lively local branch of the *Institut Canadien*, was incomparably more cultured and sophisticated than its English-speaking counterpart and even produced its own local literary periodical, *Le Foyer domestique*. This circle included historian Benjamin Sulte, soon to embark on his mammoth, eight-volume *Histoire des canadians-français*, the distinguished poet Louis Frèchette, who was also a Liberal Member of Parliament, and Frèchette's younger brother, the House of Commons translator Achille, whom we first met in 1876 at the Dufferins' Ball. By now, the younger Frèchette and his journalist bride from New England, Annie Howells, had succeeded George and Lucianne Desbarats as virtually the only couple in town to move easily within both French and English circles. "Whenever either the Governor General or the Princess are in company with French Canadians," wrote Annie Howells Frèchette in an article titled "Life at Rideau Hall" published in *Harper's*, "they enter into conversation in French as both speak it well and fluently." Indeed, as the historian MacNutt recounts, it was Louise's preference for French Canadians that caused the first flutterings in Official Society. On one occasion while entertaining a group of ladies, it was said, she gave her undivided attention to the beautiful and cultivated wife of a senator from Quebec, while all the others sat frigid and silent. One of them at last could bear it no longer and implored an equerry: "Do, I beg you, take pity on us and talk with us in English." This predilection for French was also said to have been responsible for the banishment of John Ronald Macdonald, the Rideau Hall piper, for a French lady had remarked to the Princess that his Highland music made her unhappy because it reminded her of the death of Montcalm.

In between official functions, Louise busied herself sprucing up Rideau Hall. "L. has everyone working their arms off," wrote Lorne to his father. At Louise's command, workmen cut a "Princess Vista" through the woods to afford a view of the Ottawa River, and constructed a portable "sketching box" that could be transported round the grounds to protect her from the icy winds as she drew. She herself decorated the door of her elegant blue boudoir with a *trompe l'oeil* pattern of blossoming apple boughs that can be seen at Rideau Hall to this day. Out from London to visit the first winter, came a pair of artist friends, Henrietta and Clara Montalba: while Henrietta modelled a bust of Lorne in fur collar and cap, Louise painted a splendid portrait of Clara. Another friend from overseas, Marie von Bunsen, the granddaughter of a former Prussian Ambassador to London, marvelled at the new, contented Louise:

> All honours were paid to Lorne as Governor General. Louise played second fiddle on every occasion. She walked on his left, entered the room behind him, rose with all the rest of us when he came in and like

Princess Louise's studio at Rideau Hall.

all the rest, remained standing until he was seated. In England, only on rare occasions was he commanded to join the family at table – the daughter took meals with her mother and he as a general rule with the household at the Lord Chamberlain's table.

According to Annie Howells Frèchette, Louise even took up cooking during this halcyon interlude. "A friend of mine was lately dining at Rideau Hall," Frèchette wrote in *Harper's*, "and during the dinner she remarked on the excellence of the oyster pâtés to one of the ladies-in-waiting. 'Yes,' she replied, 'they were made by Her Royal Highness.'"

The following autumn, the first cracks in this pleasant façade began to show. "The Princess Louise returns to England on the 18th," wrote Janet Hall on October 1, 1879, "having been ordered by her physicians." Few others in Ottawa accepted this news at face value, for rumours by now were rampant that Louise, after her initial enthusiasm, had become bored to tears by her rustic northern playground. In particular, according to the gossip, Louise had come to loathe the very sight of those two individuals into whose company Official Society most frequently thrust her: Sir John and Lady Macdonald. He, it was said, had appeared drunk at a ball at Rideau, and had "taken a liberty." Lady Macdonald, for her part, could not resist from continually trying to upstage the Princess as Ottawa's first lady.

The truth of such stories is impossible now to pin down – all the more because, apart from newspaper hearsay in such gossip sheets as London's *Truth* and the New York *World*, the only factual account that survives is contained in the 1912 *Reminiscences* of Sir Richard Cartwright, a former Liberal finance minster who was one of Macdonald's bitterest political enemies.* According to Cartwright, the Premier "had given the Princess very just cause for his offence by his conduct on the occasion of a state function, so much so, in fact, that she was obliged to request her retirement from his presence." Meredith, so much more unbiased as an informant, does not report this incident. Still, as evidence for the prosecution, we know that as early as the spring of 1879, Macdonald and Lorne were on bad terms as a result of the Governor General's having dragged his heels about accepting his prime minister's advice to dismiss the Lieutenant-Governor of Quebec, a Liberal appointee with the imposing name of Luc de Letellier de St. Just, on the grounds of political misconduct. (Letellier, as he was known for short, had taken it upon himself to dismiss his Quebec ministry.)

* When Cartwright's book appeared, and the *Montreal Star* cabled a query about its allegations to Lorne (or the Duke of Argyll as he had long since become), the answer came back in the form of a one-word telegram: "Rubbish."

The truth is, if Macdonald did indeed disgrace himself at Rideau Hall, so did many another Official Ottawan of the day – the Merediths, naturally, excepted. Beneath a thin veneer of *politesse*, the town was still a rough and boozy one. Just two years earlier, a closing session of Parliament, over which Dufferin had presided, had been marred by a most unfortunate incident involving a member of one of Ottawa's oldest families, one Captain Sparks of the Ottawa Cavalry Troop. According to Janet Hall's diary entry, "Captain Sparks behaved so badly at the closing that the Governor General ordered his sword to be taken from him." According to Edmund Meredith: "Captain Sparks was hopelessly drunk while escorting the Governor General to the House; he fell from his horse while essaying to draw his sword." A year later, in April 1878, just before the passage of the Canada Temperance Act, there'd been an uproarious all-night booze-up in the House after which Sir John had to be taken off quietly at 7:30A.M. by the Tory whip and stowed away in the rooms of the Deputy Sergeant at Arms. In the course of this debate, one member had risen to speak only to be greeted by shouts of ribald laughter from friend and foe alike – "Button up your pants!"

All of this escalated under the Lornes. So mesmerized were Ottawans by having a real live princess in their midst that, much in the manner of children admonished once too often to be on their best behaviour, they seemed unable to avoid behaving at their worst. In his diary note on the Lornes' first state ball on February 19, 1879,

Meredith provides this account of the behaviour of some stellar members of Ottawa society:

> A tremendous crush. All kinds of people there. Several persons drunk before it was over; some of the Guard put under arrest. . . . It is said that Senator Carroll kicked aside the Princess' train – if he did not actually push her aside by the shoulder. It is also said that Chief Justice Ritchie under the influence no doubt of the champagne, made himself somewhat conspicuous in the Dressing Room, standing on his dignity as Chief Justice of Canada, and saying that he had been standing 10 minutes and that no one had brought him his clothes. At last, in some despair, he thrust his ticket (which up to then he had kept in his pocket) through the hole – like any common mortal – and got his clothes.

In the case of Lady Macdonald, whatever she may or may not have done to offend Louise, it was quite certainly not because she ever appeared tipsy. As early as 1868, in a doomed attempt to set a good example at home, Agnes Macdonald, as she reports in her own diary, had forsworn even so much as a glass of wine at dinner. But whether or not the London (Ontario) *Advertiser*, a Liberal organ, was correct in its report that their hostilities dated from a joint appearance in the royal box at the Grand Opera House when Louise, having graciously risen to acknowledge the applause of the audience, was infuriated to discover that Lady Macdonald had brazenly risen alongside her, there is little doubt these two strong-willed women detested each other. In 1883 when Louise wrote a personal letter to Macdonald to deny any difficulties between herself and Agnes, it was only because Macdonald himself had written an agonized, almost begging letter to the Governor General's secretary. The words that Louise chose to use in her disclaimer were less than warm. "You must know in how many ways I admire Lady Macdonald and think her a worthy example to every wife."

That autumn of 1879, with Louise out of sight and out of mind in England, and with Lady Macdonald, after the Mackenzie interlude, firmly reinstated as wife of the prime minister, the role in which she revelled and would continue now to occupy uninterruptedly until Macdonald's death in 1891, seems a good moment to stand back and take a closer look at the woman who remains by far the most complex, most gifted, and, ultimately, the most tragic of all Canadian prime-ministerial wives.

CHAPTER 14

Agnes Macdonald: the Lady or the Tiger?

I also know that my love of Power is strong, so strong that sometimes I dread; it influences me when I imagine I am influenced by a sense of right. . . .

Agnes Macdonald;
diary entry; April 19, 1868.

As the historian Donald Creighton was the first to point out, the difficulty in coming to terms with Agnes Macdonald is that there were really *two* Agnes Macdonalds, each of whom had almost nothing in common with the other.

To begin with, there was the sensitive, high-spirited, late-blooming bride of thirty-one who, soon after she arrived in Ottawa in the spring of 1867 as Macdonald's second wife,* began keeping a diary that captivates the reader with its vivacity and its witty turn of phrase. "It has been a hot dusty day but these are dusty times," she wrote in her very first entry on July 5, 1867. "This new Dominion of ours came noisily into existence on the 1st, and the very newspapers look hot and tired with the weight of announcements and cabinet lists. Here – in this house – the atmosphere is so awfully political that sometimes I think the very flies hold Parliament on the kitchen tablecloths."

This first Agnes possessed the eye for telling detail, the gift for

* Macdonald's first wife, whom he married in 1843 when he was twenty-eight, was his first cousin, Isabella Clark. She died in 1857. There were two children; "little John A." his father's namesake, died as an infant; Hugh John (1850-1929) became a considerable political figure in his own right, serving as a Minister of the Interior in Sir Charles Tupper's ministry of 1896 and as Premier of Manitoba, 1899-1900.

total recall and the evocative writing style, all demonstrated in her account of the trial of McGee's assassin quoted earlier, that could have made her a journalist of considerable accomplishment. Indeed, every now and then she did write for public consumption, most notably in 1884 when, on a cross-country trip via the newly-completed CPR, she insisted on riding through the Rockies on the cow-catcher and composed a delightful account that was published in *Murray's Magazine*.

> Emerging from one tunnel, we saw a party of young English sportsmen, standing and looking in understandable amazement at the sight of a lady, bareheaded with an umbrella, seated in front of an engine at the mouth of a tunnel in the Gold Range of British Columbia.
>
> I am sorely afraid I laughed outright at the blank amazement . . . and longed to tell them what fun it was; but not being "introduced, you know" contented myself with a solemn little bow – which was quite irrepressible under the circumstances.

Agnes Macdonald. She was the most interesting of all prime-ministerial wives – and also the most tragic.

This first Agnes, as she reveals herself in her diary, was also a woman of a passionate and sensual nature, as much head over heels in love with her brilliant husband as Lady Dufferin was with hers, but unlike that awestruck consort, not above sending him up a little: "In theory I regard my husband with much awe," she tells us in that first 1867 diary entry, "in practice I tease the life out of him. Today he rebelled, poor man, and ordered me out of the room. I went at once but he relented, the good old boy, and called me back." The glimpses Agnes provides us of Sir John as husband and lover are a welcome counterpoint to the boozy, Machiavellian Macdonald that Edmund Meredith knew. Here, for instance, are the two of them alone together, in the stone terrace house with the smelly drains on Daly Street that was their first home in Ottawa, on the swelteringly hot night of July 6, 1867:

> My husband devoted himself to Patience, his much-beloved game. I think I shall ever think of him sitting absorbed in the cards, leaning on the large green table in my dressing-room. He says it rests his mind and changes the current of his thoughts more than anything else.

Here, on the following day, is Sir John coming home from the office:

> He comes in with a very moody brow, tired and oppressed, his voice weak, his step slow, and ten minutes after, he is making clever jokes and laughing like a schoolboy with his hands in his pockets, and his head thrown back . . . I think he likes me to be near him; he is so equable and good natured that being near him is always refreshing. . . .

Six months later, on a bleak November evening, she sketches in a tender, fireside scene:

> As I write, the clock is striking ten; the house is very quiet. John lies reading near me on the sofa. Do you think it was very wicked of me to rest my head on his shoulder while he read me *Locksley Hall*?

And the following January, an entry that evokes in a few sentences, all that was magic in Ottawa in the early post-Confederation years:

> My darling's birthday, and he is fifty three; I think no one could guess him as much as that, he is so bright and active. . . . At home til 3, then to the Dept with my husband and then to drive with him across the ice, such smooth sleighing; the whole country is a sheet of unbroken snow, dazzling to look upon; the air is rare with cold; the lightness of the atmosphere quite remarkable. My house is warm and cosy with the blazing fire and the bright gaslights as we trundled in after our cold drive, and John said, "How comfortable this is."

Most poignantly of all, in the pre-dawn hours of February 7, 1869, Agnes feels the first labour pains occasioned by her only child:

> My darling held me in his arms until just now when I feared to disturb his precious sleep and I got up softly turning out the gas and left him. . . . O God, My Father and every constant blessed comforter, help me patiently to bear my pains and to be prepared for all things. . . .

A woman, in other words, who was young in heart, full of natural coltish optimism, and of the fearless exuberance that comes so naturally to women who are in love and are certain of being loved in return.

The other Agnes was the stern-visaged Lady Macdonald whom we first encountered in Chapter four, making mincemeat out of the hapless Reverend Bedford-Jones. Tall, rawboned to the point of ugliness, always "execrably dressed" in Meredith's opinion, and much given to standing on her dignity as the wife of the prime minister, this other Agnes came quickly to frown on balls and theatricals, outlawed all card games except Sir John's beloved Patience, "which we read that Albert the Good was fond of," and came to rule Official Society unsmilingly and with a rod of iron.

This other Agnes was also a woman who, in Creighton's words, "looked back upon her own – and other people's – frivolities with grave disapproval." Within a few months of arriving in Ottawa, she beleaguered Sir John into banning all political visitors on Sundays, and was bemoaning his distinct lack of interest in instituting family prayers. "The want is a grief to me and yet how to arrange it I know not; Sir John rises late." But on Sunday mornings, even he rarely dared risk what must have been a very pained look indeed by refusing to go to church. "He said he was weary and would not," she writes on April 26, 1868, "but when I looked ever so little sad he got up at once and dressed in a hurry . . . I dare say many would laugh at my being so particular about his going with me, and perhaps some would say that when he was tired it was cruel, but I do not see it in that light."

A disappointed woman in other words, hewing to the straight and the narrow and the puritanical because only there did she feel confident of being in control.

These opposed personalities developed out of Agnes's background and were amplified by the circumstances of her marriage.

She was born in Spanish Town, Jamaica, in 1836, the only daughter among five children of a sugar plantation owner named Thomas Bernard and his wife, Theodora. A perfervidly pious, not to say sanctimonious woman, Theodora exerted the dominant influence over Agnes until the day of her own death in 1875. During the first eight years of their married life, Theodora lived with the Macdonalds. "John is reading *Nature's Nobleman* in bed and I hear Mama brushing out her hair next door," writes Agnes in 1869. This constant heavy-breathing, hair-brushing presence of his mother-in-law may have been one of the reasons Sir John so often sought solace in the bottle. But so devoted was Agnes to Theodora that when the Reverend Bedford-Jones had the unhappy task of breaking the news of her mother's sudden death to her, he tells us that he "feared for Lady Macdonald's sanity."

In 1851, a year after her father's death from cholera when she was fifteen, Agnes and Theodora left Jamaica for England. In 1854, they set sail across the Atlantic again, this time *en route* to Barrie, Ontario, where Agnes's elder brother, Hewitt Bernard, had established a law practice. In 1858, after Hewitt had accepted a position as private secretary to Macdonald, then a forty-two-year-old recently bereaved lawyer from Kingston who had just become head of the Liberal-Conservative Party, they moved to Toronto. Sometime that year, at a concert, Agnes first glimpsed her future husband, by now a much-sought-after widower, sitting in the front gallery with a group of ladies. "I remember distinctly how he looked," she wrote in later years. "A forcible, yet changeful face, with such a mixture of strength and vivacity, and his bushy, dark peculiar hair as he leaned on his elbows and looked down."

In 1859, like everyone else connected with government, including the Merediths, the Bernard household moved with the rotating capital to Quebec. Here, though Agnes lacked the looks and the flirtatious disposition to be a muffin, she had a perfectly splendid time. Like Fanny Meredith before her, she enjoyed the wondrous winter picnics at Montmorency Falls with the requisite visit to the hollowed-out ice cone. "Once entered, we found ourselves in a wondrous fairy cavern," she wrote, "there, on ice-carved sofas were stretched out dark rugs of fur; and on the icy buffet, no end of good things were spread."

On Valentine's Day, 1860, Agnes, along with the Merediths, was among the eight hundred guests at a magnificent ball hosted by the merry widower Macdonald himself, where the decorations featured a life-sized statue of Cupid carved from ice, and a bubbling fountain of eau de cologne.

Sometime during these Quebec years, Agnes came to know Macdonald as more than a friend, though alas, this was long before she began keeping her diary. As a charmer and as a rising politician, he was a considerable catch, much pursued by ladies far more beautiful and incomparably more worldly; what must have drawn him to her was a quick, informed intelligence and, all the more so because his first wife had been, although beautiful, an invalid, her physical vitality. Although we do not know for certain, he probably proposed. The trouble seems to have been that Macdonald, during these Quebec years was known to be drinking extremely heavily. "It must have been impossible for her to come to terms with his problem," Louise Reynolds has written in her authoritative and richly detailed biography, *Agnes*, from which much of the information in this account is drawn. "Agnes, with no informed opinion available to her as to how to cope with alcoholism must have made up her mind that she could not risk her future as his wife." In 1865, when the capital moved to Ottawa, Agnes and Theodora, having listened to all the horror stories about the backwoods capital, decided not to go, and instead moved back to London. Just over a year later, one noonday in December 1866, while out strolling with Theodora on Bond Street, Agnes bumped into Macdonald who was in London to see the British North America Act through Westminster. Perhaps she believed he had mended his ways. Perhaps, now that she'd turned thirty, she was ready to risk much to escape spinsterhood. By the New Year the two were engaged and on February 16, 1867, they were married at St. George's, Hanover Square, in a splashy ceremony in which Jessie McDougall and Emma Tupper, the daughters of two other Fathers of Confederation acted as bridesmaids. At the reception at the Westminster Palace Hotel, the plate of every guest boasted a nosegay of violets mixed with snowdrops.

When Agnes arrived in Ottawa in the spring of 1867, there was no doubt whatever in her mind about the role she would play. "I do so like to identify myself with all my husband's pursuits and occupations," she wrote. "I would soon fall out of his life if I went my own ways." Yet in the beginning, she was uncertain how to proceed. The constant round of official entertaining, which Sir John so much relished and was so good at, did not come to her naturally: in the manner of so many nervous political brides, she fussed endlessly over the details without much success in the results. "John says the dinner last night was a failure," she wrote sadly that first year. "Perhaps my having ordered it to be ready an hour too soon might have had something to do with it." A surviving Macdonald menu of that era – mock turtle soup followed by mutton and apple pudding – suggests a certain stolidity in the cooking. As a hostess, moreover, Agnes was both psychologically and physically awkward. "I pour tea very untidily," she lamented. Describing a party given for Macdonald's teenage son Hughie, up from Queen's on vacation, she was even more cast down. "Tea and games and supper, but it was very stupid, I could do nothing to promote gaiety." It scarcely helped her self-confidence that at the instant Macdonald came in, the party took off. "He was charming, and we could never have done without him." Not surprisingly, except for the "reading parties" for similarly serious-minded women who gathered one morning each week to plough determinedly through works like Parkman's *Jesuits in America* and Stanhope's *Life of Pitt*, few of those who came to Lady Macdonald's parties much enjoyed them. "Rather boring," wrote Lucianne Desbarats, wife of the Queen's Printer, of a musicale on May 9, 1868, that Agnes herself ranked as one of her rare successes. "No dancing, only music."

Pretty, flirtatious Lucianne Desbarats, with her bobbing curls and her silk dresses that rivalled even Lady Lisgar's, was exactly the kind of woman certain to make plain, ungainly Agnes feel uncomfortable.* So, also was her next-door neighbour Charlotte Rose –

* One of Lucianne's dresses rivalled so closely a dress of Lady Lisgar's that it got her into trouble. In her book of reminiscences, her daughter-in-law, Lilian Desbarats, reveals the following contretemps.

> She had a sewing woman who made her dresses, this woman pleaded with Mrs. Desbarats to let her make a grand ballgown for her. At last my mother-in-law consented. It was a lovely gown of mauve and pale green with a very full skirt. One evening, Mr. and Mrs. Desbarats were invited to dinner at Government House. Madame Desbarats was delighted with this occasion to wear her beautiful new toilette, but what was the matter with Lady Lisgar? She hardly took any notice of Madame Desbarats, in fact she haughtily turned away from her. Madam Desbarats was completely dumbfounded. Next morning the woman who had made the dress came in great distress. "Madame, Madame, you did a terrible thing wearing that dress to Government House – Lady Lisgar's maid is a great friend of mine – she showed me all Lady Lisgar's wardrobe and I copied one of her Ladyship's dresses for you.'"

and this mattered much more, since as the wife of Sir John's oldest and dearest friend and Minister of Finance, John Rose, Agnes had no choice but to be frequently in her company and to read the *risqué* "Modern Novels," with titles like *Cometh Up as a Flower*, that Mrs. Rose was constantly pressing into her hand.*

As doubtless endeared her even less to Agnes, the life story of the elegant Charlotte read rather like a Modern Novel. In 1838, her first husband, Captain Robert Sweeny, had killed a fellow officer in a duel over her honour. Sweeny himself had died two years later, it was said from his burden of guilt. In 1843, the widowed Charlotte had married Rose, then a rising Montreal lawyer, and had promptly become the city's leading hostess. At their spacious estate, Rosemount, on the slopes of Mount Royal, the Roses entertained everyone who mattered: the Prince of Wales on his grand tour in 1860, in the course of which he'd laid the cornerstone of the Parliament Buildings at Ottawa; his younger brother, Prince Arthur; and Prince Napoleon of France.

Charlotte Rose. Agnes feared her "cosy yet cutting smile."

As a political wife, Charlotte Rose was everything that Agnes Macdonald was not: silky, elegant, and self-confident. When Charlotte was in Ottawa, society gravitated towards her as towards the sun. Edmund Meredith, among many others, was dazzled by her charm, not least because she invariably went out of her way to compliment him on his renditions of *Horatius at the Bridge*. "She told me that my reading was 'the thing' of the concert," he preened on one occasion.

Agnes Macdonald saw Charlotte otherwise. "She is so clever, but her stories savour of such worldliness that I fear she is dangerous." In truth, however, one suspects that Agnes was more intrigued than she cared to admit by the orchidaceous world personified by Mrs. Rose. Certainly, her comments on reading that "decidedly objectionable" novel, *Cometh Up as a Flower*, evoke a suspicion of someone protesting too much. "Of all things, I hate the fashionable delineation of passion in novels *à la mode*. The scenes in *Cometh Up*, especially Nellie's last interview with her lover when, herself a wife, she tells him how dearly she loves him . . . may be powerful, but in my humble opinion . . . only coarse." When the Roses left Canada at the end of 1869 to take up permanent residence in England, he to become unofficial agent for the Canadian government, Agnes confessed to her diary that she was relieved. "I think I feared her cosy yet cutting smile."

The sense of being at a social disadvantage that Agnes invariably felt in the presence of women like Charlotte Rose and Lucianne Desbarats was probably one of the reasons that very early in her

* This particular novel, by Rhoda Broughton (1840-1920) was the publishing sensation of 1887. Thanks to its steamy love scenes, sales rivalled those of *East Lynne* and *Lady Audrey's Secret*. Of more literary interest was Broughton's 1883 novel, *Belinda*, a satire set in Oxford, recently reissued by Virago Press.

married life, she decided to remove herself entirely from their circle by giving up novels, eschewing cards, and taking "a right stand about balls . . . and theatricals." On January 20, 1869, when the Desbarats gave the great fancy-dress ball described in chapter seven, Agnes's advanced state of pregnancy prevented her from attending. Even so, "I think I should have had the courage not to go even if I had been able. I trust so," she writes, all alone in her sitting-room, having presided over a dinner-party from which all the guests – and Sir John – had rushed off to the party.

However much she was influenced by her own feelings of inferiority and by Theodora's religiosity, some of the motivation for the gradual ascendancy of evangelical piety in Agnes's character lies in another direction. Her husband's incessant drinking played its part. If anything, marriage had made Sir John's weakness more pronounced. All through the summer of 1869, the Premier was more or less constantly "on the burst"; even his trusted brother-in-law, Hewitt Bernard, was confiding now to his colleagues, as Meredith reports on September 13, "that he did everything he could to dissuade his sister from the marriage." Reading Agnes's own diary during these agonizing periods is painful, as we watch her insisting on taking all the blame for herself – "I know that I troubled my darling; my over-anxiety was the cause of it" – growing more and more scrupulous in her piety, and attempting to make bargains with God: novels and wine and the theatre cast aside forever, if God will only make John give up drinking.

Never once in her diary, and this only adds to the poignancy, does Agnes mention the problem by name: instead it is always "his headaches, that grieve me so much"; or "something that happened this week which gave me pain." "I know that if my feeble faith were to fail and my eyes cease looking upwards," she writes on April 26, 1868, after a temporary surcease, "that the shadow which darkened my life would assuredly lower again." Then in November 1869, in the midst of a particularly ruinous bout, she almost flagellates herself. "I was overconfident, vain, presumptuous in my sense of power. I fancied I could do much, and I failed signally. I am more humble now."

To make all this that much sadder, Agnes's self-criticism was probably not entirely mis-directed: it is not unreasonable to speculate that Macdonald, goaded by the spur of her saintly disapproval, drank more than he otherwise might have done, knowing all the while that he was grievously wounding someone who loved him.

As if all of this were not a sufficient cross to bear, there was the

Agnes Macdonald and Mary Macdonald in June 1869. A month earlier, Agnes had realized that her only child was both mentally and physically handicapped.

tragedy of their only daughter, Mary, born on February 8, 1869, hydrocephalic, crippled both mentally and physically. The saddest entry in all of Agnes's diary comes on May 1, 1869, when Mary is three months old and her mother faces the fact that her child will never be normal. "The day has been stamped with the world's great seal, it is graven I think with the word 'disappointment.' Perhaps yesterday was one of the saddest times in my life. Let it pass, let it die. . . . Only teach me, Heavenly Father, to see the lesson it was destined to teach." Both of the Macdonalds, in fact, accepted the tragedy of Mary with surpassing courage. Thanks to their loving devotion, their retarded daughter eventually learned to speak well enough to dictate her own letters, and to take a keen interest in her surroundings.

Because neither Sir John nor Agnes would have it any other way, Mary's contemporaries in Ottawa accepted it as perfectly normal that little "Baboo" (her father's affectionate nickname), would be included in their birthday parties and that they in turn would go to hers. At Earnscliffe, in the 1880s, Macdonald personally supervised the construction of a little balcony overlooking the dining-room, that still exists, from which Mary in her wheelchair could look down on the company. But the sight of that deformed little figure in the wheelchair amid all the other healthy bouncing youngsters playing ring-around-the-rosy must have been insufferably sad. "It was a most pathetic sight," writes Lilian Desbarats. "She was just like a large rag doll with an oversized head being carried around among gay and active children." Louise Reynolds, in her biography, *Agnes*, provides the most poignant of all vignettes. "One time, as the guests were preparing to leave at the end of a dance which Mary herself had given, [Macdonald] quietly persuaded them to stay a little longer. When they had resumed the dance, he leaned over his child's chair and said, 'You see, Mary, they want a little more of your society and a little dancing by the way.' "

Because of the problems posed by Mary and by Sir John's serious illness in the spring of 1870, followed by the humiliation of the Pacific Scandal and the five-year spell in Opposition, Agnes Macdonald played only a marginal role on the Ottawa stage during the 1870s. Though she had disliked intensely the affectations of Lady Lisgar – "I think too much luxury though wonderfully pretty to look at is not healthy or wise" – she got on well with Lady Dufferin and particularly appreciated that gracious woman's tender gesture of inviting Mary to help her own teenage daughter, Lady Helen Blackwood, sell flowers at a charity bazaar. But in the autumn of 1878, when Macdonald returned triumphantly to the prime-ministership, the Dufferins were on the way home and Agnes was ready to take centre stage for herself. She was no longer a nervous gawky hostess, but a woman of a certain sombre distinction, "a very clever stern woman," in the words of a contemporary, who had long since come to terms both with herself and with "the shadow" that darkened her life. In the process, but for occasional glimpses such as the trip through the Rockies on the cow-catcher, the first coltish and indiscreet Agnes had disappeared entirely. She'd even given up keeping her diary.

The symbol of the Macdonald restoration was Earnscliffe,* the fine, gabled Gothic Revival mansion in a commanding position overlooking the Ottawa River, a mile or so upstream from Rideau Hall. As early as 1871, the Macdonalds had lived briefly as tenants at Earnscliffe, then known simply as "Reynold's House" and owned

* Earnscliffe, since the late 1920s, has been the residence of British High Commissioners to Canada. Its prospect has been damaged severely in recent years by its proximity to the Macdonald-Cartier bridge over to Hull, a four-laned thoroughfare upstream by only a couple of hundred yards that not only blocks out the view but, by its ceaseless hum of traffic, invades the serenity.

Earnscliffe, as it appeared in 1882, when the Macdonalds bought it for $10,000.

by their good friend Thomas Reynolds, an early railway magnate. Agnes at that time wrote lyrically in her diary of the "pretty, irregular large grey stone house which is now my home; the windows with their large frames glowing with lamplight looked so cosy." It was at Earnscliffe (a name suggested by Sir John and meaning "Eagle's Nest" in the Cornish dialect), on the blizzardy New Year's Day of 1871, even though Sir John "spoiled everything by having ordered a Council and going away before one single caller had rung the hall bell," that Agnes presided alone over one of her few really successful parties. "The house was thronged from noon til dinner time with men of all ages . . . some merely shook hands or bowed and exchanged a few commonplaces about the weather, but the larger part lunched at a continually replenished table in the dining room and wished me and mine all happiness for the new year between mouthfuls of hot oyster soup or sips of sherry."

In 1882, when Earnscliffe came on the market, Agnes, with so many happy memories of the place, cajoled Sir John into buying it for $10,000. "I did want him to have a really nice home and *coaxed hard*," she wrote in later years. Quickly, Agnes embarked on a renovation programme that cost the considerable sum of $7,000 and that included a new dining room, offices for Sir John and his new private secretary, Joseph Pope, a verandah overlooking the river, and, most intriguingly, two cunningly devised escape routes by which Sir John could slip out of the house and avoid unwanted callers.* In 1889, an elderly female constituent of Sir John's, Sarah Grimason, came up from Kingston to visit and described the scene in a charming Irish brogue.

> They do have a lovely place all their own, down by the Rye-do. The house has a lovely slate roof like they have in England, and beautiful grounds and a man to wait on the dure. Lady Macdonald keeps her own cow and hins and they make their own butter. . . . They have two fine cows and six servants.

As Lady Macdonald made certain everyone knew, this establishment existed to rival Rideau Hall. In 1889, when the famous Canadian-born singer, Madame Emma Albani, came to town, it was at Earnscliffe and not at Government House that she stayed, and it was Agnes, not Lady Stanley, who gave a splendid "At Home" at which Albani, in a charming gesture, sang a song especially for Mary on her twentieth birthday. Entrée to Earnscliffe, however, was not easily attained. One who was never received there, for instance, was Mrs. George Foster, wife of Sir John's Minister of Fisheries, who, though the totally innocent party, had been divorced from a previous husband. Nor, because of Lady Macdonald's interdiction, could the unfortunate Mrs. Foster be received anywhere. It wasn't until 1894, with Macdonald dead and Agnes abroad, that Lady Aberdeen, herself no lax moralist, dared lift the ban and invited Mrs. Foster to Rideau Hall.

During these years of unthreatened ascendancy, Agnes also acquired a taste for power politics. As a new bride, she had come home from a highly political dinner party and had concluded, as she wrote, that while "Sandfield Macdonald [Premier of Ontario] says he likes politically-inclined women . . . if a woman gives too much attention to politics she becomes too violent a partisan and is likely to ride her hobby to death." But in the 1880s, as all members of Macdonald's cabinet quickly discovered, crossing Agnes could be equivalent to signing their own political death warrant. "I did not speak to that molecatcher of a wife of his at Government House," wrote Sir John Thompson, Minister of Justice, to his own

* A similar escape route was installed, and can still be seen today in the office in the West Block that Sir John adopted after his return to office in 1878, instead of going back to the old southwest corner office in the East Block.

Mr & Mrs P. Sherwood

Lady Macdonald
at home
Monday February 9th
Music
9 o'clock
Earnscliffe

An invitation to the party at which the great Madame Albani sang especially for Mary Macdonald. It was preserved in the scrapbook of Mrs. Percy Sherwood, whose husband later became chief of the Dominion Police.

wife in 1887. And though Thompson was recognized by everyone, including Macdonald, as his most natural successor, Agnes wrote a heated letter to the Governor General, Lord Stanley, on the very night of Sir John's death, June 6, 1891, "begging His Excellency, in the interests of Canada and of the Conservative Party, to send for Sir Charles Tupper."

But Macdonald was gone, and with him Agnes's power. Lord Stanley ignored her advice and instead sent promptly for Thompson, who turned down the offer, at least for the moment. The crown thereby passed to Sir John Abbott, Minister without Portfolio.

Lady Macdonald in 1885. By now, she relished power and ruled Official Ottawa with a rod of iron.

Agnes now became, as she always knew would happen, a woman without a purpose. "I am in truth only a very sad old woman – with a past alas! wholly unforgotten and unforgettable," she wrote to Joseph Pope, Macdonald's former secretary, in 1897. This condition obtained until the end of her life, twenty-three years later. Though she accepted the title Baroness Macdonald of Earnscliffe within a few weeks of Sir John's death, the role of dowager empress in Ottawa did not suit her. She had come to relish power too much to sit gracefully on the sidelines and watch it being exercised by others. Nor, having invested so much of herself in Macdonald and in Mary, had she any real friends of her own. Only twice in a long acquaintanceship that stretched all the way back to pre-Confederation times in Toronto and in Quebec, does Meredith, for instance, mention Agnes with anything approaching warmth. On the first occasion, in May of 1867, during the week Agnes had come to Ottawa as a bride and a couple of days after Sir John "was carried out of the Executive Council lunchroom hopelessly drunk," he called to bid her welcome. "She looks very well, but, I thought rather worn . . . what a prospect she has before her!" The second time was twenty-three years later, in August 1890 when their paths crossed at Rivière du Loup during the last summer of Sir John's life. On this occasion, however, "Sir J was very bright and pleasant," and it was the condition of Agnes's brother Hewitt Bernard, that was giving her concern.

> The drawing room looked like a hospital ward. Poor Bernard was seated like a mummy in a chair in the centre of the room and Mary Macdonald was on a couch in the corner . . . Lady Mac as usual looked "rudely healthy" and strong. . . . When I bade goodbye, Lady Mac followed me out, talked 15 minutes at least about her brother and his illness . . . she addressed me as Dear Mr. Meredith, which touched me much. . . .

For a couple of years after Macdonald's death, Agnes, Mary, and the invalid Hewitt wandered fretfully round North America: summers at Rivière du Loup and at a cottage she'd acquired at Banff, winters in Victoria and at Lakewood, New Jersey. Then, in 1893, after Hewitt's death, she and Mary all but severed their ties with Canada to embark on a twenty-seven-year exile at a succession of pensions on the French and Italian rivieras and in English seaside towns. In 1900, she even sold Earnscliffe and all its contents in a giant auction sale that in itself, as we shall see later on, turned into a pivotal event of the social season. In 1913, she cut the last link with Canada and with the old days through a ferocious quarrel by mail with Joseph Pope, whom she accused of having mismanaged her finances. "I also hope and expect that no more correspondence between you and me will be continued by or desired by you," she wrote, cutting off in the process her last Canadian friend.

On September 5, 1920, Agnes died at Eastbourne. She was eighty-four. It was a measure of her isolation that by her own instructions she was buried there, "an ocean away from the grave of her husband whose memory she had always treasured," as Louise Reynolds writes. Mary, cared for by a faithful companion, lived on in southern England until her own death in 1933 at the age of sixty-four. In her late middle age, Mary became a remarkably independent spirit; one of her first actions was to make up the quarrel with Joseph Pope. "I should like to have news of some of the people whom I knew when we were all at Earnscliffe," she wrote to him in 1921. "What has become of Old Sarah who was my nurse when I was a little girl?"

CHAPTER 15

Lorne Alone

He is apparently happy without Louise.

Sir Henry Ponsonby,
Private Secretary to Queen Victoria
in a letter to his wife, 1882.

No record exists to suggest that at any time during their respective widowhoods, Agnes Macdonald and Princess Louise ever encountered each other while walking by the sea at Eastbourne, at Cimiez, at Ventimiglia, at Alassio, or at San Remo. Quite assuredly, had either one seen the other coming, she would have ducked into the nearest doorway. Yet the irony was, both these old enemies spent a similar old age, wandering querulously around the English, French, and Italian rivieras.

We last saw Louise in the autumn of 1879, when she was thirty-one, sailing home to England. Her stay lasted nearly four months; during the course of it, London society was agog with rumour that the Princess had begged permission of her mother to stay home permanently, and had been met by the Queen's "stern refusal."

On February 6, 1880, Louise reluctantly returned to Ottawa. "Quite a large crowd assembled at the station," Janet Hall wrote. Then, a week later, a sleighing accident just outside the gates of Rideau Hall proved a gift from fate that provided the unhappy princess with the permanent reprieve she was looking for. "We have had a narrow escape here," Lorne recorded in his diary, "having been run away with, and upset, and then dragged for four hundred yards when on our way into town for a Drawing Room. L. has been much hurt, and it is a wonder her skull was not fractured. The muscles of the neck, shoulder and back are much strained, and the lobe of one ear was cut in two."

In fact, Louise, like Queen Victoria and all of her daughters, was a robust woman and her injuries, while painful, healed quickly. In less than a month she was up and about and looking "so well and vivacious in talk," as Lorne put it in a letter to his father, "that no one will believe she suffers." Her expert capacity for malingering, however, hoodwinked everyone – Lorne in particular. "Any fatigue brings on much pain," he continued, "and I fear there will be nothing for it but long periods of rest and quiet in England and that travelling and taking part in ceremonial receptions will be quite out of the question." Out from England to cheer the convalescent came her favourite brother, the gentle young haemophiliac Prince Leopold: in June, the two embarked on a trip to Chicago which, since the movements of "Queen Vic's chicks" as the Yankee newspapers described them, were reported in minute detail, must have been anything but restful. Then, on July 31, Louise and Leopold sailed for England. "A great many believe the Princess will not return," Janet Hall informs us in her diary.

As near as makes no difference, this opinion was correct. For the next twenty months, with her marriage by now in a condition of total collapse, Louise breezed merrily round the spas of Switzerland and Germany. It was rumoured that Lorne knew so little about her whereabouts that he did not even know how to address a birthday telegram. "Louise don't care for Lorne," wrote the seasoned observer, Sir Henry Ponsonby. "The cure at the German baths was an excuse. True, she was shaken by her fall, but Canada was quite as restoring as Germany."

Not until the summer of 1882, with barely more than a year remaining in Lorne's term of office, did Louise put in another fleeting appearance in Canada, spending a summer at the Citadel at Quebec, and undertaking an autumn tour of British Columbia. Then, instead of returning to Ottawa, she proceeded to winter in Bermuda. The following October, the Lornes sailed home for good. "Princess Louise . . . hasn't been a success in Canada," noted Ponsonby, who, if only in private, was never afraid to call a spade a spade.

Lorne, for his part, can be rated a partial success as a bachelor Governor General. Though not unintelligent, he lacked the capacity for sustained concentration needed to be at home with matters of high policy: having made a hash of the Letellier affair in 1879, he never again attempted to cross Macdonald. Instead, he proved a pleasant and affable figurehead who, perhaps even more than

Dufferin, revelled in snow and ice. Under Lorne's enthusiastic patronage, the mythology of Ottawa as the capital of winter that the Dufferins had initiated was further embroidered: Rideau Hall skating and tobogganing parties became even more splendid. During these years of the early 1880s, as Annie Howells Frèchette described in her article for *Harper's*, the distinctive Canadian fashion of Hudson's Bay blanket coats became all the rage: "The toboggan slide and vicinity fairly blossoms with the merry romping company," she told her readers.

"The Marquis of Lorne Initiating Our Correspondent into the Perilous Pleasures of Tobogganing," ran the caption.

> Surplus dignity is thrown to the winds, along with streamers of ribbons, tassels and bright-hued scarves. A pretty Canadian girl never looks prettier than when clad in her cloak made of a fleecy white blanket (its gay border carefully reserved as a trimming), a red and blue tuque perched coquettishly upon her abundant hair . . . and a bright-coloured skirt just showing between her cloak and mocassined feet.

Another American journalist of the period, an unidentified reporter from *Frank Leslie's Illustrated Newspaper*, initiated by Lorne himself into the "Perilous Pleasures of Tobogganing," went on to sketch a memorable portrait of the Governor General at work in his office.

> The Marquis of Lorne was seated at a cabinet-desk close to the window, a buffalo robe enshrouding his chair. He was attired in a blue shirt with a turned-down collar; a brown scarf, a blue coat with Astrakhan collar and cuffs and braided in black silk after the fashion of a hussar-jacket. His trousers were of light plaid, his boots laced with yellow tops and india-rubber soles. He wore no ornaments save a massive gold watch-chain of the curb pattern, and two plain gold lumpy rings.

Lorne in his study at Rideau Hall, January 1880. Instead of a photographer, the reporter from Leslie's Illustrated *brought an artist with him.*

Beyond all else, the man from *Leslie's Illustrated* was riveted by the magnificent inkstand that stood on Lorne's desk. This, the Governor General explained, "was made of a hoof from Lord Clyde's charger in the Crimea."

South of the border, thanks to such glowing hyperbole, the image of Ottawa underwent a dramatic change: no longer was it a raw little lumber-town, but the glittering capital of a glamorous snow-and-ice kingdom. In 1883, Lorne's own triumphant visit to Washington embellished the picture. During these years, the British Minister to the United States, the distinguished diplomat Lionel Sackville-West, and Victoria, his ravishingly beautiful illegitimate daughter by the Spanish dancer Pepita, reigned supreme as the leading host and hostess on Embassy Row*; the magnificent ball the nineteen-year-old Victoria arranged for Lorne on January 26, 1883, constituted the event of the season. In the splendid crimson and gilt ballroom at the British Embassy, Lorne led off the first quadrille with the wife of the Minister of Sweden and Norway. But, according to the Washington papers, the Marquis enjoyed much more the romping Sir Roger de Coverley, "much like the Virginia Reel," that closed the evening.

"He is apparently happy without Louise," wrote Ponsonby of Lorne in these years. Not even during the dull spring and autumn seasons, when the Rideau Hall toboggan slide stood marooned in a sea of mud, did the Governor General complain of feeling lonely. Rather, as he wrote to his father, "I am entertaining the whole world, at the rate of about five hundred a week." Setting a fashion that would obtain until the Second World War, Rideau Hall style became the style of a country house party that knew no Monday mornings. To Rideau came the distinguished American landscape painter Albert Bierstadt, to produce an evocative oil sketch of the Parliament Buildings as they appeared from the viceregal grounds. There came also the composer Arthur Sullivan, taking time out from a North American tour of *The Pirates of Penzance* to set to music the words of "A National Hymn," an anthem to Canada composed by Lorne himself.* In the absence of his wife, one or another of Lorne's sisters and brothers was nearly always in temporary residence, though it must be said that his adoring younger sister, Lady Frances Balfour, found Canada even less to her liking than Louise had done. "I made many acquaintances," she wrote in her own memoir, "but I can only recollect one Canadian who spoke of literature, his name was Plumer." A much more enthusiastic visitor was the beautiful Victoria Sackville-West who, along with

* Those members of the British aristocracy who served as proconsuls and diplomats constituted a tight little world. This Victoria Sackville-West became the mother of the noted writer, Victoria Sackville-West, who married Harold Nicolson, Dufferin's nephew-by-marriage.

* Luckily, Sullivan's partner, the lyricist W. S. Gilbert did not accompany him. Lorne's poem opened as follows:

God bless our wide Dominion
Our father's chosen land
And bind in lasting Union
Each Ocean's distant strand

The state carriage with Ottawa's newly-formed cavalry troop: Princess Louise's Dragoon Guards. The Yankees were much impressed.

her father, returned Lord Lorne's visit to Washington late that same winter of 1883. She fell in love with sleighing and tobogganing; in return, the dashing Captain Drury, one of Lorne's aides-de-camp, fell in love with her. "I asked Lord Lorne why his ADC always told me that his favourite flower was tulips (two lips)," Victoria wrote in her *Book of Reminiscences*. "I was almost stupid in that overwhelming state of perfect innocence." Like all visitors to Rideau in that era, Victoria was initiated into the trick of using static electricity to light the gas jets – "by rubbing my feet in the carpet all along the big corridor and putting my nose in contact, at the end, with the gas-burner."

When not playing host, Lorne busied himself with attempting to raise the cultural consciousness of Canadians. His imperishable achievement was to succeed in institutionalizing some of his own enthusiasm.

To a degree, as in the case of mythologizing winter, Lorne was following in his immediate predecessor's path. As early as 1877, during a visit to Toronto, Dufferin had praised the efforts of the fledgling Ontario Society of Artists, and called on the government to establish a national gallery. Dufferin's own skill with pen and ink and charcoal had created something of a vogue for sketching; in May 1878, Edmund Meredith and his daughter Mary had much admired Dufferin's sketchbooks on public display at Rideau Hall, as well as "many interesting volumes of engravings and etchings."

For Canada's professional artists, a company that then could have been more than comfortably accommodated in a single streetcar, the arrival of Lorne and Louise as Dufferin's successors could scarcely have been more propitious. Some of the viceregal couple's best friends were the most noted British artists of the day: Landseer, Millais, F. W. Watts. "I had the feeling that the reign about to begin was full of promise for the artistic life of our nation," said Napoleon Bourassa of Montreal, an elegant goateed figure who was one of the best-known Canadian painters of the era but who is better remembered as the father of the fiery Quebec nationalist, Henri Bourassa. Early in February 1879, Lucius O'Brien of Toronto, vice-president of the Ontario Society of Artists, travelled to Ottawa to ask that the Governor General and his wife become patrons of the society. Lorne not only agreed, but spoke eagerly of his wish to found an arts school and a Dominion-wide arts society. Then in May, when he and Louise travelled to Montreal to open the new building of the local art association, Lorne waxed even more enthusiastic and, indeed, got rather carried away. "We may look forward to the time," he said, "when the influence of such associations may be expected to spread until we have here, what they formerly had in Italy, such a love of art that our Canadian painters may be allowed to wander over the land scot free of expense, because the hotel keepers will be only too happy to allow them to pay their bills by the painting of some small portrait, or some sign for 'mine host.' "

As for Ottawa, to this point, the capital could well have been accused of caring not at all about culture. But on May 29, two days after Lorne's speech in Montreal, a small group of public-spirited gentlemen assembled at the Rideau Club to discuss the establishment of an art association as prelude to the establishment of an art gallery. They included Chief Justice Ritchie and Sandford Fleming and also Colonel Allan Gilmour, one of Canada's earliest patrons of the arts, a wealthy lumber baron whose fine house on Vittoria Street boasted a private picture gallery that contained a fine collection of Victorian paintings, including several Krieghoffs. In April 1877, when Edmund Meredith visited Gilmour's gallery – by invitation – he was particularly impressed by "eight or ten very good pictures purchased at the Philadelphia Exhibition. Among the most striking to my mind are *The Rock of Gibraltar*; *A Fjord in Norway* and *Greenlanders Travelling*."

A key participant at the Rideau Club meeting of May 29, 1879 was, as we are not surprised to discover, Meredith himself. Because he was now a superannuated gentleman of leisure, he was immediately nominated to draft a constitution and by-laws for the proposed society. On June 14, having worked quickly and with his customary skill, Meredith was able to present a draft that was approved verbatim at a public meeting held at City Hall where, as he tells us, "about 50 or 60 were there, including some ladies." As defined by Meredith, the principal objective of the new Ottawa Art Association was "the encouragement of knowledge and love of the fine arts and their general advancement throughout the Dominion . . . it is also proposed to open up a school of art and design in Ottawa . . . and to use the influence of the Association in promoting the creation of a National Gallery at the seat of Ottawa." Getting this new body off the ground would be Meredith's last legacy to the capital, and he went home in an excellent mood. "The meeting was *much* more successful than I expected."

More successful yet, though Meredith was gone by then and missed it, was the event on March 6, 1880, from which the National Gallery formally traces its beginnings: the gala opening of the new Royal Canadian Academy of Artists at the Clarendon Hotel on Sussex Street, a ceremony which nearly a thousand Ottawans attended and in honour of which Lady Macdonald, Lady Tilley, and Lady Tupper all wore their best black silks. Louise, to everyone's chagrin, was still laid up from her accident, but Lorne, resplendent in the Order of the Garter, performed splendidly on his own, presiding from an ornate chair got up to look like a throne.

Lorne himself had also personally selected the twenty-five academicians and thought up the twist by which each of these artists, as a condition of membership, must donate a "Diploma Work" to the nation to form the nucleus of a national collection. From Lucius O'Brien, first President of the Academy, came *Sunrise on the Saguenay*, a huge landscape in oils which hung in pride of place directly behind Lorne's chair and which even today, is remarkable for the translucence of its colours. From Napoleon Bourassa, the first Vice-President–the Academy, at least at its outset, was resolutely bicultural – came *The Mystic Art*, an allegorical portrait in the pre-Raphaelite style. Women were eligible for membership, although they were not "required" to attend business meetings or to serve on the executive, and perhaps the single most intriguing work in the show was presented by the sole female academician, the Toronto painter Charlotte Schreiber. This was a large narrative painting, *The Croppy Boy*, suggested by an Irish revolutionary poem: a young patriot is seen confessing all to a priest who, as can easily be seen by the boots and spurs sticking out from under his cassock, is really a British officer in disguise.

As for the work of Frances Richards, which had so entranced Oscar Wilde, this was apparently judged good enough only to merit associate membership in the Academy, not full membership, so that today, alas, the collection of the National Gallery includes no "diploma work" from her hand. Perhaps, although she was considered competent enough to take charge of the Ottawa Art School for the year 1881-82 when its permanent head, the noted artist William Brymner, was off on sick leave, Frances Richards was just too young and too pretty to be taken seriously as a painter. In any event, she could console herself with the knowledge that Princess Louise admired her work; so much so that she purchased, in 1882, her portrait of a Blackfoot Indian named Po-kah-nee-ha-pee. Noteworthy too, is the fact that while the works of most anointed Founding Fathers of Canadian art remain stashed away in storage, dusted off only for such occasional events as the National Gallery's centenary exhibition of 1980, two excellent portraits by Frances Richards are on view in Ottawa at all times: her portrait of Sir George Kirkpatrick, Speaker of the House of Commons between 1880 and 1884 can be seen in the "Speakers Corridor" in the Centre Block; her portrait of her uncle, Sir William Buell Richards, Chief Justice of Canada in the 1870s is at the Supreme Court.

"If Dufferin does not get India, it is possible I think, that I may get it," wrote Lorne to his father, the Duke of Argyll, in March 1883. He was riding a crest of success at the time, having founded a sister institution for Canadian scholars, the Royal Society of Canada, barely two years after the successful establishment of the Royal Canadian Academy. The first meeting of the Royal Society, held in May 1882 at the Senate Chamber, brought most of the notable scholars of the country together for the first time: among others, Principal Dawson of McGill; Goldwin Smith, the Sage of "The Grange" at Toronto; and Principal Grant of Queen's. It added to Lorne's satisfaction that while the newly elected Fellows were still in town, he was able to take them on a tour of the National Gallery, which had just opened its first official premises in a building near the West Block that was also the first home of the Supreme Court of Canada.*

* This handsome stone building was demolished in 1956 to provide space for a parking lot – just one of a melancholy list of acts of vandalism committed in the name of progress by the Department of Public Works.

But Dufferin did indeed "get India." When Lorne sailed home to England the following autumn, still only thirty-seven, his career as proconsul was over. In contrast to Dufferin, in contrast also to his immediate successor, Lord Lansdowne, Lorne's years in Canada proved not to be an apprenticeship to greater glories. Reading between the lines of a letter that the Duke of Argyll wrote to Queen Victoria in October 1883, there is a hint that between these two, the true state of affairs in the Lorne household may well have been known. "I do not myself think that apart from his personal connection with Your Majesty's family, Lorne has, as yet, rendered such services as would ordinarily merit a dukedom," wrote his father. "If I were in his place, I would take an active part in the House of Commons."

Lorne absorbed his father's message, swallowed his disappointment and, for want of much else to occupy himself within England, sat inconsequentially as Liberal-Unionist MP until 1900, when he succeeded to the Dukedom of Argyll. He also published occasional volumes of light verse, some on Canadian themes, also lengthy treatises on the increasingly à la mode subject of Imperial Federation, and a biography of Queen Victoria. "Watching the Queen dying," he wrote in one noteworthy phrase, "was like watching a great ship going down." Only on paper and for occasional public appearances were he and Louise still presumed to be married; even so, it was widely noticed that she chose to spend their silver wedding anniversary, in 1896, travelling alone on the continent.

Lorne's last years were darkened by a scandal that, while it never became public, was common knowledge in court circles. According to the French historian, Philippe Jullian, in his 1972 study *Edward and the Edwardians*, this affair had its source in Dublin in 1907, on the occasion of an official state visit by Edward VII and Queen Alexandra. "It was discovered," writes Jullian, that the jewels belonging to the Order of St. Patrick had disappeared. . . ."

> Since these jewels were the property of the crown, the king was furious and gave orders for a thorough inquiry into the matter. It was learnt that the king-at-arms who had charge of these gems was in the habit of giving masculine parties in the room where the strong box was kept. One obvious adventurer who had been received in Society was immediately suspected, but the King's advisers warned him against pursuing the matter, as this young man had been a close friend of his brother-in-law (poor Louise's husband) and he would undoubtedly have compromised the royal family if the matter had ever come to court.

Lorne died in 1914, of pneumonia. Louise, for her part, lived on and on, only her delight in painting and sculpture* saving her from an end as bleak as that of Lady Macdonald. Whether or not her great critic Sir Henry Ponsonby had come to know more of Louise's circumstances than he cared to commit to paper, he, by the 1890s had changed his mind about her. "Whatever people say of Princess Louise," Ponsonby wrote as the Queen grew older and older and court circles stuffier and stuffier, "I must say she is charming, and I don't know what I should do at these long dreary evening parties if it were not for her. With such a sweet smile and soft language, she says such bitter things!"

For Louise, if not for Lorne, the free and easy Edwardian era came as a breath of fresh air; alone among the king's sisters she got on with him, and was frequently invited to his house parties at Windsor and at Sandringham. She also became one of the first royal ladies to take up smoking and once astonished a high-ranking Russian officer by declining the exotic Russian cigarette he offered from a silver case, with the words, "Thanks, I prefer a gasper." She was equally renowned for her mocking, irreverent sense of humour, as in the case of the dove which, one bleak January day, entered the mausoleum at Frogmore, just as the royal family gathered to mark the anniversary of the Queen's death.

In the view of Louise's brothers and sisters, the dove clearly represented, "Dear Mama's spirit." She, however, thought otherwise. "Dear Mama's spirit would never have ruined Beatrice's hat."

Louise died in December 1939 at ninety-two, a wild card to the end amid the doughty members of the House of Windsor. Contemplating her photograph taken in Ottawa by Topley, one is reminded, somehow, of her great-great niece, the irreverent Princess Margaret.

* One of Louise's most impressive sculptures, a figure of her mother, Queen Victoria, can be seen facing Sherbrooke Street West in Montreal, just in front of the Strathcona Music Building, formerly Royal Victoria College.

CHAPTER 16

Rosedale Revisited

The general idea abroad is that I have come in for a grand future!

Edmund Meredith
diary entry; July 19, 1879

As Edmund Meredith walked home from City Hall to Sandy Hill on June 14, 1879, it was not only because the founding meeting of the Art Association had gone so swimmingly that he stepped along with a spring in his stride and a sparkle in his eye. Some of his good cheer flowed from the fact that two days earlier, when he had arrived home from a garden party organized by Lady Macdonald in aid of St. Alban's Church, his daughter Mary had come rushing to meet him at the front door and had pressed a letter with a London postmark into his hand.

This letter had reached Ottawa sooner than Meredith had expected, but for some days he, and indeed the whole family, had been anticipating it. On June 9, Fanny's sharp eyes had spotted in a Dublin newspaper the death notice of an elderly and wealthy connection-by-marriage of Meredith's; one Aunt Bella. In the Augusta Street household, it must be said, this news occasioned joy rather than sorrow. "I had been schooling myself to dismiss from my thoughts the expected legacy," Meredith relates. "From what I had heard from home it seemed to me that the excellent old lady had decided to follow Uncle Richard's example and get on into the eighties . . . but the legacy I presume now will be payable immediately; certainly, it has come just in time as I had begun to despair of paying off my liabilities, especially as every last extraordinary has been spent; namely, Mary's insurance money from the Equitable Life Insurance Company."

THE PRIVATE CAPITAL

All through the decade and a half that we've been living along with Meredith, money matters have obsessed him. Now, in his company, we can savour the moment, as he describes how he accepted the London solicitor's letter from Mary and instead of ripping it open then and there, took his full time:

> I knew this was important, but did not open it until I had gone upstairs, washed my hands, and made myself quite comfortable.
>
> On reading it, I was gratified to find that Aunt Bella had exceeded my estimation by £1000 pounds . . . the whole will amount to an addition of about £300 annually to our income. This will go far towards relieving us of all money embarrassment. I am certainly thankful for this most fortunate piece of good luck, especially for the sake of Fanny and the children who have been rather ground down for some years past.

Edmund Meredith in 1878. A year later, he came into his legacy, and escaped from Sir John and from Ottawa.

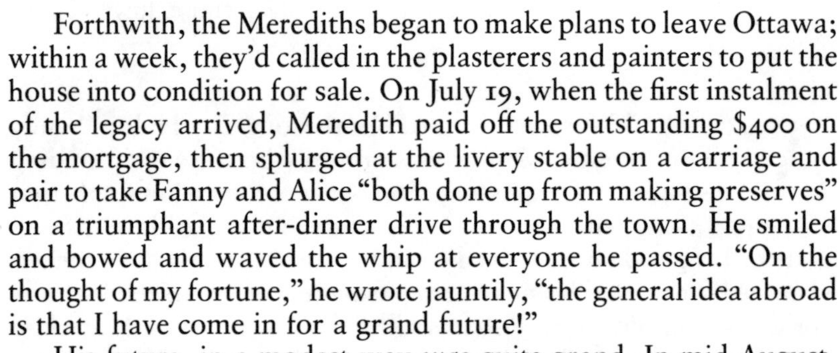

Forthwith, the Merediths began to make plans to leave Ottawa; within a week, they'd called in the plasterers and painters to put the house into condition for sale. On July 19, when the first instalment of the legacy arrived, Meredith paid off the outstanding $400 on the mortgage, then splurged at the livery stable on a carriage and pair to take Fanny and Alice "both done up from making preserves" on a triumphant after-dinner drive through the town. He smiled and bowed and waved the whip at everyone he passed. "On the thought of my fortune," he wrote jauntily, "the general idea abroad is that I have come in for a grand future!"

His future, in a modest way *was* quite grand. In mid-August, having deposited Fanny and the children at a comfortable hotel in the fashionable resort of St. Hilaire in Quebec's Eastern Townships – Fanny never having cared overmuch for bunking in with the richer Meredith relatives at Rivière du Loup – he set out alone on a trip he'd been longing to take for years: a scholarly pilgrimage through intellectual New England. At his first stop, "the old Dutch city of Albany," he could for once afford a first-class hotel, "where the arrangements were very elegant; in the glass with the napkin at dinner, there was a very recherché bouquet provided for each diner . . . mine was a beautiful damask rose; another striking feature of the room was that each of the black waiters had a very elaborate Chinese fan with which he constantly fanned the guest he was looking after." Glancing round the room, Meredith commended himself on his own smart and sensible summer-time rig. "It is singular how rigidly the Americans adhere to broadcloth; I was very remarkable on being the only person in the hotel who had the courage to wear a linen coat." Later, after "an admirable dinner," he fell asleep reading *Persuasion*.

At New York, the highlight for Meredith was a day spent admiring the wonders of the new Metropolitan Museum. Then, at Boston, where he stayed at the fashionable Parker House, he had a wonderful time rereading the classics with a scholar identified only as "Dr. Humphreys." "I found myself terribly rusty and of course, as I expected, the new way of reading Greek by the accent also added to the difficulty." Most stimulating of all, thanks to a letter of introduction from Dr. Humphreys, was an afternoon spent out at Beverley Farms with the Autocrat of the Breakfast Table himself, the great Oliver Wendell Holmes. "I had a very pleasant gossip and chat for more than an hour; he is wonderfully voluble." Throughout this trip, as a measure of the stimulation he felt after years of intellectual privation in a backwoods capital, Meredith feasted on novels in a way he hadn't done in years. "Within the last few weeks," he reports at Newport on August 20, "I have read two of the most famous novels of the last century, *Evelina* and *Tom Jones*, and if this be the best and worst of those times, I have a very great feeling of pity for my grandfather and grandmother; I do not know whether I more dislike the prudery of Evelina or the gross indecency and amorality of Tom Jones." Meredith also included in his vacation reading list *That Wonderful Woman!* "a very sensational but not unmoral novel" by the New Brunswick writer, May Agnes Fleming.

In Toronto, in September – there had never been any doubt in either his or Fanny's minds that they would retire to Toronto – the Merediths spent a hectic fortnight looking for a house. At 6 Rosedale Road, on a handsome lot that had once been the old apple orchard at Rosedale, they found exactly what they were looking for: a spacious, white-brick house with twenty-two rooms, built soon after the Jarvis estate had been subdivided in the 1860s. Then, leaving Fanny – a new, brisk, energetic, and cheerful Fanny – to clear up the last details in Ottawa and, as we already know, to be driven to the railway station by the faithful Dr. Tupper, Meredith embarked on a nostalgic pilgrimage home to Ireland and England. Just before leaving, he turned down without a second thought one last overture from Macdonald to serve, along with Hewitt Bernard and John Langton, on a new Civil Service Commission, a body that, when it reported in 1882, resulted, as the political scientist R. MacGregor Dawson has noted, "in the first important gesture towards civil service reform." In Meredith's view, "If I am to do any more real work, I should much prefer to have a fresh field of labour – fresh woods and pastures new."

Meredith being Meredith, he, in fact, worked nearly as hard in his retirement as he had done during his three decades as a civil servant. The difference was, he could afford now to concentrate on the matters that truly interested him. He kept up his interest in prison reform, attended the International Congress of 1887 at Rome at his own expense, and, in 1896, when he was seventy-nine, served on a commission of inquiry appointed to investigate the administration of Kingston Penitentiary. He also served as Vice-President of the Astronomical and Physical Society of Toronto, and kept up a voluminous correspondence with his friend Sandford Fleming about the installation of Standard Time. As if all of this were not enough, he also took a regular part-time job as a vice president of Toronto General Trusts and usually walked to the office and back every day, all the way from Rosedale Road to King Street, a distance of over two miles. One wonders, though, if Toronto General Trusts had made the wisest possible choice of vice president, for Meredith had retained his taste for financial speculation; in the late 1880s, as Coly Meredith tells us, "he took a leading part in organizing an expedition to hunt for buried treasure in the Gulf of Mexico; the treasure was not found."

"Whenever Mr. Meredith's name was mentioned," a former junior colleague at Toronto General Trusts wrote to Coly Meredith in the late 1940s, "there was always a sense of refreshment." Meredith's own sense of refreshment, during his sunset years, derived primarily from his home and family. Holding perpetual open house at Rosedale Road, he and Fanny were happier, more at peace with themselves and with each other, than they'd been since the old golden days at Quebec. Tuesday was the formal receiving day, Coly tells us, when "men, young and old were always properly dressed in morning coat and topper with high white collar and very starched cuffs and a walking stick." But any day of the week, a relative or a friend, or a friend of a friend could turn up at the house and be sure of a welcome. "People were continually arriving at the house for a meal, or the day, or for a number of days," Coly continues. "Telegrams would arrive announcing their coming, and they would be put up as a matter of course." It was above all at Christmas that Meredith truly reigned supreme as acknowledged chieftain of a Family Compact clan. "About twenty-four Merediths and Nantons could be counted on to sit down at the table," Coly tells us, that not only had been extended to its full length but with the aid of trestles and extra leaves made into an enormous dinner table. We had some really good Irish linen tablecloths. The lighting was by candles, and the napkins were properly arranged with the regulation thick square quarter-slice of bread tucked in. . . .

After dinner, we enjoyed charades, drawing room games, songs and having my father read."

Fanny, for her part, revelled in the carriage horse, Viva, that Aunt Bella's legacy enabled her to afford. Even when she was well into her sixties, according to Coly, "my mother could manage Viva better than anyone else in the family."

Except for Mary, the Meredith children married, one by one, in the late 1880s and 1890s; for Meredith in particular, his grandchildren – "sweet little mischievous pickles," as he liked to describe them – were a source of endless pleasure. One grandson whom, alas, he did not live to see, Escott Reid, the son of his youngest daughter Morna, became one of Canada's most distinguished diplomats during the 1940s and 1950s; history sometimes having its soft spots as well as its ironies, Reid fulfilled some of the hopes Meredith had once had for himself.* The one shadow that darkened Meredith's life during his last years – Fanny never recovered from the blow and forever after wrote letters on stationery edged in black – came in January 1895 when his elder son Arthur died at Edmonton.

"I am unusually fortunate in the shining love and devotion of wife and bairns, who all surround me with the most perfect and constant attention," wrote Meredith on his eighty-first birthday in 1898. He died three months later, on January 12, 1899, from the after-effects of a prostate operation. Fanny, always so much more delicate, survived him by two decades. Tended by the faithful Mary, she died on September 27, 1919.

The Meredith saga in Ottawa was not quite over. In 1898, Edmund and Fanny's youngest child, Coly, who, though born in St. Andrew's, New Brunswick, had always considered himself to be a citizen of the capital, returned there to live until his own death in 1967. Through his own lively recollections of life in Ottawa during the Edwardian era, Coly Meredith will occasionally be heard from again.

The world Coly discovered in Ottawa at the turn of the century was a very different world from the one Edmund and Fanny had

* Escott Reid's two sons, Tim and Patrick, continue the family tradition as senior civil servants.

Coly Meredith at twenty-two, in 1896. Two years later, he came back to the capital to practise architecture. In contrast to his father, he liked the city.

discovered thirty years earlier. Laurier with his "sunny way" was prime minister now; Macdonald and Agnes and the Dufferins and the Lornes and even Tupper, all were fading into memory.

The times demanded a new sort of chronicler; already, in the pages of *Saturday Night* and of the Ottawa *Free Press*, they had found one.

Part 2

THE UNCAUGHT BUTTERFLY

THE WORLD OF THE SOCIETY COLUMNIST AMARYLLIS 1897–1911

CHAPTER 17

Amaryllis, AKA The Marchioness

Le roi est mort, vive le roi *has been the cry in Ottawa since June 23, and the very people who hoped "those horrid Grits would not get in for it would ruin our society" have been among the very first to establish an* entente cordiale *with the new ascendancy.*

Amaryllis; writing in
"Society at the Capital,"
Saturday Night; March 13, 1897

Late in the winter of 1897, nine months after Wilfrid Laurier had become prime minister and in the epochal, ostrich-plumed year of the Old Queen's Diamond Jubilee, a reporter who signed herself simply "Amaryllis" began writing a regular column about Ottawa in *Saturday Night* magazine, then a fashionable weekly published in Toronto and mostly concerned with the comings and goings of society. The shrewd comment about the realities of power quoted above was her opening salvo; Amaryllis had begun as she meant to go on. Before long, we are informed that Lady Laurier "gives a card party nearly every afternoon and loves best to entertain her intimate friends, all of whom are of the feminine gender. She is, of course, always charming to men, especially men on the right side of politics, but she infinitely prefers women's society." Madame Emilie Lavergne, who was either Laurier's mistress or an exceedingly close friend, is, by contrast, "a brilliant woman called by many the Canadian Lady Chesterfield" (Lady Chesterfield having been an exceedingly close friend of Benjamin Disraeli's, as Amaryllis took for granted her readers would know).

Monsignor Merry Del Val, emissary from the Vatican sent to help solve the troublesome Manitoba Schools Question, "is a man of the world as well as a priest. He is, however, the despair of newspaper reporters, for though he receives them kindly and talks a great deal, he says absolutely nothing and they find on taking leave that they have told him all they know."

Amaryllis sketched the *mise en scène* as deftly as she limned her characters. In turn-of-the-century Ottawa, "the arrival of a new ADC at Rideau Hall carries almost the same amount of interest as a new Governor-General." This was because "there is always a great scarcity of men at all Ottawa functions. . . . Of course the House of Commons, not to mention the Senate, supplies a certain number of the necessary sex, but they, alas! are not travelling for pleasure and do bring their wives. . . ." During the summer-time exodus to Murray Bay and Rivière du Loup, "many Ottawa families living on fashionable streets close up the front of their houses and live in the back, thus giving the impression that they, too, are out of town."

Near the end of 1897, just before Christmas, a strikingly similar column – a little more long-winded, a little less acerbic – began appearing three times weekly in the daily newspaper, the Ottawa *Free Press*. Here, the first report plunges us straight into the spacious double drawing room at the Russell House hotel, where we find the illustrious Madame Lavergne holding a splendid holiday reception. "A great many people, such a chatter and clatter of tongues, so many people that it would be almost easier to say who was *not* there, than to mention names. The linen was stretched over the carpet . . . but it is difficult to make dancing a feature at afternoon teas, the young people never seem to feel up to it." One guest singled out for special mention was "Miss Cissy Fitzgerald, the ex-Gaiety Girl, who brought her dog with her, a funny little white thing that she held in her arms." Another was Mrs. Clifford Sifton, wife of Laurier's key western lieutenant: "a rather striking though pleasing figure in a handsome crimson gown, and a large black velvet hat with ostrich feathers." But the particular star, as always, was Madame Lavergne herself. "Her bright pretty manner is always delightful and she seemed so really pleased to see everyone that they all felt glad they had come."

For a few weeks, these *Free Press* columns appeared unsigned. Then, on January 13, 1898, at the end of a report on the fashionable new sport of skiing – "*skilöbning*, to be quite correct" – it is announced without fanfare that "in future, in fond remembrance of Charles Dickens, this column will be signed *The Marchioness*." This choice was interesting, because it meant that the anonymous author had adopted as namesake not a haughty leader of society, but the cheeky, cribbage-playing maidservant in *The Old Curiosity Shop*, described there by Dickens as "taking a limited view of society through the keyholes of doors." Both columns continued in *Saturday Night* and in the *Free Press* for the next half-dozen years. Then, respectively, in July 1902 and in February 1903, they ceased abruptly. Without note of explanation or word of farewell, the lady vanishes. "Surrounded by mysteries," as Dickens writes of his little Marchioness, "unacquainted with her own name."

Amaryllis and The Marchioness were of course, one and the same. Not to divulge too much too soon, the *plume* behind these *noms* was wielded by a woman who was exceptionally well-connected politically and socially, much less well-connected financially, a woman in her early thirties who had been born in Ottawa in the middle 1860s, around the same time that Edmund and Fanny Meredith had arrived. In an era when the reporting of society was coming to be at least as important as the reporting of politics, her elaborate pseudonyms were the journalistic convention. *Saturday Night*'s Toronto columnist and powerful society editor, Grace Denison, called herself "Lady Gay," after the energetic Lady Gay Spanker in Dion Boucicault's comedy of manners, *London Assurance*. Mrs. Alexander McIntyre, of the Ottawa *Daily Citizen* was "Frills"; Florence Hamilton Randal, of the Ottawa *Journal,* was "Kilmeny."

In the case of Amaryllis, AKA The Marchioness, however, there was rather more to it than that. She had not only chosen her verbal dominoes with exceptional flair, she was much more careful than her contemporaries, never (or almost never), to let them slip. Through six years and several thousand columns, she drops only one single clue that is specific enough to betray her; even this one, as we shall discover, is far from a dead giveaway.

Perhaps she was cautious because she wrote so close to the bone. More likely – Amaryllis, in *Saturday Night* with a Toronto audience, might just have gotten away with the guise, but in small and gossipy Ottawa, the real identity of The Marchioness would have escaped no one – it was a charade she enjoyed playing. Indeed, one suspects that she preferred the personae of these alter egos to her own. So for the moment, let us play along with her. For simplicity's sake, and with apologies to The Marchioness, we will call her Amaryllis throughout.

One further word of introduction. As our guide to the capital,

Amaryllis will provide a quite different point of view from Edmund Meredith. Obviously, she was a woman and he was man; as importantly crucial a distinction is that while his personal presence, thanks to his diaries, pervades every corner of the world he describes, she is a will-o'-the-wisp. She kept no diary, and left neither letters nor descendants; her true identity will be pinned down eventually, only through considerable sleuthing. Thus, instead of revealing her own character, except in glimpses, she will hold up a mirror in which her contemporaries in turn-of-the-century Ottawa will reveal themselves. Put another way, Amaryllis impales her quarry with merry abandon, yet she herself forever remains the uncaught butterfly.

The Official Ottawa that Amaryllis wrote about so knowingly was in many respects the same world that Edmund Meredith had known a generation earlier – if grown a bit larger and with more efficient

Elgin Street, in the 1890s, as it appeared from the steps of the East Block. The large building on the right is the Langevin Building, erected in 1887 to house the growing civil service. Nowadays this building, which contains the prime minister's office and the Privy Council office, is the nerve centre of Official Ottawa.

drains. In other respects, it was another world entirely. Meredith himself, returning for a brief visit in the summer of 1895, at the age of seventy-seven, found himself both at home and a stranger. On the one hand – "I was stopped again and again by men and women who all congratulated me on my looking so well" – there was the pleasure of walking familiar streets and finding familiar faces: Sir Charles Tupper in the Conservative Lounge at the House of Commons; Wilfred LeSueur, old friend from the Literary and Scientific Society, at the Rideau Club; best of all, and hale and hearty as ever, Sandford Fleming, "who seemed very glad to see me, after a grand talk, we had dinner and sat out on the lawn." On the other hand, as witnessed by Meredith from a comfortable seat on the new electric streetcars, there was "the new city that seems to have grown up": the big sprawling Langevin Building on Wellington Street, built in 1887 to accommodate a civil service that had burgeoned to over one thousand; the opulent new houses in Sandy Hill that quite dwarfed the Gothic Revival villa on Augusta Street that once had seemed so spacious. Most of all, Meredith was impressed by the new ornamental gardens at the Experimental Farm on the western edge of town. "A wonderful variety of shrubs and flowers from all over the world," he marvelled. "Mr. Saunders is always carrying on experiments in hybridization and I saw the paper bags tied around these blossoms fertilized by foreign pollen so as to prevent other pollen from reaching them."*

Other developments within the "new city" pleased Meredith somewhat less. At St. Alban's, now under a new rector, one Mr. Bogert, he found the congregation "rather slim; he, they say, has emptied the church, his sermons are very poor." Nor did he approve of the new generation and what it was coming to. Dining with his old friends, the Grant Powells, he met their granddaughter, Ethel Gormully, soon to marry Sandford Fleming's youngest son. "A pretty young girl," he remarked in his diary, "but very fast." Meredith, safe to say, would have approved even less of Amaryllis – though doubtless, like everyone else in Rosedale, he flipped quickly through *Saturday Night* to find her column on page seven, sandwiched between the advertisements for Dodd's Dyspepsia Pills and Crompton Corsets and Thistle Brand Finnan Haddies.

The years between Meredith's final departure in 1879 and the advent of Amaryllis as a journalist in 1897, had encompassed much by way of history: the completion of the CPR, highlighted by Agnes Macdonald's triumphant journey on the cowcatcher; the Riel Rebellion of 1885 that Willy Jarvis had so shrewdly foreseen; the death of Sir John A. Macdonald in 1891; the bizarre five years between

* William Saunders, a pioneer in cross-breeding techniques, had launched the Dominion Experimental Farm in 1888. In 1904, his son, Charles Saunders, developed Marquis Wheat there, thereby revolutionizing grain production on the prairies.

1891 and 1896, when four different Conservative prime ministers, of which Tupper was the last, tried unsuccessfully to hold the Tory fort. Within the capital itself, growing ever more apparent, was the dichotomy between what was still a rough-and-ready "lumber-yard," in the description of one Governor General, and a glittering viceregal society that, building upon the foundations laid by the Dufferins and the Lornes, was becoming ever more splendid and arrogant.

Consider, as through a set of the newly popular stereopticon slides, the turn-of-the-century style of the city itself. Those fine Sandy Hill houses and the gardens at the Experimental Farm were really only cosmetic touches on an urban landscape that had achieved an apogee of ugliness. For public consumption (as when setting up an Improvement Commission in 1899), Laurier spoke grandiloquently of creating a "Washington of the North." Privately (as when writing to Emilie Lavergne), he used adjectives like "dull" and "detested." On July 24, 1900, a fledgling civil servant arriving in town to begin his career tramped through the dusty streets – even at this late date, only Sparks Street was paved – and formed a similar impression. "Not interesting," William Lyon Mackenzie King noted in his diary. "Tiresome."

This was the heyday of the lumber kings. The mills at the Chaudière were churning out 200 million board feet of sawn lumber every year. Ezra Butler Eddy's match factory, not to be outdone, boasted of producing upwards of twenty thousand matches every day. As a result, the piles of timber and of sawdust were both higher and more numerous than ever before. Not until 1900, after a devastating fire had wiped out virtually the whole industrial section of the city and left fifteen thousand people homeless, was even a start made on reducing such eyesores. Almost as bad was to look overhead, for those twin modern marvels, electricity and the telephone, had been accompanied by monstrous regiments of poles, all standing askew, festooned with ugly wires. The new electric streetcars, running since 1891, had, for all their speed and efficiency, played havoc with the old tranquillity of hoofbeats and sleigh bells. "The rails tear up the roads and leave little space for carriages," noted the Countess of Aberdeen in her journal, soon after arriving at Rideau Hall in 1893. "The cars frighten the horses and they come along so swiftly and silently that they are a real danger." Ever one to call a spade a spade, the Countess concluded, "electric trams make driving a pain."*

Even Parliament Hill looked down at heel. Here, the problem lay within. None of the buildings, Amaryllis reports, had been

* As in the case of the mills at the Chaudière, electricity had been pioneered by another Yankee entrepreneur. His name was Warren Soper. Out at Rockcliffe, high on a bluff overlooking the Ottawa, Soper built himself a splendid mansion and named it Lornado, after his favourite fictional heroine, Lorna Doone. Lornado is now the residence of ambassadors of the United States.

scrubbed out properly since the government had moved in three decades earlier. Like all the other fastidious ladies who flocked in to hear the interesting debates, she was horrified. "Let us hope that the Minister of Public Works, the Honourable Israel Tarte, or 'Busy Izzy' as I have recently seen him referred to, will shortly see to the cleaning up," she wrote in 1901. "He would find no lack of deserving women willing to attack with pail and scrub-brush. There is no branch of the civil service on which the waiting list is longer than that of charwoman." But Busy Izzy, though a lion at winning elections – "they are not won by prayers," he liked to say – proved on this matter to be a mouse. "The Minister of Public Works told the House that every time he passed through the corridor he was ashamed," wrote a *Free Press* colleague of Amaryllis's a few days later. "But it was very hard, he added, to get the money from Parliament and that the Ministers in framing their estimates had been afraid to ask money enough for this purpose."*

On top of all this, and no matter the temperance movement that elsewhere across the nation was now rapidly gaining strength, Ottawa maintained its reputation as a town that, more often than not, walked with unsteady gait. When Edmund Meredith's twenty-four-year-old son Coly came back to town in 1898 to set up as an architect in an office overlooking Sparks Street, the first things he noticed were "the numerous bars, all stand-up affairs, with a brass rail to put one foot on, and the floor covered with sawdust and ample brass spittoons." The most popular Sparks Street tavern, Coly reports, rejoiced in the piratical name, The Bucket of Blood. "Here, behind the bar, the shelving was very ornate, with mirrors at the back; in the summer, these mirrors would be frosted over, I think Epsom Salts was used to do the frosting." Nor, for that matter, were the hookshops of Lower Town any fewer or less popular than before, although by now prostitutes were described rather more directly than as the "unfortunate frail ones" of Meredith's day. On January 29, 1898, in a news story that with variations only in the names of those concerned appeared more or less every day, the *Free Press* reported that one Tilly Remon, "a bad woman, dressed very loud," had been sentenced to six months for being a madam. Tilly had been convicted "on the evidence of C. Charbonneau who had seen young men well known about town going to her place in the afternoon."

Amaryllis, who was certainly not a *naïve*, never evinced in her columns the least concern about such goings-on. The bleak side of

* Tarte had plenty of other problems that session. There was, for example, the querulous Tory backbencher who kept on asking embarrassing questions about telephones. "Why should the country be paying for private telephones at the private residences of the Minister of the Interior, the Deputy and Private Secretary of the Interior Department and the Commissioner of Immigration? Why, further, should the public purse bear the cost of paying $42 for ice for the Minister of the Interior?"

Ottawa she knew only too well as a dweller in boarding-houses, shivering in winter and sweltering in summer. The Ottawa she invaded under her domino, from around teatime until the small hours, after which she sat up until dawn to write her column, was the other Ottawa, the world of Official Society, a world that had now achieved, in the words of the later historians, H. S. Ferns and Bernard Ostry, "a social hierarchy gilded and plumed . . . such as no other city in North America could display." This was a world gilded and plumed in the literal sense, a world where men wore uniforms – not just the tall silk hat and dark frock coat that were still rig of the day for Parliamentarians and deputy ministers, but the navy blue Windsor uniform encrusted with gold braid that the prime minister and his cabinet wore on formal occasions, the scarlet coats and bearskins flaunted by the young bucks who whiled away their leisure hours in the Governor General's Foot Guards, the white satin knee breeches and buckled shoes worn by the Governor General himself when he presided at state ceremonies. No less resplendent, indeed considerably more so, was the appearance of the ladies. When she arrived at the subject of fashion, Amaryllis really let herself go. This was an era when dress was more sumptuous and more ornate than at any time since the early eighteenth century, as the leg-of-mutton sleeves of the mid-nineties yielded to the bosomy, slightly top-heavy silhouette of the *fin de siècle*. From her pen, in nearly every column, mellifluous, evocative words like *aigrette* and *mousseline-de-soie* and *georgette* and *barathea* flowed as effortlessly and as gracefully as notes of music. Yet the wistful exuberance with which she described other women's clothes indicates a woman whose own dress budget was much less elastic than she would have liked. "The gown worn by Her Excellency on Wednesday afternoon has been described as grey *peau de soie*," she wrote of Lady Minto across a Rideau Hall tea table in November 1902. "It seemed to me of some softer material – *crêpe de Chine* – that is, the overblouse which fell in graceful points over a satin skirt. On the bodice of the gown, was laid a beautiful collar of real lace, fastened down here and there with diamond ornaments." Still, Amaryllis being Amaryllis, she was unable to restrain a note of *lèse-majesté*. "Her Excellency was suffering from a severe cold which the previous night had necessitated the application of linseed poultices, and she was obliged to wear layers of cotton wool under the pretty silk and lace bodice."

Yet more elaborate and intricate were the social rituals that by now had developed. Fanny Meredith had dropped in on her friends for tea on any afternoon she felt like it – but woe betide the newcomer now who did not take pains to find out that while the ladies of Sandy Hill received on Tuesday afternoons, Wednesdays, as Amaryllis put it, were "sacred to Metcalfe Street." Worse than woe betide the gentleman so gauche when calling on a lady as to give his gloves, stick, and hat to the maid in the frilly apron who answered the door, not knowing it was "the thing," as the saying went, to carry them into the drawing room and place them neatly on the floor next to his chair. It was a world of "faint implications and pale delicacies," as Edith Wharton once wrote of New York society, full of chatter and the clink of teacups, redolent of calling cards in silver cases and dance programmes with tassels. Much more than hostesses fussed over what their guests actually ate – Amaryllis, on one occasion, wrote disparagingly of "boiled mutton and turnips" – they worried about the appearance of their tea and dinner tables. "So much is written about table decorations in society columns that one gets the impression they must all be very lovely," wrote Amaryllis. "As a matter of fact, most of them are commonplace." She herself was a purist, who preferred "cut glass, solid silver and pink roses" and did not at all admire the *coup de foudre* at a luncheon given by the American consul in 1901, "a centrepiece made of broken bombshells filled with red and white flowers resting between four or five rifles stakes together." Still, she was rather a fan of the talented butler at Government House who in 1901 devised for the viceregal dinner table, "a great tract of winter country, dotted here and there with pinetrees, with straggling fences emerging out of snowdrifts, frozen lakes, rivers and small streams."

Government House, *ça va sans dire*, remained the glittering pinnacle of it all. In our own time, when, by Edward Schreyer's calculation, fewer than fifty per cent of Canadians even know who the Governor General is, it is difficult to contemplate the serene, unchallenged omnipotence of Rideau Hall at the turn of the century. That clumsy overgrown villa, already a patchwork of additions, with a couple still to come, surrounded by its eighty-eight acres of parkland, held not just the capital, but the entire nation in its thrall. For Amaryllis and her devoted readers, the date on the social calendar that mattered most was always that day in mid- to late October when the viceregal court returned from its "summer-time wanderings" and deputized a footman to run up the Union Jack. "The people know that when the flag flies over Rideau," she reports in November 1901, "the Visitors' Book is open in the vestibule below. A long procession extending perhaps over weeks can be seen of carriages in one avenue, pedestrians in the other, going up to Government House to inscribe their names in it." Inside the vestibule, "a printed notice on the wall requests ladies and gentlemen to write very plainly. That of course is from the ADC in waiting."*

Rideau Hall, as Amaryllis enjoyed rubbing in, set Ottawa apart, both from Montreal, so much more handsome and sophisticated a city, and from Toronto, so much wealthier. "Most Toronto women, apart from the few who enjoy the advantages of a visit to Ottawa during the session, have probably never made a curtsey in their lives," she wrote. "It is different with us. We have the viceregal court to keep us from growing too stiff-kneed or democratic." She herself was a court insider, which was her great strength as a columnist. Others signed their names in the book with obsessive care in the hope that the ADC, when scrutinizing it, would assign them at least a place in the outer circle, that ragtag assembly of perhaps a thousand who qualified for invitations to the big "crush" receptions and to skating parties. Amaryllis could sign if she wished with a scrawl, confident that this year, as always, she would find herself in the circle of intimates, numbering a couple of hundred, who were asked to perch on little gilt chairs in the ballroom for the most exclusive functions, those evenings of amateur theatricals when, as in the Dufferins' time, the viceregal household let down its hair. Indeed, as Amaryllis lets drop early on, as a young girl back in the eighties she had belonged to the most select Rideau Hall coterie of all, that tiny band of beaux and belles, at most never more than a dozen, who, on the strength of their good looks, their good breeding, and their passable capacity to sing and to dance, were actually invited to play small parts in these productions.

Now, in her thirties and in full pursuit of a career – even if only until something better came along – Amaryllis used her insider status to good advantage. By carving out a role as adviser and confidante, she cultivated her contacts. Thus in 1896, when the Countess of Aberdeen had terrible trouble finding someone to make imitation chain mail for a costume ball, it was Amaryllis who recommended exactly the right tinsmith, name of Jolicoeur. In 1902, when the Countess of Minto wanted to show off the new viceregal gramophone, it was Amaryllis who was invited to an intimate, firelit tea – "hot toast, muffins and bath buns" – in order to hear "a famous baritone sing the 'Toreador Song' from *Carmen*." At the same time, she was sure enough of her position to dare to be flip from time to time – even about that most glittering of events on the viceregal calendar, the annual State Drawing Room, an event that, for the

* This is probably as good a time as any to say a few words about Rideau Hall, the building itself.

The house began its life in 1838, as a bow-fronted Regency villa, built for the chief contractor of the Rideau Canal, Thomas Mackay. According to the architectural historians, Marion MacRae and Anthony Adamson, writing in the *The Ancestral Roof* in 1963, it was probably inspired by the well-known handbook, *Cottages and Villas*, published in 1793 by the British architect Sir John Soane; inspired in particular by Soane's design for Chilton Lodge in Berkshire. This original Rideau Hall contained only eleven rooms, yet, as MacRae and Adamson point out, "two of these were elliptical reception rooms of great elegance, and two more, *mirabile dictu*, contained bathrooms." Only one of these elliptical rooms survives: the original second-floor drawing room which, with all its original thistle-encrusted plasterwork intact and a handsome marble fireplace, serves as the Queen's bedroom when she is in residence.

The first important addition was made in 1865, just before the arrival of Lord Monck, the first Governor General to live in Ottawa. This was designed by the Public Works' architect, F. A. Rubidge, and consisted of a long, two-storey wing at the east side, in the style of the Second Empire. In the 1870s the light it sheds on the mannered formalities of the era, deserves to be lingered over.

By custom, the ceremony took place, in the crimson and gold Senate Chamber, on the night of the first Saturday following the Opening of Parliament. Along with a small band of other journalists, Amaryllis would look down from the gallery. Their Excellencies, "surrounded by a glittering staff of military men," would stand on the steps of a dais arranged to look like a throne, he in the full court dress that included white satin knee breeches and silver-buckled shoes, she in her best Brussels lace and a diamond tiara. Then, as the Military Secretary bawled out the names – "at first in a loud, distinct voice, but later the distinctness was not so apparent" – a long line of outwardly gorgeous but inwardly quaking citizenry would file up to be presented. There were the season's debutantes, three feathers waving and full court trains, thankful that in Ottawa, in contrast to similar occasions in Dublin, it was not the custom for His Excellency to kiss them. There were the Supreme Court judges, the senators and MPs and their ladies, and "lastly, the ladies and gentlemen of no particular position." Protocols were strict: in 1899, there was a dreadful rumour, which Amaryllis was pleased to pass on, that the American Consul, one Colonel Turner, who, as a purely commercial representative, did not qualify for the diplomatic entrée, had tried to jump his place in the queue. "There is seldom smoke without fire," she reported, "and the fact that one or two consuls in official uniform were seen before the drawing room but were not presented, leads one to the belief that something must have happened."

The journalists themselves were presented to Their Excellencies last. Amaryllis, we can imagine, was always graceful as a swan. Yet even for her, as she revealed in 1897, in one of her earliest and funniest columns, Drawing Rooms were not without terrors.

> The ordeal of making two very low curtseys gracefully, rising without falling, getting out without turning your back on Her Majesty's representative, is nothing compared to the criticism you know you are undergoing from your friends who have previously been presented, and whom you pass as you advance to the Throne. Such remarks as, "No, it's not a new gown, only done over" . . . "I think she has had it dyed" . . . "She ought to try to look more cheerful." Some ladies got frightened and hurried past Their Excellencies with a sort of nod over their shoulders, as if to say, "I'll see you later." The men on the whole did better, for they have on the whole not much to do . . . they never have.

Dufferins built two additions, one on either side of the front: the ballroom on the right, and the Tent Room on the left.

This, roughly, was the Rideau Hall that Amaryllis would have known at the start of her career as a journalist. Then, in 1899, the Mintos added a utilitarian wing at the rear, containing additional bedrooms and offices.

The last important change – and the present appearance of the building – dates from 1913 when, during the era of the Duke and Duchess of Connaught, the Public Works' architect, David Ewart, superimposed a heavy stone front, with a large coat of arms. Also at this time were added a long drawing room, just behind the Tent Room, and a formal reception hall.

No doubt because he was designing for royalty – the Duke of Connaught was Queen Victoria's son – Ewart was overawed by the challenge. His work destroyed the last vestiges of Rideau Hall's original grace. The pity is that when working on a smaller scale, he was capable of both charm and inventiveness: Ewart's own house, on Besserer Street, is probably the single prettiest house in all of Sandy Hill: a delightful Edwardian cupcake.

The Marquis of Lansdowne. The dry furnace heat at Rideau Hall, he was wont to complain, played havoc with his furniture.

Luckily for Amaryllis, she began her career as a journalist just as Government House, under the Aberdeens and later even more so under the Mintos, was livening up. The years of the later eighties and early nineties, when she had been in her teens and twenties, had been, in truth, rather a doldrum era. It wasn't so much that the immediate successors to Dufferin and to Lorne had been nonentities, as that neither had really addressed himself to the job. For the fifth Marquis of Lansdowne, a slight, dark Anglo-Irish aristocrat appointed in 1883 when he was only thirty-eight, Canada was clearly only a stepping stone to glittering prizes as Viceroy of India and Foreign Secretary. For the first Baron Stanley of Preston, a former Conservative Member of Parliament who succeeded Lansdowne in 1888 and served until 1893, the appointment was more in the nature of a retirement post.

To occupy themselves, both men had fostered the cult of winter. Lansdowne pioneered the custom of holding skating parties by night, torchlit evenings which he described as "Arctic Cremornes" after the recently defunct Cremorne pleasure gardens in London; Stanley, or rather Lady Stanley, sent out whimsical invitations to winter-sporting at-homes, enlivened by sketches of ladies and gentlemen falling off toboggans. The only time either of these gover-

An invitation to one of Lady Stanley's skating parties, again from the scrapbook of Mrs. Percy Sherwood.

nors general seemed truly to come alive, however, was when they were engaged in "killing salmon," as they put it, on the Cascapedia River near the Bay of Chaleurs, where, by fiat of the Quebec government, no one but the Governor General was allowed to fish. Over four seasons, as his biographer, Lord Newton, notes proudly, Lansdowne and his party "killed" a total of 1,245 salmon, averaging twenty-four pounds each. Stanley built for himself a cosy nineteen-bedroom fishing lodge, which he named Stanley House, and installed in it one of the first rural telephones in Canada, for the express purpose of calling to points upstream to find out how the salmon were rising.*

To this short list of achievements, it can be added that Stanley donated the Stanley Cup for hockey. However, given his own penchant for liking to have the lights out by twelve, it seems unlikely that he would have much enjoyed the spectacle of Stanley Cup winners, a century later, carousing around pouring champagne into his cup, and over each other.

On the negative side, Lansdowne, even though perhaps the ablest individual ever to occupy Rideau Hall other than Dufferin, as his later career demonstrated, committed in his term probably the most egregious act of political misjudgement of any Governor General. On November 12, 1885, considering whether or not Louis Riel should be reprieved from the death penalty, Lansdowne reported in his telegram of advice to Queen Victoria, "Lord Lansdowne believes that the grievances of the halfbreeds have been greatly exaggerated. . . . There is undoubtedly some feeling, a survival of old race antipathies, but Lord Lansdowne does not consider that it is universal or very deep-seated." Four days later, Riel was hanged at Regina. A week after that, forty thousand *Canadiens* assembled on the Champ de Mars at Montreal. Among them was the Member of Parliament for Drummond-Arthabaska, Wilfrid Laurier. "Had I been born on the banks of the Saskatchewan," he shouted from the platform, "I myself would have shouldered a musket." Lansdowne, as the British historian, Thomas Pakenham, has described him in another context, "had not the faintest spark of imagination."

There were, at Rideau Hall, a few links left over from the old days. Every winter, without fail, Dufferin's eldest son Archie, Arthur Meredith's old dancing-school chum, now Lord Ava and in the words of his awestruck young cousin, Harold Nicolson, "the handsomest man I ever met," returned to Government House to take part in the skating, tobogganing, and skilöbning, and to make every belle in the capital fall achingly in love with him. But, with Meredith gone and Amaryllis not yet writing, all that really sur-

* Stanley House now belongs to the Canada Council, which uses it for summer seminars on matters cultural.

vives to enliven the official record of these in-between viceregal years is the chapter devoted to Canada in *The Days Before Yesterday*, an exuberant memoir written in the 1920s by Lansdowne's brother-in-law, Lord Frederick Hamilton. Hamilton, who later became a distinguished British diplomat, visited often and, unlike the haughty Lansdowne, who found Ottawa "new and uninteresting" and was continually bemoaning the effects of dry furnace heat on his fine inlaid furniture, he had a fine time. "Ottawa society was very pleasant," he wrote. "There was then a note of unaffected simplicity about everything and the people were perfectly natural and free from pretence. . . . I called one afternoon on the very agreeable wife of a high official and was told at the door that Lady R ____ was not at home. Recognizing my voice, a cry went up from the kitchen stairs. 'Oh yes, I am at home to you. Come right down to the kitchen,' where I found her with sleeves rolled up making with her own hands the sweets for the dinner party she was giving that night."*

* Hamilton provides only the initial, but she was probably Lady Ritchie, wife of Sir William Ritchie, Chief Justice of the Supreme Court.

Hamilton was charmed with everything he saw. At the Rideau Hall dinner table he met Sir John A., who he thought "conveyed an impression of having an enormous reserve of latent force behind his genial manner." Once, he lingered past adjournment in the House of Commons to watch the after-hours event known as the "Pages' Parliament." "One boy, elected by the others as Speaker, puts on a gown and seats himself in the Speaker's Chair, the Prime Minister and the Leader of the Opposition take their places, and the boys hold regular debates." Also in the Commons, he heard the flamboyant transplanted Irishman, Nicholas Flood Davin, "give the most curious peroration I have ever listened to." The House was debating a dull bill on lumber, Hamilton continued, "when Davin, who may possibly have been under the influence of alcoholic excitement, insisted on speaking. He finished with these words, every one of which I remember:

> There are some who declare that Canada's trade is declining; there are some who maintain that the rich glow of health which at present mantles o'er Canada's virgin cheek will soon be replaced by the pallid hues of the corpse. To such propagandists of a preposterous pessimism, I answer Mr. Speaker with all confidence, never, never.

To add to his list of conquests, Hamilton, on accompanying his sister on a visit to an Ottawa convent, dazzled a pair of elderly nuns. "I was gazing at the piles of clothing neatly arranged on the shelves when the old nun clapped her hands. 'We will dress you up as a sister,' she cried. . . . They put on me a habit (largest size) chuckling with glee. . . . Having no moustache, I flattered myself that I made a rather saintly looking novice."

Like so many British visitors, Hamilton was enraptured by winter and by its embellishments. "In those days, all members of snow-

AMARYLLIS, AKA THE MARCHIONESS

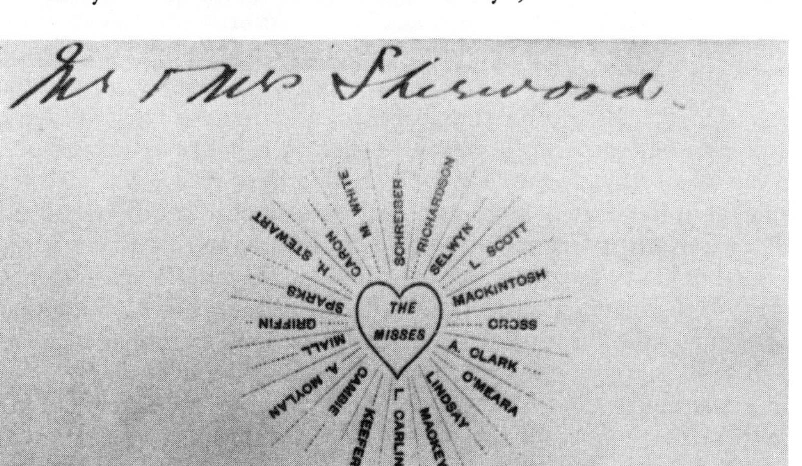

Mr & Mrs Sherwood

THE MISSES

M. WHITE
SCHREIBER
RICHARDSON
SELWYN
L. SCOTT
MACKINTOSH
CROSS
A. CLARK
O'MEARA
LINDSAY
MACKEY
L. CARLING
KEEFER
CAMBIE
A. MOYLAN
NIALL
GRIFFIN
SPARKS
H. STEWART
CARON

TWENTY OTTAWA SPINSTERS

REQUEST THE PLEASURE OF YOUR COMPANY AT A SMALL DANCE AT

THE OLD RACQUET COURT

ON WEDNESDAY EVENING, FEBRUARY 10TH, AT 8.30 O'CLOCK.

CHAPERONES:

HON. MRS. HERBERT.	MRS. TUPPER.
MRS. LAY.	MRS. WRIGHT.

"Ottawa society was very pleasant," felt Lord Frederick Hamilton. Lilian Scott, who became Lilian Desbarats and who published her recollections in the 1950s, was one of the twenty spinsters who sent out the invitation.

Until Hamilton introduced "skilöbning," snowshoeing was all the rage. This is the cover of the 1884 membership list of the most fashionable club, to which Amaryllis belonged.

shoe clubs, men and women alike, wore coloured blanket-suits, consisting of knickerbockers and long coats, with bright coloured stockings, sash and knitted tuque. . . . A collection of three hundred people in blanket-suits gave the effect of a peripatetic rainbow against the white snow." For the Arctic Cremornes at Rideau Hall, "the rinks were all fringed with coloured fairy-lamps, the curling rink and the tearoom above it were outlined with innumerable coloured electric bulbs and festoons of Japanese lanterns were stretched between the fir trees." When it came time for supper, guests were served in the long, covered curling-rink. "There was a long table elaborately set out with silver-branched candlesticks and all the Governor-General's fine collection of plates, but the servants waited in heavy fur coats and caps. Of course, no flowers could be used, so the silver vases held branches of spruce, hemlock and other Canadian firs. The French cook had to be very careful as to what dishes he prepared, for anything with moisture would freeze at once: meringues, for instance, would be frozen into uneatable cricket balls and tea, coffee and soup had to simmer perpetually over lamps."

Most intriguing of all, in Hamilton's estimation, was the ice palace, built every December to house the band. "It was usually built in what I may call a free adaptation of the Canado-Moresque style. A very necessary feature was the large stove for thawing the brass instruments. The bandsmen always had to handle the brass with woollen gloves on to prevent getting burnt."

Hamilton, endearingly, saved his personal and truly significant contribution to the Canadian winter to the last. "In January 1887, I brought my Russian skis to Ottawa, the very first pair that had ever been seen in the New World. I coasted down hills on them amidst universal jeers; everyone declared they were quite unsuitable to the Canadian conditions."

Within a decade, as Amaryllis reports, the hills around Rockcliffe were dotted with "skilöbners," ladies in thick tweed skirts, ending just above the ankle, bright berets, and long scarves, gentlemen in tuques and knickerbockers. While the social ascendancy of skating as winter-time pastime continued unquestioned, hardly anyone, any longer, went snowshoeing.

The Ice Palace at Rideau Hall. This photograph dates from 1907, but the "Canado-Moresque style" described by Frederick Hamilton had remained constant.

Amaryllis, in her salad days, had known Hamilton well and had even acted with him in a Rideau Hall theatrical. She also shared Hamilton's gift for being irrepressibly entertained by everything she saw, and for being both participant and irreverent observer. If her own particular stock in trade was a streak of elegant bitchiness, an ability to stand a little apart from her society and to send it up, she took good care to remain a member in good standing of that society. Her livelihood as a journalist depended on her being asked back by the people she sometimes lampooned. As a result, when Amaryllis felt that her society was being attacked by an outsider, she rushed ferociously to its defence. A case in point is her treatment of the "society highwaywoman" affair of 1898. At first, when rumours of a certain ladies' euchre party at which "sums of money ranging from ten to twenty dollars were abstracted from purses lying in muffs and coat pockets in the dressing room," rocketed through town, she bounced them around like shuttlecocks. "This time next week, the sum stolen will rival the national debt and in addition, one hears of silver-backed brushes, umbrellas, silver button hooks and even a cake of soap being stolen . . . I suppose it was nice scented soap." But by the next week, with anti-society watchdogs in full cry from pulpit and editorial office, she'd changed her tune: "Very little card-playing goes on for money in Ottawa society, and as for saying that the women drink too much wine, it is perfect nonsense . . . these preachers and would-be improvers of the human race who find their chief strength lies in attacking society are decidedly wearisome. There is a lot outside society that wants renovating."

Still, there were times when, even though it must have earned her some frigid glances, Amaryllis could not suppress her wicked delight in exposing the pretensions she saw around her. All these years later, the reader giggles, as Amaryllis must surely have giggled, at the sight of a coterie of panicky Sandy Hill matrons, setting out into the crisp October weather of 1899 to defend their reputations:

> Much excitement was caused in society circles last week by a rumour which found its way into the columns of a morning paper to the effect that a married lady of Sandy Hill (eminently respectable Sandy Hill) had eloped with a gentleman high in the service of the Government. The lady, it was said, was a prominent member of several charitable organizations. "Who can it be?" said everyone. Alas! for Sandy Hill, several names were mentioned, all of them connected with charitable organizations. It was shocking, but interesting. Since then, the ladies of Sandy Hill have taken to parading Sparks Street when all the world is there. Why is it? Do they want their friends to know that they are still here?

Such rollicking spirits were in tune with the times. In almost any era, Amaryllis would have been a success as a journalist, but much of the zest in her reportage flows from the fact that she was writing about Official Ottawa during one of its most bravura periods. If Rideau Hall had happened upon interesting times, so even more had Parliament Hill. These early years of Laurier were a heady, expansive time, when the long and lingering depression of the early nineties had lifted at last, and when it really did seem as if the new twentieth century might belong to Canada. These years were also, after all the stiff, formal years of Agnes Macdonald, years of social fluidity and innovation. All manner of new people were flocking into town to bang at society's doors. As we discover from Amaryllis's earliest columns, Laurier's much-heralded "cabinet of all the talents" had brought with it to the capital a number of talented hostesses: Mrs. Clifford Sifton, wife of the Minister of the Interior; Mrs. A. G. Blair, wife of the Minister of Railways and Canals; Mrs. William Fielding, wife of the Minister of Finance. Thanks to Laurier and to the enigmatic Madame Lavergne, French Canadians were, for the first time, truly a presence to be reckoned with. Thanks to the presence in government offices of a pair of promising young poets, Archibald Lampman and Duncan Campbell Scott, the capital was even experiencing a tentative literary flowering.

If Meredith, chronicling his world from a sedate masculine viewpoint, was a bit of an unpublished Trollope within the colonies, Amaryllis, bringing to bear her sophisticated, feminine eye, was more of an unsung Edith Wharton. Bold where Meredith had been hesitant, irreverent where he was earnest, her style was made to order for a capital which, although still hideously raw and provincial by international standards, was beginning at last to grow up. More than anyone else, it was the prime minister himself who had created the new ambience. *Le roi est mort. Vive le roi!*

"Not to have made some purchase at the Earnscliffe sale is what few persons with aspirations after social distinction like to own up to and not to have been there at all puts one quite outside the pale." Thus, on May 26, 1900, in a piece that *Saturday Night* considered sufficiently interesting to run as a separate news story, Amaryllis began her description of the event that, more than any other, epitomizes the transition from the Ottawa of the Merediths to her own. People still cherished the memory of Sir John and when Agnes Macdonald, after several unsatisfactory years of being an absentee landlady in far-off England, decreed that Earnscliffe and all its contents should be put on the block in a gigantic auction sale, they flocked to pay him homage – and also to pay what Amaryllis consid-

The presentation desk belonging to Sir John A. Macdonald, inscribed "Dominion SecreTORY," was the pièce de résistance *at the Earnscliffe sale.*

ered to be "absurdly high prices" for any and every object with "Macdonald associations." "The bed he slept in, and died in by the way, the wardrobe in which his clothes were kept . . . a desk made of many kinds of Canadian wood, a very hideous piece of furniture but valuable for the reason that it had been presented to Sir John by some organization or other and was much prized by him, sold for about three times its actual value. . . ." Meanwhile, she added, "a kitchen range which cost less than a year ago well over a hundred dollars was bought by a practical housekeeper for ten dollars. It had no 'associations' but few will deny that a kitchen range is better without them."

The auction at Earnscliffe lasted three days. When it was over, people had got Sir John out of their system. Thereafter, attention turned to number 335 Theodore Street in the centre of Sandy Hill, the ugly yellow brick mansion that a grateful Liberal Party had bought for the considerable sum of $9,500 to serve a residence for its triumphant, if, alas, rather impecunious, new prime minister. Here, there existed no secret passages to serve as escape hatches from importunate visitors. Laurier's house, indeed, fronted right on Ottawa's new electric streetcar line, with a stop just opposite the front door. "Sir Wilfrid's democratic principles will not allow his riding in anything aught but else but trams," Amaryllis announced approvingly to her readers.

Laurier's house on Theodore Street, now Laurier Avenue. In 1897, the Liberal Party had bought it for him from an Ottawa jeweller for $9,500. Zoë Laurier willed the house to Mackenzie King, and it is now a museum.

CHAPTER 18

The Distant Violin

Proud I am of your friendship, nay of your affection, and could I yell it on the top of houses, prouder yet would I be.

Wilfrid Laurier to Emilie Lavergne,
May 24, 1891.

When Laurier was sworn in as prime minister on July 11, 1896, he was fifty-four and in his prime, a tall, slender, consummately graceful figure with a strong yet mobile face, and a shock of chestnut hair, just silvering over, swooping down over the back of his high, starched collar. As much as Lord Salisbury at Westminster, he looked the very model of a late-Victorian prime minister. Yet the office had come to him anything but easily and not even entirely at his own behest. A quarter-century earlier, arriving in Ottawa as a new backbencher from the Eastern Townships hamlet of Arthabaskaville, he'd seemed singled out for stardom: a clever young *avocat* of *Rouge* persuasion, bookish, idealistic, overflowing with seductive charm, hampered only by a weak chest. In 1877, he'd won golden opinions for an epic speech on Political Liberalism that the Liberal Party of our own time, in its occasional reflective moments, still likes to hark back to. A year later, Alexander Mackenzie promoted him to the cabinet.

But following the Macdonald restoration, and during the long grinding years of opposition as principal Quebec lieutenant under Edward Blake, the stuffing seemed to have gone out of Laurier. Clever but indolent, said colleagues. "Lazy Laurier," jibed the newspapers. "The tall courtly figure was a familiar sight in the Chamber and in the library, particularly in the library where he could be found every day ensconced in some congenial alcove," wrote John Dafoe of the Winnipeg *Free Press* many years later, looking back on the Laurier he remembered from his own days as a young press gallery reporter. "But the golden voice was silent." When Blake, tired and ill and dispirited by 1887, proffered the leadership, not so much as it seemed then as a prize, but almost out of politeness, Laurier had to be bullied into accepting it. It was really only when Mrs. Blake, at the end of the interview, fixed him with steely gaze and said pointedly, "Yes, Mr. Laurier, you are the only man for it," that he reluctantly agreed. Even in 1896, it wasn't so much that he and his Liberals had won the election as that the Tories had lost it, by failing to pull themselves together after Macdonald's death.

"Laurier will never make a leader, he has not enough of the devil in him," a veteran Grit backbencher had once grumped to Dafoe. But power, as it so often does, energized Laurier. He in turn energized the country. Almost overnight, he became extravagantly popular. Somehow, his charm, his manner, his presence, his style, all added up to an idea whose time had come. Amaryllis abandoned her customary skepticism about politicians to let readers know that she, for one, had spotted the magic early on. "I remember going to a political gathering just before the general election where Sir Wilfrid was principal speaker," she wrote. "And though I have a suspicion that I was born a Liberal, I became a more pronounced one that night." Even more enthusiastic was Amaryllis's editor at *Saturday Night*, Grace Denison, AKA Lady Gay. "The crowd flung themselves upon the Premier and hands clawed at him," began her account of Laurier's first triumphant prime-ministerial progress to Toronto in October 1897. Her chronicle continued:

> The first girl up wore a green hat and pink roses, and one could from an alcove, watch the progress of that hat with fascinated delight. Then came two little women in red hats, almost lost amid the sea of straining, suffocating, panting men. But the red hats did the trick. Their elbows must have been sharp, for portly persons doubled up in their vicinity, and left them right of way.

During Pierre Elliott Trudeau's term in office (1968-1984), the only reminder of any previous prime minister, or of any link whatever between himself and the Liberal Party that he maintained in his Centre Block office, was a photograph of Laurier in a silver frame. The parallels between these two are almost uncanny. Each sought to make Quebec an integral part of Canada by making Canada a truly bicultural country. Each had to make their case, not only to English Canadians but also to their own, against the contrary eloquence of a nationalist champion: as René Lévesque was to Trudeau, so Henri Bourassa was to Laurier. The similarities extend to lesser matters: Laurier did not smoke and drank, at most, a couple of glasses of wine at dinner. In place of Trudeau's rose, Laurier wore, not always, but often enough to become his signature, a cravat pin in the shape of a lucky horseshoe given to him by a motherly landlady while he was studying law at McGill. When he retired, Trudeau picked a date that extended the length of his own term just beyond that of Laurier's.

Style is the man himself, as Trudeau, quoting Buffon, liked to say. A fine appreciation of this, an uncannily prescient description of the phenomenon that would later be called Trudeaumania, is contained in the collection of political profiles, *The Masques of Ottawa*, published in 1921 and written under the pseudonym "Domino" by Augustus Bridle, a one-time drama critic for the *Toronto Star* who later became a political commentator. Here is what Bridle had to say about Laurier, from the perspective of one who understands theatre:

> [He] swung in a great romantic orbit of political sentiment. We never had a statesman who could smile so potently. Never one with such mellifluous music in voice, such easy grace in his style, such a cardinal's hauteur when he wanted to be alone and such a fascinating urbanity when he wanted to impress a company, a caucus or a crowd. The Romanist whom Orangemen admired, the Frenchman who made an intellectual hobby of British democracy . . . was the kaleidoscopic enigma of Canadian public life.
>
> Laurier was nearly all things to all men . . . the kind of man to whom other people naturally happened. He was a human solar system, in which many kinds of people wanted to gravitate, even to the ragged little girl on the prairies who picked him the wildflowers he wore in his coat as far as she could see him on the train platform. . . . He was sometimes many things to himself. . . . One moment he could be as debonair as Beau Brummell, the next as forbidding and repellent as a modern Caesar. He was consistently the best-dressed public man in Canada. A misfitting coat was to him as grievous as a misplaced verb in a peroration. . . .
>
> Laurier could perform obvious tricks with consummate grace. And he performed many. There was never a moment of his waking life when he could not have been lifted into a play. His movements, his words, his accent, his clothes, his facial lineaments were never commonplace, even when his motives often may have been. He was Debussy's Afternoon of a Faun. . . .

Parallels between Trudeau and Laurier can be overdrawn. In his battles with recalcitrant opponents, Laurier was never impelled by a need to have been seen to have wrestled them into the ground. To the divisive issues of his day, such as the Manitoba Schools Question, he applied the soothing solvent of his self-described "sunny way" and his own supple personal diplomacy. Even those whom Laurier bested never held it against him, nor did he himself go in for holding grudges. His manner towards his opponents was graceful and almost comradely. "Sir John is showing signs of age at last . . . to see him gradually sink . . . conveys an impression of sadness irrepressible," he wrote to Emilie Lavergne a fortnight or so before Macdonald died in 1891.

A difference nearer to the nature of this story lies in each man's attitude towards women. Each was effortlessly attractive to women; each revelled in being an object of desire; each in his own day was mildly notorious for being a compulsive flirt. But Laurier actually *liked* women. He sought out, all his life, the company of women who were witty, educated, mature. He sought out above all Emilie Lavergne, that "brilliant woman called by many the Canadian Lady Chesterfield," whom Amaryllis so much admired. From its beginnings in Arthabaskaville in the mid-1870s to its ending in Ottawa just after the turn of the century, the liaison between them stands as perhaps the most remarkable romantic liaison in Canadian political history. Not only was Emilie central to Laurier's emotional existence for more than a quarter-century, she influenced his career profoundly.

When Emilie, as legend has it, walked across the lawn at a summer-time garden party and into Laurier's life, he had already been married for most of a decade. As if to heighten the drama, the circumstances of the marriage between Laurier and Zoë Lafontaine in 1868 had been as flamboyantly romantic as in any of the "risqué modern novels" that Charlotte Rose was pressing on Agnes Macdonald in Ottawa that same year.

Zoë and Laurier had met and fallen in love in the Montreal household of a mutual elder friend, one Dr. Sèraphin Gauthier, where Laurier, then a law student at McGill was a lodger, and Zoë, a shy, delicately pretty music teacher, was an unofficial daughter of the Gauthier family. But when Laurier moved on to the Eastern Townships in 1866 for the sake both of his career and of his weak chest, the relationship seemed to wither. Within two years, Zoë had become engaged to a young doctor from Pointe Claire. Then, on May

Wilfrid Laurier at twenty-eight, a year after his marriage to Zoë Lafontaine.

Zoë Lafontaine as a young woman. If she could not marry Laurier, she would marry no one.

12, 1868, just as Laurier was in the midst of preparing his first really important legal case, there arrived in Arthabaskaville a telegram from Gauthier in Montreal. "Come at once," it read, "a matter of urgent importance." Next day, in his examining room, Gauthier poked and prodded at Laurier's chest, and pronounced (correctly, as it turned out) that he, in fact, was not tubercular, but merely a sufferer from chronic bronchitis. Once satisfied, Gauthier revealed the real reason for his telegram. The previous day, Zoë had broken down in tears. She could not, would not, marry her fiancé. It had to be Wilfrid Laurier or no one. That same evening, at eight o'clock, the two were married by special dispensation. "There was never a moment of Laurier's waking life when he could not have been lifted into a play," as Bridle wrote.

It may have been a harbinger of things to come that instead of bedding down his bride, Laurier took a late train back to Arthabaskaville so as to appear in court next day. Yet, for the first several years of their marriage, Wilfrid and Zoë lived an idyll. "Those days of Arthabaska, how gladly I would return to them," he wrote fifty years later. "We were young then, and youth paints only *en couleur de rose*." Sadly, there were no children. But Zoë found solace in her music, in her garden, in organizing wonderful picnics and parties for other people's children, in plans for a splendid new house.

As the 1870s wore on, *la vie en rose* began to grey a little. As Laurier became less and less a simple country lawyer and more and more a man of affairs, Zoë did not grow with him. She did not care for politics. She put on weight. "She had no thought of probing or changing, no seed of her own to plant," Joseph Schull has written in his definitive biography, *Laurier*. "Perhaps he missed it."

At this point, on cue as if in a novel by Flaubert, Emilie Barthe came on the scene. She was fast approaching the fatal age of thirty, the daughter of a well-known *Rouge* politician and journalist, Joseph-Guillaume Barthe, just back from several years abroad in London and in Paris, where she had met the great Victor Hugo himself. Emilie was not the least bit beautiful but rather, as the French would say, *une jolie laide*. For Laurier, though, as for many men, "the sparkling well-stocked mind," as he later put it, "the ready flow of conversation," more than made up for a certain angularity of figure, a jutting chin, and irregular teeth. Doubtless, like all the rest of Arthabaska, he was dazzled by her marvellous Paris clothes, shown off to perfection by a flawless carriage.

Joseph Lavergne. He was resigned to the liaison between Laurier and Emilie.

Ostensibly, Emilie had come to town to make a brief visit to relatives. Instead, having met Laurier, she lingered on. Then, in November 1876, she married Joseph Lavergne, Laurier's solid, but even by Arthabaska standards unexciting, partner in law. It could only have been a *mariage de convenance* except that in this case the *convenance* was not money, but a proximity to someone else's husband.

For a time, until everyone got used to it, Arthabaska was scandalized. Far from being clandestine about their ever-deepening friendship, Lavergne's bride and Lavergne's senior partner were open about their mutual attraction. Business was rarely pressing in the small, one-storey clapboard office on the village's main street. Almost every day, either at around eleven in the morning, or at tea-time, Laurier would rise from his desk and say over his shoulder while going out the door. "Joseph, if you will permit it, I am going to chat with your wife."

Much, much later on, when grizzled old Liberals who had once been Laurier's colleagues on the back-benches reminisced about him, they could never for the life of them figure out the nature of the change that had overtaken their leader as he approached the mid-point of his career. The earlier Laurier had been promising – but dreamy and lackadaisical. The later Laurier was determined, adroit, purposeful. "How the Laurier of the early eighties developed into the Laurier of the last two decades is one of the transformations for which I can offer no explanation," George Ross, once a Liberal MP and later Premier of Ontario, wrote in 1913.

Had anyone thought to ask her, Emilie might have provided the answer. During these critical, transitional years, no one was closer to Laurier. In Arthabaska, they saw each other almost daily. During the three or four months that he spent in Ottawa each year attending Parliament, they wrote to each other at least twice a week. No problems with the postal service in those days; her letters arrived as regularly as clockwork on Wednesdays and Saturdays. He would sit down in his room at the Russell House and answer them on Sunday afternoons. For Laurier, who was no fan of physical exercise, this long-distance "intellectual conversation," as he once described it, was the high point of the week. "Again Sunday," he wrote on July 19, 1891. "A fine day for a walk but my easy chair was tempting." Then, the following week, "Heaven bless him who invented Sunday."

Sadly, none of Emilie's letters survive. But one of the most delightful historical scoops of recent years has been the discovery of some fifty-six of Laurier's letters to her, dated between the years 1890 and 1903.* From these letters, some written on plain quarto notepaper, others on House of Commons letterhead, and usually signed "Of all your friends the truest, WL" in Laurier's bold, declarative hand, it is possible to piece together, if not the entirety of their relationship, then much of its spirit and temper. And although the letters do not cover the earliest years of their friendship, the world wagged slowly in those days and it is reasonable to suppose that the kinds of the things they were writing to each other about in the 1890s were much the same kinds of things they had talked about a decade before.

The first unexpected discovery in these letters is that it was Emilie, far from rich, far from a beauty, certain to be the butt of blame if their intimacy became the cause of social scandal, who held the upper hand. "If you only knew what your affection is to me," Laurier wrote to her in 1891, "if you had for me the same unique affection that I have for you." It is clear that she frequently chastised him for being neglectful, for being moody, for flirting with other women, and although he occasionally struck back – "Who of us is the moody one? . . . I think it is you . . . " – his answers, even when defending himself, were usually beseeching. "I would like to see you my dear, dear friend . . . simply to see you, to be near you, to look into your eyes, to listen to your voice . . . *Cher injust*, this is an expression which you once applied to me, and which I would like to utter to you in so many words. . . . "

Clearly, Emilie was well educated and well travelled; she had seen London and Paris, while Laurier had seen only Arthabaska

* In fact, two separate caches of letters exist. The larger group, comprising forty-one letters, all dated between 1891 and 1893, were given to the Quebec historian Marc La Terreur in 1963 by a nephew of Emilie's, Louis-Renaud La Vergne. La Terreur unveiled his scoop in a celebrated paper presented to the Canadian Historical Association the following year. But the more ambitious work he planned to write on the relationship between the Lauriers and Lavergnes was never completed, for La Terreur died tragically in a plane crash in 1978.

The second cache, consisting of fifteen letters dated between 1890 and 1903 were discovered later among the Mackenzie King papers.

Emilie Lavergne. Perhaps the letter she is reading is one from Laurier.

and Ottawa. More than that, she was ambitious, for Laurier and also for herself. Although the letters available to us all date from the years after she had completed her task, it is evident that early on, she spotted something special in Laurier, but spotted also, in his *naïveté*, his laziness, above all in his gaucheries, much that needed correcting. So she set out to transform this back-country politician into a sophisticated one whose soaring career would pull her along with him. "When I bound myself in friendship to Wilfrid Laurier," she told her nephew, Louis-Renaud La Vergne, when she was an old woman, "I saw very quickly that this young deputy was still, in certain ways, only the little greenhorn. His wife was not the person who could teach him even those elements of etiquette that a man of the world should know. He did not even know the correct way to eat an orange at table. I made him understand that this lack of etiquette would hamper him among the English elite, with whom he would be called to mingle at Ottawa. I taught him then to eat, to dress with taste, in a word, all that a gentleman should know. As he was a man of wit, he understood it."

If this comment sounds not just patronizing, but more than a little cold-blooded, it is to be remembered that at the time that Emilie made it, she and Laurier had been estranged for many years, and on Emilie's part, quite bitterly estranged. It is also to be remembered that for a clever and ambitious woman in mid-Victorian Quebec, there were very few doorways open to self-advancement.

She began, all grace and laughter, by turning her well-appointed Arthabaska parlour into a salon and a college of one. "Oh Madame de Staël," Laurier reminisced to her in later years of those golden Arthabaska afternoons. "How much I find her in my own dear friend . . . you have, as no one has, the happy faculty of inspiring the flow of mind and soul." Of poetry, philosophy, and religion they could already talk as equals, for Laurier, from boyhood on, had been the kind of voracious reader who thought nothing of gobbling up half a dozen books on a lazy Sunday. She doted on historical biography, the biographies of notable women in particular: along with Madame de Staël, the great literary and intellectual hostess of eighteenth- and early nineteenth-century Paris, they discussed Madame de Staël's mother, Madame Necker, and Mary Wollstonecraft Shelley, the wife of the poet, and the author of *Frankenstein*. Above all, Emilie admired Josephine Bonaparte and liked to see herself in her, a conceit that Laurier encouraged. "Do you remember my dearest friend," he wrote in later years, "the words which Napoleon used to say of her, *Quelle gracieuse en tout*." Clearly, Emilie responded to this enthusiastically. "You go into very nice disquisitions and comparisons suggested by the early married life of N and J," he told her a few letters later. "This would be a very suggestive subject, but I have no time to write all I would wish and therefore refrain completely." At times, they would argue about religion, for Emilie, while worldly, was a devout Catholic and Laurier was not. "I am not a believer," he told her. "I most fervently believe in the justice of Him from whom we proceed and to whom we owe all. I believe in the justice of his laws, eternal like himself . . . further my faith goes not, and I regret it."

Emilie, as her nephew Louis-Renaud recounted in an unpublished memoir, always made a graceful little ritual of "*le thé à l'anglaise*." As the evening began to draw in, she would strike a match to a neat little pyramid of birch logs in the fireplace. Next would appear a maid in a white cap, bearing a grand silver tea service. Then, Emilie would light the alcohol flame under the silver kettle, and once the water had come to a rolling boil, pour it into a pot that contained the best China tea that Arthabaska could provide. Probably when Laurier was present, this was the *quatre d'heure* in their conversations when intellectual subjects were supplemented with practical hints. "It is an insult to one's tea to blow on it." "There is, dare I mention it, something awry in the cut of that coat." By such hints, and asides, and quite likely the occasional outright nag, Emilie coaxed and goaded Laurier, as poor Zoë could never have done, into transforming himself from a country politician into a metropolitan one, and eventually, since his manners were to dazzle London, into a cosmopolitan one.

In matters that extended well beyond tea, Emilie, despite her *Rouge* heritage, was a passionate anglophile. "For her," recalled nephew Louis-Renaud, "it was only the English who knew table manners, knew how to dress elegantly, knew how to enter and how to hold forth in the salon." Almost always, probably at her instigation, Laurier wrote to her in English. More likely that not, they usually talked to each other in English. So that it was through her, perhaps even more than through his great friend and mentor, Edward Blake, that Laurier first came to comprehend the English mindset, so different from his own nature, but one that he had to come to terms with if he aspired to become anything more than just another local Quebec politician. In this regard, Emilie, as tutor, succeeded far beyond even her own wildest dreams. In 1897, when Laurier, wearing the cocked hat, gold lace, and white silk stockings of an Imperial Privy Councillor, scored a personal triumph at the Queen's Jubilee celebrations in London – cheered nearly as loudly as Queen Victoria, the Fleet Street papers said, the only colonial statesman with real panache – it was equally Emilie's triumph, no matter that it was Zoë who rode next to him in the open carriage, and Zoë who came home no longer Madame Laurier but Lady Laurier. Perhaps it occurred to the newly-dubbed Knight Commander of St. Michael and St. George, that all those imperialist duchesses he had discovered he could dazzle so effortlessly were, despite their glittering tiaras and titles, only weak reeds next to his demanding and mercurial Emilie. "She was a terror to argue with," Louis-Renaud recalled. "She always knew how to find your weak point – and how to make fun of it."

Since Emilie also possessed a broad streak of Gallic practicality, she did not confine her sphere of influence to the intellectual and to the social. As early as 1879, as an intriguing letter written to her by the senior member of the Quebec legislature, George Irvine, reveals, she was lobbying hard with men of influence to promote Laurier's career. "Laurier is here," Irvine informed her on July 26. "I am glad that I have been able to get him the money required. Your speaking to me about it made me look out for an opportunity for him and I assure you that without me, he would have found it difficult. You see what a useful friend you are."

Most probably, Emilie deserves some of the credit (along with Mrs. Edward Blake) for persuading Laurier to accept the Liberal leadership in 1887, and thus to take the first crucial step that led to his becoming prime minister. The letters that have survived tell us nothing about this. But this act of ambition was entirely out of keeping with Laurier's character until that time, and entirely in tune with Emilie's own purposefulness.

Sometimes, to be sure, she seems to have had second thoughts – most often during spells when Laurier's letters contained too little of her and too much of the small change of politics. "So, my dearest friend is drawn . . . involuntarily against her will into that vortex of politics which she cordially hates," he wrote to her in 1890. "You persist in believing that I am carried away by this life." Still, it is difficult to believe that Emilie did not enjoy being his political confidante. In February 1890, on the eve of making his first really important speech as Opposition Leader, he revealed in complete confidence his nervousness. "My room has been crowded all day by anxious men rushing in with long faces, men with advice, men with a prayer and then again with different advice and a different prayer." When the speech went off well, he uninhibitedly allowed his self-satisfaction to show. "I am not displeased . . . when I have the pleasure of conversing with you . . . I will tell you the whole inside story." In fact, this particular speech, delivered on February 17,

1890, was one of the most significant of Laurier's career. The issue, which prefigured the Manitoba Schools crisis of 1896, was a motion introduced by the fanatic anti-French, anti-Papist Ontario Member of Parliament, D'Alton McCarthy, calling for the abolition of French in the legislatures and courts of the Northwest Territories, as the future provinces of Saskatchewan and Alberta were still described. Laurier, as he would do again in 1896, spoke for moderation.

> We are here a nation, or we want to be a nation. The honourable gentleman will revert to the cold, dry argument that after all a duality of race will produce friction and that friction will produce danger. But where is the remedy? The true remedy . . . is mutual forbearance and respect.

Emilie, on at least one occasion, also acted as Laurier's political operative. Through the summer of 1891, the summer after Macdonald's death, the summer after his own battering at the hands of the Tories in the general election of the previous March, the problem that nagged at Laurier, through a parliamentary session that dragged on interminably, was how to repair the breach between himself and his predecessor as Liberal leader, the brilliant but difficult Edward Blake – for Blake, next only to Emilie, was his closest confidante and friend. The substance of their quarrel – free trade with the United States – was one of those gut issues that, like Manitoba Schools, run as leitmotiv through Canadian history and, indeed, if in a negative way, help make Canada, Canada.

Blake, with his Ontario base and his linkages with the Toronto establishment, was much more of a protectionist than Laurier. During the election, Blake, at the last moment, had withdrawn as a candidate; instead he had done all but campaign openly for the Tories by writing an open letter to his former electors in West Durham denouncing Laurier's reciprocity platform as only a hop, skip, and jump away from the dreaded spectre of "Political Union." That the Tories had overwhelmingly won the election on the slogan, "The old leader, the old flag, the old policy," had scarcely improved relations.

"A slap in the face of the party and of me particularly," Laurier had described Blake's action in a letter to Emilie. Four months after the vote, the two were still not speaking. Then, in July, the fact that the Blakes, like the Lavergnes, were accustomed to vacationing at Murray Bay gave him an opening. On July 19, he sent a conciliatory letter to Blake, addressed to his summer home. Then he despatched a letter to Emilie that seemed to contain mixed signals. Clearly, he hoped she would take an initiative. "You will of course see E.B. Remember my dear friend, that though very moody, he is a very sensitive heart. I do not know how we stand . . . I cannot be angry with him, I know him too well and love him too well." At the same time, he fretted that she might be indiscreet. "I tell you all this because I am sure when you meet him, I must come in for a share of your conversation but under no circumstances, and for no reason, show him a letter from me. . . . "

Emilie, as diplomat, most likely relied on her own instincts. In any event, by August 9, after she had spent a social evening with the Blakes, matters were much improved. "We are now good friends again," wrote Laurier cheerfully. "I received from him a most affectionate letter." Then he added playfully, "I see by your own letter that you have made the conquest of the whole household. Why should I think you might exaggerate when you tell me that your host neglected all his other guests and gave you the whole of his time? Do you really believe that I am surprised by this?"

Friendship and admiration. Trust and tenderness. And, as in all such quasi-political relationships, a liberal dash of mutual self-interest. But was there more? Beyond a doubt, there was love. "Proud I am . . . of your affection," Laurier wrote Emilie on one occasion, "and could I yell it on the top of houses, prouder yet would I be." Another time, he confessed that he could hardly bear to say goodbye because "my heart clings to the paper." But did their relationship extend to its natural physical conclusion? Or was it always merely platonic? About this tantalizing question, the letters are ambiguous. It becomes necessary not just to read between the lines, but to address allusive references that one suspects were intended as a code.

"I send you a book," Laurier told Emilie on May 21, 1891. "I do not ask you to read it all." There was nothing unusual about this, for almost as frequently as letters, books sped back and forth between them. But in this particular instance, most unusually, Laurier chose to disclose neither author nor title and suggested that she read only one section. "Read the chapter, St. Anne's Hill, and you will understand that when I read it, my heart was full of images often indulged in, never realized." Twice more in further letters, both times equally obliquely, he referred to St. Anne's Hill. "Keep the book, do not send it back," he told her on May 24. "I want to pore over it with you, and go over some of the passages which struck me." On May 29: "Have you read St. Anne's Hill? Put the book aside, keep it in readiness that I may point out to you what would be my dream, what picture now haunts me."

Still more evocative is the musical imagery they sometimes used. "How often have I pictured to myself that I was sitting by your piano, listening to your voice," Laurier wrote on August 23, 1891. "I heard you once last summer from the open window of my room, I heard your voice, faint it is true in the distance, still audible. My heart was big that night and the words went deep into my heart, though I could hardly respond to the sentiment they gave expression to . . . it was the Barcarolle." By the following spring, the piano and the *Barcarolle* had given way to another instrument and, perhaps, to a more discreet symbolism. "Should I listen to her verbiage," he teased Emilie, referring to some woman who was trying to flirt with him, "hearing only the distant violin?" A few days later, he chided Emilie for a long delay in writing. "What was the cause of your silence? Had you forgotten, or failed to listen, to the distant strains of the violin?"

Laurier in April 1874, when he was thirty-two.

Armand Lavergne in his late teens. The resemblance about which everyone gossiped was most evident around the eyes, the mouth and the forehead, and in the set of the ears to the head.

Was it all only innocent, late-Victorian folderol? Or were St. Anne's Hill, the *Barcarolle*, the distant violin, all protective devices to hide from Joseph Lavergne, from Zoë, and also from the prying eyes of servants and postmistresses and other potential blackmailers the proof positive that he and Emilie were lovers? For speculation was one thing, words on paper quite another, and almost from their first meeting, excited chatter that Emilie was his mistress had been widespread. In 1880, when she gave birth to a son, to whom she gave the excessively romantic name Armand, straight out of *La Dame aux Camellias* by Alexandre Dumas, the gossip intensified. As the years went by, and *le petit Armand* developed an uncanny likeness to Laurier, gossip hardened into conventional wisdom. Indeed, there were some who professed to believe that Emilie's other child, a daughter named Gabrielle, two years older than Armand, was also Laurier's. In the case of Bielle, as everyone called her, the physical resemblance was not so noticeable. It was rather the fact that Laurier, though far from a rich man, paid for her education at a Quebec City convent.

However much all these insinuations may have wounded the quiet, self-effacing Zoë, she never, that we know, made any comment. Clearly, though, the gossip got to Joseph. "I must confirm that my uncle was troubled by the resemblance of his son to M. Laurier," wrote Louis-Renaud La Vergne in his memoir, "a resemblance of which my aunt was proud." On one dramatic occasion, as Louis-Renaud further recounts, he and Armand came home from school to find Emilie and Joseph in the parlour, staring intently at a photograph of Laurier as a young man. Emilie, however, found precisely the right words to ward off embarrassment. "We arrived at the moment when she said, 'It cannot be otherwise, it is M. Laurier who resembles *Armand*.'" Joseph, in any event, appears to have believed in peace at any price. On another occasion, when his brother, father of the observant young Louis-Renaud, arrived angrily with yet another crop of rumours, Joseph responded wearily. "What do you want me to do? . . . I have a good wife. Why humiliate her unjustly? She admires him as I admire him myself. All things considered, I prefer to live in peace and let people talk."

As to the substance of the rumours, if we ourselves make a comparison of photographs of Armand Lavergne and of Laurier taken at similar ages, we find a resemblance that however coincidental, is striking to a degree – especially around the eyes and the mouth and, in a way most suggestive of all, in the set of the ears to the head. As striking are the numerous references to Armand in Laurier's letters to Emilie, references he took no trouble to conceal, references that, coupled with the almost as frequent references to Gabrielle, account for perhaps a third of all the thousands of words. "Tomorrow is the little man's birthday," he writes on February 20, 1890. "He will be ten years old. Kiss him again and again for me." A year later, when Armand came to spend a week with him at the Russell House in Ottawa, he could hardly wait to tell Emilie all about it. "That little man is full of magnetism, winning and attractive and at the same time so frank, so outspoken, so clever also and so readily witted. . . . Yesterday at dinner my old neighbour Mrs. S. asked me to remark, 'What beautiful eyes that child has.' . . . On the morning of his arrival he scarcely ate anything, but this morning at breakfast he ate four, yes four, muttonchops. What do you think of this?" But during this visit, Laurier also picked up a warning of trouble ahead. Armand, now a student at *Le Séminaire du Québec*, showed disturbing signs of becoming a fervid *nationaliste*. "At college they have put the most absurd ideas in his head. . . . Tell him that above all else he must apply himself to learn English, that it is absolutely essential for such an intense French Canadian as he is; it is the absolute condition which will enable him, some day, to defend the rights and privileges of his race." In 1901, even though the liaison between him and Emilie was now all but over, Laurier continued to fret about Armand, now a law student at Laval. "He is a fine boy, but on certain things his ideas are very much stuck. He seemed, if opportunity occurs, ready to throw the whole English population in the St. Lawrence . . . this Anglophobia becomes

Gabrielle Lavergne. Laurier paid for her education.

more serious when he refused to write or study English. Could you not alter his mind?"

As for Gabrielle, if anything, when writing of her, Laurier's tone sounds even more fatherly. In September 1892, shortly after sending Emilie the money for tuition fees, he worried whether or not, given the nuns' habit of opening the mail, he ought to write to Gabrielle at the convent. "The rule is sometimes very capricious and rather than cause even the slightest trouble to the child, I will forgo the pleasure." Then, a few weeks later, when he did decide to write, he addressed "Ma chère Bielle," in the most affectionate of terms. "If you look at the signature you will see the name of your friend above all, the oldest of your friends, who has loved you since you came into the world." Seven years later, as Bielle reached her twenty-first birthday, Laurier remembered it with a flourish. "I have just written a word, my dear friend, to your lovely daughter to offer her a small souvenir," he told Emilie. "How time flies." More revealing of the depths of his affection, Laurier on that particular day, October 9, 1899, was agonizing over the single most critical decision of his entire prime-ministership: whether or not to send Canadian troops to the war in South Africa. "I suppose it is a worry to reflect that someday Gabrielle will be taken from her mother's side," he mused on to Emilie. "I have this great advantage, my life is a constant struggle and worry; all my energies have to be concentrated to perform the task which is before me and the difficulties of which are increasing."

Were these the words of a lover and of a father? Or were they words incomparably more wistful, those of a man whose hidden, unspoken tragedy was never to have been capable of being anything other than a vicarious lover and a vicarious father? The ultimate truth of their relationship remains a secret that Emilie and Laurier took with them to their separate graves. But one explanation can be advanced, however tentatively, however much it may seem voyeuristic and even disloyal to Laurier to suggest it.

It is a fact that Zoë and Laurier had no children. It is also a fact that on their wedding night, he, for whatever reason, found prior business in Arthabaska pressing. It is further a fact that, as Marc La Terreur, discoverer of their correspondence, remarked in his 1964 paper, whenever Laurier touched on matters physical when writing to Emilie, he seemed to do so with extreme distaste. Writing on the court of Louis XV he complained, "*Tout etait chez lui dominée par la sensualité.*" He dismissed Pompadour as "a vile woman." Even the splendid Josephine, when Laurier chanced upon some unflattering references to her in a biography of Napoleon became "an inveterate coquette, and had I been in N's place, I would have been unmerciful." Most telling of all, perhaps, is a reference in another letter to a mutual friend of his and of Emilie's who was having an affair. "He must learn the lesson that after all there is such a thing as chastity among women and honour among men, that human actions can have another inspiration than vile appetites."

"I do not believe that their relationship was . . . intimate," wrote La Terreur, summing up his evidence. Basing his judgement on the correspondence alone, La Terreur left it at that. But Emilie's nephew, Louis-Renaud La Vergne, in his own chatty memoir (which another historian, Maurice Carrier, drew on heavily for a 1961 thesis, *Laurier, citoyen d'Arthabaska*) adds a further piece of information. Describing how Laurier's supporters dealt with the rumours that swirled round their leader and Emilie, La Vergne wrote:

> Judge Marc-Aurèle Plamondon, great friend and neighbour of Laurier's, defended him in a fashion so singular that Laurier probably wished he had kept silent.
>
> "I know for a fact that Laurier is impotent!"

A happier explanation to the riddle exists, a solution entirely in keeping with Emilie's and Laurier's time. In the Victorian and Edwardian eras, non-physical, spiritual, and intellectual relationships between male and female kindred spirits, as between George Bernard Shaw and the actress Ellen Terry for instance, were not the least bit unusual. Arthur Balfour loved the Countess of Elcho, but appears to have done nothing about it. Even during the worst moments of the Gallipoli campaign of the First World War, Prime Minister Asquith sat at the cabinet table writing love letters to Venetia Stanley who, when she chose to have a physical affair, chose to have it with Beaverbrook. Much closer to home, Sir Robert Borden of all people, Laurier's staid and supposedly unconscionably dull successor, wrote in rapturous vein during the 1930s to the British Columbia poet Audrey Alexandra Brown when he was nearly eighty and she was barely out of her twenties.

All things considered, it may well have been Amaryllis, writing in haste to meet a deadline, who came closer to the mark than anyone else when she described Emilie as "the Canadian Lady Chesterfield." For, although it was to Lady Chesterfield that Disraeli wrote many of his most brilliant and incisive letters – once, in fact, even proposing to her when grief-stricken over the death of his wife Mary Ann – the two were never physical lovers.

However matters truly stood between them, and whatever

barcarolles Wilfrid and Emilie may have played on that distant violin, their relationship influenced our history. But for her tutoring of him, it is inconceivable that so recently after Confederation, and at a time, moreover, when the Macdonald-Cartier *modus vivendi* between French and English Canadians seemed on the brink of breaking down, the country would have been prepared to elect a French Canadian as its prime minister. Undoubtedly, Emilie helped to spark ambition within Laurier. Her imperishable contribution was to have shown her own beloved "*cher injust*" how to be more graceful, more sophisticated, more accomplished than any of the English Canadians around him – and to show him how to understand them so that he could use them.

CHAPTER 19

Emilie and Zoë

Madame Lavergne and Mlle Lavergne have arrived in town and taken apartments at the Russell. Judge Lavergne is also staying at the Russell.

Amaryllis;
"Society at the Capital," *Saturday Night*;
September 15, 1897

Laurier's attitude towards his astonishing victory in the election of June 23, 1896, was equivocal. "The victory that provokes so much enthusiasm and so much excitement causes me an irreducible sentiment of sadness," he confided to Emilie the following September, in one of his rare letters in French. "Many others before me have found in the triumph more bitterness than joy." Emilie's own response seems to have been wistful. "In your last letter, there was a note of sadness that impressed me singularly, my dear friend," he remarked.

Quickly though, they themselves became excited by the new possibilities that had been opened up to them by the voters. "There is no life for you but in the city," he had told her years earlier. "You must have about you not only society, but congenial society." Yet for nearly two decades, but for occasional visits to Ottawa, Quebec City, and Murray Bay, she had been suffocating away in Arthabaska, "a fixed and commonplace abode . . . where the atmosphere is heavy and friends are few." As prime minister, it was now readily within Laurier's power to transport her to the capital, to share with him the excitement of a new political era. To do that, all he needed was find a suitable sinecure for Joseph.

Not even for Laurier, could the universe unfold quite as expeditiously as planned. "Everything I had projected for Joseph has to start again," he wrote her crossly on September 30, 1896. Still, by the following summer, he'd found the perfect slot, combining ample prestige with limited responsibility: a judgeship in the Quebec Superior Court for the Division of Hull. No one in Ottawa had the slightest doubt which member of the Lavergne household it really was who was being summoned to the capital. "Madame Lavergne . . . [has] arrived in town and taken apartments at the Russell," reported Amaryllis on September 15, 1897, and then added wickedly, "Judge Lavergne is also staying at the Russell."

Emilie Lavergne. In the first years of Laurier's prime-ministership, she dazzled Official Ottawa. She dressed superbly, and, as is also evident in the photograph on page 250, chose styles that showed off her magnificent shoulders.

Emilie swept into Ottawa as a ship in full sail. She had never looked better; handsomer by far, at forty-nine, than she had ever been at twenty. She had never been more determined to succeed. Her ambition now, as the columns of Amaryllis leave no doubt, was to establish herself as *the* political hostess, queening over Official Society as a consort in all but name. It is easy to picture her settling into the Russell that first autumn, humming the *Barcarolle* as she unpacks, and happening upon, in a stack of old letters from Laurier that she is about to stash away in her writing table, a phrase that for a moment or two, she lingers over. "My dear friend, whose chief enjoyment is, like Madame de Staël's, to meet her friends, to have them about her and then let the mind open its wings and fly about in the *arabesques* of improvised conversations." Emilie smiles fondly. Wilfrid has the most charming way of expressing his sentiments, but he will mix his metaphors. Then she clicks the drawer shut, and from another pulls out a long sheet of paper. She dips her pen in the ink and begins to compose a list of names.

One of the invitations that Emilie sent to more than six hundred people for her first big Ottawa party. It is preserved in the scrapbook kept by Mrs. Duncan Campbell Scott, the first wife of the Ottawa poet. Emilie's handwriting, it can be observed, was bold and assertive.

Mr & Mrs Duncan C. Scott

Madame Lavergne

At Home

on Saturday 18th

4 to 7. o'clock.

Emilie began her campaign to conquer the capital with just the right combination of understatement and flamboyance. The invitation cards she sent out for her first big party, on December 18, 1897, were unassuming to a degree – a simple engraved card, "Madame Lavergne," with "At Home 4 to 7" written neatly below; nothing there to indicate that the hostess was anything other than the unassuming wife of an obscure new judge in Hull. The difference was, as Amaryllis later reckoned, Emilie sent out these cards to more than six hundred people and that, even more astonishing, almost everyone answered her summons, "Senators, judges and cabinet ministers. . . . All kinds of great and prominent people." A more important difference was that Amaryllis not only made Emilie's party the lead item for that first of her columns for the *Free Press*, but that the newspaper gave it six inches of space. A few fragments of that report were quoted in chapter seventeen, but let us now stand back for a moment and take a closer look. It is gathering dusk on a chilly December evening; outside the Russell, as the guests come flocking in, the sound of sleigh bells and the clanging of streetcars fills the air. Amaryllis takes us inside:

> The drawing room of the Russell House is a capital place to hold a reception, especially if it be an afternoon reception and the invitation list is not any shorter than one's visiting list. The Russell drawing room is so large that two or three combined visiting lists, even should they be as long as I am sure popular Madame Lavergne's must be, would not make it disagreeably crowded.
>
> There were a great many people in it on Saturday afternoon, and such a chatter and clatter of tongues. At first, the noise had the effect of making one feel a little deaf, but one got used to it as one does to most things in this mundane sphere, and soon one was chattering away just like the rest in a very high key, so as to be heard above the noise and the din.
>
> The drawing room looked very pretty, that is, the ceilings and walls of it. Only the first comers saw any more of it. It was brilliantly lighted and in the corridor there were many comfortable sofas and chairs which were not long left unoccupied. Half way down the corridor, in the large alcove, refreshments were served. The Guards band was there, and it added greatly to the general brilliancy and merriment of the affair. . . .
>
> Miss Lavergne, whose pretty Christian name is Gabrielle, received with her mother, looking so nice in a light blue dress and a white hat with ostrich plumes.

Like any good society columnist, Amaryllis saved her best line for the last:

Madame Lavergne, like the capable hostess she is, managed to collect any quantity of men, so that very few ladies were left without cavaliers.

That was only the beginning. In January, arrayed in "a handsome gown of black satin trimmed with jet," Emilie presided over "a brilliant progressive euchre party" in aid of St. Luke's Hospital, which, as she had quickly cottoned on, was the most fashionable charity of the moment. ("Clever doctors to have made your hospital the fashion," noted Amaryllis in an aside. "I hope it will not also extend to the privilege of being there.") In March, again in aid of St. Luke's, she commandeered the whole of the adjoining Russell Theatre for a bravura display of "Living Pictures." Pretty Gabrielle Lavergne stole the show in the final tableau, "Our Lady of the Snows," as "a sweet, fresh Young Canada." And there were other goings-on to be noticed. "One found one's gaze straying over to the balcony to see how the Premier was taking it all."

By now, the message was clear. The way to get Laurier to lend his presence to an occasion was to ask Madame Lavergne to organize it or to play a prominent part in it. Anyway, Emilie was so much fun. All the innumerable entertainments that were the stock in trade of the era were enlived by her presence: the endless progressive euchre parties; studio tea parties at which Hamilton MacCarthy, RCA, showed off the maquettes for his latest sculptures; driving parties to Aylmer, sleighs assembled in front of the East Block to leave at seven sharp; afternoon musicales where, as Amaryllis reported deadpan, the company was sometimes treated to "the marvellous whistling performances" of Mrs. Smart, wife of the Deputy Minister of the Interior, whose *pièce de résistance* was the "Intermezzo" from *Cavalleria Rusticana*.

One of the most splendid of all the parties where Emilie was a star guest was a cruise down the Ottawa River to Rockland on a soft May afternoon in 1898, to visit the estate of the lumber king W. C. Edwards.

> Charting a palace steamer like the *Empress*, taking all your friends and many acquaintances twenty-three miles down the river to a gorgeous country residence and there entertaining them in princely style, is hospitality on a broad scale. Only people of great wealth would do it, and many people of great wealth would not do it. But such was the party of which Mr. and Mrs. Edwards were the host and hostess on Saturday afternoon. The steamer left the wharf pretty sharp on time. Mr. Edwards, the very embodiment of a genial host, stood just inside

the gangway cordially shaking his guests by the hand as each one entered. The decks were quickly sought, and here were met almost everyone of one's acquaintance. . . .

Soft fleecy clouds softened the glare of the sun, and there was a pleasant breeze. . . . The music was splendid. It was an orchestra of the 43rd Rifles and it played all the best tunes in *The Geisha*, besides any number of popular airs which set people ahumming. . . . The dancing was in the aft part of the saloon and notwithstanding the up and down motion it went with a vim. . . . But there were others who preferred sitting out on deck enjoying the delicious fresh air and watching the ever moving shore, where the trees were just putting on the new green leaves of early summer, noting here and there a neat white farmhouse standing in the clearing with cows grazing on the hillside. Then it would be a summer hotel with shady grove of pine trees nearby, and again woods and brushwood, that impenetrable jungle of brushwood skirting so much of the shore of the noble Ottawa. "Great place for ducks in there" one heard a sportsman say as the brushwood gave way to tall river grasses, and little bays and marshes that suggested Pauline Johnson's canoe song. . . .

Then the white mills of Rockland hove into sight. These mills turned out on closer view to be enormous places. . . . To go through would have been interesting, but that is another story. This was a garden party at the beautiful red brick mansion up on the hill surrounded by tall pine trees, and with soft grassy lawns spread about it.

There were all sorts of conveyances to meet the guests and take them up the hill, from two-wheeled haycarts drawn by horses evidently suffering from that tired feeling, to elegant four-wheeled double-seated carriages, whose restive steeds on reaching the main entrance did some fine work in the way of a "pas de deux" to the music of the 43rd Rifles.

Mrs. Edwards, the chatelaine of this fine domain, met her guests at the steps of the verandah. . . . Marquees were erected on the lawn and small tables were arranged for guests to have tea. The table in the dining room opening onto the lawn was spread with everything imaginable in the way of edibles from boned turkey on down, or up, to strawberries and cream. There was a good deal of disporting on the lawn, some croquet, which everybody is learning how to play, nobody, of course, being old enough to remember it before it went out, oh so many years ago. There was an old-fashioned swing which held two comfortably and which seemed popular even when not swinging. . . .

But in spite of the beautiful weather and lovely lawns, tea was the chief feature of the afternoon. Fortunately the supply was greater than the demand. As a meditative man remarked, "will the time ever come when polite society can amuse itself without eating?" Echo answers "Never." The most ravenous among the guests always explained that they had missed their lunch. It was surprising how many had missed their lunch. . . . "*

* In 1903, shortly after Edwards was appointed a Senator, he purchased an additional mansion in town, to which he commuted aboard his splendid steam yacht. "It is a beautiful stone residence set like Earnscliffe on a bluff overhanging the Ottawa River, just at the gates of Rideau Hall," Amaryllis reported. "The Welsh name Gorphwysfa means 'the abode of peace.' " Gorphwysfa today is 24 Sussex, the official residence of the prime minister.

Whatever may have been whispered privately, everyone, in public, seems to have accepted the existence of a prime-ministerial *pas de trois*. "Dinner party for 30 tonight, very bright," wrote the Countess of Aberdeen in her diary. "Mr. Laurier took me in, and His Excellency had Mme. Laurier and Mme. Lavergne." So far as it is possible now to judge, the inevitable excited speculation as to what that relationship actually encompassed only came to a head whenever the dashing young Armand Lavergne, now in his late teens and looking more every day like Laurier, came to town. One piece of Ottawa folklore has it that a certain religious-minded matron, observing Laurier and Armand together, remarked that their resemblance could only be "the finger of God." Her friend, a more worldly lady, replied: "I've heard it called many things, but never that."

In fact, Armand, now studying at Laval, came seldom to the capital. As a burgeoning Quebec nationalist, forays into a society that talked almost exclusively in English were scarcely his style. He was there at Easter 1900, however, entertaining the ladies of the Morning Music Club at his mama's behest, with a rendition of "the very popular college song, *Malbrouk*, popular not only in France but in Quebec." We can chuckle, as Amaryllis must have chuckled, as she described this scene. "Mr. Lavergne sang very nicely and everyone was very sorry when he ended it somewhat abruptly, muttering that there were twenty more verses." No doubt the real trouble was that the mistress of ceremonies at that particular concert was Mrs. Lawrence Drummond, wife of the Military Secretary at Rideau Hall, whose husband was now on leave of absence to fight in South Africa. And Armand, that season, as we know from his own correspondence, was adding as postscript in letters to Emilie: "*Vive les Boers! Mort aux Anglais.*"

Meanwhile, at 335 Theodore Street, there was Zoë. Her courtiers, in the big echoing drawing room resplendent with à la mode copies of Louis Quinze were, as Amaryllis reports, "three cages of birds, two cats and two tiny Pomeranians who sit on the most luxurious chairs and sofas and to whom she feeds chocolates." For Zoë, these first heady years of the Laurier era, so radiant with fulfilment for

Zoë Laurier, and an unidentified group of friends, on the steps of 335 Theodore Street circa *1898. In this case, the dog she is holding is not a Pomeranian, but a King Charles spaniel.*

Wilfrid and for Emilie, must have been the most bitter years of all her marriage. She had grown quite formidably stout, and indeed she looked considerably older than Laurier. She was still painfully shy, still far from at ease in English, which Emilie spoke so easily and so usefully to the wives of Laurier's key ministers: Sifton, Fielding, Blair. Her most painful burden, surely, was that her rival was always so near. For the Lavergnes, who soon abandoned the Russell House for a red brick house just two blocks east on Theodore Street, were almost permanent fixtures at the Lauriers', guests at all their most intimate gatherings. On December 11, 1897, for instance, we find them sharing a table with D'Alton McCarthy and the Joseph Popes at "a most exclusive dinner party in honour of the Lieutenant Governor of Manitoba." It must have been equally hurtful that Amaryllis, when divulging the guest lists for social affairs, made it her sly practice to mention Madame Lavergne immediately after Lady Laurier, thus giving her an order of precedence ahead of Mrs. Sifton, Mrs. Blair, Mrs. Fielding, and all the other "cabinet ladies." An account of June 1900 is typical. "Lady Laurier left yesterday for Arthabaskaville, where she will spend the month of July . . . Madame Lavergne left on Tuesday for Murray Bay." Indeed one feels almost guilty for having smiled so readily at Amaryllis's knowing aside: "Lady Laurier infinitely prefers the society of women to that of men."

Amaryllis can be forgiven. Emilie, after all, was playing a role that needed to be played and one that Zoë could not play. The ladies-only card parties undoubtedly *were* quite unspeakably boring, "ghastly affairs where women dressed up in their stiffest afternoon frocks meet," as Amaryllis described the genre, carefully not specifying whose parties, exactly, she had in mind. Only slightly less tedious were the evening musicales, centred round the huge grand piano in Zoë's drawing room, at which whichever faulty soprano was next on the seemingly bottomless list of Zoë's musical protégées was called on to perform. Sometimes, those who, like Amaryllis, could not afford to lose the entrée to 335 Theodore, had to get up at the crack of dawn. "On Sunday, at the Basilica, Miss Helen Le Bouthillier recently from Paris sang an Ava Maria of Saint-Saëns," she noted wearily in June 1901. "Shortly before leaving for Paris under the patronage of Lady Laurier, she gave a concert at the Russell Theatre. Those who heard her at the Basilica say she has improved greatly . . . "*

It took a woman further removed from the scene than Amaryllis – and with a softer heart – to find the hidden agenda masked by the yapping Pomeranians and the off-key singers. "Madame Laurier looks sad," wrote Lady Aberdeen of their first meeting in 1894. "She feels having no children."

And yet. Even during the years that Zoë seemed to have settled into being that most poignant of all female figures, the wife a successful politician happened to have married when he was young, she proved to have more steel in her than either Laurier or Emilie suspected. Late in life, she taught herself to be fluent in English. She got herself a first-rate dressmaker, much skilled not so much at disguising embonpoint as in setting it off with lots of appliqué embroidery and furbelows. By around the spring of 1902, Amaryllis's reporting on Zoë began to take on a different tone. At the prorogation of Parliament, "Lady Laurier wore a beautiful gown of black satin, embroidered with white silk, and in this embroidery were glints of gold; her hat was a flower tocque, centre of pale green

* To be fair to Zoë, one of her musical judgements proved inspired. The mezzo-soprano Eva Gauthier (1885-1958), whom she sponsored to study in Paris in 1902, became one of Canada's most distinguished concert singers, an artist of "rare eclecticism," as *Encyclopedia of Music in Canada* remarks, who gave the North American premiere of Stravinsky's *Trois poésies de la lyrique japonaise* in 1917, and in 1926 performed at a memorable New York concert at which George Gershwin accompanied her at the piano. During her own farewell tour of Canada in 1906, Emma Albani declared, "As an artistic legacy to my country, I leave you Eva Gauthier."

foliage and border of pink roses." A few weeks later, as the Lauriers prepared to sail off to England for the coronation of Edward VII: "I hear that Lady Laurier is going armed with a diamond tiara. Moreover, the wife of the Premier has shown her patriotism by entrusting the construction to a jeweller of our own city."

Sometime during this period, Zoë, for all that she would have preferred to have remained in Arthabaska – "I would rather be the wife of a simple *avocat*," she wrote sadly to a friend, "I belong to everyone and no-one" – seems to have decided to make the best of politics. Somewhat like Agnes Macdonald before her, she gradually began to develop an appetite for the exercise of power and of patronage. "She had a good old-fashioned idea about power, that it existed to be used," Joseph Schull has written. To the ranks of the indigent postmistresses and widowed stenographers and musical protégées whom she had always fostered, there began to be added a select list of promising young men whose claims she advanced and upon whom she could look as surrogate sons. There was Sydney Fisher, for instance, the stylish bachelor Minister of Agriculture; and the personable widower, Henry R. Emmerson, Minister of Railways; both of whom she was forever trying to marry off. There was another bachelor, the Deputy Minister of Labour, William Lyon Mackenzie King, to whom, it was discovered on Zoë's death in 1921, two years after Laurier's, she had willed the house on Laurier Avenue, as Theodore Street had long since been renamed, as testament of her affection.

Zoë Laurier around the turn of the century. By now, she too had acquired a good dress-maker.

Since life doesn't unfold in straight lines, it is simplistic to suggest that Zoë's rising star pushed Emilie's into eclipse. All his life, Laurier would need a feminine intellectual anchor; in 1916, at the age of seventy-five, he was writing Marie-Louise Pacaud, the widow of his closest friend in Arthabaska, in much the same vein he had once written to Emilie. "Your beautiful fair hair has turned to wonderful white," he told Marie-Louise. "Did you believe that with the fair hair, your charm had disappeared? Do not make this mistake."

Rather, although we cannot know for certain, what seems to have happened is that somewhere around the turn of the century, Emilie began to overplay her hand. Perhaps she presumed too much, offering Laurier advice he did not need and trying to intrude into the running of the government. It may even have been, as Amaryllis drops a fleeting hint, that the two disagreed sharply over Laurier's decision to send troops to South Africa during the Boer War. The story of this decision, and of its effects upon Ottawa, belongs in a later chapter. But it is possible, indeed is probable, that Emilie was, in Amaryllis's words, "the brilliant French Canadian lady who for love of notoriety pretends to entertain pro-Boer sentiments," who in December 1900 caused a fearful contretemps at a viceregal dinner party by haranguing the visiting young war hero, Winston Churchill. As corroborative evidence, Armand, in one of his "*Vive les Boers!*" letters to Emilie, dated June 18, 1901, tossed out the phrase, "*Comment est Kruger?*" which suggests that Emilie had named a pet dog or cat or canary after the South African prime minister.

In any event, sometime during this period, Laurier sent a messenger from his office to Emilie, with a package containing all the letters that she had written to him. It is also at this time that references to Emilie in the columns of Amaryllis begin to thin out noticeably. Befittingly, on the very last night of the old century, December 31, 1900, we find her shining in all her old glory, "wearing a smart gown of black crêpe de Chine over cerise satin," chaperoning a gala debutante ball, along with five other prominent society ladies. We do not find her again until the following June 15, in an entry that, knowing what we know now, and as perhaps Amaryllis knew at the time, reads almost as an epitaph:

> Mr. Justice Lavergne and his family are leaving next week to take up their residence permanently in Montreal. Mme Lavergne is one of the most charming women in Ottawa society, and everyone laments her departure.

Laurier, in what must have been a deliberate act of disentanglement, had transferred Joseph to the Montreal bench. The move was designed to look like a promotion and it increased Joseph's salary by $1000 annually. In the parting from Emilie, no lover could have been gentler. "May you be happy in this new place which you now enter," Laurier wrote to her on September 18, 1901. "If it be in my power to help, never fail to come to me as a friend, an ever true, warm and sincere friend." On November 29, in a letter occasioned by his sixtieth birthday, he sounded as if he regretted the new arrangement. "Though there is now a long distance between us, my dear friend, I do not for one single moment forget you. . . . The friendship of the past has been too close to be followed by an absolute separation . . . I cannot help regretting the good old times."

Yet those times were irrevocably over. Relations between him and Emilie now grew increasingly sour. By 1903, as the last surviving letters reveal, they were squabbling over money and Laurier's manner had changed unmistakably. "It is not an agreeable thing to have to give a negative response to a demand advanced for so many good reasons as you have made . . . but, for this year, there cannot be an addition to the salaries of judges."

Relations broke off entirely in 1909, when despite Emilie's confident expectations, a candidate other than Joseph was appointed Chief Justice of Quebec. This time it was Armand who wrote furiously to Laurier to protest "the humiliation done to my poor father."

Joseph Lavergne died in 1922, and in her own last years, Emilie retired to a convent on Drummond Street in Montreal. One of her last acts, before her death in 1930, was to entrust the packet of letters from Laurier to her beloved nephew, Louis-Renaud La Vergne. Near his own death in 1963, La Vergne passed these on to the historian Marc La Terreur. This slim bundle of letters, along with those discovered later in Mackenzie King's personal papers and the corroborative evidence provided by Amaryllis, have provided the framework upon which it has been possible to reconstruct, if only partially, this remarkable tale of love and ambition.

A postscript about Armand Lavergne. He lived all his life with a question mark over his head. "Whether I be the son of Laurier or of Lavergne," he once said enigmatically, "I have good reason to be proud."

If he was indeed Laurier's son, he reacted as the sons of famous men so often do – by fighting his father. As a young man, though wilful and rebellious, Armand seemed bursting with promise, destined to become "not one in a thousand, but one in a million," as Laurier once promised Emilie. In 1904, at the age of only twenty-four, he was elected to the House of Commons as Liberal member for Montmagny. Laurier himself led him across the floor of the Commons to introduce him to the Speaker.

Armand Lavergne as a young Member of Parliament. He and Laurier quarrelled bitterly over the issue of minority rights in Alberta and Saskatchewan.

But within a year, the main source of conflict between them – Armand's ferociously intense Quebec nationalism versus Laurier's pragmatic pan-Canadianism – could no longer be suppressed; the two quarrelled bitterly over the issue of minority rights in the new provinces of Alberta and Saskatchewan. Armand now found his father-figure and hero in the nationalist leader, Henri Bourassa, twelve years older than he.

In 1908, he quit federal politics to enter the Quebec Assembly. As one of Bourassa's chief lieutenants (certainly his loudest one), Armand helped found *Le Devoir* and fought bitterly against Laurier's naval policy and Canada's entry into the First World War, even going to the theatrical extent of taking out a commission in the militia to make the point that while prepared to defend Canada, he would not fight in foreign wars. In 1930, now a Conservative, he surfaced again in Ottawa, once more as member for Montmagny. But it was a measure of how little he had fulfilled his promise that instead of being invited to join R. B. Bennett's cabinet, he was given only the sinecure of Deputy Speaker. He died of pneumonia in 1935, aged fifty-five, leaving no children. "I wish the simplest of funerals," he wrote in his will, "a pauper's casket, and I ask all those who have loved me to pray for my poor soul which is in need of it. . . . I have tried to serve my country and my race, that our English compatriots do not forget the pact of honour they have made with us. Canada will be bilingual, or it will be American."

A year after his death, Armand Lavergne's admirers organized a pilgrimage to his grave in Arthabaska. Among *Québécois*, he remains a hallowed memory, even today. "At heart he was a man of Opposition," wrote the historian La Terreur, "of easy opposition, unable to submit to party policy. But in spite of all his vagaries, one finds one constant, *l'amour de sa race*." Perhaps Armand's tragedy, *au fond*, was always to have been torn. "Only one thing pains me," he wrote to Laurier in 1909. "It is that you should believe I love you the less and that the past does not count. . . . It is above all when I fight you that I feel how strong it is . . . God is my witness that I love you, but forgive me, I love my country too."

CHAPTER 20

The Remarkable Ishbel

It is not so much what is done or what is said. It will be the tone *which will make itself felt, and in this every member of the Household, even down to the smallest child, will have a share.*

The Countess of Aberdeen;
diary entry; September 17, 1893

A remarkable characteristic of the world in which Amaryllis operated was the freedom it afforded to women. In other Canadian cities, ladies were relegated to knitting by the fireside, or entertaining themselves over teacups. But in turn-of-the-century Ottawa, thanks to the style established by Laurier and Emilie Lavergne, women were actually allowed, even encouraged, to wield influence. "It is curious what a fascination politics have for a woman, once she is allowed to pretend she understands them," wrote Amaryllis. "She cannot vote yet, but she is allowed to have an opinion, and at times, even to flatter herself that she has influenced brothers or husbands to vote as they did."

Official Ottawa had always been supportive of the feminine principle to a degree. The business of government, like all other kinds of business, was supposed to be a world in which men went unchallenged. But while women in commercial offices were unthinkable, except as humble "typewriters," and quite unimaginable in the men's clubs where so much of the real business was done, it was more difficult to keep them entirely out of politics. Anyone could attend debates; even Fanny Meredith, though little interested in the affairs of state, had gone to the Commons galleries frequently,

If only for social reasons, turn-of-the-century women flocked to the House of Commons. This "Lady's Ticket" for the Opening of Parliament in 1895 is contained in the scrap-book of Mrs. Duncan Campbell Scott.

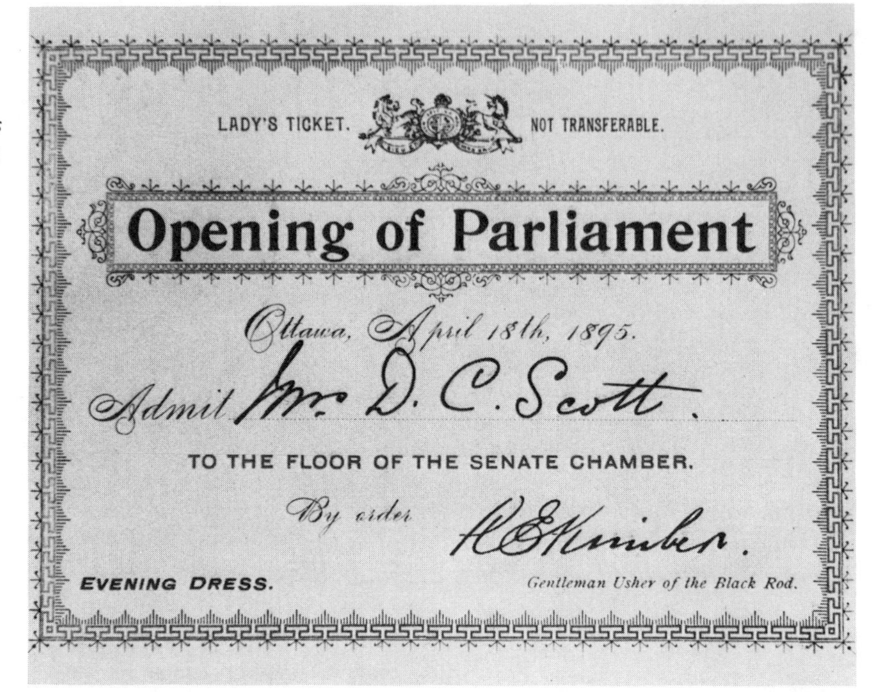

LADY'S TICKET. NOT TRANSFERABLE.

Opening of Parliament

Ottawa, April 18th, 1895.

Admit Mrs. D. C. Scott.

TO THE FLOOR OF THE SENATE CHAMBER.

By order

EVENING DRESS.

Gentleman Usher of the Black Rod.

with her daughters in tow, rather in the manner of taking them to a matinée. More important, for all the cigars and spittoons that were its stage props, politics had a distinctly feminine context, for it involved emotion and nuance and intuitive judgement. During the Pacific Scandal, Dufferin had cheerfully sent off his wife to act as his eyes and ears, knowing that her reports of how Macdonald was handling himself would be as astute as his own. During the 1880s, if only as antidote to boredom, the feminine fascination with politics intensified, and by now women reporters had arrived on the scene to record the phenomenon. Here, for instance, is the twenty-eight-year-old journalist, Sara Jeannette Duncan, on April 19, 1888, describing a late-night Commons sitting for the Toronto publication, *The Week*, in a tongue-in-cheek style that prefigures Amaryllis.

> The extent to which people will permit themselves to be bored in a good cause is phenomenal. . . . Scores of ladies, who might be suspected of about as much interest in a dry debate as a kitten might take in the theory of evolution sit til midnight. . . . It is especially the correct thing to spend an hour or two in the Speakers Gallery, in such radiance of apparel as is naturally reflected from Government House. There is something strong-minded, demi-aesthetic in it, that is agreeable

to the feminine sense of the fitness of things: it is said to be an admirable soporific, moreover, after the effect of Viceroyalty and champagne upon one's excited nerves. . . . *

* Duncan, alas, spent only a single season in Ottawa. She moved on from there to a wider world and eventually, having married an Imperial civil servant, spent most of her later life in India. She is best remembered, however, for her witty novel of small-town Canadian mores and manners, *The Imperialist*, published in 1905.

It helped further that an additional phenomenon had arrived by the time Amaryllis turned up. The later 1890s and the early 1900s were the heyday of the "New Woman," as she was known. As early as 1879, in an article in *Rose-Belford's Canadian Monthly* that was probably inspired by John Stuart Mill's 1869 essay, *The Subjection of Women*, a writer named Agnes Machar, daughter of the principal of Queen's University, had argued that the days of the "clinging vine" were over, that this child-like woman had been superseded by a woman capable of making her own contribution to society. "She has a right to share in the world's work," wrote Machar. "There is little doubt that in the long run, women will find themselves permitted to do whatever they should prove themselves able to do well." In Ottawa, as everywhere else, this New Woman had her detractors. "Her folly is rampant," wrote one R. Preston Robinson in the local magazine, *The Lounger*, in 1898. "The science of physiology demonstrates clearly that woman is the weaker vessel. The average constitution of a woman is about 20 percent less enduring than that of man, the blood of a woman contains fewer red blood corpuscles, and she exhales less carbonic acid." But she also had her supporters, among them the civil servant and biographer Henry J. Morgan, who, in 1903, published a four-hundred-page volume of photographs and short biographies, *Types of Canadian Women*, celebrating the achievements of some 358 women, including Agnes Macdonald and the painter, Frances Richards. "My *Types* might never have been dreamed of," Morgan noted in his introduction, "had I not been swept unconsciously into the current of the age, and felt the urgency of one of its most vital movements."

Amaryllis, as a woman out earning her living and writing a column that was at least as much about politics and social mores as it was about society, was obviously one of the New Women. Morgan indeed, had planned to include her in a second volume that, alas, was never published. Yet even Amaryllis, when she began writing in 1897, was rather taken aback by the social revolution underway now at Rideau Hall, at the hands of perhaps the most remarkable New Woman of them all: Ishbel Maria Marjoribanks Gordon, the Countess of Aberdeen.

The New Woman of the turn of the century, as depicted on the score card for a progressive euchre party. The energy and vitality of the movement was frequently symbolized by sporting images. When not playing golf, in a perfectly tailored scarlet jacket, the New Woman was often shown riding a bicycle. Invariably, she wore a straw boater and a neat collar and tie.

Into the amiable, winter carnival ambience that prevailed at Rideau Hall, the Aberdeens had arrived on a wind of change in the autumn of 1893. They were small- and large-L liberals – "horrid Grits" in the

Ottawa translation – and not just wishy-washy Liberals but earnest, moralistic Gladstonians, close friends and emissaries of the G.O.M. himself, who the previous year had won his last election victory at the age of eighty-four.

Government House was set on its ear. "It is not so much what is done or what is said," wrote Lady Aberdeen on her first evening in Canada. "It will be the *tone* which will make itself felt, and in this every member of the Household, even down to the smallest child, will have a share." Hand-in-hand with fervent Gladstonism went equally fervent Presbyterianism. "We were at one in believing that Liberalism is the Christianity of politics," she wrote, "and that those who take service under its banner must apply its principles to all relations of life both public and private." She matched actions to words. Within weeks, a small, plain wooden Presbyterian chapel replaced an old Rideau Hall conservatory. Pictures of "dear Mr. G." blossomed in every room.

One can picture, somehow, Lady Aberdeen wielding the nails, hammer, and stepladder herself. So devoted was she to Gladstone that as a young girl she had copied his example of roaming the dark alleys off London's Strand every Friday evening, in search of fallen women to reform. She was thirty-six and the mother of four when she arrived in Canada, a big, buxom woman of commanding if rather perspiring presence and limitless energy. In her marriage, as photographs leave no doubt, and as even the cautious official vice-regal historian Robert Hubbard has written in *Rideau Hall*, she was clearly "the dominant partner." Another historian, John Saywell, in his splendid introduction to the *Canadian Journal of Lady Aberdeen*, published in 1960, has gone a step further. "She seized the initiative," writes Saywell, "and retained it for the five years they remained in Canada. Aberdeen often followed where she bravely led." We can go still another step further and suggest that, in fact, between 1893 and 1898, Ishbel Maria Marjoribanks Gordon, Countess of Aberdeen, *was* Governor General in all but name and that "Gentle Johnny," as she called him, was her consort.

Indeed, save for his unfortunate habit "of trying to look as if nobody was looking at him," as Amaryllis once described him, Aberdeen, a slight, rather delicate man a decade older than his wife, was admirably suited to be a consort. He was a better than average skater, a gracious and affable host, and, if rather inclined to ramble, an excellent speaker. "Lord Aberdeen has originality," Amaryllis once noted indulgently. "It is always a pleasure to listen to him." A bit less indulgently, she remarked in the same column on Lady Aberdeen's unnerving habit of "pulling on his sleeve, and

Lord and Lady Aberdeen in 1898. In truth, she was the Governor General and he was her consort.

offering suggestions." Aberdeen was also quite spectacularly good at imitating railway whistles, and was renowned as the only peer of the realm actually capable of driving a locomotive from London to Edinburgh.

As proconsul in all but title, Lady Aberdeen was the first activist since Dufferin. But, as a Liberal and as a woman, her point of view was different. Never before and never since has anyone attempted to use the office of Governor General as an instrument for social reform. In her richly detailed journal, she revealed passionately and eloquently many of the stark realities of Canadian life that, then as now, so few comfortable citizens of Official Ottawa bothered their heads about.

It was the plight of poorer women and children that distressed her most. As she discovered early on during a visit to a hospital for foundlings in Montreal, there was the terrible practice of "baby-farming" in Quebec. "There is no registration of births necessary in this province at all – the influence of the priests keeps up a very strong feeling about illegitimate children and the consequence is that it is accepted as a belief that the kindest thing is to baptize these children and then facilitate their exit from the world . . . the babies are farmed out with the result that . . . the percentage of deaths some years has been as high as 90p.c. & one year actually 99 percent." A visit to Toronto introduced Lady Aberdeen to the appalling garment industry sweatshops. "The same old set of circumstances as at home," she noted on February 20, 1894. "Home work and married women's work underselling the work of women wholly dependent on their earnings . . . the sort of prices which prevail are 14 cents for a boy's double coat with three pockets, taking a day and a half to make – 35 cents for a grown-up coat – thread of course having to be supplied by workers. Then in factories, girls by the score earning only 2 dollars a week, afraid of giving up their work because there are hundreds of others ready to step in their places – afraid to join Protective Association – dismissed for attending meetings – fines, unsanitary conditions etc., & no women inspectors."

Lady Aberdeen's answer was to rally the women of Canada to form a lobby group. Against tremendous odds she established almost single-handedly first, in 1894, the National Council of Women and, in 1897, to celebrate the Diamond Jubilee, the Victorian Order of Nurses. The story of how Lady Aberdeen accomplished these institutions, both of which continue to flourish, has been documented by Saywell and by others. More to our own point of interest is the philosophy behind these institutions which illuminates Lady Aberdeen's remarkable personality.

Although since girlhood she had been an ardent advocate of votes for women, Ishbel Aberdeen was a suffragist, not a suffragette, as the distinction was made in those days. Her brand of feminism had little in common with that of militants like Emmeline Pankhurst and her daughters, or Emily Wilding Davison, who flung herself under the King's horse at the Derby. Indeed, in founding the National Council of Women, the Countess had been anxious to overcome "the idea that organizations of women are only meant to

Lady Aberdeen. She dared to exercise her power openly.

promote either directly religious work, or missionary work, or women's suffrage work." In her speech to the First Annual Meeting, on April 11, 1894, she made an emotional but tactful appeal to the great common denominator among women.

> How can we best describe this women's mission? Can we not best describe it as "mothering" in one way or another? We are not all called upon to be mothers of little children, but every woman is called upon to mother in some way or another, and it is impossible to be in this

country, even for a little while, and not be impressed with a sense of what a great work of "mothering" is in this sense committed to the women of Canada.

In short, Lady Aberdeen's concern was not so much to reform the condition of women as such, but to reform society, employing women as a means to this end. Women were persons, certainly, but even to Ishbel Aberdeen they were not persons of quite the same order as men.

"A pretty pickle is it not?" Thus, on July 13, 1895, Lady Aberdeen described the Manitoba Schools Question, then bursting upon the nation in all its fury. When it came to Canadian politics, which fascinated her and of which she demonstrates in her journal a remarkably clear and sympathetic if not always objective understanding, she played a role more akin to that of governess than that of mother.

She had come to Canada in the midst of exceptionally interesting if decidedly nasty times. Quite apart from Manitoba Schools and all its attendant passions, there was, not all that different from more recent history, the drama of the disintegration of the Conservative Party to be watched unfolding daily. The Tory Syndrome was being born: between Lady Aberdeen's arrival in 1893 and Laurier's election three years later, three separate Tory prime ministers – Sir John Thompson, Sir Mackenzie Bowell, and lastly, for just two months and a fortnight, Edmund and Fanny Meredith's old friend Sir Charles Tupper, now seventy-five – tried unsuccessfully to fill the awesome gap left by Macdonald's death. (Previously, for a few months in 1891-92, yet a fourth prime minister, Sir John Abbott, had already tried and failed.)

Into this morass, Ishbel Aberdeen plunged with her customary verve and energy. Powerful women exercising their power behind the scenes were scarcely strangers to the capital, but neither Agnes Macdonald nor Emilie Lavergne would have dared show their hands so openly. It was one thing for a Governor General's wife to act as her husband's operative from a discreet seat in the Commons gallery, as Lady Dufferin had done. It was quite another for a viceregal consort to ensconce herself, as Lady Aberdeen did, in a commanding position "right on the floor of the House, between the Speaker and the Treasury Bench." Easy to picture her there, day after day, listening, earnest and intent – and rather too eager to speak her mind. "It makes a wonderful difference in the knowing and understanding of men to see them as they are in the House instead of merely in dress clothes at our Parliamentary dinners," she wrote.

"Those on the side of the Ministry have to pass my chair so often that I frequently have an opportunity for a friendly word with all sorts . . . several of the Opposition members also come round behind and have a little talk."

Her forays into politics met with mixed success. With Thompson, prime minister when she arrived and a sane and generous-spirited Nova Scotian, himself happily married to a strong-minded wife, she got on famously, even to the point of clucking worriedly in her diary about his perilous habit of refusing to wear any gloves in below-zero cold. "Lady Thompson says she provides him with one pair every year, but that he lost one if not both of them on the first day." Lady Thompson, indeed, soon became Lady Aberdeen's closest Ottawa confidante and in December 1894, when Thompson died suddenly at Windsor Castle while visiting the Queen (not of pneumonia, as might have been expected, but of a heart attack) it was to Ishbel that Frances Thompson came rushing in her grief, "to burst out [saying] of old Sir Charles Tupper, 'if *he* were sent for, I should look upon it as an insult to my husband's memory.' " Ironically (as recounted in chapter fourteen), when Lady Macdonald in similar circumstances implored Lord Stanley to send for Tupper and not for Thompson, attention was not paid, but Aberdeen, as was no surprise, sent for Mackenzie Bowell.

With Laurier, always at home in the company of brainy, outspoken women, Lady Aberdeen got on equally well. "He is a brilliant man, and very agreeable socially," she wrote on their first meeting, in 1894. Before long, going far beyond the bounds of normal viceregal discretion, she had become a Laurier partisan. In January 1896, as Bowell's government lurched towards its doom, and seven ministers – "the nest of traitors" – resigned *en bloc* from the cabinet, she and Laurier indulged in an episode of intrigue. As third party and go-between, they selected Emily McCausland Cummings, another of Ottawa's New Women, a reporter for the Toronto *Globe* who, by lucky happenstance, was also an active participant in the National Council of Women. "As she is always in communication with me about the Council, her comings and goings will not be considered unnatural," the Countess confided to her diary. On January 7, Mrs. Cummings turned up both morning and evening at Rideau Hall with missives from Laurier. "He feels strongly that if Sir Mackenzie fails in reconstruction, he should be sent for." On January 11, after four more days of to-ing and fro-ing, Laurier himself turned up in the company of Mrs. Cummings under the cover of a skating party. "He says he could form his cabinet in three days."

Emily McCausland Cummings, of The Globe. *She came from Port Hope and wrote under the pseudonym, "Sama." She later became editor of "Women's Sphere," a department of* The Canadian *magazine. Journalism was proving a promising field for many of Canada's New Women.*

In the event, Bowell managed to struggle on for another three and a half months. On April 23, he dissolved the House for an election and four days later, by prior arrangement, handed the prime-ministership over to Tupper. After the election, when Laurier was commissioned at last to form his ministry – he managed the task in only two days, it turned out – Lady Aberdeen sent him a sprig of white Scottish heather for good luck.

In the long run, Ishbel had shown sound political judgement in discriminating in favour of Laurier. But, her indiscretion so infuriated Tupper that, in high dudgeon, he sent back the gold box the Aberdeens had sent him for his golden wedding anniversary. He got even with her further by leading Canadian doctors in their fight against the Victorian Order of Nurses. In 1898, when the Aberdeens departed, Tupper took the astonishing step of refusing to allow the Conservatives to join in the routine House of Commons Farewell Address.*

* Tupper was doubly infuriated by the fact that in late June 1896, after his defeat but while he was still prime minister, Aberdeen, acting on Laurier's advice, refused to allow him the privilege of making Conservative appointments to the Senate and to the Bench. No doubt Tupper surmised correctly that Laurier was not the Governor General's only adviser.

As thought Tupper, so also thought most of Ottawa Officialdom – many because they were Tories *au fond*, but many also with good reason. For all her good intentions, Lady Aberdeen had the defects of her virtues; she was bossy, meddlesome, and domineering. Even with Laurier safely in power, she was apparently unable to let well enough alone. Here, our informant is that supremely well-connected observer of the Ottawa scene, Sir Joseph Pope, now in Edmund Meredith's old job as Under-Secretary of State. "Shortly after the change of government," relates Pope in his memoir, *Public Servant*,

> there was a dinner at Rideau Hall to which Mr. J. M. Courtney, the Deputy Minister of Finance was invited. In the course of the evening, Lady Aberdeen backed Mr. Courtney into the Governor-General's private office, showed him the Treasury Minutes, passed at a recent meeting of the cabinet and asked him whether he thought they were such as His Excellency could properly be asked to sign. Mr. Courtney, a rather choleric gentleman at all times, a radical with a high sense of honour, was furious at being made the recipient of this confidence, giving the lady to understand that in the first place, she should never have seen those minutes and secondly, that if Lord Aberdeen had any doubts as to the propriety of the recommendations they contained, his proper course was to consult his Prime Minister, whose name stretched halfway across the page submitting the cases for approval, and not a permanent official like himself.

This particular story, Pope continues, "was related to me by Mr. Courtney at the time, almost word for word as it is set down here. I kept it to myself for many years. One day I told it to Sir Wilfrid. He simply laughed, and said nothing."

"It was all very funny." So Lady Aberdeen, not normally a great one for irony, described her single social coup as Governess General. The day was Monday, August 23, 1897; the setting not Ottawa, but Toronto. The scene was a lavish garden party at the handsome Georgian manor house, The Grange, arranged in the Aberdeens' honour by the Sage of the Grange himself, Professor Goldwin Smith. "On the lawn, near the roseries were spread generous buffets with dainty fare," reported *Saturday Night*'s Lady Gay. "In front of the library windows sat the Highlanders' Band, playing capitally. . . . At precisely half-past five, Their Excellencies drove up in an open landau, the only carriage permitted onto the grounds."

In venturing in through those gates, the Aberdeens were carrying the banner of Empire deep into enemy country. Goldwin Smith, author of the "sub-arctic lumber village" crack about Ottawa, was the most ardent advocate of Canada's annexation by the United States to be found in the nation. An old Etonian, a former Regius Professor of History at Oxford turned leisured man of letters, Smith had fetched up in Toronto in 1871 to marry fortune in the form of a Family Compact widow and to become, even in that citadel of Toryism, the most prominent figure in society. (An approximate contemporary parallel would have been the late Kenneth Clark choosing to settle in, say, Regina.) Torontonians, as *Saturday Night*'s editor, Hector Charlesworth, once noted, "thrust Smith into the limelight on every possible occasion." They read, or at least they bought, his books. They repeated his anecdotes. They marvelled at how he beat them at whist. They fought for invitations to the dinner parties he gave for visiting luminaries like Sir Arthur Conan Doyle, creator of Sherlock Holmes and the singer Madame Albani. Young ladies flocked to his Thursday afternoon lectures on English literature; afterwards, Mrs. Smith poured tea and there might even be tennis. "Thus is applied the antidote," noted *Saturday Night*, "to prevent any fear lest so unusual an exercise of their mental powers should turn into bluestockings so many of Toronto's brightest flowers."

From The Grange, when not engaged in the social round, Smith ridiculed the Office of the Governor General, much as he had once ridiculed Ottawa. "As useless, but as capable of giving harm as the appendix." Now, on this sunlit Jubilee Summer afternoon, as so often has happened before and since to staunch republicans when actually confronted by royalty, Smith melted as butter in the sun. "On the doorstep, hat in hand," marvelled Lady Aberdeen. "All the time ready to fetch anyone we wanted to speak to."

With a flourish, Smith got out The Grange's most treasured antiques, the famous Lord Simcoe wineglasses finished with a cut-glass ball at the end of the stem instead of a base, so that they had to be drained at a single draught. Nothing would do but he and Lord Aberdeen must drink the Queen's health from them. "Who would have thought the day would come?" the Countess continued in her diary. "It is a curious fact that the man who has been preaching annexation, should also be the man to receive us in the most absolute royal manner, every point of etiquette being most formally observed."

An invitation to one of Lady Aberdeen's skating parties. Winter sports bored her, but she bowed to the inevitable.

In Ottawa, however, Lady Aberdeen fared less well as the figurehead for capital society. The trouble was, she had a way of treating the leading lights of society as if they were ladies of the evening in need of services from Gladstone's and her Strand Rescue Mission. She did not care for skating and tobogganing, still less for all the endless talk about it. "This is a very noticeable feature of society," she complained in her diary. "Skating, curling, tobagganing etc. engrosses all the talk of the young people." Nor, like Princess Louise before her, was she much impressed with Ottawans' manners. "The ladies behaved somewhat boisterously in the cloakroom," she wrote of her first big reception on December 23, 1893. "They quite upset our calculations by vaulting over the table arranged for giving out cloaks and insisted on going for the bundles themselves." She had little patience with the pomp and circumstance that surrounded the Opening of Parliament – "too ridiculous to be driving through this very colonial town dressed up in diamonds and evening dress in broad daylight" – and to further distress local sensitivities, she did her best to undercut the intricate structure of "at-home" days and calling cards, much treasured by Ottawa ladies as an art form that distinguished them from other less-couth Canadians. "I suggested having a conference amongst the leaders of society with a view to lightening the intolerable burden imposed by the observance of strict rules about calling, leaving cards personally, and never calling except on the day 'at home' and always asking for the people," she wrote in February 1895. When this effort failed, she tried a new tack with the younger generation. "Ottawa society cannot stand for itself alone," she lectured a bevy of thirty-three young unmarried ladies assembled in flowered hats in the Rideau Hall ballroom

A bevy of Ottawa maidens, probably dressed in costume for a charity concert. The photograph is undated, but judging from the leg-of-mutton sleeves, it was probably taken around 1895. Many of these girls joined the May Court Club. Second from left in the back row is Amy Ritchie, who was the cousin and also future mother-in-law of the diplomat-diarist, Charles Ritchie. Seated on the extreme right is Lilian Scott Desbarats.

on May Day 1898. "It must represent Canada as a whole and influence Canada. . . . You can permeate social life with sweetness and beauty and intellectual stimulus . . . or you can help to make gossip the main staple of the conversation." Elsewhere in her address to this new May Court Club, reported Amaryllis, who was present both as a journalist and as a founding member, "Her Excellency spoke to the girls as John Ruskin speaks to women. Indeed, she held a copy of *Sesame and Lilies* in her hand." Afterwards, everyone went out into the garden to crown the May Queen, who would also serve as the club's president, and to dance around the Maypole. They also sang a chirpy little May Court song to the tune of "My Bonny Lies Over the Ocean."*

The traditional viceregal consort's role of playing hostess was way down on Ishbel Aberdeen's list of priorities. Even as a debutante, back in the 1870s, the pleasure of parties had eluded her. "I did not find where the wonderful attraction lay, hopping round the room, and talking about the floor, the weather and suchlike," she'd written in her diary of her very first ball. Now, as chatelaine of Rideau Hall, she seemed determined that every event there must needs be both democratic – and socially relevant.

The result, predictably, was social disaster. All of a sudden, the old select dinner parties for two dozen or so, at which, as Amaryllis remembered nostalgically, "Lady Stanley always had the pleasant, home-like fashion of making tea herself," mushroomed into huge,

* As a volunteer service club, the May Court continues to function in Ottawa, with affiliated branches in eight other Ontario cities.

overblown, unprogrammed affairs given twice or even three times weekly. "Seventy or eighty guests are bidden and assembled in the racquet court," Amaryllis explained, meaning by "racquet court," the room the Dufferins had had built and called the "Tent Room." "The staff receives the guests and it takes nearly an hour for the anxious ADC in Waiting to identify everybody, and make the necessary introductions. The scene is an amusing one – that is, if you have the man who is to take you in well in sight and have no fear of being left alone at the last minute." Worse still, Lady Aberdeen, for all her populist principles, was given to parading around like an absolute monarch. "Her Excellency always has a little page, sometimes two, dressed in the costumes of Louis XIV. They carry her train and run about during dinner carrying notes and messages." After dinner, which invariably took place at a huge horseshoe table in the ballroom that made conversation difficult, "Her Excellency

The ballroom at Rideau Hall, laid out for a state dinner in 1898. The horseshoe table made conversation difficult.

leads the way back into the racquet court where the women are neither more nor less lively than they always are during the depressing half-hour when the lords of creation are enjoying their post-prandial smoke. Lady Aberdeen used to walk about and stand talking to the ladies but hearing how so many suffered from fatigue in so doing, she now, with her usual courtesy and kindness, always sits down, thus allowing her guests to do so."

Quite often, however, it was physically impossible to sit down. After formal state dinners for Parliamentarians (Lady Aberdeen shocked Officialdom by invariably attending these herself, as the only lady present) it was standard practice for her to invite upwards of a thousand to squeeze into the racquet court for a huge "kettle-drum" reception. "An *omnium gatherum* of men and women who not only sup as if they had not dined that day," reported Amaryllis, "but as if that necessary meal had not been enjoyed for weeks." What Amaryllis was really getting at here was that, much to Official Ottawa's horror, all manner of ordinary citizens, perhaps even one's own dentist, were being included on the guest list. Moreover, since the doors to the drawing rooms were kept firmly locked, there was no escape from the chilly, drafty racquet court. To top it all off, the Aberdeen's butler, Grant, was often rude to the guests and once had the effrontery to write to the local papers complaining about colonial manners.

Once and once only, more by good luck than good management, Lady Aberdeen engineered a social success. By common consensus, her mammoth Fancy Dress ball, held in the Senate Chamber on February 17, 1896, was second only to the ball held by the Dufferins twenty years earlier. True to form, the Countess had designed the event as a learning experience, hoping, as she wrote, "to divert Ottawa gossip . . . away from the everlasting discussion of hockey and winter sports varied with society scandal." Months beforehand, guests were marshalled into groups, each group instructed to represent a period of Canadian history, each to perform a dance representative of the period. But this time, for whatever reason – maybe for once, even boorish Ottawans were bored by society scandal – her plans caught everyone's fancy. Amaryllis, unfortunately, was still a year away from formally launching her career as social columnist. Still, the anonymous correspondent who reported on the ball for the short-lived local magazine, *The Lounger*, was almost certainly she. "Never before was the study of history so ardently pursued in our Capital. Fair ladies pored over Parkman with sighs and exclamations." As in Dufferin's day, the Librarian of Parliament, now the man of letters, Martin Griffin, had thoughtfully left all his books on costume design scattered open upon the tables. "Gentleman also studied these with a semi-comical, semi-tragical air of anxiety. . . . Never again shall it be said, in Ottawa at least, that Canada has no history."

On the night itself, that ever-popular Canadian celebrity, Madame Albani, the international opera diva, was there to look on. So also was the redoubtable Mrs. Potter Palmer, doyenne of Chicago society. To start the ball rolling, a party from Government House, led by the Aberdeen's eighteen-year-old-daughter, Lady Marjorie Gordon, frolicked around pretending to be Vikings in horns and in

A group of guests at the fancy-dress ball. This group, which represented the departure of Jacques Cartier from France, danced a quadrille.

the fake chainmail made by the tinsmith that Amaryllis had recommended. Everyone laughed, no one harder than the Countess, when several helmets fell off in the course of the dance and rolled on the floor. Next, everyone watched and smiled knowingly as the party presided over by Zoë Laurier, assisted *ca va sans dire* by Emilie Lavergne, executed a slow bourrée that evoked the founding of Montreal by Maisonneuve. Amaryllis danced the Sir Roger de Coverley in the set that heralded the coming of the Loyalists, but it was Hayter Reed, the Superintendent General of Indian Affairs who stole the show. "After the State Lancers," reported *The Lounger*, "the people dressed as Indians formed in line and marched to the front, the braves first and squaws after in true Indian fashion. Mr. Reed made a speech in the Indian language to Their Excellencies. Mr. Wilfred Campbell, the poet, interpreted."

There were, however, *frissons*. *Frissons* followed Lady Aberdeen as summer followed spring. In *The Lounger*, Amaryllis was unable to resist passing them on:

> It was Her Excellency's expressed desire that too great expense should not be incurred . . . there was a great overhauling of partly worn evening gowns. But it is said that one lady, about whose costume

> certain rumours had reached Her Excellency's ears, assured her when questioned that the dress had cost only three dollars. It arrived, however, express from New York in a box that was both large and long and the brilliancy of whose contents was an astonishing illustration of what may be done with three dollars judiciously expended.

"Rumour has it that a certain titled Englishman and his wife have also secured passage aboard the *Labrador*." Thus on June 15, 1898 Amaryllis added spice to an otherwise humdrum column outlining the plans of various Ottawa notables, including Emilie Lavergne, to board that vessel *en route* to a summer in Europe. "If this be true," she went on, "there is no danger of the other passengers suffering from ennui, for the lady is warranted to keep things lively at any price." Then she added the kicker. "The only fear is that it may cause some of the other ladies to postpone their departures."

As it happened, Amaryllis had the right ship but the wrong date. It was not for another five months, not until November 12, 1898, that the Aberdeens sailed home aboard the *Labrador* for good. But, as Amaryllis leaves no doubt, many in Ottawa were perfectly delighted to see the backs of them. That Emilie Lavergne should head this list is, on reflection, no surprise. Always possessive, Emilie would have been less than pleased by the vigour and warmth of the friendship that had blossomed between Lady Aberdeen and her beloved Laurier. Emilie, it is worth noting, had been conspicuous by her absence from any involvement with the National Council of Women. Nor had Gabrielle Lavergne, though of the right age and social position, danced around the pole on the day the May Court Club was born. On the basis of no firm evidence whatever – other than that Emilie in the official photograph looks uncommonly well turned out – we can further suspect that it may well have been she who flaunted the infamous "three-dollar-gown" at the Fancy Dress ball of 1896.

For others in Ottawa society without personal axes to grind, Lady Aberdeen had quite simply taken up too much space in a little town. She lacked grace and lightness of touch; above all, she lacked the gift of humour to lighten her message. She made people feel uncomfortable. Indeed, there was something unnerving, almost threatening, about a woman who could behave as Ishbel had behaved on the afternoon of April 22, 1896. Out for a casual springtime drive along the Quebec shore of the swollen Ottawa River, her ponies, Cowslip and Buttercup, had suddenly lost their footing and been swept away into the torrent. "I found myself on my back in the water," she wrote later. "My head got under the water, I began to wonder how long one could remain conscious . . . I remembered I had been told one ought to float in such emergencies." Then, when the rescuing boat came from shore, she calmly shook herself off and walked home – feeling not the least bit sorry for herself but only for "my poor, lovely ponies, gone for a quick death" – to preside as planned over that night's dinner party.

Some in Ottawa bade farewell to Ishbel regretfully. Years later, they still remembered her compassion and her courage. "You were never outwardly discouraged," wrote Mrs. Kate Hayter Reed in 1923, looking back on the difficult days of organizing the Victorian Order of Nurses. "You forged on and on. How well I remember when Lady Ritchie and I made the canvass from shop to shop and only the coal man saw the great plan you had in view. I can hear Mrs. S. . . . railing against it at a dinner party – the idiot – but I never fail to rub it in and send her the praise it now gets in the newspapers."

For such women, Ishbel Aberdeen had served as consciousness-raiser, to borrow a phrase from our own time. One realizes further that Amaryllis herself, at heart, was another member of this company. To be sure, as a society columnist, she wrote what her readers wanted. Yet every now and then, as often as she dared, she revealed her own social conscience. As early as Christmas 1897, in the same column in which she described Emilie Lavergne's epochal reception, she wrote of the "the plight of little sick children in the hospitals." "I have not heard of any collections being made for these children, but why need there be collections? Everyone knows where the hospitals are." By June 1901, she'd grown bolder and was arguing, albeit unsuccessfully, that instead of giving the Duchess of York a mink cape on her Royal Visit that autumn, the ladies of Ottawa should build a public swimming bath for the children of Lower Town, and name it in the Duchess's honour. When it came to the National Council of Women, Amaryllis was a fervent supporter, and indeed a rather abrasive one. "The best men in the land are the men who admire and help," she wrote during the annual meeting of 1898. "It is the man – you know him – who says, 'I don't let my wife do this' and 'I don't let my wife do that!' who is loud in his condemnation of the Council. Beware of him!"

Late in October 1898, a few days before Lady Aberdeen left Ottawa, Amaryllis was one of five Ottawa women specially invited to accompany the Countess on a visit to some of her favourite Ottawa subjects, those girls and young women who worked as

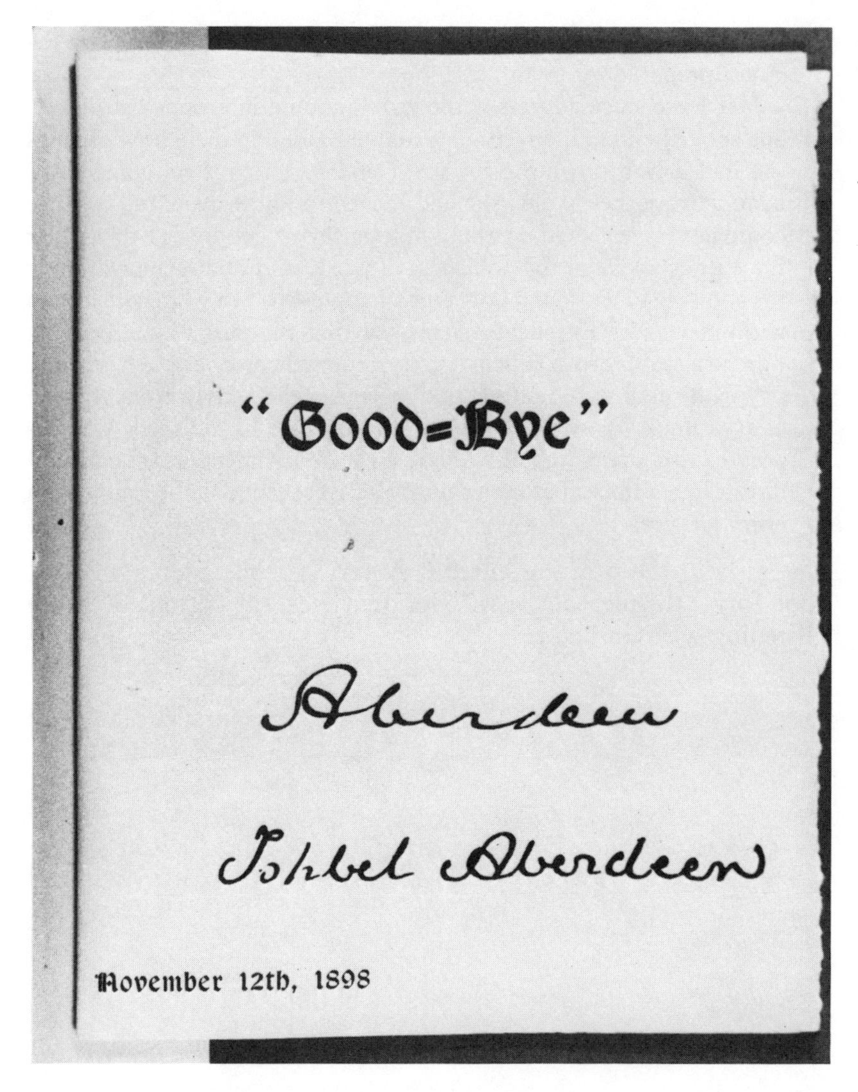

Lord and Lady Aberdeen's farewell to Canada. On their departure, they sent these cards to all their friends.

stitchers and binders in the Government Printing Bureau. Amaryllis, for once, did not report tongue-in-cheek, but as a member of a sisterhood in which she as a journalist, come to think of it, was only a slightly more privileged member.

> A large room on the third floor is where the girls work. They stitch the leaves of the books together and then bind them. In this large room, the girls received Her Excellency. It seemed as if one had reached the very heart of the work. . . . Piles of books were on the long tables and

> through rows of sewing machines, the visitors picked their way to the chairs prepared for them . . . .
>
> Her Excellency addressed the girls standing in groups before her. She spoke in a kind, affectionate manner and told them how often as she had driven down Sussex Street and had seen them going to or coming from their work, she had longed to know them and that she could not leave Canada without at least saying goodbye to them. Her Excellency spoke of the nobleness of work, and of how much power for good lay in work and how much happier women were with it than without it. Her Excellency suggested that the girls of the Printing Bureau should form a benefit society among themselves, each member paying a small sum monthly and so ensure themselves from want in case of illness or want of work. A committee of four girls was appointed to confer with Lady Aberdeen at Government House on Monday at one o'clock. Before leaving, Her Excellency shook hands with every girl present.

The girls of the printing bureau, Amaryllis concluded, "will not soon forget the pleasant visit." Her own eyes, she conceded, "were glistening with unshed tears."

CHAPTER 21

"Minto's Folly"

Her Ex. and Captain Graham are amusing themselves alone in New York. His Ex. is alone and amusing himself with a young woman you have heard of. She is generally called "Minto's Folly." It is quite charming to find people going their own way, with no concern of what other people may think or say.

Captain Agar Adamson; in a letter to his wife,
Mabel Cawthra Adamson; April 20, 1901

As everywhere else in the British Empire, the Victorian Era ended officially in Ottawa in the small hours of January 22, 1901, when the eighty-two-year-old Queen died at Osborne House. Official Society plunged immediately into mourning. Before the day was out, as Amaryllis informed her Toronto readers, the exterior of the Parliament Buildings had been draped in black. "Here and there, a white crown above the well-known letters, V.R., stands out to relieve the background. . . . It is surprising this sense of personal sorrow," she went on. "The Queen seems to have been part of our lives – a something that always was and always would be."

Yet when it came to describing the elaborate protocols of mourning, Amaryllis was her usual ironic self. For the Opening of Parliament on February 7, she reports, "all the cabinet ministers' wives, following the example of Lady Laurier, are wearing thick black veils over their faces. The French Canadians, like the people of old France, have strict ideas on the subject of mourning. They do not consider it orthodox unless the face is hidden." The viceregal court, she continued, did not go quite that far. "The mourning worn by Lady Minto is somewhat like widow's mourning, only that on closer inspection one discovers that the long veil falling from the back of the bonnet to the hem of the gown is not of crape,

The Parliament Buildings in January 1901, draped in mourning for Queen Victoria.

but of black tulle. It hangs much as the white tulle veils worn at the Drawing Room are expected to hang, and has a graceful effect." This suggestion of a certain carelessness in the official manifestations of grief was soon underscored. "The cabinet ladies have recommenced entertaining," Amaryllis reported in mid-February, "although in a manner informal as regards the invitations. On the night of the Opening of Parliament, there was a large dinner at the residence of the Prime Minister to which all the guests had been invited verbally by either Sir Wilfrid or Lady Laurier during the afternoon. It must have been rather trying for the cook. Many other ladies have commenced giving teas, which they take great care to assure all invited are not 'teas,' others give luncheons which are not 'luncheons,' and I have even heard of a skating party which was not a 'skating party.' It would appear that there is a good deal in a name."

The viceregal court was a little more subtle in its circumvention of convention. "Nothing will take place at Government House during the year of sufficient size to warrant having a band in attendance," Amaryllis warned her readers, much to the horror of all the capital's belles. "This means the stoppage of all gaiety, alas, alas," wrote an eighteen-year-old diarist named Ethel Chadwick, who had made her debut at a ball chaperoned by Emilie Lavergne just three weeks previously and who now foresaw a dull and arid season. "I am the unluckiest girl in the world," she continued. Practice, however, rather differed from theory. On February 2, the very day of the memorial service for the Queen at Christ Church Cathedral, the Governor General's house party, a company that included Lady Minto's sister, the Countess of Antrim, a Woman of the Bedchamber to the late Queen-Empress, spent the rest of the afternoon skating merrily on the rink at Rideau Hall. Lord Minto meanwhile, as we discover from Amaryllis, "has been taking advantage of the absence of state functions to spend much of his time tramping over the country on [*sic*] skees." Later that week, Ethel Chadwick's mother profited from these examples, and sent out cards for a debutante supper party.

Memorial Service
to Her late Majesty
Queen Victoria.
Christ Church Cathedral
OTTAWA, CANADA.
Saturday Feb. 2nd 1901
Admit

Card of admission for Queen Victoria's memorial service at Christ Church Cathedral. Later that afternoon, however, the viceregal court skated merrily on the Rideau Hall rink.

Such liberties did not imply any lack of respect for the late Queen. Rather they bespoke a simple fact of life. Victorianism, as a state of mind and as a defining mode of behaviour, had already passed from the capital – had gone, indeed, two years earlier, when the Aberdeens sailed home to Britain to be replaced at Rideau Hall by Gilbert John Elliott-Murray-Kynynmound, fourth Earl of Minto, and his Countess.

"You must never be persuaded to give your name to any new venture which might be criticized," Queen Victoria had warned Lady Minto on the eve of her departure for Canada, in a deliberate reference to the Aberdeens' attempts to raise the banner of the despicable Gladstone in the colonies. Yet the irony was, for all that the Queen had disliked them most thoroughly, the Aberdeens, in all their energetic high-mindedness, had been quintessential Victorians. The Mintos, by contrast, were Edwardians. They were a distinct new species of proconsul: a glossy and worldly couple entirely at home within the chic, fast, raffish Marlborough House set that surrounded the Prince of Wales. At once arrogant and elegant, they exemplified the style of the British Empire as it approached its zenith. They brought to Ottawa Edwardian style at its most seductive and evocative; the style of one of those lavish, ferociously energetic but ultimately indolent country-house parties, at which,

Lord and Lady Minto, in January 1899, three months after their arrival in Canada. They were arrogant and elegant – and quick off the mark to acquire fur coats.

just as in the opening setpiece of Victoria Sackville-West's classic novel, *The Edwardians*, the company is jabbering away to one another in a curious jargon that seems to involve – Horribilino! – Italianate endings to English words and where the King himself, accompanied by Mrs. Keppel, is expected within the hour for a spot of grouse-shooting. So close were the Mintos to this prototype that in private, they always referred to their Military Secretary, Major Lawrence Drummond, as "Lorenzo."

Edwardian style was bold, showy, and often reckless. Thus Minto, in his salad days, under the name "Mr. Rolly," had been one of the best-known gentlemen jockeys in England, riding four times in the Grand National and surviving even a broken neck in a fall from a horse. Edwardian style was by and large anti-intellectual. "They were more interested in facts than ideas," observes Anquetil, Sackville-West's outsider in *The Edwardians*. "For the life of him, he could not see that . . . their conversation was in any way worthy of exciting the interest of an eager man." Minto, in his bluff, soldierly way, fitted this description exactly. "Clever people," he once observed, "are generally so damned silly."

Edwardian style was also highly charged with sexuality. Just as King Edward VII never made any pretence of keeping secret his liaisons with Lily Langtry or with Daisy Warwick or with Alice Keppel, so Minto, while Governor General, was blazingly indiscreet about a six-year relationship with the beautiful young Ottawa woman whom those in the Rideau Hall inner circle nicknamed "Minto's Folly."

Lady Aberdeen, it will be recalled, had given her matched pair of carriage ponies the innocent, bucolic names Cowslip and Buttercup. Minto's ponies bore titles more in the Edwardian manner. They were Madam and Mistress.

While they were harbingers of the new, the Mintos were not strangers to Ottawa. In the mid-eighties, they had spent the first two years of their married life at Rideau Cottage while Minto, then Viscount Melgund, still half a decade away from succeeding his father, the third Earl, had served as Lansdowne's Military Secretary.

In 1884, Melgund had recruited and organized the contingent of Canadian boatmen despatched up the Nile to relieve the ill-fated General "Chinese" Gordon at Khartoum – alas too late. A year later, during the Northwest Rebellion, he had served as chief of staff to General Middleton, commanding officer of the Canadian militia. "Shortly before the battle of Batoche," Amaryllis reminded her readers in a foray into military history that comes as near to the truth as makes no difference, "he was sent to Ottawa with dispatches which, it has since transpired, contained a request for the ordering out of the Imperial troops at Halifax. Luckily for the *amour propre* of the Canadian people, the general wired that as Batoche was taken, he had no need of the troops. The laconic reply, 'Thank God, Melgund,' showed that our future Governor General understood what our feelings would be had our own soldiers not been allowed to win their own battles."

For a soldier who some years earlier had been forced to send in his papers to the Scots Guards as the result of an unfortunate scuffle with a superior officer over a woman known as "Baby" Ashton, this had been an excellent start to rehabilitating his career. "I shall not live to see it," John A. Macdonald had said, "but someday Canada will welcome you back as Governor General." Now, at fifty-three, the paterfamilias of three daughters and two sons, Minto was fulfilling Macdonald's prophecy. He was a crisp, erect, military figure with a carefully-waxed moustache who, because he was short, always looked to best advantage on the back of a horse; the kind of figure whom John Singer Sargent was so good at capturing in his portraits, and whom Sargent undoubtedly would have been commissioned to capture if only the Minto estates in the Scottish border country had yielded a trifle more revenue. He was in most ways, the very model of a huntin'-fishin'-shootin' aristocrat, a Liberal-Unionist in politics but a High Tory at heart, who had slight use for "goody-goody benevolent people," as he once labelled humanitarians of the dreaded Gladstonian ilk. The arts, like ideas, flew right over Minto's head; his sort of music, he once remarked in his diary, involved the band of the Coldstream Guards playing "The Lost Chord" and the "Toreador Song"; in six years in Canada, Minto's sole contribution to Canadian culture was to proffer a suggestion, which no one ever took seriously, that Rideau Hall should be turned over to the National Gallery and a new and proper residence built for the Governor General on Nepean Point.

Yet, on the evidence provided by his terse and regrettably only sporadic diary, Minto was by no means a prefiguration of Colonel Blimp. He spent much more time with his children than the average Edwardian papa; in a private family joke, he frequently referred to them as "The Picks" – probably it was short for piccaninnies – and always found the house "terribly silent" when they were away. None of the British governors general, and perhaps not even any of the Canadian ones, has been more in tune with the Canadian landscape than was Minto. He tramped round the country on his "skees"; galloped over it on his black charger, Sampson. He hunted moose on the Mattawa, shot ducks on the St. Clair flats, ran the rapids on the St. Jean, canoed almost daily up the Gatineau from April until mid-November when the ice began to form. He even climbed the ten-thousand-foot Mount Avalanche in the Yukon.

Above all, Minto felt a kinship with the Northwest. As Governor General, he travelled from Edmonton to Saskatoon by covered wagon, reliving his old battles during the Northwest Rebellion. Westerners, he thought, were "splendid people, one finds them refined, full of energy and one sighs to think of the stupid duchesses to be found in the old country." His attitude towards Canadian Indians was remarkably enlightened. In 1885, as an aide, he had disagreed profoundly with Lansdowne's advice to the Queen that Riel must be hanged. After the rebellion, as the historian Carman Miller reports in his study, *The Canadian Career of the Fourth Earl of Minto*, he was horrified and embarrassed by Lansdowne's "sneering reception of Poundmaker, the great Cree chief whom they met in captivity. . . . To Melgund, Poundmaker appeared 'all dignity,' saying through the interpreter that he was so honoured in meeting the representative of the Queen and so regretted the circumstances under which he met him." Fifteen years later, Minto was equally horrified by the efforts of the Department of the Interior to stamp out Indian culture. "I cannot help thinking of the Highlander's kilt, a far more barbaric dress than that of any Red Indian, and the

Highland Sports, conducted in a scarcity of costume positively appalling to many – followed by a dance which I can only suppose would ruin forever all reserves in the Northwest," he wrote to Laurier in 1903, in an unsuccessful attempt to have the ban on tribal dancing lifted. (In later years, as Viceroy of India, Minto treated East Indians with equal dignity and infuriated King Edward by appointing a Hindu lawyer to the Viceroy's Council.)

With French Canadians – those French Canadians at any rate who did not make rude remarks like "*mort aux Anglais*" – Minto also got on famously. Like most gentlemen of the era, he was charmed by Emilie Lavergne. On a snowy afternoon in December 1902, we find him taking tea with her at her new home in Montreal, hearing out her bitter complaints "against the nouveau riche English for the absolute cold shoulder they give the French," as he reported in his diary, where he reached the conclusion, "I must say, I do think the British very narrow." It was a measure of the considerable power that Emilie still wielded, even though now removed from the centre of affairs, that a few days later Minto summoned to his office several prominent citizens of Montreal to discuss ways of improving French-English relations.

Lady Minto, even more than her husband, deserved to have been painted by Sargent. She would have fitted perfectly into that Sargent study that, better than any other, as Barbara Tuchman has remarked, expresses the ideal of feminine aristocracy of the period, the dazzling group portrait of three of her good friends, the former Wyndham sisters, Lady Elcho, Mrs. Adeane, and Mrs. Tennant, that now hangs in the Metropolitan Museum in New York. As we can tell from a middling-good portrait that does exist, painted by Robert Harris at Rideau Hall in 1902 (the mouth was wrong, Minto thought, the hair too dark), she was "not quite beautiful [as Amaryllis put it], but an extremely pretty woman with charming manners and very bright and lively." As we can tell further from contemporary photographs, Lady Minto dressed like a dream. "The Countess has been electrifying Ottawa with the beauty of her gowns," reported Amaryllis during the week of Opening of Parliament in 1900. "At the Opening it was rose satin laid in white panels slashed half way up, showing a petticoat of cream lace beneath. . . . At the State Dinner, the gown was blue satin, fairly glowing when the light caught it. . . . At the Drawing Room, rich white satin, embroidered with maple leaves in diamond sequins."

Lady Minto in 1899. She was a fringe member of the coterie known as "The Souls," and she dressed like a dream.

Mary Minto – "Polly" as she was known to her friends – was fourteen years younger than Minto and considerably more cultured and accomplished. Her late father, Sir Charles Grey, had been first Prince Albert's and later Queen Victoria's private secretary. In her youth, she had been a fringe member of "The Souls," that celebrated coterie of languid, literate, self-consciously clever aristocrats centred round Arthur Balfour and George Curzon. Her closest friend was the celebrated Mrs. Willie Grenfell, later to become Lady Desborough, one of the central female figures among The Souls, satirized by Max Beerbohm in *Maltby and Braxton*.

Given this background, her marriage to Minto in 1883 had surprised everybody, not least Polly herself. "Melgund had made

Lady Minto's boudoir at Rideau Hall in 1901. The Edwardian style is evident in the cheerful chintz slipcovers, and the plethora of family photographs, in silver frames, scattered around artlessly. Evident too is Lady Minto's love of flowers, even though the month was November and only potted chrysanthemums seem to have been available.

many bets against his marriage," she tells us in her own memoir, *Myself When Young*, published in 1938 as one of a collection of period reminiscences edited by Margot Asquith, "and had always led me to believe he preferred to be a freelance, ready at an hour's notice to start on active service for Timbuctoo or Madagascar, so when he asked me to marry him, I was almost as surprised as were his numerous friends." Still, the Mintos seem to have gotten on with each other better than most married couples in the circles in which they travelled. In the privacy of their bedroom – or at least of such of their intimate correspondence as survives – he was always "Rolly" and she "My Loving Girl" or "Dearest Squidge." "It is quite dreadful my girl having gone and your boy hates it," wrote Rolly on October 10, 1899, after seeing her off on a trip to England. "I was told how beautiful you looked on the bridge in your sailor's hat. Your boy told you so too – and why you shd. disguise yourself with those awful cigarettes is a wonder to me." The Mintos, however, were Edwardians, and in the Edwardian scheme of things, having a lover was not the least bit incompatible with having a happy marriage.

In Ottawa, as Amaryllis noted early on, Lady Minto was "clearly not so interested in politics as Lady Aberdeen." That was putting it mildly. She was, however, much taken by Laurier – who among women was not? – and described him forty years later as "a French Canadian of exceptional charm and distinction who soon became an habitué of Government House." No doubt she saw in Laurier a figure who, thanks to Emilie's tutelage, would have fitted in splendidly among The Souls. She spent much time arranging flowers, Amaryllis reports, and redesigning the gardens at Rideau Hall. She also used her influence to improve the condition of Ottawa's deplorably muddy and potholed streets and it was largely at her instigation that, in order to provide a more attractive carriageway to Government House, a pretty new wrought-iron bridge was built across the Rideau to connect with a new tree-lined boulevard named King Edward Avenue.

Lady Minto's real passion was skating. Much to Ottawans' discomfiture, she was much better both at waltzing and at the new style of large figures than anyone in the capital. "There are not many men in Ottawa who skate sufficiently well to show Lady Minto off to advantage," Amaryllis reported. To compensate, she imported each season from the United States the professional World Champion, George Meagher, who, when not whirling around the ice with the Countess, found time to coach the locals at twenty-five cents a lesson. She founded, and left behind as a permanent legacy, the Minto Skating Club, which half a century later produced Barbara Ann Scott. Even a messy compound fracture of the right ankle suffered on the last day of the 1904 skating season failed to deter Lady Minto. The ankle was never the same again she tells us, nevertheless, in 1929, eleven years before her death in 1940, she celebrated her seventieth birthday at the Westminster Ice Club in London. "I waltzed to favourite tunes and skimmed the whole length of the rink on a back rocker, bringing back the happy remembrance of youthful pleasures."

In the way of all new tenants of Rideau Hall, the Mintos quickly set about reshaping it in their own image. Any lingering photographs of Gladstone were taken down. "The establishment was too awful," wrote Minto to his brother on Christmas Day 1898, leaving no doubt of his opinion of the previous regime. "Punctuality for anything quite unknown – dinner sometimes not til 10 P.M. – people meeting their own tradesmen here at Government House." Minto Style, in its outward manifestation, was all pomp, circumstance, and punctiliousness, for to the Edwardians, form and appearance were crucially important. "The mere smartening up of things seems to have pleased everyone," he continued to his brother the following March. "Even the people *not* now asked to state functions as far as we can judge approve." Along with purging the guest list, the Mintos reinstated strict viceregal etiquette. "For the State Dinner last Thursday," Minto went on, "we went strictly by precedence, and only men to dinner and only their wives and daughters to the reception afterwards . . . formerly, as far as I can make out, there was a huge crowd of people quite unentitled to official recognition."

Some Ottawans greeted the new order with disappointment and chagrin. "The skating people seem to be the only ones Their Excellencies care for," the Parliamentary Librarian, Martin Griffin, wrote crossly to Lady Aberdeen. "They do not seem willing or able to lead in any direction." But for those privileged few given the entrée, the Government House atmosphere had never been more salubrious. For the most part, these intimates were a youngish, sporting, unmarried set. Amaryllis was in, not because she was a working journalist but in spite of it, because back in the eighties, as a debutante, she had belonged to "The Wanderers," an exclusive snowshoeing coterie of which the Mintos had been founders. In also were the four vivacious Ritchie sisters, Beatrice, Elsie, Grace, and Amy, all daughters of a former Chief Justice, and Annie and Jessie Clarke, a merry pair of sisters who kept spinsters' hall in the pretty Gothic Revival stone house at the edge of the Rideau Hall grounds that is now the Norwegian Embassy.* The group further included a clutch of dashing militia officers, most notably Agar Adamson, from whom we heard at the beginning of this chapter and from whom, thanks to his letters and diaries, we shall later hear a good deal more.

For these lucky Ottawans, much of the fun was celebrity-watching. For fashionable Londoners and fashionable New Yorkers, a visit to Rideau Hall had become chic in a way that it had not been since Lorne and Louise had departed. According to season, there were always strolling across the lawns or skating on one of the two rinks, any number of glamorous visitors, many of whose names, indeed, ring more bells with us than they did with Canadians of the time. The house party of Christmas 1900, for instance, included the twenty-five-year-old Boer War hero Winston Churchill. Ostensibly, Churchill had come to town to give a lecture; really, he was in hot pursuit of another guest, the exquisite, shimmering Pamela Plowden,

* These Ritchie sisters were the cousins, a generation removed, of the diplomat-diarist and his brother Roland, who himself became a justice of the Supreme Court. Amy, the youngest sister, was also the mother of Charles Ritchie's wife, Sylvia.

a particular flame of Dufferin's eldest son, the glamorous Lord Ava.

The Clarke sisters, or the McLeod Clarkes as they preferred to be known, were pivotal figures in Ottawa society for many years, not least because, as the grand-daughters of Thomas MacKay, the contractor who had built Rideau Hall, they enjoyed the freedom of the viceregal grounds. In 1924, in the satirical novel, *The Land of Afternoon*, by the Ottawa writer Madge Macbeth, they were lampooned as the Angus-McCallums. "Two sisters with generous florid cheeks and rotund figures who . . . seemed to lie fatly on the surface of every function, rather like cream on a pan of milk."

"spoken of as one of the great beauties of London with many hearts at her feet," as Amaryllis reported. The other guests made equally good copy: the Scottish MP, Ian Malcolm, who would shortly marry Lily Langtry's daughter, Jeanne; Mr. Reuter, son of the founder "of the great telegram company"; Cecil Baring of the London banking Barings; not to mention Charles Dana Gibson, the great American illustrator who had long since inspired every girl in Ottawa to dress her hair in the style of his Gibson Girl and whose model was his wife, the beautiful Irene Langhorne of Virginia, elder sister of the rumbustious Nancy, who later became Lady Astor. "He is a very good-looking lion," Amaryllis reported of Gibson. "Everyone wanted to hear him roar and he wanted to go off quietly and talk to some nice girl." There was also Mrs. Mabel Dodge, the New York society hostess, who entranced Minto with her zither-playing, and who later became notorious for her flaming affair with the revolutionary journalist, John Reed.

Out of that company, in an uncharacteristic lapse of political judgement, Amaryllis picked the MP, Malcolm, "bright, jolly and clever," as the comer. "Imperial Federation is marching along surely and silently," he told her in an interview. Churchill, by contrast, was a glum and glowering young man "with a sphinx-like countenance," who seemed quite incapable of small talk. "Not the kind of man who shines at a supper party," she reported. "In fact one rather fancies he despises fashionable society."* To be fair, Churchill may have been put off by Emilie Lavergne's rudeness to him about the Boers. He may also have been depressed because Pamela Plowden had turned down his proposal of marriage yet one more time. "We had no painful discussions," he wrote to his mother, Jennie, from Ottawa, "but there is no doubt in my mind that she is the only woman I could ever live happily with." In any event, Amaryllis found the lion of the following winter, 1901, even slower going. "He is not the easiest person in the world to converse with," she wrote of the dapper young Italian inventor, Signor Guglielmo Marconi. "He has not much to say unless the subject be wireless telegraphy, and the majority of Ottawa society people have not a great deal of conversation at their disposal on that subject."

But for Amaryllis and Agar Adamson and everyone else in the inner circle, the most fun of all was keeping abreast of "Minto's Folly," the romantic intrigue being conducted right under their noses.

"Minto's Folly" was Lola Powell. She was less than half his age, twenty-five at the most when the affair began, though twenty is

* On the same page of that same issue of *Saturday Night* (January 5, 1901), that paper's drama critic, the pseudonymous *Lance*, was far more prescient. Having reviewed Churchill's lecture in Toronto the previous week, he reported: "He is a capital lecturer, there can be no doubt about that. In the first place, he has an abundant self-confidence. In the second place, he has a resonant and not unmusical voice. In the third place, he has an inexhaustible vein of humour. And in the fourth place, he is a real artist in the manipulation of a simple, old-fashioned, Anglo-Saxon vocabulary. . . . He is a youth going to make either a shining mark, or a dismal failure of the future."

probably closer to the mark. (Her birthday was April 9, Minto informs us in his diary three years running – but never says *which* birthday.) She belonged to the social ascendancy that was already coming to be known as "Old Ottawa," the third daughter of the late William Francis Powell, a former member of the Ontario legislature and later Sheriff of Carleton County. One of her elder brothers was Ottawa's Chief of Police. She lived with her mother and her younger sister, Maud, a debutante of 1898, in a grey stone house called Edgewood, just opposite the gates of Rideau Hall, a house that nowadays, much added on to, is the South African Embassy.

A skating party at Rideau Hall during the Minto era. Lola Powell, in her white coat, stands sixth from the right in the second row, looking towards Minto, seated front row centre, with Lady Minto on his left. Second from the right, in the back row, in a bowler and waistcoat, arms akimbo, is Agar Adamson.

Lola was tall and dark, with blue eyes. "She's so pretty, I admire her immensely," noted the diarist Ethel Chadwick who, though several years younger, became a close friend. From a number of surviving photographs, we can understand immediately the source of Minto's attraction to her. Amid bevies of dimpled fair-haired maidens, Lola stood out, not so much for beauty as for smouldering intensity. In a carefully-posed group photograph of a Rideau Hall skating party, one's eye fixes instantly on Lola, standing sixth from the left in the second row, wearing the only white coat in the crowd and a flamboyant hat, and, in contrast to everyone else in the picture, looking directly not towards the camera, but at Minto, wearing a fur hat in the front centre. Most revealing of all is an astonishing studio portrait of 1904, in which Lola, with her magnificent swath of hair set loose, and string after string of beads around her neck, has chosen to pose as an eastern siren, reclining on a leopard skin, much in the manner of the novelist Elinor Glyn, paramour of Lord Curzon, then serving as Viceroy of India, the office that Minto would next succeed to.

In fact, however much her looks belied it, Lola seems to have been in most of her pursuits a rather unsophisticated Ottawa girl. Following Minto's lead, one of her favourite pastimes was *skilöbning* on the hills round Rockliffe. At parties, she was always in demand

Would you like to sin
With Elinor Glyn
on a tiger skin?
Or would you prefer
To err with her
Upon some other fur?

Lola Powell, in fact, has chosen a leopard skin on which to pose. In all other respects, the demeanour of "Minto's Folly" suggests Elinor Glyn, the novelist and mistress of Lord Curzon, whom Minto succeeded as Viceroy to India in 1905. The photograph was taken in April 1904, six months before Minto left Ottawa.

to play the piano for singsongs, "choruses," as they were known in those days; she always knew all the new "coonsongs," as in "All Coons Look Alike" and "Come Back My Honey," and all the new showtunes, like "Sing Me To Sleep" and "My Little Canoe." In her more serious moments, she taught Sunday School at the viceregal church, St. Bartholomew's, just opposite the Rideau Hall grounds, and, as Minto himself tells us proudly, she organized the annual concert. In 1901, Amaryllis reports, Lola presented "a very clever paper to the May Court Club on that fascinating woman, Lady Mary Wortley Montague."

Such moments, one speculates, were out of character. Indeed, in 1908, in Ethel Chadwick's diary, we catch Lola out, as she recycles that same paper on Lady Mary Wortley Montague at the May Court Club. As described by Ethel, Lola comes across as more than a bit of a bubblehead. She was much given to fits of the giggles, talked "a blue streak," and was extremely practised in the flirtatious banter that was known at the time as "chaffing." She was also, as we discover, very good at drawing attention to herself. "Coming home in the streetcar, explosions started in the motor," Chadwick reports on one occasion. "Lola was in a wild state of real or pretended terror." Above all, though Ethel Chadwick was much too naïve to be aware of it, Lola was a totally sensual being. "She's funny, always eager about anything pertaining to men," in Ethel's innocent words.

It was not until mid-October 1899, nearly a year after he arrived in Canada, that Minto began keeping his Canadian diary regularly. Thus we have no notion of how and when his liaison with Lola began. She first pops up in the Minto Papers on June 17, 1899, in, of all places, a letter to Lady Minto, who was away at the viceregal summer retreat, Stanley House. "I haven't seen Miss Lola yet, but I only arrived this morning," reported Minto, himself just back from a military review at Niagara. Three weeks later, it becomes clear that he has been seeing Lola nearly every day – mostly in a canoe. "I took Lola out before dinner," he continues to Lady Minto. Later that same week, in a letter of July 13, Minto breezes on merrily about a "splendid" canoeing picnic down the Ottawa River that had included – safety in numbers – a dozen other guests:

> Our party went off splendidly yesterday – except that we had one heavy storm and got wet. We paddled down to Templeton 7 miles. I took Lola. We went on board the steamer at Templeton & had tea & came back in her, getting home about 9 p.m. – then supper in the dining room – and then sang songs and danced in the dining room!! Lola and Bill played by turns – and Lawless danced a cake-dance. I had visions of Lady Aberdeen emerging from under a sofa.

"I don't like entertainments without my loving girl," Minto was careful to add. Doubtless, he was convinced that by keeping everything out in the open, he could forestall trouble. By now, though, people were beginning to talk. Amaryllis herself had not been on the picnic, but at least one of her sources had been. She published a full account in the next issue of *Saturday Night*, and somehow, in cold hard print, the whole thing shrieked with innuendo:

> The young woman who had the honour of being paddled by Lord Minto was Miss Lola Powell. His Excellency has a fine little canoe and is as expert with a paddle as any Canadian. He enjoys it immensely too. While the flotilla of canoes was drifting down the river, some rain fell but "when you're in the shade with a very pretty maid, it doesn't

much matter what the weather may do" and it is much the same in a canoe. . . . A steamer hove in sight and canoes and canoeists were taken aboard. The steamer was loafing about the river by the express command of His Excellency. . . . It was moonlight that evening, so the steamer did not hasten to the city, but when the party was landed at Rockcliffe, His Excellency led the way to Government House. . . .

Lady Minto was not amused. The precise words of her reproach to Minto are lost to history, but the tone of his next few replies suggests what they may have been. *July 15*: "I can't live absolutely like a hermit – and I must go out. . . . There is absolutely no one to speak to – except of course Lola. What am I to do?" *July 17*: "I think the supper party here was a pity. . . . I don't think however there was much harm done. . . . You know your boy is idiotic about some things – but I am left quite alone here and the only individual I know well is Lola." Well into the autumn, correspondence between the Mintos on the subject of Lola continued to be heated. "I don't quite understand what you mean by watching L. at entertainments," he wrote on September 20. "I have hardly ever spoken to her at a dinner party – and at balls I thought girls were meant to be danced with – and surely if I did watch her entirely at a ball it will look very much odder than if I danced with her – the only thing I cd. do wd. be not to dance at all if I am to watch her entirely – and then no one can say anything."

Perhaps the six-week trip to Britain that Lady Minto embarked on a fortnight later, armed with a lavish cheque to spend on new gowns, represented the terms of a truce. Or perhaps "Her Ex." by then had discovered diversions of her own. Not least of her missions in London, Amaryllis informs, was to find a new aide-de-camp to replenish a household that, with Major "Lorenzo" Drummond off to the war in South Africa, had lost one of its liveliest members. In any event, some kind of *modus vivendi* had clearly been reached, for far from fading out of Minto's life, Lola continued to be part of it to the very day of his departure from Ottawa in November 1904. The staccato entries in Minto's diary describe the affair unfolding, as, for example, the following selection, taken at random from February/March 1902:

13 Feb. Op. Parliament with usual functions – was cheered very loudly for Canada where they do not as a rule cheer. . . . On getting home, went skiing with Miss Lola.

21 Feb. Skied alone to Rockliffe, such a glorious full moon and met Miss Lola on the way back, and went part of the way home with her.

24 Feb.	To see Miss Lola who is not well, with a bad cold.
25 Feb.	Five o'clock tea with Miss Lola, still not well enough to go out.
3 March	After luncheon to see Miss Lola.
6 March	To see Miss Lola after luncheon.
10 March	In the evening, the LeMoine's skating party. Polly led the march with LeMoine, self and Miss Lola the second pair.
25 March	To see Sir Wilfrid . . . to see Miss Lola for a short time.
26 March	Rode Sampson, first ride of the year . . . rode down to Edgewood, and Miss Lola walked beside me to the Keefers, where there was a maple sugar party.

Lola and Minto could scarcely bear to be out of each other's company. Earlier in that winter of 1902 when the vice-royals went to Quebec City to spend a week, we find Lola aboard the train with them, having arranged conveniently to visit friends. In 1900, Amaryllis reports, she was one of only two "locals" invited to an intimate Boxing Day dinner for the Churchill-Plowden house party.

Lola Powell in 1901. When she married, in 1911, Minto sent a bracelet made of diamonds and sapphires.

Although we cannot know for certain, it is impossible to believe they were not lovers, and certainly at the time, as Adamson's comment is witness, everyone believed them to be so. Minto was clearly aware of all the talk, and it seems inconceivable that as an ambitious man, he would have taken such risks with his reputation for a relationship that involved no more than giggles and shrieks in "My Little Canoe." Even for governors general, *droit de seigneur* extended only so far; even King Edward himself, as was well known, never trifled with young, unmarried girls. As for Lola, she, like Emilie Lavergne, seems rather to have encouraged the gossip. Plenty of Edwardian belles were only teases, for whom the chase was all and who, when quarried at last in the marriage bed, closed their eyes, as the saying went, and thought of England. But Lola, from all that we know of her, was sensual and uninhibited.

A puzzling question remains: exactly when and where did they manage to be lovers? The multi-layered clothes of the day – even the simple shirtwaists worn in canoes – made brief encounters out of the question. Lola, further, even supposing her mother and sister were broadminded, would have lived constantly under the surveillance of servants who, unlike proper British servants, could not be counted on not to talk. Minto's aides would have been discreet, and guaranteed to disappear at the right moment – still, even in say, the Cricket Pavilion at Rideau Hall with Lady Minto safely out of town, there would always have been the danger of some half-trained footman barging in with another plate of cucumber sandwiches. Even in the "Royal Shanty," in the Rockcliffe Woods, a hut built in 1901 to demonstrate to the Duke and Duchess of York how a lumber camp worked, there was always the possibility of being happened upon by a jolly party of *skilöbners*. Still less could these two have found anonymous refuge at the Russell House.

A voyeuristic scrutiny of Minto's diaries suggests a couple of possible solutions. There were, in the summers, their canoeing excursions; not the merry river picnics, but the long private excursions ten or a dozen miles up the Gatineau that occasionally, as on the afternoon of July 17, 1904, they embarked on. "Paddle with Lola," Minto wrote that day, "up to the Alonzo Wright bridge, 1 hr 45 minutes hard paddling." Quite easily, given an absence of pesky lumbermen, could they have managed a ramble into the woods. At other times, one suspects, they depended upon the discreet collusion of certain intimate friends. Lola's closest confidantes were the Clarke sisters, whose house was big and roomy with a cosy upstairs library and Minto, as we know from his diary, frequently dropped in unaccompanied for tea, and found Lola there. Indeed, in 1902, when the Clarkes rented the place to General Dundonald, the newly-appointed militia commander, Minto was decidedly put out. "Can't say how I miss the Clarkes and the possibility of dropping in for tea," he wrote on December 17.

One episode of the affair between Minto and Lola, as recorded in Minto's diary, might well have been scripted by Feydeau. The date was September 12, 1903, a sunny golden afternoon. Lady Minto, as it happened, was out of town, indeed, well out of the country, aboard a steamer that was bound for Japan. Lola, who had been visiting friends in the Thousand Islands, had taken this cue to return to town. "To my surprise, a note from Lola," wrote Minto. "She is to stay with the Clarkes at their little shack." (The Clarkes had recently built themselves a summer cottage in the Rockcliffe woods.)

The two spent most of the day on the river, sailing Minto's new clinker-built dinghy. Towards evening, dishevelled and windswept, they ambled up towards Rockcliffe from the private viceregal boathouse. As they passed Edgewood, standing shuttered and empty, they stopped for a moment, and Lola got out her key. "L. wanted to pick up some things," Minto explains. Then he continues:

> Found that Miss L's house had been burglarized. I was waiting at the door while L. went upstairs and heard her call out and went up – her things were strewn all over the room, her desk broken open.

This was a decidedly sticky wicket, Minto realized, as he heard or imagined he heard, a scuffle of footsteps downstairs. Alone with Lola in her bedroom, he was in an extremely compromising situation:

> I was not at all sure that there was not someone in the house. The whole position was so difficult, that I was not inclined to stay for too long.

How, though, could he extricate himself?

> Unfortunately, the telephone was broken. I had to go next door to telephone for her brother, the Chief of Police. In the meantime, I met a messenger boy outside and sent him up for Joe Maude [Drummond's replacement as Military Secretary] to come at once, after which the police arrived.

Luckily for all concerned, this viceregal foray into bedroom farce seems to have passed unnoticed. Amaryllis, even at her nerviest, would scarcely have dared report it. Minto, vastly relieved, adds the epilogue:

> After dinner, I walked over to the Clarkes and saw L. again. She has lost one or two things she was fond of but nothing very serious. . . . The amusing thing is, she will have it that it was only the New Edinburgh boys. I tried to explain that to me it somewhat resembled burglary, but there seems to be a distinction between the boys and the burglars, the former take only jewellery out of their New Edinburgh light-heartedness, the genuine burglar chloroforms the owner of the house, and wears a mask. . . .

As in the case of their first meeting, Minto's diary doesn't record the circumstances of his and Lola's final parting. All we know is that on November 2, 1904, she was one of the guests at "our last dinner party, a small one for friends," and that Minto at the end of it, "felt sad indeed."

Nor do we know whether, prior to Minto's death in 1914, after he had served as Curzon's successor as Viceroy of India, he and Lola ever met again. However, we learn from Ethel Chadwick's diary that far from fading into obscurity, Lola reigned as a belle for another seven years. She relished her celebrity status and considered herself, as Ethel describes it in 1906, "a sort of attaché to Government House." In 1908, we find her at the Rideau Hall skating rink vying with Ethel for the attention of Lord Lascelles, the future Earl of Harewood and future brother-in-law of King George VI, who was then serving as one of the aides to Minto's successor (and brother-in-law), Earl Grey. "Lola was getting after me for cutting her out," Ethel reports, but it was to Ethel and not to Lola that Lascelles sent a postcard of the palace at Udaipur from his next posting in India. But for Lola, as for Scarlett O'Hara, tomorrow was always another day. In 1910, we find her giving a dashing little tea in honour of one Commander Roper, an adviser sent from Britain to help establish the new defence force that Laurier's opponents described as the "tinpot navy." "They all talked about how impious they were," Ethel reports. "They gloried in it." Along with becoming impious, Lola had also become a terrible snob. In 1912, we find her married and living in Dublin, refusing to call on an old friend from Ottawa. "Lola hasn't seen Winifred," reports the reliable Ethel, "because her husband, being in trade, wouldn't go down with the people she was with."

In truth, Lola herself had married only one rung above trade. Her husband, one Captain Eric Charles, whom she appears to have met while on an extended visit to the British Isles in 1910, belonged to the Royal Engineers, rather than to a *real* regiment, like the Brigade of Guards or the Rifle Brigade. Still, even by the most tactful of estimates, Lola was beginning to "get on," as the saying went, and was by now well into her thirties. "At last she's engaged," reported Ethel who, much to her own chagrin, at twenty-nine was not. "Beautiful Lola getting married not to any Lord or title – however, a soldier is always pretty nice."

The Powell-Charles wedding, on April 20, 1911, was the event of that year's social season. A surpliced choir sang, "The Voice that Breathed O'er Eden" and "O Perfect Love," and the bride wore ivory charmeuse satin. "Christ Church Cathedral was thronged by a very interested congregation," reported Amaryllis's somewhat pedestrian successor, "all anxious to do homage to the lovely bride who has been one of the Capital's greatest favourites." The week before, in an astonishing breach of convention, Lola and Captain Charles had been dined out at the new Country Club by all the dashing bachelors of Ottawa. "After dinner there were lots of speeches," reported Ethel, "some very funny things were said. After dinner, we sang choruses, and Lola played." At Lola's trousseau tea, Ethel noted enviously, "nearly $3,000 in cheques." She noted further, but without comment, "a handsome diamond and sapphire bracelet from Lord Minto."

"The celebrated Lola Powell is no more," Ethel Chadwick concluded.

CHAPTER 22

"'Follow the ADC"

Follow the ADC,
The Wonderful ADC,
Tis twenty to one
He'll show you some fun
If you follow the ADC.

song from the musical extravaganza,
The Princess and the Pauper,
written, produced, and directed
at Rideau Hall in January 1900 by
Captain Harry Graham, Coldstream Guards.

Chacun à sa chacune, the Edwardians said. Whether Lady Minto, while Minto was canoeing with Lola, was herself canoodling with Harry Graham is a matter on which we have no more evidence than Agar Adamson's cheeky insinuations. "Her Ex. and Captain Graham are amusing themselves alone in New York," he'd written to his wife in the letter of April 1901. We have, however, plenty of evidence from countless period reminiscences that the ladies of Lady Minto's set allowed themselves a new and distinctly un-Victorian freedom. The English diarist, Cynthia Asquith, once described a conversation between herself and Lady Minto's great friend, Lady Desborough. "We discussed 'lovers,' and their compatibility with happy marriages. She said she was not monogamous in the strict sense of the word, and had never been in love in the way which excluded other personal relations. To be at her best with one man, she must see a great many others." That was putting it tactfully, for Ettie Desborough was notorious in her circle for her torrid affairs with younger men, most notably, on the eve of the First World War, with the dashing hedonist Patrick Shaw-Stewart, who was also the best friend of her eldest son, Julian Grenfell.

We know, further, that during her first sojourn at Rideau Hall during 1883-85, while Minto was an aide, Lady Minto had found the capital unspeakably boring. Largely at her urging, Minto cut his term short by two years, much to Lansdowne's fury. Thus, although it was in March 1898 that Minto began lobbying to get the governor-generalcy, it was well into June before he steeled himself to tell his wife. "My hand was forced, owing to some chance remark of Polly's about an invitation to dinner at the Chamberlains," he wrote in his diary. "She was very good about it." Although Minto does not record it, it seems likely that Polly, as quid pro quo, insisted on choosing a set of courtiers to her own liking.

Whatever the case, the aides Minto brought with him to Canada had certainly not been selected for their political acumen. In 1904, right on the eve of the American presidential election, Captain Harry Graham committed the egregious gaffe of publishing a poem lampooning Teddy Roosevelt in an American magazine. He, however, was only following the lead established a year earlier by Captain Bell who had written to the *New York Times* to complain about, of all things, Chamberlain's Imperial Preference tariff policy. And neither Bell nor Graham was a patch on the Rideau Hall comptroller, Arthur Guise, who, on a viceregal trip to the Yukon in 1900, had taken it upon himself to punch out a burly American prospector of pro-Boer sympathies in a Dawson City bar. On the same trip, during a stopover at Banff, Guise and Graham had caused a furor by skinny-dipping in the swimming pool at the Banff Springs Hotel.

Lady Minto pretended not to notice. "Our congenial staff took up their duties with a splendid *joie de vivre*," she tells us in her memoir. Her only real problem child among the aides, we learn from Amaryllis, was a certain Captain Mann, whom she had particularly sought out for his skating abilities while back in Britain in the fall of 1899. On the ice, Captain Mann did not disappoint. In March 1900, for instance, we find him performing all manner of tricks at a winter carnival. "The first figure was the paper hoop," Amaryllis reported. "A number of ladies stood at one end of the rink, men at the other, and paper hoops between, to be jumped through before the ladies were reached. Captain Mann distinguished himself by a flying leap through one of the hoops. He went headfirst, landing flat on the ice at the other side. He was on his feet in a second, and carried off Her Excellency." Nor was Mann at a loss for social aplomb. The following May, in the wake of a disastrous fire that had wiped out most of Ottawa's working-class district round the Chaudière Falls, we find him ministering to the refugees housed in the military drill shed at Cartier Square. "Captain Mann was invited by the ladies serving the evening meal to assist by pouring tea," Amaryllis reported. "He was resplendent in immaculate morning dress; it was funny to see him giving tea from a huge tin teapot, while in his other hand he held silk hat and lavender gloves." On that occasion, Mann had been accompanying the Minto children on a *noblesse oblige* mission to the fire victims; Amaryllis, in her deadpan reportage provides a period setpiece:

> These jolly young people came with a carriage-full of toys; a veritable Santa Claus carriage, and the homeless boys and girls were drawn up in a line outside the drill hall and each one was made happy by the presentation of a toy. It was worthwhile being burnt-out, some of them thought. Afterwards, they gave three cheers for their kind little friends from Government House. . . . They were led by the Sergeant-Major, which may account for the quality of the cheer.

Captain Mann, however, did disappoint by his lack of attention to his most important duties, sufficiently so to cause his early dismissal. "I believe he had a very poor memory," Amaryllis wrote. "On a certain occasion last winter, Lord and Lady Minto decided to give an extra skating party. The cards were written, and on the afternoon appointed, the viceregal host and hostess were ready to receive their guests. The band played; the tea and coffee steamed away. By four o'clock, something was known to be wrong, for nobody came. The ADCs were interrogated, and it dawned upon one of them that he had forgotten to send out the cards."

Neither Graham nor Bell nor Guise, despite their peccadilloes, would ever have been caught out in such a lapse. From the accounts of Amaryllis, from Minto's diaries, from our own first-hand inspection of them in their swords and gold braid in contemporary photographs, these three emerge as having been quintessential viceregal cavaliers, fulfilling the job description for Government House aides drafted by Amaryllis in 1900: "He should be young, not married or engaged. He should be good-looking, bright in conversation, skate well and dance well – or at least, neither too badly. And he must have a sufficiently good memory to remember names as well as faces."

Of this trio, Graham was *primus inter pares*. Whether or not there was anything to the rumours about his and Lady Minto's inclinations towards each other, he brought to his task remarkable panache. At a time when the notion of an officer of the Coldstream Guards exhibiting genuine talent as a writer and actor would have been frowned on as "middle-class," Graham liked to parody himself as a typical, "silly-ass" stage Englishman. "A Scotchman by

The Earl of Minto and his aides in May 1899. Standing, l. to r., Captain Lascelles, Arthur Guise, Major Lawrence Drummond, Captain Harry Graham.

birth, an Englishman by occupation," he wrote, "a dilettante with a turn for writing inferior doggerel, a taste for literature, an ear for music and a prodigious thirst." In fact, Graham's turn for "inferior doggerel," although not accomplished enough to win him a place in *The Oxford Book of Light Verse*, was relished by his contemporaries and remembered by them years later when they came to write their memoirs. In *Close of an Era*, a delightful 1944 exercise in nostalgia by the bon-vivant, Percy Colson, we find perhaps the best of Graham quoted, a short poem called "Grandpapa" from a collection titled *Strained Relations*:

In politics it was his rule
To be broadminded but despotic
In argument he kept quite cool
Knowing a man to be a fool
And most unpatriotic
Who differed from the views that he
Had cherished from the age of three.

Graham established himself quickly as the resident actor-manager at Rideau Hall. Each year, under the sobriquet "Col. D. Streamer," he wrote, directed, produced, and starred in a musical extravaganza presented in the ballroom to an audience of Official Ottawans who rose to the occasion by dressing as elaborately as for an opening night at Covent Garden. "No horrid theatre hats to disturb one's peace of mind," wrote Amaryllis approvingly. From surviving programmes preserved in old scrapbooks, we can tell that Graham's productions were in fact British pantomimes: classic fairy tales spruced up with plenty of local references and by the addition of new characters with names like the Prince of Kintumpoo and Miss Lottie Longsox. The Minto's three pretty daughters, Eileen, Ruby, and Violet, took turns at being principal boy. "A clever pack of nonsense, put together by an artist in that line of business," wrote Amaryllis in 1899 of Graham's first effort, *The Babes in the Woods*. "The local hits were capital, especially that little play on our Canadian idiom, 'on' instead of 'in' Sussex Street." Next year came *The Princess and the Pauper* with Graham horsing around as a character called the Duke of Karaboo. "I must say that Captain Graham is the only amateur actor I have ever seen who did not overdo a drunken part," wrote Amaryllis, who, as we shall eventually discover, had the theatre in her blood. We have Minto's word for it that

The Minto children, in costume for the pantomime, The Babes in the Woods, *in 1899. L. to r., Larry (Lord Melgund), Lady Violet, Lady Eileen, and Lady Ruby Elliott. A few years later, Mackenzie King fancied himself in love with Lady Ruby.*

A scene from The Babes in the Woods, *on the stage in the ballroom at Rideau Hall. On such occasions, the ballroom was described on the programme as the "Theatre Royal."*

Graham's final production in the spring of 1904, *Bluebeard*, which Lady Minto watched most dramatically from a stretcher, having been invalided by her broken ankle, constituted "Harry's triumph." But perhaps this was only because in Minto's estimation, Lola Powell, playing a character named Zisboombah, described on the programme as "Bluebeard's favourite niece," stole the show.

Captain Arthur Bell of the Scots Guards – "Cloche" Bell to everyone – was equally a showman. One morning in July 1903, he astonished Minto by appearing for breakfast "in a wonderful costume, trousers cut off at the knee and knickerbocker stockings." In his new plus fours, his goggles and duster coat, Cloche cut a dashing figure driving around Ottawa in his new motor-car, one of the capital's first. Cloche, it appears, did not lack for money. In 1901, he hired a private railway car, packed it with twenty-four members of Ottawa's smart set, and embarked for Montreal where, after a specially-ordered dinner in the private dining-room of the Windsor Hotel, the party enjoyed front-row seats at a production of Pinero's controversial new play, *The Gay Lord Quex*. He was also a generous soul who, later that year, treated all the servants at Rideau Hall to a picnic in the Gatineau Hills.

Above all, in Amaryllis's words, Bell was "a devotee of outdoor amusements." Among other pastimes, he introduced to Ottawa the sports of bicycle polo and of paperchasing. In the latter case, his accomplice was the lovely Lola Powell, who proved less fleet of foot than she was of fancy, as Agar Adamson reported to his wife, who had gone to her mother's place in Toronto to await the birth of their first child. "25 girls and 18 men gave Capt. Bell and Miss Lola Powell 10 minutes start with a bag of paper," he wrote on October 27, 1901, a "most beautiful" crisp clear day. "I, with the gallantry of the race, had to pull Miss Powell out of a bottomless ditch . . . I bust two of my trouser buttons."

There is also a suspicion, although neither Adamson nor Amaryllis substantiate it, that gossip may have linked Bell as well as Graham to Lady Minto. In 1903, when Graham was temporarily absent with his regiment, Cloche accompanied Her Excellency on a trip to New York and later that season went with her on a two-month trip to Japan, sponsored by the CPR to publicize its new line of steamships. "Polly had quite set her heart on it, though I have thrown cold water on it," Minto noted in his diary. "Cloche pays for his own ticket."

No such calumny, however, blotted the escutcheon of the Rideau Hall comptroller, Arthur Guise. Or rather, to let the full glory of his name unfurl, Arthur St. Valery Beauchamp Guise. Guise's brooding,

Lord and Lady Minto and their aides in November 1900. Arthur Guise, wearing a trilby, stands directly behind the Governor General. Harry Graham, in a double-breasted waist-coat, is behind Her Excellency who, demonstrating once again her marvellous sense of style, wears a beautifully cut "tailor-made."

black-Irish good looks were a match for his name; far and away the handsomest of the aides, his taste in women ran mostly to New York showgirls, in particular a certain Miss Sybil Kaye who, on the pretext of visiting her sister, often encountered him in Ottawa. Guise's political predilections were no less flamboyant. In Graham's description, he was "a wild warmhearted Irishman, a bonvivier of Bohemian tastes, an Imperialist with radical tendencies." As a consequence, no other aide caused Minto more political headaches. Having clashed with the pro-Boer Yankee in the Yukon in 1900, Guise somewhat contradictorily attended the following year a speech given in Ottawa by one John Redmond, an Irish Home Ruler who not long before had prayed publicly for the defeat of the British in South Africa. When word of this reached him in London, Joseph Chamberlain, the Colonial Secretary, was furious. Never again was Minto to permit "such improprieties," he wired. Minto, in his soldierly, chaps-together fashion, backed his own aide. "A bit of d. . . .d nonsense," he wrote in his diary. "How a big man like J.C. can fuss over it, I cannot understand."

Although Guise made no pretence about his dislike for Ottawa, he stayed with Minto for the full six-year term. In 1910, he popped up again in the capital, this time in the pages of Ethel Chadwick's diary. Ostensibly, he had come as relief comptroller to Lord Grey;

really, he was in hot – and this time honourably-intentioned – pursuit of another Ottawa belle turned sometime actress, Hazel Mackintosh, the daughter of a former governor of the Northwest Territories. Their wedding, which took place six months before Lola Powell's, was not as showy but infinitely classier. "Guise always liked the gay, larky sort of girl," Ethel wrote wistfully in her diary.

There was a darker edge to all the larkiness. All the love affairs, real or pretended, all the theatricals, all the paperchases, were diversions to channel benignly the pent-up energies with which the Edwardians were so richly endowed. Such energies had many sources: the easing of Victorian repression; the sheer self-confidence of the British at the height of the empire; the absence of demanding work needing to be done. Above all, perhaps, since Minto and his aides were soldiers all, there was a needling sense of frustration at being far removed from such splendid little wars as there existed to be fought. So, every now and then, in search of real excitement, the energies within the Minto household escalated from simple high jinks into a certain carelessness about life itself.

The first time this happened, on May 17, 1899, there were no fatalities. The second time, on December 6, 1901, two innocent bystanders, one named Bessie Blair and the other named Henry Albert Harper, paid the price. Only a well-orchestrated conspiracy of silence saved the governor-generalcy itself from being implicated.

Ever since 1861, when the Prince of Wales had visited Ottawa to lay the cornerstone for the Parliament Buildings, it had been the custom for distinguished visitors to the capital to be treated to a trip down the timber-chutes at the Chaudière Falls. Although this jaunt sounded only slightly less hazardous than going over Niagara in a barrel, it was in fact conducted in the most sedate circumstances, with visitors stowed regally aboard a massive and virtually untippable log crib. "It is great fun," wrote Amaryllis, "rather like the waterchute of the modern fairground."

For Minto, a former steeplechaser, the ride was undemanding. In the spring of 1899, with the Willy Grenfells visiting from London, he looked for something more exhilarating. Grenfell, after all, quite apart from being married to the most stylish woman in the Marlborough House set, was renowned as the most notable athlete in all of England. He had sculled across the English Channel in a rowboat and had twice swum the Niagara River, just below the falls, once during a snowstorm.

One Captain William Lawless, a militia officer in the Government House circle, came up with an inspiration. "He is a prominent young society man," Amaryllis wrote disapprovingly later, "perhaps more prominent in athletic circles than social, whose courage and daring are very near to the point of foolhardiness." An amusing way to entertain the Grenfells, Lawless suggested, would be to make the trip down the chutes in an ordinary rowboat. Amusement was not at all what Lady Minto remembered forty years later. Here is her account, from her memoir:

> A broad boat, twelve feet long, was chartered, which easily held our party of six. We sat on planks behind each other, two Mintos, two Grenfells, two Lawrence Drummonds. An old boatman, well used to the river, held the rudder and our pilot [Lawless] sat in front. The first two chutes were quite enjoyable but the boat was gaining a tremendous impetus as we raced on towards the final waterchute. Over we went, a drop of twenty feet into the turbulent waters. The bow of the boat was submerged, but righted itself, only to be tossed like a cork, helpless and sideways, out of control amongst the seething rapids. It was a miracle that we reached calm water in safety, and Willy Grenfell, with all his experience, told us he had never before lived through such an agonizing moment in any boat.

Next day, the Ottawa papers reported only that the Government House party had found the excursion "very jolly." Amaryllis was bolder. In the next issue of *Saturday Night*, she reported what everyone was saying. "Trying this, at this time of the year with the water so high has caused a sensation in social and other circles. The Earl of Minto confided to a friend that he had never been so frightened in his life." Amaryllis then arrived at the point. "No doubt they enjoyed it for in these days, when *ennui* is more dreaded than *la grippe*, a novel experience is well worth the danger."

The next lapse into carelessness again involved the Ottawa River. Again, the pursuit of novelty was the catalyst, this time the rare pleasure of skating upon the river, which was usually covered with snow December through March. An early winter in 1901 had made conditions perfect. A cold snap, coming before any snow fell, had transformed the whole eastward sweep of the Ottawa below the city into a shimmering rink. Or so, in any event, it seemed. "Old residents shook their heads and hinted at the treachery lurking under the broad expanse," wrote Amaryllis sombrely, in hindsight. "No one heeded these wise people."

The viceregal party skating on the Ottawa River, December 1901. This sequence of photographs, which may even have been taken on the day of Bert Harper's and Bessie Blair's tragic deaths, illustrates the fatal allure of the ice. Lord and Lady Minto are shown just downstream from Rideau Falls, the junction of the Rideau River with the Ottawa. Cloche Bell appears twice, looking directly towards the camera, with a white handkerchief tucked into his breast pocket, and in silhouette, showing one of the Minto daughters how to use a sail when skating. Given the prevailing westerly wind that blows in Ottawa, this would only have been useful when skating downstream, in the general direction of Montreal.

With Lord and Lady Minto setting the pace, no one in fashionable society could afford to be left behind. "I am off today with Their Ex's to skate . . . downriver," Agar Adamson wrote to his wife on the morning of Friday, December 6. He then went out, leaving the letter unfinished. At about two o'clock, a viceregal party of a dozen or more departed downriver from the Rideau Hall boathouse. Apart from "Their Ex's" and Adamson, it included Cloche Bell, the lively Ritchie sisters, and the usual jousting crew of militia officers. There was also a certain Mr. Treadgold, a wealthy young prospector from the Yukon. Treadgold had chosen for his particular partner the pretty Miss May Blair, a daughter of the Minister of Railways and Canals.

An hour or so later, a second group of four skaters set off in apparent pursuit of the viceregal party. It included Alex Creelman, a teller at the Imperial Bank, and Miss Jeannie Snowball, the daughter of a New Brunswick Senator. The other two were May Blair's nineteen-year-old sister, Bessie, and Henry Albert Harper, twenty-nine-year-old Assistant Deputy Minister of Labour.

Bert Harper was the close friend and room-mate of the Deputy Minister, twenty-eight-year-old William Lyon Mackenzie King, "Rex," as he was known to his friends. Both men were continually torn between the pleasures of being highly eligible and sought-after bachelors in Ottawa society and the serious business of being idealistic social reformers. They were drawn as moths to flame by the delights of rowing competitions, debutante balls, and preening at tea-time in front of impressionable young girls. "So awfully clever," wrote Ethel Chadwick in April 1901, after a King-Harper visitation, "Oh, so clever." Much more real and earnest, however, were the evenings they spent together by the fire in their cosy lodgings on Somerset Street, reading aloud to each other from the works of Matthew Arnold and William Morris and, above all, Tennyson.

Much of their friendship involved keeping tabs on each other. Bert might well have remained at the office that fine Friday in December if Rex had been in town. But he was away on a trip to British Columbia to mediate a labour dispute, and Harper yielded to the blandishments of Jeannie Snowball and Bessie Blair and Alex Creelman.

Both parties lingered on the river long after it was sensible. Agar Adamson got home about half-past six, and immediately resumed writing his letter to his wife. "I have just come back from our skating expedition. . . . On the way home, Grace and Elsie Ritchie, Miss LeMoine, Captain Bell, Gladwyn McDougall and Campbell all went through the ice up to their necks and had to jolly well swim for it, and then skate eight miles home. Grace Ritchie badly cut her face and head on the ice. It was great stupidity on the part of the men who had no right to take such chances after it became dark. Miss [May] Blair and Mr. Treadgold had not turned up when we left, and I should not be a bit surprised if they were drowned."

Minto himself, as host of the party, was equally concerned about the fate of May Blair and Treadgold. "I said to Polly I did not like leaving them out," he wrote in his diary. "But someone said they were a long way down and might possibly sleigh back. Just before dinner, I phoned to the Blairs to ask if they were back, and they were not." But neither Minto, nor Adamson, nor anyone else, had reason, at that point, to worry about Bessie.

Night had long since fallen. For those still out on the ice, it had become almost impossible to distinguish between ice that was solid, ice that was spread thinly over the water, and those deadly patches of open water where the current ran swift. Whether or not the Blair-Harper party of four had started out with the idea of catching up with the viceregal party, they had given up the attempt and were heading home. As they neared Gatineau Point, Creelman and Bessie Blair were in the lead, he pulling her along with his walking-stick, and both of them laughing. Suddenly, they felt their skates slushing through a patch of thin papery ice. Yet more suddenly, they pitched forward into open water. "Don't mind me, I can swim," shouted Bessie. Creelman clung to the edge of the ice. Jeannie Snowball dashed off to Gatineau Point for help. Harper, left alone on the solid ice, tried to pull Bessie up towards him. Flat on his stomach, he edged towards her, holding out his walking-stick. Each time he neared her, the ice cracked ominously. Each time he tried from another angle, it cracked again. Then Harper stood up, and threw off his gauntlets. "For God's sake, Harper, don't you come in too," shouted Creelman. Harper plunged into the water and swam towards Bessie. His last words, later reported by Creelman, were, "What else can I do?" Even before Harper had managed to reach Bessie, the two were pulled under the ice by the current.

Somehow, Creelman hung on, shouting time and again for help. Eventually, against all odds, he was rescued by May Blair and Treadgold, straggling upriver at the tail end of the Government House party. "It was not for some time that they realized that the 'Miss Blair' the half-drowned man was talking about was Miss Bessie and not Miss May Blair," Amaryllis reported in *Saturday Night*. "Then the awful truth flashed to them."

"P.S. I have just heard that Miss Bessie Blair and a chap named Harper were drowned," scribbled Adamson, in the third and final take of his letter, written around nine o'clock that night. "She was a nice little girl, just out."

The next day, the Ottawa papers carried front-page articles complete with photographs of the victims as well as interviews with Creelman and reports from eyewitnesses who earlier had seen the merry foursome whizzing down the river. References to the viceregal skating party, however, were kept to the barest minimum. No reference was made to the fact that members of the group led by Minto had also narrowly escaped drowning. Even Amaryllis went out of her way to make the point that neither Bessie nor Harper had been in any way connected with the viceregal party.

Nor did Minto, in what was for him a quite lengthy diary account, commit to paper any feelings of guilt. Indeed, unlike Adamson, he made no mention of any of the mishaps within his own party, still less did he suggest that he or any of his aides might have behaved recklessly or set a foolhardy example. Minto's actions, however, belied his words. He first despatched Lady Minto to comfort the stricken Blair household. (In fact, the senior Blairs turned out to be away.) Then, he and Cloche Bell rushed off to the boathouse, "where we found Treadgold seeing to getting Creelman home." Next, he summoned Colonel Percy Sherwood, the chief, not of the regular city police, but of the Dominion Police, the security force of the day. As Minto wrote later, "I strongly advised Sherwood to recover the bodies the next morning." Shortly after first light, Sherwood telephoned Minto to say that Bessie Blair's body had been found. "When I got there, they had also found Harper," Minto reported. "I stayed with the bodies until they were taken away. Neither of them showed any signs of struggle, and their faces were full of colour. . . . I did not know Harper but he seems to have been a most promising young fellow, and behaved most gallantly."

No inquest was held. Instead, all of fashionable Ottawa attended one or the other of the two funeral services, held on Monday, December 9. That of Bessie Blair, as the daughter of a cabinet minister, attracted both the Mintos, their senior aides, and Agar Adamson. At Harper's funeral, at St. Andrew's Church, Minto was represented by his Military Secretary, Major Maude. On December 13, the May Court Club cancelled its regular meeting out of respect for its deceased member, Bessie Blair, but the following week, Lola Powell read out her "clever paper" on Lady Mary Wortley Montague. The gala dance at Ottawa's Racquet Court, arranged by Cloche Bell and Arthur Guise to repay all their many hostesses in Ottawa, did not suffer for having been pushed forward from December 12 for another fortnight. Agar Adamson, for his part, vanished into the wilderness of northern Quebec on a long-planned moose-hunting expedition.

Mackenzie King did not forget, quickly or ever. He had lost in Harper the only real male friend of his adult life. Coming back from British Columbia, King had heard about the tragedy in the cruellest of ways. A telegram sent to him aboard the train was not delivered, instead he read the news in a paper picked up casually at the Toronto railway station. He rushed back to attend the funeral, and that same evening took part in a public meeting called to launch a subscription drive to pay for a monument in honour of Harper. He did not speak at the meeting though. Indeed, it was another three weeks before he could bring himself to continue his diary. "Bert has gone quickly, the soul of the man that I loved as I have loved no other man, my father and brother excepted," he wrote on New Year's Day. Later however, when the memorial subscription appeared in danger of flagging, he pushed it through and when the Harper Monument was unveiled at last in November 1905, he chose the inscription from his and Bert's favourite passage in Tennyson's *Idylls of the King*. "Galahad . . . cried, 'If I lose myself, I save myself,'" reads the plaque under the charming little statue of Galahad that still helps to guide the traffic along Wellington Street, just in front of the Parliament Buildings. In 1909, now Minister of Labour, King chose the eighth anniversary of Harper's death to make his maiden speech in the Commons. "Before going to the House," he wrote, "I put ten little white roses on the base of the

"FOLLOW THE ADC"

Colonel & Mrs. Sherwood.

Mr. Arthur Guise and Captain Bell
at Home
at the Racquet Court
on Thursday December twelfth
at nine-thirty o'clock.

Dancing. An answer is requested.

Invitation to the ball given by Arthur Guise and Cloche Bell in December 1901. In the event, out of respect for Bessie Blair and Bert Harper, it did not take place on December 12, but was postponed to the end of the month.

The style of the invitation conveys a good deal. The words "At Home" and "Dancing," and the hour, "nine-thirty o'clock," bespoke a formal party, at which white tie and décolletage *were* de rigueur. *Though Guise and Bell requested a reply, they felt no need to include an address, much less a telephone number. At the turn of the century,* ADCs *ranked second only to governors general on the Ottawa social scene. The "Racquet Court" that was venue for the party was a building on Metcalfe Street that served Ottawa as a kind of all-purpose assembly room.*

Harper monument. It was beautiful to leave it there to look at when I came out. It was in thinking before the debate that I was alone – no single soul to really share a discussion with, or to share a supreme hour of one's life with – that I knew the loss was irreparable."

King, however, was King. If he harboured any resentment towards Minto as the instrument, however unwitting, of the death of his friend, he set it aside in the interests of his own rising career. In the later years of Minto's term, he turned up more and more frequently at Rideau Hall and, for a while, even fancied himself in love with the Governor General's pretty middle daughter, Lady Ruby. "Such character, such strength of soul," he wrote. "She is the only woman of younger years than myself that I have ever looked to as above and beyond me." Lady Ruby, however, was not interested.

By the middle of that decade, in the era of Earl Grey, King had become almost a permanent fixture at Rideau Hall skating parties, as recounted in the diary of Ethel Chadwick. Less impressionable now than as a teenager, Ethel found him "stilted and priggish." Further, in her view, King was "a real butterer-up" who forever praised her skating outfits – "he asked where the purple one had gone to, then said he liked my dark blue awfully" – but hardly ever invited her to waltz. "Fool, if he would ask me to skate instead of jawing." Still, even the arrogant Ethel was a little touched when at Easter 1906, King sent round by special messenger a copy of *The Secret of Heroism*, the little book that he had just published in memory of Harper. "It seems very high-flown, of course, as one would expect anything of King's to be," she wrote in her diary. "Harper, though, had very high ideals and lived up to them."

In *The Secret of Heroism*, King quoted one of the idealistic expressions composed by Harper just two months before he went off on the fateful skating party on the Ottawa River. "With many people here in Ottawa, I fear the social round is becoming an end in itself, and therefore a danger to themselves, and to others."

CHAPTER 23

"Marching to Pretoria"

Old England is having a scrap with a Boer!
Not really? Yes really!
And Canada's soldiers are well to the fore.
Not really? Yes really!
One gallant contingent she's sent o'er the main
To fight for the Queen, and it's perfectly plain
She could send just as many again and again
Not really? Yes really!

song from *The Princess and the Pauper*,
by Harry Graham,
January 1900

"Ladies, study your maps," wrote Amaryllis on October 21, 1899, just ten days after the first shots had been fired in South Africa. "There is one beneficial circumstance connected with war, that relic of barbarism," she continued. "It has given us something worthwhile to talk about. Us women, I mean. Men are never at a loss for grand and ennobling subjects, but women have such an unfortunate adaptability for discussing their neighbours and their neighbours' wives, that this war is a blessed break in the monotony. . . . And there is another thing this war is going to do. It is going to teach us the geography of South Africa."

Amaryllis's tone of slight skepticism about the war, which she herself later abandoned, was quite unusual. "A martial spirit seems to have descended upon this usually prosaic capital," she wrote. "It is really impossible to talk or think of anything but the war." Quickly, it became almost impossible to hear anything but the transplanted sounds of war. Martial tunes were played at almost every corner, almost all the time. "Rather tiring," wrote Amaryllis. Ministers of the Crown and their officials came home whistling the new airs: *Goodbye Dolly Gray* and *Soldiers of the Queen*. Everyone knew at least the first ferocious lines of Rudyard Kipling's patriotic ode to the war, "The Absent-Minded Beggar": "When you've shouted 'Rule Britannia,' when you've sung 'God Save the Queen,'/When you've finished killing Kruger with your mouth." Khaki overnight became the fashionable colour, even though, as Amaryllis noted, it was not "universally becoming."

No one believed for a moment that war was hell. Rather it was glamour and glory and excitement and chivalry. So, in hindsight, everyone's attitude was extraordinarily innocent. To the seventeen-year-old Ethel Chadwick, for instance, the far-off conflict in South Africa meant collecting and swapping military buttons, doodling sketches of dashing subalterns in her diary, and confiding to its pages, "It would be rather romantic to have a beau killed in the war." For Agar Adamson, then a thirty-three-year-old summer soldier, it meant both trying to organize his impending marriage on November 15 and lobbying for a post out there in what would surely be his last chance to prove his military mettle. Adamson's fiancée, Mabel Cawthra, was, if anything, even more eager than he. "My suggestion is that you should still volunteer," she wrote him from Toronto in mid-October. "You could marry me first . . . I could go to Natal . . . we don't go to war every day."

These personal sentiments were all encompassed within a self-justifying ideological whole. The turn of the century was the heyday of the New Imperialism, the grandiose, expansive, quasi-religious concept of empire, co-invented by Cecil Rhodes and Joseph Chamberlain, and apotheosized by Kipling. Like their counterparts in Wellington and in Melbourne and in London, Ottawans saw the war in South Africa not simply as a splendid Imperial adventure, but as a crusade, undertaken among the lesser breeds without the law, for the good and the just and the true.

The main agenda of the war, as it appeared to Ottawans that autumn of 1899, was best expressed by a patriotic tableau put on at the Russell Theatre and titled "Britannia and Her Colonies, Defending Liberty." Lady Victoria Grey, niece of Lord Minto, played the lead role and electrified everyone by holding a real live flaming torch aloft, quite heedless of her gorgeous streaming hair.

Miss Lola Powell took the part of Australia.

The war itself, as even those uninformed Ottawa ladies who, as Amaryllis reported, "persist in speaking of the 'seacoast of the Transvaal,' " soon discovered, had been brewing for a long time. Its origin went back half a century, to the great mythic *Voortrek* of 1837, when most of the Boer settlers, descendants of the original

Dutch and German pioneers who had reached the Cape before the British, had migrated northwards to create the new republic of the Transvaal, beyond the reach of British overlordship. By defeating a British army at the battle of Majuba Hill in 1884, the Boers had demonstrated their determination and had reconfirmed the independence of their republic. Yet the British continued to press northwards. In the 1890s, the great gold finds within the Transvaal attracted thousands of British adventurers – *Ouitlanders*, as they as they were called. Recognizing the demographic threat they posed, the Transvaal President, Paul Kruger, a cranky and narrow yet supremely patriotic leader, refused to grant the *Ouitlanders* the rights of citizenship.

The British now had their issue, to justify their behaviour to the world and to themselves. To aid the *Ouitlanders*, Cecil Rhodes organized the Jameson Raid of 1897, a buccaneering and bungled attempt to overthrow Kruger. The cross-border skirmishing continued. The inevitable formal conflict began on October 11, 1899, when the Boers astonished the world, and Britain, by hurling their ragged armies, minus even uniforms, into the British colonies of Natal and Cape Province, and by surrounding the key railway towns of Mafeking, Ladysmith, and Kimberley with quite unexpected military skill. For a time, it seemed as though they would sweep all the way to the Cape.

Britain's response was instant and massive – not least because it had been prepared long in advance and awaited only an excuse to be unleashed. On October 14, General Sir Redvers Buller set sail from Southampton with the largest army in the history of the British Empire, twice the size of that of Wellington at Waterloo. The Boers were bound to be crushed. The only question remaining was whether Canadian troops, along with those from the other colonies, would be present for the battles, and for the victory parades. Almost unbelievably, it seemed for a time that no Canadians might go.

That decision – whether and in what form to send Canadian troops – was Laurier's to make. For the prime minister, the war in South Africa was Manitoba Schools all over again but more potent and more divisive because the issue this time was not education and minority rights, but war and national pride. Moreover, the pride of two nations was at stake. For most French Canadians, the Boer farmers in their slouch hats and their wives in their sunbonnets were a minority people much like themselves, searching for a distinctive homeland where they could follow their own language and religion and customs. Kruger, in some ways, even seemed, in his patriotic fervour, an echo of Louis Riel. English Canadians, however, had no doubts about where *their* real homeland lay. As an anonymous editorialist for *La Presse* wrote perceptively, "We French Canadians belong to one country, Canada. Canada for us is the whole world. But the English Canadians have two countries, one here and one across the sea." Reflexively, passionately, and overwhelmingly, English Canadians wanted to answer the call of their mother country. "COWARDS IN OTTAWA," trumpeted a *Montreal Star* headline when the first doubts began that Canada might not after all send troops, following it up with accounts of Boer massacres of the wives and children of *Ouitlander* settlers.

As if trying to prevent the country from splitting apart wasn't trouble enough, Laurier had also to deal with a meddlesome and muddled Governor General. Trying to figure out where Lord Minto stood on the war is next to impossible, not least because he himself never seemed to be certain. He was, as the historians John Saywell and Paul Stevens have pointed out, "an old, not a new Imperialist." Roughly, this meant that while Minto was absolutely certain that British was best, he wasn't at all certain about the new, expansive Imperialism. He was thus a bit of a Little Englander. He was also a thoroughly decent fellow. He considered Rhodes to be a blackguard, and signified his disapproval by refusing to be introduced to him at a dinner at the Rothschilds' following the Jameson Raid. In September, shortly before the actual fighting began, Minto wrote to his brother in England, "My Chief at home is thirsting for blood, all my friends here ditto, and myself, while recognizing imperial possibilities, see also the iniquity of the war, and that the time for colonial support has hardly arrived."

This last comment by Minto is especially interesting, but it is also quite unusually confusing, because by then he had already done his bit to ensure Canada's colonial support. Through the previous summer, anti-Boer agitators, supposedly free agents but in fact master-minded by Colonial Secretary Joseph Chamberlain, as Minto knew well, had organized public protest meetings all across the country against Boer "atrocities." Much more directly, on orders from Chamberlain, Minto had taken steps to prepare for Canadian military support. Without telling Laurier, Minto had instructed General Hutton, the British officer commanding the Canadian militia, to draft a contingency plan for sending a Canadian expeditionary force. The week before the first shots were actually fired, a copy of Hutton's plan was leaked to the press, perhaps by some outraged Canadian clerk. Its effect backfired, though. The quick declaration of war meant that Laurier, rather than being able to claim that the

British had been devious behind his back, would have to make a quick decision. Now that everyone knew a plan existed, he could not stall the issue until a military blueprint could be prepared.

Cabinet met on Thursday, October 12. Within it, four members (besides Laurier) were crucial. There were three hawks: Frederick Borden, the Minister of Militia; Richard Cartwright, the veteran Minister of Trade and Commerce; and William Mulock, the Postmaster General. Of these, the most combative was Mulock. At one point he stormed out of the meeting and Laurier had to send a messenger to bring him back. The most effective, probably, was Cartwright. With experience going back to Alexander Mackenzie's cabinet, when Laurier was still a green backbencher, Cartwright pointed out that with an election no more than a year away, the shaky Liberal hold on Ontario would be shattered if troops were not despatched, not only right away, but in a manner that would earn applause from Whitehall.

Standing alone, in defiant isolation, was the Minister of Public Works, the brilliant, crotchety Israel Tarte. Tarte brought to the debate not just the sentiment of his people, but his own considerable personal skill. The issue, he argued, wasn't whether or not Canada should send a contingent. It was instead whether Canada should take part in Britain's wars without a share in Britain's war councils, a perfectly reasonably quid pro quo that, as Tarte and everyone else around the table knew perfectly well, Britain would never give.

Cabinet broke up at five o'clock, still as undecided as it had been at the start of the meeting. "There has been a nice Row," Minto wrote to Polly later that evening after Laurier had briefed him. "I don't think troops will be sent. Tarte is the moving spirit against it. Sir W says there is very strong opposition in the province of Quebec, but I doubt its being nearly as strong as they say, and the excitement in Ontario in favour of troops is very great. . . . Sir W does not appear to me to appreciate the importance of his position – there is no enthusiasm about it – in fact, he is a Frenchman."

Minto had judged accurately the pressures upon Laurier, but he had misjudged his man. Sometime that evening, Laurier figured his way through to a compromise. The next morning, he described it and sold it to his cabinet. Canada would say "Ready. Aye Ready" – but with a note of reserve in its voice. A contingent of 1,000 troopers, divided into companies of 125 men each, would be recruited across the country. Canada would pay the actual and quite negligible costs of recruitment, but all the real costs – of transportation, equipment and supplies, and the shilling a day for troopers – would be paid for by Britain.

At five that afternoon, Friday, October 13, the Minister of Finance, W. S. Fielding, read out the decision to reporters. By then, Laurier had already left for Rideau Hall to inform Minto. As always, even though it was pouring rain, he travelled by streetcar. On the way home, he happened to get into a tram on which Amaryllis was already a passenger. Her observation of a prime minister who had just made the single most crucial decision of his career was her own best piece of reporting. It appeared a week later in *Saturday Night*.

> A city streetcar towards six o'clock on a rainy afternoon is a good field for the study of human nature. Various types are there represented. I was one of many in a streetcar one particularly wet afternoon last week, when two local militia men in full fighting gear, at least so it seemed to the inexperienced eye, got in and began to talk in rather loud tones of the Boer War. They had been in a firing competition and had come out on top, and they were full of enthusiasm.
>
> To make matters more interesting, who should come in then but his Right Honourable Self, Sir Wilfrid Laurier! Sir Wilfrid's democratic principles will not allow of his riding in aught else but trams, so, unlike other Prime Ministers, he eschews cabs. He wore a brown overcoat and high silk hat – not rainy day clothes. The corner at which he got in and a transfer in his hand suggested a conference with the Governor-General.
>
> What a chance for the soldiers! The Premier moving up the car dropped into a seat beside them. He buried himself behind his paper, but it was no use. "Glad to see you are going to send a contingent to fight the Boers," said one of the soldiers. "Yes," said Sir Wilfrid. "We are going to send one," and with a flicker of his sunny smile he disappeared behind the *Free Press*. "Sorry sir, you can't send artillery," and as Sir Wilfrid looked up to murmur he was sorry, a regular bombardment of questions began, til the Premier in self-defence was obliged to evacuate his seat and move to the opposite corner of the car. The militia men were most respectful, but they were interested in the war news and they wanted to get the latest from headquarters and at the same time offer a little judicious advice. They took the necessary snub, however, in a manly way and began discussing each other's boots. It is not altogether safe for great men to go about unprotected.

Laurier's decision to send troops to South Africa may or may not have marked the beginning of the end between him and Emilie. Quite certainly, as demonstrated by the angry *Vive les Boers!*

postscripts, it seriously affected his relations with nineteen-year-old Armand Lavergne.

The decision marked also the beginning of a line of French-Canadian nationalism that we can now trace all the way to René Lévesque. On the evening of October 12, in between the two crucial cabinet sessions, Tarte had assembled a delegation of the most important Quebec members at Laurier's house. Among them was the grandson of the immortal Papineau, the pale, intense, Henri Bourassa, thirty-one years old and already the idol of the young Armand.

Bourassa got right to the point. "Mr. Laurier," he said, "do you take account of opinion in the province of Quebec?" For once, Laurier was not gentle. "My dear Henri, the province of Quebec does not have opinions, it has only sentiments." As if to soften this barb, Laurier added, "the circumstances are extremely difficult."

"It is because they are difficult that I ask you to remain faithful," Bourassa shot back. "To govern is to have the courage, at a given moment, to remain faithful."

This time, Laurier retained his familiar composure. He got up from his chair and put his arm on Bourassa's shoulder. "Ah my dear young friend, you have not a practical mind."

Five days later, Bourassa resigned – as a Liberal, and from the Commons. He promptly ran again, as an independent, in his old constituency of Labelle and was re-elected overwhelmingly. For the first time since Confederation, there now existed within the nation, a political movement whose only home was Quebec.

"Bourassa is not a name to conjure with in the present state of public opinion," Amaryllis informed her readers on October 28. By now, the war was well underway and Amaryllis, *faute de mieux*, was beginning to sound like a jingo. "Everyone who could possibly manage it was at the station to wish the soldier boys Godspeed," she'd reported four days earlier, when the 125 men of Company D, who constituted Ottawa's share of "Canada's offering to the Empire," left by train for Quebec. There they embarked for the front aboard the cattleship *Sardinian* with the rest of the Canadians. "The engines were puffing and blowing, bands were playing . . . the crowd, which some numbered at 15,000, simply surged into the station and neither the thick rope nor a guard of policemen commanded by the chief in person were enough to hold it. . . . When the crowd grew wilder, I saw His Excellency himself struggling in the midst of it like an ordinary citizen. . . . Some of the soldiers got into the train and put up the windows. There was a regular scrimmage to get near. Everyone wanted to shake hands, and above the din of bands and cheering, one often caught the words, 'God bless you boys.' " Another *Free Press* reporter spotted a prominent society matron viewing the march-past from Wellington Street, where the crowds stood forty people deep, who had been "literally forced into the ranks of the band. She was alive to the situation however, and clinging to the big drum made her way along until a break in the crowd enabled her to make her escape."

Georgina Pope, sister of Joseph Pope, Under-Secretary of State and former private secretary to Sir John A. Macdonald, in the khaki uniform worn by the nurses who accompanied the first Canadian contingent.

Also in the crowd at the station, looking on with chagrin, was Agar Adamson. Among the officers of the Governor General's Foot Guards, the militia regiment from which most of Company D had been drawn, the competition had been so intense that he had missed being selected, even though he was an officer of six years seniority. "I can imagine your feelings," wrote Mabel Cawthra from Toronto. "I don't think I could have stood it. . . . Do you think if we went out to South Africa on our honeymoon, they might like to have a Canadian on the spot, should there be any casualties?"

In the bright autumn weather, as Union Jacks in their thousands supplanted the scarlet maples, the war still seemed like an adventure out of the novels of Ouida. Amaryllis closed off her account with a couple of fashion notes. The three nursing sisters who accompanied the troops, she informed readers, "wore smart uniform dresses of khaki, made with plain, neat-fitting skirts and belted jackets with brass buttons, the Red Cross badge on their arm and a red cockade in their trim little hats." The brass buttons and red cockades, she thought, "gave a jaunty soupçon of *La Vivandìere* – not that these nurses have the least desire to play the pets of the regiment – they have no thought beyond the noble duty that lies before them."

Despite all these flourishes, and despite popular expectations, the news from the front was not at all what anyone had expected it to be. The Boers proved to be well armed, and even had heavy artillery. The country was difficult and they, unlike the British, knew it very well. Above all, the Boer "commandoes" as they called themselves, were masters of – another new term – "guerrilla tactics." They were mostly mounted, so that even if repulsed, they could vanish in a cloud of dust, left behind for the British infantry to wipe out of their eyes, cursing their thick uniforms and heavy gear.

The Canadian contingent disembarked at the Cape to join a British army that, advancing ponderously towards Mafeking, Ladysmith, and Kimberley, soon suffered a trio of humiliating defeats. "There is gloom in the air," wrote Amaryllis, after the news of Magersfontein, Tugela River, and Colenso had reached the capital. "Depression is felt in Ottawa, just as it is in every British city."

Then, on the evening of January 12, 1900, the reality of war entered into Society's drawing rooms. The curtain had just rung down at Rideau Hall on the rousing finale of Harry Graham's *The Princess and the Pauper* – "the entire company marched on stage in uniform, led by Drum Major Bullbobs, played by the Honourable Esmond Elliott, seven-year-old younger son of Their Excellencies," reported Amaryllis – when the news was whispered from one group to another round the supper room: Dufferin's eldest son, Lord Ava, gallant and handsome, beau ideal of capital society, had been killed fighting with the Gordon Highlanders near Ladysmith. "It was said that a cable had come to his Excellency, so that there was little hope the news might prove untrue. It seemed strange," Amaryllis continued, "that the news of his death should come to so many of his friends at Government House, where he first learned to love Ottawa." The loss of this hero took the edge off the first good piece of news to come from the Cape, the great British victory at Paardeberg in mid-February; a battle at which the men of Company D had not only distinguished themselves sufficiently to win a battle honour for the Governor General's Foot Guards, but during which one of their members, Private "Dickie" Thompson, won a recommendation for the Victoria Cross for having lain seven hours under enemy fire, thumb and forefinger pressed round the jugular vein of a wounded comrade, to keep him from bleeding to death. (Thompson, in fact, was awarded a much rarer honour, one of only five "Queen's Scarves," for which the recipient must not only have been recommended for the VC, but must also have won subsequent citations for bravery. His scarf, made of khaki wool and crocheted by the aging Queen herself, can be seen at the Canadian War Museum.)

By now it was obvious that the war would not be quickly won. As early as December 1899, the British government sent an urgent request to Ottawa for more troops. This time, though, the War Office had at last begun to recognize that the only way to combat commandoes was with other commandoes.

To battle the Boers with a sharp-shooting rifle instead of a cuirass, and accustomed like them to riding hard over difficult terrain, sleeping out in the open, living off the country, what better men existed anywhere in the Empire than the men of the North-West Mounted Police? As Minto himself was one of the first to realize, this was an opportunity for Canada to make her own unique contribution to the war. In London, Lord Strathcona, now Canadian High Commissioner, took the political pressure off Laurier by

THEATRE ROYAL

Government House

"The Princess
AND
The Pauper."

1900

Programme for "The Princess and the Pauper," written and directed by "Col. D. Streamer," AKA *Harry Graham, in 1900. Lola Powell played a character named the Honourable Constantia Koffdrop.*

offering to pay for this new contingent out of his own immense fortune. Strathcona's Horse, as the new regiment was christened, was raised in the West in just fifteen days. Most of its 537 members were either serving or former Mounties. In command was an officer whose name was already a legend: Colonel Sam Steele, a tall, stalwart twenty-five-year veteran of the force, famous for having defended law and order in the Klondike against Soapy Smith and other notorious rascals. Years ago, as a raw recruit, during the long hard march from Roche Percée to Edmonton in the autumn of 1874, Steele had served under our old friend Willy Jarvis, Edmund Meredith's brother-in-law, and had heard his ebullient, red-haired commander spin yarns of his campaigns with the British regulars in Africa. Now, at forty-eight, it was Steele's own chance to win his spurs there.

Officers and men of Strathcona's Horse, drawn up for review at Lansdowne Park in March 1900.

In the last week of February 1900, Strathcona's Horse swept into Ottawa *en route* to the front. During the fortnight the regiment spent there, camped out in chilly barns at the agricultural exhibition grounds at Lansdowne Park in the worst of the winter weather, virtually every member of the regiment came down with a streaming cold. At Government House, Amaryllis reported, "the sneezing and coughing of the gallant troopers all but obliterated some of the best lines" during yet another performance of *The Princess and the Pauper*. None of which diminished their allure. This new breed of soldier, clad romantically in Stetsons, high yellow boots, and long sweeping greatcoats, took the city as Lochinvars. On February 24, seventeen-year-old Ethel Chadwick spent the whole afternoon strolling up and down Sparks Street ogling "these most interesting gents" through her eyelashes. Then she dashed home and drew them in her diary. At a skating party the next week, she actually got to meet some. "One, a tall one called Mr. Barber was awfully nice, and asked me to do the outside edge." Amaryllis, for her part, was almost equally smitten. "What this city will do without them, one does not really know," she wrote. "No entertainment has been considered worth going to unless some of the Horse were there." It added to the Horse's mystique, she continued, that a number of its members were that most romantic of all species of military: gentlemen rankers. "Not a few are scions of noble houses. One 'Tommy' is a lord, Lord Edward Seymour. . . . Lord Edward, however, has not been the best of Tommies, and Ottawa society, which dearly loves a lord, has not had the chance of making his acquaintance for the reason that he has been confined to barracks." In the thick of the social whirl, however, were "Mr. Beresford, a cousin of Lords Charles and William Beresford, Mr. O'Brien, who is a relative of Lord Inchquin, and a nephew of Lord Dundonald. . . . But they are only troopers now, have to groom their own horses, sleep on straw in a cattle shed."

Officers and men of Strathcona's Horse, sketched in her diary by Ethel Chadwick, February 1900. Many of the regiment's members were gentlemen rankers.

Like everyone else, though, Amaryllis reserved her greatest enthusiasm for the Horse's commanding officer. Indeed, for the first and last time in her career, Amaryllis, in describing Steele, actually gushed. "After hearing Mr. Bourassa speak on the war," she reported early in March, "I went to a tea where I had the pleasure of meeting the Colonel. He is not at all the kind of man one generally meets at teas, he must have felt rather out of his element, though he by no means showed it. His manner was of the pleasant, unassuming kind which good soldiers have in common with nice men. Looking at this gallant officer, one thought of what Mr. Bourassa had said, and it occurred to one that perhaps there was some truth in the arguments of the member for Labelle, and that Canada should not allow her bravest and best men to expatriate themselves, even for the dazzling dreams of Imperialism."

For most Ottawans, the fortnight of the Strathconas was the high point of the war. One quartet of young ladies was so reluctant to say goodbye that they persuaded a prominent society matron, Mrs. Collingwood Schreiber, to chaperone them down to Halifax to watch the regiment board ship. As late as the following May, Ethel Chadwick and her younger sisters were still getting up skits for their family's entertainment at which "Rossie came in as a Strathcona's Horse in a big coat of Papa's and last year's grey fedora."

For those Ottawans who, like Amaryllis, were in the political know, a fortnight of almost equal interest had been afforded early in February. This event, although also military, was of a quite different order. It concerned a British-Canadian confrontation as a result of which General Hutton, the commander of the Canadian militia and a figure of importance in the capital, outranked only by the Governor General, had been most unceremoniously sacked. It can be said of General Hutton that in his bluff, commanding, piercing-eyed person, he epitomized most of the reasons why Britain both won and lost an Empire. He was tough, able, and energetic, a member of that fast-track group of officers who were known as the Wolseley Ring, an innovative tactician who, while serving in Egypt in the eighties, had demonstrated that British soldiers could be trained to ride and manage camels just as well as Bedouins. He was also vain, overbearing, and pig-headed, and, in the words of a War Office official, "constitutionally deficient in every atom of tact." There was moreover, as Minto confided to his diary, "something verging on the theatrical in him."

Major-General E. T. H. Hutton, General Officer Commanding the Canadian militia, 1898-1900. His sudden departure caused a furor.

It can also be said that although Hutton brought many of his problems upon his own head, he did not create them all. As Amaryllis commented in 1897, long before Hutton arrived on the scene, "the life of a General Officer Commanding is no bed of roses." The "GOC", as he was called for short, was always a serving British officer, appointed directly by the War Office, usually without any consultation with the Canadian government, and commissioned to ensure that the colony was properly defended, most particularly against the United States. But as soon as he arrived in Canada, the GOC found himself the servant of the government, subordinate to the Minister of Militia. To complicate these tangled lines of responsibility, the militia itself, as most politicians saw it, constituted not so much Canada's first line of defence as, in the words of historian Desmond Morton, "the most comprehensive engine of patronage in the government."

All five of Hutton's immediate predecessors as GOC had been vanquished by the job – most spectacularly General Frederick Middleton, the hero of Batoche, who not long thereafter had been all but run out of the country, the victim of a nasty little trumped-up scandal concerning his supposed improper disposition of a bundle of furs confiscated from a Métis trader during the Rebellion.

Hutton arrived in Ottawa in the summer of 1898 determined to change all that. For one thing, he was an old army pal and confidant of Minto's. For another, he had been hand-picked for the job by Chamberlain, who was determined to re-establish British influence over Canadian defence policy. Lastly, Hutton had sufficient private means to rent Earnscliffe from Lady Macdonald and to set himself up in the capital with a panache no predecessor had attempted. When he wanted to be, Hutton could be charming. "He has a hearty, pleasant manner," Amaryllis reported after an early Hutton tea party, "and a merry twinkle in his eye which is conducive to merriment in others. He led the attack on the teatable with great vigour." Mrs. Hutton, who came equipped with impeccable court connections and an enviable wardrobe, proved equally charming and was soon elected President of the Women's Art Association.

Mrs. Edward Hutton. She had excellent court connections, and cut a swath through Ottawa society.

There were a few bad portents. Hutton quarrelled with Sam Hughes, the Conservative MP who was the strongest advocate of militia reform; his action in removing a Liberal MP from the command of a New Brunswick regiment scarcely endeared him to the Liberal government. Yet Hutton's energetic policies produced results. For the first time, staff college courses were established for militia officers. In 1899, the summer militia camps were the smartest and most successful in memory. "Canada at last appears to have found a perfectly satisfactory General," reported Amaryllis. "He is immensely popular with the officers and men under him, and he has not won their hearts by flattery and soft ways."

In Ottawa, that summer, the highlight of the season was a splendid ball at Earnscliffe in honour of the militia officers encamped at Rockcliffe. "The beautiful grounds were diffused with a soft glow from Chinese lanterns," Amaryllis tells us. "The air was soft and warm . . . the women wandered from the ballroom to the garden without any covering over décolleté gowns. . . . The men wore mess dress, of which the General is particularly fond, and always requests at his dances."

He was however, rather too energetic. Unlike Minto, Hutton interpreted Chamberlain's request for a contingency plan to send Canadian troops to South Africa as a mandate to try to stampede Canada into the war. Further, Hutton assumed that what Chamberlain really wanted was an *official* contingent from Canada to demonstrate that the Empire, when the call went out, would instantly respond. This provoked a ferocious row with Sam Hughes, by then well advanced in his own plan to raise a private force – a plan that a number of ministers, anxious to send troops as their constituents demanded, but not to do so officially, looked on with favour. In October, when Hutton's contingency plan was revealed in the press, he was suspected of having had a hand in leaking it, in order to apply pressure to the cabinet. Whether or not this was true, the tensions unleashed by the war itself quickly escalated the strains to the breaking point.

At Quebec City on October 30, the night before the Canadian troops sailed, Hutton and Frederick Borden got into a terrible row

The cattleship Sardinian, *with members of the First Canadian Contingent aboard, sails for the Cape on October 31, 1899.*

after a dinner at which Hutton had given a speech about the need to remove political influences from the militia. Next, Hutton quarrelled with, of all people, Minto. To meet the demand for mounted riflemen (this was before Strathcona's Horse went out) Hutton wanted to send city-trained cavalry, in order to bolster his position with the militia. Minto wanted raw northwestern recruits who could ride and shoot. "He cannot get out of his head the popular effect of the organization," wrote Minto in his diary, "and thinks a great deal about the hats they are to wear."

In January 1900, Hutton and Minto clashed over war charities. To raise money for wounded members of the Canadian contingent and their dependents, the British newspaper, *The Daily Mail*, sponsored a recital in Ottawa by the popular singer Ernest Sharpe. Minto agreed to attend on the understanding that the proceeds would go to the Red Cross Relief Fund. But Hutton, without consulting Minto, arranged that the money, approximately five thousand dollars, would go to the Soldiers Wives League, of which Mrs. Hutton was President. When Minto discovered this – over dinner just before the concert – he was furious, because the group was simply a branch of a larger Imperial league and there was no guarantee that the money would be used for Canadian soldiers. It was too late not to go, but when Hutton came to his box during intermission, "I gave him my mind straight," as Minto informed his diary, "and told him I considered I had simply been brought there under false pretence." In her account, Amaryllis only hints at this squabble. She reports that the concert included, as always, *The Absent-Minded Beggar*, that Mrs. Hutton wore black velvet, and that – as must doubly have infuriated Minto – "the young ladies selling programmes wore a red ribbon fastened across the bodice of their gowns; on the ribbon was written, in gold lettering, " 'Soldiers Wives League.' "

The final break came two weeks later, in the form of a sordid squabble between Borden and Hutton over whether, in the purchase of horses for the Second Contingent, Conservative dealers were being favoured over Liberals. Laurier informed Minto that either Borden or Hutton would have to go. Minto delayed for three weeks and then on February 7, signed the Order-in-Council cancelling Hutton's commission.

This news was "a veritable bombshell," Amaryllis reported. Neither she nor anyone else was fooled by the story that was put out that the General's services were urgently required in South Africa. "It has caused the greatest sorrow. . . . It is the same old story – the story we are beginning to know by heart, the story of politics entering into the militia of Canada and one good General after another going back to England before the expiration of his term." There was one final denouement before the Huttons left town on February 15, that she could not resist reporting. "There was a dinner for the General at the Rideau Club on Tuesday night; a dinner by the militia on Wednesday, and there would have been another dinner Thursday had not the hostess, one of the sweetest women in Ottawa, not dreaming of anything beneath the surface, invited the Minister of Militia to meet the General! The General had another engagement."

Since the Canadian politicians aspired to nothing higher than to use the militia as a source of patronage, it isn't easy to judge which side should carry more of the blame in this protracted war of the generals, the Canadians for being greedy or the British for being insensitive. All that was certain was that the system could not last. One of Hutton's successors, General Dundonald, was every bit as intemperate as he, and indeed intruded so much into Canadian politics that he planned to stand for the House of Commons as a Conservative, and was only forestalled by being fired. In 1905, the

Militia Act was revised and for the first time, an all-Canadian Militia Council was established, to replace the GOC.

The central change had taken place earlier, out on the veldt. "Canadians went to the war imperialists," Desmond Morton has written. "They came home nationalists." In all, over the two and three-quarter years that the fighting went on, Canada contributed 7,300 soldiers to this longest, bloodiest, and most humiliating of all the supposedly splendid little wars that Britain embarked on between 1815 and 1914. The events of two world wars have all but blotted South Africa out of our collective memory. But in the capital, as the curtain went up on the new century, the patriotic excitement was, if anything, even greater than in 1914 or 1939. Even for newlyweds like Agar and Mabel Adamson, it was indeed impossible "to talk or think of anything but the war."

CHAPTER 24

Horseman on the Veldt

Mabel and I paid a visit to one Professor Reis, a clairvoyant. . . . He answered questions written on pieces of paper. (1) Shall I receive a commission in the Transvaal? A. Yes, and almost at once you will succeed and not be wounded. (2) Will Mabel continue to be happy with me? A. Yes, and you have a loving wife and above all, the best companion and good friend in her (3) Should I gamble? A. Yes, though only on Mondays, Tuesdays and Fridays.

Agar Adamson; diary entry; January 28, 1900

That clairvoyant in New York, whom Agar and Mabel Adamson consulted on their way back to Ottawa from their honeymoon in Mexico, managed to get most of it right. Soon afterwards, Adamson received the commission to South Africa that by now, having been turned down once, he was almost frantic to achieve. He returned from the war unwounded. (Much later, at the end of the First World War, by then well over fifty, he emerged from three and a half years in the trenches with no worse physical scar than a shoulder wound.) He and Mabel, more often than not, were happy together, though their marriage was never a tranquil one. Lastly, Adamson continued to gamble, and to party. "Suffering from a head; sweet champagne on top of dry," he wrote on April 12, 1901, one of many such entries in his diary. A few months later, "Poker party . . . excellent supper . . . turning over a new leaf."

Adamson, whom we first encountered as a deliciously gossipy letter-writer, was the kind of man who was continually turning over new leaves. "So big a one that I am a wreck in consequence," he wrote on another occasion. "He was always either on top of the world or down in the depths," recalls his younger son, the distinguished architect-planner emeritus and author, Anthony Adamson. Adamson *fils* remembers further that his father was "almost a classic Edwardian"; sporting, energetic, given to practical jokes. But there was also a reflective and even a literary side to the man. His letters from South Africa to his new bride, frequently scribbled in pencil on the backs of spare War Office forms or whatever other pieces of paper were available, supplemented by terse entries in the *aide-mémoire* diary that he carried with him in his saddle-bag, provide perhaps the most vivid surviving descriptions of those long-ago battles on the veldt as seen through the eyes of a Canadian.

In 1899, the epochal year of his marriage and the outbreak of the Boer War, Adamson was thirty-three. For a decade, he'd been one of the most popular young bucks in the capital. He was yet another of Official Ottawa's Anglo-Irishmen; in fact, his grandfather, Dr. William Agar Adamson, a sporting parson out of Trinity College who'd come out in 1840 as Chaplain to the Governor, Lord Sydenham, and who later became both Chaplain and Librarian to the Senate, had been a good friend of Edmund Meredith's and had moved to Ottawa in the same year. Two generations later, in the way things were done in those days, the Upper Chamber had become a kind of family enterprise for the Adamsons: Agar's father, James, was employed there as a clerk from the 1850s until his death in 1890, and Agar himself, having been staked to several pleasantly happy-go-lucky years at Cambridge by a rich uncle overseas, was appointed Custodian of the Rolls in 1889. The civil service "Blue Book" for 1890 lists him as a junior clerk at a salary of $650 a year. In 1899, he was still a junior clerk and his salary had increased to only $1,000.

In the way of so many young men of the era, Adamson's real passion was for soldiering. In 1893, he was commissioned in the Governor General's Foot Guards and by 1899 he was a captain. While for some of his brother officers the militia was mostly a social club, an entrée to the Rideau Hall inner circle, Adamson took it seriously. He was a fan of General Hutton's and it may well have been that difficult but able GOC who inspired a talent for battlefield tactics that served Adamson well both in South Africa and, later, during the First World War.

When it came to good looks, Adamson was not far behind the

brooding Black-Irish benchmark established by Arthur Guise. He was, though, of a completely different type: brown-haired and smooth-faced with a fine Roman nose and – his most remarkable feature – extraordinarily bright-blue eyes. Luckily, it did not show that in one of them, as the result of a childhood encounter with a cinder, he was almost totally blind. Much to Adamson's regret, he was stocky and rather short, only about five foot eight, and, sometimes, in his letters to Mabel, he would mock himself. "Are you sorry you did not marry a big, strong, light-haired husband who would be a comfort and a strength to you instead of a no-account brown boy?" This, however, was a trifle disingenuous for, as he was perfectly well aware, Adamson was gifted with enormous charm, a man's man who got on splendidly with women. He was a superb horseman, and while a student at Cambridge, rode to victory in the Newmarket Stakes. He was a particular chum of Dufferin's son, Lord Ava, the news of whose death, in January 1900, put a damper on his honeymoon. "So few really good genuine men in this world," wrote Adamson in his diary in Jalapa, Mexico. "It seems hard a Boer bullet should find its way to him." Equally as much, he was a chum of Amaryllis, who had known him from childhood and who shared his irreverent sense of fun. Given his talent for gossip, he was probably one of her best sources. Time and again he turns up in her columns – next man through the paper hoop after Captain Mann in the skating carnival described in chapter twenty-two, organizing sleigh parties to Aylmer, and even, on one epochal occasion in April 1899, winning top prize in a charity bazaar competition, where gents trimmed ladies' hats. "Mr. Adamson has various talents," she wrote, "but one never fancied a talent for millinery among them. Some men can do almost anything. I don't believe, though, that any girl would have worn that hat."

Above all, Adamson was a man of his age. He had most of the standard prejudices; generally speaking he cared neither for Jews nor French Canadians nor Roman Catholics – although when it came to the particular, as in the case of Amaryllis and her numerous family connections, many of his best friends were in fact, Catholic Irish. Restive and unfulfilled in time of peace, he came into his own in time of war, first in South Africa and then, more spectacularly, during the First World War when, as commanding officer of the Princess Patricia's Canadian Light Infantry, he became something of a legend. "In the mess, he was a most delightful dinner companion," recalled a brother officer. "He had a resonant voice, a good accent and an excellent vocabulary. His after-dinner speeches were not the less anticipated because he could indulge in pointed irony and was not particular whose toes he trod on . . . he refused to be bored."

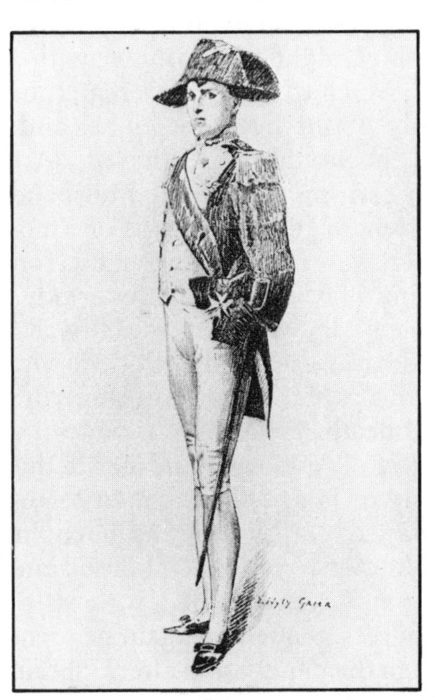

Agar Adamson as Napoleon, Mabel Cawthra as Madame Récamier, as they appeared at Lady Aberdeen's Victorian Era Ball, in Toronto, November 1897. The drawings were made by the artist Wyly Grier and published in a souvenir book, produced to raise money for the Victorian Order of Nurses, founded by Lady Aberdeen to commemorate Queen Victoria's Diamond Jubilee.

During most of the nineties, Adamson shared a house with an elderly aunt, to whom he was devoted. He seemed a perennial bachelor. Then, in 1897, he fell in love with Mabel Cawthra. Family history is fuzzy about the precise circumstances of their meeting, but by the end of that year they were being seen often in each other's company, most noticeably in November at the magnificent Victorian Era Ball in Toronto (organized by Lady Aberdeen as a kind of companion piece to the Fancy Dress ball in the Senate Chamber described in chapter twenty), to which they partnered each other as Napoleon and Madame Récamier, he scowling splendidly after the fashion of Orchardson's famous painting of the defeated Emperor aboard the *Bellerophon*, she in the style of David's equally famous portrait of Récamier reclining upon her sofa.

The following March they turned up together in Ottawa in Amaryllis's columns, as fellow guests at a "recherché little supper party" after a glittering concert at the Russell Theatre by the noted French bass, Pol Plançon, at which other guests included the Lauriers and a number of cabinet ministers and their wives.

Having dropped the names, "Mrs. Cawthra and her daughter,

Miss Cawthra," Amaryllis had no need to embroider. Known as "The Astors of Canada," the Cawthras were *primus inter pares* among the new class of merchant princes who, by the 1890s, had succeeded the Family Compact as rulers of Toronto. Mrs. John Cawthra of Devon House at 150 Beverley Street was one of the most formidable dowagers in the city; Mabel, her youngest child and only surviving daughter, was one of its most sought-after belles.

There was a good deal more to Mabel than her looks (though not conventionally beautiful, she had wonderful auburn hair and fine intelligent eyes) and her money. She was a prodigiously talented young woman who had studied painting and sculpture in Paris, and who could turn her hand to almost anything artistic, from needlework to the difficult technique of enamelling on metal. Mabel's options in choosing a husband were unlimited. She must therefore have spotted in Adamson the quality that was in short supply among all the doughty merchant princelings who courted her in Toronto: he could make her laugh. It must have been refreshing to meet someone who refused to be bored. There was also the fact that she, like him, was the very devil on horseback; indeed, on one visit to England she had even advertised successfully in *The Times* for accommodation with a family "keen on hunting." Adamson, in one of his many letters, managed to strike exactly the right combination of humour, horsiness, and swagger. "Put on all my good clothes yesterday," he wrote of equitation trials in Ottawa. "My gee was 17 hands and with a tight pair of military breeches I found it most difficult to mount with my poor short little legs. The examination included 4 jumps, one 4.6 in post and rails which was quite a new sensation with bearskin and sword. . . . We then trotted round the ring on stripped saddles without bridles on a horse prepared for the purpose, with the gait of a wild beast. . . . The result was that out of 17 candidates, only two got through, and I beat the other chap."

The winning of Mabel, however, took Adamson a while. The first time he proposed, after the "recherché" supper party in Ottawa in 1898, she turned him down. For one thing, she still considered herself engaged, if only in secrecy, to a certain Captain W. S. Sparkes, a Canadian officer of the Egyptian Camel Corps, founded by General Hutton, whom she had met on an 1896 journey up the Nile. "I am bound by a sense of decency to a man whom I could have cared for," she wrote Agar, "if only his memory was not blurred by the vision of a pair of parti-coloured blue and green eyes." For another, she herself was a free spirit, yet another New Woman of the era, who did not entirely envisage her future life in harness as a wife. "I do

Agar Adamson (l.) and Mabel Cawthra. This photograph was probably taken in Ottawa, in March 1898, at the time that he first proposed. The man on the right wearing a monocle is George Sparkes, Adamson's closest friend, and the younger brother of Captain W. S. Sparkes of the Egyptian Camel Corps, to whom Mabel had been secretly engaged.

not know what I want," she wrote in another letter. "I feel as if I were a combination of dozens of people all demanding different things. . . . You know that I am no believer in marriage ceremonies and think divorce ought to be encouraged, and marriage made a yearly contract."

Still, Mabel was head over heels in love and by the summer of 1899 – Captain Sparkes presumably having drifted into the desert aboard his camel – matters between herself and Agar had reached a head.

The first week in September, he joined the Cawthras at their summer place at Shanty Bay on Lake Simcoe. "Mr. Adamson came and Mabel drove to meet him," Mrs. Cawthra wrote in her own journal. "I had a conversation with him and consented to his engagement to Mabel." All of her own last doubts about "a terror of settling down," Mabel exorcised in an extraordinarily candid letter to Agar. "I want you to feel that Marriage is not the hard and fast hopelessly binding thing that most people think it is . . . I am simply going to live with you because I want to, and if I cease to want to I shall leave and hope that you will do the same." On November 15, 1899, they were married at St. George's Church in Toronto. "A smart wedding if there ever was one," reported Amaryllis, scissors-and-pasting the Toronto papers. "Mr. and Mrs. Adamson left by the five o'clock train for the south; their wedding trip will comprise an extensive tour of Mexico on horseback."

These two riding aficionados, she added, had left nothing to chance. They had even packed their own favourite saddles aboard the train with them.

In truth, the wedding had gone anything but smoothly. From the start of the romance, Mrs. Cawthra had been concerned that Adamson was nothing more than a fortune-hunter. A fortnight before the wedding, rumours had reached her ears of the alarming state of his gambling debts. On November 2, she despatched her son Bertie to Ottawa to check the rumours out. According to family legend, Bertie telegraphed gloomily, "Agar Owes Thousands." However determined Mrs. Cawthra now was to cancel the wedding, she encountered in her daughter Mabel a will every bit as strong as her own. In his wedding-night diary entry, written aboard the train south, Adamson gives us a hint of the rows that had gone on. "I married the dearest woman in the world who owing to a misunderstanding to put it generously, alone approved of the match. . . . The wedding guests saw a very pretty wedding, a beautifully-dressed bride. . . . No one knew the sorrow and trials the bride had gone through and all on account of a no-account husband." A few weeks later, in a private letter to Adamson, Mrs. Cawthra left no doubt of her attitude. "She just had to say she did not trust me," Agar reported to Mabel, "and could never trust me, and was cut to the heart that you should have married such a man."

Mrs. Cawthra wasn't entirely wrong in supposing that Mabel's fortune was part of her attraction to Adamson. Her error was not to recognize – as his voluminous correspondence makes plain – that he was just as much in love with Mabel as she with him, if quite often stormily. It took time, but in the end Adamson's charm conquered Mrs. Cawthra. On her deathbed in 1922, it was not her irreproachable son Bertie whom she most wished to see but that "no-account" son-in-law, Agar.

"If I depend upon you or anyone else for income, I lose my self-respect." Thus Adamson, clearly in one of his new-leaf frames of mind, wrote to Mabel in March 1900. The war in South Africa, quite apart from all the excitement, offered him a chance both for self-respect and at least a modest income. But for him and for Mabel, it was also a chance to escape from the dreary inanities of the Senate and the migrainous, accusatory atmosphere of Beverley Street. Furthermore, if he did well in battle Adamson might win their ticket to permanent freedom. "I'm sure if we could once get into an Imperial Regiment," he wrote, "it would suit us both down to the ground."

Agar and Mabel, freighted by now not only with their saddles but also with some magnificent purchases of silver that had once belonged to the Emperor Maximilian, had got back from Mexico on a thirty-degree-below-zero day at the end of January, just too late for him to enlist in Strathcona's Horse. Instead, in drizzly March, having wangled a leave of absence from the Senate, he made his way to Halifax, to take up a commission in a special service regiment raised from the militia to man the Imperial Garrison and thus relieve the British regulars for duty at the front. This was a start, but no more. The charms of Halifax, from the elegant clock-tower built by Queen Victoria's father to the books in the garrison library inherited from the abandoned British garrison at Corfu, were dampened for Adamson by the late Nova Scotia winter. "The climate is beastly," he wrote morosely to Mabel. "The wind goes right through you. . . . Soft Nova Scotia coal is very smoky and makes everything inside and out filthy . . . the town is old and very shabby, all the houses built of shingles and bespeak a long gone by past." Nor were the duties inviting, "one being to parade the lower parts of town to gather in all drunken men and search for houses of ill-fame which is done by entering them in the Queen's name back and front . . . the duty is not a pleasant one . . . the low part of town is very low." Only slightly less irksome was the task of fitting out the officers' mess. "Everything is shockingly dear and we are tied down to buy things at Grit shops without tenders. . . . Napkins $6 a dozen cheapest; tablecloths $22, red carpets for the mess room same as our red carpet, $2.40 per yard." One of the few bright spots – a consolation he would discover again in the trenches in the First World War – was a stray cat who adopted him. "She won't leave me, finished a whole box of sardines this morning and drank out of the jug."

Meanwhile, back in Ottawa, Mabel was demonstrating very effectively that their marriage was a true partnership. Equipped with looks, with confidence, and best of all with contacts – the Postmaster General, William Mulock, was her first cousin – she set out to win for her husband the chance he so desperately wanted. "Hope your dinnerparty was a success," Adamson wrote her in late March. "How I envy the PMG sitting at the head of my table, with such a sweetheart at the other end; hope the drinks did not run out; sorry you did not ask Borden, it is not incumbent on you to flirt with him." Mabel got the message. "What a morning you must have had with the PMG and Borden," Agar wrote a few days later. "Hasn't he quite a twinkle in his eye? Mrs. Kitson always used to say a clever woman could do anything with him." (Adamson was probably referring to Mrs. Gerald Kitson, wife of the Commandant of the Royal Military College at Kingston.) Then he added, a bit guiltily, "My Darling Mabel, I don't really like you knocking about Departments asking favours for your husband."

Later in the war, Mabel's attitudes would change, but this early on, she was every bit as bellicose as Agar. "Why was I not born a man?" she lamented to him in a letter. "Bertie would have made such a nice girl!" Whether her determined lobbying had its effect, or whether Adamson's own efforts achieved the same end, the golden opportunity presented itself on April 18. "Would you like me to enlist in Strathcona's Horse?" he wrote in haste. "I think I have the refusal of a position. . . . Think it over for 8 hours and wire me." Here, as so often happens both in Adamson's correspondence and in his diaries, the flow of information abruptly ceases. To continue the story, we have to turn to Amaryllis. "Captain Adamson arrived in Ottawa on Saturday," she reported on April 25. "The Strathcona's Horse reserve to which Captain Adamson will be attached will go to England and will remain there until required at the Cape. Mrs. Adamson and her mother, Mrs. Cawthra, intend accompanying Captain Adamson to England." As it happened, to get into Strathcona's Horse, Agar had had to accept a come-down in rank to Lieutenant, and the stay in Britain was less than twenty-four hours. "Arrived Liverpool at five," Adamson recounts in his diary on May 10, 1900, "special train to London docks; boarded HMS *Assaye*; Mabel slept on board, trying to buck each other up; Mabel true as steel." The *Assaye* sailed for the Cape the next afternoon, as Mabel, Mrs. Cawthra, and Lord Strathcona all waved from the jetty. Halfway across, a transport homeward bound semaphored the news of the relief of Mafeking.

Agar Adamson, newly commissioned in Strathcona's Horse. To get into the regiment, he had had to accept a come-down in rank, to Lieutenant.

"Nothing shall be hidden from you," wrote Adamson on May 27, from somewhere in the South Atlantic, "not even the fact that I am now suffering from a smashed nose, a stiff neck and a swollen wrist and a generally battered all round sort of feeling. . . . In a weak moment, I promised to go in for the Officers Boxing Contest . . . the five judges gave the battle to me and my opponent went to bed." Indeed, Adamson's candour in letters to Mabel outshone even hers to him. A fortnight later, awaiting orders at Capetown, he described how he resisted an invitation infinitely more alluring than a boxing contest:

> I dined the other night at the Mount Nelson Hotel, a very smart hotel full of v. smart people. I dined with five men of the Buffs and six grass

> widows, with husbands at the front. The pace was quite fast enough for me. And their morals not becoming, with husbands fighting for their country. I was taken upstairs after much eating and drinking by a v. smart major's wife in V lancers to look at some photos and it was not her fault that I remained faithful to you, my sweetheart. . . . My five pals did not put in an appearance until the next day. . . . The whole hotel is full of the same kind, but everything is done very quietly. . . . They say the air in Capetown is conducive to it and these women living in this state of excitement are not responsible for themselves.

By this kind of chronicle and by Agar's later detailed accounts of the fighting itself, Mabel Adamson must have become much better informed than most women about what the war was really like. Nor did Agar ever leave her in doubt about what their separation meant. In a letter thanking her for a parcel of handkerchiefs and hand-knitted helmets, he requested, "Will you while I am away adopt a scent and let everything belonging to you waft a suspicion of it?"

Adamson and his contingent of fifty men had arrived at the Cape on June 3, too late to catch up with Steele and the rest of the Strathcona's. "We only missed by six days, nobody knows where they went or what they were up to. They went in six different transports with 1500 mules on a secret mission." (In fact, the regiment had been despatched on a mission that could have significantly affected the course of the war. Its orders were to range far behind enemy lines and to cut the railway between Lourenço Marques in Portuguese East Africa and Pretoria in the Transvaal that was the landlocked Boers only link to the outside world. "Kruger got onto the game," as Adamson wrote in his next letter, and the expedition was called off. As an historical footnote, the daring plan had been devised by the Anglo-Irish secret agent Roger Casement; sixteen years later, Casement would land in Ireland from a German submarine and thereafter be executed for the high treason of trying to free his native country from British rule.)

With Mafeking, Kimberley, and Ladysmith by now all back in British hands, Adamson's worry was that there would be no battles left for him to fight. "It looks at an end, I fear," he continued in his June 3 letter, "Everybody is very selfish and looking after their own interests. All the regular officers say they do not see how I could get a look in for a [regular] commission at my age, but we shall see, and if you can conceive any little game, conceive it."

Adamson needn't have worried. Although bested in the set-

Boer scouts on the veldt. This was not a gentleman's war.

Canadian troops encamped in South Africa.

piece battles by the sheer weight of British numbers, those extraordinary Boer generals, Smuts, Botha, and De Wet, hadn't the least intention of surrendering. They presented to the British, and to the rest of the world that watched, at first with amazement and then increasingly with admiration, a new form of war – guerrilla war. Operating in their own country and among their own people, the Boers performed like fish in water. It was an unusual war: small groups of men, riding hard, shooting fast, and then vanishing again to live by their wits and off the land. It was also a brutal war of tricks, ruses, and deceits. Between a peaceable Boer farmer and a ruthless Boer commando the dividing line was fine, and increasingly it was crossed by both sides. The war had ceased to be a gentlemen's war. It had become, instead, the war of *Breaker Morant.*

Adamson went off to war jauntily. "The main body of the Strathconas have joined Buller at last," he wrote on June 23, setting off with his men to catch the Regiment up. He was now at Pietermaritzburg in Natal, having travelled up from the Cape by troop-ship. Here they'd picked up their horses and their equipment, and Adamson accompanied this letter with a sketch. "We carry on our saddles many things I will try to show you . . . 2 blankets, waterproof sheets, rubber coat, saddle bag, waterproof saddle cover, shoe case, great coat, rifle, bucket, pistol. We ask a great deal of our horses." The horses, however, demanded even more of their riders. "Most of them are Argentines or Walers, most had little or no breaking. I gathered all the bad ones together and put the bronco busters on them and they proved a marvel."

From Pietermaritzburg – attached for the time being to another Mounted Regiment, The South Africa Light Horse, which was mostly comprised of *Ouitlander* refugees ("a fine lot," he considered) – Adamson and company travelled northwards by train to Newcastle, just below the Transvaal border. Their ultimate destination was Buller's massive camp at Standerton, some hundred miles further north, inside the Transvaal. On the way there, riding through the Drakensberg Mountains, past flat-topped Majuba Hill, somber and majestic, and into the rolling country of the high veldt, Adamson had his first taste of war.

"There are 10,000 Boers within three miles of us," he wrote from Newcastle on June 26. "We start tomorrow to Charleston, alone to scout the country, if nothing found to report, and go on north. They are asking a good deal of me. They offered me the job, asked me if I could do it which of course I said I could, my one chance. I have one white guide. My darling, I mean to do my best. We carry nothing but our haversacks, and your photo taken in Ottawa."

Scouting, above all, scouting in unfamiliar territory, is one of the most demanding of the martial arts. It isn't a job for amateurs. Something about Adamson must have caught the eye of his superiors. Out on the veldt, in the gathering South African winter, he was a chocolate soldier of the militia no longer.

> *June 27*: Drew 10 mules and wagon, two days fodder and rations, and took a flanking party four miles out on the right flank. . . . The coun-

try is very hilly and it is jolly easy to lose your way. . . . The days are delightful, like a Canadian October day, but the nights are bitterly cold. . . . We slept in the open, one blanket and waterproof sheet each man and I in my Klondike bag. . . . The mules are wonderful little beasts and generally are treated kindly. We have 2 black drivers with orders to shoot them if they go further than 100 feet from their wagons, make signs or speak to anyone on the roads.

June 29: Started ahead early with the advance guard of 20, six miles ahead of convoy with orders to search every house with or without a white flag and take all white men without passes prisoners. . . . We did a lot of riding, entering many houses, finding nothing.

July 1: Went ahead with authority to sack a certain rebel's house, which we did most thoroughly. At another house we commandeered one mule, three horses and some geese. The Boers, although popping up all around us did not show fight and I did not attack being in too small numbers and fearing being led into an ambush.

July 2: Commandeered a most excellent lunch at a farmhouse. The good woman said she had nothing to eat but corn. We searched and found every luxury. . . . Arrived at Standerton, joining Buller's force. The Light Horse go out at night, and have promised me a run next time; they captured last night two important Boers in a house playing billiards in the middle of the night.

Steele and the rest of the Strathcona's, as Adamson quickly discovered at Standerton, were by now miles off on the veldt, scouting for General Dundonald's flying column, the advance guard of Buller's army. For another two weeks, he and his men stayed attached to the Light Horse. "My own darling," he wrote to Mabel on July 6, "the enemy did their best to make you my sweetheart a widow [yesterday], but only succeeded in wounding my horse. McDougall of Ottawa shot through knee and poor old Sparkes of Ottawa clean through the neck . . . a most wonderful escape."*

Adamson's note, scribbled in smudgy blue pencil as soon as he reached the sanctuary of camp, conveys instantly, eight and a half decades later, the state of high excitement in which he wrote it. After all those years of firing blank cartridges in summer militia camps, he had at last fired the real things, and had had them fired back at him. "The sensation was most new to me," he wrote in a later, longer letter describing the action. "A bullet makes a most curious sound as it passes you, very much like an Elephantine humming bee. I do not think I was afraid. I should have left two very unhappy people behind, a strong spirit of revenge and hatred of the enemy filled me."

* This was George Sparkes of Ottawa, one of Adamson's closest friends, and brother of W. S. Sparkes of the Camel Corps, Mabel's former fiancé. McDougall was Gladwyn McDougall, son of William McDougall, Edmund Meredith's Minister just prior to Confederation.

In fact, as both Adamson's longer letter and the comments of others make clear, he and his men not only survived their first action, but distinguished themselves. Out of this small engagement in the Transvaal came Canada's first Victoria Cross of the war. Here is Adamson's account, the only comprehensive account that exists, as he wrote it but for the excision of a few details for clarity's sake.

> Strathcona draft 32 strong; Light Horse 350 strong, started from Standerton at 8:30 a.m. and advanced towards Enemy who was showing in small numbers at top of hill. Enemy vanished, with the supposed idea of drawing us into a trap.

Having spotted the Boer trap, the British troops halted, as they themselves attempted to trap the Boers. Most of the Light Horse withdrew back towards Standerton, leaving behind as bait Adamson and his small company of Canadians. The trick worked. But only to a point.

> Enemy fired at 3,000 yards and advanced to within 1000 yards. Had my horse shot in leg slightly, dismounted and advanced, firing. More enemy appeared and put us under cross-fire. Advanced to 300 yards, firing, horses following behind without being led, wonderfully well, there being no cover to put them in of any kind. Fire became very hot from front and flank. No sign of Light Horse. Three horses already being shot, three men down wounded, withdrew, with enemy coming on, about 200 all told I should think. Swung around my men to avoid crossfire. Stringer and Isbester, not seeing movement, advanced straight in old direction and were captured. . . . Held our position until too hot and more enemy appearing, so routed horses and advanced, finally gaining new position which we held till dark. . . . After dark we withdrew leaving McArthur and McDougall (wounded) under white flag at a Boer House.
>
> My men were wonderfully cool. . . . The bullets simply flew all around your head and boy, it is wonderful how any escaped; I was dressed as a trooper without a bandolier, but they were on to me. Another time, I do not see how I escaped, and the brutes were using exploding bullets that burst on your head like the report of a cannon. . . .
>
> It is most unfortunate that the Light Horse did not connect. I obeyed orders and the CO of the Light Horse congratulated me. My orders were to engage the enemy and wait til reinforcements, none of which arrived or we would have had them.

Adamson never makes clear why the Light Horse failed to return to trap the Boers; we can only assume that they lost their way on the way back. Still the engagement had been a success. Although under fire all day and greatly outnumbered, Adamson had not lost a single man, other than the two who were taken prisoner. Moreover, he had brought back all his wounded. "Richardson carried McArthur out of range of his own horse," he reported. "I have forwarded an account of the action to headquarters. It would be a great thing if we could get him a V.C. for Canada, the Strathconas and the Mounted Police to which he belongs." In September, Adamson learned that Sergeant Arthur Richardson had indeed been awarded the V.C. for his gallantry in rescuing a wounded colleague under fire in open country. Adamson himself won a mention in despatches.

"My nerves today are a bit trying and feel very restless," he wrote the day after the engagement. Aside from the psychological effects of coming down from his high, Adamson seems to have drawn from the experience a realization of just how difficult this war would be. "The whole country is full of Boers and spies, all orders are issued only a quarter-hour before they are required," he wrote. Nor did all the spies wear moustaches. On July 12,

> Entered a very smart Boer farm, three women, one a very pretty young girl, took their horses, drank their health in a most excellent cup of tea; they are Old Dutch, beautiful clothes as is the custom with Old Dutch families. . . . They said their brothers, father and nephew were not fighting against us but tending their cattle up north. Poor women, it is very hard on them, but it is impossible to believe any word a Boer says. . . . The Light Horse keeps finding hidden treasures and arms in what look like new-made graves, over which are crosses, and even inscriptions.

On July 16, six weeks after arriving in South Africa, Adamson and his men at last joined the Strathcona's. "Have been given my draft as a separate command," he wrote in delight. With the rest of the regiment, he was to do "all the advance and flanking work for Dundonald's column. The enemy snipe at us every day, whom we hold, sending back for artillery." The dangerous and lonely days and nights followed each other and more and more often in his letters, Adamson allowed the strain to show:

> *July 23*: We are on short rations, three dog biscuits and a little bully beef. Bitterly cold. Night and day work, all hands done to a turn. It is wonderful what power the mind has over the fatigues of the body. We bury poor devils every day.
>
> *July 24*: We make a move before it is light every day. Washing impossible,

> one night in bed out of every three, with the marrow of one's bones almost frozen; thoroughly done out and half starved is at present the condition of your husband, to say nothing of dirt and want of clothes. I think if some of your over-educated and unbelieving friends found themselves on top of a Kop at 4 a.m. with a Maxim with smokeless powder peppering them and could see decent, brave little Tommies giving messages to their mothers that they were dying like men and hoped to meet them in heaven, it might put the fear of God in them, but I don't think this is the breed of dog that is helping England to take this Godforsaken country.

In Adamson's final remark, we can glimpse a distant early warning signal. It seems clear that Mabel, waiting for him in England, had by now been rethinking, quite fundamentally, her own attitudes towards the war. Always more intellectual than he, she was also considerably more of a liberal. We can guess that within the cultural and social circles she was part of in London, she met many people who, if not actually pro-Boer, dared to question the morality of the war, and that she had passed some of their comments on to Adamson who, for his part – "your over-educated and unbelieving friends" – had not received them well. Thus far, though, there was no serious rift between them. "I see a parcel waiting for me," he wrote hastily on August 1, while back at Standerton. "If I look at it, you won't get this. I hope there is also a letter, even abuse from you is sweetness to me." The next day, having unwrapped the parcel, he teased her. "The socks are very nice and fit with a little hauling in of the slack." He also brought Mabel close to him by describing the life he was living in vivid detail. "Water is scarce and undrinkable. I have quite cured myself of wanting water; chewing a stone or a piece of wood is a great help." He told her how, as a substitute for wood to light campfires, they used "cattle droppings, which by digging a hole in the ground about half a foot deep makes a good fire." Repeatedly, he referred to the cold of the nights: "One ounce of rum is served out, it warms you up for an hour or so but soon goes off . . . as soon as you wake up you are too cold to go to sleep again so up we get, which is generally about 5." As discomforting was the "dirt and want of clothes. . . . I have not had my breeches off for six days." And the sheer exhaustion. "Ten hours in the saddle with your eyes cocked for Mausers, then out all night on picquet, and off again in the morning."

Adamson managed to write almost daily, in the form of a running diary, and these letters were collected once a week. Another four and sometimes six weeks passed before they reached Mabel in England. This meant that by the time she received them, that long-awaited "final engagement" that Adamson and everyone else took for granted would soon happen, would indeed long since have happened. In that set-piece battle, Adamson might be killed, and his letters would not reach her until long after the fatal telegram had been delivered. "The Boers have some game but I have no idea what it is," he told her. "A big show I fancy will come sooner or later. And now, my darling, have no fear of me. I have made arrangements that you are to be telegraphed fully, and the truth, if anything comes my way."

In fact, the Boers had no intention of changing their game of lurking in the hills, dashing down to ambush scouts and convoys. Buller's hope of drawing them down upon him proved futile. So instead, he had to go after them.

Early in August, the big push began. Separate armies, under Generals Buller, Roberts, Cleary, Dundonald, and French moved north, trying to force Botha's and De Wet's commandoes to make a stand by trapping them between British forces and, if that failed, to drive the remaining Boer fighters into the northern Transvaal wilderness. "The ultimate end will be a gathering together of all their forces north of the Crocodile River, in very hilly country where I hear one man with a rifle is equal to 100 trying to catch him," wrote Adamson on August 15 from his campsite on the Komatic River, a hundred miles north of Standerton.

For him and the Strathcona's, the push north had begun on August 3, when they reached the small town of Paardekop. From there, they pushed on to Amersfoort and then on to the larger town of Ermelo and on up to Belfast on the railway line. Adamson described the engagements in his long letter of August 15, the first chance he'd had in ten days to put pencil to paper:

> We have entered and taken three towns, the first was Amersfoort. I had the advance guard and two small gallopping guns, with orders to enter if possible, if not to hold for main columns to come up. We were not fired upon until about within 1000 yards of the town, when we charged in open order from three sides. We rode very hard, the bullets simply rained in upon us, some of the escapes were simply marvellous, saddle horses and water bottles suffered but not one man actually killed. . . . We dismounted and drove the brutes out of town. We held the town until the Flying Column came up. . . .
>
> The town was given over to loot, which was most thorough and perhaps a mistake. Two big shops were sacked of everything, bicycles, baby carriages, pianos, organs, smashed to pieces; silk stockings and woman's underclothes by the hundreds found happier homes on Tommies' legs . . . many a valuable house was pulled to pieces simply

to build huge fires. . . . Our parson's wife we protected but all her sheep, chickens, geese, pigs were either stolen or smashed. . . . I have always been under the impression that we did not loot, but in this case it was general, and no attempt was made to prevent it. . . .

Two days later, Adamson entered Ermelo, once again doing so with the advance guard, and this time almost without resistance.

We rushed to the Town Hall, pulled down the Transvaal Flag* . . . the town was not badly looted as the orders were against it, although a great deal was done by our men and the Light Horse. I commandeered the largest house in town, put a guard around it, and sent 3 men to cook dinner for us and make arrangements for 10 officers to sleep there; it turned out to belong to a very rich Hungarian merchant whom I found to be a Mason. He had been out with the Commando but wished to surrender. I promised to do my best for him; he got his pass and is now living with his most charming wife. He did us very well – 12 dined with him as he produced a most excellent claret (Chateau Margaux) and sweet champagne.

We remained two nights. On the second night about 3 in the morning I heard a great racket at the front door and in a short blue shirt went round the verandah to see the cause and was met by a maiden whose language was German. My brother Mason appeared in night robe and translated, while my legs grew stiff and cold, which was that three soldiers had entered her house which was close by and were in bed with her two sisters trying to rape them. . . . I had to tackle the job myself, after I had my breeches on, for to be caught without one's breeches on any occasion is not comfortable and in that case circumstantial evidence might implicate me. . . . At any rate, I did what I could and the brutes made their escape in double short order, but I greatly fear they were our men.

* Adamson brought this flag back to Canada. On a morning in June, eighty-three years later, Anthony Adamson unrolled it on the floor of his study in Toronto, still in perfect condition. Agar had also intended to bring Mabel home a more astonishing treasure; a live zebra, commandeered in October 1900 from the farm belonging to the Boer commander, General Daniel Erasmus. Sadly, the zebra died before it could be shipped to Canada, and Mabel had to make do with the skin.

After Ermelo, the Strathcona's moved on through Carolina, and then into the high veldt, together with the Light Horse and the 19th Lancers. "We are now, I believe, 6,000 feet above the sea. . . . The country is very bare, no wood. . . . Horse sickness, a disease particular to South Africa is doing its work; a horse starts out perfectly well and is dead by noon." This was the region, he continued, "where cattle are sent for the winter but they cannot live much after this month, which is considered one of the chief reasons why [the Boers] will come to terms shortly." The sun, the dust, and the wind were all relentless. There, camped by the Komatic River, Adamson completed his ten-page letter. "I hope this will reach you. It is being written tonight under difficulties, in bed with a sputtering candle. . . . It is too cold to write more and alas, your sleeping cap was stolen from my haversack."

Here, Adamson's letters to Mabel from the high veldt abruptly ceased. After this, he stopped writing daily, and those letters he did write – "a most unhappy letter" on August 31, as he noted in his diary, others on September 14 and October 28 – she did not choose to keep. Something had gone badly wrong between them, its beginnings perhaps an anti-jingoist letter from Mabel that festered into that most destructive form of marital warfare, a row by long distance, and then lapsed into sullen stalemate. For Adamson, as a traditionalist husband, the last straw, certainly, would have been Mabel's astonishing decision to abandon waiting for him in fashionable Belgravia to embark on a nursing course in a remote hospital in Yorkshire. "Letter from Mabel, giving address of her beastly hospital," he wrote in his diary on September 18. "Hardly the occupation a husband would choose!"

Being married to a New Woman was one thing. To compound the strains upon Adamson, his own splendid little war was no longer proceeding as satisfactorily as before. Relations between him and his commanding officer, Colonel Sam Steele, were deteriorating by now, close to the breaking point. Here a certain revisionist view of Canadian history may have to be taken. Steele, a pioneer of the North-West Mounted Police and a genuine war hero, has passed into our history as a minor icon, a *Lion of the Frontier*, in the title of an admiring 1979 biography by Robert Stewart. Yet, in Adamson's view, Steele was a coarse bully. Both views may be correct. But Adamson's, which he was by no means the only one to hold, has never before been expressed in public print.

Colonel Sam Steele, Commanding Officer, Strathcona's Horse. He was both a hero and a bully.

Adamson's doubts about Steele had begun as early as July 16, 1900, the day he and his troop linked up with the Strathcona's at Waterval. Steele was "doing good work," he told Mabel, but "lacks polish and is generally rude to everybody." Nor, for that matter, was Adamson much impressed with his brother officers, "a mixed lot" who, by implication, fell far short of the fine fellows of the South Africa Light Horse. By August 2, Steele had become "a failure . . . a good fighter but selfish and most inconsiderate to his men." On August 15, Steele "is most thoroughly hated. It is a great pity, and hard on old Lord Strathcona. Steele's language and general handling of his men is Billingsgate personified, and although I said in my last letter a good fighter, I have my doubts if he is not too excitable." As if then trying to be fair, Adamson added, "I tell you this not as a complaint or a growl. I personally have not spoken a word to him except officially. His only confidants are his batmen with whom he is on most friendly terms and I hear when able gets beastly drunk with them."

In the absence of any more letters to Mabel, we have only a few terse entries in Adamson's diary to tell us of what was clearly a deepening animosity as the Strathcona's pushed on ever northwards into the high veldt, pursuing Botha's army. On September 1, he was outraged at having been sent out to risk his men on what he considered to be a foolhardy and ill-conceived scouting mission. "Tried to capture three Boer wagons, we were surrounded, almost cut off from our horses, one man missing, was sent without support and with absurdly few men for the job, very lucky to get back." On October 7, put in charge of a dismounted troop, he was appalled at Steele's callousness towards the men. "Men suffering terribly from bad boots, the O.C. will not allow a single man to ride on wagons, most unjust." On October 18, as the regiment moved into rest camp at Pretoria: "C.O and most of the officers disgracefully drunk, making idiots of themselves at the club. The men left absolutely alone."

The truth of the matter remains elusive. Adamson's opinion stands in direct opposition to the entrenched Steele legend. In his biography, drawing on first-hand accounts by Strathcona's, Stewart sketches a picture of Steele as a severe disciplinarian, but not as the almost brutal figure Adamson saw. "He would brook no slackness. He demoted incompetent NCO's and tongue-lashed officers for drifting out of touch while on patrol. . . . [he once] sentenced a trooper to fourteen days field punishment for stealing some jam." And of course, while they may have clashed in the field, Adamson said nothing publicly. Steele in his own memoir of the war, written in 1913, reports only that Adamson and his men were "a very good lot."

Clearly, the core of Adamson's dislike for Steele was his most ungentlemanly behaviour: his foul language and his drunkenness and, even more, his negligent and callous treatment of his men, treatment that in Adamson's view, sometimes verged on the sadistic. Years later, he recounted to his sons how on one occasion, Steele ordered a dozen men suffering from piles to gallop flat out for five miles, his cure being to burst them and make them bleed. A Steele apologist would probably say that this apparent brutality hardened his men so that they could survive the war. However, Adamson's gentler approach appears to have yielded as many or more dividends, both in South Africa and later during the First World War.

It is possible also that something more was involved. Adamson's distaste for Steele may have resided in his knowledge of some incident involving the shooting of prisoners, as in the celebrated case of Lieutenant Harry "Breaker" Morant of the Bushveldt Carbineers. "I am afraid that when the truth gets out in Canada, there will be a great deal of dirty linen-washing about the Strathcona's Horse," he wrote to Mabel on August 15, in what may or may not have been a veiled allusion. In his biography, Stewart reports, without comment, rumours to this effect. "The Strathcona's were said to have lynched Boer prisoners, and when a British staff officer remonstrated, they threatened to lynch him too." In his own memoir, Steele sounded defensive on the subject. "There may have been men in South Africa who would have done this, but they were not in Strathcona's Horse."

Whatever the case, Adamson's experiences with the Strathcona's left him with a bitter taste in his mouth. The following year, learning that the man who he had lost on the ill-fated scouting party of September 1, 1900, and had presumed dead, had turned up as a prisoner of the Boers, "has helped make my reminiscences of South Africa less unpleasant than they were," as he wrote Mabel. In a succeeding letter, he recounted with quite uncharacteristic venom a piece of gossip concerning Steele's behaviour in London in February 1901, when the Strathcona's, *en route* back to Canada, were being fêted as heros.

> I got the full story of Lord Strathcona's lunch at the Savoy. Bobs [Lord Roberts], Wolseley, Chamberlain present. Steele arrived a bit tight and grew tighter, insisting on making a speech in the middle of which Lord S. pulled him up and said that they would have speeches on other occasions. He insisted upon continuing, in the middle of which he wanted to pump ship. He left the table. He was found to have lost his way, and found himself in a kitchen, on the stove of which he relaxed nature. He then returned, and wound up being sick on the carpet.

"All of this need go no further for it will do no good," Adamson wound up this account to Mabel. "I did my duty, while playing the game under the most trying circumstances." But he never forgave nor forgot. In May 1919, with Steele by then in his grave, and with Adamson now the hero of the hour for having brought home in triumph the remnants of the Princess Patricia's, the regiment he had commanded in the trenches, he was unable, writing to Mabel, to resist getting in one last dig at Steele.

> I had a long talk with Sir Frederick Williams-Taylor. . . . He told me many things about Strathcona's Horse I often wanted to know. Lord

S. went to the dinner in London with a cheque in his pocket for $10,000 to give to Sam Steele but he was so drunk and insulted Bobs [Lord Roberts] that he decided not to. He was also so drunk when landing in Halifax that the GG called off the reception in Ottawa.

Despite these rumours about his conduct, Steele's career prospered. In South Africa, he found an enthusiastic mentor in, of all people, Sir Robert Baden-Powell, hero of the relief of Mafeking, and better known to history as the simon-pure founder of the Boy Scouts. Under Baden-Powell's patronage, Steele returned to South Africa in 1901 to help found the South African Constabulary, a force modelled on the Mounties. Later, in Britain, when Baden-Powell was Inspector-General of Cavalry for the British Army, Steele served as his adjutant-general. He was too old to serve in the First World War and died in 1918 as a Knight Commander of the Order of the Bath and as one of the most honoured Canadians of his time.

Steele, clearly, was an extraordinary individual and some of his failings were simply human ones. Yet it is hard not to believe that Adamson was onto something in his distaste for Steele as a bully. One reason for concluding the argument his way is, very simply, that Adamson himself was so likeable a person and such an exemplary officer, that it is hard not to agree with him. The other reason is that the Sir Frederick Williams-Taylor who in 1919 "told me many things about Strathcona's Horse I often wanted to know," was, during the Boer War, Inspector-General of the Bank of Montreal, which was, for most practical purposes, Lord Strathcona's private bank, and so was better placed than almost anyone to know what had actually happened.

"I am sending you a book which I think is rather pretty," wrote Adamson to Mabel on November 7, 1900, in the first letter since August 15 to survive. "The lines on page 3 hark back to my sentiments of a year ago." He had not forgotten their first wedding anniversary but at this point, flat on his back at the Princess Christian Hospital, just outside Durban, he could attempt no more than a single paragraph. "Expect to be allright," he reassured her, but as his quivering, almost indecipherable scrawl would have told her, typhoid fever – the dreaded "enteric" that was endemic to the veldt – had come much closer than Boer bullets to making her a widow.

Or so, at any rate, Adamson wished Mabel to believe. He was ill, certainly, not only with fever but also from an unromantic case of piles that, during his last weeks in the saddle, had made riding

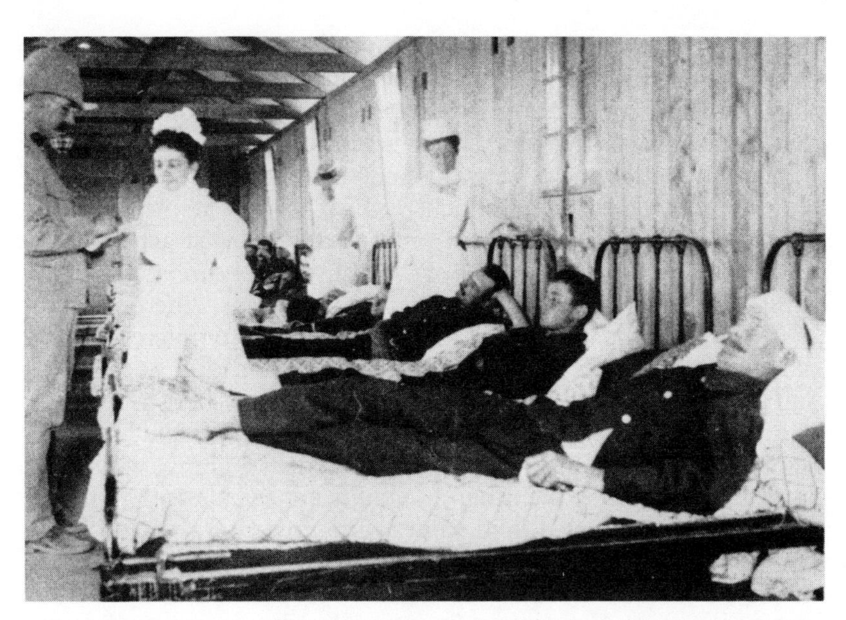

A military hospital in South Africa. Typhoid fever was as deadly an enemy as Boer bullets.

excruciating. But, as the perfectly normal handwriting in his diary written in hospital during the same period tells us, neither then nor earlier was he anywhere near as close to death's door as he made out. Indeed, on October 27, less than a week after coming down sick, he had "attempted a flirtation with a fair-haired nurse." He had not, however, "had the heart to go on with it, my mind too full of the beastliness of Kidderminster," Kidderminster Infirmary being the hospital where Mabel herself was studying nursing.

Whether or not Mabel ever saw through it, the ruse of male fragility worked. Six weeks later, when Adamson was invalided back to Britain, she was waiting on the dockside. "After five months of doubt, a misunderstanding . . . is cleared up," wrote Adamson triumphantly. "We are again happy!"

Immediately, Mabel whisked him off on a long, recuperative second honeymoon in the south of France. Here – at first the news came as an unwelcome surprise, but soon they were pleased – they conceived their first child. At Mentone and at Monte Carlo, it did not seem to matter that typhoid, by removing Adamson from the war, had ended his and Mabel's hopes of winning a place in an Imperial regiment – or even that somewhere *en route* to the Durban Hospital he had lost all his baggage, a serious matter, since without the precious War Office forms it contained, he would have the devil's own time getting paid. In March 1901, when the next batch of letters begins – from Adamson, now in London, hunting down the labyrinth of his back pay and booking passage to Canada, to Mabel in Switzerland, where she had gone to spend some time with the ever-demanding Mrs. Cawthra – he was once again fit as a fiddle and in the highest of spirits. "Drew £100 at the War Office," he told her triumphantly on March 14. "Sent you a cheque and will send another . . . unless you think it foolish to buy an Athol motor which weighs 25 lbs., is very small and can be attached to the rudder of any canoe, skiff or boat . . . it would be most useful this summer." He also visited motorcar showrooms – "the only thing that would suit us would cost £250" – bought a "complete outfit for playing ping pong," "an excellent small billiards table at the Army and Navy," and even, in search of a present for his cherished Ottawa aunt, rehoned his skills at millinery. "A nice little girl and I invented two bonnets – both black, to one we added an aigrette, white, and some violets, and to the other a magnificent buckle and an osprey which had to be curled, and some white flowers."

Adamson's mood of ebullience lasted nearly a year. In Ottawa, where he arrived in early April, six weeks ahead of Mabel, he received a hero's welcome. "Everyone has been very kind to me, although the maudlin rot they talk about South Africa is wearying." The Masonic Lodge presented him with a set of silver-backed hairbrushes. The city itself, thanks to Lady Minto's efforts was looking sprightlier. "They have built six new bridges . . . also a drive of 6 miles all round the town that cuts clean through Cartier Square and through our old tennis pavilion." Even the Senate seemed more amusing. "We have had two very long and one most trying divorce cases," he wrote Mabel shortly before she sailed to join him. "If they are printed in time, will send you a copy to read on board." Best of all, there seemed even some hope of advancement. "They have asked me to allow my name to go before the committee for an increase." In September, when the Duke and Duchess of York visited Ottawa, Adamson was selected to command the guard of honour on Parliament Hill. He not only received his South Africa medals from the Heir to the Throne in person, but also spent a splendid Sunday afternoon playing bicycle polo with him, in a game got up by Cloche Bell. (Years later, during the First World War, in which the fun-loving Cloche had perished early on, Adamson used this memory as a code to inform Mabel that King George V had visited behind the lines. "The gentleman who rode my silver-plated bicycle in Ottawa paid a call to us yesterday," he wrote on August 7, 1918.)

Later that autumn of 1901, he was still riding the crest, this time because the prestigious position of Gentleman Usher of the Black

Rod had opened up and, what with his excellent war record, he had high hopes of getting it. "I have made Sir Richard Cartwright solid, this now gives me four ministers," he wrote on October 30 to Mabel who, because her pregnancy had proved more difficult than expected, had gone to Toronto to have their baby, a son whom they named Rodney. The only serious stumbling block appeared to be Richard Scott, the crusty and venerable Secretary of State; even so, Scott's vivacious daughter Minnie, who acted as his political hostess, was an old flame of Adamson's. "Minnie told her father he had not treated her fairly after promising to support me and if he continued not to, she would give over to her sister the job of entertaining all his stupid sessional people, and go her own way." As late as December 9, the day of Bessie Blair's funeral following the fateful viceregal skating party, the job still seemed within his grasp but for one worrisome fly in the ointment. "Minnie Scott received a letter from Mrs. Forester asking her what chances Forester would have for the Black Rod – not to tell Mr. Adamson."

Minnie Scott's lobbying notwithstanding, the job of Black Rod went neither to him nor to Forester, but to a third candidate, one Molyneux St. John, a former Liberal journalist. Worse still, he and Mabel soon became embroiled in the second flaming row of their marriage after he refused to abandon his elderly aunt at Christmastime to join Mabel and the baby in Toronto, and she refused to abandon Mrs. Cawthra to join him in Ottawa. "Found a letter from Mabel in same tenor as one once written to South Africa," he noted bleakly in his diary on December 23.

In the winter of 1902, with his career going nowhere, and now with a wife and a child to be thinking of, Adamson's thoughts turned once again to South Africa, where the war was still dragging on. By dint of much lobbying (this time round, the Senate, by a vote of 32-18, and after more than an hour of heated debate, agreed only to subsidize an unpaid leave) he and Mabel managed to secure for him a Senior Captaincy in the 6th Canadian Mounted Rifles, a regiment raised in Canada but paid for by the War Office. Adamson set off with the highest hopes. This time, in contrast to Steele, his commanding officer, one Colonel Irving, was "a really charming old boy," as he reported to Mabel. Better still, the Regiment was taking its own horses along, and Adamson was delighted to commandeer for himself, "a thoroughbred, and also a very fine black." He sailed for the Cape aboard the troop-ship *Winifredian* on May 17, 1902; Mabel, having kissed him goodbye at Halifax, closed up the house in Ottawa and embarked with the baby for England; from there, she intended shortly to sail for South Africa herself, "to

The troopship Winifredian sails for the Cape on May 17, 1902. Adamson was aboard, once again on his way to the war.

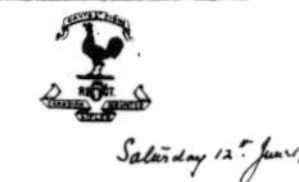

Saturday 12th June/02.

My dear Mabel.

Note our Regimental paper. Hamilton our genial Q.M. is sending you a prayer book emblazoned with Regimental Arms. We ought to sight the Cape lights tonight and by this time tomorrow will know something about our movements. [illegible] fancy it will be Durban. We have had a most delightful voyage, never at all rough, and only for

One of Adamson's letters from South Africa. He wrote to Mabel almost every day.

start life afresh under the Southern Cross" as Adamson grandiloquently put it in a letter. With the greatest good luck, he might yet find himself a place in "an Imperial regiment." Given moderate luck, and armed with a letter of recommendation from Lord Minto, he could find an appointment on the Governor's staff, or perhaps even become a gentleman farmer.

Adamson, however, had no luck at all. He and the rest of his regiment disembarked from the *Winifredian* at Durban in mid-June 1902, amid murderously stormy seas, a fortnight after peace had been declared. His attempts to find a job all foundered. "I have tried in vain, but they are firm," he wrote Mabel, of his efforts to join the Regulars. "They will not employ overseas Colonials." Back from Capetown came a brusque reply from the Governor's ADC. "He regretted that there were no vacancies of any kind and that for over a year there had been a waiting list outnumbering the possible jobs." The single firm offer came from an old army pal in the Bengal Lancers, now running a military remount station. "He offered me a job at 9/3 a day, but as the entrance to the mess is £10 and daily messing 7/6, besides polo 3 afternoons and hounds 3 mornings a week, I did not consider it for a moment."

Instead, he and Mabel dragged gloomily back to Ottawa, and

the Senate. Judging from the tenor of Adamson's diary entries, the years between 1903 and 1905 constituted one long "down-in-the-depths" period punctuated by too many splitting headaches, too many marital spats, and too few "new leaves" turned over. He and his superior officers existed most of the time at daggers drawn; in June 1903 he was actually suspended for a few days after a row with the Chief Clerk. Two years later, when a new political appointee was hired at a salary $200 higher than his own, Adamson resigned in a huff, and as Mabel had been urging all along, agreed at last to move to Toronto. There, matters improved considerably. They had a second son, whom they named Anthony; they also established a business, the Thornton-Smith Company, a pioneer firm in the field of interior decoration. While it was rather more her business than his, and a peculiar one for a captain of cavalry to be engaged in, it was streets ahead of the Senate. When not involved in decorating the new Royal Alexandra Theatre and the Senate Chamber, as well as numerous private houses, they lived as most Toronto aristocrats of the period lived, riding to hounds and giving dinner parties. It was a measure, though, of Agar's and Mabel's expansive, eclectic style that their circle of friends also included such figures as Professor James Mavor, the political economist and former socialist, and the literary critic Pelham Edgar.

Neither his work nor his social life was really enough to occupy Adamson. In August 1914, a chance to demonstrate his martial prowess came a second time. He was pushing forty-nine, yet within a fortnight, testament to the excellent repair both of his physique and of his friendships in high places, he had been accepted at his old rank of captain in a new regiment, the Princess Patricia's Canadian Light Infantry, composed mostly of officers and men who had already seen active service, financed by the Montreal millionaire, Hamilton Gault, and commanded by Colonel Francis Farquhar, Military Secretary to the Governor General.

Through nearly four years in the trenches, Adamson served with singular gallantry and distinction. His gripping accounts of that war, contained in letters written daily to Mabel, who was living in London and running an organization for Belgian Relief, belong to another story. Enough to say here that in 1915, after Farquhar had been killed and Gault disabled, he took temporary command of the regiment and won the DSO at Bellewaerde Ridge for directing the defence "with the utmost coolness" though in great pain from a severe shrapnel wound. The next year, he was promoted Lieutenant-Colonel and took formal command of the regiment, a position he held until February 1918, leaving then not because, as the story was put out, he had been passed unfit by a medical board, but because Mabel was about to undergo a major operation for cancer (diagnosed falsely, as it turned out) and he was determined to be with her. "I once told you that the only thing in the world worth living for was love," he wrote her. "To this, I have since added a sense of duty to one's country . . . added to which the good luck of finding the opportunity to make other people happy."

After the war, Adamson, as ever, refused to be bored. One of his new enthusiasms was flying and it was this that in the end was the death of him. Having survived a crash-landing in the Irish Sea and a three-hour wait to be picked up by a trawler, he succumbed to pneumonia a few weeks later. The date was November 21, 1929; Adamson was just a month short of his sixty-fourth birthday. Mabel lived on to see the start of another war; she died in Toronto in 1943. Of their two sons, Rodney, the elder, became a mining engineer and a celebrated mountaineer. From 1940 until his death in 1954 in the crash of a TCA North Star, he kept up the Ottawa connection by sitting as Conservative MP for York West, and was a member of George Drew's shadow cabinet. Anthony, born in 1906, whose buoyant memory has greatly enlivened this story, grew up to become a noted architect and town planner, best known for his achievements in the field of architectural preservation: he was chief design consultant for Upper Canada Village and, in partnership with Marion MacRae, has co-authored three definitive books on heritage architecture. He and his wife, Augusta, live in Toronto, in a Victorian house that in itself provides a link with yet another era we have known. "Rose Cottage," built in 1860, is only a block or so away from the site of Rosedale House, where Fanny Meredith grew up; it was one of the first houses to rise after the debt-ridden Sheriff Jarvis began to subdivide his property.

Always, when Adamson reminisced to his sons about South Africa, it was the rough, male war that he remembered: the bullying indignities of Steele; an epic race with a British officer, one Captain Birdwood, who later became a Field Marshal, to be first to haul down the Transvaal flag at Ermelo. But that war out on the veldt was also the first modern war to involve large numbers of women and civilians. A handful of these were Canadians; one was a young woman with whom Adamson, in his days as a young buck around Ottawa, would have had a nodding acquaintance. Her name was Florence Hamilton Randal. Like Amaryllis, she was, of all things, a society columnist.

CHAPTER 25

Moonlight in the Transvaal

The May Court Club is losing one of its most popular members in Miss Florence Hamilton Randal. She leaves Ottawa about April 12 for South Africa. All who know her will agree that the little Boer children who are placed under her charge will be very fortunate. . . . She is eminently fitted for the teaching profession and has more of those charming natural qualities which are not mentioned on school certificates, but which are quite as necessary as any book-learning.

Amaryllis; The Ottawa *Free Press*;
April 2, 1902

Coming from Amaryllis, such effusion towards a rival was unusual. Only a fortnight earlier, a bit of mild plagiarism on the part of her opposite number on the *Citizen* had provoked a fit of pique in print. "When the compiler of a column devoted to womankind and things social cribs one's comments and well-told anecdotes and puts them into her columns without a word of reference or apology, then one feels anything but flattered," she wrote. "I do not see any reason for women journalists doing what would be considered quite unorthodox for men."

But when contemplating Florence Randal, her counterpart on the Ottawa *Journal*, Amaryllis's tone was invariably supportive. "The May Court presented Miss Randal with a silver-handled umbrella and silver chain," she reported the following week. During the twelve months Florence was in South Africa, Amaryllis went out of her way to encourage her own readers not to miss the "long and excellent" accounts she sent back to the *Journal*.

Perhaps Amaryllis's generosity was motivated by a sense of relief. While the *Journal* itself, as the most serious-minded paper in the capital, did not go in for expansive society reporting, thus constraining Florence to keep her accounts to short, unsigned factual notes, some of her free-lance reporting was as pungent as Amaryllis's own. In October 1898, she had produced a dashing and even daring article on Rideau Hall under the Aberdeens for the prestigious monthly, *The Canadian*. Why were the chairs in the drawing room covered with such cheap and flimsy chintz? Florence had asked the "courteous official" who was showing her around. " 'Well,' he said gravely, 'it's this way you see, each Governor's lady likes different colours, and the Government – especially this one – is most practical, they can get what they want by changing the colours of the chintz.' " She also revealed an eye for the telling detail. "In LadyAberdeen's study are several good pictures; a grandfather clock, and Gladstone's face looks down benignly from the wall." In the schoolroom, "the wall is decorated with hockey-sticks, dumb-bells and tennis racquets and of course, the ever-necessary maps. A huge poster calls attention to the fact that A. and M. Gordon are able and willing to take photographs 'unrivalled for delicacy and finish' for such as will pay five cents a sitting."

Florence Hamilton Randal.

It may have occurred to Amaryllis, who, truth to tell, was not a beauty, how unfair it was that someone who was so pretty should also be so good a journalist.Florence Randal was quite strikingly lovely, with fair curling hair, a delicate oval face, and, her best feature, luminous cornflower-blue eyes. She was twenty-seven that spring of 1902, a native of Compton in Quebec's Eastern Townships where her father had been a merchant and real estate agent. After graduating from the genteel ladies' college, King's Hall, she became a governess and for a time worked in New York City. Later, during the mid-nineties, she taught school in Montreal and in the town of Buckingham, Quebec, twenty miles east of Ottawa, where one of her brothers was employed in the paper mill. During these years, she had begun to write: poems and whimsical little stories that were published in, among other outlets, *Massey's Magazine* in Toronto. She also put her fluent bilingualism to good use, trading lessons in French for lessons in shorthand and typing. In 1897, the same year Amaryllis began writing for *Saturday Night*, P. D. Ross of the Ottawa *Journal*, one of the most influential editors of the day, hired Florence as the paper's first society editor. To the Rosses, who were childless, she quickly became both daughter and protégée.

By 1902, though, "The Social Round," as Florence's column was titled, had begun to pall. Nor did free-lancing and occasional book reviews provide enough of a challenge for an ambitious girl. There is also evidence in Florence's diary for the early months of 1902, that there was a man in the picture, a certain "J.R.L."who appears to have been pressing her for an answer that she was not inclined to give. In any event, early that March, when the Department of the Secretary of State sent round a circular inviting young women with a teaching background to go out to South Africa on a mission of Imperial unity, she, along with more than three hundred others, submitted her name. "Before I hardly knew where I was, I found myself on the list," she records in her diary on March 5. A week later, she'd passed the medical. "Dr. C. saying my lung power and heart action were excellent." By March 24, the announcement of her selection was in the papers, and there was no going back. "I dread it a good deal, and yet I am not at all sorry. . . . It does not really come home to me at all that I am going to leave everything that I know. . . ."

As Florence kept telling herself, "I should consider myself very lucky." In her diary, she makes it clear that she regarded teaching only as a means to advance her career as a journalist. "Mr. Ross advises it, and I would love the trip and the writing of it."

Events that had unfolded in South Africa soon after Agar Adamson had been invalided home had given Florence Randal her chance. The culminatory set-piece battle that Adamson had been awaiting had never arrived; instead, the Boers had retreated into the almost limitless high veldt, from which they emerged to make occasional raids while waiting and hoping for the steady rise of anger in Europe to force the British to a peace settlement. In retaliation, the British, now under Lord Kitchener, developed a new, strange, and brutal form of warfare that was directly aimed at civilians. All across the veldt, squat and ugly blockhouses ringed with barbed wire were constructed: here the captured Boer commandoes were penned. Meanwhile, their wives and children, having first watched their farms and houses put to the torch, were herded into centres that by their title, "concentration camps," introduced an ugly new phrase to the language. By March 1902, about a hundred and twenty thousand Boers, or about half the total population, were inmates of some fifty camps. Conditions were fearful; the death rate, mostly from typhoid, an appalling 12 per cent.

Statistics like these, and the accompanying cry of genocide that went up all over Europe, horrified British liberals: Lord and Lady

Aberdeen; the up-and-coming member of Parliament David Lloyd George; Beatrice and Sidney Webb. Above all, they horrified an extraordinary, forty-one-year-old British spinster named Emily Hobhouse – "that bloody woman," as Kitchener described her. "I call this camp system wholesale cruelty," wrote Hobhouse, after a tour of the camps in 1901. "It presses hardest upon the children. . . . Entire villages and districts rooted out and dumped in a strange, bare place. . . . Of course, by judicious management, they could be improved."

One of Hobhouses's recommendations, backed by the prestigious, non-partisan committee of ladies who had followed her out to the veldt, had been that the informal schools that had been started in some camps should be regularized and expanded. Accordingly, the British Governor of the Cape, Lord Milner, appointed a young, idealistic teacher, C. B. Sargent, as his educational adviser. By the end of 1901, with more than thirty thousand Boer children enrolled in the concentration camp schools – far more than ever before had had any formal education – Sargent sent out the call for reinforcements. From more than two thousand applicants, two hundred were selected from Britain and another hundred from the white colonies. Florence Hamilton Randal, stepping smartly aboard the Allan liner *Corinthian* at Halifax on April 14, 1902, was one of forty Canadians chosen. In her lapel she wore as talisman a bright shiny maple leaf pin. As important to her as her mission as teacher was her commission from Ross to send back fortnightly letters to the Ottawa *Journal*, which he promised to display prominently.

The trip commenced more like an all-expenses-paid holiday than a solemn Imperial progress. In Britain, where the Canadian party spent a fortnight, Florence was enchanted by the greenness and, above all, the neatness of the English countryside. "All washed and combed . . . one could play tennis anywhere, with no expense for the rolling." As intriguing were the bizarre English customs. "They always push the babies backwards, when wheeling them in perambulators." "On May Day, I saw Jack-in-the-Green in the London streets, while men in all sorts of costumes danced around him for money." While in London, she and the others met Joseph Chamberlain, the Colonial Secretary, in a special audience; he gave them "a keen glance" and called them "Daughters of the Empire," but otherwise, "the aggressiveness of 'Pushful Joe' did not seem to mark him." Of much more interest to Ottawa readers was an invitation to a tea at Kensington Palace at which those figures from the capital's past, Princess Louise and Lorne, now Duke of Argyll, actually appeared together. "The Princess asked many questions about Ottawa," Florence reported, "but not so many as her husband." Louise looked "very well indeed," she continued, "in a rich gown of violet velvet, with lace at her throat and a hint of turquoise."

Best of all was the long, dream-like voyage out to the Cape, aboard a liner on which the Canadian girls were almost the only women passengers. "The piano was brought up on deck, and we danced and sang each night." One particularly pleasing partner was the Third Officer, "who writes poetry and yet knows very little about girls, a delightful combination, since he was willing to learn." At the Canary Islands, where Florence and the others all bought wide-brimmed straw hats, "small boys turned handsprings on the dock and sang the ridiculously incongruous 'Ta-ra-ra boom-de-ay' in hopes of a penny."

On May 25, Florence awoke at sunrise off Capetown to find "Table Mountain looming cold and barren in the early dawn." For a moment, she and the other girls were reminded of Quebec. "But the city that lay at the mountain's foot could never have been Canadian." Then, she added, feeling goose-bumps, "If we only knew what the next few weeks in a foreign land would bring forth."

The same week that Florence stepped off the boat at Capetown, Smuts, Botha, and De Wet were facing Kitchener and Milner across a bargaining table in the little Transvaal town of Veeringning. But, since peace had so often been promised before, she found in Capetown the same feverish war capital that Agar Adamson had described two years earlier. "The men seem to tumble over one another on the streets, so thick are they compared with women, khaki-coloured officers are everywhere, and very smart they look. . . . The women, I am told, practically live in white silk and wear feathers on their hats, reckoning a cost of five pounds a trifle. Those who cannot make a show in dress stay indoors." She was too good a reporter not to see another side. "The blacks outnumber the whites four to one and they seem to be regarded as a menace to the law-abidingness and comfort of the colony." Not that Florence herself, in contemplating blacks, was anything but a child of her age. "A cupid done in stove polish," was her description of one Kaffir child.

On the following day, the party set off by freight train on the jolting, thousand-mile, four-day journey to the Transvaal. Passing through the desert-like Great Karoo – "the dry bones of the continent showing through," she wrote poetically – they giggled, ate picnic lunches, and told one another's fortunes by candlelight. Then as they moved into the fighting districts, everyone turned serious. "For miles on miles, there was a network of barbed wire . . . hour after hour, one passes by blockhouses . . . at De Aar, where we stopped for lunch, some of us went into the graveyard on the chance of seeing some graves of Canadian soldiers . . . we found three . . . Oh, the ache of the heart one had to see row on row of white cross headboards, and to note how young were some of the Never-Grow-Olds." Other stops were more cheerful. "We chatted with some Canadian members of the South African Constabulary. . . . In their khaki, relieved by dark green and hats resembling those of the Strathconas, they presented a splendid appearance." On May 31, late at night, they reached Camp Irene near Pretoria: from this largest of the camps, they were shortly to be despatched to smaller camps throughout the Transvaal.

The next day, Sunday, June 1, just after church services, came the news that everyone had been awaiting so long. "We were sitting in the drawing-room tent when Colonel Pickwood came in and asked the Headmaster to read out a telegram. At last, at last, the long looked for Peace! Owing to there being some Boer teachers on the staff, there was no open celebration. The only thing we did, beyond being full of a quiet delight, was the singing of the National Anthem. The Boers in the camp sang their wailing, droning hymns of thanksgiving, and some of the women wept, either for joy, or because their former fatherland was no more."*

But there were many in South Africa, as Florence shortly realized, who did not greet the news of peace with hymns of joy. "For many of the men one meets," she wrote reflectively a few weeks later, "the war had come to be a personal possession . . . now all experiences look tame and of no moment. Before them stretches out a drab, bourgeois vista." Florence might well have been describing the sentiments of Agar Adamson and all the rest of his regiment – but for her, as a teacher, and more particularly as a journalist, the real drama of life out on the veldt was just beginning.

By early August 1902, just as Adamson, all hopes dashed for a "new life under the Southern Cross," was embarking dejectedly for England *en route* home, Florence was well on her way to becoming an old South Africa Hand. She had been to Pretoria, where Colonel Sam Steele, now of the South African Constabulary and presumably wearing his best tea-party manners had taken her and a group of other teachers on a "most interesting" tour of Kruger's old house.

* On that same Sunday, back in Ottawa, the Governor General found out about the peace in the most casual of ways. As Minto reports in his diary:

> At about 5 P.M. I found a pencil "phone" on my table from CPR announcing peace, taken off the phone by some of the servants . . . phoned at once to Sir Wilfrid telling him the news, and sent note to Hanington [Rector of St. Bartholomew's] telling him he could set his own bells going . . . soon the noise was terrible, Cloche ringing our own bells and all the New Edinburgh boys taking at a turn at St. Bartholomew's.

She had been down a gold mine – "I was glad I did it for the sake of saying so, but I did not enjoy it" – and had seen the gold capital of Johannesburg. "In some ways it reminds me of Ottawa," she informed readers back home, except that instead of streetcars there were rickshaws. "The runners delight me every time I see them, each with a varying head-dress, tufts of grass, or horns of animals, or great crowns of flapping feathers." She had also discovered, much to her chagrin, that a dim-witted adviser had recommended bringing all the wrong kinds of clothes to South Africa. "No white gowns, we were told, on account of the difficulty in washing. Brown holland would be most suitable." In the event, there was not the least difficulty in the washing, and next to the elegant rig worn by South African women, brown holland looked dingy indeed. "What made us crosser than anything else with our mentor in dress was that, when we met her, she looked so excessively smart herself."

In mid-June, Florence, along with one other Canadian teacher, was assigned to Camp Middleburgh. This was one of the larger enclaves, just a mile across the veldt from Middleburgh itself, "a very pretty little town with a large, imposing Dutch Church," on the Pretoria–Lourenço Marques railway line. The insanitary conditions that had so shocked Emily Hobhouse had long since been set right, yet the camp itself was "monotonous, with rows of tents and ugly buildings of corrugated iron." Florence was assigned to a spacious, comfortably furnished room in a "canvas house," that contained, "an iron bedstead with a white counterpane, an earthen floor carpeted fairly well with rugs, two camp reclining chairs, two large tables, a portable washstand and a mirror." By the greatest good luck, she had arrived on the epochal day that the first Boer commandoes came straggling in from the high veldt to reclaim their wives and children. For the *Journal* of July 21, 1902, Florence sketched this word-picture:

> As we neared the confines, we noted that the wire fences were lined with "kapjes," or sunbonnets, ruffled pink, white, and the rusty black of long-worn mourning. This was a great day for Boer womenkind, for a "commandi" was even then sighted coming down the road, husband, brother and son coming back after the weary months of hill fighting.
>
> None were allowed within the camp that day, but wildly joyful were the greetings over that open-meshed boundary. "These," said one young girl proudly, "are the knights of the Transvaal." Sorry looking knights perhaps they were in their patched clothes and dirty brown hats, but they received as great a measure of feminine admir-

ation that day as ever did the Jouster at a tourney, crowned by the Queen of Beauty. The young girls were tricked out in their gayest – but they grew shy when bearded men who had been slips of boys a while gone came up for their welcome . . . and some of the little band of fighters broke down utterly when they found no mother, wife or sweetheart to thrill and gladden at their coming. . . .

There was one boy of thirteen who was sadly in need of the clothing at once supplied by the British government. He said he had been living for months on mealies; that long before, he would have surrendered had not the veldt cornet threatened to shoot all who turned their horse's heads in the direction of any English garrison.

During the next few days, Florence set up her classes – "the hours are from nine til a quarter past one, with a short intermission when the teachers take tiffin in the mess tent," and experienced her first dust storm. "We lay awake for hours, fearing we should be blown away into the lonely veldt. Indeed, in the morning we found two of the school tents had blown down. It is really horrible, everything is covered with grime."

Middleburgh, though, had begun to change for the better. Renamed a "Burgher Camp" now that the former commandoes had joined their womenfolk and were waiting to be returned to their ruined farms, it soon began to function much as refugee camps would after the Second World War. One of the first things Florence remarked on, with some surprise, was what seemed a total absence of hostility between Britons and Boers. "One good result of the war being so long and drawn out has been that both sides were so tired of it . . . Boer and British teachers are on the best of terms and one generally breathes much easier when delicate subjects are broached than in many other places." Indeed, there were several occasions on which Florence found herself flirting with pro-Boer attitudes. "One likes to see old feuds die, but I could not help sympathizing with the little Boer teacher who said apropos of a dance, that she would take anyone for a partner as long as he was not a 'hands-upper.' " ("Hands-uppers" were those Boers who had surrendered and then worked as scouts for the British.) Another time, she confessed to "being consumed with desire" to do as the Boer teachers did and start wearing a "kapje." "These ruffled hoods are most picturesque, especially the white embroidered ones, but the other teachers seemed to think it would be *infra dig* to don one." Or perhaps it was not so much peer-group pressure as medical opinion that dissuaded her. "A doctor inveighed against them to me . . . as a rule, the Boer girls have very thin straggly hair, and the kapje habit may have something to do with it."

Every fortnight, without fail, Florence sat down to compose her long report, bristling with evocative detail, to the *Journal*. Ross, true to his word, nearly always ran these as a two-column spread on page three. Most often she wrote of the daily routine of the camp. "I have allowed my affections to be captured," she wrote early on of her students. "I had had visions of uncleanly little wretches. As to the reality, Piet's clothes are patched but not ragged. . . . From half-wild colts who have never gone to school the children have become respectful and most eager to learn. Their knowledge of English is wonderfully good. . . . One of the teachers told me that in clay-modelling they excelled, the boys being especially well up in the making of guns, knowing the difference between a Lee-Medford, Mauser, etc. 'What are they for?' a teacher asked a proud exhibitor. 'To shoot the English with,' came the prompt reply." As beguiling as watching the children was watching their proud, shy papas. "It was most interesting to watch the men coming in from surrender looking into the school tents at their little ones, going through the motions of the Swedish drill with the utmost precision, while a Scotch teacher gave quick orders and a Boer teacher struck the chords of a piano. For hour after hour, the men hung about enthralled."

By contrast, Florence found Boer women considerably harder to deal with. "Nearly all are long and lank and lean, dressed in rusty black and faded calico and none too clean in appearance." At first, she thought the bread they baked in their mud ovens flaky and delicious – but after a bit of investigative reporting, she was horrified. "In the mornings, when the members of the family have just left their warm beds, the sheets are made into a sort of tent, and the dough is tucked inside." Still, there was one aspect of male-female relationships in the Transvaal that intrigued her. "Womankind is rather spoiled by men out here, the latter seeming to live in wholesome awe of their wives. Indeed, the Women's Rights question would never need to be raised; the *vrouw* has long since seen to that. Her 'man' helps her with the housework . . . and generally 'flakes' around at her behest."

Unexpectedly, life in the "Burgher Camp," also involved a considerable degree of social reporting. Middleburgh itself was still a garrison town, awash with handsome officers who, as she tells us, "did

Florence Randal at Middleburgh Camp in the Transvaal, in 1902. Dressed as if for a garden party, and holding a bunch of marguerites from the veldt, she stands in front of the "canvas house" that contained her living quarters. In the background is one of the "ugly buildings of corrugated iron" noted in her columns.

not put on any airs at all." On July 31, 1902, she attended "the loveliest dance I have ever been to," put on by the Bachelor Officers. "They knew how to make us enjoy ourselves. We stayed til nearly three and I had every dance." Another "element to be reckoned with in one's social life," and not to be sneezed at, was the South African

Constabulary officer, "delightfully spic and span in his khaki and green, and plumed Australian hat." There were also the gallant fellows known to us simply, from Florence's accounts, as "The Repatriation Men," mostly former British and colonial officers saddled now with the paperwork involved in compensating former commandoes for their destroyed property, as stipulated by the peace terms. In the company of various bachelor officers, SAC constables, and Repatriation Men (but always with another couple along to play gooseberry), she enjoyed many a Sunday afternoon cricket match, and many a merry midnight picnic. "South African moonlight is a true gift of the gods," she wrote of one magic night on the veldt. "We drove out, after an hour and a half the valley was reached, and there at twelve o'clock the campfire was lighted, the coffee made and stirred with a burnt stick, and the alfresco table laid. Afterwards came cigar smoke, and songs and repartée. Then home in the dawning hours and rubbing of sleepy eyes in the school tent."

As delightful were the long leisurely daylight drives across the "trackless veldt," that with the coming of spring was transformed from an endless breeder of dust storms into a wondrous green carpet. "Large-eyed, short-stemmed marguerites are scattered over it, and all other manner of foreign blooms in purple and yellow. No one can tell you the names of the flowers, everything being 'blomen' with the exception of the 'heuning-bloisel' whose breath is all of honey." One afternoon in November 1902, Florence and another teacher "in the company of a former officer in a Canadian Mounted Regiment, and an Australian," drove out fifteen miles on a special mission. "We went to the scene of a sharp skirmish two years before . . . we had come to take a photograph of a grave. It was easily found, close by the main road, a cairn of stones and above it, a wooden cross with the words in black, 'Corporal Thomas Taylor, C.M.R., killed in action August 19th, 1900.' 'The handsomest boy of them all,' said his old comrade, 'and sent to his death by a fool officer.' "

Then, as Florence recounted it, the "former Canadian officer," alas un-named, spoke of an even more painful occurrence. "He harbours in his keen blue eyes that lust for vengeance of the slayers of another friend of his – Gat Howard. It gained so much more in the telling – the actual hills where 'we' got into a tight corner – the ridge from which 'we' lit out very lively." Whoever Florence's companion was, he held the key to a riddle, for the events that followed the 1901 shooting by Boers of Major Gat Howard – his nickname was from "Gatling Gun" – have never to this day been fully revealed. In his definitive work, *The Boer War*, the British historian Thomas Pakenham has provided the clearest account to date:

> It was an open secret that some of the irregular colonial troops made it a principle not to take prisoners. "Hold up your hands men," said Charlie Ross. Captain Ross was second in command of a corps of scouts raised by Major "Gat" Howard. We held up our hands. "I want you to take an oath with me not to take another prisoner," said Charlie. We held up our hands. These Canadians, according to one of the sergeants, had just found the bullet-riddled body of Gat Howard, shot after capture.

Major Gat Howard. The events surrounding his death in 1901 have never been fully revealed.

Perhaps Florence's companion was Captain Charlie Ross himself. If not, he must have been another officer from the same corps of scouts. Although she never wrote about it, Florence may have known the truth about how Howard was shot in cold blood, and about how his men then despatched those Boers they subsequently captured.*

On a lighter note, Florence later that summer accompanied an SAC officer when he set out on a patrol to search for proscribed stills in an African village, or "Kaffir Kraal." That bit of venturesomeness provided her with the material for an intriguing report that appeared in the *Journal* on May 26, 1903:

* Agar Adamson, during his time in South Africa, encountered Howard once, in late October 1900; they dined together in Pretoria. Adamson, however, was coming down with typhoid, "too seedy to cheer up," and did not describe the meeting in any further detail, either in his diary or in letters to Mabel.

The Chief of the Kraal, by name Abraham, was rich – and therefore disappointing. He wasn't a child of nature. He looked like a cullu'd gentleman ready to do a turn at whitewashing your fence. He had even got to the point of wearing a white man's neglige, and he lived in a tin shanty, and slept on a brass bedstead. His wife, a Cape Malay, was yellowing towards whiteness. She was kneading coffee over a brazier and she spoke very good English.

I asked the corporal in disgust if I had come to a Kaffir-Kraal for this; so he took me into a bee-hive dwelling, with a mud floor like asphalt, and thick walls fringed with bamboo palisades; then he fumbled at what looked like a Dutch oven, opened a door in it about a yard high, and stooping down drew me after him into the darkness. It was clean and of no disagreeable odor. It belonged to one of the four wives of a Kaffir who lounged somewhere about. Whichever of the quartet gave him the best "scoff" was treated with the greatest approach to consideration.

There was one very grand hut which we entered at the last. The walls were frescoed in an odd pattern of red, white and blue triangles on an orange foundation, crudely done yet most characteristic and pleasing to the eye in the half-light. A young woman sat at the door patiently stringing endless blue beads with thread of sinew, straining her eyes in the dusk. The corporal felt round the walls, seeking what he might "attach" in the way of beads, but she wouldn't sell much. I don't think it would have lain heavily on his conscience if he had stolen a few. But he did not get the chance, for she watched him closely. I fancy perhaps that he had been there before.

As we came out, she looked at me curiously. And then she turned to the corporal. "Baas" – she said – "Missis?" And she pointed to me. He wasn't in the least embarrassed. "Ikone!" he said stoutly. I think it's the only Kaffir word he knows. But it seems to answer. It has such an emphasis though, that I felt as if I had been definitely and absolutely rejected.

Not all of Florence's experiences in South Africa provided material for public consumption. "This is a queer land," she confided to her diary in June 1902, "I don't think I will ever feel less than a wayfarer and a sojourner." Florence was much too much a product of her time to say so even in private but reading between the lines of her diary it is clear that between two sets of restless sojourners – the dashing military bachelors of Middleburgh and the "daughters of empire" up the road at the Burgher Camp, there quickly developed an atmosphere of highly-charged sexual tension. Thus Florence devotes a good third of her diary entries from September 1902 to February 1903 to recording, in horrified fascination, the perilous adventures of one of the younger, flightier teachers, a certain "Olive T." who, in her afternoon gallops on horseback across the veldt with one "Mr. Ludgate" of the Repatriation Men, got deeper and deeper into trouble. "I can't realize that those two are living out so much of what one has read in books," wrote Florence on December 11. On January 26: "It is too late to save Olive now. Yesterday, she told me of what had happened the night before. She says he will marry her." Florence, at this point, was perhaps not the best possible person to come to for advice. Having spurned much earlier the moonlight picnic advances of a certain Captain Van Campau – "he asked me to kiss him . . . on a few hours acquaintance, but I am still hopelessly Canadian enough to prefer to know a little more about the man" – she was at that very moment deep in the toils of a less fleshly but no less complicated romance with one of Mr. Ludgate's colleagues among the Repatriation Men, a Mr. Thomas Wakeford.

Beyond the fact that she did not marry him in the end, and that in the privacy of her diary, she called him either "Wacky" or "Sentimental Tommy," not much is left to posterity of Wakeford. Still, as he emerges from the diary, it is clear that he shared much of the roguish charm of Agar Adamson in the days before he met Mabel and settled down. In September, for instance, Wacky began his courtship by telling Florence soulfully that although apparently in the pink of condition and a topnotch cricketer, he had "only a few more months to live." "It is ghastly," she wrote. "The other day we laughed and joked about going to his funeral. His underlip quivered in an odd way, but he was so reckless and gay that we thought nothing of it. He was watching my face yesterday . . . I came very close to crying." Three months later, on New Year's Day, the wicked Wacky confessed to Florence that "he had made up that yarn about his illness . . . his success astonished him." The first time he proposed, she thought he was fooling again – except that he was so persistent. "He didn't see why I was so unkind to him," she wrote on January 11, 1903. "Why did I take my hand away the moment he touched it?" "Strange to say," she reported the following day, "he really seems in earnest, he wants me for his wife. . . . It is queer to think a man would propose out here to a girl of whom he knows absolutely nothing, as to family and real character." As Florence's time in South Africa began to run out, Wakeford became increasingly insistent. "He said he intended to *make* me understand, if only the time left to him were long enough," she wrote on February 16. "Then I said, 'It's no use, Mr. Wakeford.' 'No use,' he repeated, and then he sat very still in the shadows with his hand up to his mouth for so long that I grew nervous and had to make some trivial remark." On April 26, a week before Florence sailed home to Canada, came the final parting. "He won't give up even now . . . I was sad at leaving him."

Although she spurned Wakeford, Florence was curiously ambivalent about their relationship. "I like him very much, and more each time I see him, but not enough to marry," she told her diary. The explanation for her rejection of him – an easy answer to suggest today but then almost unheard of – may have been that she was an ambitious woman prepared to put her own career ahead of marriage to someone who, no matter how charming, could never have come to terms with her sense of herself.

Early in 1903, as the camps began to wind down, Florence, with fewer and fewer pupils to teach, was given the chance to renew her contract for another two years and to teach at one of the new "farm schools" being established out on the veldt. But she had had enough of "this queer old country." She sailed back to Canada in May.

Instead of returning to Ottawa, and the cushy job awaiting her there, Florence Randal once again demonstrated her independence by heading off to Winnipeg, the boom town of the era, where two of her brothers were already working. There, for a time, she held down two jobs simultaneously on the Winnipeg *Telegram*, as women's page editor, and as secretary to the editor, Sanford Evans. Later, at the *Free Press*, she wrote her own column under the pseudonym, "Kilmeny." Society reporting by now was far behind her; she wrote often of such serious matters as the suffrage movement, and on one occasion, "the problems of a lady dentist."

In 1908, after a two-year courtship, Florence Randal married a former colleague on the *Telegram*, exactly the kind of man she seemed to have been holding herself in reserve for: the clever, iconoclastic political journalist and recent gentleman emigrant from Britain, J. F. B. Livesay. Two daughters were born of the marriage, one of whom, the elder and more rambunctious, became one of the most distinguished Canadian poets of our own time, Dorothy Livesay. In 1921, when Dorothy was thirteen, it was Florence who sent one of her earliest poems to the Vancouver *Province* where, to Dorothy's great astonishment, it was actually published and she was paid $2 for it.

Once married, Florence continued her own career; she pub-

Florence Randal in Winnipeg, shortly before her marriage to J. F. B. Livesay. Once married, she continued her own career.

lished a book of verse, *Shepherd's Purse*, and a volume of short stories, *The Savour of Salt*, and, as her most notable achievement, a volume called *Songs of Ukraina*, painstakingly translated from the original language, which she'd learned from her young housemaids.* To the end of her life, Florence Randal Livesay, as she now signed herself, continued to write poetry and to work as a journalist. Her last article, a short piece on the revival of Gaelic in Ireland, titled, "And Now, that Irish Question," was published in *Saturday Night* in May 1950, only three years before her death, at the age of seventy-nine, in Toronto.

Florence paid a price for her single-mindedness. J. F. B. Livesay became the pre-eminent journalist of his day, a war correspondent in the First World War, and later founder and first general manager of the Canadian Press. Together, the Livesays, who eventually settled in a handsome country house at Clarkson, just outside Toronto, became Canada's foremost journalistic couple, "the writing Livesays," as *Saturday Night* described them in 1944. Yet, as Dorothy Livesay recalls today, their marriage was not a happy one. One problem was that Florence was no hand as a housekeeper. There was also a deeper difficulty. "She didn't shine socially and she didn't entertain. She was too busy with her writing, and with her translations from the Ukraine. It was very evident that my father was jealous of her interests from the beginning." In a poem, "The Tears of Women," written in 1978 when she herself was nearly seventy, Dorothy Livesay wrote poignantly about her mother, from whom she had been estranged most of her life; perhaps also, she was writing about herself:

> . . . Was it
> praise
> she craved?
> Recognition of *the one thing*
> her talent?
> Or was it only a finger to rub her cheek
> a word of surprise
> at the Irish sapphire
> of her eyes?. . . .

In the summer of 1903, as Florence was setting off for the west in search of new challenges, another ambitious young journalist arrived in Ottawa. His name was M. O. Hammond and, as the new parliamentary correspondent for *The Globe*, he was about to take up the biggest challenge of his own career. In years to come, he and Florence would meet and come to be good friends. No evidence, however, exists to suggest that at any time during the eighteen months that Hammond spent in Ottawa, stretched over four Parliamentary

* A further group of Florence's translations from the Ukrainian, assembled and edited by Dorothy Livesay and Louisa Loeb from an unpublished manuscript in the collection of the National Museum of Man, was published by Hyperion Press of Winnipeg in 1981, with an introduction by the then Governor General, Edward Schreyer. Its title is *Down Singing Centuries*.

sessions, 1903 to 1906, he and Amaryllis ever encountered each other. Nor for that matter, unlike everyone else in this story but the wistful Janet Anna Hall, did Hammond ever once dine at Rideau Hall.

The capital Hammond takes us into is a capital that we have not yet properly explored: the jostling, untidy and slightly grubby world of the "Sessional People" – those who lived in Ottawa only during the three or four months when Parliament was sitting. If this world lacks the high drama of viceregal and prime-ministerial love affairs, it was a world much more in tune with the Canadian realities of the day.

CHAPTER 26

Sessional Person

This was the day which seemed to mark another transition stage of my career, for I was officially notified of my promotion to the Ottawa work. . . . Met Clara at the office . . . after an ice cream soda at Patterson's, got laundry, watered the garden and took the car to the beach . . .
M. O. Hammond; diary entry; August 22, 1903

Everyone addressed M.O. Hammond by his initials only – even, so far as we can tell, his loving wife Clara. This was probably by his own request, and for a simple reason. "Melvin" and "Ormond," Hammond's given names, might have done nicely for a curate or for a writer of romantic novels. But, as he surely reckoned, they did not do at all for a young gentleman from *The Globe*, determined to go places in the cut-and-thrust world of journalism.

Hammond, who had just turned twenty-seven that summer of 1903, was clearly going places. "Have made no New Year's resolution," he'd written in his diary on New Year's day, "unless it is to be further up the ladder at the end of the year than I am now." In March, when Joseph Flavelle's rival paper, *The News*, had offered him a job at the excellent salary of $20 weekly, his superiors at *The Globe* had almost matched the offer with $19 and – as mattered much more – had promised the next opening at Ottawa. Then as now, a posting to the Parliamentary Press Gallery was a plum for an aspiring reporter; it was sugar on the plum that *The Globe*'s news editor, Stewart Lyon, had taken him aside and put a confidential word in his ear. "He was very nice and rather flattering," recorded Hammond. "He warned me against disagreements with my partner at Ottawa. He also said my judgement was the better, and I was to use it in the work wherever possible, although appearing and acting under the direction of my senior."

M. O. Hammond, his wife Clara, and their son Harold, picking wild-flowers near Ottawa in 1905. The friend on the right is unidentified.

As bonus to his good fortune, Hammond was a good-looking man; dark and sturdy, with crisply waving hair and a jaunty, carefully-trimmed mustache. He was not at all a bumptious young man, though; his manner, then and always, was quiet and soft-spoken, friends recalled, and even a little self-effacing. Perhaps he worried that if he ever allowed himself the luxury of cockiness, the bright glittering world of all his prospects would suddenly vanish. Quite apart from being only a humble "Sessional," another characteristic of Hammond distinguishes him from Meredith and Amaryllis and Adamson, and from all the other people we have so far encountered. They were colonials and none of them would really have quibbled at that description, but he, quintessentially, is a *Canadian* figure. In hindsight we can see in him a harbinger of all the keen young men from small Ontario towns and farms who in years to come would set out for Ottawa in droves and who, in the process of finding their own futures, would establish in the capital a new and distinctively Canadian governing style. Eventually, this new Ottawa style would come to be apotheosized in the person of a young man from Newtonbrook, Ontario, who was also burdened with an overly-fussy pair of first names, Lester Bowles Pearson. There was also, come to think of it, the man who hired Pearson at External Affairs, Oscar Douglas Skelton, from Orangeville, a man who belonged to the same generation as Hammond and who, like him, chose to be known – "O.D." – by his initials only.

Hammond's boyhood home at Clarkson, Ontario. His background was quintessentially Canadian.

Hammond, for his part, came from Clarkson, about twenty miles west of Toronto. His origins were humble; his parents simple farmfolk of Late Loyalist extraction, his boyhood home an unpainted clapboard farmhouse. Reading the one-line entries in the tiny pocket diary he kept sporadically during 1890, the year he was fourteen, it is easy to picture the senior Hammonds regarding with pride, certainly, but perhaps also with a gathering sense of dismay, this precocious only child who, it was already clear, was not cut out to be a farmer. Other lads from Clarkson quit school thankfully at the end of the Sixth Reader; Hammond, rain or shine, rode a plough-horse into Oakville to the high school, and brought home such astonishing marks as "100 in Euclid!" Other Clarkson boys played scrub hockey on Saturday afternoons; Hammond, more often than not, "stayed in house and read and talked." Nevertheless, he was a cheerful, obliging boy who did not grudge his share of the farmwork. On June 26, 1890, he "loaded and unloaded and spread manure all day." On June 30, he "picked 92 quarts of strawberries." On July 15 he "helped set up the binder, which took us all day." In later years, as Hammond made his way in the world, it was one of his most endearing qualities that he never pretended that his background was anything other than classic Ontario Gothic. Thus in 1903, just before going to Ottawa, he spent one of his two precious holiday weeks at Clarkson, helping his father bring in the oat harvest. "In my old clothing and brown skin, I was surely a sight for Millet," he noted. Recognizing, with a start, that his parents were growing older, he felt a pang of guilt. "For the first time I realized what a sacrifice it had been for them to raise me, to go and live away from them."

Hammond had left home for good in 1893, when he was seventeen. His first stop was the Central Business College at the corner of Yonge and Gerrard in Toronto, for a course in shorthand and typing. From there – 80 WPM in the former, and 45 in the latter – he went to a job as clerk-stenographer at the Union Loan Company. But the world of high finance held no attraction. "Will have to stay until I get another one, which I hope will be on a newspaper," he noted on New Year's day, 1894.

The next year, on November 5, 1895, by coincidence on precisely the same day that another precocious type, William Lyon Mackenzie King, was hired for a short stint as a cub reporter, came the golden opportunity: the chance to be private secretary to *The Globe*'s managing editor, J. D. Willison, close friend of Laurier and the most notable journalist of the day. Willison, who had an eye for spotting talent and was himself a former farm boy from Huron County, saw in this eager nineteen-year-old the two qualities that make a good reporter: an easy, fluid way with words, and an insatiable curiosity. Within a year, Hammond was out in the field with a notebook conducting the annual crop investigation; by 1899, he had been entrusted with the much more intricate task of "looking into the state of people throughout the province." In 1901, he began covering the Ontario Legislature. It was the best job in the world, he thought, for *The Globe*, soon to celebrate the sixtieth anniversary of its founding by the legendary George Brown, was the most renowned newspaper in the land, with a circulation of nearly fifty thousand and a bumper Saturday edition that sometimes ran to thirty-two pages. There was even a special "*Globe* train," that arrived every morning at London on the dot of 6:45, to connect with the early morning trains radiating throughout the western

Ontario peninsula. An early public relations man had made up a song:

> Come see the Globe train passing, boys,
> she's snorting on the line
> And running round the mountainside
> A race that baffles time!

During these early Toronto years, as he was learning his trade as a journalist, Hammond was also beginning to cultivate in earnest the habit of keeping a meticulous record of everything that happened to him personally. He started in 1897, still much in the manner of a schoolboy, with a notebook that listed every boarding house that had ever housed him in Toronto – Jarvis Street, Shuter Street, Carlton Street – and of all the books he had ever read. *Ben Hur*, *Adam Bede*, and *Lorna Doone*, we discover, constituted the menu for March 1896. The rest of the notebook soon turned into a "commonplace book," as the phrase went, titled *Epigrams and Pearls of Expression*, into which Hammond transcribed passages that appealed to him – an eclectic selection that ranged from Robert Louis Stevenson, through Marie Corelli and Rudyard Kipling, to Lord Acton and Goldwin Smith.

At the beginning of 1903, the year that we catch up with him, Hammond started keeping a voluminous diary. From then on, until the end of his life in 1934, he wrote in it virtually every day. Like Edmund Meredith, he was fussy about the format: always in Hammond's case, a red leather notebook about six inches by four, a total in all of fifty-two. Much more so than Meredith, though, Hammond leaves us with the impression that someday, far down the road, he intended Doing Something with his diary, perhaps using it as the basis for a memoir. Almost always he wrote in full sentences, and he meticulously indexed each separate notebook on the inside front and back covers. In later years, as he began to ascend to the title of Canada's foremost literary journalist, Hammond more and more often used his journal as a means of setting down the first draft for set pieces that he might or might not get around to writing up later. But in these first years, he wrote much closer to his own bone: a naïve and idealistic young man, brimming over with intellectual curiosity, intrigued with everything and everyone he saw, from celebrities like Laurier and Borden to the nameless but interesting people he chanced to sit next to on trams. "I noticed a young mother with a babe in her arms and a fat boy about 3 years old," he wrote in February 1903. "The latter seemed stupid and emotionless while the mother was well-dressed, goodlooking and active, so that I thought the father must be a nerveless block of wood."

As fortuitously, Hammond also used these years of journalistic apprenticeship to cultivate a hobby, a passion indeed, that would sustain him throughout his life. At a time when the technology of photography was becoming widespread and affordable, he became a camera buff. Although he never referred to himself as anything but an "amateur," Hammond was a good deal more than that. His albums (which together with his diaries are deposited in the Archives of Ontario) constitute a priceless visual record of the era. It adds to the pleasure of looking at Hammond's photographs that in almost every case, we can identify from his diaries the date and circumstances – even the mood in which he took them. One of the very few things he does not tell us is exactly the kind of camera he used: most probably, it was a Kodak, perhaps a No. 4 Bull's Eye Special, a model that came out in 1898 and soon became highly popular.

Hammond was a gifted amateur photographer, particularly skilled at capturing children. His son Harold paddles at Britannia Bay on the Ottawa River, just west of the capital; an unidentified girl drinks from a fountain on Parliament Hill.

Pleased though he was to be going to Ottawa, Hammond's joy was not total. "I am a homebird," he wrote in his diary on August 23, aboard the overnight train, "and greatly dislike leaving my family." Although shy, he was not at all a loner, but rather a sociable young man who had cultivated a wide circle of friends, both male and female. At *The Globe*, a certain "typewriter" named Miss Jarrett had quite clearly had her eye on him. Instead on September 15, 1900, he had married Clara Williams, the pretty high-spirited daughter of a Methodist preacher. "Notable was the bombardment of rice just before we left the Union Station," he wrote on his wedding day, aboard the train for New York. "Honeymoon now supposed to be over," he wrote a fortnight later, as he and Clara returned to Toronto. "But I don't think it really is, believe it has only begun."

Time proved Hammond right. All his life, he would be a supremely happy family man. By 1903, he and Clara were the parents of a son, a rambunctious twenty-month-old named Harold, whom Hammond dearly loved to photograph, in his smart new overalls or his sailor suit. Such photographs, and Hammond's diary of his early married life, sketch a charming period picture of a kind of Mr. Pooter writing his *Diary of a Nobody*, in Toronto. He was proud of their trim little red-brick semi-detached at 704 Ontario Street in Cabbagetown, with its neat little garden planted with geraniums and sweet-scented verbena and phlox, and the "cosy red shade" that hung low over the dining-room table. He loved the "ideal evenings" they spent there together, he reading aloud from the essays of his twin heros, Robert Louis Stevenson and Goldwin Smith, while she sat sewing beside him; evenings that not infrequently ended up in "a jolly good romp" as Hammond, with surprising candour, was wont to record. Proudly, he shared with Clara the fruits of his growing success: the $6 a month necessary, after the staggering coal bill of $30 was paid, to splurge on the salary for a hired girl; another $6 for six yards of green crêpe de Chine to make Clara a spring dress in 1903, even though she herself would have been happy to settle for material at half the price. Somewhat disingenuously, Hammond recounted this purchase to Miss Jarrett back at the office. She, with evident wistfulness, remarked, "It must be a lovely thing to have someone want you to have the best, and be prepared to pay for it." Miss Jarrett was no doubt speechless a month later, when Hammond splurged the astonishing sum of $625 on a walnut upright piano for Clara.

In later years, the Hammonds would become renowned among the Toronto culturati for their cheery musical and literary evenings. In these early years, they were just beginning to get the hang of entertaining, she with with her "thimble teas"; "ice cream, salad, sandwiches flying, talk buzzing," as Hammond reported proudly; the two of them together at cosy evenings of euchre with fellow reporters and their wives where, although no money changed hands, husbands and wives racily switched partners to play against each other. There were the Sunday-night suppers at Hammond's in-laws, the languorous summer evenings out at Balmy Beach, the Saturday afternoons spent pushing Harold round Riverdale Zoo in his perambulator, Hammond stopping frequently to photograph the polar bear, the elephant, and his favourite subjects, the storks; the occasional strolls downtown to ogle Toronto society disporting itself in the brand new, and in Hammond's opinion, "gorgeous" King Edward Hotel, "the Alhambra Palace of the West," as the advertisements described it.

All of which made packing "a rather sorrowful proceeding," even though Hammond would be away just for a few months, until the end of the Parliamentary Session. "There were lumps in my throat while I gathered my clothes and books into my trunk," he wrote. "Took Clara to the station and said goodbye with as much sorrow as if I were going to the Pacific Coast."

Next morning, Hammond was wakened abruptly by the sleeping car shunting and jolting in the Ottawa yards. "It was a lovely morning, and with the return of daylight my courage and spirits revived." He heaved his luggage aboard a streetcar, and set out briskly to conquer the capital.

"Had a good breakfast in the Senate Restaurant and met my partner, Charlie Matthews," wrote Hammond of that all-important first morning in Ottawa, August 24, 1903. He'd been summoned to the Press Gallery in the middle of the Parliamentary Session, and so had a great deal of catching-up to do. The first item on his agenda, though, was the one that was always top priority for Sessional People: "Set out to find a room." This was always a challenge, no less than in Edmund Meredith's day. Unless one were a wealthy enough Sessional to be able to book, long in advance, one of the renowned feather-beds at the Russell House, the problem was to select not so much the best possible anchorage among the dingy flotillas of downtown boarding houses, but the least horrid one. "The usual old trouble," wrote Hammond in 1906, demonstrating during his last season in Ottawa, the wisdom of experience. "Dirt, bad smells, dark halls, dirty women."

As a rule, Hammond did better by way of lodging than most of his colleagues. His upright appearance and winning ingenuous manner usually cajoled the better sort of landladies into unlocking the doors of rooms that were already bespoken, or even dislodging other more obnoxious tenants. That first year, he quickly found a comfortable, "parlour bedroom" at Miss Finn's on O'Connor Street for $12 a week. The next year, when he brought Clara and Harold up to join him, he was even luckier and engaged "two splendid front rooms" at Mrs. Robinson's on Nepean Street, $50 a month, with three meals included. Indeed, the Hammonds became so friendly with Mrs. Robinson that when the 1904 session ended, they gave her a "Wedgwood fern bowl." "Poor soul, she will be lonesome with a neglectful husband and an unsociable son," he wrote. But in 1905, with Mrs. Robinson's establishment already full up, Hammond experienced the same travails as everyone else. "Today will long be remembered because of furnishing my first good-sized row with anybody," he wrote on April 26 of a certain Mrs. Hall. "The end was our packing up to leave tomorrow." The problem was a common one: not enough heat. "Clara went to the kitchen to get hardwood for the grate, it would not burn . . . I said to Mrs. Hall, there was nothing to do but change; she said we had taken the rooms for the session and would have to pay for the session. . . . As we were moving, she ordered the wagon driver to stop and told me she had consulted her lawyer. . . . I was so poor a talker compared to her, I fear I did not say much, and we settled for $5." But it

The Russell House hotel. For Hammond, and for all other "Sessional People," this was an extension of government.

was not in Hammond's nature to part with anyone in anger. "In the end, I shouted back over my shoulder, and said I hoped she would have good luck." The Hammonds in any event were lucky: it turned out that space had freed up suddenly at Mrs. Robinson's.

Where Sessionals actually had the misfortune of sleeping was one thing. What they did with the rest of their leisure hours was quite another. Hammond, like everyone else, soon made it part of his daily routine to check out the action at the Russell House, and not only because *The Globe*, like most other major newspapers, maintained a small telegraphic office there. The Russell, like the legendary Willard's in Washington, was much more than just an hotel. It was the capital's great meeting place and central promenade. "A little city within a city," as a Quebec journalist had written in the

1880s. "It is like the Pont d'Avignon, all the world passes by. Would you like to meet the big and little people of politics and journalism? Go to the Russell." At the Russell, back in the 1860s, Edmund Meredith had been delighted by the cuisine in the big noisy dining room, where guests clustered round long tables. At the Russell, in the 1890s, Laurier had sat down to write to Emilie on Sunday afternoons in his musty bed-sitting room, all cluttered with papers and books. Here it was, in the spacious ground-floor reception rooms, that Emilie had held her bravura Christmas reception of 1897.

By the turn of the century, the Russell's days were already numbered; plans were on the drawing-boards for a much larger, much grander hotel that, in 1912, emerged as the Chateau Laurier. Yet, as if in defiance, under its bustling, showman-like manager, one M. St-Jacques, the Russell flourished as never before: a vast, rambling four-storey pile that occupied nearly a full city block at the corner of Sparks and Elgin, with bright red-and-white-striped awnings, a vast lobby with a gleaming floor of tile, and – a startling innovation for 1903 – a brand-new candlelit café of which even the soignée Amaryllis approved. "A gorgeous little place," she wrote. "There are some *cabinets-particulières*, the cutest little cubicles in brown and soft green, with little tables and chairs for two or four or six for supper or dinner."

The Russell functioned as an extension of government. Into the famous "Hotel Bar," at the back of the lobby just off to the right, flocked MPs, Senators, job-hunters, and lobbyists, to be swallowed up instantly in a cloud of blue cigar smoke.

A Press Gallery colleague of Hammond's, Paul Bilkey of the rival Toronto *Telegram*, summed up the Hotel Bar in his 1940 memoir, *Persons, Papers and Things*. "If any single individual could have known and written it, it would have been the history of Canada over a very long period, and some of it would have been unprintable."

As a Methodist teetotaller, Hammond seldom if ever entered the bar. Nor did he dine at the Russell Café; his kind of eating places were the small, hole-in-the-wall lunch parlours that flourished all over the business district, Cassidy's and the London and the Uwanta, where a beefsteak with onions, or an oyster stew could be had for a quarter, with an occasional seasonal splurge on peaches and cream at the restaurant in Bryson's and Graham's on Sparks Street, the leading department store of the day. But Hammond greatly enjoyed lingering in the Russell lobby watching "the world and his wife" parading by. In September 1903, soon after he arrived, the star guest was the legendary Lily Langtry, come to perform in a play called "The Captain's Divorce" at the adjoining Russell Theatre. Unlike the Earl of Minto, who caused tongues to wag by coming without Lady Minto and by visiting Langtry backstage in her dressing-room, Hammond was not much impressed. He was, however, much taken by the ubiquitous Signor Guglielmo Marconi, in town to lobby for funding for his wireless telegraphy station in Cape Breton, whom he spied across the lobby on September 13, and asked for an interview. "He was courteous to a degree and showed none of the impatience characteristic of many men under such circumstances, but said he had no news as yet. . . . He wore the insignia of some order, and it was a mass of diamonds, while his whole person was redolent of rare perfumes."

The original Centre Block, photographed by Hammond in the winter of 1905. It was a much more human and welcoming place than its modern replacement.

For Hammond, as for all Sessional People, the focus of life during the four or five months they spent annually in the capital was, naturally, Parliament Hill. While cabinet ministers maintained their offices in the East and West blocks, with their civil servants in close attendance, all of the MPs and the Senators and the Press Gallery reporters lived and worked and played in the Centre Block, or, as it was more often known, "The House of Commons Building."

This original centrepiece of the tryptych, destroyed by fire in 1916 but for the Library, has been all but blotted out of our history, which is a pity. Hammond himself, although a lover of fine architecture, gives us almost no impressions of the original building in his diary; instead, he let his camera do the work. From his photographs, and from the descriptions of others, it is clear that this first "House of Commons Building" was a much more human and welcoming place than its much grander later replacement. "I hear talk of a 'much larger, more imposing, up-to-date building,' " wrote the poet Duncan Campbell Scott to his friend, the Toronto literary critic, Pelham Edgar, a few days after the 1916 fire. "The very phrase makes one shudder. We had a building that was beautiful, and harmonized with the site. . . . If they can put up a more beautiful building, let them put it up somewhere else."

The original House of Commons Chamber. The Press Gallery, in which Hammond spent so many of his working hours, was just behind the Speaker's Chair.

Many agreed with Scott. "The construction is better . . . the accommodation is incomparably superior," wrote Senator Charlie Bishop, a one-time reporter on the Ottawa *Citizen*, of the new building, in a long, nostalgic article published in 1945. "But that vague and indefinable thing known as 'atmosphere' is much less attractive." The central spire of the original building, suggested by that of the Cloth Hall at Ypres, in Belgium (later to have its own tragic place within Canadian history), was much lower, much less intimidating, than that of the modern Peace Tower. "From it came the harmony of beauty and of dignity," wrote Bilkey of the *Telegram*. "It was restful to the eye, and soothing to the soul."

Inside, the atmosphere was much clubbier than within the replacement. There were no private offices, and members had to make do with an individual locker for their coats, hats, and umbrellas. The Commons Chamber itself, located in the middle of the building instead of, as today, at the extreme west, was much cosier, a square-shaped room, quite small, and with rows of seats that rose more abruptly, more in the manner of the Commons at Westminster. "The speaker now faces south," wrote Bishop. "He used to face east, in the direction from which the wise men came." The Press Gallery, in which Hammond and Bishop and Bilkey spent so much of their working day, was a mezzanine, swooping dangerously low over the Speaker's chair. "Compared with the present one, it was atrociously inadequate, on big days especially," wrote Bishop. "It never collapsed, but the support seemed none too strong and one felt as if it were liable to crash at any time."

The Senate Chamber in 1911, decorated in crimson and gold by Thornton-Smith, the firm established by Agar and Mabel Adamson. Unfortunately the snuff box on the clerk's table is not visible.

Much grander than the Commons, much larger than its counterpart today and in Bishop's opinion, much more attractive, was the Senate Chamber, located then as now, at the east end. "The spacious outer lobby was a show place, deeply carpeted in crimson and with crimson and gold draperies," he informs us. "It was a sort of vale of Beulah, a vestibule to the sanctum sanctorum. Inside was more of crimson and gold. The spacious senatorial chairs were richly upholstered in silk. . . . Reposing on the clerk's table was a small rosewood box, not overly conspicuous. The attendant, calling attention to it, said softly, 'This is the snuff box.' When the Senate was sitting, some venerable members would be seen in habitual approach to the treasured receptable. They would take a pinch of snuff, inhaling deeply, and probably producing at once a mild gale of sneezing. It was supposed to be good for the circulation.

Much the most convivial rooms in the House of Commons building were the members' lounges: Number 16 for government supporters; Number 6 for the Opposition. Here, in the absence of private offices, the politicians gathered to gossip and to do their constituency work at long writing tables that ringed the walls, assisted by "sessional clerks" who, in that era, were still uniformly male. Number 9 was the smoking room, but in Bishop's description it might equally well have been called the poker room. "The atmosphere was usually redolent of shag tobacco. . . . When the hour got late, and spirits became restless, resort was often made to the high stakes of 'stud.' The members smoked pipes. A few were given to cigars. One never saw a member smoking a cigarette." Downstairs, in the basement, were to be found the restaurants of both the Senate and of the Commons; for some long-forgotten reason, the latter was always known as "The Ark." For MPs and Senators alike, in an era when the salary of the prime minister was $12,000, that of the Opposition Leader $7,000, and that of run-of-the-mill backbenchers $2,500, the flat rate of $20 a month took care of three meals a day, seven days a week. "There were bars in the vicinity," we learn from Paul Bilkey, "one for the stimulation of the Commoners and one where the elder statesmen assuaged a thirst which, considered collectively, would have shamed a camel. The port on the Senate side was somewhat celebrated, but the Commons bar could produce in an emergency a decoction of rum which was very comforting to the wounded heart." In the case of the Senate Bar, a certain degree of circumlocution was always involved. "It was not considered proper to invite a friend or a colleague down to have a drink," Bilkey relates. "There was a prescribed ritual which was rigidly observed. 'Let us,' the hospitable one would say, 'go down and see the cornerstone.' "

Hammond, the non-drinker, spent little time in any of these haunts. He enjoyed the camaraderie of the press room, a small square chamber with a cosy grate fireplace on the ground floor at the back of the western end; he loved browsing in the library and the reading room to which, as he noted, "Access is a privilege that a king, if he be a literary person, might envy"; as a boarding-house dweller he was everlastingly grateful for the splendid marble bathtubs provided for Parliamentarians. But when not actually taking rapid-fire shorthand notes in the Press Gallery he loved to slip off to the spot at the back of the western end of the building overlooking the Ottawa River that in those days – the name has long since vanished – was known as "Sunset Point." Here, as part of the Ottawa Improvement Commission's attempts at beautification, there had recently been built a pretty pagoda-like pavilion that made a delightful place to sit. It is easy, from any number of Hammond's

"Sunset Point." Here, on the bluff behind the Parliament Buildings, Hammond loved to linger. The pavilion was demolished around 1950.

diaries and photographs to picture him there with a book on his knee, or perhaps a half-finished letter to Clara in front of him, a straw boater on the bench beside him, in shirt-sleeves and a suit that as Clara would surely remark, could do with a bit of a press. The golden, late-summer evening of August 31, 1903, will do as well as any. "Went out on the Hill and read Paul's *Men and Letters* and watched a man and a woman in a small boat dodging about on the river, picking up driftwood from the sawmills, apparently for fuel. . . . As the night descended, and the lights glimmered in Hull and Western Ottawa reflecting on the inky darkness of the river, it was beautiful."

For most Sessional People, the trek between their boarding houses and the House of Commons building, with a short spur eastwards in the direction of the Russell House, defined the perimeter of the only capital they ever knew. Hammond was different. He possessed both a powerful visual sense and an insatiable instinct to learn. For a southern Ontario farm-boy, Ottawa was a new and intriguing environment, and he was determined to wring out of it as much as he possibly could. From the beginning, he was an habitué of the National Gallery, which at that stage of its shifting fortunes, shared a building on O'Connor Street with the Dominion Fisheries Exhibit. "The pictures have a perpetual fascination for me, particularly, 'The Bay of Naples,' " he wrote. Perhaps, when contemplating this particular picture, the proximity of the other tenants only added to the verisimilitude. "The fish smelled bad, although the young fry recently hatched were very active and interesting."

Hammond, above all, found the capital an endless source of inspiration for taking photographs. On his first morning, right after finding a room at Mrs. Finn's, he made a beeline for the establishments of the leading photographers, Topley and Jarvis. To his great delight, Jarvis, after looking over Hammond's portfolio, suggested he enter a competition for "amateurs." In the event, he won top prize – although for which particular picture he does not say.

The view across to Hull from Sunset Point. Hammond was fascinated by the French Fact.

On August 27, 1903, Hammond set out on his first Ottawa shoot. "Took 3 pictures on the Hill, one of Victoria's statue, one of the Library and one of the northeast elevation of the Commons building." On September 2, in between takes of reporting a railway debate in the House, he rushed out to take "several pictures round Parliament Hill and Lovers Walk, coming back in time for the 3-4:30 take." Soon, in the company of another Press Gallery member called Dunbar who was also a camera buff, he began venturing further afield. At Rockcliffe, "we found beautiful vistas in abundance and we fairly revelled as we spied the Gatineau Point church through frameworks and traceries of beautiful trees and branches, and afterwards, we took the sun on the water."

Cemetery in Hull with Angel Gabriel Arch

Beyond the tinge of exoticism suggested by the Gatineau Point church lay something that, almost uniquely among Hammond's contemporaries, attracted his attention. This was the French Fact, although no one then called it that. On Thanksgiving Day, alone, for "everyone who would have been available went to the football match," he "determined to explore the Quebec side a bit, so walked across the bridge to Hull and turned east along the main road. . . . I came to a cemetery, the extraordinary entrance to which attracted my attention. It was a huge stone arch surmounted by a statue of the Angel Gabriel blowing a trumpet." Having stopped to take a picture, he walked on eastward to the Gatineau River. "Here is the splendid church whose spire is visible from Ottawa. . . . I walked

An old house in Hull. The carriages in the yard suggest the home of a cab-driver.

up the riverbank along the very narrow street. The houses are very plain exteriorly, but open doors frequently revealed taste and cleanliness inside. Everyone seems to have a boat, and a big woodpile stands in front of each house." The following June, he spent a Sunday morning photographing the annual Corpus Christi procession in Ottawa's Lower Town. "This old world festival appealed to my artistic impulses . . . a most unique outdoor ceremony, conducted by the Papal Delegate, Monsignor Sbarretti, conducted under a canopy to the front steps of the Church, and there he elevated the Host, the candles burned in the daylight and incense was burned, Latin hymns sung and prayers chanted; the little girls confirmed today knelt in a V shape behind the Delegate, while hundreds of devout Catholics on the lawns, the sidewalk and even in the muddy street knelt in a semi-circle."

Two views of the Corpus Christi procession in Lower Town, June 5, 1904.

As a proper Methodist, Hammond may have felt a bit guilty about flirting with Popery. Most Ottawa Sundays found him dutifully taking in the lengthy, Yorkshire-accented sermons of the Reverend G. F. Salton, pastor of the Dominion Methodist Church – "popular church for swell people," as he noted – where the Clifford Siftons and the Frederick Bordens were fellow-worshippers. But for a young man with an open mind, these brushes with another culture, along with meetings with a number of politicians from Quebec whom he came to admire, inspired a feeling of empathy with French Canadians that even in our own time would be unusual for someone from his background, and which in Hammond's time was quite astonishing.

In 1903, Official Bilingualism was still at least six decades in the future. Yet that autumn, we find him investing in a French grammar, and poring over it religiously out on Sunset Point. "Learning to conjugate the verb *avoir*": he wrote in October. "There might be some hope for me." He kept at it. "Studied nouns and pronouns for 1½ hours" he reported the following March. "I am making good progress." In 1905, during the ferocious debate over minority education rights in the new provinces of Alberta and Saskatchewan, we find him in heated argument with a former colleage on *The Globe*. "I told him he argued as a Protestant and I as a Canadian, that the RCs are here, and we have to recognize that." Later that summer, preparing for a photographic trip to the Papineau seigneurie at Montebello, we find him falling under the spell of Papineau's grandson, the independent member for Labelle, Henri Bourassa. "He is most charming and talked to me most freely. He is quick as a flash, has all the courtesy and wit of the old school, together with keen intelligence and the ability to impart it readily; altogether, he is a likeable man." Mind you, Hammond never cared much for Bourassa's younger disciple Armand Lavergne, whom he described on one occasion as "the smart-alec from Montmagny" and on another as "a squirt."

The Chateau at Montebello, photographed by Hammond on June 24, 1905. At this time, the estate was still owned by the Papineau family. When Hammond arrived with his camera, he had much the same kind of experience as Edmund Meredith had on his natural history society excursion in 1868. As Hammond recorded,

> *Sought the man of the house, young Mr. Papineau, about 20 years old, who is a grandson of the late rebel leader, he at first declined admission to the house but afterwards followed us out and said he would make an exception. . . . Young P is at the developing stage, but bright and talkative, though not overly posted on his distinguished ancestor's history. . . .*

This was probably Talbot Papineau, Henri Bourassa's first cousin. He was a figure of great promise, killed at Passchendaele during the First World War. In later years, the Papineau estate became the exclusive Siegniory Club; since 1970 it has been a resort hotel. In 1981, it was the site of the annual summit conference of the industrial powers.

Nor was Hammond, although a devoted husband, entirely immune to another aspect of Gallic charm. In 1905, when he and Clara attended a "Government Wives" reception at the Russell House, they spent most of the evening as "wall ornaments, watching the dancers dance," for neither of them, as strictly brought up Methodists, had ever learned the polka or the lancers, much less the wicked waltz. Instead, he observed the scene with interest. "The contrast was quite apparent between the warmblooded French girls and the more stolid Englishwomen," he noted in his diary.

There was more to Hammond's fellow feeling with French Canadians than just a passing fancy of his idealistic youth. A decade later, in a thoughtful essay, *Ontario and Quebec: A Contrast in Backgrounds*, published in *The Canadian* in October 1913, he expressed opinions well ahead of the conventional attitudes of the day.

> Ontario and Quebec cannot be expected to think alike on all public questions affecting Canadian nationality or Imperial relations. . . . Ontario looks well afield, is progressive in ideas and has constant reminders through immigration and agitation of her Imperial relations and responsibilities. . . . The French Canadians being cohesive and unchanging, seem destined to be the conservative leavening proportion of the Dominion's population. . . . Ontario people are apt to forget that residents of Quebec go back two or two and a half centuries on Canadian soil, and that the family pride of a de Boucherville or a Joly de Lotbinière has just as much basis as that of a Ryerson or a Denison.

Not all of Hammond's perambulations around Ottawa were designed as learning experiences. Many were just good fun. By great good fortune, his arrival in the capital had coincided with the extension of the streetcar system into the outlying countryside on both sides of the river, a cheap and easy way of broadening one's horizons. In March 1904, on a golden late-winter Sunday afternoon, he and a reporter friend, Horace Boultbee, ventured down to Rockcliffe with their cameras. "There was lovely bright sunshine

Skilöbners *at Rockcliffe Park, March 1904.*

and clear still air, a number of buxom young girls were out skiing, and this sport, which I now saw for the first time, appealed to me as being very desirable." Certainly neither of the "buxom young ladies" whom Hammond snapped wickedly while their backs were turned would have thanked him. From their heft, we can guess that these two may well have been Annie and Jessie Clarke, those *skilöbners par excellence* and great friends of Minto and of Lola Powell.

Later that spring, when Clara and Harold arrived to join him, there were yet more delightful excursions. The first Sunday in May, they set off in search of wildflowers at Aylmer, on the Quebec shore. "Got off at Blueberry Point, a wild parklike wood greatly famed for its trailing arbutus . . . they are so sweet and fragrant and so elusive that they seem to be the best wildflowers growing. The Ottawa River is close by and the roar of the rapids, the soughing of the wind through the pines and the restful silences of the woods were conditions of never-ending delight. Our baby was greatly interested in gathering 'lowers." A week later, "so warm and July-like that I donned my summer underwear," they stayed on the Ontario side and headed for Britannia-on-the-Bay, about eight miles west of the city, at the point where the Ottawa widens into Lake Deschenes. "It was a lovely cool ride . . . over hill and dells past cozy farmhouses," and while Clara and Harold went paddling, Hammond took some of his most evocative photographs. One

Harold and Clara Hammond at Britannia-on-the-Bay, July 1904.

magic day at the end of July, they set out on a twenty-mile cruise on the Ottawa aboard the excursion paddlewheeler, *G. B. Greene*. "Lovely ride. The two riverbanks are generally wooded and mostly wilderness. The blue Laurentians parallel the river all the way up on the Quebec side . . . Ate our luncheon of canned chicken and bread and butter; a most agreeable outing for 50 cents a head."

Ah Wilderness! It seems a dreamy, idyllic sort of existence and in many ways, it no doubt was. It is hard not to envy M. O. and Clara who loved each other, had no particular career or money worries, and who made their way through life unthreatened by war or rumours of war. It is tempting to see in this pair, pursuing their own sunny way onward and upward, a metaphor for the life of the nation itself, in these pleasant and prosperous middle years of Laurier.

But of course it was not that simple – nothing ever is. Than M. O. Hammond, the earth had seldom produced a more honourable and upright character. Yet Hammond, like everyone else in this story, was a product of his times. As a political journalist, he sometimes behaved in a manner that we would find astonishing.

CHAPTER 27

"'Drill Ye Tarriers, Drill'"

As their work is carried on by night, little is known of their methods.

from *The Beaver and His Works*, by Henry J. Morgan.
A quote selected by M. O. Hammond for the programme
of the annual Press Gallery dinner; April 16, 1904

Few reporters in any era, much less in our own, have come to the capital as buoyed up by optimism as M. O. Hammond. "The Press Gallery is in fact a school in national affairs for journalists," he wrote in 1907, summing up his experiences in an article for the Toronto magazine, *The Westminster*. "At Ottawa, the man who receives his early training in a small city or a provincial capital first looks upon the Dominion as a whole." Then he sketched a cheery picture. "Perhaps his atmosphere has encouraged suspicion of the French, or some other large section of people. There he fraternizes with French Canadian reporters, and learns to love them for their innate courtesy, their sparkling wit and their mastery of the English language. . . . He learns that the questions which excite one province are but a fragment of the problems of the nation. He appreciates the fact, even if some members do not, that Dominion appropriations are as necessary for harbours of refuge for Nova Scotia fishermen, and for the payment of judges in Alberta, as they are for deepening the channel at Port Colborne, or for surveys on the Trent Canal."

Other reporters perceived the scene differently. One was Paul Bilkey of the Toronto *Telegram*, who arrived that same year of 1903, a few months earlier than Hammond. "The Press Gallery was divided on party lines almost as distinctly as the House of Commons," he wrote in his own memoir. "For a long time, the Gallery was divided into two bitterly hostile camps, so that men who should have been friends hardly spoke to each other."

Both views were probably correct. But Bilkey, in some ways, saw things the more accurately. This was an era when even the best and most high-minded of journalists functioned not as adversaries to politicians, but as their alter egos. Hammond himself was the truest of Grits, as ferocious a partisan as anyone else. He had to be to work on *The Globe*. True, that paper was no longer quite the

Two leading journalists of the day, Hammond's superiors at The Globe, *proudly displaying the nation's leading newspaper. Standing is J. A. Macdonald, who had succeeded J. A. Willison as editor in 1903, and Stewart Lyon, News Editor.*

indivisible organism of Liberalism it had been in George Brown's time, when, as Goldwin Smith had remarked acidly, "The Grits are singular . . . in being the party of a newspaper." Under the editorship of Willison, it had quite often infuriated Grit politicians by insisting on reporting the speeches of their opponents, if only on the back pages. But as it had happened, Willison had quit *The Globe* at the end of 1902 to edit the more independent-minded *News*. "If you would have a free and energetic public opinion," he told the Toronto Canadian Club, "you must encourage its expression, and discourage party servitude." These words fell on deaf ears. Under its new editor, a former clergyman named J. A. Macdonald, *The Globe* remained in most respects a party instrument, the senior Liberal organ in the Dominion, recipient of the lion's share of federal government advertising, about $4,400 annually. So Hammond and all other reporters knew exactly what was expected of them. "When the Liberals of North Grey enter a contest which invites comparisons they so far surpass their opponents as to make it a contrast," began his account of a provincial by-election rally at Owen Sound on January 2, 1903, when he was still covering the Ontario Legislature. So pleased were the Grits by this story, and by other reports of Hammond's that a few days later the Premier himself, the former federal member George Ross, Laurier's old friend, presented him with a cheque for $25. "I protested," Hammond recorded in his diary. "But he said, 'You do your work so well that you deserve it.' I then accepted it."

More incestuous still were certain other aspects of the journalist-politician relationship that Hammond describes without batting an eye. On January 28, 1903, for instance, he was summoned to the office of the Ontario Provincial Secretary, there to be granted an exclusive interview with a Tory member who was about to defect to the Grits. This interview, however, involved not a single line of spoken dialogue. Instead, Hammond was handed a complete script of questions and answers which he published, without a second thought, in next day's newspaper. Later, when the affair backfired, and the supposedly defecting Tory dramatically accused the Liberals of having attempted to bribe him, Hammond was summoned to testify at a Royal Commission of Inquiry. Far from being humiliated, he emerged from the witness box with his reputation, if anything, enhanced. "This is the manner in which we get interviews," he'd told the courtroom, with a candour that charmed everyone. Indeed, even the commission counsel, S. H. Blake, brother of the great Edward Blake, was full of praise. "He shook hands and congratulated me on having told such a straight, truthful story." Nor did

Hammond's career suffer for having allowed himself to be used as a dupe. A few months later, he was promoted to "the Ottawa work."

On Parliament Hill as at Queen's Park, Hammond's job involved at least as much flackery as actual reporting. Still, if one were cast in the role of P.R. man, that summer of 1903 was an excellent time to begin. The sheer scope of the session itself, the longest and busiest on record, stretching all the way from May to October, was witness to a burgeoning nation that could no longer afford to have all of its affairs dealt with in the space of three or four desultory months. Reaching at last full maturity at thirty-six, the Dominion seemed to have taken a grasp on its own future. In "New Ontario" and in northern Quebec, the great mining booms at Cobalt and at Noranda were soon to get underway. The peopling of the prairies, the filling up of the "last, best West," was on the brink of beginning; soon, two new provinces, Alberta and Saskatchewan, would be created out of the old Northwest Territories, to stretch the nation continuously from sea to sea. In a few months time, in January 1904, Laurier would tell the Canadian Club of Ottawa, "As the nineteenth century was that of the United States, so, I think, the twentieth century shall be filled by Canada."

The premier, that summer, was at the mid-point of his stewardship. As Hammond found him, he was at the peak of his power and authority. "His bare, boyish face, his quick artistic temperament, his commanding grace and intellect and his polished speech make him the one to whom all members look up," Hammond wrote in his diary of his first impressions. On July 30, 1903, three weeks before Hammond arrived in Ottawa, Laurier had unveiled his own National Dream, the Grand Trunk Pacific, a new railway that, by arching into uncharted territory far to the north of the CPR, would serve to move wheat and mineral resources ever more quickly to international markets. "The flood of tide is upon us that leads to fortune. . . . We cannot wait, because time does not wait," Laurier had told a hushed Commons in a speech that Hammond, reading it after a hard day of oat-harvesting on the family farm at Clarkson, had pronounced as "great."

Laurier in 1906. He was no longer the invigorating presence of his first years in office.

Hammond, if anything, was even more of a Laurier-worshipper than Amaryllis. Yet even cynical Tory reporters like Bilkey admired the premier. "I don't think anyone ever extracted any news out of Laurier," he wrote. [But] he was kind and courteous to all." Like Macdonald before him, Laurier understood how to make the humblest and greenest reporter feel important by seeming to take him into his confidence. "Went over to the Premier's Office to inquire about Council," recorded Hammond on September 19. "Though he had no news, he walked out with me and asked where I lived, and where I was born. He remarked that R. Blair, MP for our county, was a type of Christian who was very cantankerous and also rather undesirable. 'I am sorry Joe Featherston was defeated,' he said." There were also Laurier's sudden flashes of fire, all the more impressive because they were unexpected. On October 20, 1903, after news had reached Ottawa that Canada, thanks to bungling by the Imperial Government, had lost nine-tenths of her case in the Alaska Boundary Dispute, Hammond went round to the East Block and found the premier "on his knees on the floor studying a map. He was very indignant at the decision and said it was 'a damned injustice' and 'utterly indefensible.' " A few days later, on October 23, much to Hammond's approval, Laurier created "more or less of a sensation" with "a strong speech, full of unified national spirit in which he demanded treaty-making power for Canada."

In the general election of November 3, 1904, Laurier achieved the apogee of his career: a stunning majority of seventy-four seats; Opposition Leader Robert Borden was defeated in his own riding. Out on the campaign trail in southern Ontario a few weeks earlier, Hammond had been one of a handful of political reporters summoned into the premier's private car. Ever observant, and perhaps knowing more of the rumours about Laurier's private life than he let on, he focused in his diary account on Zoë Laurier, and captured her at precisely the moment when, with Emilie Lavergne chafing in exile at Montreal, she was beginning to emerge as a political personality in her own right:

> Lady Laurier is a very stout woman, rather short and quite talkative. She talks in a loud voice, but uses good English. The most lasting impression I have of her is that of a good wife. She refers to him always as "my husband," not as "the Premier" or "Sir Wilfrid." . . . She told us that Sir W. had been to see a Tory dentist in London that A.M. I asked him afterwards if he had done as he always does in Ottawa, walk out, say nothing about pay, let the bill be sent in, but he said that he had asked and that the man would not take anything.
>
> Supper was at 6. Sir W. invited us; they served fish and broiled chicken, Sir W. doing the carving as any family man. Someone said they proposed 2 meetings at Guelph that night. "I hope not," Lady L. said, "It would not be fair to my husband to let him address 2 meetings." She spoke in French to the [premier's] secretary. "Speak English," was Sir W's gentle admonition."

Zoë Laurier in 1905. She appears much as Hammond would have found her on the campaign train.

And yet. However deftly "Sir W." may have attacked the broiled chicken and the fish – perhaps we can decipher traces of Emilie's tutelage in the efficient despatch of wings and drumsticks and in the filleting – the truth was that, as even an acolyte like Hammond could not fail to notice, Laurier, by now well into his sixties, was no longer the invigorating, forceful presence of his first years in office. His hair was snowy white now, and his face was often haggard, sometimes even "of a deathly hue," as Hammond worried in his diary. He found the premier's handshake "rather weak, I must say." In the summer of 1902, Laurier had been taken gravely ill in London, while attending the coronation of Edward VII. For a while his life was feared for, and the dreaded word *cancer* flashed around. Cancer it was not, but, which was almost the next worst thing, during this period one of his oldest lieutenants, Israel Tarte of Public Works, "Busy Izzy" of yore, had seized the opportunity to stab his leader in the back. Perhaps Tarte had never got over his personal defeat about sending troops to South Africa in 1899. In any event, in Laurier's absence, Tarte, the Quebec nationalist, had made an unnatural alliance with the industrialists of Ontario and had toured the country arguing for a high protective tariff, directly opposed to the government's modified free-trade policy. When Laurier returned to Canada in the autumn of 1902, debarking at Rimouski to avoid the rest of the river, and leaning heavily on Zoë's arm, he despatched Tarte a frigid letter. "My first duty was to wait upon the Governor-General, to inform him that I was obliged to demand the resignation of your portfolio."

In his diary entry of May 19, 1904, Hammond, thanks to a conversation with his next-door neighbour at the Speaker's Dinner, one A. A. Wright, "the old man of long whiskers from Renfrew," adds a gloss to this story. "He said Tarte's son-in-law is studying medicine with a specialist in Paris who was consulted by Laurier while in Paris. . . . The young man heard the specialist tell Laurier he could not live 6 weeks. He at once cabled Tarte, and Tarte, seeing Laurier's finish, believed he could become Premier and started his high protection campaign."

Tarte quite apart, the famous "cabinet of all the talents" was long gone. David Mills, Edmund Meredith's old friend, had retired to the bench. Oliver Mowat, ex-premier of Ontario, had gone to the grave. Some talents had fizzled out with a whimper: in July 1903, for murky and mysterious reasons, A. G. Blair of Railways and Canals had resigned over the new railway policy. "Blair never expected his resignation to be accepted," recounted Hammond in his diary, of another profitable off-the-record conversation, "but in reality, Laurier was glad to get it." Some years later, in October 1908, Hammond acquired a richer story. "When Blair was still Minister of Railways, he went to J. R. Booth [Ottawa's richest lumber baron] and proposed Booth sell the Canadian Atlantic Railway [Booth's private railway] to the government, and that he (Blair) would recommend the government buying it at a price $1 million higher than Booth's price, he (Blair) to get the million. Booth went and told Laurier. The latter made no charge but waited . . . when Blair resigned, Laurier sent for him and told him he was welcome to his personal views but if he fought the government, he, Laurier, would have to fight him and go into personal matters. Then, when he told Blair his knowledge of the Booth affair, Blair collapsed and went out a humble, broken man."

Nor was it a secret, even without a million at stake, that two of the premier's most senior ministers, Clifford Sifton of the Interior, staunch Protestant from Manitoba, and Charles Fitzpatrick of Justice, doughty Irish Catholic from Quebec, could scarcely stand the sight of each other. "As long as Sifton is in the cabinet, we are sitting on a powderkeg," Fitzpatrick was said to have said in the Commons' smoking room. "I have always known that Fitzpatrick carries a knife in his boot for me," Sifton was said to have replied. Fitzpatrick won in the short run. In 1905, Sifton quit the cabinet after a bitter quarrel about the issue of separate schools in the new provinces of Alberta and Saskatchewan. But the loss of Sifton, a man of energy and vision however unappealing his personality, was a serious blow to the government.

All this was bad enough. Yet more damaging to the government's image were the unpleasant rumours that gathered like swarms of buzzing wasps over the heads of a number of newer cabinet recruits. In the view of many opinion-makers, the odour of corruption was now as all-pervasive over Parliament Hill as it had been during say, the Pacific Scandal. "Citizenship is decaying rapidly, with a canker worm of vice eating into its vital parts," a noted Methodist preacher, the Reverend D. S. Chown, had informed his congregation in February 1904. "It is almost impossible for a man of large ideas, of noble ideals and of honour to obtain a seat in Parliament. . . . The political atmosphere has become so offensive to moral and intellectual men that many prefer to remain free from its pollution rather than inhale it." The Ottawa poet William Wilfred Campbell went Chown one better, and read out a poem about corruption to an entranced audience at the Ottawa Canadian Club, just a month after Laurier had spoken of the twentieth century belonging to Canada. "Franchise but a bartered power/Freedom, thought and honour gone." And while the opinions of these two could be shrugged off, those of the Governor General could not. In November 1902, as he recorded in his diary, the Earl of Minto was horrified at having to preside over the swearing-in of two men whom he clearly considered to be a couple of blackguards. "[He] comes with a very evil reputation," he wrote of the new Minister of Marine and Fisheries, Joseph Prefontaine, and of Tarte's successor at Public Works, James Sutherland, "He is not reckoned clean-handed." Soon afterwards, as we discover from Agar Adamson's *aide-mémoire*, there was a terrible foofaraw at the Rideau Club when Prefontaine and another new minister, Louis Brodeur of Inland Revenue, were blackballed, a humiliation that never before had befallen a member of cabinet.

The most damaging rumours of all, and certainly the most titillating, concerned bizarre goings-on in the bedrooms of state. "The tales which were bandied about by scandal-mongers, a term which in this instance would have to include the whole adult population of the capital, would have made a new *Decameron*," Paul Bilkey tells us. One of the most lurid stories involved Clifford Sifton; an alleged scuffle occurred between the Minister of the Interior and a cuckolded husband that, because it was well publicized, may have helped trigger his sudden resignation.* Others attached to Frederick Borden, Minister of Militia, "tall, debonair and fruity-voiced," in Bilkey's description, and with whom, in Agar Adamson's words, "a clever woman could do anything." Hammond, being a rather innocent fellow, only hints at such goings-on. "It is said there are other reasons for his retirement," he notes of Sifton on March 2, 1905, "the reports of his . . . none too moral character . . . though his wife was with him on his recent stay in London." Later, on July 26, 1907, recounting a conversation with J. A. Mackay, business manager of *The Globe* and a close personal confidant of Laurier, Hammond grew bolder. "He saw Laurier, the question of personal scandals came up. 'I can't go into my ministers' bedrooms and see whether they are sleeping with their own wives or not,' said Laurier. 'Yes, but that is hardly a conclusive answer for the people,' Mr. M. replied."

The most sensational and by far the most bizarre story of them all amounted to a sex scandal in which Canada, for once, may have established an international precedent. This story – the reasons why it was kept so close a secret at the time will soon become evident – was set down by Edmund Meredith's son, the popular and fashionable young architect, Coly, in the last set of notes he made for his

* In The Promised Land (1984), Pierre Berton describes this incident in detail.

unpublished memoir, in 1959, at the age of eighty-five. Here, exactly as he wrote it, is Coly Meredith's account:

> THE DOCTOR, HIS WIFE, AND A CABINET MINISTER
>
> Among my clients were several Cabinet ministers, one of whom, I have discreetly forgotten his name, bought a large house in a fashionable part of Ottawa and arranged with me to make very extensive alterations. When the work was far on, I was directed to stop it.
>
> I knew the Doctor in the case, our both being in the Militia. The Doctor's wife was young and very beautiful; the Doctor was frequently away for a few days. After a time he became uneasy about affairs at home, and said he would be away for a day or so. He returned very late at night and took chloroform and some surgical instruments and then went quietly upstairs.
>
> Some days later, I was called to the Minister's office and instructed to stop the work. In all my life, I have never seen such a deflated and sad wreck of what had been a man. He resigned from the Cabinet, and disappeared from Ottawa.

Coly Meredith's own upright character, together with the fact that he both knew the cabinet minister personally and was apparently told of it by his brother officer in the militia, the doctor, who would have had no interest in deceiving him, indeed quite the opposite, make it certain that this astonishing Boccaccio-like story is correct. Coly, though, took care in his memoir to provide no clues to the identity of the politician. From some corroborative evidence, and by a process of elimination, we can suggest that the gelded minister was almost certainly Henry R. Emmerson, who succeeded Blair at Railways and Canals in 1904 and who resigned abruptly from Cabinet on April 2, 1907. He was well-known as a ladies' man, and was even the subject of a pamphlet denouncing him as a skirt-chaser. Even the innocent Hammond makes a veiled reference to Emmerson's unsavoury reputation. "He was there," Hammond reports of a Russell House reception in 1905, "the Beau Brummell with all the girls he could find to talk or dance with. . . . It would take a pretty long search to find anything brilliant in Emmerson." Paul Bilkey, in his memoir, goes much further, and by way of a long rambling parable involving a cow moose, a bull moose, and a hunter, all but recreates the scene described by Coly Meredith:

> The hunter, armed with an undersized megaphone succeeds in making a noise very like that of a cow moose of exceptionally friendly

disposition. The distant bull, without pausing to reflect upon the forwardness of the female, comes rampaging through the bush full of high domestic resolve, only to experience the bitterest kind of disappointment and disillusionment. . . . Instead of a compliant cow, there is a hunter with a high-powered rifle. . . . Mr. Emmerson left the cabinet soon after.

"I believe we are making history these days," wrote Hammond on May 17, 1904, as the House plodded its way through the last of the umpteen Opposition amendments to Laurier's railway bill, "but it is pretty dull as a rule." Even for this wearer of rose-coloured glasses, there were clearly many moments when the job of being a Press Gallery reporter proved a bit of a letdown. Much of the work was routine, far more so than nowadays. Only the debates in the House of Commons mattered; much of the time the Press Gallery did little more than copy down speeches in shorthand. In fact, the nine reporters of the *Hansard* staff had rather more prestige, and certainly more pay. Hammond had been summoned to Ottawa in mid-session, 1903, only because another *Globe* man had suddenly been given the nod to join *Hansard*.

Nor, except when Clara and Harold were with him, was boarding-house life as rewarding as tending his own garden in Cabbagetown. Most days, Hammond lingered in his bed until ten – "something in the Ottawa air induces sleep," he noted, and then went up to "The Ark" in the Commons basement for breakfast. At eleven, he went into the House to do the first shorthand "take" of the day. Each "take" lasted an hour and a half; he and his partner Charlie Matthews generally did three each. In the evening, they would edit down their copy into a manageable three or four thousand words for the full-page report on the day's proceedings that *The Globe* usually carried. Then, more often than not, he would go back into the Commons to take a late-night sitting. Laurier, Hammond tells us, was "a hard man to take. He speaks rapidly, and sometimes obscures some of his syllables by his French accent." Opposition Leader Borden enunciated every word – but Borden, even allowing for Hammond's bias, was quite clearly a terrible bore. "He often speaks on trivial matters, whether he has anything to say or not."

Hammond by now was also beginning to realize that being a Grit reporter put him at a considerable disadvantage. Unlike Tory reporters such as Paul Bilkey, he had no leeway for initiative. He was thus, in Bilkey's blunt description of his Grit counterparts, "bound and gagged . . . unable to indulge in intelligent anticipation or indeed any kind of anticipation." Certain stories could not be reported at all; others required extreme delicacy. In July 1904, for instance, when Lord Dundonald, the last of the imperious British generals, was sacked, Hammond would much rather not have had to cover the general's stagy departure. "The Tories and militiamen had done their best to make a big demonstration," he tells us. "It fell to me to write it up and the controversial nature of the subject made it a job to be dreaded." Eventually, after much chewing of the pen, he drafted what he considered to be a "fair report." It was certainly a skilful one. "It was the period of the Boer War successes over again," Hammond began. "The hero of Ladysmith was the hero of the night." Then he got to the point. "The event was promoted by the military and by the enthusiasts of the Conservative Party, two forces who can be counted on to assemble crowds and make cheers." Even at that, *The Globe* of July 27, 1904, buried Dundonald down with the livestock market report on page nine.

There were exceptions to this rule of partisanship. In 1905, *The Globe* broke with the government on the separate school provisions in the Autonomy Bill, as the bill establishing Alberta and Saskatchewan was known, and a new editorial policy of "independence within party lines," as Hammond described it, was decreed. However, it developed that the independence doctrine had been motivated more by financial concerns than strict Protestant principle. "If we stood for the Bill, there are 1000s of Libs in Western Ontario who would flood over to the *News*," the editor of *The Globe*, J. A. Macdonald, remarked to Hammond.

Laurier. The horseshoe stickpin that was his signature gleams in the sun.

Despite these constraints, the job was mostly fun. Hammond hobnobbed daily with men whose names were household words, yet who knew him by name. On a fine spring morning in 1906, he set up his tripod on the Commons laws and snapped many of them in candid poses: Laurier with his fine silk hat shining like patent leather, and with his legendary horseshoe pin catching the sun; Sir Frederick Borden, the dandy, with dundreary whiskers freshly laundered and brushed, clutching an umbrella in kid-gloved hand; Sir William Mulock, with his magnificent watch-chain; and, bringing up the rear, that most choleric of all Tory members, Sam Hughes, stomping along in a tall stovepipe hat. One evening that season, Hammond and a fellow reporter dined with Hughes at a Chinese restaurant. "He pumped hot air into us for over an hour; told of how Sifton's downfall was the result of an RC plot headed by Laurier and Fitzpatrick." Aboard the train to Ottawa, he encountered that

THE PRIVATE CAPITAL

Sir Frederick Borden, left, Minister of Militia. To win Agar his commission to South Africa, Mabel Adamson had flirted with him. On the right is Sydney Fisher, the bachelor Minister of Agriculture whom Zoë Laurier was forever trying to marry off.

Sam Hughes, MP. The most choleric member of the House.

On the left, William Paterson, Minister of Customs, next to an unidentified politician. On the right is the notorious Henry Emmerson. Less than a year later, he resigned under mysterious circumstances.

Sir Robert Laird Borden, Leader of the Opposition. Hammond found him a dull speaker.

rising star within the Department of Labour, Mackenzie King, who used the occasion to butter him up. "King said he had been asked to enter politics and asked my view. I said to wait a few years and he said, 'I think you're right.' "

As interesting were many of the lesser lights whom Hammond encountered. This was the era of the great Commons characters, who although they did not carry field-marshal's batons in their Gladstone bags, were gifted with tongues capable of clipping hedges. There was George W. Fowler, the Tory from New Brunswick, who had flung out the famous description of the cabinet, "Wine, Women and Graft." There was Thomas Mackie of the Grits, said to have said at the time of the Manitoba Schools Controversy, "What is this Remedial Bill? I'll pay it myself." Hammond's own favourite was one Seymour Eugene Gourley of Colchester, Nova Scotia, famous for his fire-eating speeches and also for sartorial eccentricities."White duck trousers and a black frock coat would never have surprised his colleagues, even to an accompaniment of tan boots and a sombrero," Paul Bilkey wrote of Gourley. (Gourley may well have been the anonymous Parliamentarian whom Amaryllis, in one of her rare forays into the world of the Sessionals spied sitting on a bench at a Commons garden party wearing "a white straw hat on top of full evening regalia.")

Then as now, the big day in Parliament was Opening Day. Describing this in his diary on March 8, 1906, Hammond got rather carried away. "Lord Grey resplendent in scarlet and gold, and Laurier and Cartwright nearby in Windsor Uniforms. Floor gay with Supreme Court judges, back to back on woolsack, wearing scarlet and ermine. Church dignitaries in purple and women in lovely heaving chests bared to the admiring public and panting galleries above, bursting with curiosity." But the more important event was Budget Night. Unlike today's advance lockup for reporters, with officials present to explain the fine print, everyone had to listen to the speech itself, and do their own addition as the Minister droned along. "Mr. Fielding's budget speeches are so compact that the writer of even the shortest report must pay close attention," Hammond reports. "On such days, the correspondents help each other, then the old hand has the advantage over a younger man for the mysteries of a tariff exposition are almost beyond understanding." More riveting, though, were the hijinks on the floor when epochal bills were passed. On July 5, 1905, when the bill creating Alberta and Saskatchewan went through, "papers flew and hats were smashed by the wild Irishmen and Frenchmen," Hammond tell us. "Some had evidently visited the cellar restaurant frequently and were feeling gay and festive, there was a general abandon on all sides."

Hammond's own Press Gallery colleagues also captured his interest. There were then only about thirty gallery members, and occasion-

The Parliamentary Press Gallery at Montmorency Falls. May 11, 1906.

Immigrants at Quebec. Scenes like this fascinated Hammond.

ally, as Hammond recorded with his camera on May 11, 1906, the company embarked as a body on pleasurable junkets, in this case to Quebec City, to meet the splendid new Canadian Pacific liner, the *Empress of Britain*, arriving on her maiden voyage. (Hammond being Hammond, he soon wandered off to photograph the immigration sheds. "They are a never-ending source of interest to me, to watch the newcomers as they adjust themselves to the new condition," he noted in his diary.) Among his colleagues, he admired the grizzled old veterans who remembered Macdonald and Cartier: William Mackenzie of the Winnipeg *Free Press*, Fred Cook of the *Mail and Empire*, and John Garvin of the Ottawa *Journal*, renowned at the Friday night press-room singsongs for his ringing rendition of "Drill Ye Tarriers, Drill." He was intrigued by the caustic and iconoclastic Bilkey, though the two were never friends. "He has a happy indifference to any and all political idols and the freedom with which he smashes them is always entertaining." Most of all he admired the handsome and fearless Ernest Cinqmars of *La Presse*, who on June 7, 1906, as has never before or since befallen a political reporter, was called to the bar of the House to answer for an attack he had made in print on George Foster, the Tory finance critic. "There was a crowded house and galleries and general elecric air." Thereafter, the occasion became almost festive. Hammond was granted special permission to photograph Cinqmars during his ordeal, and the "culprit" "bore himself with calmness and nerve;

Ernest Cinqmars of La Presse *at the bar of the House of Commons, to the left of the Speaker, on June 7, 1906. Hammond had received special permission to take this picture. Cinqmars had attacked Sir George Foster, the Tory finance critic, for slandering French Canadians. "He has only one desire, the desire to insult. He belongs to the school of lying, hypocrisy and cowardice." The reporter appeared wearing a silk hat and frock coat, and was discharged with a mild rap over the knuckles for having passed "the bounds of reasonable criticism."*

there were a few incidents to cause roars of laughter and applause, as they went through the ancient formula." So far as the records show, no punishment of any kind was imposed upon Cinqmars.

Gallery members enjoyed a number of agreeable perks. One was known simply as "the trunk." From Hammond's first mention of applying for this, in September 1903, it is clear that "the trunk" was the official insignia of gallery membership. But not until the following April, when, following some shilly-shallying by the Tory-dominated Executive, his was actually delivered, do we discover that a "trunk" was precisely that: a leather-bound trunk full of stationery, "worth about $40 I guess."

One other consideration from which Hammond and his colleagues benefited was far more valuable, and by our own standards, far more unusual. In those days, the Parliamentary *Hansard* men covered only the debates of the Commons and of the Senate. By custom, the Commons committees were covered by moonlighting journalists – always those of the government persuasion. On top of their regular work, it made for a long and harrowing day, but the harvest was rich. In 1904, thanks to his work recording the Agriculture and Railway Committees, Hammond, who by now could handle "138 WPM" like a breeze, added more than $800 to his salary – enough to take him and Clara off to the St. Louis World's Fair. In 1905, "chiefly reporting the Telephone Committee," he made $1400, and the Hammonds each acquired a new fur coat. In 1906, his last year in the Gallery, he made $1650 – enough for them to move out of Cabbagetown onto Albany Avenue in the much more fashionable Annex district of Toronto, where an attractive half-double, in which he and Clara remained for the rest of their lives, cost Hammond $4600.

Two programmes for the Annual Press Gallery Dinner. Hammond chose the art nouveau scroll shown in 1904. His colleague on the Toronto Telegram, *Paul Bilkey illustrated the programme for 1905. This quintessential Ottawa event has changed remarkably little down the years.*

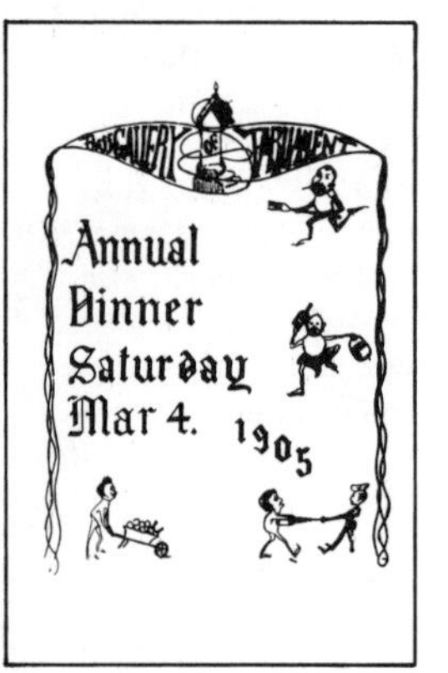

For all that he stuck to Radnor Water – "I tried some claret and some white wine and disliked both," he reported on one occasion – Hammond was popular with his colleagues, and in 1906, was elected to the Press Gallery Executive. "This was not all," he reported proudly in his diary. "I headed the roll. I had to say something, and somehow had enough grease on my tongue to let loose." As early as 1904, he was on the Committee for the annual Gallery dinner, in charge of "drafting the menu card." From this card, which happily survives, we can see that with his eye for the visual, Hammond took pains to order up from the printer a splendid art nouveau scroll for the cover. For the inside pages, he chose appropriate quotations from Shakespeare, Robbie Burns, and the Bible, not forgetting one in French. As for the dinner itself, Hammond recorded it in detail in his diary, demonstrating that this quintessential Ottawa event has changed little down the years – even to the patronizing puffery that the politicians, in their speeches, tend to bestow on reporters.

It was in the House of Commons restaurant and was one of the most enjoyable table functions I was ever at. There were 70 or 75 people there, the tickets costing $3.50 each. A most distinguished array of guests: Sir W. Laurier, R. L. Borden, Speakers Belcourt and Power, Sir Wm. Mulock, Sir Fred Borden. . . .

L's speech was a little jewel. He spoke briefly as they all did. He referred to us as of a higher order, who looked down on the members and improved on the imperfections in their speech. If he were 30 years younger, there was nothing he would rather be than a member of the P.G. (a voice, "you've done pretty well"). He looked upon our work as of great importance. He saw many new faces every year, and he had been looking at the Gallery for 20 years. As he sat down, he said, "With great pleasure I drink the health of the Canadian Parliament as revised and improved by the Press Gallery."

The Premier's reception was very enthusiastic and he seemed to enjoy the sallies and shafts all through. Equally warm was the reception given to R. L. Borden. As in L.'s case, all stood to cheer as he rose and sang, "He's a Daisy." B.'s speech was also happy. His chief point was that he had early learned it did not pay to argue with an editor in his own paper, for the editor always has the last word.

Speaker Belcourt was happy and gave a satirical curriculum for a school of journalism. Sir Wm. Mulock was happy, and threw off his brusqueness. An exceedingly funny incident later was when he made knives and forks into "bones" and kept time with one of the sugars. Sir Fred Borden showed that he was one of the boys and was given a fine reception, towards the end he consented to play the violin, on which he is quite skilled, but it was found the orchestra men were all gone. "The Minister of Militia has come unarmed," was one of the comments hurled at him amid great laughter. . . .

The songs were very good and included "Bedelia," "Big Chief," "Bedouin Love Song," "The Stein Song," "Goodbye Liza Jane." There were constant interruptions, many of them very apt and which caused great laughter. Mulock told the story of the man who had been warned by his wife to take sarsaparilla when he had had too much whiskey but who explained that when he'd had too much whiskey he could not say sarsaparilla.

The whole spirit of the banquet was one of good natured abandon and yet temperate indulgence. A good deal was drunk, but there was very little effect of it to be seen.

During these years in the Press Gallery, Hammond continued to be *The Globe*'s fair-haired boy. Even the fact that he was elected spokesman for a group of reporters demanding higher pay – "I said we did not want a union, but to be dealt with on our own merits" – did not prevent him from snaffling all the juiciest assignments. In November 1903, he was despatched to Boston to meet A. B. Aylesworth, Canadian Commissioner in the ill-fated Alaska Boundary negotiations, now coming home crestfallen aboard the S. S. *Mayflower*. "If he gets past Hammond, it's all right," remarked the news editor. "No one else will get him." Hammond not only landed an exclusive interview, he found time to pass a profitable afternoon in Boston's Museum of Fine Arts. "There were 2 works by Turner and when I saw them, I wondered not at Ruskin's uphill task in interesting the world in his work." On December 30 – "oh rarity!" – he called round at The Grange, camera in hand, to meet with Goldwin Smith. "What a dear old mansion it is and what a lovely

Goldwin Smith, Sage of The Grange, photographed by Hammond.

L. to r.: Arnold Haultain, the journalist, Goldwin Smith, and M. O. Hammond on the steps of The Grange, Goldwin Smith's residence in Toronto. The house is now part of the Art Gallery of Ontario.

hospitable old Englishman he is. . . . He wore a black silk cap to cover his bald spot, that grim sternness that adorns his countenance on the street was entirely absent." In the early autumn of 1905 came the most exhilarating story of all, all the way out to the prairies – "oh how limitless and lonesome they were" – to cover the official inauguration of the new provinces. At Edmonton, a parade highlighted by hundreds of schoolchildren cheering and waving flags "gave me a thrill and brought tears to my eyes." At Regina, "the procession was the finest show of Indians in warpaint, they gallopped along on horses, their wierd impassive faces a sight to behold."

On September 11, 1904, still only twenty-eight, Hammond had been offered the city editorship of *The Globe*. He was flattered, but declined it as not quite the right step on his "career ladder." Then, two years later, on September 6, 1906, came an offer he couldn't refuse, the chance to be both literary editor and editor of the weekly *Globe* magazine, the most important cultural and literary supplement in the country. "I started home in a kind of daze and walked on air," he tells us. He realized he would miss the Press Gallery. "But the more I think, the more it seems my opportunity." An opportunity, moreover, to earn a dazzling $30 a week.

During the next three decades, as *Globe* literary editor, and columnist and also as an author, Hammond came to occupy a pre-eminent position in Canada's cultural firmament. "He was a very careful editor with a sensitive appreciation of words," an admirer remembered later. "Many a well-known Canadian writer was helped in the earlier stages of his or her work by his kindly and discerning criticism." He remained an avid photographer and, as one of the founders of Toronto's legendary Arts and Letters Club, he got to know all the charter members of the Group of Seven, and championed their work. He and Clara – or "Sue," as sometime during the First World War she decided she preferred to be called, for reasons that Hammond never explains – were now the parents of a daughter, Helen Isabel, as well as of Harold; during the teens and twenties they became renowned, in the words of a friend, as "the souls of simple and unostentatious hospitality. Literary folk and artists always found much pleasure in the little parties at 148 Albany Avenue." Bliss Carman's line, "I always like to go to the Hammonds," was quoted in Hammond's obituary.

Hammond published three books: a short monograph, *Painting and Sculpture in Canada* (1932); a charming travel book, *Canadian Footprints* (1926), illustrated with his own photographs; and his major work, *Confederation and its Leaders*, which appeared in 1917 to mark the fiftieth anniversary of Confederation and which contains many passages that, for their pith and richness of imagery, command our interest today. Of Edmund and Fanny Meredith's old friend, Sir Charles Tupper: "No speaker could still him, no audience terrify this veteran of a hundred battles. Now he used a stream of invective, again he tripped an enemy with fox-like cunning . . . his energy and bluster were as invigorating as a northwest wind." Of George Brown, founder of *The Globe*, "A steam engine in trousers, and had he lived in more recent times, he would no doubt be called a human dynamo."

Like Brown of *The Globe*, Hammond of *The Globe* died while still in his prime, in October 1934 at the age of only fifty-eight, apparently of a heart attack. He left behind an unfinished history of his beloved newspaper that survives among his papers. All the Toronto culturati attended his funeral, including someone we know well, Florence Randal Livesay, whose work he had often published. Soon afterwards, Hammond's friends organized the kind of memorial that they knew he would much have preferred, a retrospective exhibition of all his best photographs at The Art Gallery of Toronto.

During his years as literary editor of *The Globe*, one of Hammond's most rewarding associations was his ripening friendship with the Ottawa poet, Duncan Campbell Scott, whose work he frequently commissioned and published. They first met in December 1908, when Scott was in Toronto and Hammond dropped around to see him at the King Edward Hotel. "He was friendly in his quiet way, and we adjourned to the bar-room, where over a little wine we chatted."

Then, as always, their conversation turned quickly to Scott's fellow poet, Archibald Lampman, now nearly a decade in his grave. "He and L. had many walks together," Hammond recorded. They spoke also of the old golden days of the eighties and nineties, when these two young civil servants had begun to create in their off-hours the foundations of a national literature, of an era when Ottawa had been not just the political capital of the Dominion, but also its cultural capital.

CHAPTER 28

"An Oxygenic Essence"

. . . . I venture to say that Ottawa will become in the course of ages the Florence of Canada, and the plain of the Ottawa its Val D'Arno. Perched upon its crown of rock, a certain atmosphere flows about its walls, borne upon the breath of the prevailing northwest wind, an intellectual elixir, an oxygenic essence, thrown off by the immeasurable tracts of pine-clad mountain and crystal lake. In this air, the mind becomes conscious of a vital energy, a buoyant swiftness of movement rarely experienced in like degree elsewhere . . . as the years go on . . . it will become an ideal city for the artist.

Archibald Lampman; *The Globe*; February 4, 1893

Lampman was always a great one for hyperbole, but on this occasion, even he was pushing it a bit. Amaryllis, who, unlike him, had actually been to Florence, saw the city she'd been born in with a more ironic eye. In April 1902, when the German pianist Arthur Friedheim, a pupil of Liszt's, whose international fame was eclipsed only by Paderewski's, came to Ottawa at the tag end of a North American tour, she attended his recital and described it for readers:

> Friedheim's audience was too small to be enthusiastic – he described it as colder than the weather. Earlier, I heard two men discussing the concert and one said to the other, "Are you going to hear this man play?" "No," came the reply. "I think it perfect cheek of one man to think he can come here and charge two dollars and do nothing else all evening but play the piano."

She wrote in like vein a month later of the ceremonies held in the Parliament Buildings to unveil the official portrait of Laurier:

> In the course of his remarks, Sir Wilfrid said that sometime he might ask that the walls of the House of Commons be adorned with scenes of the history of our country, painted by Canadian artists. He evidently had it in mind to flatter Canadian artists, for he also alluded to the *Prix de Rome* given by the *Academie des Beaux Arts* in Paris. Sir Wilfrid said that Canada was as yet too young a country to think of such an undertaking as that, but he spoke in such a way that much excitement will be felt throughout the country by those who are anxious to see Canada come a little more to the fore in matters of art. No doubt both in Montreal and Toronto, Sir Wilfrid's words will be heard with much pleasure. But I fear the subject is not a burning one in Ottawa.

For all his excesses – on reflection he may only have been spinning out words to fill his weekly column – Lampman yet was onto something. From its earliest days as capital, there had existed in Ottawa a cadre of culturati, even though the place was small and unsophisticated. As early as 1868, the eager young cultural nationalists of the Canada First movement – the poet Charles Mair, the biographer Henry J. Morgan, the literary lawyers George Denison and Robert Haliburton and William Foster – had held their founding meetings in the city, in a small corner room in Matthews Hotel. In 1870, Edmund Meredith had taken time out from digging up his drains to be the moving spirit behind the Literary and Scientific Society where he had listened, a few years later, to his colleague at the Post Office, W. D. LeSueur, expound about that most difficult of all the new philosophers, Herbert Spencer.

Parliament itself brought to the capital a number of individuals of intellectual and literary bent. While neither Macdonald nor Laurier ever attempted to emulate Disraeli by churning out novels in their off hours, both were cultivated men who read widely and voraciously. In an era when politics was far from being a full-time profession, some of their colleagues were pleased to wear alternative hats as poets and belletrists. Thomas D'Arcy McGee was the author of both a popular history of Ireland and of a volume of poetry, *Canadian Ballads and Other Verses*. J. D. Edgar, Speaker of the House during Laurier's first administration, was also a poet whose patriotic hymn, "This Canada of Ours," was just too far ahead of its time to be considered as a national anthem. John Bourinot, Clerk of the Commons from 1880 to 1902 and author of the epochal manual, *Parliamentary Procedure and Practice in Canada*, that is still referred to today, found time to write the first serious works of literary criticism to be published in Canada: *The Intellectual Development of the Canadian People* (1881) and *Our Intellectual Strengths and Weaknesses* (1896).

Far and away the most interesting of the literary gents whom voters had sent to the capital was Nicholas Flood Davin, a one-time Irish journalist and Franco-Prussian war correspondent who had emigrated in 1872, had got into various scrapes, and who, in 1887, had become the Conservative member for West Assiniboia in the Northwest Territories. Davin was a devil. "He wound up an impromptu Blackfoot dance in the Commons smoking room by springing up on the long table, laden with bottles and glasses, and jigging down the centre, kicking over everything in sight," Lady Aberdeen recorded disapprovingly in her diary in 1897. He was also devilishly attractive though bald as an egg. Amaryllis, among many other ladies was quite smitten by him and on two occasions went out of her way to follow him to her own Alma Mater, Rideau Street Convent, where he was a popular guest lecturer, and to sit spellbound as he recited "The Assyrian came down like the wolf on the fold," from *The Destruction of Sennacherib* by Lord Byron. In the Commons, Davin's was the first effective voice from the West. But although full of promise, he never fulfilled it, and, after his defeat in the election of 1900, depressed further by a tangled personal life that included a wife, a mistress, and two illegitimate children, he put a bullet through his head in the Clarendon Hotel in Regina. In happier times, Davin produced among other volumes, *Eos: An Epic of the Dawn*, the first literary work to come out of the Northwest. No doubt it also endeared him to Amaryllis that, in 1895, Davin had introduced a Private Member's bill calling for votes for women.

"AN OXYGENIC ESSENCE"

A quite separate centre of intellectual energy was generated by *Le Cercle des Dix*, an exclusive francophone society limited to ten members who met every Wednesday evening at one another's houses to discuss history, literature, music, and archaeology and indeed just about every intellectual topic except politics, which was *proscrit*. Among its members were the historian Benjamin Sulte and the poets Alphonse Lusignan, Alfred Garneau, and Achille Fréchette, all employed as translators in the Commons and Senate, and another historian, Alfred-Duclos DeCelles, who was Assistant Librarian of Parliament. Amaryllis, who, unusually for the set she moved in, seems to have spoken French fluently, was openly envious of the sparkling conversation from which she was excluded. "These are worldly men, who can claim distinction as *litterateurs*," she noted wistfully in March 1901.*

The centre of cultural energy from which the "oxygenic essence" really emanated was comprised of just two members. One was Archie Lampman and the other was his close friend and kindred spirit, Duncan Campbell Scott. They were only humble, ill-paid

* Another fluently bilingual member of Official Society was, of all people, Colonel Hubert Foster, an Imperial Officer who served as Quartermaster General to the militia between 1898 and 1901 and who emerges from most accounts as having been even more heavy-handed than General Hutton in his attitude towards colonials. "It may surprise many to learn that Colonel Foster is a member of Les Dix," writes Amaryllis in the same column – but maddeningly, leaves it at that.

civil service clerks and neither in retrospect can be ranked as a great poet. Yet together they achieved a level and a quality of creativity that no other city in the Dominion could match. Earlier poets in Canada had written as expatriates, describing the Canadian landscape in language and imagery derived from English poetry: Lampman and Scott were unmistakably Canadians, who perceived from the inside out.

"This place had a wild time last night. The sharpshooters came home, and were paraded all over the town with music, waving of hats, and large cheering. . . . Fine fellows they looked, dusty and brown and ready for anything. . . . I, rambling about in the multitude, got a few looks at them. The city was hung with flags innumerable, there were surely never so many up before."

Decorations on Sparks Street, July 1885, welcoming home troops from the Northwest Rebellion. Lampman described this scene in a letter to Maud.

The writer was Archie Lampman; the date was July 25, 1885. He was twenty-three years old that tumultuous summer after Cut Knife Hill and Batoche, and in this letter, the first of a small cache of Lampman family letters, quoted from here for the first time, he was writing to the girl with whom he was already madly in love, and who he would marry two years later: Maud Playter, the sixteen-year-old daughter of an Ottawa physician, out of town that week on a visit to Toronto. By then, Lampman had been living and working in the capital for two and a half years. From a photograph taken around this time, we have a clear impression of how he looked: a strikingly handsome young man with finely chiselled features, large limpid brown eyes, and a high, intellectual brow. Not until the early nineties would he allow his chestnut hair to grow into a sweeping Tennysonian shock, but already he looked just as a poet should. No wonder Maud fell in love with him, although he was undeniably on the short side and far from robust, having been weakened by a childhood bout of rheumatic fever.

Archibald Lampman about 1885.

Lampman had come to Ottawa for an uncomplicated reason. For a young man poor as a church mouse whose single burning ambition was to be a poet, a government job – "easy, monotonous work, the same thing over and over from January to December," as he wrote to another friend – offered an ideal financial foundation. In those days, getting such a position depended entirely upon who one knew; luckily for Lampman, one of his closest friends at Trinity College in Toronto had been Archie Campbell, son of the Postmaster General Alexander Campbell, the great friend of Edmund Meredith. In appointing the young poet to a third-class clerkship in the Savings Branch division of the Post Office, Campbell was in fact using his gift of patronage rather in the manner of an unofficial Canada Council. However, such culturally supportive arrangements were not unknown. In 1866, another poet, Charles Sangster, had been given a post office job, and another, Charles Mair, worked for the Department of the Interior. Later, Lampman would come to despise his job, but in the beginning he was happy enough. "I like the Civil Service," he wrote. "I go to work at 9:30, taking lunch with me and get away at four. . . . Hours easy, and time to myself, Thank God."

Lampman in the mid-nineties, in a classic poetic pose.

Far from having to get by on his own, in the approved poetic style, in a garret room in an impersonal, unfriendly boarding house, Lampman was surrounded by a large and affectionate clan. Within a year or so of his arrival in Ottawa, his parents and three younger sisters had moved up from Cobourg, on Lake Ontario. Writing to Maud that steamy July night, he was most likely sitting in a snug upstairs bedroom-study in the family's small frame cottage on Nicholas Street, at the western edge of Sandy Hill. It was a cluttered, cheerful household that puts one somehow in mind of the establishment of the Bronson Alcotts in Concord, Massachusetts; for the Lampmans, who traced their ancestry back to Loyalists of German extraction, were a brood of intellectuals. It must be said that

Lampman's father, the Reverend Peter Lampman, does not appear to have been an outstanding success as an Anglican clergyman. No doubt it was his reputation for being "disputatious" that led to his early retirement. But he was also a scholarly fellow who delighted in seventeenth-century literature and an amateur poet who, as Lampman once put it, "first instructed me in the art of verse." His mother, Susanna Gesner Lampman, was a cultured and spirited woman, an excellent pianist who taught music to eke out expenses. Belle, the eldest daughter, was studying art. Nineteen-year-old Annie, a girl of a dark, gypsy-like beauty who will play her own cameo role in this story, was already demonstrating a brilliant musical talent. In the manner of happy Victorian families, every member had a nickname. To her children, Susanna was "Possum." Annie was sometimes "Gretchen," sometimes "Birdie," sometimes "Nipper." Archie, for reasons unknown, was most frequently "Bear." "Bear," as his sisters later remembered, would sometimes announce at the breakfast table, "Well, I've writ a pome."

Annie Lampman. She was a talented pianist who studied at Leipzig.

As the eldest child and the precious and delicate only son, he was the apple of everyone's eye. A star scholarship pupil at Trinity College School, Port Hope, he had done not quite so well – only a second – studying the classics at Trinity College in Toronto, having spent rather too much time writing for the college literary magazine, *Rouge et Noir*, and organizing practical jokes.

By Lampman's own account, the inspiration to become a serious poet had come to him in a flash on an evening in May 1881, during his last year at Trinity. A fellow student had lent him a copy of *Orion, and Other Poems*, by the New Brunswick nature poet, Charles G. D. Roberts. "Like most of the young fellows about me, I had been under the impression that we were situated hopelessly on the outskirts of civilization," he recalled for the Ottawa Literary and Scientific Society nearly two decades later. "I sat up reading and rereading *Orion* in a state of the wildest excitement, and when I went to bed, I could not sleep. It seemed to me a wonderful thing that such work could be done by a Canadian, by a young man, one of ourselves. It was like a voice from a new paradise of art, calling us to be up and doing."

"*August* 1, 1885. Duncan Scott and I tried the birchbark canoe again yesterday," wrote Lampman to Maud. "I am getting perfectly used to it and can skim along in it quite at my ease." With the entry of Scott, a tall, bony figure wielding a paddle, we arrive at the nub of our story. Already these two have been friends for some time. The circumstances of their first meeting are lost to history – quite likely, they bumped into each other at the Literary and Scientific Society. Lampman, continuing his letter to Maud, conveys some of the early flavour of their relationship.

> Next Saturday, we are going to make a little trip in the afternoon. We shall go up in the canoe to the first lock, then carry the canoe over to the Rideau and paddle down til we come to that bridge at the end of Nicholas Street. When we get there, we will carry the canoe over again to the canal, and come home. I am rather better in the canoe than Scott. His legs are too long and his feet get asleep, but I fit into it as neat as a pin.

Lampman, as is evident, was already the dominant partner. Indeed, since his tragic early death at thirty-seven in 1899 is part of our literary legend, it is not giving this story away to recount that even from beyond the grave he would dominate the relationship for nearly another half-century. Scott, though in fact nine months Lampman's junior, seemed somehow much older and more careworn: a spare, austere, and rather forbidding-looking figure, whose eyes alone gave notice of a dry, self-deprecating wit that Lampman, despite his ebullient pleasure in jokes, did not really share. Scott was painfully shy and reserved, a disability that neither time nor a long and distinguished career did much to erase. "The moment I endeavour to write or speak anything about myself something intervenes, I become shy and inarticulate, and anything that I write or say seems affected and banal," he wrote to a friend, in his eightieth year. "I suppose this makes ordinary intercourse with me difficult, but I cannot change my spots now."

A disconnected and rather chilly childhood had contributed to this remoteness. Like Lampman, Scott was a child of the manse, the son of an itinerant Methodist preacher, William Scott, best known for his work among the Indians. Born in Ottawa, he grew up in a succession of small towns and villages in eastern Ontario and in Quebec's Eastern Townships, picking up a random education from whatever common schools and Wesleyan colleges were available. He dreamed of studying medicine at McGill, but in the absence of money for tuition, bowed to the inevitable and, in December 1879, when he was not quite eighteen, accepted a job as a copying clerk in the Bureau of Indian Affairs. It was a considerable point of pride that Sir John A. himself, after a personal interview stage-managed by the Reverend William Scott, proffered the appointment. "Approved," the Premier had scribbled hurriedly. "Employ Mr. Scott at $1.50."

It was central to the friendship that developed between Lampman and Scott that Scott, during his earliest years in Ottawa, had had no thought of becoming a poet. In his early teens, at the high school in Smith's Falls, he had first felt what he later described as "the pang of poetry" when a teacher wrote some lines from Tennyson's *Dream of Fair Women* on the blackboard. But at this point, he was much more deeply interested in music. Though largely self-taught, he was by all accounts a reasonably accomplished pianist, and he had also lately taken up the viola. Then he met Archie. "It never occurred to me to write a line of prose or poetry until after I had met Lampman," he remarked in later years.

August afternoons in Ottawa have a quality of timelessness. Even a century later, it is easy to happen upon the shades of Archie and Duncan as they would have been that Saturday half-holiday, paddling up the canal, wearing floppy Panama hats and bandannas tied round their necks. True enough, that "first lock" mentioned by Lampman would have been well out in wooded countryside while nowadays it is well within city limits, opposite Carleton University. Even so, it occurs to the literary pilgrim that the "little trip" Lampman sketched out was quite an ambitious venture for a couple of novice canoeists to squeeze into a single afternoon: a round trip of about seven miles, with another couple of miles of portaging. Thinking of the heavy serge trousers and thick cotton shirts they were probably wearing, one hopes that that particular August Saturday was not a typical Ottawa Valley roaster. For Lampman, though, it was usually a case of the hotter the better. "He was the greatest man for heat I ever knew," Scott remarked years later to M.O. Hammond. "On the hottest days, when I could barely stand, he wanted to go walking." One of his most evocative and most frequently anthologized poems was titled simply, "Heat." Its last lines are: "In the full furnace of this hour/My thoughts grow keen and clear."

That first golden summer of the birchbark canoe was a pivotal summer for two poetic careers. At the end of August, Archie and Duncan set off on the first of the many long canoeing expeditions into the wilderness that they would undertake together and that so materially influenced their poetry. They went to the Lièvre, a river that flows into the Ottawa at Buckingham, Quebec, about twenty miles downstream from the capital. "We had an excellent time and got strong and brown and gluttonous," Lampman reported to Maud. "I grew a beard which I have not shaved off yet, and which has excited immense disgust at home . . . I had only one collar with me and that had got covered with mud, so I came home without one."

"AN OXYGENIC ESSENCE"

As he probably saved up to tell Maud in person, Lampman had also come home with the idea for one of the finest poems he would ever write. His true gift as a poet, as the critic E. K. Brown has remarked in his landmark 1943 study, *On Canadian Poetry*, was the gift of rendering the moment. "Lampman *watches* . . . with an eye which appreciates not only the contours and colours of particular objects but just as sharply the relations between objects, and Lampman *dreams*, he does not merely record but also feels the essence of the scene in which he finds himself." Later in his career, Lampman would write poems of weightier content. But it is difficult to find in his entire *oeuvre*, lines more evocative of the man and of his nature than the wonderful middle stanza of "Morning on the Lièvre."*

Softly as a cloud we go,
Sky above and sky below,
Down the river; and the dip
Of the paddles scarcely breaks,
With the little silvery drip
Of the water as it shakes
From the blades, the crystal deep
Of the silence of the morn,
Of the forest yet asleep;
And the river reaches borne
In a mirror, purple gray,
Sheer away
To the misty line of light,
Where the forest and the stream,
In the shadow meet and plight,
Like a dream. . . .

In the case of Scott, the fruits of the trip were less immediately apparent. Another three years passed before his first poems were published, in a volume titled *Songs of the Great Dominion*, edited by the Montreal man of letters, W. D. Lighthall. But it may well have been that one of these earliest poems, a short, stark narrative titled "At the Cedars," was first envisioned on the Lièvre. Scott's work, denser and more original than Lampman's, contains, in Brown's words, "a mixture of restraint and intensity which grasps and will not let go . . . as one reads, it is to be struck by the predominance of the dark and the powerful – night, storm, the wilderness." His finest poems, a series of dreampieces on Indian themes, would be written much later but already, in "At the Cedars,"

* In 1961, David Bairstow of the National Film Board used this poem as the basis for a prize-winning short film.

the nature of Scott's imagination is apparent, as is also a characteristic, spare, staccato rhyme scheme that prefigures the Imagist poets of the 1900s.

"At the Cedars" tells of a log-jam on the Ottawa River in which a man is caught and killed as his sweetheart looks on. In the most compelling sequence:

> He went up like a block
> With the shock,
> And when he was there
> In the air,
> Kissed his hand
> to the land
> When he dropped
> My heart stopped,
> For the logs had caught him
> and crushed him;
> When he rose in his place
> There was blood on his face.

"Restraint and intensity." Contemplating the nature of the friendship that developed between them, E. K. Brown's splendid phrase seems to apply not just to Scott, but equally to Lampman and to both of them together. Nearly half a century later, when speaking of Lampman, Scott would sometimes say, in a whisper, "Poor Archie," and suddenly fall silent. Brown, Scott's closest friend of his later years, goes on to comment: "It is impossible to convey how much feeling he put into the simple phrase." The relationship between Scott and Lampman prefigured that between Mackenzie King and Bert Harper, a Tennysonian kinship of shared interests and high ideals. Just as King erected the statue of Galahad in front of the Parliament Buildings to commemorate Harper, so Scott, during the half-century by which he outlived Lampman, devoted himself almost obsessively to keeping Archie's memory alive and his work in print.

The kinship between Scott and Lampman, however, unlike that between King and Harper, was by no means always sweetness and light. Their marriages complicated things, as did the fact that while Lampman began to bite the civil service hand that fed him, Scott, discovering administrative talents within himself, began to clasp it firmly. In 1889, he was made a first-class clerk at $1,400 a year, and in 1896 Secretary of the Department. Eventually, in 1913, he made it all the way to the top as Deputy Minister. Lampman, by contrast, received only one promotion in seventeen years, to second-class clerk in 1893. Much to the dismay of his supervisor at the Post

Office, the man of letters W. D. LeSueur, who appears on many occasions to have covered for him nobly, Archie became a bit of a troublemaker, the kind of dissatisfied office worker who considers himself several cuts above his job and who gripes endlessly about working conditions. "We are all crammed together like sardines," he wrote to Maud in 1890, when the department shifted into the new Langevin Block. "There are 13 persons in my room intended for 8." That same summer, there was a squabble over holidays. "I fear I shall only get three weeks after all; they have got into one of their strict fits and there is no doing anything with them. . . . Mr. LeSueur says he would like to grant me four weeks but he did not feel that he could."

Even more, Lampman had grown to detest the chicanery and grubbiness of politics. In a grim little verse scribbled down for his own satisfaction, he compared "the politician" to "the pimp." He referred to his Minister, Mabel Adamson's doughty kinsman, William Mulock, as "Moloch." Unlike Scott, who, as a natural conservative, did not question the social order, Archie became a passionate socialist and wrote a long poem about a mythical *Land of Pallas*, a Utopian kingdom where "all the earth was common" and "no coined gold was needed there or known."

Where it counted, none of this mattered. Just as easy as finding Archie and Duncan in their birchbark canoe in the long-lost summer of 1885, is finding them together any time after office hours during those last years of the eighties and early years of the nineties. The Experimental Farm in autumn is a good place, or Rockcliffe in the winter, or, at all seasons, Beechwood Cemetery (where both are buried now, within a stone's throw of each other), for all of these were favourite haunts. From each of these spots, they could view the city from a different angle, the fantastical spires of the Parliament Buildings in sharp relief against the blue hills of the Gatineau and the great sweeping river. Lampman, in his "oxygenic essence" period, came up with the most flowery descriptions. "Bell-tongued city with its glorious towers," he wrote on one occasion, and on another, "Yon city, glimmering in its smoky shroud." But Scott, when need be, could also reach for the purple, as in "Imperious towers pierce and possess the sky." At Christmas, it became a tradition for each to write a poem and to send these to friends and relatives as a joint greeting card.

Their enthusiasm attracted others to them. On chilly winter evenings, in front of a blazing log fire, primed with a bottle or two of sherry and a few dozen oysters, the conversation in either the cosy Lampman establishment or at the fine new brick house on Lisgar

Lampman and Scott and their circle, circa *1890. Scott is on the left in the front row. Lampman wearing a hat, is second from left in the back row. The woman directly in front of him is possibly Maud Playter.*

Street that Scott, as a measure of his growing affluence, had had built for himself in 1887, was often every bit as lively as within *Les Dix*. In the winter of 1887, when Lampman was laid up with an ulcerated knee, he gives us a few glimpses of this circle of friends in letters to Maud. Along with Duncan, "who comes in to see me every day," bearing armloads of Henry James and Trollope, we find the Ottawa painters William Brymner and Charles Moss; the literary lawyer J. A. Ritchie,* an old chum from Trinity days; James Macoun, a distinguished naturalist with the Geological Survey; and, of all people, Lampman's attendant physician, Dr. James Grant, whom Fanny Meredith had so detested. "He comes in every day to bandage my leg and then sits down and smokes a cigarette while we talk of various things." Lampman and Scott were also regulars at the literary salons held frequently in the pleasant New Edinburgh parlour of Achille and Annie Howells Fréchette: it was probably this connection that caused Lampman's first book of poetry, *Among the Millet*, to be given an excellent review in *Harper's* by Annie Fréchette's brother, the famous American novelist, William Dean Howells. Lampman, according to Howells, seemed "always to have the right word on his lips."

The most dramatic and certainly the most obstreperous of their literary friends whizzed into their lives like an angry comet in the spring of 1891. His name was William Wilfred Campbell, and right from the beginning they were a little dubious about him. But Scott

* Ritchie, who was the son of the first Chief Justice, Sir William Ritchie, and brother of the popular Ritchie sisters, was Crown Prosecutor in Ottawa for many years. He was well known as an amateur playwright, but is best remembered as author of the lines inscribed over the entrance to the Centre Block: "The wholesome sea is at her gates, her gates both east and west."

Scott and William Wilfred Campbell. Campbell was a difficult friend.

and Lampman were above all else generous spirits, and if there was one thing they could not bear to see, it was a fellow poet in trouble.

"One of my next door neighbours is the poet William Wilfred Campbell," wrote Lampman to his close friend, the Boston journalist E. W. Thomson, in February 1892. "His first impression is unsatisfactory, but I find myself genuine in respect for him as I know him better. His mind is erratic, but there is some good stuff in it, which comes out now and then in an accidental kind of way."

This was an excellent description. To it can be added an equally good physical description of Campbell, provided by M. O. Hammond a decade or so later. "Rather a squat figure with a nervous twitch to his face and blink to his eyes which give individuality if they do not add to his personal charm." Truth to tell, Campbell's personal charm at the best of times was of negative quantity. An Anglican minister a few years older than Scott and Lampman, he was high-minded, energetic, and intelligent. Though much less gifted than they, he was in his way a good enough poet of nature and at that time his literary reputation was, if anything, larger. He was also, unfortunately, cranky, bombastic, and thin-skinned almost to the point of paranoia. Having abandoned the pulpit to concentrate on writing, Campbell had arrived in Ottawa determined to make a test case of himself. So gifted a poet, he informed everyone who would listen, must be given a job. Macdonald, who seems indeed to have been somewhat taken aback, found him a spot at $1.50 a day in the Department of Railways and Canals, with a promise of something much better to open up soon in the Parliamentary Library.

Macdonald, alas, was in his grave within a month, and Campbell, with a wife and children to support, was almost destitute. "In comparison with him," Lampman continued to Thomson, "I am a small Croesus." He and Scott devised a rescue operation. "We decided to see if we could not get the Toronto *Globe* to give space for a couple of columns and short articles weekly, at whatever pay we could get from them. They agreed to it."

What the editors had agreed to, it developed, was a weekly half-page, "At the Mermaid Inn," the title suggested by a line from Keats. This began appearing in *The Globe's* Saturday literary section on February 6, 1892, and continued for almost eighteen months, until July 1, 1893. Scott, Lampman, and Campbell all contributed: each was paid $3 a week. Lampman, whose pen was the most agile, produced the most copy, a total of eighty-eight individual entries; Scott and Campbell wrote respectively, sixty-seven and sixty-six.*

Within the framework of these columns, Lampman and Scott did some of their liveliest prose writing. In Lampman's case, the topics ranged from his affection for cats – "all people who have a fine and subtle sense of humour love cats" – and for tobacco – "it is most conducive to meditation" – to his remarkably advanced opinions on the status of women. "Give them perfect independence, place them upon an exactly equal footing with men." Scott, always more politic, stuck mostly to literary criticism, although on one occasion – "It is not often that the consideration of tariffs and their problems concerns a literary man" – he worked himself into a fine lather of indignation about the prohibitive import duty on books. On one occasion in April 1892, the two joined forces to write a review of the current Royal Canadian Academy exhibition and concluded that it was even tougher to be a Canadian painter than a Canadian poet. "His art depends more than any other on the culture, the experience of the past, and in a land like Canada, where we have practically no great pictures available, and no eminent resident artists, the young painter finds himself without the means of overcoming the technical difficulties of his profession." A year later – some aspects of Official Culture never change – Lampman pushed these thoughts further. "One of the things that might be done by the Dominion Government would be the improvement and increase of the so-called National Gallery at Ottawa."

* In recent years, "At the Mermaid Inn" has been revived by *The Globe and Mail* as a weekly column of comment on matters cultural and literary, on the Saturday editorial page.

Of the three, Campbell's contributions were far and away the most inflammatory. In the very first month, he nearly scuppered the column by referring offhandedly to the Crucifixion as "a myth . . . connected with the old phallic worship of some of our most remote ancestors." Not the least contrite, he went on from there to attack organized religion, "a tool of capitalism, indifferent to destitution, misery and degradation." In those days an ardent nationalist of the "Canada First" persuasion, though later he would nail quite different colours to his mast, he made mincemeat of Canadian universities. "To be direct, what are they doing for a national literature? . . . We shall never have a true nationality while this miserable condition of things lasts."

Then, on July 1, 1893, Campbell stepped beyond all bounds. For reasons quite inexplicable, he attacked his friend and benefactor Lampman, by way of a merciless parody of a "flabgaster in rhyme" named by Campbell, "John Pensive Bangs," who was given to writing poems that led off in such vein as:

> I sit me moanless in the sombre fields
> The cows come with large udders down the dusk,
> One cudless, the other chewing of a husk . . .

For *The Globe* and presumably also for Lampman (he did not respond in public and what he may have said privately has not been recorded) this was the last straw. No further columns appeared. Relations soon deteriorated further: When a critic for *Munsey's* magazine in New York surveyed Canadian poetry in 1895 and praised Lampman and Scott to the skies but dismissed Campbell as "a rhetorician rather than a poet," he became convinced that the two of them, along with the New Brunswick poet Bliss Carman who had been praised highest of all, were engaged in a conspiracy to wreck his reputation. Nor did it help that in an ensuing literary brouhaha dubbed by the press as, "The War of the Poets," Campbell publicly accused Carman of plagiarism. Shortly thereafter, he abandoned Canadian nationalism and nature poetry for the new and much more modish cause of Imperialism, or "Vaster Britain," as he preferred to describe it, and found a new friend in the General Officer Commanding the militia, Lord Dundonald. Later still, though they argued politically, he found an excellent patron in Mackenzie King; the two were particularly known for strolling through the National Gallery of a Sunday afternoon, declaiming poetry aloud.

Nothing, though, is ever quite as simple as it seems, much less in the tangled lives of poets. Perhaps the best poem that Campbell ever wrote was an elegy to Lampman, which he read aloud at a memorial service soon after Archie's death in 1899. It was titled, "Bereavement of the Fields."

> . . . Soft fall the February snows, and soft
> He sleeps in peace upon the breast of her
> He loved the truest; where, by wood and croft,
> The wintry silence folds in fleecy blur
> About his silence, while in glooms aloft
> The mighty forest fathers, without stir
> Guard well the rest of him, their rare sweet worshipper. . . .

Lampman had been right all along. There was "some good" in Campbell.

CHAPTER 29

Wives of the Poets

A room full of whist players is a spectacle to make a philosopher weep, and a progressive euchre party will turn the head of a sensitive man grey in a single night . . .
Archibald Lampman; *The Globe*; December 3, 1892

During the middle and later years of the nineties, Scott and Lampman drew apart a certain distance. *Frissons* developed between their two households: their wives, to put it bluntly, did not get on. This information we draw from a source as revealing as letters: the two huge social scrapbooks, now at the National Library, in which Belle Warner Botsford of Boston, who Scott had married on October 3, 1894, kept a meticulous record of her every move. From a carefully tabulated list of wedding gifts received, we learn that Archie and Maud Lampman had squeezed their slender resources to come up with *two* presents: a table gong and a silver mustard pot. But, as we learn further from Belle's listing of social engagements pasted in neatly at the end of each year, the Lampmans were never thereafter invited to the Scotts. Nor, for that matter, did the Scotts ever go to the Lampmans.

Perhaps it was as simple as mutual antipathy: two strong-willed women who, from the first glance, did not care for each other and who, moreover, were jealous of a friendship between their husbands. Perhaps also, Belle Scott was touchy about the fact that Duncan had once been more than a little in love with Archie's sister, the dark and lovely Annie. It may also have been the case that in the exalted social circles that Belle was determined to conquer, the Lampmans, scrabbling along on a clerk's wages in a succession of rented houses, were not considered quite the thing.

Perhaps the root problem lay deeper. By the time Scott married

Belle, the Lampmans' marriage was disintegrating and Archie had embarked on a stormy and secret affair which for whatever reason, he was determined to keep secret even from his greatest friend.

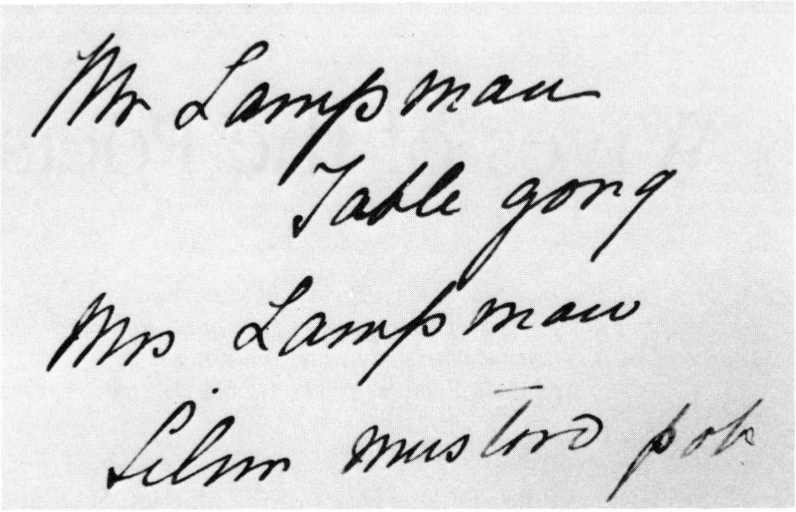

Card from Belle Scott's scrapbook.

Lampman's first volume of poetry, *Among the Millet*, published in 1888, contained on the title page under a charming little quatrain, the dedication, "To My Wife." It also contained a number of delightful sonnets written to Maud during their courtship. "Faint rose-curves . . . flit about her child-sweet mouth and innocent cheek," he wrote. Maud possessed, in Lampman's view, "a saint's pale grace . . . eyes like a prayer from some quiet window under minster towers." In those heady days of infatuation, it seemed only to add to Maud's charm that "my lady is not versed in many books/Nor hath much love for grave discourse." No matter that she loved frills and furbelows and waltzing, while for Lampman, as he phrased it later in "At the Mermaid Inn," "More misery can be got out of a common dancing party than from an hour's outpour of one of our popular preachers" – they were manifestly and splendidly in love. Maud indeed was wonderful to look at, tall and slender in the manner of a pre-Raphaelite portrait, with a magnificent cloud of curly hair.

Lampman's only other sequence of love-poems, titled "A Portrait in Six Sonnets," although written in the nineties, was not published until forty-four years after his death. Indeed, these sonnets might never have seen the light of day but for the gentle but insistent prodding of the critic E. K. Brown, who was determined to include them in *At the Long Sault*, a volume of Lampman's unpublished poetry that he and Scott were co-editing. The sequence was addressed to a woman named Kate Waddell and, as somehow lifts Lampman out of the ranks of the late Victorians and into our own time, theirs was an office romance. Kate was a co-worker at the Post Office; indeed, when it came to the job, she was rather more upwardly mobile than he. She was in her middle twenties when they met, and it is clear from her photograph that she was a woman at the opposite end of the spectrum from Maud; rangy and intelligent-looking, if a bit severe, almost a prototypical New Woman, perhaps even the inspiration for the feminist attitudes that Lampman espoused in "At the Mermaid Inn." In expressing his love for her, he treated her accordingly:

Maud Playter Lampman, and her daughter Natalie, 1895. "A saint's pale grace."

> Grey-eyed, for grey is wisdom – yet with eyes
> Mobile and deep and quick for thought or flame
> A voice of many notes that breaks and changes
> And fits each meaning with its vital chord
> A speech, true to the heart, that lightly ranges
> From jocund laughter to the serious word,
> And over all, a bearing proud and free,
> A noble grace, a conscious dignity.

Scott, who discovered this last great love of Archie's only after his death, when going through his papers and from conversations with W. D. LeSueur, could never quite come to terms with it, even at the end of his own life. "DCS says the girl was far from attractive in his opinion," wrote Brown in a memo to himself, following a long talk with Scott in the summer of 1942. "He considers that Lampman found his wife unsympathetic to poetry . . . and thought in this girl he would find a spiritual mate. The idea of spiritual affinities was very important to Lampman, and he often spoke about it in general terms to Scott. His wife was not such an affinity."

Kate Waddell in November 1898. "A noble grace, a conscious dignity."

Back in the eighties, Scott may or may not have tried to persuade Archie that Maud Playter was not the right girl for him. Certainly, plenty of other people tried, with Dr. Edward Playter, Lampman's future father-in-law, at the head of the list. Far from disliking Archie, Playter had been one of his earliest fans and patrons and indeed, had stretched an editorial point or two to include Lampman's only known work of fiction, a fairytale named "Hans Fingerhuit's Frog Lesson," in the November 1885 issue of *Man*, a medical journal that he published. But Playter, who had spoiled and indulged Maud, understood his daughter as Lampman did not. Or, putting this another way, Playter conceded certain truths about Maud's character that Archie in his besotted condition could not recognize. Even in Lampman's earliest letters to Maud, we find the first hints of trouble ahead. "I was sorry that after ten days silence you could afford me only two pages," he wrote on August 14, 1885. "You let me know how you are enjoying yourself and of the people you meet but never tell me whether you ever think of me. . . . If you love me, when you get this letter, sit right down and write one in return, not a cold one . . . but a dear, kind one." A letter written eighteen months later, in the winter of 1887, when Lampman was laid up with his bad leg is even more revealing of future incompatibility. "You recount the many gaieties (I call them miseries) which you have endured (I should say enjoyed). What amuses me, O Strange Little One, is that you commiserate with me for having missed all these things. I assure you, Dear, I am heartily thankful that I had nothing to do with them. I would much rather be laid up with a sore leg any day."

Quite simply, Maud Playter, soon to become Maud Lampman was a bubblehead–even though an exceedingly beautiful one. That winter, Playter seems to have made a last-ditch effort to put an end to the romance. The Lampman house on Nicholas Street was less than a quarter of an hour's walk from the Playter establishment on Stewart Street, but during the whole six weeks of Archie's enforced idleness, Maud was forbidden to visit him, even though plenty of chaperones were available to ensure the niceties. But Playter failed. On September 3, 1887, shortly after Maud had turned eighteen, she and Archie were married in a small, intimate ceremony at St. Alban's, the church so well beloved by Edmund Meredith. The bride was "attired in a grey travelling dress," the Ottawa *Journal* recorded. The groomsman, of course, was "Mr. D. C. Scott."

For a time, so far as we can piece it together from a handful of letters, all went well enough. She called him "Spunker" and he called her "Dear Chick." They doted on each other, and on a fat tomcat they called "Master Picken." It seems not to have mattered that on Archie's salary of $700 a year, they had no choice but to bunk in alternately with the Lampmans senior and with the Playters senior. Maud proudly channelled a small legacy of her own into getting *Among the Millet* published. In the summer of 1889, we run into the first signs of discord. "How are the girls?" writes Maud, recently embarked on a visit to Toronto, in a clear reference to Lampman's sisters, "I suppose they would rather do the work, and have me away. . . . I am having a lovely time, they want me to stay as long as possible . . . they are all crazy for us to come and live in Toronto, oh how I wish I could, you must keep your eyes open for something here for my sake." Around the same time, in an angry little poem, Lampman hints obliquely that Maud is turning into a self-centred little whiner. "O canst thou not be still thou foolish tongue/That makes this life one gust of sheer despair, of shallow rage, and rankling bitterness." Still, in the summer of 1891 as Maud once more entrains for Toronto, we find Lampman writing to her in the manner of a devoted bridegroom. "Felt very sad when I left you in the train. . . . We are always together so steadily, thou dear old puss, that it seems quite an awful thing for us to be separated for even a few days." Perhaps, though, he was feeling a bit guilty about embarking a few days later on a bachelor holiday of his own, to Nantucket Island, in the company of his friend, E. W. Thomson who, because he was also involved in an extra-marital affair was beginning to supplant Duncan as a confidant in these years. By now, Maud was pregnant: In January 1892, their daughter Natalie was born. A few months later, with the extra money from *The Globe* coming in and Lampman's promotion to a salary of $1100 in the cards, they moved into their first real home: a handsome stone house in Philemon Terrace on fashionable Daly Street, where Lampman was able to enjoy for the first time, as he wrote to Thomson, "a room where I can shut myself up to my work in solitude and silence."

Duncan Scott sometimes argued that all Lampmans' subsequent difficulties could somehow be anthropomorphically attached to this elegant but awkward and hard-to-heat house. On a hot August morning in 1915, shepherding the journalist M. O. Hammond around town on a Lampman pilgrimage, Scott stood outside the front door and remarked, as Hammond recorded in his diary: "Here, Lampman began a heap of troubles. It was a damp house, and he got it cheap. The kitchen was in the basement, and Mrs. L. contracted woman trouble from which she never recovered. The dampness was also bad for L." The real truth, though, was that well before the move to Philemon Terrace and perhaps even before Natalie was conceived, Lampman had fallen in love with Kate.

Exactly how the affair began, and how it proceeded and ended, we cannot be certain. Some of the pivotal letters concerning it, between Lampman and E. W. Thomson in Boston, have disappeared. All we really know is that Kate, around 1888, had abandoned her first career as a teacher to work in the Post Office, and that, as no one ever denied, a warm friendship had blossomed between them. A couple of stray sentences in a letter to Thomson in 1895 make it plain that the two spent much of their time at the office discussing books. "I think I told you that I had lent *Old Man Savarin* to Miss Waddell," Lampman wrote, commenting on a book of short stories that Thomson himself had recently published. "She was very much pleased with it . . . I think her opinion is worth having. She has a very good head and a very sound heart." Sometime during these years, most likely at Christmas 1893, Lampman presented to Kate the most eloquent testament of his affections he could bestow: a handsome leather-bound volume containing ninety-two of his own poems, painstakingly transcribed in his own hand.* By now, his style of address in writing to Maud, when she was out of town, had changed markedly. Instead of "My Dearest Chick" she was "Dear Madam." "You ought to stay the month out if possible," he wrote to her in Toronto on March 20, 1896. "If you don't, you will get no benefit, and the thing will be a sheer expense."

* The existence of this volume came to light in 1945, when a niece of Kate's presented it for sale to the University of Toronto Library, at a price of $100. The Library knew a bargain when it saw one.

Lampman, a month previously, had written to Thomson that he intended "to give up housekeeping on the 1st of May and board. This will give greater ease and less worry to Maud. . . . In a little while, I shall no longer care whether people pay any attention to me or not, whether those I love return the affection or not. . . ." On the basis of this evidence, one Lampman scholar, Margaret Coulby Whitredge, has suggested that he and Kate were probably physical lovers, and perhaps, during that summer of 1896, may even have lived together briefly. To make historical detection a good deal more difficult, and even after allowing for the inconsistencies of human behaviour, it is a fact that Maud and Kate seem to have been on remarkably good terms with each other during the whole of the affair. Thus, in his letter to Maud of March 20, 1896, Lampman continued either bravely or blithely: "You will be glad to know that since you left, I have not been sitting and moping over books in that high room of mine. . . . On Tuesday evening I went down to the Waddells (very improper, but I was invited) last night I dined with Duncan. . . ." Again, the following summer, when Maud was staying at a summer cottage on Britannia Bay on the Ottawa River, and Lampman was keeping bachelor's hall with his long-suffering father-in-law: "By the way, I told Miss Waddell yesterday that you would like to go the Browns with her someday. She said she would call for you about this the end of this week, some afternoon."

Whether or not this affair was more than platonic – on balance, it seems more likely than not that they were lovers – one fact is inarguable. Kate, and not Maud, inspired from Lampman the full intensity of his poetic feeling. As he wrote towards the end of his life:

> To her forever like storm-stained ships
> To the old havens, all my thoughts return –
> Return and lie close-moored, to rest a while
> By some stored look, or some long-treasured smile.

By 1897, their affair had probably run its course. Perhaps, as Margaret Whitredge suggests in her introduction to *Lampman's Kate*, her 1975 edition of his late love poems, "his wife refused him the divorce he wanted, and his 'lady' refused to share permanently a scandalous liaison." Always careless of his frail frame, Lampman now began to drive himself harder, physically, than ever before. There are many ways of committing suicide and certainly, as Scott always seems to have felt guilty about, his and Archie's last canoe trip to Lake Achigan, in the summer of 1897, a longer and harder excursion than they had ever ventured before, was an act of folly for a man beginning to be increasingly troubled by his rheumatic heart. Nor was it sensible, earlier that summer, for Lampman to pedal a borrowed bicycle hell-bent for leather over an embankment "into a mass of raspberry briars," as he recounted to Thomson, and then to set off alone to paddle ten miles with a pair of canoe portages "on my sole shoulders." The following winter, all this over-exertion caught up with him. "I reached the point where I could not walk a hundred feet without being compelled to stop until the pain subsided," he told Thomson. The two months he then spent in bed might have done the trick – except that in the summer of 1898, ostensibly on sick leave, he was again out paddling, this time on the St. Maurice River north of Trois Rivières. He died six months later. The official prognosis was pneumonia, complicated by a weak heart.

Many epitaphs were written. The most eloquent did not appear until the fiftieth anniversary of his death, in the February 8, 1949 issue of *Saturday Night*. It was written by E. K. Brown who, as the confidant of Scott in his later years, had come to appreciate Lampman better than did most of Archie's own contemporaries:

> The night of February 9, 1899, was cold and still in Ottawa. Snow fell steadily and heavily. In a house at the corner of Bay and Slater Streets, within a few minutes walk of Parliament Hill, a clerk in the Post Office department was dying at the age of thirty-seven. His death at one

> o'clock on the morning of the tenth is, I believe, the most grievous loss our poetry has ever sustained.

Along with Maud and seven-year-old Natalie, Lampman left behind a baby son named Archibald Otto, born in June 1898, after his reconciliation with Maud. (Another son, born in 1894, had lived for only a few months.) Scott helped the family out by arranging the publication of a memorial edition of Archie's poems and by assisting Maud, by now also bereft of her beloved father, to find a job in the Parliamentary Library. After her death in 1910, also of heart failure, he organized a clerical post for Natalie in the National Gallery and arranged for the teenaged Archibald Otto – "Otto" he was known as as a child, but he dropped the name after the outbreak of the First World War – to get into the Royal Military College. Later, Lampman *fils* became a police reporter for the Toronto *Star*. Sadly, though, neither of Lampman's children was particularly close to Scott, even though Natalie, in 1915, married one of his own Indian Affairs subordinates, T. R. Loftus MacInnes, son of the noted British Columbia poet, Tom MacInnes. Both Natalie and Archibald Otto seem to have made the decision that the less they were reminded of their father, the better. In his 1980 memoir, *Literary Friends*, the literary journalist Wilfrid Eggleston recounts how as a cub reporter, he ran into the younger Lampman in the cafeteria frequented by journalists, and inquired if he were related to the poet. "Yes I am his son," came the reply. "Worse luck." Like his father, Archibald Otto died young, at forty. Natalie, an increasingly difficult and reclusive woman, lived on in Ottawa until the mid-1970s.

February 15, 1899. "No one was allowed to forget that it was St. Valentine's Day at the progressive euchre party give by Mrs. D. C. Scott," Amaryllis recorded in her column. Lampman had died five days earlier. Yet this long-planned party proceeded as if nothing had happened. As recounted by Amaryllis, in a clipping carefully pasted into Belle Scott's scrapbook:

> In [St. Valentine's] honour, the rooms were wreathed with hearts, transfixed with golden darts. These ranged from large ones on the centre of the ceiling to tiny but just as expressive-looking hearts in the wreaths irradiating from it. . . . There were ten tables and there too, the tally-cards were heart-shaped.

"After such knowledge, what forgiveness?" This line from T. S. Eliot, a poet with whom Archie did not live to reckon and who Duncan could never stomach, try as he might, is the line that seems to apply best.

"A progressive euchre party will turn the head of a sensible man grey in a single night," Lampman had once written in jest. One wonders if the words flashed into Scott's mind as he came home full of sorrows in the wintry dusk and found the house packed full of ladies laughing and chattering at the tables. Belle's insensitivity to Duncan's grief – not a single entry in the scrapbook for 1899 marks Archie's passing – is hard to credit. One wonders indeed if Amaryllis herself was shocked, if by ladling so much uncharacteristic syrup over her writing, she was in fact making a comment.

How to cope with Belle Scott? A number of people remain who still remember Duncan and who remember, even better, his second wife Elise. But recollections of Belle, who died in 1929, are slipping away from living memory. A group photograph, taken in the summer of 1913, when the Scotts were entertaining the visiting British poet, Rupert Brooke, shows her as a handsome woman of commanding presence, dressed simply in black, who somehow dominates even the Apollo-like Brooke. Writing in 1951, on the basis of information provided by Scott himself and by close friends, E. K. Brown was tactful – but to the point. "She was energetic, highstrung and imperious. She had much of the characteristic New England zeal to remould persons and circumstances nearer to her heart's desire. . . . A man of Duncan Scott's disposition, shy and slow to mature, might sooner have come to full self-understanding, if he had not lived under the shadow of so dominant a wife." After their marriage, it was not only the Lampmans who lacked for invitations to tea and supper parties. Neither Scott's mother nor his sisters were ever invited either.

The wedding, in the autumn of 1894, had taken everyone by surprise. Some people no doubt whispered that Duncan was marrying on the rebound, for his attachment to Archie's beautiful sister Annie was well known. Indeed, when Scott built his handsome house on Lisgar Street, which included a music room, it may have been in the hope that Annie, who was then just about to embark on two years of piano study at Leipzig would come back and share it with him. As late as January 1891, the two were still very close: from a letter written to her by Scott that survives among Annie's own papers, we know that she had recently give him "a fine pen" and that he had used it, for the first time, to write her a pretty sonnet with the title, "For Remembrance" – one of the very few sonnets he ever wrote. But, for whatever reason, the romance withered: in 1892 Annie married a fellow Ottawa musician, the organist and choral society

Scott's house on Lisgar Street. He had it built in 1887. It was demolished in 1957, to be replaced by a modern office building.

director F. M. S. Jenkins and settled down to a long and fruitful professional and domestic life.* Instead, it was the red-haired and volatile Belle Botsford who came with her violin to share the music room.

Belle was not just a strong-minded lady from Boston with an interest in music. She was also a considerable celebrity. A talented virtuoso, she had studied at the Paris Conservatory, and had appeared as a concert soloist in Britain, the United States, and Europe. As surviving programmes in her scrapbooks reveal, she went in mostly for the swooping romantic sonatas of the Spaniard, Sarasate, and the Polish composer, Wieniawski, with the occasional bit of Vivaldi and of Mendelssohn. In the winter of 1894, as Lady Aberdeen noted *en passant* in her diary, Belle arrived in Ottawa to play a series of engagements and was straightaway invited to attend the Saturday afternoon skating parties at Rideau Hall. She first met Scott when he filled in for her regular accompanist. They were married the following October, at Belle's mother's house in Greenfield Massachusetts, in a simple but graceful Unitarian service in which Mrs. Botsford, in a break with tradition, gave her daughter away. In an account in the Boston *Globe*, Scott was described as "a man

* For many years, Annie Lampman Jenkins was organist and choir-director at St. George's Anglican Church and she later founded the Palestrina Choir. In the *Encyclopedia of Music in Canada*, she is described as having been "Canada's first outstanding woman pianist." But as the *Encyclopedia* also notes, "the life of an Ottawa woman of her day inhibited the development of her gifts in full." She died in 1952.

of distinguished bearing and manner as well as of sterling character . . . devoted to music, and very proud of his wife's talent." Curiously enough, no mention was made of the fact that he was a poet who had already been published in *Harper's* and in *Scribner's*, only as "head of the Indian Department, the youngest man in the service to receive such a position" – something of an exaggeration. The couple set off for Ottawa, continued the *Globe*, "accompanied by the bride's pet cat. The handsome black feline, Coquelicot, wore a white satin ribbon."

The puzzle is why she married him rather than the other way around. At a guess, by 1894 Belle was well into her thirties, considerably older than Scott, who was thirty-two. Perhaps also, as an entire season spent performing in Ottawa suggests, her best years on the international concert circuit were behind her.

Duncan, in any event, seems to have been dazzled by his luck. Belle arrived in Ottawa determined to conquer the capital, much in the manner of Emilie Lavergne a few years later. As documented by her scrapbooks, a priceless map of social behaviour for the period, crammed with invitation cards and menus and programmes, the next decade was a bewildering welter of dinner parties and teas and luncheons, and recitals and river-cruises. Indeed, it is here that we discover with delight what is probably the only surviving invitation to that first pivotal reception of Emilie Lavergne's, held at the Russell House in December 1897.

Belle Botsford as a young violinist.

Like Emilie, Belle had quickly seized on the fact that the charity of the moment was St. Luke's Hospital. Since, unlike Emilie, she could not guarantee the presence of the prime minister at a display of "Living Pictures," she went the down-home route, and introduced to Ottawa that staple of New England fund-raising, the bake sale. "The most appetizing cakes that were ever made were arranged temptingly on tables at Mrs. D. C. Scott's," reported Amaryllis in 1897. "Fat brown chocolate cakes and white ones with chopped almonds." As deftly, Belle exploited the fact that in a capital in which the "American Colony" of lumber barons continued to be acknowledged as kingpins, her own Yankee heritage could be used to good advantage. On Washington's Birthday in 1897, we find her stealing the show at a luncheon party given by Mrs. William Perley, at which all of the guests were ladies transplanted from south of the border. "Mrs. Duncan Campbell Scott's loyalty showed itself in a massive brooch, holding a miniature of George Washington, in the form of a hatchet," recounts Amaryllis. "The frills on her shoulders were adorned with small stars and stripes." Almost as soon as she was past the toddling stage, the

Scott's only daughter, Elizabeth, a precocious little red-haired girl born in 1895, was introduced to the social round. "After playing Round the Mulberry Bush and Little Sallie Waters, all adjourned to the library where a beautiful tree shining with half a hundred tapers held a brave array of presents," wrote Amaryllis of a child's Christmas party in 1901. Whatever one makes of Belle, it is difficult not to admire her awesome mastery of detail. "Mothers and fathers were not forgotten either, for the gilded walnuts disclosed 'the thing they most liked': in one lay a tiny pen, in another a dainty triolet written by the poet-host himself, in a third, a pipe and cards."

Belle's most important ticket to social success was her violin. Music was the fashionable art in Ottawa, then as now, and if her talent was not quite enough to win her a place in the most exalted social firmament – the bright glittering world of Lola Powell, Agar Adamson, and the sisters Ritchie – it was certainly sufficient to ensconce her in the next best one: the circle presided over at Earnscliffe by the redoubtable Mrs. C. A. E. Harriss.

In any social chronicle of Ottawa, Ella Beatty Harriss really deserves a chapter all her own. A native of Cobourg, Ontario, possessed of rather more ambition than beauty, she had had the good luck to marry, in 1883, an aging Pittsburgh steel baron, one George K. Shoenberger, and the greater luck, in 1892, to be left a rich widow while still young enough to enjoy life.

She arrived in the capital in 1897 to join her sisters, one of whom, Mary Adelaide, had become the second wife of William McDougall, Edmund Meredith's crotchety minister, and another of whom, Edith Bertha, was the third wife of Desiré Girouard, a justice of the Supreme Court. By now grown stout and voluble, Ella had come equipped with a new husband some years her junior, the penniless but talented British-born conductor Charles Harriss, whom she set out to establish as a kind of colonial adaptation of Sir Edward Elgar. "'I saw him first at a concert,' she was wont to remark," wrote the Ottawa novelist Madge Macbeth, in her thinly-veiled portrait of Mrs. Harriss as "Mrs. Hudson" in her 1924 satirical *tour de force*, *The Land of Afternoon*. "And the moment my eyes fell upon his dear, unsuspecting head, I said to myself, 'Thank God! I have found the man I intend to marry and need look no further.'"*

Mrs. Hudson, or Ella Harriss, as Macbeth comments further, "made Society her tool. . . . Never a move, an invitation, an acceptance, a salutation on the street, was made without forethought." Ella Harriss it was who had given the "recherché little

* Harriss certainly did not take life easy on his wife's money. According to the *Encyclopedia of Music in Canada*, he was "an ambitious and indefatigable musician whose lifelong purpose was the promotion of reciprocity within the British Empire; in 1902, his Coronation Mass was performed at the Coronation of Edward VII." He was also a pioneer of music festivals. Harriss was further an enthusiastic sportsman who, on the day of Bessie Blair's funeral in 1901, took Agar Adamson home for tea and lent him a pair of rifles for a moose-hunting expedition. Further, we learn from Adamson, Harriss was a great hand at poker.

supper party" of March 1898 after which Agar Adamson had first proposed to Mabel Cawthra. In 1900, she purchased Earnscliffe from Lady Macdonald, and employed the promising young architect, Coly Meredith, to remodel it "to the point of being almost a different house," as Amaryllis reported. At the gigantic Earnscliffe auction, she purchased most of the choicest items of furniture, including Agnes's favourite sofa, and marble busts of both Sir John and Agnes, which she placed on either side of the dining-room door. The highlight of the auction, as Lilian Scott Desbarats recounts in her memoir, "was that Dr. and Mrs. Harriss bid against each other without realizing it, for they were at different sides of the room. The articles they wanted soared in price."

Ella Beatty Harriss. She ruled the social roost in Ottawa for the first quarter of the twentieth century.

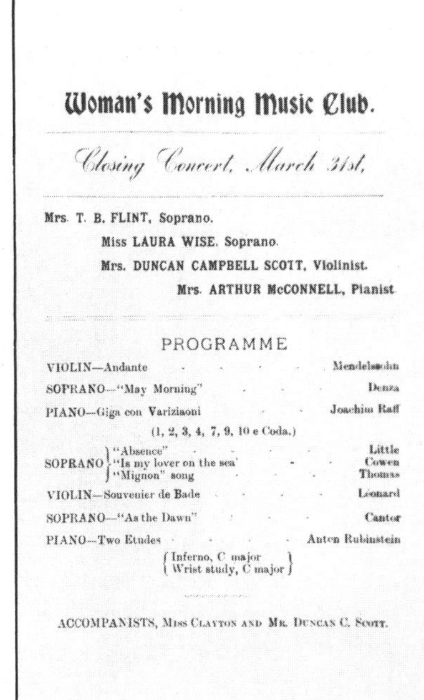

Woman's Morning Music Club.

Closing Concert, March 31st,

Mrs. T. B. FLINT, Soprano.
Miss LAURA WISE, Soprano.
Mrs. DUNCAN CAMPBELL SCOTT, Violinist.
Mrs. ARTHUR McCONNELL, Pianist

PROGRAMME

VIOLIN—Andante	Mendelssohn
SOPRANO—"May Morning"	Denza
PIANO—Giga con Varizizoni (1, 2, 3, 4, 7, 9, 10 e Coda.)	Joachim Raff
SOPRANO "Absence"	Little
SOPRANO "Is my lover on the sea"	Cowen
SOPRANO "Mignon" song	Thomas
VIOLIN—Souvenier de Bade	Léonard
SOPRANO—"As the Dawn"	Cantor
PIANO—Two Etudes (Inferno, C major; Wrist study, C major)	Anton Rubinstein

ACCOMPANISTS, Miss Clayton and Mr. Duncan C. Scott.

Programme from the Woman's Morning Music Club. Frequently, as on this occasion, Duncan Campbell Scott played the accompaniment for his wife.

With equal determination, Ella Harriss quickly developed excellent connections to both Grits and Tories and upon those three pillars – politics, the arts, and money – proceeded to rule the social roost for the next quarter-century. It was a measure of her power that the instant after patrons of the Russell Theatre checked to see who was sitting in the viceregal box, they looked to the right to check out the guests in Mrs. Harriss's permanent box. As founder and president of the Woman's Morning Music Club, an institution that lasted until the 1950s, Mrs. Harriss was shrewd enough to spot in the energetic and ambitious Belle Scott an excellent flag-lieutenant. "Mrs. D. C. Scott arranged the entire programme for the opening concert of the season," reported Amaryllis's somewhat insipid successor in November 1905, "and it reflected credit on her usual good taste and judgement."

Most of the time, Scott observed his wife's socializing, both in co-operation with and – occasionally – in competition with Ella Harriss, from a position of emotional detachment. Only once, in a novel produced in a white heat of energy in 1905 but which mouldered unpublished until 1979, did he provide a few insights into what he may really have been thinking during these years. *Untitled Novel* ca. *1905*, as the Penumbra Press edition is titled, is a truly extraordinary work.

At one level, the book is a comedy of manners as deftly observed as Madge Macbeth's, in which, knowing what we do of turn-of-the-century Ottawa, characters soar off the page as recognizable types. Here is Purcell Shortreed, for instance, handsome young British aristocrat with excellent connections at Rideau Hall, whose ability on horseback is exceeded only by his ability to lose money at cards, arriving in the capital with the express purpose of marrying the richest girl in town, one Barbara Applegarth. Here is the *nouveau riche* Mrs. Applegarth, mother to Barbara, at first dubious about Shortreed – "I would pass a *law* to compel every Englishman who came to this country to produce a certificate from a *Bishop*, saying who and what he was" – and then later, when she has discovered that Shortreed is indeed only one brother away from a baronetcy, pushing Barbara straight into his arms. "I always *said* Mr. Shortreed was a perfect gentleman." Here is Robin Garrabrant, idealistic young politician, discovering to his horror from his campaign manager that his election has been won by the dirtiest of tricks, "by means of a piece of lead from a soft pencil firmly fixed and glued under the thumbnail of the Deputy Returning Officer. Mysteriously, pencil marks had appeared on them, crosses and lines that would invalidate any ballot." (Scott, no doubt, was drawing from an actual election incident.)

But at another level, *Untitled Novel* is a work of quite different order, lurid, sensational, replete with murders, suicides, and illegitimate children, in some ways almost a parody of a melodrama of the period, and yet also strangely moving. Purcell Shortreed, far from being merely an amiable fortune hunter, becomes a metaphor for evil, a "Mephistophelean rogue" who corrupts, among others, the gentle pianist, Cornelia. Cornelia, for her part, seems to play a double role; a minister's daughter, she is described as "lovely, with an uncommon loveliness . . . something even exotic in the bloom of her face," which suggests Scott's first love, Annie Lampman. Then, a few chapters later, when Cornelia dies young of a lingering illness, we are reminded abruptly of Archie himself. Far and away the most arresting figure in the story is Adrienne Godchere, in her late thirties, "a woman of sudden and unaccountable humours," who may or may not have been intended to represent Belle. A powerful and manipulative woman, Adrienne dominates everyone else in the book – including the wicked Shortreed, who becomes her lover – until she ends up a suicide.

Whether or not Scott wrote this novel as therapy, he was much too circumspect to try to get it published. His marriage aside, these early years of the 1900s were years of swift ascendancy. Not merely a capable administrator, he possessed, as Edmund Meredith had never done, a shrewd and supple political sense. As second-in-command at Indian Affairs, and after 1913 as Deputy, he defended his department's territory against all comers, in the way of all the best bureaucrats, or at any rate, of all the most successful ones. Once, in an epic battle over office space, he even bested that most consummate of bureaucrats, Joseph Pope. As E. K. Brown later wrote, he was "gifted with that mixture of guile and idealism that is the mark of the highest sort of civil servant."

For a vigorous man in his forties who was also a poet of nature, Scott's was the perfect job. Nearly every summer, he could escape from his desk – and from Belle – to journey far into the wilds to

Scott on a treaty-making trip in 1906. He is seated at right.

The treaty-making trip of 1906. Scott, in the centre of the canoe, is looking at the camera. He frequently composed poetry while canoeing.

inspect his Indian charges. In 1906, taking along his close friend Pelham Edgar, the Toronto literary critic who had come to fill part of the gap left by Archie's death, he travelled by canoe all the way to James Bay to negotiate treaties with the Indians of northwestern Ontario. As a government official, although he was a humane and sensitive administrator, his attitudes towards the Indians were the assimilationist ones of his time. "Final results may be attained only by the merging of the Indian race with the whites," he wrote in one report. But reading the vivid and sometimes angry poetry inspired by those long canoe trips, we can suspect that Scott, as a private person, felt rather differently. In "Watkwenies," for instance, a portrait of an Iroquois woman in youth and old age, Scott contrasts the triumphant freedoms of the past with the demoralized dependency of the present:

> Vengeance was once her nation's lore and law
> When the tired sentry stooped above the rill,
> Her long knife flashed, and hissed, and drank its fill;
> Dimly below her dripping wrist she saw,
> One wild hand, pale as death and weak as straw,
> Clutch at the ripple in the pool; while shrill

Sprang through the dreaming hamlet on the hill,
the war-cry of the triumphant Iroquois.

Now clothed with many an ancient flap and fold,
And wrinkled like an apple kept til May,
she weighs the interest-money in her palm,
And, when the Agent calls her valiant name,
Hears, like the war-whoops of her perished day,
The lads playing snow-snake in the stinging cold . . .

Elizabeth Duncan Scott, 1895-1907.

Scott's own energies, in those years, were boundless. Every half dozen years or so, he published a volume of his own work; he also co-edited with Pelham Edgar a series of biographies, *The Makers of Canada*, and himself wrote the volume which dealt with the life of Lord Simcoe. One of his most evocative and mysterious poems, a dreampiece of the sea called "The Piper of Arll" served to inspire another poet, who went on to become far more famous than he. As Scott loved to recount in later years, one day in 1905 he received a most astonishing letter from the British poet John Masefield, then already becoming renowned for "Sea Fever." "Ten years ago when I was in America, as a factory hand in New York, I read "The Piper of Arll" in a Christmas number of a paper called *Truth*," wrote Masefield. "I had never (till that time) cared very much for poetry but your poem impressed me deeply and set me on fire. Since then poetry has been the one deep influence in my life." Masefield remembered the debt. In his 1941 autobiography, he described "The Piper of Arll" as "the poem which has moved me more than any other I have ever read . . . even now, I often repeat it to myself."

In May 1907, this happy, productive period ended abruptly. Since Archie had died, nothing had given Scott more pleasure than watching his cherished only child growing up. Elizabeth, as we can tell from her photograph and the charming little valentines and birthday cards preserved in Belle's scrapbooks, was a quicksilver little girl, the image of Belle, who could print very legibly at four and who, in a most avant-garde manner, addressed her parents, not as Mummy and Daddy, but as Duncan and Belle. During his trips in the wilderness, he would often write her little nonsense verses:

The Indian said "There's a bear."
And the Indian Agent said, "Where?"
Why he's in for a swim
Don't you meddle with him
Till he's absent and safe in his lair.

In the autumn of 1906, Belle took Elizabeth to Paris and enrolled her in a convent, to ensure that she had the very best of education. The following spring, Scott took a four-month leave of absence from the office, and he and Belle sailed for Europe. Their first stop was Paris, and a visit to the convent. After the happiest of get-togethers with Elizabeth, they went on to Spain, intending to return to Paris and take Elizabeth home at the end of their holiday. At the hotel in Madrid, they were greeted with a telegram. It consisted of two words: "*Elizabeth Morte*." Rushing back to Paris, the Scotts discovered that she had died of the lethally high temperature induced by an attack of scarlet fever.

From the depths of his grief, Scott wrote a single poem to commemorate Elizabeth. It was titled, "The Closed Door." Four years passed before he could bring himself to write again on any subject save bureaucratic necessity. He rarely spoke of her again, even to the closest of friends, although until the end of his life he kept some playthings of hers in front of the hearth in the music room. A letter among the papers of Annie Lampman Jenkins, acknowledging her own note of sympathy at the time, expresses the full depths of his sorrow: "Our dear child was life and the world and everything for us. I found that she had developed so finely, was so full of life and spirit and with evidences of such a noble nature shining through her actions. I was very proud of her – my mind was filled with glimpses

Duncan and Belle Scott and friends with Rupert Brooke, July 1913. Belle, dressed in black, sits on the grass. Brooke stands directly behind Duncan. Brooke understood their tragedy.

of a bright future. My dear wife who loved her with passion and idolatry – how can she exist without her?"

Belle never played the violin again. Not until 1912 could she bring herself to insert another programme or invitation into her scrapbook. In 1913, both Scotts put on cheerful faces to do their best for Rupert Brooke, who had appeared in Ottawa with an introduction from John Masefield. But Brooke was sensitive enough to see, under the pleasant veneer of tea parties in the garden and motor-car drives into the Gatineau Hills, the tragedy of a pair of lives now bereft both of love and of companionship, and in a letter to the British poet Wilfred Gibson, he described it:

> The only poet in Canada was very nice to me. . . . Poor devil, he's so lonely and dried there: no one to talk to. They had a child – daughter – who died. . . . And it knocked them out. She, a violinist, never played since; he hasn't written, till the last few months. Their house was queerly desolate. It rather went to my heart. Canada's a *bloody* place for a sensitive – in a way 2nd rate – real, slight poet like that to live all his life. Nobody cares if he writes or if he doesn't. He took me out to a Club in the country near, and we drank whisky and soda, and he said "Well, here's to your youth!" and drank its health, and I nearly burst into tears. He's a very nice chap (especially away from his wife, who's nice enough) and he's *thirsty* to talk literature. . . .*

Another visitor, M. O. Hammond, happening by Scott's office on Sparks Street in the hot summer of 1915, found the same lonely figure "thirsty to talk literature," and the fact that Hammond, though only a humble journalist, was eager and willing to hear about Lampman made him an even better listening-post than Brooke. "He closed up and went out with me, most generously, on a Lampman pilgrimage," Hammond recorded in his diary on August 7. "We took the car to the house on Bay Street where Lampman died . . . then to two others, on Stewart Street and Daly Avenue. . . .

> Next, we made for Beechwood Cemetery, where Lampman is buried. It was a long hot walk, through a winding street with ugly new French houses, followed by a shacktown in a lovely wood, the thought of which brought violent indignation from Scott. "It is a disgrace these shacks should have been permitted here," he said. He and L. used to come there early in the spring for wildflowers. . . .
>
> Beechwood is a lovely natural forest, so that almost every grave seems shaded. There is also a lovely ravine. We wound around to the grave which lay among many others, shaded by hydrangea in rich flowering. A large boulder stands at one end of the small plot and on

* It somehow adds to the poignancy of this scene that the youth that was toasted by Scott and Brooke in whisky and soda at the new Ottawa Country Club, just across the river in Quebec, had less than two years still to be lived. In April 1915, Brooke died on the island of Skyros in the early stages of the Gallipoli campaign, not in the heat of battle as he would have wished, but of blood-poisoning occasioned probably by a simple insect bite.

it, simply the word, Lampman. Scott was not overcome by emotion, nor was I as we were both perspiring freely, and Scott was indignant at the florist who had failed to plant flowers as ordered by him. "You know, Lampman's family never do anything to keep the grave in order, and never come near it."

Towards the end of this decade, and through the nineteen-twenties, Scott emerged partially from under his cloud of grief and plunged enthusiastically into founding first the Ottawa Drama League and later the Ottawa Little Theatre, for which he composed in 1928 a witty and mellifluous curtain-raising ode. But the life-force within Belle, though she went through the motions of taking an interest, had died in Paris in 1907. She grew more difficult and more querulous, and took to smoking like a chimney. Her death in 1929, after many years of on-again, off-again invalidism, was probably a happy release for them both. Two years later, on the eve of his retirement from the government, Scott once again astonished everyone by embarking upon an improbable marriage.

He was sixty-nine. The woman he took for his bride, Elise Aylen, was twenty-seven – young enough, Ottawa whispered, to be his granddaughter. Against all reason, this was the most blissful of unions. During his marriage to Elise, Scott came alive as he had not been alive since Elizabeth had died, had not been alive, in some ways, since Archie Lampman had died. Elise was a poet in her own right, a rather taciturn and withdrawn woman by most accounts, given to looking off into the middle distance in the midst of conversations. Nor was she anything like as good-looking as Belle had been; indeed she was dumpy, and quite dowdy. Yet, by whatever magic, she created within the house on Lisgar Street that was fast becoming an Ottawa landmark, the conditions in which Scott could grow old, not just gracefully, but vigorously and productively.

Elise was Old Ottawa on both sides of her family. Her maternal grandfather had been Sir John Bourinot, Clerk of the Commons and critic of literature. On the paternal side, she could trace her ancestry back to the earliest days of Bytown and the rumbustious pioneer lumber baron, Peter Aylen. She and Scott had met at the Ottawa Poetry Club soon after or perhaps even before Belle had died. In 1930, he contributed the preface to her first slender volume of verses, titled *Roses of Shadow*. "Melancholy is a luxury of youth and is fully enjoyed in these pages," he wrote. This was an understatement, for the poetry was that of an exceedingly solemn young woman, derivative of Edna St. Vincent Millay and of Sara Teasdale but without the redeeming irony, replete with such opening lines as, "The stark boards of the dance pavilion/Creak wanly," and, "Rent is the tepee of my heart that sheltered you." Still, here and there, not so much in the imagery as in the spirit behind it, Scott found reason to justify giving the book his imprimatur. "Here is one of the children of this troubled time, whose sensibility to things personal and general is acute, who suffers on both grounds and who communicates her moody interest in the beauty of life."

The nature of this marriage was a source of endless speculation for Ottawa's culturati. Some argued it was mostly a business arrangement. Scott had money, a comfortable house, and needed companionship. Elise, for all the excellence of her lineage, had scant resources. Clearly, though, there was more to it than that on both sides. Most probably, theirs was not a sexual relationship, and yet in 1943, on their twelfth wedding anniversary, Duncan poured out his poetic heart to Elise as he had never done for Belle:

> This word – this "love," so hardened by misuse
> How can it serve to tell my "love" for you
> That is too deep for thought; how can a truce
> Be made between the war of shallow and true
> In that small word . . . How can I deal
> With things intangible yet so intense
> That they are all the best of all my life,
> Implicit in my breathing and my sense?

His work was testament of his happiness. All through the thirties and forties Scott was writing as well as he had ever written: a volume of poems, *The Green Cloister*, his own favourite among his collections, inspired by a trip he and Elise made to Florence in 1932; a miscellaneous collection of new and old poems, articles, and short stories published in 1947, of which the title, *The Circle of Affection*, expresses splendidly the peace and serenity of his advancing years.

Grace of Elise, Scott became once again a social being. Back into the "Circle of Affection" were welcomed old friends like Annie Lampman Jenkins and even Scott's own sisters, not seen at Lisgar Street since his marriage to Belle. There were also all manner of new friends: the young Armenian photographer, Yousuf Karsh; the fledgling poet, Elizabeth Smart; Kathleen Fenwick, the brilliant young curator of prints at the National Gallery; and – let the circle be unbroken – Harry McCurry, Director of the National Gallery, and his wife, Dorothy, who were Annie Lampman Jenkins's son-in-law and daughter and who thereby carried the link with Archie into

Duncan Scott, photographed by M. O. Hammond on August 7, 1915. Later that day, Scott took Hammond on the Lampman pilgrimage described on page 465. The style of this photograph – the harsh lighting, and wreathing cigarette smoke, prefigures the style of Karsh portraits of the 1940s. Yousuf Karsh, in fact, became a good friend of Scott's.

a second generation. Most rewarding of all for Scott during the very last years of his life was his rich friendship with the young scholar-critic E. K. Brown who, in his brilliant study, *On Canadian Poetry*, not only ranked Scott among the major poets of Canada but was anxious to relive with him the old green years with Archie. In his essay on Scott in *On Canadian Poetry*, Brown sketched a memorable portrait of him as he appeared during one of their long conversations in the summer of 1942, in the music room at Lisgar

Street, with the landscapes of Milne and of Emily Carr and of the Group of Seven looking down. "Scott took down battered old volumes of early Canadian poets. . . . He spoke of his arduous canoe trips long ago up the Nipigon and Achigan. . . . He sought to make clear the change in the fibre of human nature that has occurred in the past half century. . . . The grave, gentle voice was that of an old man but what he had to say reflected not old age, but exquisite maturity."

After Scott's death, on December 19, 1947, many of his friends limned their own portraits. Madge Macbeth, the witty Ottawa journalist and novelist who had first met him through the Ottawa Drama League during the First World War, enjoyed recalling how he was once so much taken by a dish of sweetbreads and white wine that she served him, that he composed an ode to her cook. Yousuf Karsh remembers that Scott, no admirer of Mackenzie King's, loved telling the story of how, after inviting him to read at a literary evening at Kingsmere, King first hushed the company to listen as his little dog Pat beat out a series of horrible dischords on the piano, and then turned brightly to the elderly poet, saying, "Now, Scott, it's your turn."

Elise Aylen Scott, however, sketched no word-portraits. During their marriage, she had continued to write and occasionally to publish poetry and short stories and she had also begun work on a series of novels on mystical themes. Most of her creative energies, though, had been sublimated into looking after Scott. Now, within weeks of his death, an entirely new Elise came into being. It was not that she did not mourn her husband; it was rather that she had closed one door of her life and instantly opened another. "The change in her was fantastic," one acquaintance has recalled. "It was hard to believe . . . she was like a schoolgirl let out on holiday, bubbling with excitement, barely able to contain herself." She rented the house on Lisgar Street and left almost immediately on a trip to England. From there, she went on to Ceylon. Here, as Elise herself later explained in a brief, episodic memoir, *The Night of the Lord*, published in 1967, a chance meeting with a *kapuwa*, or holy man, at the great Buddhist temple of Maha Dewale, transformed her life:

> He stopped before me, and quickly a little circle formed around us. The drum beat faster and the kapuwa took a little of the sacred ashes from the jar he held in his hand and sprinkled it over my head. With his body continually swaying, his eyes sought my face, then suddenly he laid his hand on my forehead. A strong shudder ran through him, and like an electric shock, I felt it through my own body. At last, still

swaying, he spoke a few words which someone translated. "He says you have come very far and he knows what it is you seek." I wished he would tell me, for I scarcely knew myself, but he only mumbled something. "He says you must go on."

Elise Aylen never came back to Ottawa. She sold 108 Lisgar Street and its contents by long distance – Scott's pictures went to the National Gallery; his library to Carleton University; the house itself, sadly, was demolished in 1957 – and made a new life for herself in the ashrams of India. For a decade, she lived in the high Himalayas, up beyond Almora, later she moved to Coonoor, in the Nilgiri Hills between Bombay and Madras, under the spiritual guidance of a guru, Swami Yogeshwarananda, to whom she dedicated her memoir.

She died at Coonoor on December 18, 1972, a quarter of a century less a day after Scott. The extraordinary circumstances of her life after their marriage, circumstances that carry a story that begins with the birth of Scott in pre-Confederation Ottawa into the world of the flower children of the late 1960s, make the success of their marriage all the more extraordinary. Perhaps though, he had been a guru to her and she in a curious way, a guru to him. In his "Twelfth Anniversary Ode," Scott had written:

How can my keenest thinking hope to find
In this bright shade of a creative sphere
The essential strength and compass of your mind?

CHAPTER 30

But Who Was She, Really?

She is a person of rarely bright mentality, and savoir-faire.
Lady Gay; in an envoi to Amaryllis in
Saturday Night; March 1903

Amaryllis wrote the last of her weekly columns for *Saturday Night* at the end of July 1902. Six months later, on February 28, 1903, she produced her final piece for the Ottawa *Free Press* under her other pseudonym, "The Marchioness." She gave readers no hint of her impending departure, save that towards the end, she wrote ever more uninhibitedly, ever more tartly. In her very last column, which appeared on the eve of the Opening of Parliament, she inserted a verbal hatpin deftly between the shoulder blades of the Gentleman Usher of the Black Rod, Molyneux St. John, who a year earlier had edged out her own preferred candidate, the charming Agar Adamson:

> Cards for the floor of the Senate Chamber have been received by a number of prominent ladies, and it is certain that the coming opening will be as well attended as any. Let us hope that the Gentleman Usher will not have such an agitated quarter of an hour as he had last year. On that occasion, he blamed the misunderstanding and mistakes as to reserved seats on the Senators and they blamed them back upon him. This is really a very good plan to go upon, it lets both partners out of the difficulty.

Few chroniclers of society, whether in Ottawa or anywhere else in the country, have ever matched Amaryllis's ability to make her victims quiver with laughter even as she was leading them to the stake. The time has come to remove her domino, but let us do so delicately. If Amaryllis herself, through six years of writing columns, has revealed much of the sociology of her times, the task of discovering her true identity reveals a bit more.

Begin with the fact that as one reads Amaryllis one keeps on wondering how on earth she managed to write as she did without being barred from most drawing rooms. The simplest answer is, she sang for her supper. Early in the game, she grasped an essential and never-changing truth about Ottawa: information is power. She was a conduit through which other people could pass along gossip they'd picked up, and she could in turn entertain her sources by giving in exchange the gossip she'd already heard. She was, further, a kind of establishment rebel – a precursor, in a way, of writers like Allan Fotheringham and Sondra Gotlieb in our own day – who could poke fun at the social establishment and at the same time sustain its sense of importance by expending so much effort on it.

Amaryllis, however, was also a creation of her own time. All over the English-speaking world, the turn of the century was the gilded age of society reporting. Society figures had become the new celebrities, displacing generals and admirals. In the United States, Ward McAllister, a rather dubious hanger-on of Mrs. William Astor, had escalated himself into instant fame by promulgating the list of New York's select "Four Hundred," the number, it was said, that Mrs. Astor could squeeze into her ballroom. In Britain, the aristocratic ladies of the Prince of Wales's circle – Jennie Churchill, Daisy Warwick, Lily Langtry – were renowned as "professional beauties" and their photographs sold by the million on postcards. In Canada, a raw little colonial society with a viceregal court perched on top as a coronet among pinecones, this obsession was intensified. As we have seen, that aloof intellectual arbiter, Goldwin Smith, conveniently forgot all his republican principles in the year of the Queen's Jubilee for the sake of the biggest celebrities on the Canadian social scene, the Earl and Countess of Aberdeen. Parties in those days were almost as important as meetings of cabinet – witness Emilie Lavergne's efforts to improve Laurier's table manners – so that society columnists like Amaryllis performed much of the function that political columnists perform nowadays. "All sensible people see that what the public wants, the newspapers are bound to supply," wrote Amaryllis in 1899, in a paragraph that was as close as she ever came to delineating her philosophy. "They are thankful that the important work of telling of the doings of society is placed in competent hands where good judgement and dignified methods will be used. No underhand means are resorted to, no news is sought for at the back door. . . ."

It was further a factor in Amaryllis's success that, as we have also seen, the turn of the century was the heyday of the New Woman and that in Ottawa in particular, the feminine principle was dominant, grace of Laurier's own preference for women and the presence of such high-profile figures as Emilie Lavergne and Ishbel Aberdeen. Women like Emilie and Ishbel, however much they may have disliked each other personally, created an ambience in which other women could flourish, the iron hand in the velvet glove as the saying went: Mabel Adamson flirting with the Minister of Militia to win Agar his commission to South Africa; Ella Harriss providing neutral ground for politicians of both parties in her drawing-room at Earnscliffe, even pretty, silly Lola Powell quite turning the head of a Governor General in a canoe.

As a woman out earning her living, Amaryllis, while not exactly the norm, was a long way from being unique. Indeed, as the field of journalism began rapidly to open up for women, she, in her genteel groove of society columnist, was much less adventurous than some of her contemporaries. Kit Coleman, of the *Mail and Empire*, covered the Spanish-American War; Faith Fenton of *The Globe* went to the Klondike; Lally Bernard, a niece of Agnes Macdonald's, covered the coronation of Edward VII; Sara Jeannette Duncan, whose pungent and acerbic style, of all women journalists of the period most resembles Amaryllis's, travelled round the world reporting and wrote novels besides. Even in Quebec, where by and large the ideals of the New Woman did not much penetrate, Robertine Barry, who wrote as "Françoise," was an outstanding political reporter who founded her own newspaper, *Le Journal de Françoise*. In Ottawa itself, Amaryllis's counterpart on the *Journal*, Florence Hamilton Randal, had gone all the way out to South Africa. Sometimes, reading Amaryllis's approving comments on the exploits of her sisters, one senses a note of regret that she does not quite have the gumption to be so bold. Perhaps, as her choice of pseudonym suggests, she was aware that her own gift as a writer was better suited for the hothouse-like drawing rooms of the period than for the winds of destiny.

BUT WHO WAS SHE, REALLY?

But who was she, really? Having established a context, the moment of truth has arrived – and yet Amaryllis, to the last, insists upon playing her charade. This much we know for certain, from the clues that she has dropped: Amaryllis had impeccable social and political connections – but no money. She thought of herself as a

Three turn-of-the-century women journalists, contemporaries of Amaryllis.

Kit Coleman. She covered the Spanish-American war, and went round the world.

Sara Jeannette Duncan. She is best known for her 1905 novel, The Imperialist.

Robertine Barry. She founded her own newspaper.

Liberal, and she hero-worshipped Laurier. She was a Catholic. She knew a good deal, far more than most people in Ottawa, about music and the theatre. She had travelled quite widely in Europe and in the United States. One puzzle in her past, contained in her *Free Press* column of December 26, 1902, is that "the first Christmases of my recollection were spent in Germany, that land of the Christmas Tree and the delight of Christmas Eve, of being brought into a room in the centre of which was a splendid fir tree, brilliant with tiny red and green candles and coloured paper."

Amaryllis, further, was a long way from being a beauty. This she lets us know quite candidly, employing a detached ruefulness to conceal her envy, in a *Free Press* column of 1900, titled, "The Childlike Woman, a type quite opposed to the New Woman."

> I mean of course the small, dimpled, sweet and smiling-mouthed type. As a girl, she wears her dresses to fasten in the back, wears also broad hats and sashes that would be ridiculous on her tall, dark-browed cousin. . . . She comes out from her bath looking like a pink and white rosebud, with all that is dewy and virginal and utterly guileless about her. . . .
>
> Such a girl is certain to be petted and given cakes at luncheon by all the older girls in the school. . . . Such, in fact, is her career through life, to be given sweet cakes of all sorts, the highly-spiced cakes of the world, cakes of social success, matrimonial cakes. . . . Young ladies who were all ahead of her in class and who never paid much attention to what she had to say, did you never foresee that that "little head running over with curls" would possess a more tangible brightness than your own ready conversation and neatly turned phrases?

Other columns provide deeper insights into her character. As we already know, unlike most society columnists, Amaryllis possessed a considerable social conscience. As early as 1897, (as noted in chapter seventeen), she was concerned about "the plight of little sick children in the hospitals." She was also, on behalf "of the people who live in small overheated houses in crowded streets with no place for their children to play but on the sidewalk," a strong supporter of Sunday streetcars. "Think what a comfort it would be for those poor fathers and mothers to gather up their little ones and go off in a breezy electric car to the woods on the river shore." Her concern for Canadian Indians nowadays seems patronizing, but by the standards of her own day, it was remarkably enlightened – if only that Indians intruded at all into a column about society. "One cannot but feel that the Indian boys and girls educated at the Government Industrial Schools should not be allowed to go back to their blankets and the narrow limits of their reserve when there is no reason whatever against their being trained to become happy homemakers in the civilized world."

More unusual yet, for a society columnist, was Amaryllis's keen interest in feminism. In the pages of *Saturday Night*, her editor Grace Denison AKA Lady Gay, inveighed time and again against votes for women but Amaryllis herself, though she would never have chained herself to the railings of Parliament Hill, was considerably more than just a closet suffragette. She was not, *faute de mieux* for her readers, above shooting the occasional verbal barb in the direction of Ishbel Aberdeen, but when it came to Ishbel's National Council of Women, no one could have been a more ardent supporter. "This is a power in the land which even the male legislators are forced to take into consideration," she wrote in 1902. "Women are particularly clever at agitating and so as each new subject was brought to their attention, the aged poor, sweating practices and so on, the National Council agitated, and new by-laws were passed."

So that, fittingly enough, it is Lady Aberdeen who leads us at last to the only real clue to her identity that Amaryllis, in all her years of churning out columns, ever let slip. Late in October 1898 (as described in chapter twenty), the Countess invited five Ottawa women to accompany her on a farewell visit to the girls who worked as stitchers and binders in the Government Printing Bureau. Amaryllis, it will be recalled, wrote about that meeting with an immediacy that could only have come from being on the spot. Rereading that column we notice something that we did not notice before: Amaryllis has actually listed the names of these five women. The first four names are familiar, having appeared frequently in other columns. The fifth name is new. This name is Agnes Scott.

The paperchase begins. A determined re-reading of five more years of *Saturday Night* and of the *Free Press* yields no further mention of this name. Then at last, on February 25, 1903, an innocuous little item in the next-to-last of the *Free Press* columns suddenly becomes charged with importance.

> Mr. and Mrs. M. P. Davis entertained at a dinner-dance last night given for Miss Agnes Scott, whose engagement to Mr. Will Davis has been announced.

The following weekend, in *Saturday Night*, Lady Gay makes an intriguing comment:

> The engagement of Miss Agnes Scott is announced in Ottawa. Miss

Scott is a niece of the Hon. R. W. Scott, and she is a person of rarely bright mentality, and *savoir-faire*.

On and on, through yellowing newsprint. On Friday, April 29, 1903, the last piece of the puzzle slips into place. On page one of the *Free Press* we find an unbylined story that only Amaryllis herself could have written, as a triumphant Last Hurrah. Agnes Scott's marriage to Will Davis, we learn, was celebrated "very quietly, in St. Joseph's Church." The bride did not choose to wear white. But not even Lady Minto at her most dazzling had ever been described as dressing more ravishingly:

> The bride, given away by her uncle, the Secretary of State, wore a smart and becoming costume of pale pastel blue broadcloth. The skirt, which was plainly cut, rippled into a short train, the lower edge being trimmed with a very wide applique of ecru Russian lace, in a pattern design, which rose to the waist in front and engirdled the hips. The bodice was lavishly trimmed with the Russian lace. It opened over a vest of white lace mounted on chiffon, and the wide bell sleeves were slashed over a bouffant undersleeve of white chiffon. The French hat was of pleated tulle and fancy straw in a Gainsborough shape and trimmed with a magnificent white ostrich plume.

On her right wrist the bride wore "the groom's gift, an elegant Egyptian gold bracelet, studded with baroque pearls." Among the scores of wedding presents were "a jewel box lined with gold from Lady Minto, a painting by Jules Breton from Sir Sandford Fleming, silver salt cellars and a mustard pot from Mrs. C. A. E. Harriss." Ottawa society, clearly, had done its very best for its Boswell.

The couple left immediately "*en route* to New York, Naples and an extended tour through Italy and central Germany."

After the marriage of Agnes Scott, both Amaryllis and The Marchioness disappeared forever. Yet, right to the last, she refused to give herself away. In their fulsome accounts of the wedding, neither *Saturday Night* nor the *Free Press* remark that the ostrich-plumed bride had indeed been their best-read columnist. But Agnes was Amaryllis and no mistake. The Ottawa City Directory for 1902 lists Miss Agnes Scott, of 274 Daly Street, as a "journalist."

Having discovered at last who she really was, we quickly realize that no one could have been a more appropriate guide to Official Ottawa, through some of its liveliest years. But for the Scott family, Ottawa might never have been the capital at all.

The Scotts, by the 1890s, were one of the most consequential families in the city. They were not as rich as the lumbering dynasties of Booth and Edwards and Gilmour; in fact, they were not rich at all. "It was only in 1896, when my father was made Secretary of State, that we could afford a telephone," Agnes's first cousin, Lilian Scott Desbarats, tells us in her own memoir. As Irish Catholics, the Scotts were not of quite the same social order as the Ritchies and the Adamsons and the Merediths before them. Yet by the force of their personalities and of their wit, they earned their way in both politics and society: a rollicking noisy clan of sisters and brothers and cousins and aunts and uncles, who all but overflowed onto the sidewalk from the big square red-brick house on Daly that had once housed Sir Charles Tupper. "We all loved parties," continues Lilian, as she proceeds to give the menu for a magnificent Christmas dinner in 1892. "Meat soup, lamb rissoles, fricassee chicken, turkey, roast beef, spiced beef, peas, potatoes, plum pudding, brandy sauce, whipped cream, chocolate jelly, orange jelly, cheese and celery, pears and peaches, both preserved whole, grapes, apples, oranges, crystallized fruits, *sucre à la creme*, chocolates, stuffed dates, Christmas crackers, one dollars worth of flowers."

Among those who sat down to this feast, in the Daly Street dining room with its handsome marble fireplace, were Lilian's elder brother Willie, a serious-minded lawyer, and her other brother D'Arcy, also a lawyer but less serious, a sporting gent rather given to philandering. There was her younger sister Mary, always known as "Minnie," Agar Adamson's great friend who had lobbied so hard to have him made Black Rod and who perhaps carried a torch for him all her life, since she never married and since, when he returned a conquering hero from the First World War, leaving Mabel in England, she was the woman he chose to partner to a gala Country Club dinner. There were Fanny and Saney, the eldest sisters, who could remember only too vividly, as recounted in chapter seven, the day D'Arcy McGee had been murdered. And there was also, standing a little apart from the crowd, cousin Agnes, our Amaryllis. "We always thought of her as our sister," Lilian explains. Yet Lilian, one suspects, was always just a little in awe of Agnes. On the day of her wedding, Lilian recounts, "Agnes had very emphatically requested no children, so my children were left upstairs and not dressed up. My father brought them down. I was so ashamed to see my son, aged 3, in a crumpled playsuit, guzzling ice cream."

Agnes, clearly, had had no choice but to bow to superior male power. R. W. Scott, patriarch, senator, and cabinet minister, was not a man with whom one argued, even on one's own wedding day. He had a patriarchal long white beard, he was also crusty and choleric, a vegetarian (though, given that Christmas feast, he seems not to have imposed his views on the rest of the household) and also a teetotaller who, back in 1878, in the last days of the Mackenzie government, had railroaded the famous Scott Temperance Act through the Commons. He had been a good friend of Edmund Meredith's and, in 1877, had put Meredith's name forward to attend the prison conference at Stockholm. Now in his late seventies, he was one of Laurier's most activist ministers, a blunt and plain-spoken man who, better than anyone else, could put those arrogant British generals, Hutton and Dundonald, in their places.

Hon. R. W. Scott, with an unidentified grandchild, in 1894. He had helped put Ottawa on the map.

This was the same R. W. Scott who, earlier in our story, put Ottawa on the map. An eager young lawyer from Prescott, the son of an Irish doctor who had served in the Peninsular Wars, he had arrived in Bytown, as it then was, in 1848, and had promptly plunged into public affairs. As Mayor of Bytown, he had written the memorandum describing Ottawa in glowing terms as the best possible site for the capital. In 1857, by now a Member of Parliament, he had delicately suggested to Lady Head that she paint a picture of Barracks Hill to show to Queen Victoria. In 1858, when the Parliament of the Province of Canada had astonishingly voted to reject the Queen's choice, it was Scott who once again had stepped into the breach. In advance of a second vote, he mounted a ferocious lobbying campaign and persuaded a sufficient majority of members to switch sides. "The Ottawa men shout hurrah!" ran one newspaper account "Scott goes into exstacies of joy. . . ."

Scott's wife Mary was as remarkable a figure as her husband. By the 1890s, she was growing frail of limb and wandery of mind, a victim of what seems to have been Parkinson's disease. But in the sixties and seventies, Mary Heron Scott had been one of the most dazzling and high-spirited women in the city, a favourite dancing partner of Lord Dufferin, a gifted singer whose lilting rendition of "The Low-Backed Car" was always the hit at charity concerts. The Herons had been a family of Irish actors, a troupe of strolling players, and Mary, from her debut in a Dublin pantomine at the age of six, had been their star. According to family legend, the great Daniel O'Connell had been besotted by her.

Mary Heron Scott. She had belonged to a troupe of strolling players.

In 1847, fleeing the potato famine, the Herons had left Ireland forever. They played in the West Indies and Bermuda, in Boston and New York, in the Maritimes and even in Newfoundland. Then, in 1850, at the peak of their success, when Mary was just eighteen, they played a week in Bytown. At a supper party after the opening performance, she was introduced to the young Richard Scott. For him, it was a case of love at first sight. "On the following evening," according to a family history written by Willie Scott in the 1920s, "he occupied a seat in the front row of the hall, carrying a huge bouquet of flowers, which at an appropriate stage of the performance, he proceeded to present to Mary, and despite the vollies of chaff with which his friends assailed him, he repeated the performance on each of the remaining nights." The next year, when the Herons were returning from a West Indies tour, Scott turned up to greet them on the jetty in New York. Eventually, "his persistence was rewarded." The two were married in Philadelphia in 1853.

After Mary's marriage, the Heron troupe began to disintegrate. One sister married a wealthy German banker, William Rahe, who she met on a tour of Cuba. Another married Enrico Testa, an Italian-American tenor. Most important to this story, on November 28, 1861, Mary Heron's youngest sister Margaret married Allan John Scott of Ottawa, the younger brother of Richard Scott. Agnes was their daughter.

Family history now becomes hazy. We do not even know for certain the year of Agnes's birth. We do know, however, that Allan Scott died young, in 1868, so she was probably born around 1865. From Lilian's memoir, we know that after being widowed, Margaret Scott, known as "Aunt Moggie," lived with Agnes and various other members of the Heron family in a "queer house with five stories" at the corner of Daly and Nicholas streets, bought for them by the wealthy banker Rahe, who, as Agnes's uncle by marriage, surely also accounted for those mysterious Christmases in Germany she later wrote of in her columns. But when not visiting the Rahes in Germany, or the Testas in New York, her childhood was austere. "Aunt Moggie," to be sure, was "kind and good-natured and very amusing," as Lilian remembered. But at 47 Daly, as she also remembered, "there was no furnace in the house and no heat except the kitchen stove. . . . There was no bathroom and the only water was in the basement."

On the one hand, Amaryllis, the delicate but flamboyant flower of the drawing rooms. On the other, The Marchioness, Dickens's shabby and cheeky little servant girl, "taking a limited view of society through the keyholes of doors." Even from sketchy information, it is easy to see these two aspects of Agnes's character developing. Never mind – except that Agnes clearly minded – that her dresses were often hand-me-downs, her connections and her wit and her acting ability were enough to win her a place, early on, in the Government House circle. The only surviving photographs date from these years of the eighties: Agnes in a costume designed

Three photographs of Agnes Scott, when she was in her early twenties.

May 1887. Dressed in costume, probably for a Rideau Hall theatrical.

March 1887. Dressed for a ball.

April 1889. She was rueful about her looks.

to resemble a deck of cards for a Rideau Hall theatrical; Agnes in a fancy ballgown trimmed with ostrich feathers and clutching a spray of roses. The furbelows and frills do not disguise the plainness of features of which she later wrote so ruefully; the best that could be said of Agnes is that she had an excellent figure, and looked extremely intelligent.

It is entirely likely that Agnes had begun writing about the parties she attended long before her formal embarcation on her career as a columnist. Certainly, in 1896, she wrote about Lady Aberdeen's ball in *The Lounger* magazine. After her mother's death in 1898, she lived briefly in a boarding house on Wilbrod Street and the following year she moved into 274 Daly, bedroom space having opened up there following the marriages of both Lilian Scott and her brother D'Arcy. It may even have been at D'Arcy's wedding to Miss "Queenie" Davis, daughter of a wealthy building contractor with excellent connections to Laurier, described lavishly by Amaryllis as *the* event of June 1898, that her eye first turned speculatively towards the elder brother of the bride, the good-looking but rather rakish young man-about-town, Will Davis.

Beyond his family fortune, Davis had little to recommend him. He did not even have a proper job; instead he had a considerable reputation for liking to while his afternoons away in the gaudier salons of Lower Town. He was also much younger than Agnes, only twenty-nine when they married, while she by then was about thirty-eight. Yet continuing to be a "New Woman" had little to recommend it now that she was undeniably "getting on."

Given that the Scott and Davis clans had much in common: both Irish, both Liberal, both pillars of St. Joseph's Church, there was probably a considerable degree of family pressure applied to the making of this marriage of convenience. Davis, as anyone could see, needed a mature and sensible woman to settle him down; Agnes, just as obviously, needed a home of her own, and financial security.

Will Davis, in January 1903, three months before his marriage to Agnes Scott.

For her honeymoon as for her wedding, Agnes chose the kind of clothes she had so often written about, had so often longed for, and now, at long last, could afford. "A travelling gown of grey homespun," was her description of her going-away dress in the *Free Press*, "the skirt severely cut and the Russian bodice trimmed with applique of white and tiny blue velveteen bows. It opened over a blouse of pale pink silk with Dresden stripe. The hat was black straw, trimmed with pink roses."

After their tour of Italy and Germany, the couple returned to a brand new and magnificent red-brick house at 407 Wilbrod Street, built to Agnes's specifications as the wedding gift of her father-in-law.* She gave birth to two daughters, Margaret and Mary and, despite the increasingly frequent absences of Will Davis from the premises, established herself as a *grande dame*. The diarist, Ethel Chadwick, who had always referred to her simply as "Aggie Scott" soon changed her nomenclature and even in the privacy of her journal wrote respectfully of "Mrs. W. P. Davis." Mrs. W. P. Davis, as we learn further from Ethel, was a woman who, having always admired the *beau geste* when made by others, now indulged in it herself. In 1908, she bought at a high price the heirloom teapot that Ethel's mother had donated to a charity auction and graciously returned it to her. Occasionally, she dusted off her writing skills to prepare papers for the Women's Historical Society. While those delivered by other members were usually muddled together out of family folklore and hearsay, hers, including a detailed study of the

* This house is now the High Commission of Australia.

Reciprocity Treaty of 1854, were always gracefully written and carefully researched. During the First World War, when in honour of beleaguered Belgium a fashion for giving tea parties at which only French was spoken swept through town, she was at the forefront: "Mrs. W. P. Davis *recevra Le Cercle Littéraire Musical*" reads a card in her own handwriting in Belle Botsford Scott's invaluable scrapbook. But she also is remembered for having been a bit of a Bohemian and rather vague about mealtimes.

Card to a "French tea" of 1915. Probably the only surviving example of Amaryllis's handwriting.

Mrs. W. P. Davis
recevra le Cercle Littéraire et Musical
le vendredi 26 mars. à 4 heures.
Conférence par Madame Faribault
Gouget — Paul Déroulède.
407 Wilbrod Street. ~~Thursday~~

Agnes may have been happy enough. Better anyway, to be unhappy and rich than unhappy and poor. But abruptly the elegant façade collapsed around her. "Mr. W. P. Davis dies very suddenly," ran the heading on stories displayed prominently in both the *Citizen* and the Ottawa *Journal* on Boxing Day, 1916. The accompanying copy, worded identically in both papers, went on to say that on the morning of Christmas Eve, which that year had fallen on Sunday, Davis "had risen about 7:30, with the intention of attending 8 o'clock mass. In the process of dressing, he became suddenly ill, falling to the floor of his bedroom. Members of his household heard him fall, but by the time they had rushed to his assistance, he had expired."

All of which was suspiciously uninformative. Whether or not it was Agnes herself who had written the press handout, this was in fact a cover-up. Davis had succumbed to a heart attack, all right, but not at 407 Wilbrod. Instead, he was taken suddenly ill in the flat in which for years he had been keeping his mistress. The scandal leaked out; so also did the fact that the improvident Davis, having set himself up as an on-again, off-again stockbroker, had managed to leave Agnes virtually penniless.

Our Amaryllis was now both unhappy and poor. For a time, she moved back in with the Scotts. Then, in 1921, when the Daly Avenue house was sold, she moved to a small cottage in Sandy Hill on which her father-in-law paid the rent. "She was still bright and entertaining," recalls a member of the Davis family, who remembers her from his boyhood "A small elegant woman who dressed smartly, but rather severely." Sometime in the late 1920s, she, with her daughters, moved to France, where living was cheaper. "She was terrible about money," remembers another nephew. "Once, she horrified the family by writing home a breezy letter explaining how she always set aside a portion of the allowance we sent to buy lottery tickets." Sometime in the early 1930s – to add to the poignancy of Agnes's fate, no one can quite recall the year, let alone the date – she died in France. Neither of her daughters outlived her for long; neither married.

Her ending was sad. So one senses, was most of her life, save for those half-dozen years when, as Amaryllis, her wit and flair had made her influential, sought after, a celebrity almost, even if only in the reflected glory of those she wrote about. Agnes Scott's story is her own, yet it applies to a wider context. Others of our New Women – Florence Randal, Kate Waddell, even Emilie Lavergne at the end – paid a price for being ahead of their time. Soon, in any event, their time was behind them.

At about the same time Amaryllis stopped writing, Ottawa began to decline noticeably as an environment favourable to women. Here, as elsewhere in the country, women reverted more and more to being the "Childlike Woman," about whom Amaryllis had written so scathingly. In the capital, the descent was particularly steep and continuous, all the way down to about the mid-1970s, when the women's movement began to assert itself. "This is a terrible town for women," a 1971 issue of *Saturday Night* quotes the wife of a deputy minister as saying. "I'm sure there are more discontented women per square inch in Ottawa than anywhere else in the country."

Most of the reasons for the withering away of the feminine principle in the capital lie outside the chronological scope of this book. There was the cataclysmic effect of the First World War, which thrust masculine affairs to the forefront, followed in turn by the Depression and the Second World War. There was, further, the succession of bachelor prime ministers: Mackenzie King and R. B. Bennett. More pernicious still was the arrival, in the 1930s, of professional civil servants, the earnest and intellectual Ottawa Men, who took what they were doing terribly seriously and told their wives little or nothing about their office lives, so that these wives couldn't function as in-the-know hostesses. Indeed, even if they had tried to power-broke behind the scenes, wives of Ottawa Men would have been reprimanded for relying on frivolous intuition instead of objective bureaucratic logic.

Closer to Amaryllis's era, the role models who had been so important to women's pre-eminence were already beginning to disappear. Never again at Rideau Hall would there be a consort like Lady Aberdeen nor, until our own time, and then only very briefly in the person of Maureen McTeer, a prime minister's wife as influential as Lady Macdonald; still less would there be, in the wings, a prime-ministerial adviser comparable to Emilie Lavergne. Thus for close on three-quarters of a century, from shortly after the turn of the century, Ottawa became overwhelmingly a masculine citadel.

Thursday, September 21, 1911. On this epochal election day, it rained cats and dogs in the capital. Whether or not Amaryllis abandoned the comforts of her fine house on Wilbrod Street to go down to her old haunts at the *Free Press* office to watch the returns coming in, to see at first hand the news of the defeat of her great hero, Laurier, over the issue of reciprocity, is a matter lost to history. But in Toronto, as we know from his diary, the equally devoted M. O. Hammond spent the long bleak election night in *The Globe*'s offices, writing out the bulletins that, placed in the windows for the edification of the crowd outside, spelled out the government's quickening end. Later that week, Hammond recorded verbatim an account given to him by *The Globe*'s business manager, J. F. Mackay, of an encounter in Ottawa with their fallen hero. "I was going along the street," Mackay recounted, "when Laurier came along, jumped out of his carriage, and came to the sidewalk to greet me.

> He said, "come on up," so I went to his office, my it was hard for me to be there with him for the last time and to think of the many talks I have had with him there. He talked freely, he said he had thought he could win until the day he left for the Simcoe meeting. He said, 'that day, I sat down and talked it over with my wife. I said, 'If I am defeated, I will come back and we will spend the rest of our lives quietly together, as we have so long wanted to do.' Alas, I am defeated, but I cannot spend the rest of my life quietly," and his eyes filled with tears.

Thus closed an era.

We can picture the setting: the westering sun of an early autumn evening slanting into Laurier's office through the venetian blinds that Cartier, back in the 1860s, had installed, lingering on half-filled packing cases, half-emptied bookcases, and all the other signatures of departure.

For us also, forty-six years since we joined Edmund and Fanny Meredith, this is an appropriate moment to take our leave. The capital we leave behind is one that Edmund and Fanny would scarcely have recognized. It is still far from being a beautiful city and yet, in the words of the poet Rupert Brooke, there is "an atmosphere of safeness and honour and massive buildings and well-shaded walks." There is further, as Brooke continues, "a certain graciousness – dim, for it expresses a barely materialized national spirit."

On September 26, just five days after Laurier's defeat, the new premier-elect, Robert Borden, arrived in the capital to begin his own eight-year term of office. Borden was pulled through the streets in a carriage drawn by sixty sweating, cheering men instead of horses. He was followed by more carriages, and by motor-cars, and by a procession of foot soldiers, waving banners. "Rule Britannia Is Good Enough For Us," read one of these. An onlooker who still remembers the scene vividly was the seven-year-old grandson of one of the senior House of Commons clerks. His name was Eugene Forsey, and he grew up to become a Senator, a constitutional expert, and Canada's most vociferous writer of letters to the editor.

"It looked as if the whole country were Conservative, and Conservative only," recorded another observer, Ethel Chadwick, now twenty-nine. Ethel duly went on to remark the occasion as "very exciting." What excited her far more was the impending arrival in less than a fortnight of the Duke of Connaught, Queen Victoria's third son, to become Governor General. "I wonder what they will be like, the Connaughts and their aides," she wrote. "Will I meet them? Will I know them?"

But that, as they say, is another story.

THE END OF THE
BEGINNING

ACKNOWLEDGMENTS

It must be said straightaway – this book could never have been written, or even attempted, without the loving support and encouragement and occasionally the outright bullying of my husband, best friend, and professional partner, Richard Gwyn. He is not only a brilliant built-in editor with a remarkable flair for structure, but a master catalyst, whose energy, enthusiasm, and humour inform everything he touches. Above all over the last four years, I have been grateful to Richard for the gift of energy and of time diverted from the production of what otherwise would have been a book or books of his own; evenings innumerable, in the early stages, given over to sharing my discoveries and hearing out that day's findings; yet more evenings and weekends spent talking out the best possible ways of making it all come alive on the typewriter and, on several occasions, when certain passages seemed to be eluding me totally, taking over on the typewriter and showing me how they might happen. As writer to writer, as wife to husband, the best I can do is to say in return: Thank you, my love, now it's your turn.

My thanks otherwise are many and various. At the very beginning, Robert Fulford, who helped start me on the path to becoming a writer by buying my first magazine article and who since then has been my editor and mentor at *Saturday Night* for many years, set the whole process in motion by commissioning the piece that inspired this book, and then encouraging me to build on it. So also did Professor Peter Neary of the Department of History at the University of Western Ontario and Dr. R. L. McDougall, founding director of the Institute of Canadian Studies at Carleton University. To Rob McDougall, one of those rare academics who welcomes a non-academic trespassing on his territory, I owe an additional debt. He steered me towards a marvellous source, the scrapbooks of Belle Botsford Scott at the National Library, and he read in manuscript the two chapters dealing with the poets Duncan Campbell Scott and Archibald Lampman, making a number of valuable suggestions.

Most of the research has been conducted at one or the other of two great research institutions in Ottawa: the Library of Parliament and the Public Archives of Canada. In the case of the former, I am most grateful to the Librarian of Parliament, Erik Spicer, not only for allowing me the privilege of burrowing around in the stacks, but also for the privilege of just being able to work in what is surely the most exhilarating ambience of all research repositories in North America, all the more because in its Gothic Revival splendour, the Library so richly evoked the period I was writing about. The courtesy and efficiency of the Library staff is legendary, and I would like to thank in particular Robert Sheehan. At the Public

Archives, the physical atmosphere is more in the nature of bureaucratic grandiose, but not so the mood and temper of the staff, of which every member I encountered went out of his or her way not just to be helpful, but to be imaginative. For creative assistance, I am grateful to Jerry O'Brien, Barbara Wilson, Carman Carroll, Tom Nesmith, and Dan Moore, and especially to Glenn Wright for his suggestion that the diaries of M. O. Hammond, held at the Archives of Ontario, might prove a good source. (These provided me with a new and unexpected character.) Individuals at other institutions proved equally helpful. At the National Library, Linda Hoad, Librarian of Literary Manuscripts, set out the Belle Scott scrapbooks time and again for me to pore over and suggested a number of other useful sources. At the National Gallery, Charles C. Hill, Curator of Canadian Art, made available to me his own unpublished research on events that led up to the Gallery's founding, and also led me to the painting that appears on the dust jacket. At the Department of Public Works, Richard Raycraft, designer in charge of the restoration of the East Block, provided much information on the layout and on the fine detail of the building as it was during the 1860s and also took me on a personally conducted tour.

I must also register my thanks and appreciation to T. C. Dobb, University Librarian at Simon Fraser University, Burnaby, B. C., for granting me permission to quote excerpts from the correspondence of Archibald Lampman in the holdings of the W. A. C. Bennett Library at Simon Fraser, and to Percilla Groves, Special Collections Librarian, for her help in expediting this request.

Perhaps the most serendipitous byway of research was the opportunity first to meet and then to begin to count as friends the descendants of some of the characters who appear in this book. Anthony Adamson of Toronto granted me open sesame to the diaries of his father, Agar Adamson, and to other family papers, and then added, in lengthy conversations, a candid and witty gloss. He and his wife, Augusta, were equally generous with their hospitality. Dorothy Livesay, of Galiano Island, B.C., stopped off in the midst of a hectic poetry-reading tour to talk to me at length about her mother, Florence Hamilton Randal, and arranged to have sent to me a copy of the diary her mother had kept in South Africa, now held at the University of Manitoba. Here in Ottawa, Mr. and Mrs. Henry Davis, Colonel and Mrs. Cuthbert Scott, and their daughter Martha Scott, all helped me to solve the riddle of their mysterious kinswoman, the journalist Amaryllis. Colonel Scott, in particular, provided me with a number of family documents, both illuminative and entertaining. What struck me in all these cases, in contrast to the experience of many biographers, was that no one wished in the least to have their relatives canonized, or asked to approve the final product, but simply took it on trust that I would render their heritage as truthfully as possible. For additional personal reminiscences and helpful documentation, I would futher like to thank Mr. and Mrs. Knox Thomson and Barry Steers.

Writers take for granted that they live in a vacuum. Writing these notes, I become more and more conscious of how much I have not been alone. Judy McGrath, friend and colleague on adventures numerous and eclectic, helped enormously with the picture research and turned her skills with a camera to bringing to life many fuzzy old snapshots and documents. Helen O'Brien, an equally old friend, typed much of the manuscript with despatch; Allison Taylor helped in the preliminary stages of research. I would also like to mention, either for having provided useful leads and / or nuggets of information, or for giving me constant encouragement, Jean Bruce, Ramsay Cook, Edythe Goodridge, John Gray, David and Donalda Hilton, Paddye Mann, Lucy Booth Martyn, John McGrath, Elizabeth Smart, Irene Spry and the late Graham Spry, Alastair Sweeny, Elizabeth Waddell, my cousin-by-marriage Julian Gwyn, and my brother Nicholas Fraser. I must mention also, as an important support network before we all spun off in different directions, the group of writers who used to meet weekly for Ladies' Lunch, *circa* 1980-81; Doris Anderson, Nicole Belanger, Stevie Cameron, Sondra Gotlieb, Elizabeth Gray, Pamela Wallin, and, in particular, Charlotte Gray, who read much of the manuscript in its early stages.

Last, but a long way from least, I would like to thank my agent, Nancy Colbert, for seeing in an outline the germ of a book and for constantly, and in the most tactful of ways, encouraging me to get on with it; and my editor, Ramsay Derry, for identifying, always eruditely and with a consummate understanding both of the period and of an author's *amour propre*, all manner of ways in which the manuscript could be pruned, honed, and polished. It speaks volumes that the production of the final draft turned out to be much less of a grind than it was fun. Sarah Reid, in her turn, proved a skilled and sensitive copy editor, and John Lee an imaginative designer. At McClelland and Stewart, I am grateful to Linda McKnight and especially to Jan Walter, not only for tender, loving care but also for a certain degree of risk-taking.

As in the case of so many books Canadian, this one would not have been possible at all but for the financial assistance of the Canada Council through its Explorations Programme, and of the Ontario Arts Council.

S.G.
Ottawa
October 1980 – August 1984

SOURCES

In quilting together this story, my aim has been to keep the stitches from showing. Now, in these notes, the process is reversed: I would like to share with readers who may be interested some of the historical patchwork that was involved. I also want to acknowledge my many debts to other writers. Since this is not an academic history, I have not peppered the text with numerals, nor provided batteries of line-by-line references. However, the sources of direct quotations and of key pieces of information have more often than not been identified directly within the text.

Most of the book has been produced from primary sources: diaries, letters, scrapbooks and, in the case of Amaryllis, first-hand newspaper accounts that really count as a primary source. (The deeper I delved, the more I became grateful to those who had the foresight to preserve their family papers and to donate these to research institutions; the more also, I began to wonder how much we, in the age of instant communications and home computers, will leave behind. Rather late in the day, I began preserving minutiae of my own, thinking ahead to some *alter ego* of the year 2084, trying to piece together a picture of life as it was lived in this capital, in the era of Trudeau, Turner, and Mulroney.) But I have also drawn from scores of published works. In the case of each of the two main sections of the book, I have first listed all the sources, whether primary or secondary, of which I have made repeated use. Other sources are listed under the headings of the chapters in which they have been mainly used.

PART ONE: PIONEER MANDARIN

The foundation for this entire section is a major manuscript collection in the Public Archives of Canada, the papers of Edmund Allen Meredith (PAC MG29 E15), in particular, Volumes 7 and 8, which contain Meredith's diaries. I first encountered Meredith in Robert Hubbard's socio-architectural history, *Rideau Hall* (McGill-Queen's, 1977), where he turned up half a dozen times as an observer of viceregal society. As well, in *The Old Chieftain*, the second volume of Donald Creighton's epic biography of Sir John A. Macdonald (Macmillan, 1955), Meredith makes an appearance as a purveyor of political gossip. Meredith's diaries comprise twenty-five small, matched, leather-bound volumes: the work of a lifetime, written in spiky Victorian handwriting, the ink long faded to brown, that begins in the 1840s, when he was in his twenties, and continues on up to the week of his death in 1899. For the fourteen years Meredith lived in Ottawa, 1865-79, roughly five thousand individual entries exist. The diaries covering Meredith's later years, 1880-99, provide a richly detailed portrait of the life of a gentleman's family in Toronto in late Victorian times.

Next in importance has been the manuscript collection of Meredith's son, Colborne Powell "Coly" Meredith (PAC MG 29 E62), in particular Volume 8, files 9 and 10, and Volume 9, file 12, in which are contained unpublished reminiscences written during the 1940s and 1950s, encompassing his childhood in Ottawa and in Toronto, and his later life in Ottawa as a practising architect and prominent figure in capital society until his death in 1967. Included in this collection (Volume 9, file 14) is yet another key document; the "Rambling Recollections" written around 1910 by Edmund's wife and Coly's mother, Fanny Jarvis Meredith.

Among the surviving diaries and/or letters of Meredith's friends and acquaintances, I have made extensive use of the diaries of Agnes Macdonald (PAC MG26A Vol. 559A), of Lucianne Desbarats (PAC MG31 D34), and the aide-mémoire of Sandford Fleming (PAC MG29 B1, Vols. 80-92). Valuable also has been the correspondence between the first Earl of Dufferin, the Governor General from 1872 to 1876, and the Colonial Secretary, Lord Carnarvon, published in 1955 by the Champlain Society with an introduction by F. H. Underhill.

To fill out the historical background of the period, and to the specific events described, I relied upon a number of relevant books. Apart from those by Hubbard and by Creighton already cited, these include: *Arduous Destiny: Canada 1874-96* (McClelland & Stewart, 1971), P. B. Waite's lively and authoritative chronicle of the eras of Macdonald and Mackenzie; *George-Etienne Cartier* by Alastair Sweeny (McClelland & Stewart, 1976); *Alexander Mackenzie; Clear Grit* by Dale C. Thomson (Macmillan, 1960); and *Edward Blake* by Joseph Schull (Macmillan, 1975). Detail on the composition and workings of the pre-Confederation and early post-Confederation civil service has come from *Pioneer Public Service* by J.E. Hodgetts (University of Toronto Press, 1955), and from *The Civil Service of Canada* by R. MacGregor Dawson (London, 1929). For information about the history of Ottawa, as a lumbertown and as capital, I am indebted mainly to *The Queen's Choice* by Wilfrid Eggleston (Queen's Printer, 1961) and *Ottawa, Capital of Canada* by Shirley E. Woods (Doubleday, 1981).

As useful have been a number of period reminiscences and works of social history. *Gentleman Emigrants* by Patrick Dunae (Douglas & McIntyre, 1981), provided many insights into the world of Edmund and Fanny Meredith and led me also to a primary source that I have several times quoted: *Canada for Gentlemen: Being Letters from James Seton Cockburn* (London, Army and Navy Co-operative Society, 1885). *Getting Into Parliament & After* by George W. Ross (Toronto 1913), provided a gossipy gloss to many of the political figures of the day, and *Confederation and Its Leaders* by M. O. Hammond (Toronto, 1917), contained vivid descriptions of them, gleaned from first-hand memories. Not only for this section but for use all through the book, I discovered a little goldmine of descriptive anecdote in *Recollections*, by Lilian Scott Desbarats, privately published in Ottawa in 1957. Almost as useful, again from start to finish, has been *Types of Canadian Women* by Henry J. Morgan, a biographical dictionary published in Toronto in 1903, still quite easily available in most major reference libraries.

Helpful background on the customs and living conditions of the period has been provided by *God Bless Our Home: Domestic Life in Nineteenth-Century Canada* by Una Abrahamson (Burns & MacEachern, 1967); *At Home in Upper Canada* by Jeanne Minhinnick (Clarke Irwin, 1970); and *The Ancestral Roof* by Marion MacRae and Anthony Adamson (Clarke Irwin, 1963).

CHAPTER ONE / EDMUND AND FANNY

The main source is family papers. Additional information on the Jarvis family and on Rosedale House has been taken from *Toronto: 100 Years of Grandeur* by Lucy Booth Martyn (Pagurian, 1978), and from *Mary's Rosedale* (Ottawa, 1928), a family history of the Jarvises, based upon family correspondence and written by Coly Meredith's wife, Alden Griffin Meredith.

For the descriptions of pre-Confederation society at Quebec, I am indebted to perhaps the most engaging and informative work of Canadian social history ever written, *The Elegant Canadians* by Luella Creighton (McClelland & Stewart, 1967), now sadly out of print, and also to the *Monck Letters and Journals, 1863-68: Canada from Government House at Confederation*, edited by W. L. Morton (McClelland & Stewart, 1971).

CHAPTER TWO / AN IDEA IN THE WILDERNESS

The quote used as epigraph is from *My Canadian Leaves*, by Frances Monck, a gossipy diary contained in the *Monck Journals* particularly valuable for its descriptions of pre-Confederation society in Quebec. The quote from Trollope is from *North America*, an edition published by Penguin in 1968. Additional information comes from early city directories of Ottawa (always a rich and reliable source) and from contemporary newspaper accounts. Of particular value has been a short, pungent, and fact-filled article, "The Canadian Government Comes to Ottawa" by Courtney C. J. Bond, published in *Ontario History* (No. 55, 1963).

The comment about the quality of Irishness in Official Ottawa in its earliest years is my own observation, flowing from many sources and underscored by Luella Creighton in *The Elegant Canadians*. Despite the stranglehold grip on our history by Loyalists and by Calvinist Scots, I was struck time and again in my research by the influence of the Anglo-Irish gentry within the Canadian establishment during the post-Confederation period. These included, other than Meredith himself: Liberal leader Edward Blake; Fennings Taylor, Clerk of the Senate; Dr. William Agar Adamson, Librarian and Chaplain to the Senate; Dr. Thomas Bedford-Jones, Rector of St. Alban's Church; and the flamboyant journalist and member of parliament, Nicholas Flood Davin, who in 1877 wrote a book on the subject, *The Irishman in Canada*. Another Anglo-Irishman, the London-based lawyer Francis S. Reilly, played a vital role in Canadian history without ever setting foot in the country by drafting the British North America Act, as I discovered several years ago in the course of researching a magazine article: "Francis S. *Who?*" (*Saturday Night*, September 1980). Fittingly, during 1981-82, Reeves Haggan, a senior public servant also of Anglo-Irish heritage acted as constitutional lobbyist on behalf of the federal government in London, helping to get the new constitution through Westminster.

CHAPTERS THREE AND FOUR/"DRAINS, DRAINS, NOTHING BUT DRAINS"; "GOOD KIND DR. TUPPER"

These two chapters, describing the texture of immediate post-Confederation daily life in Ottawa, are drawn mainly from the Meredith family papers, with help from the letters of James Seton Cockburn, and the diary of Agnes Macdonald. Information about the *Peerless* and other paddlewheel steamers comes from *Ottawa Waterway* by Robert Leggett (University of Toronto Press, 1975). The letters of Sir John A. Macdonald, complaining about drains and about servants, are quoted in *Affectionately Yours, Letters of John A. Macdonald and His Family*, edited by J. K. Johnson (Macmillan, 1969).

Many of the most intriguing references in Meredith's diaries and in Fanny's memoir are those that involve their attitudes towards sex, marriage, and childbirth. In interpreting these, I found many helpful insights in *The Bourgeois Experience*, a recent brilliant study of Victorian sensuality by Peter Gay (Oxford University Press, 1984). The quoted descriptions of Tupper are provided by George Ross in *Getting Into Parliament & After* and by M. O. Hammond in *Confederation and its Leaders*. Tupper's flirtation with Lucianne Desbarats is recorded by Lilian Desbarats in her *Recollections*.

CHAPTER FIVE/"THE ASHES OF HIS FATHERS, THE TEMPLES OF HIS GODS"

The set-piece description of St. Alban's Church is based on the accounts of Edmund and Fanny Meredith, on Lady Macdonald's diary, and on a personal pilgrimage to St. Alban's, made on a wintry Sunday morning in February 1982. The memoir of the Reverend Thomas Bedford-Jones is titled, "How St. Alban's Church in Ottawa Had Its Beginning," and it was reprinted in the *Journal of the Canadian Church Historical Society* (Vol. III, No. 3, May 1957).

Information about the Jarvis family and about the education of Meredith's children is drawn entirely from the family papers.

CHAPTER SIX/OFFICE POLITICS

The pastiche of Meredith's working day on the eve of Confederation has been amassed from a number of sources other than his own diary. Detail about styles of dress comes mainly from period photographs; details about the appearance of the East Block from *The East Block*, a comprehensive history of the building by R. A. J. Phillips (Queen's Printer, 1967). It helped further that much of this building, including the cabinet chamber and the offices of Macdonald and Cartier, have been lovingly restored to their appearance of the 1870s and were opened officially to public view by Queen Elizabeth in April 1982, shortly after she had signed the new constitution. From a detailed floor-plan, *circa* 1865, I was able to ascertain the precise location of Meredith's office; so inclusive are the records of the Department of Public Works that Richard Raycraft, restoration designer, was able to produce the information that in Meredith's day, this office had been painted yellow. It is currently occupied by Senator J-P. Guay of Manitoba, who graciously invited me in to take a good look. The fascinating nugget that Meredith's minister, William McDougall, was determined to have the exterior stone of the building painted is contained in the diary of Sir Stafford Northcote for April 23, 1870. Northcote, then governor of the Hudson's Bay Company, was visiting Ottawa at the time, and heard the story from Augustus Laver, architect of the East Block. This reference was kindly brought to my attention by Dr. Irene Biss Spry and is contained in the collection, *Manitoba: The Birth of a Province*, edited by W. L. Morton (University of Toronto Press, 1967)

Information about Macdonald's friendship with Cartier, and about Cartier's affair with Luce Cuvillier is taken from *George-Etienne Cartier* by Alastair Sweeny. Notes about civil service salaries and practices come mainly from *Pioneer Public Service* by J. E. Hodgetts, including the quoted letter of John Langton, Auditor General. The comment about Langton in the Toronto *Telegraph* was reprinted in the Ottawa *Citizen* on May 7, 1869. Readers who would like to know more about this commanding founder of the public service are directed to *Early Days in Upper Canada*, a collection of his letters published in 1926. The trial of the genial embezzler, G. C. Reiffenstein, was covered extensively by contemporary newspapers; I used the account in the Ottawa *Citizen* for April 14, 1870.

CHAPTER SEVEN/"THE SHIELD OF ACHILLES"

Detail about the Civil Service Rifle Corps, the volunteer unit in which Meredith served, was obtained from *The Regimental History of the Governor-General's Foot Guards* (Ottawa, 1948). Extant photographs in the Public Archives indicate the appearance of the uniform. The biographical sketch of Thomas D'Arcy McGee and information about the Fenian crisis has been drawn mainly from Josephine Phelan's excellent biography, *The Ardent Exile* (Macmillan, 1951). Also useful was *The Fenian Movement* by Mabel Gregory Walker (Myles, Colorado, 1969). A fascinating account of the activities of the British secret agent, Henri LeCaron, is contained in *Prince of Spies* by J. A. Cole (Penguin, 1984).

For descriptions of the warlike atmosphere in Ottawa, I am indebted once again to Courtney Bond's excellent article, "The Canadian Government Comes to Ottawa," and to Lilian Scott Desbarats's *Recollections*. Lady Macdonald's brilliant account of the trial of McGee's putative assassin has been condensed, only slightly, from her diaries.

CHAPTER EIGHT / UNDONE BY SIR JOHN

Meredith himself is the chief informant. The anecdote about Macdonald and John Rose is taken from *The Young Politician* by Donald Creighton (Macmillan, 1952, p. 243). McDougall's comment about Joseph Howe and Howe's riposte comes from *Confederation and Its Leaders*, by M. O. Hammond. For notes on Sandford Fleming, I relied on Fleming's own aide-mémoire and on the accounts of Lilian Desbarats; the anecdote about Fleming's liking for marmalade in his porridge was provided to the Montreal *Gazette* columnist Nick Auf Der Maur by the Viscountess Hardinge, Fleming's only surviving granddaughter, and was published in the *Gazette* on December 9, 1981.

CHAPTER NINE / "THE SUPERANNUATED MAN"

Much of the historical background to the events of 1873-78, including the information about treaty-making, is taken from *Arduous Destiny* by P. B. Waite. Alexander Mackenzie's letter of November 11, 1873, "All the offices are crammed with hostile people," is quoted in *Alexander Mackenzie: Clear Grit*, by Dale C. Thomson. Information about Willy Jarvis's career in the North-West Mounted Police and the quotation from his report of the march to Edmonton is taken from *The Royal North-West Mounted Police*, a corps history by Captain Ernest J. Chambers. (Montreal, 1906). Apart from Meredith's diary, I have also drawn from the Dufferin–Carnarvon correspondence, and from the invaluable *Getting Into Parliament & After*, by George Ross.

CHAPTER TEN / "O, WHAT A MERRY COMPANY WE WERE!"

Along with accounts by Edmund and Fanny Meredith, I have used here the diary of Janet Anna Hall, an Ottawa woman who kept a daily diary, of which a six-year segment, covering the years 1876-82, is held at the Public Archives (MG29 C70). Otherwise, except for a couple of references to accounts in *The Canadian Illustrated News*, the description of the fancy-dress ball, and of the social demarcation lines that had now begun to prevail, is drawn almost entirely from the three-and-a-half-page account in the Ottawa *Citizen* on February 24, 1876. So complete was the *Citizen's* coverage that it included minute descriptions of each of the costumes, and reproduced the menu card. It was a measure of the growing importance of Rideau Hall as social arbiter that this sort of reportage of viceregal functions remained standard practice until after the Second World War.

The letter of Achille Frèchette to his fiancee Annie Howells is quoted in *Annie Howells and Achille Frèchette*, an interesting study of cultural life in the capital by James Doyle (University of Toronto Press, 1979).

CHAPTER ELEVEN/THE DUFFERIN STYLE

To comprehend the nature of the governor-generalcy as reinvented by Lord Dufferin, I drew upon many sources. Especially valuable for its information about the style of the viceregal court at Dublin was *The Victorians*, by Sir Charles Petrie (Eyre & Spottiswoode, 1960) and, for its evocative description of nascent Imperialism, *At Heaven's Command* by James Morris (Faber and Faber, 1973), the first volume of *The Imperial Trilogy*. Equally helpful, for insights into the Imperial style as it began to manifest itself within the Canadian context, was the introduction to the Champlain Society edition of the Dufferin–Carnarvon correspondence by F. H. Underhill. Descriptions of the style of the White House during the 1870s are taken from *Lady Sackville*, Susan Mary Alsop's sparkling biography of one of Washington's most remarkable hostesses, the illegitimate daughter of the distinguished British diplomat, Lionel Sackville-West by the Spanish dancer Pepita (Doubleday, 1978). For the biographical sketch of Dufferin, I relied mainly upon the anecdotal memoir *Helen's Tower* by Harold Nicolson (London, 1937) but referred also to the official *Life of Lord Dufferin* by Sir Alfred Lyall (London, 1905). Interesting insights into Dufferin's predilection for the trappings of chivalry are contained in a recent study by Marc Girouard: *The Return to Camelot: Chivalry and the English Gentleman* (Yale University Press, 1981).

CHAPTER TWELVE/"BOMBASTO FURIOSO"

Macdonald's comment about Dufferin, and also those of George Grant and Goldwin Smith, are quoted by F. H. Underhill in the introduction to the Dufferin–Carnarvon correspondence. Along with this collection, I have used additional correspondence of Dufferin's quoted in Lyall's biography. The most important source for this chapter, however, is *My Canadian Journal* by Lady Dufferin, a collection of her letters home, published in London in 1891.

CHAPTER THIRTEEN/THE GAY GOVERNOR GENERAL

Kevin O'Brien's book, *Oscar Wilde in Canada* (Personal, 1982), provides a detailed description of Wilde's visit to Ottawa in 1882 and of his meeting with Frances Richards. (O'Brien's exhaustive research explodes the myth, repeated as recently as 1976 by H. Montgomery Hyde in his definitive biography, *Oscar Wilde*, that Wilde was wined and dined at Rideau Hall.) Additional information about Frances Richards was obtained from the biographical note in *Types of Canadian Women*.

Two other books were central to this chapter. *Days of Lorne* by W. S. MacNutt (Fredericton, 1955), is a lively account of the ups and downs of this viceregal tenure, including the quarrel with Lady Macdonald. *Queen Victoria and Her Daughters* by Nina Epton (Weidenfeld and Nicolson, 1971), sheds much light on the difficult personality of Louise, and on the circumstances of her marriage. Epton's book also contains the revealing comments by Sir Henry Ponsonby. Important too, for insights into Lorne's probable homosexuality, is *Love in Earnest*, a study of the shadowy side of Victorian sensuality by Timothy D'Arch Smith (Routledge and Kegan Paul, 1970), and *Edward and the Edwardians* by Philippe Jullian (Viking, 1960). I have also drawn from *Ne Obliviscaris* (London, 1930), a memoir written by Lorne's sister, Lady Frances Balfour. The article by Annie Howells Frèchette quoted was titled "Life at Rideau Hall" and appeared in *Harper's New Monthly Magazine*, No. 63, 1881. Princess Louise's conversation with Alexander Mackenzie is quoted by Dale C. Thomson in his biography *Clear Grit*.

CHAPTER FOURTEEN/AGNES MACDONALD: THE LADY OR THE TIGER?

Donald Creighton's insightful comment about Agnes Macdonald is contained in *The Old Chieftain* (p. 7). Otherwise, this chapter is drawn mainly from Agnes's own diaries and from the authoritative biography, *Agnes*, by Louise Reynolds (Samuel Stevens, 1979). Additional information about Charlotte Rose is taken from *Types of Canadian Women* and from *George-Etienne Cartier* by Alastair Sweeny, who is a collateral descendant of the unfortunate Captain Sweeny, Charlotte Rose's first husband. For information about Mary Macdonald, Lilian Scott Desbarats's *Recollections* have been useful. Lady Macdonald's relations with Mrs. George Foster are described by the Countess of Aberdeen in her diary entries for November 19 and December 1, 1893.

CHAPTER FIFTEEN/LORNE ALONE

As it was in chapter thirteen, *Queen Victoria and Her Daughters* by Nina Epton was an important source here, as was *Days of Lorne* by W. S.

MacNutt. The description of Lorne in *Leslie's Illustrated* is quoted by Robert Hubbard in *Rideau Hall*; this is also the source for the account of the visit to Ottawa by Sir Arthur Sullivan. The description of Lorne's 1883 visit to Washington and of Victoria Sackville-West's return visit to Ottawa comes from *Lady Sackville*, by Susan Mary Alsop. The account of the founding of the National Gallery is drawn from "To Found a National Gallery," an essay by Charles C. Hill, published in the *Journal* of the National Gallery (No. 36, March 6, 1980), a special edition commemorating the centenary of that institution, and also from additional research that Mr. Hill kindly made available. The anecdote about Louise as a smoker is contained in her official biography, *Princess Louise*, by David Duff (London, 1940); the delicious anecdote about the dove at Frogmore is recounted by Philip Ziegler in his biography, *Diana Cooper* (Hamish Hamilton, 1981).

CHAPTER SIXTEEN / ROSEDALE REVISITED

This chapter is drawn entirely from the Meredith family papers.

PART TWO / THE UNCAUGHT BUTTERFLY

The key sources for this section are the columns that Agnes Scott wrote under the pseudonym Amaryllis, which appeared weekly in *Saturday Night* between March 1897 and July 1902, and the columns published under her other pseudonym The Marchioness, which she wrote thrice-weekly, on Tuesdays, Thursdays, and Saturdays, for the Ottawa *Free Press*, beginning in December 1897 and ending in March 1903. As related in the Preface, it was my discovery of Amaryllis that gave me the idea for this book; in chapter thirty, I have described how, at last, I was able to establish her identity. Readers interested in the fun and the frustration of historical detective work may like to have a fuller description of this process.

I started out with the instinct – one writer about Ottawa empathizing with another across the years – that someone free-lancing a column for a Toronto weekly might well also have been employed regularly by an Ottawa paper. This hunch led me directly to Florence Hamilton Randal of the Ottawa *Journal*. Having discovered, with a growing sense of excitement, that Florence Randal had later become the mother of the poet, Dorothy Livesay, I dashed off a letter: did that pseudonym, Amaryllis, ring any kind of bell? Livesay, who responded with a phone call instead of a letter, was intrigued with the possibility, but when she produced the information that Florence had in fact left Ottawa for good in April 1902, well before Amaryllis had stopped writing, that possibility had to be discarded. The consolation was that Livesay arranged to have sent to me a copy of the diary that her mother had kept in South Africa.

I now had the material for a new, and quite unexpected, chapter. Yet Amaryllis remained an unknown quantity. I kept on searching the back files of Ottawa newspapers, and eventually, within the pages of the *Free Press*, a paper that existed from Confederation days until 1917 when it merged with the Ottawa *Journal*, discovered the columns of The Marchioness. From internal evidence – matching structure of sentences; occasional identical errors of fact having to be retracted – it was clear that The Marchioness and Amaryllis were one and the same.

This discovery encouraged me to narrow my search to women journalists who had lived in the capital for a number of years. One possibility was Madge Macbeth, a spirited young woman from Philadelphia who came to the capital on her marriage and, having been left widowed early, turned to journalism to support her young family. By the time of her death in 1965, Macbeth had long become a folkloric figure, described by B. K. Sandwell in *Saturday Night* as "a professional diner out, who knows everybody, and has always known everybody." In 1924, she caused a tremendous furore by publishing, under the pseudonym Gilbert Knox, a *roman-à-clef* about Official Ottawa, *The Land of Afternoon*, in which such figures as the Clarke sisters and Mrs. C. A. E. Harriss were satirized mercilessly. Sadly though, it became apparent that Macbeth had arrived in Ottawa only well after Amaryllis first began writing.

Other possibilities survived a longer scrutiny. The literary Barry sisters, like Amaryllis, were both alumnae of Rideau Street Convent, and as the daughters of a senior civil servant, they had the entry to the right social circles. Kate Barry, the elder, published two romances set in Ottawa in the early 1880s when she was not yet out of her teens: *Honor Edgeworth* and *The Doctor's Daughter*. Kate, however, faded from the field when an account of her marriage appeared in the columns of Amaryllis in 1900. But Lily Barry lingered longer, for a 1955 obituary revealed that she had gone on to a long and distinguished career as a journalist. All the more intriguingly, during the summer of 1900, Lily Barry was in Paris providing the Montreal *Star* with reports on the great "Universal Exhibition" that are almost interchangeable with the accounts that Amaryllis, also in Paris, was sending back to the *Free Press*.

No doubt, touring the site on the electrically-powered "moving platform" that, as they both noted, was the wonder of that fair, Amaryllis and Lily Barry bumped into each other. But they were not the same person, for Lily Barry, as I learned eventually, was by then not just a free-lancer for the *Star*, but a full-time reporter, based in Montreal.

In the end, all possible leads having been exhausted, there was nothing for it but to turn back to the internal evidence; to the clues that Amaryllis AKA The Marchioness had let slip in her writing. Thus it was that, as described in chapter thirty, I eventually happened upon the trail of Agnes Scott.

Because of the elusive quality of Amaryllis, I relied in this section, even more heavily than in the previous one, upon additional primary sources. Those which contained information used in more than one or two chapters include that magnificent social document, *The Canadian Journal of Lady Aberdeen*, published by the Champlain Society in 1960; *The Canadian Papers of the Fourth Earl of Minto* – for the years 1898-1900, I relied upon the Champlain Society edition published in 1981, otherwise I referred to copies of the originals held in the Public Archives (MG27 II B1); the letters of Agar Adamson (PAC MG30 E149, Vol. 1), and Adamson's diaries, still in the keeping of Anthony Adamson; and the diaries of Ethel Chadwick (PAC MG30 D258). Another invaluable source for the period is the two-volume social scrapbook kept by Belle Botsford Scott, held in the Rare Book Room at the National Library.

Among printed sources, I referred frequently to *A Nation Transformed: Canada 1896-1921* by Robert Craig Brown and Ramsay Cook (McClelland & Stewart, 1974), to *Laurier: The First Canadian* by Joseph Schull (Macmillan, 1965), and to *Laurier, His Life and World* by Richard Clippingdale (McGraw Hill, 1979). Other key guides to the period were the excellent introduction to the Champlain Society edition of the Aberdeen Journal, by John Saywell, and the introduction to the Champlain's Minto Papers, co-authored by Saywell and Paul Stevens.

CHAPTER SEVENTEEN / AMARYLLIS AKA THE MARCHIONESS

This pastiche of Ottawa Style at the turn of the century has been amassed from many sources: the columns of Amaryllis and of The Marchioness; the diaries of Edmund Meredith and the notes that Coly Meredith kept for a memoir; the diary of Lady Aberdeen; and an evocative description, based on the reminiscences of figures of the period, by H. S. Ferns and Bernard Ostry in *The Age of Mackenzie King* (Lorimer, 1976). Particularly helpful in filling in the gap between the departure of Edmund Meredith in 1879 and the advent of Amaryllis in 1897 were *The Days Before Yesterday* (London, 1920), a rollicking memoir by Lord Frederick Hamilton, and *Lord Lansdowne*, a biography by Lord Newton (Macmillan, 1929).

CHAPTERS EIGHTEEN AND NINETEEN / THE DISTANT VIOLIN; EMILIE AND ZOË

For the biographical sketch of Laurier, I relied mainly on Joseph Schull's definitive *Laurier*, also on *Laurier: A Study in Canadian Politics* by J. W. Dafoe (McClelland & Stewart, New Canadian Library, 1963), and on *Laurier: His Life and World* by Richard Clippingdale. Clippingdale's book led me to the wonderful description of Laurier contained in *The Masques of Ottawa*, by Augustus Bridle (Macmillan, 1921).

The key source for the description of the relationship between Laurier and Emilie Lavergne is the letters written to Emilie by Laurier (PAC MG27 I 42, Vols. 1 and 2). These letters fall into two categories. The larger group, contained in Volume 1, comprise forty-one letters, all dated between 1891 and 1893. These were given to the Quebec historian, Marc La Terreur, in 1963 by a nephew of Emilie's by marriage, Louis-Renaud La Vergne. (For reasons unknown, La Vergne embellished the spelling of the name.) La Terreur unveiled his find in a celebrated paper presented to the Canadian Historical Association in 1964. But the more ambitious work he planned to write on the relationship between the Lauriers and the Lavergnes was not completed, for La Terreur died tragically in a plane crash in Newfoundland in 1978. The second cache, contained in Volume 2, were discovered later, in 1967, among the papers of Mackenzie King. These comprise fifteen letters dated between 1890 and 1903.

Another important source is the unpublished memoir of Louis-Renaud La Vergne, quoted extensively by the historian Marc Carrier in his M.A. thesis, *Laurier, citoyen d'Arthabaska*, held at the University of Ottawa. Further information, including the telling letter to Emilie from George Irvine and the letters of Armand Lavergne that contain the post-scripts, "*Vive les Boers!*" and "*Comment est Kruger?*" was obtained from the papers of Armand Lavergne (PAC MG27 II E12) Additional biographical information about Emilie, including the fact that she had met Victor Hugo and the date of her marriage, was obtained from that invaluable if unscholarly reference work, *Types of Canadian Women*. The invitation to Emilie's remarkable reception of December 1897 was found in the scrapbooks of Belle Botsford Scott; Laurier's letter to Marie-Louise Pacaud is quoted in *Sir Wilfrid Laurier: Letters to My Mother and Father*, a collection edited by Lucien Pacaud (Ryerson, 1935). Sir Robert Borden's letter to Audrey Alexandra Brown is quoted in *As the World Wags On*, by Arthur Ford (Ryerson, 1950).

Of the many questions that remain unanswered about the relationship between Laurier and Emilie, two are particularly tantalizing: the fate of the letters that Emilie wrote to Laurier and the name of the book that contains the chapter "St. Anne's Hill," that Laurier, on three separate occasions, urged Emilie to read and of which he wrote, "When I read it, my heart was full of images often indulged in, never realized."

In the first instance, Louis-Renaud La Vergne, in his memoir, reports that Emilie passed these letters on to her daughter, Gabrielle, by then the wife of a House of Commons translator; how, or where, Gabrielle disposed of them is unknown. In the second instance, I was unable to unravel the mystery of Laurier's reference to "St. Anne's Hill." One thinks readily of the great shrine of St Anne de Beaupré in Quebec, much to the fore during these years, for the Cathedral was consecrated in 1889. Yet Laurier was not at all a religious man. One hint that I pursued without success was that, as Carl F. Klinck has noted in the *Literary History of Canada*, many writers during the eighties and nineties used the French-Canadian past as backdrop for romantic novels and melodramas. However, a search through some of the novels of the day (*e.g., Marie Gourdon* and *The Keeper of Bic Lighthouse*, both by Maud Ogilvy) proved fruitless. I hope that some other researcher will one day discover the key to the riddle.

For additional information about Armand Lavergne, I am indebted once again to Marc La Terreur for his biographical monograph, *Armand Lavergne* (Fides, Montreal and Paris, 1968).

CHAPTER TWENTY/THE REMARKABLE ISHBEL

For useful background information on the "New Woman" of the 1890s, I drew from *The Widening Sphere: Women in Canada 1870-1940* by Jeanne L'Esperance of the Public Archives (Canada, Supply and Services, 1982). This excellent catalogue accompanied the exhibition of the same title, shown at the Public Archives in 1982. The quote attributed to R. Preston Robinson comes from an article in the local Ottawa magazine, *The Lounger*, for July 1896; this same issue also contains a lengthy article on Lady Aberdeen's historical fancy-dress ball, almost certainly written by Amaryllis. The quote from Joseph Pope is from his memoir, *Public Servant*, edited by his son, Maurice Pope (University of Toronto Press, 1960).

Elsewhere in this chapter, the Countess of Aberdeen, through her own magnificent *Journal* was her own best informant. A superb gloss to the woman and to the era is provided by John Saywell's introduction to the Champlain Society edition of 1960. Helpful also was *A Bonnie Fechter* (London, 1952), a memoir of Lady Aberdeen by her daughter, Lady Marjorie Pentland.

CHAPTERS TWENTY-ONE AND TWENTY-TWO/ "MINTO'S FOLLY"; "FOLLOW THE ADC"

The theme of these two chapters, the Earl and Countess of Minto as quintessential Edwardians, was crystallized by the cheeky comment of Agar Adamson, which appears as epigraph to chapter twenty-one. As in the case of the discovery of Florence Hamilton Randal, the discovery of Adamson's letters (PAC MG30 E149, Vol. 1) came about serendipitously. I had sought out this collection only with the thought that Adamson, as an Ottawa man who had fought in the Boer War, might shed some light on the mood and temper of the capital as war fever swept through it. The first letter I looked at, however, was the "Minto's Folly" letter, and it set me off on an entirely new train of thought.

To establish further the Edwardian context, I drew on a wide range of printed sources: Victoria Sackville-West's classic novel, *The Edwardians* (London, 1930); *The Proud Tower* by Barbara Tuchman (Macmillan, 1962); *Edwardians in Love* by Anita Leslie (Hutchinson, 1972); *The Edwardians* by J. B. Priestley (Heinemann, 1970); *The Diaries of Cynthia Asquith* (London 1968); and *The Souls*, by Jane Abdy and Charlotte Gere (Sidgwick and Jackson, 1984).

As in the case of Lady Aberdeen, the fourth Earl of Minto was his own best informant through his diaries and letters (PAC MG27 II B1), as was Lady Minto in her memoir, *Myself When Young* (London, 1938). In further describing the career of this interesting Governor General, I referred to the official biography, *Lord Minto, a Memoir*, by John Buchan (London, 1924), but relied mainly on two much more recent works: the excellent introduction by John Saywell and Paul Stevens to the Champlain Society edition of *Lord Minto's Canadian Papers* (1981), and the comprehensive study by Carman Miller, *The Canadian Career of the Fourth Earl of Minto* (Wilfrid Laurier Press, 1980). The delicious comment by Lord Minto, "Clever people are generally so damned silly," is quoted by Percy Colson in *Close of an Era* (London, 1944).

For additional information about Lola Powell, I used the voluminous diaries of one of her best friends, Ethel Chadwick (PAC MG30 D258). Information about the King–Harper friendship was drawn mainly from *A Very Double Life* by C. P. Stacey (Macmillan, 1976). The lyrics composed by Harry Graham for his musical productions at Rideau Hall were published in the Ottawa newspapers; I used clippings preserved in the scrapbooks of Belle Botsford Scott, which also contains the programmes for most of these events. Graham's own word-portrait of himself and also the portrait of Arthur Guise are contained in *Across Canada to the Klondike*, an unpublished narrative of a viceregal tour by "Col. D. Streamer," contained in the Minto Papers.

CHAPTER TWENTY-THREE/"MARCHING TO PRETORIA"

For background detail on the origins of the Boer War, I relied mainly on two excellent recent accounts: Thomas Pakenham's masterful history, *The Boer War* (Random House, 1979), and *The Great Anglo-Boer War* by Byron Farwell (Fitzhenry & Whiteside, 1972). For accounts of the Canadian response, I used *The Canadian Career of the Fourth Earl of Minto* by Carman Miller, and the Saywell–Stevens introduction to the Champlain Society edition of the Minto papers. The account of the epochal exchange between Laurier and Henri Bourassa is taken from *Laurier*, by Joseph Schull. A comprehensive account of the long drawn-out battle between Canadian politicians and the Imperial officers commanding the Canadian militia, including the sacking of General Hutton, is contained in *Ministers and Generals* by Desmond Morton (University of Toronto Press, 1970).

CHAPTER TWENTY-FOUR/HORSEMAN ON THE VELDT

Having discovered Adamson as a lively commentator on Ottawa society, it was impossible not to follow him out to South Africa. His accounts of the war are mostly contained in his letters, and I have also drawn from his diaries and from a number of letters written to him by his wife still in the possession of their son, Anthony Adamson. Additional information was obtained from two long conversations with Anthony Adamson. Information about Colonel Sam Steele has been taken from *Sam Steele, Lion of the Frontier* by Robert Stewart (Doubleday, 1979) and from Steele's own memoir, *Forty Years in Canada* (London, 1914). As a general guide to the action described by Adamson, by Stewart, and by Steele, I relied once again on *The Boer War*, by Thomas Pakenham.

CHAPTER TWENTY-FIVE / MOONLIGHT IN THE TRANSVAAL

Background information about the concentration camps of the Transvaal and about Emily Hobhouse has been taken from *The Great Anglo-Boer War* by Byron Farwell. Otherwise, this chapter is based upon the diary that Florence Hamilton Randal kept in South Africa, now held at the University of Manitoba, and upon the reports she sent back to the Ottawa *Journal* during 1902 and 1903. Information about her later life and career was provided by conversations with Dorothy Livesay.

CHAPTERS TWENTY-SIX AND TWENTY-SEVEN / SESSIONAL PERSON; "DRILL YE TARRIERS, DRILL"

The major manuscript collection of M. O. Hammond, on which these chapters are based, is held at the Archives of Ontario. It includes his diaries, many letters, an unpublished history of *The Globe*, and clippings of articles he wrote for other publications. Hammond's photograph albums are also to be found at the Ontario Archives.

Additional information has been taken from *Persons, Papers and Things* (Ryerson, 1940), a memoir by Hammond's Press Gallery contemporary, Paul Bilkey, and from "Years Around Parliament," by Charles Bishop, a series of articles published in the Ottawa *Citizen*, beginning on September 15, 1945. Background detail on the journalistic practices of the day, including the quote by Goldwin Smith, has been taken from "Partisanship, Patronage and the Press in Ontario, 1880-1914," an article by Brian P. N. Beaven, published in the *Canadian Historical Review*, September 1983. Useful also has been the memoir of the former *Globe* editor, Sir John Willison, *Reminiscences, Personal and Political* (McClelland & Stewart, 1919).

Among specific references, information about the quarrel between Clifford Sifton and Charles Fitzpatrick is recorded in *Laurier*, by Joseph Schull, and the quotes by the Reverend D. S. Chown and the poet Wilfred Campbell are contained in *The Canadian Annual Review* for 1903. The startling information provided by Coly Meredith is contained in his papers; further comment about Henry Emmerson is drawn from *Laurier*, by Schull and from *Persons, Papers and Things*, by Paul Bilkey.

THE PRIVATE CAPITAL

CHAPTERS TWENTY-EIGHT AND TWENTY-NINE/ "AN OXYGENIC ESSENCE"; "WIVES OF THE POETS"

Those in search of the cultural ambience in the capital around the turn of the century will find rich pickings. The two most important original sources that I have used, both for the first time so far as I am aware, are the social scrapbooks of Belle Botsford Scott, held at the National Library, and a cache of Lampman family correspondence purchased in 1971 from Natalie Lampman MacInnes by Simon Fraser University. Important also – a source that extends far beyond the chronological scope of this book all the way up to the nineteen-fifties – were the letters and diaries of Annie Lampman Jenkins (PAC MG30 D183). I have also drawn extensively from three collections of letters written by Scott and Lampman, edited and published privately a generation ago by their younger friend and colleague, the Ottawa poet Arthur S. Bourinot: *Letters of Lampman to E. W. Thomson* (1956); *Some Letters of D. C. Scott* (1959); *More Letters of D. C. Scott* (1960).

Beyond this, I have culled from a wide range of secondary sources. Pride of place must be given to the critic E. K. Brown, both for the critical commentary and for the biographical essays on Lampman and Scott contained in his landmark study, *On Canadian Poetry* (Ryerson, 1944). Later, in his introduction to the *Selected Poems of Duncan Campbell Scott* (Ryerson, 1951), Brown provided a fuller biographical study of the latter poet. A brilliantly evocative sketch of the friendship that developed between these two towards the end of Scott's life is contained in the introduction to *The Poet and the Critic* (Carleton University Press, 1983), a definitive edition of their correspondence edited by R. L. McDougall. Impressions of Scott's second wife, Elise Aylen, are drawn from *Literary Friends*, a memoir by Wilfred Eggleston (Borealis, 1980); particularly helpful were the observations by Lena Raskevitch Eggleston. Elise Aylen Scott's own memoir, *The Night of the Lord*, was published in 1967 by Bharatiya Vidya Bhavan (Bombay).

In the case of Archibald Lampman, biographical information has also been drawn from *Archibald Lampman: Canadian Poet of Nature* by C. Y. Connor (New York, 1929). Of most interest were the first-hand memories of the poet gleaned from many of Lampman's relatives and contemporaries. For the light shed on Lampman's relationship with Kate Waddell, I am indebted to two essays by Margaret Coulby Whitredge: her introduction to the *Collected Poems of Archibald Lampman* (University of Toronto Press, 1974) and to *Lampman's Kate*, an edition of late love poems published by Borealis in 1975. Helpful also have been D. M. Bentley's introduction to a recent edition of *Lyrics of Earth* (Tecumseh Press, 1978) and an earlier essay on Lampman by Munro Beattie, which appeared in *Our Living Tradition* (Carleton University Press, 1957). For biographical information about William Wilfred Campbell I have drawn from *Wilfred Campbell: A Study in Late Victorian Provincialism* by Carl F. Klinck (Ryerson, 1942).

All of the quotations from "At the Mermaid Inn," and the background information on the column, have been taken from the definitive collection, *At the Mermaid Inn*, edited and introduced by Barrie Davies (University of Toronto Press, 1979). Additional information about Ottawa cultural circles has been taken from a number of sources: notes on Nicholas Flood Davin come from *Mr. Davin M.P.*, a biography by C. B. Koester (Western Producer Prairie Books, 1980); notes on *Les Dix* from *Annie Howells and Achille Frèchette* by James Doyle; information about Ella Beatty Harriss comes from *Types of Canadian Women*; the thinly-veiled fictional portrait of Mrs. Harriss is contained in *The Land of Afternoon* by Madge Macbeth (Ottawa, 1924). Macbeth, in her episodic memoir, *Over My Shoulder* (Ryerson, 1953), provided the anecdote about Scott's liking for white wine and sweetbreads; Yousuf Karsh, in a conversation, produced the anecdote about Scott and Mackenzie King. For the account of Rupert Brooke's meeting with the Scotts in 1913, I am indebted to *Rupert Brooke in Canada*, edited by Sandra Martin and Roger Hall (PMA Books, 1978).

CHAPTER THIRTY / BUT WHO WAS SHE, REALLY?

The detective work involved in establishing the identity of Amaryllis has already been described. For information about other women journalists of the day, I relied on *Types of Canadian Women* and also, once again, on *The Widening Sphere* by Jeanne L'Esperance. Information about the Scott family was provided by Lilian Scott Desbarats in her invaluable *Recollections*, and by Colonel Cuthbert Scott, who loaned me a number of family documents, most notably a lively unpublished history of the Heron family.

For personal recollections of Agnes Scott Davis, AKA Amaryllis, I am indebted to Colonel Scott, who was her cousin once removed, and also to Henry Davis, who was her half-brother-in-law. (The contractor M. P. Davis, who was Agnes's father-in-law, lived to a hearty old age: Will Davis, born in 1874, who became her husband, was the eldest child of a first marriage; Henry Davis, born in 1914, the son of a second.) Cuthbert Scott, the present-day head of the Ottawa clan of Scotts, is a distinguished lawyer emeritus. Henry Davis, having served with distinction in the Royal Canadian Air Force and later in the Department of External Affairs, retired in 1982 as Secretary of the Canadian Intergovernmental Conference Secretariat, and continues to serve as the Queen's private secretary in Canada. It is a further grace-note to this story that Davis's wife, the former Isobel Margaret O'Reilly, is a great-granddaughter of Edmund and Fanny Meredith through their elder son Arthur, who died young at Edmonton in 1895.

To finish on a contemporary note, the *Saturday Night* article that contains the quote, "Ottawa is a terrible town for women," was my own first attempt to describe the ambience of Official Ottawa; it was titled "Twilight of the Ottawa Man," and appeared in January 1971. The deputy minister's wife quoted anonymously was in fact Sondra Gotlieb, who soon became a shrewd and acerbic writer about society both at Ottawa and at Washington. A few years later, in an interview for a 1976 profile, Senator Eugene Forsey reminisced to me about Sir Robert Borden's triumphant arrival in Ottawa in 1911; this kinetic link between past and present, along with my discovery of Amaryllis, catalysed my own serendipitous journey into our capital's past.

INDEX

Italicized page numbers indicate a page on which a picture appears.